feria (fair) at some time during this period. Alon[...] happen in July or August; inland, the cooler m[...] summer peak are favoured. See p432 and the sect[...] and towns for more on the timing of Andaluci[...]

COSTS & MONEY

Andalucía is refreshingly economical by European standards. Accommodation, meals, drinks, transport, car hire and entertainment generally cost noticeably less than in the UK or France. All prices listed in this book are for the high season, so if travelling outside this time you might be pleasantly surprised.

If you are very frugal, it's possible to scrape by on €40 a day by staying in the cheapest accommodation, avoiding restaurants except for an inexpensive set lunch, and keeping a close eye on what you spend on museums, entertainment and bars. A comfortable midrange budget would be €70 to €130 a day. This would allow you €30 to €60 for accommodation; €3 or €4 for a light breakfast; €15 to €30 for one full meal and one lighter one; €8 to €15 for public transport, the odd taxi and admission fees; and the rest for a drink or two, intercity travel and some shopping. If you have €200 a day, you can stay in excellent accommodation and eat some of the best food Andalucía has to offer.

Two people can travel more cheaply (per person) than one by sharing rooms. Rooms, apartments and villas for up to six people, available in many places, work out even cheaper per person – good value for families, especially when they have a kitchen where you can prepare meals. You'll also save by avoiding the peak tourist seasons, when most room prices go up.

Children benefit from reduced admission fees at many museums, monuments and attractions, as do, in fewer cases, students and seniors. A few museums have free-admission days – worth bearing in mind if you're taking the whole family.

TRAVEL LITERATURE

Andalucía has fascinated foreign writers for two centuries, giving rise to a wealth of literature in English and other languages.

South from Granada (1957) In the 1920s Englishman Gerald Brenan settled in the remote village of Yegen in Las Alpujarras, Granada province, aiming to educate himself unimpeded by British traditions. His classic book is an acutely perceptive, humorous account of village life punctuated by visits from the Bloomsbury set.

Driving Over Lemons (1999) The entertaining, anecdotal, bestselling tale of taking on a small Andalucian farm by a more recent British migrant to Las Alpujarras, amiable drummer/sheepshearer/writer Chris Stewart.

Tales of the Alhambra (1832) American Washington Irving took up residence in Granada's abandoned Alhambra palace in the 1820s. His book weaves a series of enchanting stories around the folk with whom he shared his life there, and contributed much to romantic notions of Andalucía which persist to this day.

Andalus (2004) Jason Webster uncovers what's left of the medieval Islamic legacy today as he travels across contemporary Andalucía with an illegal immigrant from Morocco – a book both comical and serious that combines adventure, travel and history.

Getting to Mañana (2003) Amid the welter of 'The First Year of My New Life in an Old Farmhouse on the Continent' books, Miranda Innes' tale stands out for telling us about the troubles as well as the dreams of the real people who did it (in this case in the hills of Málaga province). Good on food and plants too.

The Sierras of the South (1992) It's instructive to read the stories of foreigners who settled in Andalucía before everyone else was doing it. Alastair Boyd evokes life in the hills around Ronda in the 1950s and '60s, when foreigners were a rarity.

LONELY PLANET INDEX

1L petrol €1

1.5L bottled water €0.50

Bottle of San Miguel beer €1.50

Souvenir T-shirt €10

Tapas €1.80

HOW MUCH?

Two-hour bus or regional train ride €10

Admission to major monument or museum €6-12

Midrange double room in high season €65-120

Decorative fan €10

Three-course lunch or dinner with drinks €20-30

TOP TENS

Festivals & Events

Andalucians love to celebrate, and there's always something exciting going on somewhere. For more festivals and events around Andalucía, see p432 and individual destination sections.

- Carnaval (Carnival) February or March; wildest in Cádiz (p179)
- Semana Santa (Holy Week) March or April; grandest in Seville (p113)
- Feria de Abril (April Fair; p114) April or early May; Seville
- Motorcycle Grand Prix (p199) April or May; Jerez de la Frontera
- Feria del Caballo (Horse Fair; p195) early May; Jerez de la Frontera
- Concurso de Patios Cordobeses (Patio Competition; p308) first half of May; Córdoba
- Romería del Rocío (Pilgrimage to El Rocío; p157) May or June; El Rocío
- Festival Internacional de Música y Danza (International Music & Dance Festival; p372) late June and early July; Granada
- Feria de Málaga (Málaga Fair; p257) mid-August; Málaga
- Bienal de Flamenco (p114) September of even-numbered years; Seville

Outdoor Adventures

Andalucía has no shortage of challenges to set the adrenaline pumping – for plenty more ideas see the Andalucía Outdoors chapter (p71).

- Canyoning the Garganta Verde (p207)
- Climbing the sheer walls of El Chorro gorge (p287)
- Paragliding over the Mediterranean coast at La Herradura (p395)
- Windsurfing Tarifa (p218)
- Kitesurfing Tarifa (p218)
- Dolphin- and whale-watching in the Strait of Gibraltar (p219)
- Walking Las Alpujarras (p386) and the Sierra Nevada (p382)
- Skiing at Europe's southernmost ski station, Sierra Nevada (p383)
- Horse riding in Las Alpujarras (p389)
- Watching for deer, ibex, boar and mouflon as you walk in the verdant Parque Natural Sierras de Cazorla, Segura y las Villas (p347)

Hotel Conversions

Some of Andalucía's most charming hotels used to be urban palaces or country farmhouses.

- Las Navezuelas, Cazalla de la Sierra (p141) 16th-century farm, winery, olive mill
- La Casa Grande, Arcos de la Frontera (p202) Rambling cliffside mansion
- Alquería de Morayma, Cádiar (p392) Alpujarras farmstead
- Casa de Carmona, Carmona (p134) 16th-century town palace
- Sierra y Mar, Ferreirola (p391) Alpujarras village houses
- Parador de Granada, Granada (p375) 16th-century monastery within the Alhambra; original burial place of the Reyes Católicos (Catholic Monarchs)
- Hotel Carmen de Santa Inés, Granada (p373) Islamic house in the Albayzín
- Las Casas del Rey de Baeza, Seville (p117) 18th-century communal-housing patios
- Hospedería Las Cortes de Cádiz, Cádiz (p180) Elegant 1850s mansion
- Hospedería de la Cartuja, Cazalla de la Sierra (p141) 15th-century country monastery

Andalucía: A Portrait of Southern Spain (1984) Naturalist Nicholas Luard does a similar job for the country behind Tarifa and Algeciras in the 1960s and '70s.

The Almond Blossom Appreciation Society (2006) Chris Stewart's third book about his quirky life in Las Alpujarras (and before) – this time with a Moroccan angle too.

INTERNET RESOURCES

Andalucía te Quiere (Andalucía Loves You; www.andalucia.org) Encyclopedic official tourism site of Turismo Andaluz, with detailed information on every city, town and village, directories of everything from accommodation to recommended hikes, and around 100 maps.

British Embassy in Madrid (www.ukinspain.com) Good practical information.

Lonely Planet (www.lonelyplanet.com) Succinct summaries on travel in Andalucía; the popular Thorn Tree forum; travel features; services for travellers; downloads and lots more.

OKSpain (www.okspain.org) Site of the Spanish tourist offices in the USA, with good links.

Welcome to Spain (www.spain.info) Site of Turespaña, Spain's national tourism authority: tons of useful stuff.

Itineraries

CLASSIC ROUTES

THE BIG THREE
10 Days to Two Weeks

Capture the essence of Andalucía's culture and history by visiting its three great World Heritage cities: **Seville** (p91), **Córdoba** (p300) and **Granada** (p356), home to Andalucía's most outstanding medieval Islamic monuments. You can fly in or out of Seville or Granada, or take a return flight to Málaga and journey overland to Seville at the start of the trip.

Seville's great monument is the glittering **Alcázar** palace (p99), but don't miss the city's monumental Gothic **cathedral** (p97) and its great flowering of baroque churches. Or head to Andalucía's finest Roman site at nearby **Itálica** (p130). From Seville, move northeast to Córdoba, home of Spain's most influential and magnificent Islamic building, the **Mezquita** (p301), as well as the Christian **Alcázar de los Reyes Cristianos** (p307). Get out of the city to visit the vast caliphs' palace **Medina Azahara** (p306). From Córdoba, head southeast to the fabled city of Granada, overlooked by the magnificent jewel of the **Alhambra** palace (p359) and its exquisite **Generalife** gardens (p364). Move on to explore Andalucía's best-preserved old Islamic quarter, the **Albayzín** (p367), but don't neglect Granada's great Christian heritage, at its most evocative in the historic **Capilla Real** (p365). For a change of pace, head out of Granada to mainland Spain's highest mountains, the **Sierra Nevada** (p382).

Seville to Granada via Córdoba is only 300km. Allowing for one night in Málaga at the start or end of the trip, and half a day for travel on each leg of the route, you can see heaps with four nights in Seville, two in Córdoba and three in Granada. If you have extra days, so much the better.

EASTERN DELIGHTS   Three Weeks

If you're travelling through eastern Andalucía, it's a perfect opportunity to explore the remains of the region's two principal historical eras: the eight centuries of Islamic rule (AD 711–1492) and the subsequent Reconquista (Christian reconquest). There are moody castles, vibrant fortresses and elegant architecture, and we've added an opportunity for some beach time.

Start in Málaga, with its monumental **Castillo de Gibralfaro** (p245), delightful **Alcazaba palace** (p247) and massive post-reconquest **cathedral** (p244). Head north to the architectural gem of **Antequera** (p288), home to some 30 churches and a history that reaches back nearly 5000 years to its prehistoric **dolmens** (p289). Carrying on north brings you to Córdoba, whose famous **Mezquita** (p301) is all about the architectural clash between Islamic simplicity and Christian flamboyance. Explore the dramatic hilltop castles that stood near the Muslim-Christian frontier in later Islamic times, such as those at **Almodóvar del Río** (p317) and **Zuheros** (p319), and Jaén's all-seeing **Castillo de Santa Catalina** (p330). The rolling countryside you pass through once nurtured wealthy rural towns such as **Priego de Córdoba** (p320) and the exquisitely unique Renaissance towns of **Úbeda** (p339) and **Baeza** (p334).

Turning south, go to Granada, home to the incomparable **Alhambra** (p359), the last Islamic fortress to fall in the Reconquista. Then make for Almería, overlooked by one of Andalucía's finest fortresses, the **Alcazaba** (p401). Before returning to Málaga take a few relaxing days to enjoy the unspoilt beaches along the unique **Cabo de Gata** (p410) coastline.

Three weeks should be plenty of time for this circuit. Public transport links most of the towns but timetables can be restrictive, making travel by your own car preferable.

Driving through olive fields, Europe's only desert and down the Mediterranean coast, while stopping along the way for the best of eastern Andalucía's fantastic architecture, plus swimming at some of Spain's best beaches – it's a dream trip. The 850km can be done leisurely in three weeks, giving you extra time to explore off the beaten track.

BEST OF THE WEST
Three to Four Weeks

Start this loop of western Andalucía with a couple of nights in **Málaga** (p242), a vivacious city whose recently opened **Museo Picasso** (p245) is drawing attention to its cultural depths. Then head across to spectacular, historic **Ronda** (p277) and move on west into Cádiz province to the little village of **Grazalema** (p204), a good base for some marvellous walks through the area's verdant, undulating landscapes.

Continuing westward, stop off at the dramatic and ancient cliff-top town of **Arcos de la Frontera** (p200), before you reach **Jerez de la Frontera** (p191), home of sherry and fine horses, and a hotbed of flamenco. Move north for a few days to experience the buzzing and beautiful regional capital, **Seville** (p91), then back south to another of the highly individual towns of the 'sherry triangle', **Sanlúcar de Barrameda** (p188), to enjoy the town's famed succulent seafood and sherrylike wine, manzanilla. From Sanlúcar take a trip to the vast and incomparably vital wetlands of the **Parque Nacional de Doñana** (p154), then plunge into the historic, atmospheric port city of **Cádiz** (p174). Now head down the Costa de la Luz, where Andalucía's most glorious stretches of sand front the Atlantic Ocean. The small coastal getaways of **Los Caños de Meca** (p211), **Zahara de los Atunes** (p213) and **Bolonia** (p214) are all ideal for chilling out before you reach **Tarifa** (p215) at Spain's southern tip, an ancient town with a hip international scene based loosely around windsurfing and kitesurfing.

En route back to Málaga, stop at the spectacular historical anomaly that is **Gibraltar** (p228) and, if the Costa del Sol tweaks your curiosity, **Marbella** (p270).

This western circuit around some of Andalucía's best natural and cultural attractions is 800km. Three weeks gives time to enjoy it but four weeks allows you to really savour the spectacular scenery, explore the historic towns and cities in depth, linger in the sherry houses and truly lie back on the beaches.

TAILORED TRIPS

LANDSCAPES TO DREAM ON

Andalucía's landscapes both pamper and shock the senses. Lovers of the hills will adore the little-trumpeted **Sierra de Aracena** (p167) at the western extremity of the rolling Sierra Morena with its evergreen oak forests and timeless villages, and the large **Parque Natural Sierras de Cazorla, Segura y las Villas** (p347) in the northeast, with its majestic topography and Andalucía's greatest numbers of visible large mammals – deer, boar, mouflon and ibex. The summit, though, is the **Sierra Nevada** (p382). Here rises mainland Spain's highest peak, **Mulhacén** (3479m; p385) in the midst of an awesome high-altitude wilderness with a population of some 5000 ibex. By contrast the Sierra Nevada's southern flank harbours one of Europe's most harmoniously human-influenced landscapes – the ancient white villages of **Las Alpujarras** (p386), among green hillside orchards, thick woodlands and rapid streams.

Andalucian beachscapes are by far their best along the sandy Atlantic littoral, and nowhere more attractive than on the massive sand dunes of **Ensenada de Valdevaqueros** (p218) and **Bolonia** (p214). A little further up this coast are the infinite wetlands of the **Parque Nacional de Doñana** (p154), teeming with deer, wild boar and birdlife.

Over at Andalucía's southeastern tip you'll find its most otherworldly landscape, **Cabo de Gata** (p410), Europe's driest area, with near-deserts running down to a coast of turquoise waters and beautiful beaches strung between fearsome cliffs.

ANDALUCÍA FOR KIDS

Beaches, beaches everywhere, but away from the salt water, kids of most ages won't fail to be excited by the attractions along the Costa del Sol west of Málaga: **Aquapark** (p268) and **Crocodile Park** (p268) in Torremolinos; **Tivoli World** (p268) amusement park, **SeaLife** (p268) aquarium and the **Selwo Marina** (p268) dolphinarium at Benalmádena; **Parque Acuático Mijas** (p268) in Fuengirola; and **Selwo Aventura** (p268) wildlife park near Estepona.

In **Gibraltar** (p228) kids love the cable car, the apes and the caves of the upper rock. Next stop: Jerez de la Frontera for its **zoo** (p195) and the prancing horses of the **Real Escuela Andaluza del Arte Ecuestre** (p194). In Seville, **Isla Mágica** (p111) is a highlight for all white-knuckle thrill-seekers.

Head west to visit the old metal mines and vintage train at **Minas de Riotinto** (p162) and enjoy another subterranean experience at Aracena's **Gruta de las Maravillas** (p166). Call in at the **Reserva Natural Castillo de las Guardas** wildlife park (p113) on your way east to Granada's hands-on science museum, the **Parque de las Ciencias** (p371), and **Mini Hollywood** (p407), a Wild West movie town in the desert north of Almería. En route back to Málaga, stop in at the **Parque Ornitológico Loro-Sexi** (p394), Almuñécar's tropical bird aviary, and the spectacular **Cueva de Nerja** (p297).

EATING FOR EPICURES

Work up a good appetite swimming on Málaga's beaches and dine on octopus and beetroot rice in **Café de Paris** (p261). Famished after schlepping around the Alhambra? Grab fantastic seafood at Granada's **Los Diamantes** (p375), North African tapas in **Om-Khalsum** (p376), or drool over a lamb *tagine* in **Restaurante Arrayanes** (p376). Following a day of swimming on the spectacular Cabo de Gata, replenish in Almería city on delicious deer cutlets with caramel treacle at **La Encina Restaurante** (p405). The elegance of Úbeda's architecture is complemented by the food at **Taberna La Imprenta** (p344) where the prawns are saucy, the asparagus is wild and the chocolate cake positively dangerous. Celebrate Córdoba's abundance in good food with a slice of famed **Bar Santos** (p313) tortilla. Tapas are excellent at the **Taberna San Miguel** (p313). Dine at **Bodega Campos** (p314) where royals, stars and presidents have eaten. Taste Seville's best tapas at **Los Coloniales** (p121) where the *churrasco* (cutlets) are the size of a small African country. Explosive, inventive dishes by the world's best chef, Ferrán Adriá, are at **Hacienda Benazuza** (p118). The best of Huelva province is Alájar's **Casa Padrino** (p169), where scrambled eggs with freshly picked wild herbs go splendidly with wine. And finally, Cádiz city is master of seafood: **El Aljibe** (p181) plays with tradition, stuffing halibut with seafood and burying it in puff pastry. *¡Buen provecho!*

A BEACH HOLIDAY

Andalucía's best beaches are undoubtedly along **Costa de la Luz** in Cádiz and Huelva provinces. **Tarifa** (p215) has tiny, popular **Playa Chica**, and the 10km white-sand **Playa de los Lances**, at the end of which stands a dreamy sand dune. **El Palmar** (p210) is a popular spot with trendy *madrileños*, who flock here for the peace and lack of development. **Los Caños de Meca** (p211) has beautiful sandy bays overlooked by a pine forest, and gets busy with a relaxed, shabby-chic crowd and plenty of surfers. One of the top beaches along this coast is at the fashionable **Zahara de los Atunes** (p213).

The coast of Huelva province is one long, wide sandy beach over 100km long, whose peace is being threatened by holiday development, so tread lightly. Sixty kilometres of beach and windswept dunes with a thick, protective barrier of pines run southeast from the outskirts of Huelva. Check out the 100m-high dunes at **Cuesta de Maneli** (p153) and, going towards the Portuguese border, the superb beaches at **Isla Cristina** (p160) and **Punta Umbría** (p159), where some adventurous beachgoers try their hand at kitesurfing the coast. More languorous beach bums will love the perfect beaches of **Parque Natural de Cabo de Gata-Níjar** (p410). Charming little coves, such as Cala del Barranco, Cala Grande and Cala Chica, are excellent for a day of beach hopping and picnicking.

Snapshot

Andalucians continue to bask in their biggest economic boom since Christopher Columbus found America and turned Seville into the richest city on earth. Thanks to a decade of growth in tourism and construction and two decades of EU subsidies and finance for agriculture and infrastructure, unemployment in Andalucía is at its lowest levels in memory (14% in 2006 – a figure that ignores the many Andalucians who work while registered as unemployed).

Since the left-of-centre Partido Socialista Obrero Español (PSOE; Spanish Socialist Workers' Party) regained power at national level in 2004, Andalucía – whose regional government is also in the hands of the PSOE – has enjoyed improved cooperation with Madrid on a range of issues, from strategies to save the Iberian lynx (see p64) to renegotiation of the regional autonomy statute that defines the separation of powers between Madrid and Seville (Sevilla in Spanish).

Andalucía is also at last (albeit far too late) taking some steps to check the rampant overdevelopment of its coasts and some of the corruption, international crime and environmental degradation that feeds on this. A series of big police operations in 2005 and 2006 saw dozens of people arrested in crackdowns on international money laundering on the Costa del Sol, and the mayor, deputy mayor and over 50 others arrested in the notorious resort town of Marbella in connection with a web of bribery and illegal building permits (see p34).

Meanwhile Andalucía continues successfully to meet another new challenge thrown up by the 21st century in the form of unprecedentedly high levels of immigration – not just sun-seeking, wealth-bringing northern Europeans but also economic migrants from impoverished Africa (especially from nearby Morocco), Latin America and Eastern Europe (see p39). Ethnic harmony is something all Spain is striving doubly hard to maintain and Andalucía, historically a crossroads and meeting place of so many cultures, seems to be maintaining its traditions of racial integration.

In the half-century since tourism was launched on the Costa del Sol, Andalucía has transformed itself from an impoverished, hungry, rural backwater with a barren coastline to a prosperous region with increasingly cosmopolitan, fashionable and cultured cities, high levels of consumption, a coast lined with international holiday resorts, universal schooling, large universities and much more relaxed social codes. Wages, educational standards and employment levels still lag below the Spanish average, but the air of confidence and progress is palpable. There are, however, one or two little clouds on the economic horizon that may make the late 2000s slightly less golden. The construction and property boom finally showed signs of plateauing in 2005–06, and the enlargement of the EU to 25 countries in 2004 means that Spain will become a net contributor to the EU budget after two decades as a large-scale recipient of funds. Meanwhile, in contrast to its overweight construction and tourism industries and still large agricultural sector, Andalucía lags in technological industries. With 18% of Spain's population, it produces only 5.4% of the national output from technologically advanced industry. Diversification has to be a key to its future.

FAST FACTS

Area: 87,000 sq km
(Portugal: 92,000 sq km)

Human population:
7.9 million
(Spain: 44 million)

Lynx population: under 200 (Spain: under 200)

Thoroughbred horses confiscated in 2006 Marbella corruption investigation: 103

Wolf population: 60 to 80 (Spain: 2000 to 2500)

Olive trees: 80 million (Spain: 120 million)

Registered unemployment (2006): 14% (Spain: 9%)

Average monthly wage (2005): €1482 (Spain: €1682)

Annual visitors to Alhambra: 2 million

Half-bottles of manzanilla consumed in Seville's Feria de Abril: 800,000

History

Andalucía stands where the Mediterranean Sea meets the Atlantic Ocean and Europe gives way to Africa. From prehistoric times to the 17th century, this location put it at the forefront of Spanish history and at times made it a mover in world history. Then centuries of economic management turned Andalucía into a backwater, a condition from which it only started to emerge in the 1960s.

IN THE BEGINNING

A bone fragment found in 1982 near Orce (Granada province) could be the oldest known human remnant in Europe. It is probably one to two million years old and is believed to be from the skull of an ancestor of the modern *Homo sapiens*.

The Palaeolithic or Old Stone Age, which lasted beyond the end of the last Ice Age to about 8000 BC, was not as cold in Andalucía as in more northerly regions, permitting hunter-gatherers to live here in reasonable numbers. They left impressive rock paintings at the Cueva de Ardales (p286), the Cueva de la Pileta (p284) near Ronda, and elsewhere.

The Neolithic or New Stone Age reached eastern Spain from Egypt and Mesopotamia around 6000 BC, bringing innovations such as the plough, crops, domesticated livestock, pottery, textiles and villages. Between 3000 and 2000 BC, metalworking culture arose at Los Millares (p407), near Almería. This Copper Age gave rise to a megalithic culture, during which tombs known as dolmens were built of large rocks. Spain's best dolmens are near Antequera (p289), Málaga province.

Around 1900 BC the people of El Argar in Almería province learned to make bronze, an alloy of copper and tin that is stronger than copper. El Argar was probably the first Bronze Age settlement on the Iberian Peninsula.

The olive tree, the vine, the donkey and writing were all brought to Andalucía by the Phoenicians and the Greeks.

TARTESSOS

By about 1000 BC, a flourishing culture rich in agriculture, animals and metals arose in western Andalucía. Phoenician traders, from present-day Lebanon, arrived to exchange perfumes, ivory, jewellery, oil, wine and textiles for Andalucian silver and bronze. They set up coastal trading settlements at Adra (west of Almería), Almuñécar (which they called Ex or Sex), Málaga (Malaca), Cádiz (Gadir) and Huelva (Onuba). In the 7th century BC the Greeks came too, trading much the same goods.

The Phoenician- and Greek-influenced culture of western Andalucía in the 8th and 7th centuries BC, with Phoenician-type gods and advanced methods of working gold, is known as the Tartessos culture. Iron replaced bronze as the most important metal. Tartessos was described centuries later by Greek, Roman and biblical writers as the source of fabulous riches. Whether Tartessos was a city, a state or just a region no-one knows. Some argue that it was a trading settlement near modern Huelva; others believe it may lie beneath the marshes near the mouth of the Río Guadalquivir.

TIMELINE	8th & 7th centuries BC	206 BC
	Phoenician- and Greek-influenced Tartessos culture flourishes in western Andalucía	Itálica, first Roman town in Spain, founded near modern Seville

CARTHAGINIAN & ROMAN ANDALUCÍA

From the 6th century BC the Phoenicians and Greeks were pushed out of the western Mediterranean by a former Phoenician colony in modern Tunisia – Carthage. Around the same time the people known as Iberians, from further north in Spain, set up a number of small, often one-village statelets in Andalucía.

The Carthaginians inevitably came into conflict with the next new Mediterranean power, Rome. After losing out to Rome in the First Punic War (264–241 BC), fought for control of Sicily, Carthage conquered southern Spain. The Second Punic War (218–201 BC) brought Roman legions to fight Carthage in Spain. Rome's victory at Ilipa, near modern Seville, in 206 BC, was conclusive. The first Roman town in Spain, Itálica (p130), was founded near the battlefield soon afterwards.

Andalucía quickly became one of the most civilised and wealthiest areas of the Roman Empire. Rome imported Andalucian wheat, vegetables, grapes, olives, copper, silver, lead, fish and *garum* (a spicy seasoning derived from fish, made in factories whose remains can be seen at Bolonia, p214, and Almuñécar, p394). Andalucía also gave Rome two emperors, Trajan and Hadrian, both from Itálica. Rome brought Spain aqueducts, temples, theatres, amphitheatres, baths, its main language (Spanish is basically colloquial Latin 2000 years on), a sizable Jewish population (Jews spread throughout the Mediterranean part of the Roman Empire) and, in the 3rd century AD, Christianity.

> 'Andalucía quickly became one of the most civilised and wealthiest areas of the Roman Empire'

THE VISIGOTHS

When the Huns arrived in Europe from Asia in the late 4th century AD, displaced Germanic peoples moved westwards across the weakening Roman Empire, some overrunning the Iberian Peninsula. One Germanic group, the Visigoths, eventually made it their own in the 6th century, with Toledo, in central Spain, as their capital.

The long-haired Visigoths, numbering about 200,000, had little culture of their own and their precarious rule over the relatively sophisticated Hispano-Romans was undermined by strife among their own nobility. But ties between the Visigothic monarchy and the Hispano-Romans were strengthened in 587 when King Reccared converted to Roman Christianity from the Visigoths' Arian version (which denied that Christ was God).

AL-ANDALUS: ISLAMIC RULE

Following the death of the prophet Mohammed in 632, Arabs carried the religion he founded, Islam, through the Middle East and North Africa. If you believe the myth, they were ushered onto the Iberian Peninsula by the sexual exploits of the last Visigothic king, Roderic. Chronicles relate how Roderic seduced young Florinda, the daughter of Julian, the Visigothic governor of Ceuta in North Africa; Julian allegedly sought revenge by approaching the Muslims with a plan to invade Spain. In reality, Roderic's rivals probably just sought help in the ongoing struggle for the Visigothic throne.

In 711 Tariq ibn Ziyad, the Muslim governor of Tangier, landed at Gibraltar with around 10,000 men, mostly Berbers (indigenous North

6th century AD	**AD 711**
Visigoths, a Christian Germanic people, take control of the Iberian Peninsula	Muslim invaders land at Gibraltar and overrun the Iberian Peninsula within a few years

Africans). Roderic's army was decimated, probably near the Río Guadalete or Río Barbate in Cádiz province, and he is thought to have drowned as he fled. Within a few years, the Muslims had taken over the whole Iberian Peninsula except for small areas in the Asturian mountains in the far north. The Muslims (sometimes referred to as the Moors) were to be the dominant force on the Iberian Peninsula for nearly four centuries and a potent force for a further four. Between wars and rebellions, the Islamic areas of the peninsula developed the most cultured society in medieval Europe. The name given to these Muslim territories as a whole was Al-Andalus, which lives on today in the modern name of what was always the Muslim heartland – Andalucía.

Moorish Spain by Richard Fletcher is an excellent short history of Al-Andalus, concentrating to a large extent on Andalucía.

Al-Andalus' frontiers were constantly shifting as the Christians strove to regain territory in the stuttering 800-year Reconquista (Christian reconquest), but up to the mid-11th century the small Christian states developing in northern Spain were too weak and quarrelsome to pose much of a threat to Al-Andalus, even though the Muslims had their internal conflicts too.

Islamic political power and culture centred first on Córdoba (756–1031), then Seville (c 1040–1248) and lastly Granada (1248–1492). In the main cities, the Muslims built beautiful palaces, mosques and gardens, established bustling *zocos* (markets) and public bathhouses (which most people attended about once a week), and opened universities.

Although military campaigns against the northern Christians could be bloodthirsty affairs, the rulers of Al-Andalus allowed freedom of worship to Jews and Christians under their rule. Jews, on the whole, flourished, but Christians in Muslim territory (Mozarabs; *mozárabes* in Spanish) had to pay a special tax, so most either converted to Islam (to become known as *muladíes*, or Muwallads) or left for the Christian north.

The Muslim ruling class was composed of various Arab groups prone to factional friction. Below them was a larger group of Berbers, living mostly on second-grade land, who rebelled on numerous occasions. Before long, Muslim and local blood merged in Spain and most Spaniards today are partly descended from the Muslims.

The Muslim period left a profound stamp on Andalucía, and not only in terms of architecture. The region's predilection for fountains, running water and decorative plants goes back to Muslim times, and many of the foods eaten in Andalucía today – and even their names, such as *arroz* (rice), *naranja* (orange) and *azúcar* (sugar) – were introduced by the Muslims. And they're still grown on irrigated terracing systems created in Muslim times.

The 9th-century 'Andalucian Robin Hood', Omar ibn Hafsun, waged prolonged rebellion against the Cordoban emirate from his hilltop hideout, Bobastro.

The Cordoban Emirate (756–929)

Initially, Muslim Spain was a province of the emirate of North Africa. In 750 the Omayyad dynasty of caliphs in Damascus, supreme rulers of the Muslim world, was overthrown by a group of non-Arab revolutionaries, the Abbasids, who shifted the caliphate to Baghdad. One of the Omayyad family, Abd ar-Rahman, escaped the slaughter and somehow made his way to Morocco and thence to Córdoba, where in 756 he set himself up as an independent ruler. Abd ar-Rahman I's Omayyad dynasty more or less unified Al-Andalus for 2½ centuries.

756–929	929–1031
Muslim Emirate of Córdoba rules most of the Iberian Peninsula	Caliphate of Córdoba, the political and cultural apogee of Al-Andalus (Muslim-ruled parts of Spain and Portugal)

The Cordoban Caliphate (929–1031)

In 929 Abd ar-Rahman III (r 912–61) gave himself the title caliph (meaning deputy to Mohammed and therefore supreme leader of the Muslim
world) to assert his authority in the face of the Fatimids, a growing
Muslim power in North Africa. Thus Abd ar-Rahman III launched the
caliphate of Córdoba, which at its peak encompassed three-quarters of
the Iberian Peninsula and some of North Africa. Córdoba became the
biggest, most dazzling and most cultured city in Western Europe. Its
Mezquita (Mosque; p301) is one of the wonders of Islamic architecture
anywhere on the planet. Astronomy, medicine, mathematics, philosophy,
history and botany flourished, and Abd ar-Rahman III's court was frequented by Jewish, Arabian and Christian scholars.

The famous 10th-century
Córdoba caliph Abd
ar-Rahman III had red
hair and blue eyes; one of
his grandmothers was a
Basque princess.

Later in the 10th century, the fearsome Cordoban general Al-Mansur (or
Almanzor) terrorised the Christian north with 50-odd *razzias* (forays) in
20 years. In 997 he destroyed the cathedral at Santiago de Compostela in
northwestern Spain – home of the cult of Santiago Matamoros (St James
the Moor-Slayer), a crucial inspiration to Christian warriors. But after
Al-Mansur's death, the caliphate disintegrated into dozens of *taifas* (small
kingdoms), ruled by local potentates, who were often Berber generals.

The Almoravids & Almohads

In the 1040s Seville, located in the wealthy lower Guadalquivir Valley,
emerged as the strongest *taifa* in Andalucía. By 1078 the writ of its Abbasid dynasty ran all the way from southern Portugal to Murcia, restoring
a measure of peace and prosperity to Andalucía.

Meanwhile, the northern Christian states were starting to threaten.
When one of them, Castile, captured Toledo in 1085, a scared Seville
begged for help from the Almoravids, a strict Muslim sect of Saharan
Berbers who had conquered Morocco. The Almoravids came, defeated
Castile's Alfonso VI, and ended up taking over Al-Andalus too, ruling
it from Marrakesh as a colony and persecuting Jews and Christians. But
the charms of Al-Andalus seemed to relax the Almoravids' austere grip:
revolts spread across the territory from 1143 and within a few years it
had again split into *taifas*.

In Morocco, the Almoravids were displaced by a new, strict Muslim
Berber sect, the Almohads, who in turn invaded Al-Andalus in 1160,
bringing it under full control by 1173. Al-Andalus was by now considerably reduced from its 10th-century heyday: the frontier now ran from
south of Lisbon to north of Valencia. The Almohads made Seville capital
of their whole realm and revived arts and learning in Al-Andalus.

In 1195, King Yusuf Yacub al-Mansur thrashed Castile's army at Alar-
cos, south of Toledo, but this only spurred the northern Christian states
to join forces against him. In 1212 the combined armies of Castile,
Aragón and Navarra routed a large Almohad force at Las Navas de Tolosa
(p333) in northeastern Andalucía. Then, with the Almohad state riven
by a succession dispute after 1224, the Christian kingdoms of Portugal,
León and Aragón moved down the southwest, central west and east of
the Iberian Peninsula respectively, and Castile's Fernando III (El Santo,
the Saint) moved into Andalucía, taking strategic Baeza in 1227, Córdoba
in 1236 and Seville, after a two-year siege, in 1248.

1212	1248–1492
Battle of Las Navas de Tolosa: northern Spanish Christian army defeats Almohad rulers of Al-Andalus	Emirate of Granada remains as last Muslim state on the Iberian Peninsula

The Nasrid Emirate of Granada

The Granada emirate was a wedge of territory carved out of the disintegrating Almohad realm by Mohammed ibn Yusuf ibn Nasr, after whom it's known as the Nasrid emirate. Comprising primarily the modern provinces of Granada, Málaga and Almería, with a population of about 300,000, it held out for nearly 250 years as the last Muslim state on the Iberian Peninsula.

Spanish History Index (http://vlib.iue.it/hist -spain/Index.html) provides countless internet leads for those who want to dig deeper.

The Nasrids ruled from the lavish Alhambra palace (p359), which witnessed the final flowering of Islamic culture in Spain. The emirate reached its peak in the 14th century under Yusuf I and Mohammed V, creators of the greatest splendours of the Alhambra. Its final downfall was precipitated by two incidents. One was Emir Abu al-Hasan's refusal in 1476 to pay any further tribute to Castile; the other was the unification in 1479 of Castile and Aragón, the peninsula's biggest Christian states, through the marriage of their monarchs Isabel and Fernando (Isabella and Ferdinand). The Reyes Católicos (Catholic Monarchs), as the pair are known, launched the final crusade of the Reconquista, against Granada, in 1482.

Harem jealousies and other feuds between Granada's rulers degenerated into a civil war which allowed the Christians to push across the emirate, devastating the countryside. They captured Málaga in 1487, and Granada itself, after an eight-month siege, on 2 January 1492.

The surrender terms were fairly generous to the last emir, Boabdil (p356), who received Las Alpujarras valleys, south of Granada, as a personal fiefdom. He stayed only a year, however, before leaving for Africa. The Muslims were promised respect for their religion, culture and property, but this didn't last long.

Pious Isabel and Machiavellian Fernando succeeded in uniting Spain under one rule for the first time since the Visigothic days. Both are buried in Granada's Capilla Real (p365) – an indication of the importance they attached to their conquest of the city.

CHRISTIAN CONTROL

In areas that fell under Christian control in the 13th century, many of the Muslim population fled to Granada or North Africa. Those who remained became known as Mudejars. The new Christian rulers handed large tracts of land to their nobility and knights who had played a vital part in the Reconquista. Muslim raids from Granada caused lesser Christian settlers to sell their smallholdings to the nobility and knightly orders, whose holdings thereby increased. The landowners turned much of their vast estates over to sheep, ruining former food-growing land, and by 1300, rural Christian Andalucía was almost empty.

Fernando III's son Alfonso X (El Sabio, the Learned; r 1252–84) made Seville one of Castile's capitals and launched something of a cultural revival there, gathering scholars around him, particularly Jews, who could translate ancient texts into Castilian Spanish. With the Castilian nobility content to sit back and count their profits from wool production, Jews and foreigners, especially Genoese, came to dominate Castilian commerce and finance.

1481	1492
First tribunal of the Spanish Inquisition, held in Seville	Spain's Catholic Monarchs, Isabel and Fernando, conquer Granada, expel Jews and fund Columbus' voyage to the Americas

Persecution of the Jews

After the Black Death and a series of bad harvests in the 14th century, discontent found its scapegoat in the Jews, who were subjected to pogroms around the peninsula in the 1390s. As a result, some Jews converted to Christianity (they became known as *conversos*); others found refuge in Muslim Granada. In the 1480s the *conversos* became the main target of the Spanish Inquisition, founded by the Catholic Monarchs. Many *conversos* were accused of continuing to practise Judaism in secret. Of the estimated 12,000 deaths for which the Inquisition was responsible in its three centuries of existence, 2000 took place in the 1480s.

In 1492 Isabel and Fernando ordered the expulsion of every Jew who refused Christian baptism. Around 50,000 to 100,000 converted, but some 200,000, the first Sephardic Jews (Jews of Spanish origin), left for other Mediterranean destinations. A talented middle class was decimated.

For a colourful and not overly long survey of the whole saga of Spanish history, read The Story of Spain by Mark Williams.

Morisco Revolts & Expulsion

The task of converting the Muslims of Granada to Christianity was handed to Cardinal Cisneros, overseer of the Inquisition. He carried out forced mass baptisms, burnt Islamic books and banned the Arabic language. As Muslims found their land being expropriated too, a revolt in Las Alpujarras in 1500 spread right across the former emirate, from Ronda to Almería. Afterwards, Muslims were ordered to convert to Christianity or leave. Most, an estimated 300,000, converted, becoming known as Moriscos (converted Muslims), but they never assimilated to Christian culture. When the fanatically Catholic King Felipe II (Philip II; r 1556–98) forbade them in 1567 to use the Arabic language, Arabic names or Morisco dress, a new revolt in Las Alpujarras spread across southern Andalucía and took two years to put down. The Moriscos were then deported to western Andalucía and more northerly parts of Spain, before being expelled altogether from Spain by Felipe III between 1609 and 1614.

SEVILLE & THE AMERICAS: BOOM & BUST

In April 1492 the Catholic Monarchs granted the Genoese sailor Christopher Columbus (Cristóbal Colón to Spaniards) funds for a voyage across the Atlantic in search of a new trade route to the Orient. Columbus instead found the Americas (see p151) and opened up a whole new hemisphere of opportunity for Spain, especially the river port of Seville.

During the reign of Carlos I (Charles I; r 1516–56), the first of Spain's new Habsburg dynasty, the ruthless but brilliant conquerors Hernán Cortés and Francisco Pizarro subdued the Aztec and Inca empires respectively with small bands of adventurers, and other Spanish conquerors and colonists occupied vast tracts of the American mainland. The new colonies sent huge quantities of silver, gold and other treasure back to Spain, where the crown was entitled to one-fifth of the bullion (the *quinto real,* or royal fifth).

Seville became the hub of world trade, a cosmopolitan melting pot of money-seekers, and remained the major city in Spain until late in the 17th century, even though a small country town called Madrid was named the national capital in 1561. New European ideas and artistic movements reached Seville and made it a focus of Spain's artistic Siglo

Ghosts of Spain (2006) by Giles Tremlett of the Guardian gets right under the skin of contemporary Spain, and its roots in the recent past. If you read only one book on Spain, make it this one.

16th century	17th century
Most remaining Muslims convert to Christianity to avoid expulsion; Seville grows into one of Europe's biggest and richest cities	Moriscos (Muslims converted to Christianity) expelled from Spain (1609–14); economic depression, epidemics and famines

de Oro (Golden Century; p49). The prosperity was shared to some extent by Cádiz, and less so by cities such as Jaén, Córdoba and Granada. But in rural Andalucía a small number of big landowners continued to do little with large tracts of territory except run sheep on them. Most Andalucians owned no land or property.

Spain never developed any strategy for absorbing the American wealth, spending too much on European wars and wasting any chance of becoming an early industrial power. Grain had to be imported while sheep and cattle roamed the countryside.

In the 17th century, silver shipments from the Americas shrank disastrously and epidemics and bad harvests killed some 300,000 people, including half of Seville in 1649. The lower Guadalquivir, Seville's lifeline to the Atlantic, became increasingly silted up and in 1717 control of commerce with the Americas was transferred to the seaport of Cádiz.

THE BOURBONS

Felipe V's (Philip V's) accession to the throne in 1701 marked the beginning of the Spanish Bourbon dynasty, still in place today. In the 18th century Spain made a limited recovery from the social and economic ravages of the previous century. The monarchy financed incipient industries, such as Seville's tobacco factory (p108). A new road, the Carretera General de Andalucía, was built from Madrid to Seville and Cádiz. New land was opened up for wheat and barley, and trade through Cádiz (which was in its heyday) grew. New settlers from other parts of Spain boosted Andalucía's population to about 1.8 million by 1787.

NAPOLEONIC INVASION

When Louis XVI of France (a cousin of Spain's Carlos IV) was guillotined in 1793, Spain declared war on France. Two years later, Spain switched sides, pledging military support for France against Britain in return for French withdrawal from northern Spain. In 1805 a combined Spanish-French navy was defeated by a British fleet under Admiral Nelson off Cape Trafalgar (p211), terminating Spanish sea power.

Two years later, France (under Napoleon Bonaparte) and Spain agreed to divide Portugal, Britain's ally, between the two of them. French forces poured into Spain, supposedly on the way to Portugal, but by 1808 this had become a French occupation of Spain. In the ensuing Spanish War of Independence, or Peninsular War, the Spanish populace took up arms guerrilla-style and, with help from British and Portuguese forces led by the Duke of Wellington, drove the French out by 1813. The city of Cádiz withstood a two-year siege from 1810 to 1812, during which a national parliament convening in the city adopted a new constitution for Spain, proclaiming sovereignty of the people and reducing the rights of the monarchy, nobility and church.

SOCIAL POLARISATION

The Cádiz constitution set the scene for a century of struggle in Spain between liberals, who wanted vaguely democratic reforms, and conservatives who liked the old status quo. King Fernando VII (r 1814–33) revoked

'Spain never developed any strategy for absorbing the American wealth, spending too much on European wars'

1717	1810–12
Control of commerce with the Americas transferred from Seville to Cádiz	Cortes de Cádiz: Spanish parliament meets in Cádiz, holding out under French siege

the new constitution, persecuted opponents and even temporarily re-established the Inquisition. During his reign most of Spain's American colonies seized their independence – desperate news for Cádiz, which had been totally reliant on trade with the colonies.

The Disentailments of 1836 and 1855, when liberal governments auctioned off church and municipal lands to reduce the national debt, were a disaster for the peasants, who lost municipal grazing lands. Andalucía declined into one of Europe's most backward, socially polarised areas. At one social extreme were the few bourgeoisie and rich aristocratic landowners; at the other, a very large number of impoverished *jornaleros* – landless agricultural day labourers who were without work for a good half of the year. Illiteracy, disease and hunger were rife.

In 1873 a liberal government proclaimed Spain a republic – a federal grouping of 17 states – but this 'First Republic' was totally unable to control its provinces and lasted only 11 months, with the army ultimately restoring the monarchy.

Andalucian peasants began to stage uprisings, always brutally quashed. The anarchist ideas of the Russian Mikhail Bakunin, who advocated strikes, sabotage and revolts as the path to spontaneous revolution and a free society governed by voluntary cooperation, gained a big following. The powerful anarchist union, the Confederación Nacional del Trabajo (CNT; National Labour Confederation), was founded in Seville in 1910. By 1919, it had 93,000 members in Andalucía.

In 1923 an eccentric Andalucian general from Jerez de la Frontera, Miguel Primo de Rivera, launched a comparatively moderate military dictatorship for Spain, which won the cooperation of the big socialist union the Unión General de Trabajadores (UGT; General Union of Workers), while the anarchists went underground. Primo was unseated in 1930 as a result of an economic downturn and discontent in the army.

> The Cádiz constitution is nicknamed La Pepa because it was proclaimed (in 1812) on 19 March, the Día de San José (St Joseph's Day). Pepa is the feminine form of Pepe, which is the familiar form of José.

THE SECOND REPUBLIC

When the republican movement scored sweeping victories in Spain's municipal elections in April 1931, King Alfonso XIII departed to exile in Italy. The ensuing Second Republic (1931–36) was an idealistic, tumultuous period that ended in civil war. Leftists and the poor welcomed the republican system; conservatives were alarmed. Elections in 1931 brought in a mixed government, including socialists, centrists and Republicans, but anarchist disruption, an economic slump and disunity on the left all helped the right win new elections in 1933. The left, including the emerging Communists, called increasingly for revolution and by 1934 violence was spiralling out of control.

In the February 1936 elections a left-wing coalition narrowly defeated the right-wing National Front. Society polarised into left and right and violence continued on both sides of the political divide. The anarchist CNT had over one million members and the peasants were on the verge of revolution.

On 17 July 1936 the Spanish garrison at Melilla in North Africa revolted against the leftist government, followed the next day by some garrisons on the mainland. The leaders of the plot were five generals. The Spanish Civil War had begun.

1891–1918	**1936–39**
Impoverished Andalucian rural workers launch waves of anarchist strikes	Spanish Civil War: right-wing Nationalists led by General Franco rebel against left-wing Republican government and win control

THE CIVIL WAR

The civil war split communities, families and friends. Both sides committed atrocious massacres and reprisals, especially in the early weeks. The rebels, who called themselves Nationalists, shot or hanged tens of thousands of supporters of the Republic. Republicans did likewise to those they considered Nationalist sympathisers, including some 7000 priests,

---

FERNANDA LA POTAJA   *Susan Forsyth & Antonio Luque*

Like most Andalucians, Fernanda Navas Arroyo is known by her nickname. Everyone in her village of Cómpeta knows her as La Potaja ('po-*ta*-ha'), a nickname acquired via her husband, who loved the type of stew known as *potaje*. A woman with bright eyes, the hands of a worker and a ready smile, she was born in 1939, just weeks after the end of the civil war.

Since the 1990s Cómpeta, in Málaga province's Axarquía district, has garnered previously unimaginable wealth from building houses for foreigners who choose to live or buy holiday homes in what is a very picturesque corner of the hills. But back in the *años de hambre* (years of hunger) after the civil war, Cómpeta was just another poor, isolated hill village.

Back then, Fernanda's family – Fernanda, her mother, father and four brothers and sisters – all lived in one room. Quarrels broke out every other day with so many hungry people in such a constricted space. Fernanda has early recollections of her father being locked up by the Guardia Civil, accused of taking some sacks of flour.

Then in 1948 her father died. One day soon afterwards, Fernanda remembers, she went to gather some potatoes from a *bancal* (irrigated terrace) near the village. ('To steal to eat is not theft,' she comments.) A man looking after the *bancal* caught her, knocked her to the ground and left her there.

From another incident those in authority don't emerge so badly. When the provincial governor visited Cómpeta in 1950, Fernanda's mother took her badly-dressed, shoeless children out to see him and tugged at his sleeve, asking 'What is going to become of us?' He pulled out 200 pesetas for her – a fortune for the family at that time, and Fernanda recalls that they had food for a month.

Fernanda was sent to live with a family who kept their own goatherd and were able to spare some food for her. 'I ceased to be hungry and my health problems disappeared. Everyone worked. I carried water, washed plates and clothes: there are always things to do in a house. I never went to school: I can't read but I can spell some things.'

At 18 she left the village to work two summers with an aunt in hotels in Galicia, and she was paid well. Each week, she sent her mother an envelope containing 100 pesetas.

She married at 21, after five years' courtship, at six in the morning (at that early hour because she didn't have the required white dress). She soon bore children. Two of the five died. Today two work in construction and the third is a dance teacher. Fernanda was widowed at 35, two months after she and her husband had bought a small *finca* (rural property) for 200,000 pesetas. She went to work, and finished paying off the *finca* in 1993. Fernanda shows us her hands and tells us with pride that in 1999 they collected 7000kg of olives from the *finca's* trees.

We asked her how life was for women in the 1960s and '70s.

'Women were discriminated against and had little freedom. Few clothes, not much furniture and less freedom. We couldn't talk with men, much less kiss them for fear of being treated as a whore. And a woman go into a bar? Never ever!'

Today Fernanda is happy: happy with her three children and five grandchildren, and very happy with her home, an attic apartment from which she can see the blue sea, and which speaks of work, much work and happiness.

1939–75	1975–78
Spain under Franco's dictatorship; civil war followed by the 'years of hunger'; mass tourism launched on Costa del Sol	Transition to democracy following Franco's death

monks and nuns. Political affiliation often provided a convenient cover for settling old scores. Altogether, an estimated 350,000 Spaniards died in the war (some writers put the figure as high as 500,000).

In Republican-controlled areas, anarchists, Communists or socialists ended up running many towns and cities. Social revolution followed. In Andalucía this tended to be anarchic, with private property abolished and churches and convents often burned and wrecked. Large estates were occupied by the peasants and around 100 agrarian communes were established. The Nationalist campaign, meanwhile, quickly took on overtones of a holy crusade against the enemies of God.

The basic battle lines were drawn very early. Cities whose garrisons backed the rebels (most did) and were strong enough to overcome any resistance fell immediately into Nationalist hands – as happened at Cádiz, Córdoba and Jerez. Seville was in Nationalist hands within three days and Granada within a few more. The Nationalists executed an estimated 4000 people in and around Granada after they took the city, including the great writer Federico García Lorca (see p48). There was slaughter in Republican-controlled areas, too. An estimated 2500 were murdered in a few months in anarchic Málaga. But the Nationalists executed thousands there in reprisals when they and their Fascist Italian allies took the city in February 1937. Much of eastern Andalucía – Almería and Jaén provinces, eastern Granada province and northern Córdoba province – remained in Republican hands until the end of the war.

By late 1936 General Francisco Franco emerged as the undisputed Nationalist leader, styling himself as the Generalísimo (Supreme General). Before long, he also adopted the title Caudillo, roughly equivalent to the German Führer. The scales of the war were tipped in the Nationalists' favour by support from Nazi Germany and Fascist Italy in the form of weapons, planes and 92,000 men (mostly from Italy). The Republicans had some Soviet planes, tanks, artillery and advisers, and 25,000 or so French soldiers fought with them, along with a similar number of other foreigners in the International Brigades.

The Republican government moved from besieged Madrid to Valencia in late 1936, then to Barcelona in autumn 1937. In 1938 Franco swept eastwards, isolating Barcelona, and the USSR withdrew from the war. The Nationalists took Barcelona in January 1939 and Madrid in March. Franco declared the war won on 1 April 1939.

FRANCO'S SPAIN

After the civil war, instead of reconciliation, more blood-letting ensued and the jails filled up with political prisoners. An estimated 100,000 Spaniards were killed, or died in prison, after the war. A few Communists and Republicans continued their hopeless struggle in small guerrilla units in the Andalucian mountains and elsewhere until the 1950s.

Spain stayed out of WWII, but was afterwards excluded from the UN until 1955 and suffered a UN-sponsored trade boycott which helped turn the late 1940s into the años de hambre (years of hunger) – particularly in poor areas such as Andalucía where, at times, peasants subsisted on soup made from wild herbs.

25 Años sin Franco (25 Years without Franco; www.elmundo.es /nacional/XXV_aniversario) is a special 2000 supplement of *El Mundo* newspaper published online – in Spanish, but the photos and graphics tell their own story.

<table>
<tr><td>1982–96</td><td>1982</td></tr>
<tr><td>Sevillan Felipe González, of the left-of-centre Partido Socialista Obrero Español (PSOE) party, is Spain's prime minister</td><td>Under Spain's new regional autonomy system, Andalucía gets its own regional parliament, dominated ever since by PSOE</td></tr>
</table>

COSTA DEL CRIME

The Costa del Sol west of Málaga was long ago nicknamed the Costa del Crime for the fact that crooks from the UK could find refuge there thanks to cumbersome extradition agreements between Spain and Britain. Extradition improved when Spain and Britain signed a Fast Track Judicial Surrender treaty in 2001, but other breeds of criminal continue to find the Costa a happy hunting ground – chiefly thanks to its tourism-based building boom.

The crux of the problem is that Spanish town halls charge fees for granting building permits, and many town halls, especially along the tourism-dominated coast, have become addicted to this income, which can amount to 50% or more of their revenue. Town halls are also keen to encourage construction because it boosts local economies. At the same time, the temptation to municipal corruption is high since developers are so keen to obtain building permits and open up new land for building.

Town halls thus face strong temptations to grant illegal building permits that contravene planning laws by, for example, being within environmentally protected rural areas or green zones within towns, or by cramming too many dwellings into a small area. The consequences of half a century of such development are that huge stretches of Andalucian coast have become ugly concrete jungles, unsightly development has sprawled inland, a culture of corruption has developed in many town halls, and the construction lobby has become almost all-powerful.

A perfect scenario for heavier crime to move into. The Costa del Sol resort town of Marbella has become a byword not only for glitzy ostentation but also for overdevelopment, municipal corruption and international Mafia activity. In 2005, in the so-called Ballena Blanca (White Whale) case, 41 people were arrested in Marbella on suspicion of organising Europe's biggest money-laundering network, worth at least €250 million. Proceeds from drug dealing, contract murders, kidnappings, arms trafficking, prostitution and more had allegedly been 'laundered' and reinvested in Costa del Sol property, via a Marbella law firm.

Then in spring 2006 Marbella's mayor, deputy mayor and several other town-hall officials and associates were among over 50 people arrested in connection with a web of bribery and illegal building permits. They were accused of offences ranging from bribery and misappropriation of public funds to collusion to profit from inflating land prices. Among the property worth €2.4 billion seized by police were 275 works of art, 103 thoroughbred horses, a helicopter and 200 fighting bulls. A caretaking committee appointed to run the town's affairs immediately started sealing off building sites that had been ordered to stop work by Andalucía's supreme court. Up to 30,000 of Marbella's 80,000 homes may have been built illegally, and as many as 5000 of them could face demolition.

Marbella's problems had really begun in the 1990s during the mayoralty of Jesús Gil y Gil, a populist, right-wing construction magnate who perfected the art of running a town for the benefit of himself and his henchmen. He died in 2004.

Marbella is only the worst case. A former mayor of nearby Estepona is doing a five-year jail term for helping a Turkish heroin-trafficking syndicate launder its ill-gotten gains. In another operation in 2005, police arrested 28 alleged Mafia bosses from former Soviet republics on the Costa del Sol and in other Mediterranean Spanish towns. According to police, the mobsters laundered the proceeds of crimes committed back home through a network of property, restaurants and bars in Spain.

The Junta de Andalucía (Andalucía's regional government) at last made some effort to bring construction and corruption under control in 2005 and 2006 by negotiating a series of district plans to control future development and by putting a stop to the worst cases such as Marbella. Files on alleged illegal planning permissions in numerous Andalucian towns and villages were in the hands of public prosecutors at the time of writing. The Junta also plans to dynamite a hotel built on Playa Algarrobico, within the Cabo de Gata natural park in Almería province – a sign that the days of uncontrolled development along Andalucía's coasts may at last be drawing to a close.

1992	1996–2004
Expo '92 world fair in Seville; high-speed AVE Madrid–Seville rail link opens	Spain governed by right-of-centre Partido Popular (PP) party; Andalucía enjoys economic progress fuelled by construction boom

Franco ruled absolutely. He was commander of the army and leader of the sole political party, the Movimiento Nacional (National Movement). Army garrisons were maintained outside every large city, strikes and divorce were banned and church weddings became compulsory.

In Andalucía, some new industries were founded and mass foreign tourism was launched on the Costa del Sol in the late 1950s, but by the 1970s many villages still lacked electricity, reliable water supplies and paved roads – and the education system was pathetically inadequate: today many Andalucians over 50, especially in rural areas, are illiterate.

NEW DEMOCRACY

Franco's chosen successor, Alfonso XIII's grandson Prince Juan Carlos, took the throne, aged 37, two days after Franco's death in 1975. Much of the credit for Spain's ensuing transition to democracy goes to the king. The man he appointed prime minister, Adolfo Suárez, pushed through the Cortes (Spain's parliament) a proposal for a new, two-chamber parliamentary system. In 1977 political parties, trade unions and strikes were legalised and Suárez' centrist party won nearly half the seats in elections to the new Cortes. The left-of-centre Partido Socialista Obrero Español (PSOE; Spanish Socialist Workers' Party), led by a young lawyer from Seville, Felipe González, came second.

Spain enjoyed a sudden social liberation after Franco. Contraceptives, homosexuality, adultery and divorce were legalised, and a vein of hedonism was unleashed that still looms large today.

In 1982 Spain made a final break with the past by voting the PSOE into power. Felipe González was to be prime minister for 14 years, and his party's young, educated leadership included several other Andalucians. The PSOE made big improvements in education, launched a national health system and basked in an economic boom after Spain joined the European Community (now the EU) in 1986.

The PSOE has also dominated Andalucía's regional government in Seville ever since it was inaugurated in 1982, as part of a devolution of limited autonomy to the 17 Spanish regions. Manuel Chaves of the PSOE has headed the Andalucian executive, known as the Junta de Andalucía, since 1990. The PSOE government at the national and regional level eradicated the worst of Andalucian poverty in the 1980s and early 1990s with grants, community works schemes and a generous dole system. Education and health provision have steadily improved and the PSOE government has given Andalucía Spain's biggest network of environmentally protected areas (see p66).

The PSOE lost power nationally in 1996 to the centre-right Partido Popular (PP; People's Party), led by former tax inspector José María Aznar, who presided over eight years of steady economic progress for Spain. Registered unemployment in Andalucía remains the highest in Spain (14% in 2006), but the rate almost halved in the PP years. The Andalucian economy benefited from steady growth in tourism and industry, massive EU subsidies for agriculture (which still provides one job in eight), and a decade-long construction boom.

The early years of the 21st century also saw an important shift in Andalucía's ethnic balance with the arrival of not just more northern

Between 1950 and 1970, 1.5 million Andalucians left to find work in other Spanish regions or other European countries.

You can find Juan Carlos I and the Spanish royal family on the web at www.lacasareal.es.

The Junta de Andalucía has its site at www .juntadeandalucia.es in Spanish, and the Spanish national government at www.la-moncloa.es.

2004	2005
Andalucians stage massive peace marches following Madrid train bombings; PSOE wins national and Andalucian regional elections	Spain legalises gay marriage, with the same adoption and inheritance rights as heterosexual couples

European sun-seekers but also economic migrants, legal and illegal, from Latin America, Morocco, sub-Saharan Africa and Eastern Europe. See p39 for more on this phenomenon.

José María Aznar's high-handed style of governing did not go down well with a lot of Spaniards. His support for the 2003 US-led invasion of Iraq was unpopular, as was his decision to send 1300 Spanish troops to Iraq after the war. The PP was unseated by the PSOE in the 2004 national election, which took place three days after the Madrid train bombings of 11 March in which 191 people were killed and 1755 injured. The new PSOE government pulled Spain's troops out of Iraq within two weeks of taking office. In April 2006, 29 accused, many of them Moroccan, were ordered to stand trial for involvement in the bombings. A two-year investigation by Judge Juan del Olmo had concluded that Islamic extremists inspired by, but not directed by, Osama bin Laden, were responsible for the attacks.

In *The British on the Costa del Sol* (2000), Karen O'Reilly takes an anthropologist's approach to this unusual community (if it can be called that) that hangs between two cultures.

The PSOE's national victory in 2004 was good news for the Junta de Andalucía, still controlled by the PSOE, for which working with Madrid suddenly became a lot easier. Perhaps emboldened by this, the Junta and the police at last took some steps to rein in the rampant overdevelopment of the Andalucian coast and some of the corruption, crime and environmental degradation that went with it (see p34).

2006
Smoking banned in many public places throughout Spain

2006
Mayor, deputy mayor and police chief of Marbella and over 50 others arrested over bribery, corruption and illegal building permits

The Culture

REGIONAL IDENTITY

Andalucians have a huge capacity for enjoying themselves, but that doesn't mean they don't like to work. As someone put it, they work but they don't have a work ethic. Work simply takes its allotted place alongside other equally important aspects of life, such as socialising, entertainment and relaxation. Timetables and organisation are a little less important than in many other Western cultures, but things that Andalucians consider important do get done, and if anything really needs a fixed time (eg trains, cinemas, weddings, sporting events), it gets one.

These are enormously gregarious people, to whom the family is of paramount importance (children are always a good talking point). Andalucians who live away from home – students, people with jobs in other cities – make frequent visits back home at weekends and for the numerous fiestas and public holidays scattered generously through the calendar. Local fairs, religious festivals and family fiestas such as baptisms, first communions and weddings are all important opportunities for families and communities to get together and mark the rhythms of the seasons and of their lives. Andalucians get high on fun, noise, colour, movement, music, emotion and each other's company, and can turn even the most casual of meetings into a party.

With some exceptions – think of the elaborate dress donned by Sevillan society for its fiestas and bullfights – Andalucians are fairly informal in both dress and etiquette, the more so as you move away from the cultured classes of the cities. The Spanish 'gracias' for example is heard far less than 'thank you' in English-speaking countries. While warm smiles and greetings are the norm to visitors and friends alike, and much as Andalucians welcome the fact that millions of foreigners come to spend their money in Andalucía each year, you can't expect the average local to display too much personal interest in the average tourist stuttering out a few syllables of Spanish. Invitations to Andalucian homes are something special.

In terms of its identity within Spain, Andalucía has no serious yearnings for independence or greater autonomy as some Basques and Catalans do. Andalucians are aware of what makes them different within the broader Spanish community – including particularly strong Islamic, Arabic and African influences from their history, yielding perhaps a more instinctive understanding of the north African cultures on their doorstep today, and a greater *gitano* (Roma) influence too, yielding flamenco music and dance – but they still consider themselves very much part of the Castilian nation whose capital is Madrid.

LIFESTYLE

Home for most Andalucians is an apartment in a city or town, furnished in the most modern style its occupants can afford. Many middle-class families live in modern terraced or detached houses in the suburbs or in dormitory towns. Lifestyle progress is generally considered to be a matter of getting away from the rural backwardness of parents and grandparents, even though people maintain personal ties to villages or country towns, and often a small *finca* (country property) where they go for weekends. It's only in the last decade or so that rural tourism has taken off, as city-dwellers rediscover the pleasures of fresh air, greenery and open space.

The underside of Andalucian society is vividly portrayed in Sevillan Alberto Rodríguez's 2005 film *7 Vírgenes* (7 Virgins), about a teenager living 48 hours of intense freedom on leave from a juvenile reform centre. The film has the realism of a documentary and an evocative hip-hop/techno soundtrack.

In 1975 the average An-
dalucian woman would
give birth to 3.1 children;
today she has just 1.4
(slightly above Spain's
national average).

Andalucians – not, as a rule, great travellers – typically opt for a week or so at a seaside resort for their annual holiday.

Though they still attach great importance to their extended families, Andalucians increasingly live in small nuclear groups. The birth rate has fallen dramatically in the last 30 years, and divorces, illegal under Franco, exceeded 14,000 in Andalucía in 2005.

Social life is vitally important to any Andalucian, and especially to those in their teens and 20s, for most of whom it's *de rigueur* to stay out partying deep into the *madrugada* (early hours) on weekends. Teenagers like to gather in large groups in squares and plazas, bringing their own booze to avoid age restrictions and the high cost of drinks in bars – a phenomenon known as the *botellón* (literally, 'big bottle').

Gender roles tend to be more traditionally defined here than in northern Europe and North America. Though many women have paid jobs, their wages are only around 70% of men's and they tend to do most of the domestic work, too. In the villages it's still unusual to see men shopping for food or women standing at bars.

To find out more about
Spanish *gitanos*, start
with the trilingual
(English, Spanish and
Romany) website,
Unión Romaní (www
.unionromani.org).

Openly gay and lesbian life is easier in the bigger cities where gay scenes are bigger and attitudes more cosmopolitan. Spain legalised gay marriage in 2005, giving gay couples the same adoption and inheritance rights as heterosexuals, despite strong opposition from the Catholic church.

POPULATION

Andalucía's population of 7.9 million comprises 18% of the Spanish total. The population is very much weighted to the provincial capitals. Seville (population 710,000), Málaga (558,000), Córdoba (319,000), Granada (238,000) and Huelva (145,000) are all five times as big as any other town in their provinces. About one-fifth of Andalucians live in villages or small towns.

Andalucians have an incredibly diverse bunch of ancestors, including prehistoric hunters from Africa; Phoenicians, Jews and Arabs from the Middle East; Carthaginians and Berbers from North Africa; Visigoths from the Balkans; Celts from central Europe; Romans; and northern Spaniards, themselves descended from a similar mix of ancient peoples. All these influences were deeply intermingled by late medieval times. The *gitanos* probably reached Spain in the 15th century, having headed west from India in about the 9th century. Spain has around 600,000 *gitanos* – more than any other country in Western Europe – and about half of them live in Andalucía, where they have made a distinctive contribution to the culture, notably through flamenco.

The late 20th century brought the first big wave of migration into Andalucía for many centuries and by 2005 Andalucía had a record 420,000 foreign residents, about 11% of the foreign population in Spain (see the boxed text, opposite).

Upcoming soccer fixtures
can be found in the
local press or the sports
papers *AS* or *Marca*, or on
websites such as
BBC Sport (news.bbc
.co.uk/sport) and Planet
Fútbol (planetfutbol
.diariosur.es).

SPORT
Football

Every weekend from September to May, millions follow the national Primera División (First Division) on TV, which devotes acres of airtime to every game.

Andalucía's top clubs are Sevilla and Real Betis (both of Seville; see p127), both usually found around the middle of the Primera División table. Sevilla won the UEFA Cup in 2006. Málaga were relegated from the Primera División in 2006, to be replaced by another Andalucian club (and the oldest in Spain), Recreativo de Huelva (p148). The Segunda División (Second Division) usually has a further half-dozen Andalucian teams. League games are mostly played on Sunday, with a few on Saturday.

Bullfighting

Incomprehensibly cruel though it seems to many, the *corrida de toros* (bullfight) is also a pageant with a long history and many rules, considered a sport-cum-art-cum-fiesta by its aficionados. Many people feel ill at the sight of the kill, and the preceding few minutes' torture is undoubtedly cruel, but aficionados will say that fighting bulls have been bred for conflict and that before the fateful day they are treated like kings. The *corrida* is also about many other things – bravery, skill, performance and a direct confrontation with death. So deeply ingrained in Spanish culture

It was in Huelva, Andalucía, that soccer was introduced to Spain in the 1870s by British sailors; Recreativo de Huelva (founded in 1899) is the oldest club in the country.

THE NEW ANDALUCIANS

British expats are not the only ones trying to forge new lives in Andalucía today. Far from it. Andalucía has undergone an amazing about-face in population movements in just a few decades. The impoverished 1950s and '60s saw 1.5 million hungry Andalucians leave home for Madrid, northern Spain and other European countries in search of work. Today Andalucía has become an importer of people from almost all continents as its growing economy offers the hope of a better life to people of multiple religions, nationalities, aspirations and languages. By 2005, Andalucía had a record 420,000 foreign residents according to official figures. The real figure may be 50% or 100% higher but one thing is certain: the numbers are growing ever faster, and the 2005 total was 30% up on 2004.

About one-third of the foreigners in Andalucía are from Western Europe (principally Britain, Germany, Scandinavia, France and Italy). Those from the north – with Britons the most numerous – are no longer only retired folk seeking a quiet, sunny bolt hole on the coast. Many new arrivals from these countries today are in their 20s, 30s or 40s, often families with children, looking for new opportunities in a sunnier, less expensive environment, encouraged by TV programmes such as *A Place in the Sun*. They'll often settle in villages and towns inland, where property prices are lower than on the coast. They may start off working as builders or in estate agents' offices, or set up small businesses or trades serving other foreigners – shops, restaurants, bakeries, building, decorating or plumbing businesses, tourism services, looking after holiday homes, new estate agencies. Such newcomers are generally welcomed by the local populace for the money and economic activity they bring to an area, even though social integration is erratic. Their kids will usually go to local Spanish schools, speak fluent Spanish with a strong Andalucian accent, and integrate more easily than their parents. Some villages have gained a new lease of life from the construction and property boom engendered by the numbers of northern Europeans moving in (as well as a rash of unsightly and/or illegal housing scattered across the countryside).

Not everyone manages to carve out a living in their place in the sun, of course; plenty return whence they came after a year or two, a pattern that may accelerate if the recent slowdown of the Andalucian property market continues.

At the same time Andalucía is attracting more and more economic migrants of a different kind – Moroccans and sub-Saharan Africans (Africans comprise a quarter of the foreigners living in Andalucía), Latin Americans (another quarter, chiefly from Argentina, Bolivia and Ecuador) and Eastern Europeans (about 15%, mainly from Romania, Bulgaria, the Ukraine and Russia), all desperate to earn higher wages than they can get back home. These migrants flock to fill gaps in the Spanish labour force by doing low-paid jobs such as building and agricultural labour and restaurant work.

So don't be surprised if your Andalucian holiday guesthouse is owned by a Scot, your room is cleaned by a Bolivian chambermaid, your meal is served by an Argentine waiter, the stalls in the local market are run by Bulgarians and Moroccans, and the voices at the building site along the street are Arabic and Russian.

is bullfighting that the question of whether it's cruel just doesn't frame itself to many people. Plenty of people are uninterested in the activity, but relatively few actively oppose it, especially in southern Spain. The anti-bullfighting lobby is bigger and more influential in parts of northern Spain: in Catalonia, stop-bullfighting petitions signed by 549,000 people were presented to the regional president in 2005. Spanish anti-bullfighting organisations include the Barcelona-based **Asociación para la Defensa de los Derechos del Animal** (ADDA; Association for the Defence of Animal Rights; www.addaong.org). The London-based **World Society for the Protection of Animals** (www.wspa.org.uk) also campaigns against bullfighting.

It was probably the Romans who staged Spain's first bullfights. *La lidia*, as the modern art of bullfighting on foot is known, took off in an organised fashion in the 18th century. The Romero family from Ronda, in Málaga province, established most of the basics of bullfighting on foot, and Andalucía has been one of its hotbeds ever since. Previously, bullfighting had been done on horseback, as a kind of cavalry-training-cum-sport for the gentry.

THE FIGHT

If you're interested in exploring Andalucian culture, attending a *corrida* (bullfight) will certainly display one side of this – though it's not for the squeamish, and you may leave little wiser as to why some people get so excited about it all.

Bullfights usually begin at about 6pm and, as a rule, three different matadors will fight two bulls each. Each fight takes about 15 minutes.

After entering the arena, the bull is first moved about by junior bullfighters known as *peones*, wielding great capes. The colourfully attired matador (killer) then puts in an initial appearance and makes *faenas* (moves) with the bull, such as pivoting before its horns. The more closely and calmly the matador works with the bull, the greater the crowd's approbation. The matador leaves the stage to the banderilleros, who attempt to goad the bull into action by plunging a pair of banderillas (short prods with harpoon-style ends) into his withers. Next, the horseback picadors take over, to shove a lance into the withers, greatly weakening the bull. The matador then returns for the final session. When the bull seems tired out and unlikely to give a lot more, the matador chooses the moment for the kill. Facing the animal head-on, the matador aims to sink a sword cleanly into its neck for an instant kill – the *estocada*.

A skilful, daring performance followed by a clean kill will have the crowd on its feet waving handkerchiefs in appeal to the fight president to award the matador an ear of the animal. The president usually waits to gauge the crowd's enthusiasm before finally flopping a white handkerchief onto his balcony.

If you're spoiling for a fight, it's worth looking out for the big names among the matadors. They are no guarantee you'll see an exciting *corrida*, as that also depends on the animals themselves. But names to look for include: Enrique Ponce, a class act from Valnecia; Julián 'El Juli' López, born in Madrid in 1982 (who graduated to senior matador status at the extraordinarily early age of 15); David 'El Fandi' Fandila from Granada, who topped the 2005 *escalafón* (matadors' league table) with 210 ears; Rivera Ordóñez, the son and grandson of celebrated matadors; Manual Díaz 'El Cordobés', son of Manuel Benítez 'El Cordobés', an internationally famous bullfighter of the 1960s; and macho sex symbol Jesulín de Ubrique.

The best bullfighting book for a long time, Edward Lewine's *Death and the Sun* (2005) follows matador Rivera Ordóñez and his supporting team through a whole season, revealing much about why bullfighting evokes such passion and also about the mundane reality behind the moments of high drama.

WHEN & WHERE

The main bullfighting season in Andalucía runs from Easter Sunday to October. Most *corridas* are held as part of a city or town fiesta. A few bullrings (Seville's is one) have regular fights right through the season.

The big bang that launches Andalucía's bullfighting year is Seville's Feria de Abril (April Fair; p114), with fights almost daily during the week of the fair and the week before it. It's Seville, too, where the year ends with a *corrida* on 12 October, Spain's National Day. Here are some of the other major fight seasons on the Andalusian bullfight calendar:

For the latest information on the next bullfight near you, biographies of toreros and more, check out www.portalt aurino.com.

Feria de Nuestra Señora de la Salud Held in Córdoba, a big bullfighting stronghold, in late May/early June (see p310).

Feria de Corpus Christi In Granada in early June 2007, mid-May 2008 (see p372).

Bullfight Season in El Puerto de Santa María Held on most Sundays June to August.

Fiestas Colombinas In Huelva, 3 to 9 August (see p145)

Feria de Málaga Nine-day fair in Málaga, held in mid-August (see p257).

Feria de la Virgen del Mar In Almería in the last week of August (see p403).

Corrida Goyesca Held in Ronda in early September (see p281), with select matadors fighting in costumes such as those shown in bullfight engravings by Francisco de Goya.

Bullfighting magazines such as the weekly *6 Toros 6* carry details of who's fighting where and when, and posters advertise upcoming fights locally. In addition to the top *corridas*, there are plenty of lesser ones in cities, towns and villages. Some of these are *novilladas*, fought by *novilleros* (junior matadors).

Other Sports

The annual motorcycle Grand Prix at Jerez de la Frontera, in May, is one of Spain's biggest sporting events, attracting around 150,000 spectators (see p199).

Baloncesto (basketball) is also popular. Andalucía's best teams in the national professional Liga ACB are Unicaja of Málaga and Caja San Fernando of Seville.

Andalucía's excellent golf courses stage several major professional tournaments each year. The Volvo Masters, played in November in recent years at Valderrama, near Sotogrande (northeast of Gibraltar), is traditionally the final tournament of the season on the European circuit.

MULTICULTURALISM

As elsewhere in Spain, Andalucía's *gitanos* were victims of discrimination and official persecution until at least the 18th century and have always been on the fringes of society – a position that inspired them to invent flamenco music and dance (see p43). Today, most *gitanos* lead a settled life in cities, towns and villages, but often in the poorest parts of town. *Gitanos* rub along all right with other Spaniards, but still tend to keep to themselves.

The number of more recent immigrants in Andalucía, from other European countries and from the developing world, is rising rapidly (see p38 and the boxed text, p39). A few isolated incidents aside, Andalucía has risen successfully to the challenges presented by this wave of migration. The worst outbreak of ethnic conflict occurred in 2000 in the El Ejido area of Almería province, when tensions between Moroccan workers and local residents boiled over in a wave of violent attacks on Moroccans after three Spaniards were murdered by Moroccans. An estimated 30,000 migrants, chiefly North African males in their 20s, work in Almería province's plastic-sheeted greenhouses, often in extremely poor conditions and for wages for which most Spaniards wouldn't get out of bed.

Immigration also raises serious humanitarian problems. Despite an amnesty in 2005, in which some 500,000 non-EU citizens in Spain had their situation legalised, around 40% of non-EU citizens in the country are still there illegally. Many illegal migrants take huge risks to get to Spain: every year dozens, some years hundreds, of people drown attempting to cross the Strait of Gibraltar from Morocco to Andalucía, or the Atlantic Ocean to the Canary Islands, in small boats to gain clandestine entry to Spain. Thousands more each year are intercepted by coastguards or police and sent back. Almost certainly, even higher numbers escape capture. In Andalucía the beaches of Cádiz province, near towns such as Tarifa and Algeciras, are favoured drop-off points. In 2005 desperate sub-Saharan Africans made a series of attempts to breach the fences surrounding Ceuta and Melilla, Spain's enclaves on the Moroccan coast. Many who got across were deported back to Morocco, which then dumped them on its border with Algeria in the Sahara Desert.

If they reach Spain, illegal migrants are particularly vulnerable to exploitation such as low wages, poor living conditions, enforced prostitution, and debt slavery to the criminal organisations that brought them to the country.

RELIGION

Medieval Andalucía under Islamic rule is renowned for its 'three cultures' tolerance in which Muslims, Christians and Jews supposedly lived together in harmony. In reality, Christians and Jews did at times suffer persecution or discriminatory taxes and Christian rebellions were not unknown. But there's no doubt that different religions were able to coexist and that fruitful cooperation took place under such rulers as Abd ar-Rahman III of Córdoba. The 13th-century Christian king Alfonso X kept this going, albeit briefly, but later Christian rulers subjected Muslims and Jews to forced conversions, persecutions and eventually mass expulsions. By the 17th century Spain had been turned into a one-religion state. The Protestant version of Christianity, too, was firmly stamped on before it could get a toehold in the 16th century.

'Today, people appear ever more irreligious, yet the great majority of Andalucians still have church baptisms, weddings and funerals'

Today 90% of Andalucians say they are Catholics but only 20% consider themselves churchgoers. Andalucía also has a deep-rooted anticlerical tradition. Anarchists and other 19th-century revolutionaries considered the church one of their main enemies. This hostility reached a bloody crescendo in the Spanish Civil War (1936–39), when some 7000 priests, nuns and monks were killed in Spain. Today, people appear ever more irreligious, yet the great majority of Andalucians still have church baptisms, weddings and funerals, and families spend an average of €2000 on special clothes and festivities for a child's first communion. As the 20th-century philosopher Miguel de Unamuno quipped: 'Here in Spain we are all Catholics, even the atheists.'

The number of Muslims in Spain is growing fast and now numbers around 600,000, of whom perhaps 100,000 are in Andalucía – predominantly Moroccan migrant workers. Apart from the El Ejido area in Almería province, where many Moroccans work in agriculture, Andalucía's largest Muslim community, about 20,000 strong, is in Granada.

The Jewish community numbers a few thousand people, many of them from Morocco.

ARTS

Flamenco

The constellation of intense singing, dancing and instrumental arts that forms flamenco is Andalucía's most unique gift to the world. It's not one that's appreciated by everybody – to the unsympathetic ear flamenco song can sound like someone suffering from unbearable toothache. But a flamenco performer who successfully communicates their passion will have you unwittingly on the edge of your seat, oblivious to all else. The gift of sparking this kind of response is known as *duende* (spirit).

Flamenco's origins may go back to songs brought to Spain by the *gitanos*, to music and verses of medieval Muslim Andalucía, and even to the Byzantine chant used in Visigothic churches, but flamenco first took recognisable form in the late 18th and early 19th centuries among *gitanos* in the lower Guadalquivir Valley in western Andalucía. The Seville–Jerez de la Frontera–Cádiz axis is still the heartland of flamenco. Early flamenco was *cante jondo* (deep song), an anguished form of expression for a people on the margins of society. *Jondura* (depth) is still the essence of flamenco.

A flamenco singer is known as a *cantaor* (male) or *cantaora* (female); a dancer is a *bailaor/a*. Most songs and dances are performed to a blood-rush of guitar from the *tocaor/a*. Percussion is provided by tapping feet, clapping hands and sometimes castanets. Flamenco songs come in many different styles, from the anguished *soleá* and the despairing *siguiriya* to the livelier *alegría* or the upbeat *bulería*. The traditional flamenco costume – shawl, fan and long, frilly *bata de cola* (tail gown) for women; flat Cordoban hats and tight black trousers for men – dates from Andalucian fashions in the late 19th century.

The *sevillana*, a popular dance with high, twirling arm movements, is not, despite superficial appearances, flamenco at all. Consisting of four parts, each coming to an abrupt halt, the *sevillana* is probably an Andalucian version of a Castilian dance, the *seguidilla*.

FLAMENCO LEGENDS

The great singers of the early 20th century were Seville's La Niña de los Peines, and Manuel Torre from Jerez, whose singing, legend has it, could drive people to rip their shirts open and upturn tables – real *duende*.

La Macarrona, from Jerez, and Pastora Imperio, from Seville, took flamenco dance to Paris and South America. Their successors, La Argentina and La Argentinita, formed dance troupes and turned flamenco dance into a theatrical show. The fast, dynamic, unfeminine dancing and wild lifestyle of Carmen Amaya (1913–63), from Barcelona, made her *the* flamenco dance legend of all time. Her long-time partner Sabicas was the father of the modern solo flamenco guitar.

In the mid-20th century it seemed that the lightweight flamenco of the *tablaos* – touristy shows emphasising the sexy and the jolly – was at risk of taking over the real thing, but *flamenco puro* got a new lease of life in the 1970s through singers such as Terremoto and La Paquera from Jerez, Enrique Morente from Granada and, above all, El Camarón de la Isla from San Fernando near Cádiz. Camarón's incredible vocal range and his wayward lifestyle made him a legend well before his tragically early death in 1992.

Paco de Lucía (1947–), from Algeciras, has transformed the guitar, formerly the junior partner of the flamenco trinity, into an instrument of solo expression far beyond traditional limits. De Lucía can sound like two or three people playing together. The double album *Paco de Lucía Antología* is a great introduction to his work. He vowed that his 2004 world tour would be his last tour, but he still performs.

In the hard-to-put-down *Duende* (2003), young author Jason Webster immerses his body and soul for two years in Spain's passionate and dangerous flamenco world in search of the true flamenco spirit.

Catalan actor Óscar Jaenada won the best actor award at Spain's top film awards, the Goyas, in 2006 for his portrayal of legendary Andalucian flamenco singer El Camarón de la Isla in the 2005 movie *Camarón*.

FLAMENCO TODAY

Flamenco is as popular as it has ever been and probably more innovative. While established singers such as Enrique Morente, José Menese, Chano Lobato and Carmen Linares (see p339) remain at the top of the profession, new generations continue to broaden flamenco's audience. Perhaps most popular is José Mercé from Jerez, whose exciting albums *Del Amanecer* (Of the Dawn; 1999), *Aire* (Air; 2000) and *Lío* (Entanglement; 2002) were all big sellers. El Barrio, a 21st-century urban poet from Cádiz, Estrella Morente from Granada (Enrique's daughter), Arcángel from Huelva and La Tana from Seville have carved out big followings among the young.

Flamenco dance has reached its most adventurous horizons in the person of Joaquín Cortés, born in Córdoba in 1969. Cortés fuses flamenco with contemporary dance, ballet and jazz, to music at rock-concert amplification. He tours frequently both in Spain and all over the world with spectacular solo or ensemble shows. The most exciting young dance talent is Farruquito from Seville (b 1983), grandson of the late legendary flamenco dancer Farruco.

On the guitar, keep an ear open for Manolo Sanlúcar from Cádiz, Tomatito from Almería (who used to accompany El Camarón de la Isla), and Vicente Amigo from Córdoba and Moraíto Chico from Jerez who both accompany today's top singers.

Flamenco World (www .flamenco-world.com), Flama (www.guiaflama .com), Centro Andaluz de Flamenco (caf.cica.es), esflamenco.com (www .esflamenco.com) and Deflamenco.com (www .deflamenco.com) are all great resources on flamenco, with calendars of upcoming concerts and festivals, background on artists and much more.

FLAMENCO FUSION

In the 1970s musicians began mixing flamenco with jazz, rock, blues, rap and other genres. This *nuevo flamenco* (new flamenco) greatly broadened flamenco's appeal. The seminal recording was a 1977 flamenco-folk-rock album, *Veneno* (Poison), by the group of the same name centred on Kiko Veneno (see opposite) and Raimundo Amador, both from Seville. Amador and his brother Rafael then formed Pata Negra, which produced four fine flamenco-jazz-blues albums culminating in *Blues de la Frontera* (1986). Amador is now a solo artist. The group Ketama, whose key members are all from Granada's Montoya flamenco family, mix flamenco with African, Cuban, Brazilian and other rhythms. Two of their best albums are *Songhai* (1987) and *Songhai 2* (1995).

The latest generation is headed up by artists such as Cádiz's Niña Pastori, who arrived in the late 1990s singing jazz- and Latin-influenced flamenco. All her albums, such as *Entre dos Puertos* (Between Two Ports; 1997), *María* (2002) and *Joyas Prestadas* (Borrowed Jewels; 2006) are great listening. The Málaga group Chambao successfully combines flamenco with electronic beats on *Flamenco Chill* (2002), *Endorfinas en la*

---

10 TO EXCITE

For the most exciting flamenco dance, keep an eye open for performances by any of these 10 top stars. Some lead dance companies named after them, others perform solo:

- Joaquín Cortés
- Manuela Carrasco
- Cristina Hoyos
- Sara Baras
- Antonio Canales
- Antonio Gades
- Belé n Maya
- Eva La Hierbabuena
- Israel Galván

For an interview with Sara Baras, see the boxed text, p112.

BIRTHPLACE OF THE GUITAR

The 9th-century Córdoba court musician Ziryab added a fifth string to the four-string Arab lute, producing an instrument that was widespread in Spain for centuries. Around the 1790s a sixth string was added, probably by a Cádiz guitar maker called Pagés. In the 1870s Antonio de Torres of Almería brought the guitar to its modern shape by enlarging its two bulges and placing the bridge centrally over the lower one to give the instrument its acoustic power.

Mente (Endorphins in the Mind; 2004) and *Pokito a Poko* (Little by Little; 2005). Another big crossover triumph was the collaboration between flamenco singer Diego El Cigala and the octogenarian Cuban pianist Bebo Valdés on *Lágrimas Negras* (Black Tears; 2003).

SEEING FLAMENCO

Flamenco is easiest to catch in the summer when many fiestas include flamenco performances, and some places stage special flamenco festivals (see the boxed text, p46). The rest of the year there are intermittent big-name performances in theatres, occasional seasons of concerts, and regular flamenco nights at some bars and clubs for the price of your drinks. Flamenco fans also band together in clubs called *peñas*, which stage performance nights – most will welcome interested visitors and the atmosphere here can be very intimate. Seville, Jerez de la Frontera, Cádiz and Granada are flamenco hotbeds, but you'll often be able to find something in Málaga, Córdoba or Almería – and, erratically, in other places too.

Tablaos are regular shows put on for largely undiscriminating tourist audiences, usually with high prices. Tourist offices may steer you towards these unless asked otherwise.

Other Music

In this intensely musical land all the major cities have full calendars of musical events from classical to jazz to rock to pop to electronic, and there's usually quite a choice of musical entertainment at weekends. Live music of many types is also an essential ingredient of many Andalucian fiestas.

Few Andalucian performers of any genre are completely untouched by the flamenco tradition. One of the most interesting characters is singer-songwriter Kiko Veneno, who has spent most of his life around Seville and Cádiz. Though also a practitioner of flamenco fusion (see opposite), he's more in a rock-R&B camp now, mixing rock, blues, African and flamenco rhythms with lyrics that range from humorous, simpatico snatches of everyday life to Lorca poems. His compilations *Puro Veneno* (Pure Poison; 1997) and *Un Ratito de Gloria* (A Moment of Glory; 2001) are excellent introductions to his music.

Another evergreen is the iconoclastic Joaquín Sabina from Úbeda (Jaén province), a prolific producer of protest rock-folk for more than two decades. 'I'll always be against those in power' and 'I feel like vomiting every time I sit in front of a telly', he has observed. *Nos Sobran Los Motivos* (More Reasons Than We Need) is a good album to start with.

In the realm of *canción española* (Spanish song), a melodic, romantic genre most popular with an older generation, the undoubted rising star is Pasión Vega from Málaga, whose beguiling voice may draw you in even if you don't normally go for this kind of thing. Vega incorporates

For all the gigs and festivals, log on to Indy Rock (www.indyrock.es). Clubbing Spain (www.clubbingspain.com) has the knowledge on house and techno events.

---

10 TOP ANDALUCIAN MUSIC FESTIVALS

Andalucía hosts some great music events, especially in summer. These are some of the best regular happenings:

Festival de Jerez (www.festivaldejerez.com) Two-week flamenco bash in Jerez de la Frontera in late February/early March (see p195).

Festival Internacional de Música y Danza Ciudad de Úbeda (www.festivaldeubeda.com) Mainly classical music performed in Úbeda's beautiful historic buildings in May and the first half of June (see p343).

Potaje Gitano (www.potajegitano.com) Big Saturday-night flamenco fest held in June in Utrera, Sevilla province.

Festival Internacional de la Guitarra (www.guitarracordoba.com) Two-week celebration of the guitar in late June and early July in Córdoba (see p310).

Festival Internacional de Música y Danza (www.granadafestival.org) A 2½-week international festival of mainly classical music and dance held in Granada in late June to early July (see p372).

Caracolá Lebrijana Another big Saturday-night flamenco festival held in Lebrija, Sevilla province, in June/July.

Noches en los Jardines del Real Alcázar (www.actidea.com) Eclectic concert season in Seville's beautiful Alcázar gardens, held in July and August.

Bienal de Flamenco Month-long Seville megafest held in September in even-numbered years featuring just about every big star of the flamenco world (see p113).

Festival Internacional de Jazz Jazz festival held in November in several Andalucian cities including Almería, Granada, Jaén and Málaga.

Fiesta Mayor de Verdiales Celebration of an exhilarating brand of folk music unique to the Málaga area, at Puerto de la Torre on 28 December (see p257).

---

influences including flamenco, pop, blues, Portuguese *fado*, jazz and bossa nova. Her two 2005 albums, *Flaca de Amor* and the live *Pasión Vega en el Maestranza*, are both well worth hearing.

Other original Andalucian performers to listen for include female rapper La Mala Rodríguez and combative rock band Reincidentes, from Seville; Tabletom, a hippy band that has been mixing blues, jazz, Frank Zappa influences and Málaga hedonism since the 1970s; Granada techno-punks Lagartija Nick, purveyors of 'a tyrannical storm of sound'; and everlasting Córdoba heavy rockers Medina Azahara.

On the classical front, arguably the finest Spanish composer of all, Manuel de Falla, was born in Cádiz in 1876. He grew up in Andalucía before heading off to Madrid and Paris, then returned to live in Granada until the end of the civil war, when he left for Argentina. De Falla's three major works, all intended as ballet scores, have deep Andalucian roots: *Noches en los Jardines de España* (Nights in the Gardens of Spain) evokes the Muslim past and the sounds and sensations of a hot Andalucian night, while *El Amor Brujo* (Love, the Magician) and *El Sombrero de Tres Picos* (The Three-Cornered Hat) are rooted in flamenco. Andrés Segovia from Jaén province was one of the major classical guitarists of the 20th century, and Málaga's Carlos Álvarez ranks among the top baritones of the opera world today.

Literature
ISLAMIC PERIOD
The 11th century saw a flowering of both Arabic and Hebrew poetry in Andalucía. The Arabic one is chiefly love poetry, by the likes of Ibn Hazm and Ibn Zaydún from Córdoba, and Ibn Ammar and Al-Mutamid, a king, from Seville. Jewish poet Judah Ha-Levi, one of the greatest of all postbiblical writers in Hebrew, divided his life between Granada, Seville, Toledo and Córdoba, before deciding that a return to Palestine was the only solution for Spanish Jews.

The philosopher Averroës, or Ibn Rushd (1126–98), from Córdoba, wrote commentaries on Aristotle that tried to reconcile science with religious faith, and had enormous influence on European Christian thought in the 13th and 14th centuries. This remarkable polymath was also a judge, astronomer, mathematician and personal physician and adviser to two Almohad rulers.

SIGLO DE ORO
Spain's literary Siglo de Oro (Golden Century) lasted from the mid-16th to the mid-17th centuries. In Andalucía things got moving with the circle that gathered in Seville around Christopher Columbus' great-grandson Álvaro Colón. This group included the playwrights Juan de la Cueva and Lope de Rueda.

Córdoba's Luis de Góngora (1561–1627) is considered by many the greatest Spanish poet. His metaphorical, descriptive verses, some of them celebrating the more idyllic aspects of the Guadalquivir Valley, are above all intended as a source of sensuous pleasure.

Miguel de Cervantes (1547–1616) was no Andalucian but he did spend 10 troubled years in Andalucía collecting unpaid taxes and procuring oil and wheat for the Spanish navy, as well as several lawsuits, spells in jail and even excommunications – no doubt grist to the mill of one of the inventors of the novel. His *Don Quijote* appeared in 1605. The comically insane knight Quijote and his comically dim companion, Sancho Panza, conducted most of their deranged ramblings on the plains of La Mancha, but some of Cervantes' short *Novelas Ejemplares* (Exemplary Novels) chronicle turbulent 16th-century Seville.

THE GENERATIONS OF '98 & '27
Andalucian literary creativity didn't seriously flower again until the late 19th century. The Generation of '98 was a loose grouping of Spanish intellectuals who shared a deep disturbance about national decline. Antonio Machado (1875–1939), the group's leading poet, was born in Seville and later spent some years as a teacher in Baeza, where he completed *Campos de Castilla* (Fields of Castilla), a set of melancholy poems evoking the landscape of Castilla. Juan Ramón Jiménez (1881–1958), the 1956 Nobel literature laureate from Moguer near Huelva (see p151), touchingly and amusingly brought to life his home town in *Platero y Yo* (Platero and I), a prose poem that tells of his childhood wanderings with his donkey and confidant, Platero.

The loose-knit Generation of '27 included the poets Rafael Alberti, from El Puerto de Santa María (see p184), and Vicente Aleixandre (the 1977 Nobel literature laureate) and Luis Cernuda, both from Seville. Artist Salvador Dalí, film-maker Luis Buñuel and composer Manuel de Falla were also associated with them, but the outstanding literary figure was Federico García Lorca, from Granada (see the boxed text, p48).

RECENT WRITING
Antonio Muñoz Molina (born in Úbeda, Jaén province, in 1956) is one of Spain's leading contemporary novelists, a writer of depth, imagination, social concern and great storytelling ability. One of his best novels is *El Jinete Polaco* (The Polish Jockey; 1991), set in 'Mágina', a fictionalised Úbeda, in the mid-20th century. *Sefarad* (Sepharad; 2003) weaves 17 separate stories into a multilayered exploration of themes raised by the expulsion of Spain's Jews in the 15th century, the Soviet gulag and the Nazi holocaust.

Ian Gibson's *Federico García Lorca* (1990) is an excellent biography of Andalucía's most celebrated writer. Gibson also penned *The Assassination of Federico García Lorca* (1979), revealing the murky story of Lorca's murder near Granada during the civil war.

FEDERICO GARCÍA LORCA

For many the most important Spanish writer since Cervantes, Federico García Lorca (1898–1936) was a poet, playwright, musician, artist, theatre director and much more. Though charming and popular, he felt alienated – by his homosexuality, his leftish outlook and, probably, his talent itself – from his home town of Granada (which he called 'a wasteland populated by the worst bourgeoisie in Spain') and from Spanish society at large. Lorca identified with Andalucía's marginalised *gitanos* and empathised with women stifled by conventional mores. He longed for spontaneity and vivacity and eulogised both Granada's Islamic past and what he considered the 'authentic' Andalucía (to be found in Málaga, Córdoba, Cádiz – anywhere except Granada).

Lorca first won major popularity with *El Romancero Gitano* (Gypsy Ballads), a colourful 1928 collection of verses on *gitano* themes, full of startling metaphors and with the simplicity of flamenco song. Between 1933 and 1936 he wrote the three tragic plays for which he is best known: *Bodas de Sangre* (Blood Wedding), *Yerma* (Barren) and *La Casa de Bernarda Alba* (The House of Bernarda Alba) – brooding, dark but dramatic works dealing with themes of entrapment and liberation, passion and repression. Lorca was executed by the Nationalists early in the civil war, but his passionate, free, genial and troubled spirit lives on in the many productions of his plays and other creative work he still inspires. Travellers can gain a sense of the man by visiting his summer home in Granada, Huerta de San Vicente (p371) and his birthplace outside the city (p380). For those who want to follow the Lorca trail to the bitter end, the place he was killed outside Granada is now a memorial park (p380).

Antonio Soler (b 1956) from Málaga is building a reputation as a perceptive drawer of character and atmosphere and weaver of good plots. His *El Camino de los Ingleses* (The Way of the English; 2004), tracking a group of friends' summer of transition from adolescence to adulthood, has been filmed by Antonio Banderas (see p50).

Poet, novelist and essayist José Manuel Caballero Bonald was born in Jerez de la Frontera in 1926. His *Ágata Ojo de Gato* (Agate, Cat's Eye; 1974) is an almost magical-realist work that's set in Andalucía although not in any recognisable time or place.

The highly popular playwright, poet and novelist Antonio Gala (b 1930), from Córdoba, sets much of his work in the past, which he uses to illuminate the present. *La Pasión Turca* (Turkish Passion; 1993) is his best-known novel.

Painting & Sculpture

Andalucians have been artists since the Stone Age and the region reached its greatest peaks of creativity during the 17th century.

PRE-CHRISTIAN ART

Stone Age hunter-gatherers left impressive rock paintings of animals, people and mythical figures in caves such as the Cueva de la Pileta (p284) and Cueva de Los Letreros (p422). The later Iberians carved stone sculptures of animals, deities and other figures, often with Carthaginian or Greek influence. The archaeological museums in Seville (p108) and Córdoba (p301), and Jaén's Museo Provincial (p327) all have good Iberian collections.

The Romans' artistic legacy is at its most exciting in mosaics and sculpture, with some wonderful examples in Itálica (p130), Écija (p135) and Carmona (p132), and in Seville's Palacio de la Condesa de Lebrija (p107) and the archaeological museums in Córdoba and Seville .

In Andalucía's Islamic era (AD 711–1492) the decorative arts reached marvellous heights in the service of architecture – see p52.

GOTHIC & RENAISSANCE ART

Seville has been Andalucía's artistic epicentre ever since the Reconquista (Christian reconquest). Seville cathedral's huge main retable (1482), designed by a Flemish sculptor, Pieter Dancart, is carved with more than 1000 biblical figures and is one of the finest pieces of Gothic sculpture in Spain (see p98). Then Seville's 16th-century boom threw it open to the humanist and classical trends of the Renaissance. Alejo Fernández (1470–1545) ushered in the Renaissance in painting; the Italian Pietro Torrigiano (1472–1528) did the same for sculpture.

A 16th-century master artisan known as Maestro Bartolomé created some of Spain's loveliest *rejas* (wrought-iron grilles) in churches such as Granada's Capilla Real (p365) and Baeza cathedral (p335).

SIGLO DE ORO

Early in the 17th century Sevillan artists such as Francisco Pacheco (1564–1644) and Juan de Roelas (1560–1625) began to paint in a more naturalistic style, heralding the baroque. Pacheco's studio was the centre of a humanist circle that influenced most significant Andalucian artists of the century. He advised his pupils to 'go to nature for everything'.

Though the greatest Spanish artist of the era, Diego Velázquez (1599–1660), left Seville in his 20s to become a court painter in Madrid, Andalucía and especially Seville still played a full and vital part in the the country's Siglo de Oro (Golden Century). Seville's Museo de Bellas Artes (p106) has a particularly fine collection from this era.

Velázquez' friend Alonso Cano (1601–77), a gifted painter, sculptor and architect, did some of his best work at Granada and Málaga cathedrals. Mystical Francisco de Zurbarán (1598–1664) lived most of his life in and around Seville. His clear, spiritual paintings of saints, churchmen and monastic life often utilise strong chiaroscuro as did two Italy-based contemporaries, Caravaggio and José de Ribera.

THE ROMANCE OF ANDALUCÍA

Chris 'Driving Over Lemons' Stewart was not the first foreigner inspired to successful literary endeavours by Andalucía. Back in the 19th century, the picturesque decay of Andalucía's cities, its flamenco music and dance, its legend-filled past, its people's love of fiesta, fun and bullfighting, its rugged, brigand-haunted mountains, its heat, its dark-haired, dark-eyed people – all this inspired writers to conjure up a romantic image of Andalucía that will probably never die.

One of the first Romantic writings set in Andalucía (Seville, in this case) was Lord Byron's *Don Juan*. Byron visited Andalucía in 1809 and wrote the mock-epic poetic masterpiece in the early 1820s. In 1826 France's Viscount Chateaubriand published an influential melancholic novella, *Les Aventures du Dernier Abencerage* (The Adventures of the Last Abencerraj), in which a Muslim prince returns to Granada after the Christian reconquest. The Alhambra (p359) was then established as the quintessential symbol of exotic Andalucía by *Les Orientales* (1829) by Victor Hugo (who didn't visit Granada), and *Tales of the Alhambra* (1832) by the American Washington Irving (who lived there for a few months). *Carmen*, a violent novella of *gitano* love and revenge, written in the 1840s by Frenchman Prosper Mérimée, added subtropical sensuality to the Andalucian mystique.

Composers, too, felt the pull of Andalucian images. The Don Juan story (originally a play by 17th-century Spaniard Tirso de Molina) inspired an operatic version, *Don Giovanni*, by Mozart in the 18th century. Then Georges Bizet's 1875 opera *Carmen* finally fixed the stereotype of Andalucian women as full of fire, guile and flashing beauty.

Alexandre Dumas came close to summing it up when he characterised Andalucía as a 'gay, lovely land with castanets in her hand and a garland on her brow'. The spell has hardly faded with the passing of more than a century.

Bartolomé Esteban Murillo (1617–82) and his friend Juan de Valdés Leal (1622–94), both Seville-born, led the way to full-blown baroque art. With its large, colourful, accessible images, the baroque movement took deep root in Andalucía. Murillo's soft-focus children and religious scenes emphasising the optimism of biblical stories made him highly popular in a time of economic decline. Valdés Leal could be both humorous and bitterly pessimistic. His greatest works hang alongside several Murillos in Seville's Hospital de la Caridad (p105).

Sevillan sculptor Juan Martínez Montañés (1568–1649) carved such dramatic and lifelike wooden images that contemporaries called him 'El Dios de la Madera' (The God of Wood). You'll find his carvings in many Andalucian churches, and many of the statues still carried in Seville's Semana Santa (Holy Week) processions are his work. The leading Sevillan sculptor of the later 17th century was Pedro Roldán (1624–99), whose best work is also in the Hospital de la Caridad.

18TH & 19TH CENTURIES

Andalucía's supreme representation of the grieving mother of Christ, the sculpture *La Macarena* which takes pride of place in Seville's Easter processions, is believed to be have been created by the hand of a woman – Pedro Roldán's daughter María Luisa, known as La Roldana.

An impoverished Spain in this period produced just one outstanding artist – Francisco de Goya (1746–1828), from Aragón in northern Spain. Goya recorded Andalucian bullfights at Ronda, and tradition has it that he painted his famous *La Maja Vestida* and *La Maja Desnuda* – near-identical portraits of one woman, clothed and unclothed – at a royal hunting lodge in what is now the Parque Nacional de Doñana. A few Goyas are on view in Andalucía including in Seville's cathedral and Cádiz's Oratorio de la Santa Cueva (p178).

20TH CENTURY

Maverick genius Pablo Picasso (1881–1973) was born in Málaga, but moved to northern Spain when he was nine. Picasso's career involved many abrupt changes. His sombre Blue Period (1901–04) was followed by the cheerier Pink Period; later, with Georges Braque, Picasso pioneered cubism. Since 2003 the city of his birth has at last had a fine Picasso museum (see p245), with a large collection of his works donated by his family.

Granada-born abstract expressionist José Guerrero (1914–91; see p365) followed Picasso's footsteps out of Andalucía, finding fame in New York in the 1950s. Seville-born Luis Gordillo (b 1934) spent time in Paris, Madrid and elsewhere, becoming Spain's leading exponent of pop art. Later he veered towards postmodern abstraction.

Top artists who worked primarily in Andalucía were Córdoba's Julio Romero de Torres (1880–1930), a painter of dark, sensual female nudes – not to everyone's liking (see p309) – and portraitist Daniel Vázquez Díaz (1882–1969) from Huelva.

Picasso revisited Málaga for annual holidays from 1891 to 1900, but never returned thereafter, settling in France for good in 1904.

Cinema

Spain's creative but short-of-funds cinema industry is heavily concentrated in Madrid, but a few good films are still coming out of Andalucía even if they're not generally reaching vast international audiences. One of the most successful Andalucian productions has been Pablo Carbonell's comic *Atún y Chocolate* (Tuna and Chocolate; 2004), filmed in the fishing town of Barbate (p212), with a plot revolving around weddings, tuna fishing and hashish smuggling.

Non-Andalucian productions with Andalucian themes have included Fernando Colomo's charming *Al Sur de Granada* (South from Granada; 2003), a version of English writer Gerald Brenan's life in an Andalucian village in the 1920s. Look out for Agustín Díaz Yanes' *Alatriste*, the biggest-budget Spanish movie ever, shot on several Andalucian locations with Viggo Mortensen playing the hero of the title, a soldier-cum-mercenary from Spain's 17th-century imperial wars.

The one Andalucian movie name that everyone today knows is Antonio Banderas. Born in Málaga in 1960, the dashing and talented Banderas made his name with some very challenging parts under the doyen of modern Spanish cinema, Pedro Almodóvar, including in *Women on the Verge of a Nervous Breakdown* and *Tie Me Up! Tie Me Down!*, before moving to Hollywood and a string of hits such as *Philadelphia*, *The Mask of Zorro* and *Spy Kids*. Banderas turned to directing with *Crazy in Alabama* (1999), a successful comedy starring his wife Melanie Griffith. He remains devoted to his home city, where he is setting up a drama school. He filmed much of his second directing venture, the Spanish-language *El Camino de los Ingleses* (The Way of the English; 2006), in and around Málaga. This tale of transition from adolescence to adulthood has a largely Andalucian cast including stars Juan Diego and Fran Perea.

The rising Andalucian acting star is highly versatile Paz Vega, from Seville, Cannes' best new actress of 2001 for her lead in the steamy but serious *Lucía y el Sexo* (Sex and Lucía). She made a Hollywood mark in the American-Mexican culture-clash comedy *Spanglish* (2004), and was back on Spanish soil to play the 16th-century religious mystic Santa Teresa de Ávila in Ray Loriga's *Teresa, Vida y Muerte* (Teresa, Life and Death; 2006).

Andalucian director Benito Zambrano, from Lebrija (Sevilla province), has won acclaim with two highly contrasting films: *Solas* (Alone; 1999), about a country woman surviving in a city; and *Habana Blues* (Havana Blues; 2005), a comedy of relationships and musical careers with a great Cuban music soundtrack. In between, Zambrano directed a terrific TV miniseries, *Padre Coraje* (Father Courage), about a father (Juan Diego) tracking down his son's murderer among the druggies, winos and prostitutes of the marginal suburbs of Jerez de la Frontera.

Andalucía's greatest claim to cinematic fame used to be – and maybe still is – spaghetti Westerns. It was in the early 1960s that movie-makers realised that the desert landscape around Tabernas, Almería, provided them with a perfect Wild West location and that filming there was much cheaper than in Hollywood. The Clint Eastwood trilogy of *A Fistful of Dollars*, *For a Few Dollars More* and *The Good, the Bad and the Ugly*, directed by Italian Sergio Leone (hence the 'spaghetti' label), were the most celebrated of over 150 films made in 10 years in Almería. Three Wild West town sets remain today as tourist attractions (see the boxed text, p407).

The 1960s saw several other celebrated films shot, or partly shot, in Andalucía – notably *Lawrence of Arabia*, in which Seville buildings such as the Casa de Pilatos (p108) and Plaza de España (p108) were used for scenes set in Cairo, Jerusalem and Damascus. The Tabernas desert and Almería's Cabo de Gata provided the backdrop for parts of such classics as *Cleopatra*, *Dr Zhivago* and *Indiana Jones and the Last Crusade*.

Andalucía stages several film festivals every year, the most important being Málaga's **Festival de Cine Español** (www.festivaldemalaga.com in Spanish) in late April/early May. Launched in 1998, this event grows in size and importance each year.

For Lawrence of Arabia's movie attack on Aqaba, a whole fake town was built on the Almería coast near Carboneras.

Andalucian Architecture

One of the great highlights of travelling in Andalucía is the chance to set eyes on so many beautiful and unusual buildings. The many cultures that have passed through Andalucía have yielded a fabulous diversity of constructions, from Granada's Islamic palace-fortress, the Alhambra, and Córdoba's Mezquita (Mosque) to beautiful Christian churches like Granada's Capilla Real and gaudy 20th-century confections like Seville's Plaza de España. Equally beguiling are some of the less monumental aspects of Andalucian building: the tangled street plans and impossibly mountainous settings of the white villages, the beautifully cool, tranquil patios hidden behind the façades of city houses, the gorgeous gardens filled with scents and the sound of water, and the castles sitting precariously atop almost every defensible elevation that comes into view.

Traces of some of the earliest dwellings in Andalucía can be seen at the Copper Age site Los Millares (p407), near Almería. The oldest surviving monuments are the 2nd-millennium-BC dolmens (large rock-built tombs) at places like Antequera (p289). But it was the Romans who left us the most impressive structures from before the Islamic architectural golden age. At Itálica (p130), near Seville, is the third biggest of all Roman amphitheatres in the world; at Baelo Claudia (p214) in Bolonia village, you can see an impressively intact Roman theatre; and at Carmona (p133), a necropolis with tombs the size of temples. The Romans also bequeathed Andalucía the happy invention of the interior patio, an idea later taken up by the Muslims.

The wonderfully illustrated *Moorish Architecture in Andalusia* by Marianne Barrucand and Achim Bednorz, with a learned but readable text, will whet your appetite for the region's Islamic heritage.

ISLAMIC ARCHITECTURE

Spain's Islamic centuries (AD 711–1492) left a particularly rich heritage of exotic and beautiful palaces, mosques, minarets and fortresses in Andalucía, which was always the heartland of Al-Andalus (as the Muslim-ruled areas of the Iberian Peninsula were known). These buildings make Andalucía visually unique in Europe and have to be classed as its greatest architectural glory. Nor is the legacy of the Islamic era just a matter of the big, eye-catching monuments: after the Christian reconquest of Andalucía (1227–1492), many Islamic buildings were simply repurposed for Christian ends. As a result, many of today's Andalucian churches are simply converted mosques (most famously at Córdoba), many church towers began life as minarets, and the zig-zagging streets of many an old town – Granada's Albayzín district (p367) is just one famous example– originated in labyrinthine Islamic-era street plans.

THE OMAYYADS

Islam – the word means 'Surrender' or 'Acceptance' (to the will of Allah, the Arabic name for God) – was founded by the prophet Mohammed in the Arabian city of Mecca in the 7th century AD. It spread rapidly to the north, east and west, reaching Spain in 711. In 750 the Damascus-based Omayyad dynasty of caliphs, rulers of the Muslim world, were overthrown by the revolutionary Abbasids, who shifted the caliphate to Baghdad. Just one of the Omayyad family, Abu'l-Mutarrif Abd ar-Rahman bin Muawiya, escaped. Aged only 20, he made for Morocco and thence Spain. In 756 he managed to set himself up as an independent emir, Abd

THE HORSESHOE ARCH

Omayyad architecture in Spain was enriched by styles and techniques taken up from the Christian Visigoths, whom the Omayyads replaced as rulers of the Iberian Peninsula. Chief among these was what became almost the hallmark of Spanish Islamic architecture – the horseshoe arch – so called because it narrows at the bottom like a horseshoe, rather than being a simple semicircle.

ar-Rahman I, in Córdoba, launching a dynasty based in that city that lasted until 1009 and made Al-Andalus, at the western extremity of the Islamic world, the last outpost of Omayyad culture.

The Mezquita of Córdoba

The oldest significant surviving Spanish Islamic building is also arguably the most magnificent and the most influential. The great Mezquita (p301) of Córdoba was founded by Abd ar-Rahman I in AD 785 and underwent major extensions under his successors Abd ar-Rahman II in the first half of the 9th century, Al-Hakim II in the 960s and Al-Mansur in the 970s.

Abd ar-Rahman I's initial mosque was a square split into two rectangular halves: a covered prayer hall, and an open ablutions courtyard where the faithful would wash before entering the prayer hall. The Mezquita's prayer hall broke away from the verticality of earlier great Islamic buildings such as the Great Mosque of Damascus and the Dome of the Rock in Jerusalem. Instead it created a broad horizontal space recalling the yards of desert homes that formed the original Islamic prayer spaces, and conjured up visions of palm groves with mesmerising lines of two-tier, red-and-white-striped arches in the prayer hall. The prayer hall maintained a reminder of the 'basilical' plan of some early Islamic buildings in having a central 'nave' of arches, broader than the others, leading to the mihrab, the niche indicating the direction of Mecca (and thus of prayer) that is key to the layout of any mosque.

The Mezquita's later enlargements extended the lines of arches to cover an area of nearly 120 sq metres, making it one of the biggest of all mosques. These arcades afford ever-changing perspectives, vistas disappearing into infinity and plays of light and rhythm that rank among the Mezquita's most mesmerising and unique features. The most important enlargement was carried out in the 960s by Al-Hakim II, who created a magnificent new mihrab, decorated with superb Byzantine mosaics imitating those of the Great Mosque of Damascus, one of the outstanding 8th-century Syrian Omayyad buildings. In front of the mihrab Al-Hakim II added a new royal prayer enclosure, the *maksura*. The *maksura's* multiple interwoven arches and lavishly decorated domes were much more intricate and technically advanced than anything previously seen in Europe. The *maksura* formed part of a second axis to the building, an aisle running along in front of the wall containing the mihrab – known as the qibla wall because it indicates the qibla, the direction of Mecca. This transverse axis, at right angles to the central nave, creates the T-plan that features strongly in many mosques.

Al-Hakim's Mezquita is the high point of the splendid 10th-century 'caliphal' phase of Spanish Islamic architecture – so called because this was the era of the Cordoban caliphate founded by Al-Hakim's father, Abd ar-Rahman III. The plan of Al-Hakim II's building is obscured by the Christian cathedral that was plonked right in the middle of the mosque in the 16th century, but when you are in the Mezquita it is still quite possible to work out the dimensions of each phase of its construction.

In its final 10th-century form the Córdoba Mezquita's roof was supported by 1293 columns.

ISLAMIC DECORATIVE MOTIFS

The mosaic decoration around Al-Hakim II's 10th-century mihrab portal exhibits all three of the decorative types permissible in Islamic holy places: stylised inscriptions in classical Arabic, geometric patterns, and stylised plant and floral patterns.

At this early stage of Hispano-Islamic art, the plant and floral decorations were still relatively naturalistic: later they become more stylised, more geometrical and more repetitive, adopting the mathematically conceived patterns known as arabesques. By the time Granada's Alhambra was built in the 14th century, vegetal and geometric decorative forms had become almost indistinguishable.

Other Omayyad Buildings

In AD 936 Abd ar-Rahman III built himself a new capital just west of Córdoba. Medina Azahara (see the boxed text Pleasure Dome & Powerhouse, p306), named after his favourite wife, Az-Zahra, was planned as a royal residence, palace and seat of government, set away from the hubbub of the city in the same manner as the Abbasid royal city of Samarra, north of Baghdad. Its chief architect was Abd ar-Rahman III's son, Al-Hakim II, who later embellished the Córdoba Mezquita so superbly. In contrast to Middle Eastern palaces, whose typical reception hall was a domed *iwan* (hall opening to a forecourt), Medina Azahara's reception halls had a 'basilical' plan, each with three or more parallel naves – similar to mosque architecture.

Though Medina Azahara was wrecked during the collapse of the Córdoba caliphate less than a century after it was built, it has now been partly reconstructed. From its imposing horseshoe arches, exquisite stucco work and extensive gardens, it's easy to see that it was a large and lavish place.

Relatively few other buildings survive from the Omayyad era in Spain, but the little 10th-century *mezquita* in remote Almonaster la Real (p172) is one of the loveliest Islamic buildings in the country. Though later converted into a church, the mosque remains more or less intact. It's like a miniature version of the Córdoba Mezquita, with rows of arches forming five naves, the central one leading to a semicircular mihrab.

11TH-CENTURY PALACES

Most of the 'petty kings' of the turbulent *taifa* (small kingdoms) period lived in palaces of some kind, but only a few of these remain. The Alcazaba (p247) at Málaga, though rebuilt later, still has a group of 11th-century rooms with a caliphate-style row of horseshoe arches. Within Almería's Alcazaba (p401) is the Palacio de Almotacín, constructed by the city's strongest *taifa* ruler.

THE ALMORAVIDS & ALMOHADS

The rule of the Berber Almoravids from Morocco, from the late 11th to mid-12th centuries, yielded few notable buildings in Spain, but the second wave of Moroccan Berbers to conquer Al-Andalus, the Almohads, constructed huge Friday mosques in the main cities of their empire, among them Seville. The design of the mosques was simple and purist, with large prayer halls conforming to the T-plan of the Córdoba Mezquita, but the Almohads introduced some important and beautiful decorative innovations. The bays where the naves meet the qibla wall were surmounted by cupolas or stucco *muqarnas* (stalactite

Houses and Palaces of Andalucía by Patricia Espinosa De Los Monteros and Francesco Ventura is a coffee-table tome full of beautiful photography that just might inspire some design ideas for your own palace.

or honeycomb vaulting composed of hundreds or thousands of tiny cells or niches). On walls, large brick panels with designs of interwoven lozenges were created.

From the late 12th century, tall, square, richly decorated minarets started to appear. The Giralda (p97), the minaret of the Seville mosque, is the masterpiece of surviving Almohad buildings in Spain, with its beautiful brick panels. The Seville mosque's prayer hall was demolished in the 15th century to make way for the city's cathedral, but its ablutions courtyard, Patio de los Naranjos (p99), and its northern gate, the handsome Puerta del Perdón (p99), survive.

Muqarnas (honeycomb or stalactite vaulting) originated in Syria or Iran: the Almoravid mosque at Tlemcen, Morocco, was the first western Islamic building to feature it.

Another Almohad mosque, more palace-chapel than large congregational affair, stands inside the Alcázar (p193) at Jerez de la Frontera. This tall, austere brick building is based on an unusual octagonal plan inscribed within a square.

Many rooms and patios in Seville's Alcázar palace-fortress (p99) date from Almohad times, but only the Patio del Yeso, with its superbly delicate trelliswork of multiple interlocking arches, still has substantial Almohad remains.

THE NASRIDS

The Nasrid emirate of Granada, named after its founder, Mohammed ibn Yusuf ibn Nasr, was the last Muslim redoubt on the Iberian Peninsula, enduring for 2½ centuries (1249–1492) after all the rest of Spain had been taken by the Christians. The Nasrid rulers lavished most of their art-and-architecture budget on one single palace complex of their very own – but what a palace complex it is.

BATHHOUSES

Cleanliness and the public *hammam* (bathhouse) were such features of life in Al-Andalus – Córdoba had 60 public baths – that the Muslims' Christian enemies believed bathhouses to be dens of wild orgies and came to view even simple washing with huge suspicion. To make their point, some Spanish monks took pride in wearing the same woollen habit uninterrupted for a whole year, and the phrase 'Olor de Santidad' (Odour of Sanctity) became a euphemism for the stench of the unwashed. After the Christian reconquest of Andalucía, the Moriscos (Muslims who converted to Christianity) were expressly forbidden to take baths.

Nevertheless medieval Islamic bathhouses have managed to survive in some Andalucian towns to this day. Their layout generally comprises a changing room, cold room, temperate room and hot room, in succession, with the heat in the hot rooms being provided by underfloor systems called hypocausts. Beautiful original bathhouses that you can admire today, their rooms lined by arched galleries and lit by star-shaped skylights, include the following:

- Baño de Comares (p364) Alhambra, Granada
- Baños Árabes El Bañuelo (p368) Albayzín, Granada
- Baños Árabes (p193) Alcázar, Jerez de la Frontera
- Baños Árabes (p327) Palacio de Villardompardo, Jaén
- Baños Árabes (p280) Ronda
- Baño Moro (p350) Segura de la Sierra
- Hammam Baños Árabes (p310) Córdoba

The Córdoba baths have been restored so you can luxuriate in the *hammam* experience there yourself – as you can at modern medieval-style bathhouses that have opened in several other Andalucian cities in recent years (see p78 for more information).

The Alhambra

Robert Irwin's *The Alhambra* rubbishes the myths that have gathered around this most famous of Spanish buildings and brings the place to life in a genuine way.

Granada's magnificent palace-fortress, the Alhambra (p359), is the only surviving large medieval Islamic palace complex in the world. It's a palace-city in the tradition of Medina Azahara but is also a fortress, with 2km of walls, 23 towers and a fort-within-a-fort, the Alcazaba. Within the Alhambra's walls were seven separate palaces, mosques, garrisons, houses, offices, baths, a summer residence (the Generalife) and exquisite gardens.

The Alhambra's designers were supremely gifted landscape architects, integrating nature and buildings through the use of pools, running water, meticulously clipped trees and bushes, windows framing vistas, carefully placed lookout points, interplay between light and dark, and contrasts between heat and cool. The juxtaposition of fountains, pools and gardens with domed reception halls reached a degree of perfection suggestive of the paradise described in the Quran. In keeping with the Alhambra's partial role as a sybarite's delight, many of its defensive towers also functioned as miniature summer palaces.

A huge variety of densely ornamented arches adorns the Alhambra. The Nasrid architects refined existing decorative techniques to new peaks of delicacy, elegance and harmony. Their media included sculptured stucco, marble panels, carved and inlaid wood, epigraphy (with endlessly repeated inscriptions of 'There is no conqueror but Allah') and colourful tiles. Plaited star patterns in tile mosaic have since covered walls the length and breadth of the Islamic world, and Nasrid Granada is the dominant artistic influence in the Maghreb (Northwest Africa) even today.

The marquetry ceiling of the Alhambra's Salón de Comares employs more than 8000 tiny wooden panels.

Granada's splendour reached its peak under emirs Yusuf I (r 1333–54) and Mohammed V (r 1354–59 and 1362–91). Each was responsible for one of the Alhambra's two main palaces. Yusuf created the Palacio de Comares (Comares Palace). The brilliant marquetry ceiling of the Salón de Comares (Comares Hall) here, representing the seven levels of the Islamic heavens and capped by a cupola representing the throne of Allah, served as the model for Islamic-style ceilings in state rooms for centuries afterwards. Mohammed V takes credit for the Palacio de los Leones (Palace of the Lions), focused on the famed Patio de los Leones (Patio of the Lions), with its colonnaded gallery and pavilions and a central fountain channelling water through the mouths of 12 stone lions. This palace's Sala de Dos Hermanas (Hall of Two Sisters) features a fantastic *muqarnas* dome of 5000 tiny cells, recalling the constellations.

MUDEJAR & MOZARABIC ARCHITECTURE

The label Mudejar – from Arabic *mudayan* (domesticated) – was given to Muslims who stayed on in areas reconquered by the Christians, who often employed the talents of gifted Muslim artisans. Mudejar buildings are effectively part of Spain's Islamic heritage. You'll find Mudejar or part-Mudejar churches and monasteries all over Andalucía (Mudejar is often found side by side with the Christian Gothic style), but the classic Mudejar building is the exotic Palacio de Don Pedro (p100), built in the 14th century inside the Alcázar of Seville for the Christian King Pedro I of Castile. Pedro's friend Mohammed V, the Muslim emir of Granada, sent many of his best artisans to work on Pedro's palace, and as a result the Palacio de Don Pedro is effectively a Nasrid building, and one of the best of its kind – especially the beautiful Patio de las Doncellas at its heart, with a sunken garden surrounded by exquisite arches, tiling and plasterwork.

ISLAMIC FORTIFICATIONS

With its borders constantly under threat and its subjects often rebellious, it's hardly surprising that Al-Andalus boasts more Islamic castles and forts than any comparably sized territory in the world.

Caliphate Era

The 10th century saw heaps of forts built in Al-Andalus' border regions, and many fortified garrisons constructed in the interior. Designs were fairly simple, with low, rectangular towers and no outer rings of walls. Two of the finest caliphate-era forts are the oval one at Baños de la Encina (p334) in Jaén province and the hilltop Alcazaba (p401) dominating Almería.

Taifa Period

In this 11th-century era of internal strife, many towns bolstered their defences. A fine example is Niebla (p159) in Huelva province, which was enclosed by walls with massive round and rectangular towers. So was the Albayzín area of Granada (p367). Niebla's gates show a new sophistication, with barbicans (double towers defending the gates) and bends in their passageways to impede attackers.

Almohad Fortifications

In the 12th and early 13th centuries the Almohads rebuilt many city defences, such as those at Córdoba, Seville and Jerez de la Frontera. Córdoba's Torre de la Calahorra (p307) and Seville's Torre del Oro (p105) are both well-constructed bridgehead towers from this era.

Nasrid Fortifications

Many defensive fortifications – as at Antequera (p289) and Ronda (p278), and Málaga's Castillo de Gibralfaro (p245) – were restored as the Granada emirate strove to survive in the 13th, 14th and 15th centuries. Big rectangular corner towers such as those at Málaga and Antequera suggest the influence of the Christian enemy. The most spectacular fort of the era – though better known as a palace – is Granada's Alhambra (p359).

One hallmark of Mudejar style is geometric decorative designs in brick or stucco, often further embellished with tiles. Elaborately carved timber ceilings are also a mark of the Mudejar hand. *Artesonado* is the word used to describe ceilings with interlaced beams leaving regular spaces for decorative insertions. True Mudejar *artesonados* generally bear floral or simple geometric patterns.

The term Mozarabic, from *musta'rib* (Arabised), refers to Christians who lived, or had lived, in Muslim-controlled territories in the Iberian Peninsula. Mozarabic architecture was, unsurprisingly, much influenced by Islamic styles. It includes, for instance, the horseshoe arch. The majority of Mozarabic architecture is found in northern Spain: the only significant remaining Mozarabic structure in Andalucía – but well worth seeking out for its picturesque setting and poignant history – is the rock-cut church at Bobastro (p288).

POST-ISLAMIC ARCHITECTURE

Though less world-famous than the celebrated creations of Andalucía's Muslim-era architects and builders, the region's buildings from later eras – notably the churches and monasteries built by the Christian conquerors and the palaces and mansions of their nobility – are a superb part of Andalucía's heritage.

ANDALUCÍA'S TOP FIVE FORMAL GARDENS

Some of Andalucía's loveliest buildings are greatly enhanced by the gorgeous gardens around them, full of colour, fragrances and the tinkle of water.

- Generalife gardens, Alhambra, Granada (p364)
- Alcázar gardens, Seville (p101)
- Gardens of the Alcázar de los Reyes Cristianos, Córdoba (p307)
- Parque de María Luisa, Seville (p108)
- Palacio de Viana gardens, Córdoba (p309)

GOTHIC

Christian architecture reached northern and western Andalucía with the Reconquista (Christian reconquest) during the 13th century. The prevailing architectural style at the time was Gothic, with its distinctive pointed arches, ribbed ceilings, flying buttresses and fancy window tracery. Seville's enormous, five-naved cathedral (p97), the biggest in Spain, is almost entirely Gothic. Dozens of Gothic or part-Gothic churches, castles and mansions are dotted throughout Andalucía. Some of these buildings combine Gothic with Mudejar style (see p56), others have mixed Gothic with later styles and ended up as a stylistic hotchpotch. Such are the cathedrals at Jerez de la Frontera (Gothic, Mudejar, baroque and neoclassical; p193) and Málaga (Gothic, Renaissance and baroque; p244).

The final flourish of Spanish Gothic was Isabelline Gothic, from the time of Queen Isabel la Católica, whose own burial chapel – the beautiful Capilla Real (p365) in Granada – is the supreme work in this style. Isabelline Gothic features sinuously curved arches and tracery, and façades with lacelike ornament and low-relief sculptures (including lots of heraldic shields). Another lovely Isabelline building is the Palacio de Jabalquinto (p337) in Baeza.

RENAISSANCE

The Renaissance in architecture was an Italian-originated return to classical ideals of harmony and proportion, dominated by columns and shapes such as the square, circle and triangle. Many Andalucian Renaissance buildings feature elegant interior courtyards lined by two tiers of wide, rounded arcades.

Spanish Renaissance architecture had three phases. First came plateresque, taking its name from the Spanish for silversmith, *platero,* because it was primarily a decorative genre, with effects resembling those of silverware. Round-arched portals were framed by classical columns and stone sculpture.

Next came a more purist style whose ultimate expression is the Palacio de Carlos V (p364) inside Granada's Alhambra, designed by the Rome-trained Pedro Machuca.

The last and plainest phase was Herreresque, after Juan de Herrera (1530–97), creator of the austere palace-monastery complex of El Escorial, near Madrid, and Seville's Archivo de Indias (p105).

All three phases of Renaissance architecture were spanned in Jaén province by the legendary master architect Andrés de Vandelvira (1509–75), who gave the town of Úbeda one of the finest ensembles of Renaissance buildings in Spain (see p342). Vandelvira was much

The 16th-century white-marble Renaissance patio of the Castillo de los Fajardo in Vélez Blanco (p422) was sold whole to an American millionaire and now resides in New York's Metropolitan Museum of Art.

influenced by Burgos-born Diego de Siloé (1495–1563), who was primarily responsible for the cathedrals of Granada (p365), Málaga (p244) and Guadix (p381).

This was an era in which the gentry could build themselves gorgeous urban palaces with delightful patios surrounded by harmonious arched galleries – don't miss the Palacio de la Condesa de Lebrija (p107) and Casa de Pilatos (p108) in Seville, or Úbeda's Palacio de Vázquez de Molina (p341).

BAROQUE

The reaction to Renaissance sobriety came in the colours and dramatic sense of motion of baroque. This style really seemed to catch the Andalucian imagination, and this was one of the places where baroque blossomed most brilliantly, reaching its peak of elaboration in the 18th century.

Baroque style was at root classical, but it crammed a great deal of ornament onto façades and stuffed interiors full of ornate stucco sculpture and gilt paint. Retables – the large, sculptural altarpieces that adorn many Spanish churches to illustrate Christian stories and teachings – reached extremes of gilded extravagance. The most hyperbolic baroque work is termed Churrigueresque after a Barcelona family of sculptors and architects named Churriguera.

Before full-blown baroque there was a kind of transitional stage, exemplified by more sober works such as Alonso Cano's 17th-century façade for Granada's cathedral (p365).

Seville has probably as many baroque churches per square kilometre as any city in the world. However, the church at Granada's Monasterio de La Cartuja (p370), by Francisco Hurtado Izquierdo (1669–1728), is one of the most lavish baroque creations in all Spain with its multicoloured marble, golden capitals and profuse sculpture. Hurtado's followers also adorned the small town of Priego de Córdoba (p320) with seven or eight baroque churches.

NEOCLASSICISM

The cleaner, restrained lines of neoclassicism came into fashion throughout Europe in the mid-18th century – another return to Greek and Roman ideals, expressing the Enlightenment philosophy of the era. Cádiz, whose golden age this was, has the biggest collection of neoclassical buildings in Andalucía, but the single grandest neoclassical building is Seville's enormous, almost monastic Antigua Fábrica de Tabacos (Old Tobacco Factory; p108), built to house an early state-supported industry.

Seville's Casa de Pilatos and Plaza de España both featured as Middle Eastern palaces in *Lawrence of Arabia* (1962). The Casa de Pilatos reappeared, along with the Seville Alcázar, in the medieval-Jerusalem sequences in *The Kingdom of Heaven* (2005).

HIDDEN GEMS

These off-the-beaten-track architectural highlights will have you exploring some of Andalucía's most intriguing back country as you hunt them down.

■ Mezquita, Almonaster la Real (p172)

■ Castillo de La Calahorra (p382)

■ Baroque churches, Priego de Córdoba (p320)

■ La Cartuja de Cazalla (p140)

■ Castillo de Burgalimar, Baños de la Encina (p334)

19TH & 20TH CENTURIES

The 19th century spawned revivals of a plethora of earlier styles: Andalucía acquired some neo-Gothic, even a bit of neobaroque, but most prevalent were neo-Mudejar and neo-Islamic, harking back to an age that was now catching the fancy of the Romantic movement. Mansions such as the Palacio de Orleans y Borbón (p189), in Sanlúcar de Barrameda, and public buildings ranging from train stations in Seville to markets in Málaga and Tarifa, were constructed in colourful and pleasing imitation of past Islamic architectural styles. For the 1929 Exposición Iberoamericana, fancy buildings in almost every past Andalucian style were concocted in Seville – chief among them the Hotel Alfonso XIII (p116), built to lodge visiting heads of state, and the gaudy Plaza de España ensemble (p108) by local architect Aníbal González.

Since then, sad to say, Andalucian architects and builders have displayed an uncharacteristic lack of imagination. During the Franco dictatorship, drab, Soviet-style blocks of workers' housing were erected in many cities. Andalucía's tourism boom, which began under Franco and is still going strong, has engendered more new building than any other period in its history. Unfortunately the hotels, villas and holiday apartment blocks have been thrown up with an eye primarily to speed and profit, and their impact on the landscape is often plain awful. Where architects and builders have demonstrated greater flair is in restoring older edifices to serve as hotels, museums or other public buildings. Projects like Málaga's Museo Picasso (p245) and Jaén's Palacio de Villardompardo (p327), are both 16th-century urban palaces turned into top-class modern museums. Las Casas del Rey de Baeza (p117), a hotel created out of 18th-century communal housing in Seville, and the Alquería de Morayma at Cádiar (p392), a country hotel developed from an old farmstead, have been carried out with great flair and sensitivity to the values of the old as well as the needs of the present. See p16 for our list of Top 10 Andalucian hotel conversions.

The most positive impetus to brand-new building in the past 20 years was Expo '92 in Seville, which brought a sea of avant-garde exhibition pavilions and several spectacular new bridges over the Guadalquivir.

Environment

THE LAND

Andalucía has four main geographic regions, all running roughly east–west across it: the Sierra Morena, the Guadalquivir Valley, the mountains and the coastal plain.

The Sierra Morena, a range of hills that rarely tops 1000m, rolls across the north of Andalucía. It's a beautiful area divided between evergreen oak woodlands, scrub, rough grazing pasture and scattered old stone villages.

The fertile valley of the 660km-long Río Guadalquivir, Andalucía's longest river, stretches across Andalucía south of the Sierra Morena. The Guadalquivir rises in the Cazorla mountains of Jaén province, flows westward through Córdoba and Seville and enters the Atlantic at Sanlúcar de Barrameda. Its lower reaches are straddled by a broad plain, and before entering the ocean the river splits into a marshy delta known as Las Marismas del Guadalquivir, which includes the Parque Nacional de Doñana. The Guadalquivir is navigable as far upstream as Seville.

Between the Guadalquivir Valley and the Mediterranean coast rises the Cordillera Bética, a band of rugged mountains that widens out from its beginnings in southwest Andalucía to a breadth of 125km or so in the east. The Cordillera Bética continues east from Andalucía across Spain's Murcia and Valencia regions, then re-emerges from the Mediterranean as the Balearic Islands of Ibiza and Mallorca. It was pushed up by pressure of the African tectonic plate on the Iberian subplate 15 to 20 million years ago. Much of it is composed of limestone, yielding some wonderful karstic rock formations.

The name Guadalquivir derives from the Arabic Wadi al-Kabir (Great River). The Romans called it the Betis and the ancient Greeks the Tartessos.

In Andalucía, the Cordillera Bética divides into two main chains: the more northerly Sistema Subbético and the southerly Sistema Penibético, separated by a series of valleys, plains and basins. The Sistema Penibético includes the 75km-long Sierra Nevada southeast of Granada, with a series of 3000m-plus peaks, including Mulhacén (3479m), the highest mountain on mainland Spain.

Andalucía's coastal plain varies in width from 50km in the far west to virtually nothing in parts of Granada and Almería provinces, where the Sierra de la Contraviesa and Sierra de Cabo de Gata drop away in sheer cliffs to the Mediterranean.

WILDLIFE

Andalucía's wildlife is among the most diverse in Europe, thanks to its varied, often untamed terrain, which has allowed the survival of several species that have died out elsewhere.

Animals

Many animals are nocturnal but if you want to see wildlife, and know where to look, you're unlikely to go home disappointed (see Top 10 Wildlife-Spotting Sites, p62).

MAMMALS

Andalucía has an estimated 15,000 ibex (cabra montés), a stocky wild mountain goat whose males have distinctive long horns. The ibex spends its summer hopping with amazing agility around high-altitude precipices and descends to lower elevations in winter. The largest numbers are found in the Sierra Nevada, Parque Natural Sierras de Cazorla, Segura y Las Villas, Sierras de Tejeda y Almijara and Sierra de las Nieves.

An estimated 60 to 80 wolves *(lobos)* survive in the Sierra Morena, mostly in Jaén province's Parque Natural Sierra de Andújar. In 1986 the wolf was declared in danger of extinction in Andalucía and, in an effort to protect it from hunters and farmers, farmers are now awarded compensation if their animals are attacked by wolves. But the wolf population has still sunk to levels that are probably fatally low. Around 1500 to 2000 wolves survive in northern Spain. Andalucía's other famously endangered mammal is the Iberian lynx – see the boxed text Missing Lynx? (p64).

The mouflon *(muflón)*, a wild sheep, has been introduced to the Parque Natural Sierras de Cazorla, Segura y Las Villas and a couple of other areas to help satisfy rural Andalucians' passion for hunting. Gibraltar is famous for its colony of Barbary apes (see p233), the only wild primates in Europe. More common beasts (or at least signs of them) that you may come across include the following:

- wild boar *(jabalí)* – mainly nocturnal and mostly found in thick woods and marshes; likes farmers' root crops
- red deer *(ciervo)*, roe deer *(corzo)* and fallow deer *(gamo)* – in forests and woodlands
- genet *(gineta)* – rather like a nocturnal, short-legged cat with a black-spotted white coat and a long, striped tail; inhabits woodland and scrub
- Egyptian mongoose *(meloncillo)* – another mainly nocturnal animal, found in woods, scrub and marshes, especially in southwestern Andalucía
- red squirrel *(ardilla)* – inhabits mountain forests
- badger *(tejón)* – nocturnal animal found in woods with thick undergrowth,
- otter *(nutria)* – along some rivers.

The Bahía de Algeciras and Strait of Gibraltar harbour plenty of dolphins *(delfines;* common, striped and bottlenose) as well as some whales *(ballenas;* pilot, killer and even sperm) – see p236 and p219 for more information.

> Wolves have killed over 1500 head of livestock in Andalucía since 1990; farmers complain that compensation from the regional government is insufficient and takes years to be paid.

TOP 10 WILDLIFE-SPOTTING SITES

- Parque Natural Sierras de Cazorla, Segura y Las Villas (p347) – Andalucía's greatest numbers of visible large mammals: red and fallow deer, wild boar, mouflon and ibex
- Parque Nacional de Doñana (p154) – deer, boar, millions of birds
- Gibraltar (p228) – apes on the rock, dolphins in the bay
- Parque Natural Sierra de Grazalema (p203) – a spectacular griffon vulture colony, plus ibex
- Tarifa (p219) – dolphin- and whale-watching
- Reserva Natural Laguna de Fuente de Piedra (p291) – the glorious greater flamingo
- Parque Nacional Sierra Nevada (p382) – 5000 ibex
- Dehesa de Abajo (p131) – large woodland colony of white storks
- Paraje Natural Marismas del Odiel (p149) – wetlands alive with water birds
- Strait of Gibraltar (p220) – big spring and autumn bird migrations

BIRDS

Andalucía is a magnet for bird-watchers. The forests, rugged mountain ranges and many coastal wetlands provide ideal habitats for many species.

Raptors

Andalucía has 13 resident raptor (bird-of-prey) species and several other summer visitors from Africa. You'll see some of them circling or hovering over the hills in many areas.

Europe's biggest bird, the rare and endangered black vulture (*buitre negro*), has a stronghold in the Sierra Morena, with around 230 pairs scattered from Huelva's Sierra Pelada to Jaén's Sierra de Andújar. The several hundred pairs in Spain are probably the world's biggest population.

Another emblematic and extremely rare bird is the Spanish imperial eagle (*águila imperial ibérica*), found in no other country. Its white shoulders distinguish it from other imperial eagles. Its total numbers have increased from about 50 pairs in the 1960s to some 200 pairs today, helped by an active government protection plan operative since 2001. About 50 pairs are in Andalucía – most of them in the Sierra Morena and about eight pairs in the Doñana area. Poisoned bait put out by farmers or hunters is the imperial's greatest enemy.

Another breeding centre based in the Parque Natural Sierras de Cazorla, Segura y Las Villas aims to reintroduce the bearded vulture or lammergeier (*quebrantahuesos*), with its majestic 2m-plus wingspan, to this area, from which it disappeared in 1986 (its last redoubt in Spain except the Pyrenees). Three young bearded vultures were released into the wild in 2006.

Other large birds of prey in Andalucía include the golden eagle (*águila real*) and several other eagles, the griffon vulture (*buitre leonado*) and the Egyptian vulture (*alimoche*), all found in mountain regions.

Storks

The large, ungainly white stork (*cigüeña blanca*), actually black and white, nests from spring to summer on electricity pylons, trees and towers – sometimes right in the middle of towns – in western Andalucía. Your attention will be drawn by the loud clacking of beaks from these lofty perches. A few pairs of the much rarer black stork (*cigüeña negra*), which is actually all black, also nest in western Andalucía, typically on cliff ledges. In spring both types of stork migrate north from Africa across the Strait of Gibraltar (see p220).

Water Birds

Andalucía is a haven for water birds, mainly thanks to extensive wetlands along the Atlantic coast, such as those at the mouths of the Guadalquivir and Odiel rivers. Hundreds of thousands of migratory birds, including an estimated 80% of Western Europe's wild ducks, winter in the Doñana wetlands at the mouth of the Guadalquivir, and many more call in during spring and autumn migrations.

Laguna de Fuente de Piedra, near Antequera, is Europe's main breeding site for the greater flamingo (*flamenco*), with as many as 20,000 pairs rearing chicks in spring and summer. This beautiful pink bird can also be seen in several other places, including Cabo de Gata, Doñana and the Marismas del Odiel.

Other Birds

Among the more common and visible of Andalucía's many other colourful birds are the golden oriole (*oropéndola*), seen in orchards and deciduous

Birdwatching on Spain's Southern Coast by John R Butler and Where to Watch Birds in Southern & Western Spain by Ernest Garcia and Andrew Paterson are invaluable bird-watching guides, with plenty of recommended viewing spots.

Bird-watchers will also need a field guide such as the Collins Field Guide: Birds of Britain and Europe by Roger Tory Peterson, Guy Mountfort and PAD Hollom, or the slimmer Collins Pocket Guide: Birds of Britain & Europe.

MISSING LYNX?

The Iberian (or pardel) lynx (*lince ibérico* to Spaniards, *Lynx pardina* to scientists) is a beautiful feline unique to the Iberian Peninsula. It's twice the size of a domestic cat, with a black-spotted brown coat, a short, black-tipped tail, and ears with distinctively pointed black tufts. It lives for up to 15 years and eats little but rabbit, which it catches with great agility and a burst of light-ning speed. The lynx likes to inhabit thick Mediterranean woodland interspersed with patches of scrub and open ground; however, it's on the verge of becoming the first extinct feline since the sabre-toothed tiger.

The lynx was still common enough to be legally hunted until 1966, but by the late 1980s its numbers were down to around 1000. Today, most estimates put the lynx population at less than 200. The only proven breeding populations are in two areas of Andalucía: one is the eastern Sierra Morena, with perhaps 100 lynxes; the other is the Parque Nacional de Doñana and adjoining Parque Natural de Doñana, with 30 to 50 lynxes.

The reasons for this sad decline are several:

- epidemics that have decimated the rabbit population
- loss of habitat due to new farmland, roads, dams and pine or eucalyptus plantations
- illegal traps and snares set for other animals
- road accidents.

It took Spain's politicians an extremely long time to face up to the emergency at hand. Research, conferences and strategy proposals abounded, but on the ground action was palpably scarce and uncoordinated. From 1996 to 2004 the national environment ministry in Madrid and the Andalucian environment department in Seville were in the hands of opposing political par-ties – the Partido Popular (PP; People's Party) and the Partido Socialista Obrero Español (PSOE; Spanish Socialist Workers' Party) respectively – which seemed to be incapable of cooperating on anything.

Special facilities for an in-captivity breeding programme were built at El Acebuche in Parque Nacional de Doñana back in 1992, but not until 2003 did Seville and Madrid sign a coordination agreement and decide to accelerate the captive-breeding programme – jolted into action by a shock announcement from Nicolás Guzmán, coordinator of the National Lynx Conservation Strategy, that recent studies indicated there were only 160 lynxes left.

By mid-2006 five adult males and five adult females had been gathered at the El Acebuche breeding centre, and nine cubs had been born, of which six survived – four of them mothered by a Sierra Morena lynx named Saliega and two by a Doñana lynx named Esperanza (Hope). The father of all the surviving cubs was a lusty Sierra Morena lynx by the name of Garfio (Hook). Live film of lynxes in the breeding programme is displayed on a screen at the Parque Nacional de Doñana's El Acebuche visitors centre (p155), though the breeding centre itself is closed to the public.

Meanwhile efforts continue to try to help the wild lynx population re-establish itself. Since most lynxes live on privately owned land, the national and regional governments and some conservation organisations have signed over 100 agreements with landowners to improve lynx habitat and to allow the local rabbit populations to grow. Further good news came in 2005 and 2006 with several reports of lynxes present in four areas of Spain where they were not known to have survived: Andalucía's Sierra Norte (Sevilla province) and Sierra de Aracena (Huelva province), and the Montes de Toledo and the Comunidad de Madrid, both in central Spain.

The captive breeding programme aims to create a pool of up to 80 breeding lynxes in cap-tivity, with lynxes being released into the wild from 2010 on. Experts are sounding the alarm however over the number of unnatural deaths still being suffered by wild lynxes – especially in road accidents in the Doñana area, where at least 30 lynxes have been run over in the past decade. Despite Doñana's fame and history as a lynx habitat, some experts are suggesting that reintroduction should focus on other areas.

woodlands in summer (the male has an unmistakable bright-yellow body); the orange-and-black hoopoe (abubilla), with its distinctive crest, common in open woodlands, on farmland and golf courses; and the gold, brown and turquoise bee-eater (abejaruco), which nests in sandy banks in summer.

Plants

The variety of Andalucian flora is astonishing, as anyone who witnesses the spectacular wild-flower displays in spring and early summer can easily testify. Andalucía has around 5000 plant species, some 150 of them unique. This abundance is largely due to the fact that during the last Ice Age many plants that died out further north were able to survive at this southerly latitude.

HIGH-ALTITUDE PLANTS

The Sierra Nevada, southeast of Granada, with several 3000m-plus peaks, is home to 2100 plant species. About 60 of these are unique to the Sierra Nevada. The mountainous Parque Natural Sierras de Cazorla, Segura y Las Villas in northeast Andalucía has 2300 plant species, 24 of them found nowhere else. When the snows melt, the alpine and subalpine zones above the tree line bloom with small, rock-clinging plants and high pastures full of gentians, orchids, crocuses and narcissi.

> A great source of up-to-date information on Andalucian fauna and flora is the English-language Iberianature (www .iberianature.com).

FOREST & WOODLANDS

Many mountain slopes are clothed in pine forests, often commercially grown. The tall black pine (pino laricio), with its horizontally spreading branches clustering near the top, likes terrain above 1300m. The maritime pine (pino resinero or pino marítimo), with a rounded top, can grow all the way up to elevations of 1500m. The Aleppo pine (pino carrasco), with a bushy top and separated, often bare branches, flourishes below 1000m. The lovely umbrella pine (pino piñonero), with its broad, umbrella-like top and edible kernels, prefers low-lying and coastal areas – it's characteristic of the Doñana area.

The natural vegetation of many lower slopes and gentler hill country is Mediterranean woodland, with trees adapted to a warm, fairly dry climate, such as the wild olive (acebuche), carob (algarrobo), the holm or ilex oak (encina), the cork oak (alcornoque) and the gall oak (quejigo). These oaks are more gnarled, with smaller and pricklier leaves than the tall oaks of more temperate regions. The best surviving stands of Mediterranean woodland are in the Parques Naturales Sierra de Grazalema and Los Alcornocales in Cádiz province. Large expanses of woodland in these areas, and in the Sierra Morena, have been converted over the centuries into woodland pastures known as dehesas, which provide a great example of sustainable symbiosis between humans, plants and animals. The cork oak's thick outer bark is stripped every ninth summer for cork; you'll see the visible scars – a bright terracotta colour if they're new – on some trees. The holm oak can be pruned about every four years and the offcuts used for charcoal. Meanwhile, livestock can graze the pastures, and in autumn pigs are turned out to gobble up the fallen acorns, a diet considered to produce the tastiest ham of all.

The rare Spanish fir (pinsapo), a handsome, dark-green relic of the extensive fir forests around the Mediterranean in the Tertiary period (which ended approximately 2.5 million years ago), survives in significant numbers only in the Sierra de Grazalema, Sierra de las Nieves and Sierra Bermeja, all in southwest Andalucía, and in northern Morocco. It likes north-facing slopes up to 1800m, can grow to 30m high and lives for up to 500 years.

At ground level Andalucía's forests sprout some 2000 species of fungi (*setas*) in autumn. Many are edible and appear in markets and restaurants; others are poisonous – and the decisions on which are which are best left to the local experts!

Definitely not wild but in some areas the dominant feature of the landscape – especially in Jaén and Córdoba provinces – are the lines upon lines of olive trees (*olivos*), rolling over the horizon and far beyond. Andalucía produces about 20% of the world's olive oil (see p330). Other food-bearing trees grown in many parts of Andalucía are the almond (*almendro*), with beautiful pink winter blossom, and the chestnut (*castaño*), with incredible star-bursts of catkins in midsummer. Also highly eye-catching are the unmistakable bright pink flowers of oleander (*adelfa*) bushes, which in summer line many watercourses. Widely cultivated for timber, though now unfashionable because of its insatiable thirst, is the eucalyptus (*eucalipto*).

Flower lovers should carry Betty Molesworth Allen's *A Selection of Wildflowers of Southern Spain* and, if possible, the classic *Flowers of South-West Europe* by Oleg Polunin and BE Smythies.

SCRUB & STEPPE

Where there are no trees and no agriculture, the land is likely to be either scrub (*matorral*) or steppe (*estepa*). Typical scrub plants include gorse (*tojo*), juniper (*enebro*), shrubs of the cistus (*jara*) family, and herbs such as lavender (*lavanda*), rosemary (*romero*), fennel (*hinojo*) and thyme (*tomillo*). Orchids, gladioli and irises may flower beneath these shrubs.

Steppe is either produced by overgrazing or occurs naturally in hot, very dry areas such as the southeast of Almería province. Plant life here is sparse, often mostly cacti, but can explode in colourful bloom after rain.

PARKS & OTHER PROTECTED AREAS

Much of Andalucía remains wilderness barely touched by human hand, or countryside managed in traditional and sustainable ways. Its landscapes never cease to surprise with their beauty, and nearly all of the most spectacular and ecologically important country is under official protection.

Andalucía has the biggest environmental protection programme in Spain, possessing more than 90 protected areas covering some 17,000 sq km. This amounts to 20% of Andalucian territory and more than 60% of the total protected area in Spain.

Spain, by Teresa Farino and Mike Lockwood, in the Travellers' Nature Guides series, is an excellent practical guide to 200 sites for viewing flora and fauna, with good photos, drawings and information on species.

Along with official protection (largely an achievement of the regional government, the Junta de Andalucía, since the 1980s) have come infinitely improved levels of public information and access to these often remote and challenging areas – visitors centres and information points, better maps, marked footpaths, more (and better) rural accommodation, and active-tourism firms that will take you walking, riding, wildlife watching, climbing, caving, canyoning and more.

Responsibility for most nature conservation in Spain is in the hands of the country's 17 regional governments such as the Junta de Andalucía. There are at least 17 different categories of protected area. All of them can be visited, but degrees of access vary. So does the reality of protection: some parks still lack a proper legal framework for their management, and environmentalists and dedicated officials wage an endless struggle against illicit building, quarrying and hunting in protected areas.

Parques nacionales (national parks), declared by the national government but managed by regional governments (since 2004), are areas of exceptional importance for their fauna, flora, geomorphology or landscape, whose conservation is considered to be in the national interest, and are the most strictly controlled protected areas. They tend to have suffered little human impact, and may include reserve areas closed to the public, or restricted areas that can only be visited with permission. Some unscrupulous or ignorant tourism operators will make out that every little nature reserve on their doorstep is a 'national park'. Tell them they're wrong: Spain has just 13 *parques nacionales* (14 when Monfragüe in Extremadura is added to the list, by 2007), and only two of them – Doñana and Sierra Nevada – are in Andalucía.

Parques naturales (natural parks) are declared and administered by regional governments. Andalucía's 24 natural parks account for most of its protected territory and include nearly all of its most spectacular country.

ANDALUCÍA'S TOP PARKS & PROTECTED AREAS

Park	Features	Activities	Best Time to Visit	Page
Parque Nacional de Doñana	wetlands, dunes, beaches, woodlands; vital to birds & mammals	4WD tours & bird-watching	any	p154
Parque Natural de Doñana	buffer zone for Parque Nacional de Doñana with similar habitats & wildlife	wildlife watching, 4WD trips, horse riding & walking	any	p154
Parque Nacional Sierra Nevada	spectacular high-mountain wilderness with many ibex & endemic plants	walking	Jul–early Sep	p382
Parque Natural Sierra Nevada	Sierra Nevada's lower slopes; timeless villages & tumbling streams	walking, horse riding, mountain biking, skiing & climbing	depends on activity	p382, p386
Parque Natural Cabo de Gata-Níjar	sandy beaches, volcanic cliffs, flamingo colony & semidesert vegetation	swimming, bird-watching, walking, horse riding, diving & snorkelling	any	p410
Parque Natural Los Alcornocales	rolling hills covered in great cork-oak forests	walking	Apr–Oct	p223
Parque Natural Sierra de Aracena y Picos de Aroche	rolling, green Sierra Morena country with old stone villages	walking & horse riding	Apr–Oct	p167
Parque Natural Sierra de Grazalema	beautiful, damp, hilly region with vultures, Mediterranean woodlands & Spanish firs	walking, wildlife watching, climbing, caving, canyoning & paragliding	Oct–Jun	p203
Parque Natural Sierra de las Nieves	mountain region with deep valleys, ibex, Spanish firs & spectacular vistas	walking	Apr–Jun, Sep–Nov	p285
Parque Natural Sierra Norte	rolling Sierra Morena country, ancient villages, long panoramas & gorgeous spring wild flowers	walking & horse riding	Mar–Oct	p139
Parque Natural Sierras de Cazorla, Segura y Las Villas	craggy mountains, deep valleys, thick forests & abundant visible wildlife	walking, horse riding & 4WD tours	Mar–Nov	p347
Paraje Natural Torcal de Antequera	mountain covered in spectacular limestone formations	walking & climbing	Mar–Nov	p291
Reserva Natural Laguna de Fuente de Piedra	shallow lake with Spain's biggest flamingo population	bird-watching	Feb–Aug	p291

PARKS & OTHER PROTECTED AREAS

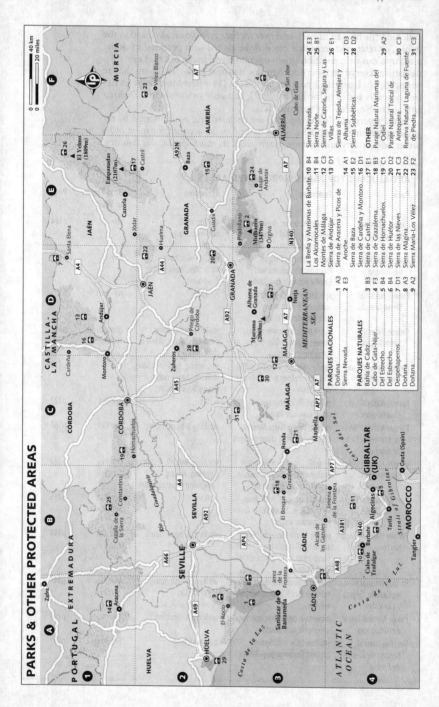

PARQUES NACIONALES	
Doñana................................	1 A3
Sierra Nevada.......................	2 E3

PARQUES NATURALES	
Bahía de Cádiz......................	3 B3
Cabo de Gata-Níjar...............	4 F3
Del Estrecho.........................	5 B4
Del Estrecho.........................	6 B4
Despeñaperros......................	7 D1
Doñana................................	8 A3
Doñana................................	9 A2

La Breña y Marismas de Barbate.	10 B4
Los Alcornocales..................	11 B4
Montes de Málaga...............	12 C3
Sierra de Andújar................	13 D1
Sierra de Aracena y Picos de Aroche.	14 A1
Sierra de Baza.....................	15 E2
Sierra de Cardeña y Montoro..	16 D1
Sierra de Castril..................	17 E1
Sierra de Grazalema............	18 B3
Sierra de Hornachuelos........	19 C1
Sierra de Huétor.................	20 D2
Sierra de las Nieves.............	21 C3
Sierra Mágina.....................	22 D2
Sierra María-Los Vélez.........	23 F2

Sierra Nevada......................	24 E3
Sierra Norte........................	25 B1
Sierras de Cazorla, Segura y Las Villas.	26 E1
Sierras de Tejeda, Almijara y Alhama.	27 D3
Sierras Subbéticas...............	28 D2

OTHER	
Paraje Natural Marismas del Odiel.	29 A2
Paraje Natural Torcal de Antequera.	30 C3
Reserva Natural Laguna de Fuente de Piedra.	31 C3

They are intended to protect cultural heritage as well as nature, and to promote economic development that's compatible with conservation. Many of them include roads, networks of walking trails, villages and even small towns, with accommodation often available within the park. Like national parks, they may include areas which can only be visited with permission.

Other types of protected areas in Andalucía include *parajes naturales* (natural areas; there are 31 of these), *reservas naturales* (nature reserves; numbering 29). These are generally smaller, little-inhabited areas, with much the same goals as natural parks. There are also 37 *monumentos naturales* (natural monuments), protecting specific features such as waterfalls, forests, dunes or forests. Some Spanish wilderness areas – about 900 sq km in Andalucía – are *reservas nacionales de caza* (national hunting reserves). Hunting, though subject to restrictions, is a deeply ingrained aspect of Spanish life. Hunting reserves are often located inside protected areas such as *parques naturales,* and you might walk or drive across one without even knowing it. If you hear gunshots, exercise caution!

ENVIRONMENTAL ISSUES

Andalucía's relative lack of industry and, until recently, its fairly traditional agriculture have left it with a pretty clean environment. Environmental awareness in Andalucía and Spain in general took a leap forward in the 1980s under the Partido Socialista Obrero Español (PSOE; Spanish Socialist Workers' Party) national government, which gave regional administrations responsibility for most environmental matters. In 1981 Spain had just 35 environmentally protected areas, covering 2200 sq km. Today there are over 400, covering more than 25,000 sq km, and Andalucía is the leader in this field (see p66).

There are problem areas nonetheless. Potentially, Andalucía's worst environmental problem is drought, which struck in the 1950s, 1960s and early 1990s, and is threatening again in the late 2000s. This is despite huge investment in reservoirs (which cover a higher proportion of Spain than of any other country in the world). The coastal building boom and the proliferation of golf courses increase demand for water, but inefficient irrigation methods and the very low price of water also lead to much waste.

The construction and property industries, as in so many places, present a variety of threats to the Andalucian environment. There's particular pressure near the coasts, where tourism multiplies the value of land and property. Slack controls on construction and widespread municipal corruption have led to unsightly, overcrowded and haphazard development, destruction of woodlands, wetlands and other coastal ecosystems, pressure on water supplies and pollution of the seas. An amazing 59% of Andalucía's coastline is already urbanised. The rampant overdevelopment of the Costa del Sol, which has been going on since the 1960s, is only the worst example. Vital wildernesses such as the Parque Nacional de Doñana and Parque Natural Cabo de Gata-Níjar are under constant pressure from mainly tourism-related schemes. Town halls and the all-powerful building and property industry say, correctly, that construction and tourism bring jobs, but environmentalists and the Junta de Andalucía argue that development must take place in a controlled and sustainable manner. The Junta is at last starting to put its money where its mouth is, with, for example, its withdrawal of planning powers in 2005 from the scandalous Marbella town hall (see p34) and the decision in 2006 to dynamite a hotel built on a beach within the Parque Natural Cabo de Gata-Níjar near Carboneras.

For official information on protected areas, visit the websites of the Ministerio de Medio Ambiente, Spain's environment ministry (www.mma .es), or the Junta de Andalucía's environmental department (www .juntadeandalucia.es /medioambiente/site /web).

Andalucía aims to generate 15% of its electricity from renewable sources by 2015. Wind will be the biggest source of this, with thousands of new windmills being constructed at wind farms around the region.

Visit Blue Flag (www
.blueflag.org) for the list
of blue-flag beaches, and
Ecologistas en Acción
(www.ecologistasen
accion.org in Spanish)
for the list of unsavoury
black-flag beaches.

The condition of Andalucía's beaches – so crucial to the tourism industry – is mixed. In 2005, 62 of them proudly flew the blue flag of the Foundation for Environmental Education, an international body that annually awards the flags to beaches that satisfy certain criteria of water quality, safety and services, including that 'no industrial or sewage-related discharges may affect the beach area'. On the other hand 34 Andalucian beaches, mainly in Almería and Cádiz provinces, were given *banderas negras* (black flags) by the Spanish environmental group Ecologistas en Acción, mainly for pollution by raw sewage entering the sea or for counter-ecological coastal building developments. According to Ecologistas en Acción, in Cádiz province, for example, there were no purification facilities for sewage entering the sea anywhere in the municipalities of Algeciras, Tarifa, Barbate, Vejer de la Frontera or Chipiona.

Air pollution by the petrochemical industry is a concern in the Huelva area. Intensive vegetable growing under enormous expanses (around 300 sq km) of ugly plastic greenhouses in the arid Almería region (see p410) is drying up the underground aquifers on which it depends, produces enormous quantities of nonbiodegradable rubbish and has sent hundreds of workers to hospital with pesticide poisoning.

Andalucía's largest and most active environmental organisation is **Ecologistas en Acción** (www.ecologistasenaccion.org in Spanish). **SEO/BirdLife** (Spanish Ornithological Society; www.seo.org in Spanish) is also active in conservation. International organisations involved in Andalucía include **Greenpeace** (www.greenpeace.org) and **WWF** (www.panda.org).

Andalucía Outdoors

Andalucía's hugely varied terrain and long coastline beckon action-lovers with endless adventures. Here we introduce some of the most popular and exciting activities you can pursue in the region. You'll also find our Top 10 Andalucian adventures on p16, and further detail in destination sections.

WALKING IN ANDALUCÍA

The thousands of kilometres of paths and tracks wending their way along Andalucía's verdant valleys and across its rugged hills provide marvellous walking of any length or difficulty you like. In some areas you can string together day walks into a trek of several days, sleeping along the way in a variety of hotels, *hostales* (budget hotels), camping grounds or occasionally mountain refuges or wild camping. For about half the year the climate is ideal, and in most areas the best months for walking are May, June, September and October. Walking in Andalucía is increasingly popular among both Spaniards and foreigners (and a growing number of specialist firms in northern Europe offer walking holidays here), but you'll rarely encounter anything like a crowd on any walk.

Trail marking is erratic: some routes are well signed with route numbers, on others just the odd dab of red paint might tell you you're heading in the right direction, and on yet others you're left entirely to your own devices. You certainly have opportunities to put your navigational skills to the test!

The two main categories of marked walking routes in Spain (even so, not always well marked) are *senderos de gran recorrido* (GRs, long-distance footpaths) and *senderos de pequeño recorrido* (PRs, shorter routes of a few hours or one or two days). The GR-7 long-distance path runs the length of Spain from Andorra in the north to Tarifa in the south, part of the European E-4 route from Greece to Andalucía. It enters Andalucía near Almaciles in northeast Granada province, then divides at Puebla de Don Fadrique, with one branch heading through Jaén and Córdoba provinces and the other through Las Alpujarras southeast of Granada before the two rejoin near Antequera in Málaga province. Signposting of this path throughout Andalucía is still in progress. There are also plenty of paths that are neither GRs nor PRs.

Further information on walks is given in this book's regional chapters. Tourist offices and visitors centres often have plenty of information on routes and conditions. The best in-depth walking guides to regions of Andalucía in English (and probably any language) are those published by **Discovery Walking Guides** (www.walking.demon.co.uk) on Las Alpujarras, the Sierra de Aracena and La Axarquía – terrifically detailed but also entertaining. The first two are accompanied by excellent maps, which you can buy separately if you wish. Further walking guides to specific areas are often available locally. For information on maps, see p435.

Walking in Andalucía by Guy Hunter-Watts has detailed descriptions and maps of 34 good day walks.

La Axarquía

Hill villages such as Cómpeta, Canillas de Albaida, Canillas de Aceituno and Alfarnate, in the eastern district of Málaga province known as La Axarquía (p292), give access to many good tracks and paths. You can choose from gentle valley strolls close to the villages or climbs to summits with majestic views.

Access cities, towns and villages: Málaga (p242), Vélez Málaga (p292), Cómpeta (p293), Nerja (p294).

Las Alpujarras

One of the most picturesque corners of Andalucía, Las Alpujarras (p386) is a 70km-long jumble of valleys along the south flank of the Sierra Nevada, stretching from Granada province into neighbouring Almería. Arid hillsides split by deep ravines alternate with oasis-like white villages surrounded by vegetable gardens, orchards, rapid streams and woodlands. Ancient paths wind up and down through constantly changing scenery between labyrinthine, Berber-style villages. Many villages have hotels, *hostales* or camping grounds, enabling you to string together routes of several days or do a number of day walks from a single base.

Access cities and towns: Granada (p356), Órgiva (p388), Laujar de Andarax (p409).

Parque Natural Cabo de Gata-Níjar

'The combination of a dry, desert climate with volcanic cliffs plunging into azure Mediterranean waters produces a landscape of stark grandeur around the Cabo de Gata promontory'

The combination of a dry, desert climate with volcanic cliffs plunging into azure Mediterranean waters produces a landscape of stark grandeur around the Cabo de Gata promontory (p410), southeast of Almería. Between the cliffs and headlands are strung some of Spain's best and least crowded beaches, and by combining paths, dirt roads and occasional sections of paved road, you can walk right round the 60km coast in three or four days. There's plenty of accommodation, including four camping grounds, along the way. September and October are good months to walk here: the searing temperatures of July and August have abated, but the sea is still warm (it's warmer in October than in June).

Access city: Almería (p398).

Parque Natural Sierras de Cazorla, Segura y Las Villas

The Parque Natural Sierras de Cazorla, Segura y Las Villas (p347) is the largest protected area in Spain (2143 sq km), a crinkled, pinnacled region of several complicated mountain ranges – not extraordinarily high, but memorably beautiful – divided by high plains and deep river valleys. Much of the park is thickly forested and wild animals are abundant and visible. The ideal way to explore it is with a vehicle to reach day walks in some of its more remote areas. Camping in wilderness areas is not permitted and with accommodation and camping grounds concentrated in certain areas, multiday walks are not really feasible.

Main access town: Cazorla (p345).

Parque Natural Sierra de Aracena y Picos de Aroche

This verdant, sometimes lush, sometimes severe region (p167), in Huelva province in far northwest Andalucía, is dotted with timeless stone villages and strung with an extensive network of well-maintained trails. It's a lovely area to spend a few days. Many villages have accommodation, enabling you to string together routes of several days. And the local food is notably scrumptious.

Main access town: Aracena (p164).

Parque Natural Sierra de Grazalema

The hills of the Parque Natural Sierra de Grazalema (p203) in Cádiz province encompass a variety of beautiful landscapes, from pastoral river valleys and dense Mediterranean woodlands to rocky summits and precipitous gorges. Some of the best walks are within a reserve area for which permits or guides are required: you may need to arrange these a few days ahead. There's plenty of accommodation in nearby villages.

Access villages: Grazalema (p204), El Bosque (p204), Zahara de la Sierra (p207), Villaluenga del Rosario (p208).

Parque Natural Sierra de las Nieves

Southeast of the interesting old town of Ronda, the Sierra de las Nieves (p285) includes the highest peak in the western half of Andalucía, Torrecilla (1919m), climbable in a day trip from Ronda. Lower altitudes have extensive evergreen woodlands.

Access towns: Ronda (p277), Yunquera (p285), El Burgo (p285).

Parque Natural Sierra Norte

The rolling Sierra Morena country (p139) in the north of Sevilla province presents ever-changing vistas of green valleys and hills, woodlands, rivers and atmospheric old towns and villages. The spring wild flowers are spectacular here. There are a variety of day and half-day walks marked around the region and, with a range of attractive accommodation, it's a delightful area to spend a few days.

Access towns: Cazalla de la Sierra (p140), Constantina (p142), El Pedroso (p140).

Sierra Nevada

This snowcapped mountain range southeast of Granada includes mainland Spain's highest peak, Mulhacén (3479m), and many other summits over 3000m. The Sierra Nevada (p382) is Andalucía's ultimate walking experience in terms of altitude and climatic conditions and also for its forbidding, wild aspect: large tracts are a rugged wilderness of black rock and stones, with plenty of sheer faces and jagged crags. During July, August and early September – the best months for walking up here, though high-altitude weather is never predictable – a national park bus service gives walkers access to the upper reaches of the range from both the north and south sides. It's quite feasible to cap Mulhacén or the second-highest peak, Veleta (3395m), in a day trip. There are many other possible routes, plus a number of refuges if you want to stay the night in the mountains. Camping is allowed above 1600m, subject to certain conditions (see p385).

Main access towns: Granada (p356), Estación de Esquí Sierra Nevada (p383), Capileira (p388), Trevélez (p391).

WATER SPORTS
Windsurfing

Tarifa, a surfers' paradise on the Strait of Gibraltar (see the boxed text p218), is one of *the* top spots in Europe for windsurfing, thanks to the strong breezes blowing one way or the other through the strait almost year-round. The long, sandy beaches are an added attraction and there's a hip international scene to go with the boards and waves. Rental of a board, sail and wetsuit costs around €35 per hour or €75 per day, with a six-hour beginner's course at around €120.

Kitesurfing

Kitesurfers (also known as flysurfers or kiteboarders) use boards like windsurfers but they catch the wind by means of a kitelike sail high in the air, to which they're attached by a harness and long strings. This fast-growing sport can be enjoyed in lighter winds than are needed for windsurfing. Experts reach high speeds and perform tricky manoeuvres

'The rolling Sierra Morena country presents ever-changing vistas of green valleys and hills, woodlands, rivers and atmospheric old towns and villages'

NOT JUST TARIFA: 10 MORE TOP ANDALUCIAN WINDSURFING SPOTS

Some pretty good winds blow further up the Atlantic coast, too:

- Bolonia (p214)
- Los Caños de Meca (p211)
- Sancti Petri (p209)
- El Puerto de Santa María (p183)
- Punta Umbría (p159)
- Isla Cristina (p160)

Along the Mediterranean coast conditions are generally less exciting, though often better for beginners, and there are facilities at several Costa del Sol resorts and places further east:

- La Herradura (p395)
- Almerimar (p410)
- Almería (p402)
- Mojácar (p417)

while 'hanging' in the air. Tarifa is the hub (see the boxed text, p218), with equipment rental and sales, and classes available. Costs are a bit higher than for windsurfing. Beginners definitely need tuition, as out-of-control kitesurfers can be a danger to themselves and everyone else. A six-hour beginner's course should cost about €120. Punta Umbría (p159) is another place with good winds. On the Mediterranean coast there are facilities at places such as Marbella (p271) and La Herradura (p395).

Surfing

Andalucía's waves don't rival those of northern Spain, but the surf can be good in winter on the Atlantic coast of Cádiz province, especially at El Palmar (p210), where waves can reach 3m, and Los Caños de Meca (p211). Some of the Mediterranean beaches are good for beginners, and bodyboarding (boogie-boarding) is popular all along the Andalucian coasts, with boards for sale everywhere.

Diving & Snorkelling

Andalucía's coasts don't provide all the spectacular sights of tropical waters but there is still some interesting diving here and plenty of dive schools and shops in the coastal resorts to help you enjoy it. Most establishments offer courses under the aegis of international diving organisations such as **PADI** (www.padi.com) or **NAUI** (www.nauiww.org), as well as dives for qualified divers and 'baptism' dives. A single dive with full equipment costs around €40. Introductory 'baptism' and 'discover scuba diving' courses for up to three hours run from about €35 to €75. The five-day PADI open-water certification course will cost you around €400.

The following are Andalucía's best diving areas, from west to east:

Tarifa (p218) Wrecks and varied marine fauna, but low temperatures and some strong currents – better for experienced divers.

Gibraltar (p236) Great for wrecks.

Coast of Granada province Especially La Herradura/Marina del Este (p395) and around the towns of Calahonda and Castell de Ferro (p392); steep cliffs, deep water, some caves.

Cabo de Gata (p413) Sea floors of seagrass, sand and rocks, often with caves, crevices or passages; grouper and conger or moray eels at some sites.

Andalucía (www.andalucia.org) and Buceo XXI (www.buceo21.com in Spanish) both list over 20 dive outfits.

Snorkelling is best along the rockier parts of the Mediterranean coast – between Nerja and Adra, and from Cabo de Gata to Mojácar.

Sailing

Some 40 marinas and mooring places are strung along Andalucía's coast from Ayamonte on the Portuguese border to Garrucha in Almería province. Voyages along the Mediterranean coast, through the Strait of Gibraltar to Costa de la Luz or Portugal, or across to Morocco, are all popular. The biggest marinas are the flashy Puerto Banús (p276) and Benalmádena (p264) on Costa del Sol, and Almerimar near Almería, each with over 900 moorings, but there are plenty of smaller, more relaxed ports such as San José (p413) on Cabo de Gata, Marina del Este (p395) near La Herradura and Mazagón (p152) near Huelva. Information on marinas, moorings and sailing clubs is available from Andalucía's official tourism website, **Andalucía te Quiere** (Andalucía Loves You; www.andalucia.org) and the **Federación Andaluza de Vela** (Andalucian Sailing Federation; www.fav.es in Spanish). Boat hire is possible at many marinas. For yacht charter, check **Costa del Sol Charter** (www.costadelsolcharter.com), **Yachting Sotogrande** (www.yachtingsotogrande .com) or **Viento y Mar** (www.vientoymar.com in Spanish).

You can learn to sail too. Beginners' classes are offered at Isla Cristina (p160). Five-day courses approved by the UK's Royal Yachting Association are given by Yachting Sotogrande, in Sotogrande between Estepona and Gibraltar, and **Allabroad Sailing Academy** (www.sailing.gi) and **Alfer Sea School** (www.alferseaschool.com), both in Gibraltar. A 'competent crew', 'day skipper' or 'coastal skipper' course costs around €700 or UK£500.

Canoeing & Kayaking

Both coastal waters and inland reservoirs are good for flat-water canoeing and kayaking. For some recommended operators, see our sections on Zahara de la Sierra (p207) and Isla Cristina (p160) in western Andalucía, and La Herradura (p395), Parque Natural Sierras de Cazorla, Segura y las Villas (p351), Almería (p402) and Mojácar (p417), dotted around eastern Andalucía.

HORSE RIDING

Andalucía is steeped in equestrian tradition. The horse has been part of rural life since time immemorial and Andalucía is the home of the elegant and internationally esteemed Spanish thoroughbred horse, also known as the Cartujano or Andalusian. Countless good riding tracks crisscross the region's marvellous landscapes, and an ever-growing number of *picaderos* (stables) are ready to take you on a guided ride for any duration between an hour and a week, or give you classes. Many of the mounts are Andalusians or Andalusian-Arab crosses – medium-sized, intelligent, good in traffic and, as a rule, easy to handle and sure-footed.

Typical prices for a ride or lesson are €25 to €30 for one hour, €60 to €70 for a half day and around €100 for a full day. Most stables cater for all levels of experience, from lessons for beginners or children to trail rides for more competent riders. The ideal months to ride in Andalucía are May, June, September and October, when the weather is likely to be good but not too hot.

The provinces of Sevilla and Cádiz have perhaps the highest horse populations and concentrations of stables, but there are riding opportunities throughout the region. **Andalucía te Quiere** (www.andalucia.org) has a directory of over 100 stables and other equestrian establishments.

Andalucian saddles are bigger than British ones, with high front and rear pieces, and a sheepskin cover for more comfort, while the stirrups are heavy and triangular, with room for the whole foot.

For a wry account of what long-distance riding across Andalucía was like not so long ago, dig out Penelope Chetwode's amusing *Two Middle-aged Ladies in Andalusia*.

Two of the many highlights of riding experiences in Andalucía are trail rides in the Alpujarras (p389) and Sierra Nevada (p383), and beach and dune riding just out of Tarifa on Cádiz's Costa de la Luz (p219). For recommended stables, see this book's sections on Alájar (p169), Aracena (p166), Arcos de la Frontera (p200), Castaño del Robledo (p169), Cazalla de la Sierra (p141), Cómpeta (p293), El Rocío (p157), Galaroza (p170), Parque Natural de las Sierras de Cazorla, Segura y las Villas (p351 and p351), Parque Natural Sierra de Hornachuelos (p317), Ronda (p281) and San José (p413).

All horse-lovers should put Jerez de la Frontera (p191) high on their itinerary. The town stages several exciting annual equine events – especially its Feria del Caballo (Horse Fair) in May – and its famous Real Escuela Andaluza del Arte Ecuestre (Royal Andalucian School of Equestrian Art) and the nearby Yeguada de la Cartuja – Hierro del Bocado (p200) breeding centre are fascinating to visit at any time.

Andalusian Rock Climbs by Chris Craggs is still a useful guide, though published in 1992.

CLIMBING

Mountainous Andalucía is full of crags, walls and slabs that invite *escalada* (climbing), now a popular sport here. Thanks to the southern Mediterranean climate, this is a good region for winter climbing. In fact there's good climbing year-round, though July and August temperatures are too high for some spots. Most of the climbing is on limestone and there's more sport climbing than classical.

The sheer walls of El Chorro gorge (p287), one of several great sites in the north of Málaga province, are the biggest magnet, with some 600 routes of almost every grade of difficulty. El Chorro presents a great variety of both classical and sport climbing, from slab climbs to towering walls to bolted multipitch routes. If this isn't enough, several nearby spots provide fine climbing too. There's accommodation for all budgets in the El Chorro area, and a climbers' scene at Bar Isabel at El Chorro train station. British publisher Rockfax's successful *Costa Blanca, Mallorca & El Chorro* climbing guide is now out of print (you might still find a few copies in bookshops) but you can obtain its El Chorro section online at www.rockfax.com.

The following are among Andalucía's other top climbing sites:

El Torcal (p291; Málaga province) Two hundred sport and classical pitches of grade V-8 in weird limestone landscape, best from spring to autumn.

Desnivel (www.escuelas deescalada.com) has comprehensive listings of Andalucian climbing sites with lots of detail in Spanish and automatic-translation English.

La Cueva de Archidona (Archidona, northern Málaga province) Superb grade 7-9 sport climbing, spring and autumn.

Loja (Granada province) Has 175 grade 6-7 mainly sport routes, best in autumn and spring.

Los Cahorros (p386; near Monachil, Granada province) Over 250 sport and classical routes, grades V-8, climbable year-round.

Mijas (p269; Málaga province) Around 80 grade V-7 climbs, good for winter.

Parque Natural Sierra de Grazalema (p204; Cádiz province) Fine classical climbs on Peñón Grande crag, spring to autumn.

San Bartolo (p214; near Bolonia, Cádiz province) Rare sandstone crag with 280 pitches up to grade 8, good for winter.

Villanueva del Rosario (Málaga province) Best boulder climbing in Andalucía; also sport and classical routes.

Short courses for beginners are available at **Finca La Campana** (p287; www.el-chorro.com) and **Girasol Outdoor Company** (p219; www.girasol-adventure.com) in Tarifa. You can also purchase climbing equipment at sports shops in most major cities; try **Deportes La Trucha** (Map p246; ☎ 952 21 22 03; Calle Carretería 100) in Málaga.

SKIING & SNOWBOARDING

Andalucía's only ski station, the very popular Estación de Esquí Sierra Nevada (Sierra Nevada Ski Station; p383), 33km southeast of Granada, is the most southerly ski resort in Europe, and its runs and facilities are of championship quality. The season normally runs from December to April, and it gets pretty crowded (with a thriving nightlife) at weekends for most of that period and around the Christmas–New Year and Día de Andalucía (28 February) holidays.

The resort has over 70 marked downhill runs of varied difficulty, totalling over 80km, plus cross-country routes and a dedicated snowboarding area. Some runs start almost at the top of Veleta (3395m), the second highest peak in the Sierra Nevada.

A single-day pass plus rental of skis, boots and poles, or snowboard and boots, costs between €50 and €65, depending on when you go. Six hours of group classes at ski school are €63.

There's plenty of accommodation at the station, but reservations are always advisable: double rooms start at about €80. The best deals are ski packages, bookable through the station's website or phone number; they start at around €150 for two days and two nights with lift passes and half-board.

CYCLING & MOUNTAIN BIKING

Andalucía's combination of plains, rolling hills and mountain ranges makes all kinds of cycling trips possible, from cruises along the *carriles de cicloturismo* (roads adapted for cycle touring) in the flat lands surrounding the Parque Nacional de Doñana (see p131 for more information about the Carril de Cicloturismo Pinares de Aznalcázar–La Puebla) to tough off-road mountain routes. Road cycling has always been popular in Spain, and mountain biking is ever more popular. Thousands of off-road kilometres await the adventurous, while the relatively little-trafficked country roads offer some great cycle touring. Spring and autumn, with their moderate temperatures, are the best seasons.

Many tourist offices have route information and **Andalucía te Quiere** (www.andalucia.org) details up to 15 mountain-bike routes in each of Andalucía's eight provinces, with sketch maps. The same routes are covered in the *Mountain Bike* booklet sold by Junta de Andalucía tourist offices.

Plenty of places rent out mountain bikes for around €10 to €12 a day, and you can join guided group rides in a number of places.

Some recommended bike-hire and tour firms can be found in Monachil (p386), the Sierra Nevada (p383), Las Alpujarras (p389) and La Herradura (p395) in Granada province; Vejer de la Frontera (p209) and Tarifa (p219) in Cádiz province; Ronda (p281), Marbella (p271) and El Chorro (p287) in Málaga province; and San José (p413) in Almería.

Wild Spain (www.wild-spain.com) includes articles and lists of guides and companies for many outdoor activities.

GOLF

Over 700,000 people a year come to Andalucía primarily to play golf, and more and more Andalucians are taking to the fairways. Andalucía has 84 golf courses (with more on the way). Over half the courses are dotted along the Costa del Sol between Málaga and Gibraltar. The fine climate and the many beautifully landscaped, well-kept courses designed by top golf-course designers are among the special pleasures of golf here. There's even one completely floodlit night-time course (mercifully without rough), La Dama de Noche at Marbella. Flat terrain is fairly rare in Andalucía, so most courses have a certain amount of slope to contend with. Green fees are comparable to Britain: between €50 and

ESCAPE

If you just feel like pampering yourself after a spot of exertion (or just feel like pampering yourself on holiday anyway), you can do so and at the same time get a feel for life in medieval Andalucía at one of the modern-day *Baños Árabes* (Arab Baths) that have opened in Granada (p371), Córdoba (p310), Jerez de la Frontera (p196) and Málaga (p248). These baths, in beautiful traditional style, re-create the experience and atmosphere of a key institution of old Islamic Andalucía (medieval Córdoba had 60 bathhouses). The scent of herbal oils and the sound of ethereal background music waft through the air as you move between pools of varied temperatures. For a full account of a visit to the Jerez baths, see the boxed text, p196.

€75 at most clubs. Top courses on the Costa del Sol, such as Valderrama (proud host to the Ryder Cup in 1997), Sotogrande, and Las Brisas and Aloha at Marbella, are more costly (€260 to €290 at Valderrama, the most expensive). Professional tuition (typically around €25 to €30 an hour) and hire of clubs (around €15 to €20 per round), trolleys (around €5, or €10 to €15 for an electric one) and buggies (around €30) are available at almost every course.

For help with planning your golf holiday, consult *The Pocket Guide to Golf Courses: Spain & Portugal*, or David J Whyte's *Spain: Over 100 Courses & Facilities*.

Useful information sources include **Andalucía te Quiere** (www.andalucia.org) and the **Federación Andaluza de Golf** (www.fga.org), both with directories of the region's courses, and the free paper *Andalucía Costa del Golf,* available from some tourist offices. Many golfers from other countries come on organised golf holidays, with tee times, accommodation and everything else booked in advance, but it's perfectly feasible to organise your own golf: English-speakers are available almost everywhere. **Golf Service** (www .golf-service.com) offers discounted green fees and tee-off time reservations.

OTHER ACTIVITIES

Andalucía's rugged limestone geology makes for some exciting caving, especially in the Ronda/Grazalema area around Villaluenga del Rosario (p208), Grazalema (p206), Zahara de la Sierra (p207) and Ronda (p281). There's some exhilarating canyoning to be had in the Garganta Verde (p207 and p206) and the hills behind La Herradura (p395). Or take to the skies in a paraglider from Zahara de la Sierra (p207), Valle de Abdalajís (p286) or La Herradura (p395). Tennis, fishing and paintball are some of the other fun things you can do in Andalucía. For introductory information on many activities see websites such as **Andalucía te Quiere** (www.andalucia .org) and **Galería Marbella** (www.galeriamarbella.com; go to 'Sports'). The region is also exciting for those who like watching birds and other wildlife – for information about wildlife and wildlife watching in Andalucía see p61.

Food & Drink

One of Andalucía's most prominent draws is just this: food and drink. In the whole of Spain, and especially in the south, lunch and dinner times are holy hours, obeyed by all. Food here is a social occasion best experienced in the tradition of *tapear*, or eating tapas. This is one of the most wonderful ways to eat: sharing and tasting new dishes all the time, adoring some, detesting others and commenting how your mother's recipe might taste much better. In Granada, Jaén and Almería, the age-old tradition of free tapas with a drink still persists, and the citizens of those regions are proud and indeed feel superior for their generosity over places like Seville and Cádiz or Córdoba where you have to pay for each tapa.

Andalucian cuisine has many influences, such as Roman, Jewish, *gitano* (Roma) and New World, but like its history, much of its architecture and general aesthetic, it is the North African influence that is most present and potent. Delicious Mediterranean ingredients such as oranges, lemons, apricots, aubergines (eggplant) and spinach are mixed with beans, pulps and grains; many dishes have spices such as cinnamon or cumin and herbs like mint and coriander. A glass of icy *fino* sherry or a cool *caña* (beer) can be accompanied by simple things like *jamón y pan* (ham and bread), or *almendras con pimentón* (roast almonds with paprika), or more elaborate dishes like *garbanzos con espinacas* (chickpeas and spinach) spiced up with turmeric and cumin. There is, of course, a wealth of fish and seafood, eaten simply, like grilled sardines with sea salt, or fried king prawns that make anyone drool just at the thought.

Spanish food, like Spanish culture has two poles: the traditional and the modern, and in the last decade there has been a new wave of contemporary cuisine, spearheaded by top chefs like the wonderfully eccentric Catalan Ferrán Adrià, or the Basque Martín Berasategui and Juan Mari Arzak. They take traditional cuisine, blow it apart and put it back together to create a revolution in Spanish cooking. Although Andalucía has been slow to get into the groove of contemporary cuisine, restaurants that cook and serve traditional ingredients in a modern way are emerging like snails on a rainy day. Mr Adrià has honoured Andalucía by opening Hacienda Benazuza (p118) near Seville, and designing the menu in one of its three restaurants with his experimental dishes that may literally blow you away. Needless to say, the famed elBulli restaurant already has two Michelin stars, though you might need to wait three lifetimes to get a reservation to actually taste Adrià's legendary cuisine. And, in places such as Restaurante Tragabuches (p283) and Café de Paris (p261), both in Málaga province, regional dishes have been given a radical twist, breathing exciting new life into provincial cooking.

Lonely Planet's *World Food Spain* by Richard Sterling is a trip into Spain's culinary soul, from tapas to *postres* (desserts), with a comprehensive culinary dictionary.

STAPLES & SPECIALITIES

You'll find all things Mediterranean dominating the region's ingredient list: creamy olive oil, dynamite garlic, teary onions, smashing tomatoes and a variety of peppers, accompanied by chickpeas, beans and rice. It's what the Spanish have been eating for centuries, and what's cooked in traditional bars and restaurants is what will be simmering in any Andalucian family kitchen. But the kings of all kitchens, bars and restaurants are four things: *jamón*, chorizo, *queso* and *pan* – ham, spicy sausage, cheese and bread. The further you go into the mountainous regions, the more tasty game dishes and stews will abound, whereas by the sea, ravishing seafood predominates.

Bread

No meal is eaten in Spain without *pan*. Every district has a *panadería* (bakery) where bread of all shapes and sizes is produced daily. For breakfast, *bollos* or *molletes* (small, soft rolls) are consumed as well as *tostadas* (toasted bread), served with a choice of finely chopped tomatoes, olive oil, *jamón* or foie gras. Simple country bread, *pan de campo*, is the perfect companion for any meal. What isn't eaten is then used to thicken soups and sauces.

Cheese

Spain's most famous cheese, Manchego, originates from the central region of La Mancha. Traditionally made from ewe's milk, it is salty and full of flavour and is frequently served as a tapa. When still fresh, Manchego cheese has a creamy and mild consistency; semicured ones are firmer and have a stronger flavour, while those aged more than three months have a distinctive tang. Typical Andalucian cheeses include Grazalema, from the mountains of Cádiz, made from ewe's milk and similar to Manchego; Málaga, a goat's milk cheese preserved in olive oil; and Cádiz, a strong, fresh goat's milk cheese made in the countryside around Cádiz. Another cheese found throughout Spain is Burgos, a very mild ewe's milk cheese, delicious when served as a dessert with honey, nuts and fruit.

One of the top books on Andalucian cooking is *Moro*, by Samuel and Samantha Clark, the cookbook of the renowned London-based restaurant of the same name. The book also explores North African influences on Spanish cooking.

Fish & Seafood

You'll be excused for feeling like a king or queen when presented with the incredible variety of fish and seafood in the coastal towns of Andalucía. Never be afraid to ask what something is, and use the tradition of eating tapas to work out what you like without overdosing on any one dish. *Boquerones* (anchovies) are the most popular. They are served either fried (*fritos*) or marinated in garlic, olive oil and vinegar. Sardines come grilled (*a la plancha*), and *gambas* (prawns) and *langostinos* (king prawns) are served grilled, fried or cold with a bowl of fresh mayonnaise. *Gambas* are also used in paellas or soups. The most bizarre are *camarones*, tiny shrimps that you can see in markets, sold while still alive and jumping around the bucket. They are used in *tortilla de camarones*, a delicious, crispy frittata embedded with the tiny prawns. Other Andalucian obsessions include *chipirones* or *chopitos* (baby squid), and in Málaga they would also add *chanquetes* (similar to whitebait and served deep-fried) to the list. *Ostras* (oysters) are plentiful in and around Cádiz.

Fruit & Vegetables

Andalucía has arguably the finest fruits and vegetables in Spain due to its generous climate. And the good news is that this fantastic produce is eaten in season and generally bought fresh and in open-air morning markets.

Along the subtropical coastal plains you can find *plátanos* (bananas), *aguacates* (avocadoes), *mangos* (mangoes) and even *caña de azúcar* (sugar cane). Almería province, east of Málaga, is Europe's winter garden, with miles of plastic-covered hothouses of intensively grown vegetables. Fruit and almond trees cover the lower slopes of the sierras alongside the famous bitter *naranjas* (oranges) – used solely to produce marmalade – introduced by the Arabs. *Higos* (figs) and *granadas* (pomegranates – get those antioxidants!) abound in the summer and early autumn months.

Córdoba province is famous for its vegetable dishes such as *alcachofas con almejas* (artichokes with clams), *revueltos de esparragos trigueros* (wild asparagus with scrambled eggs), and lots of deep-purple *berenjenas* (aubergines).

Jamón & Sausages

There is no more tastebud-teasing prospect than a few paper-thin, succulent slices of *jamón*. Most of these hams are *jamón serrano* (mountain-cured ham). *Jamón ibérico*, also called *pata negra* (black leg), comes from the black Iberian breed of pig. The outstanding *jamón ibérico de bellota* comes from pigs fed on *bellotas* (acorns). Considered to be the best *jamón* of all is the *jamón ibérico* of Jabugo, in Andalucía's Huelva province (see p170), which comes from pigs free-ranging in the Sierra Morena oak forests. The best Jabugo hams are graded from one to five *jotas* (Js), and *cinco jotas* (JJJJJ) hams come from pigs that have never eaten anything but acorns.

Don't confuse this with uncured ham, *jamón York*, which is the uninspiring, British supermarket ham variety.

Morcilla is a blood sausage with rice or onions, best eaten lightly grilled. Chorizo, another essential ingredient, is a spicy pork sausage with paprika, which can come *crudo* (raw) – good for cooking.

Olive Oil

The endless olive groves of Córdoba, Jaén and Sevilla were originally planted by the Romans, but the production of *az-zait* (juice of the olive), from which the modern generic word for olive oil, *aceite,* is derived, was further developed by the Muslims. The three most olivy Andalucian provinces are among the main contributors to Spain's standing as the world's largest olive-oil producer, and both olives and olive oil continue to be a staple of the Andalucian kitchen. For quality-control purposes there are now six accredited Denominación de Origen (DO; a designation that indicates the unique geographic origins, production processes and quality of the product) labels in Spain and four of these are in Andalucía: Baena and Priego de Córdoba in Córdoba, and Sierra de Segura and Sierra Mágina in Jaén. The absolute finest of these, such as Núñez de Prado (see p318), have nearly zero acidity.

Spain is the world's largest producer of olive oil.

Paella & Other Rice Dishes

Apart from olive oil and other crucial elements of the Spanish larder, the Arabs also brought *arroz* (rice), a staple that became the base for Spain's most famous dish, paella (pronounced *pa-eh-ya*). Although paella's home is out of Andalucía, in Valencia, this excellent dish is a Sunday-lunch must in most Andalucian restaurants.

Paella is prepared in a *paellera*, a wide, two-handled metal pan, and tastes best when cooked over a wood fire outdoors. The flavour of the *arroz* comes from the *sofrito* – a mix of softened onions, garlic and peppers – and the meat or fish it's cooked with. The yellow colour traditionally comes from saffron, although this is sometimes substituted by the cheaper *pimentón* (paprika). Andalucian versions of paella often include seafood and/or chicken. On the Costa del Sol, peas, clams, mussels and prawns, and a garnish of red peppers and lemon slices is a popular combination. In Sevilla and Cádiz provinces, big prawns and sometimes lobster are added.

You'll know a good paella when you taste one, but an indicator of whether it's done from scratch (and therefore hopefully good) is usually the preparation time: if you wait for five minutes, it's been warmed up and probably won't taste that great; if you wait for 45 minutes and are already tipsy on wine by the time it arrives, prepare for a feast.

Other rice dishes are *arroz a la Sevillana,* a seafood rice from Sevilla with crab, sausage and ham; *arroz con almejas* (rice with clams); and *arroz negro* (rice cooked in squid ink).

www.spaingourmetour .com is the most authoritative and comprehensive periodical on Spanish gastronomy.

Stews

In the past the *cocido,* a one-pot feast of meat, sausage, beans and vegetables, was a mainstay of the local diet. It's time-consuming to prepare, but in Andalucian villages the smell still wafts through the streets. A *cocido* can actually provide a three-course meal, with the broth eaten first, followed by the vegetables and then the meat.

More usual nowadays is a simpler kind of stew, the *guiso,* which comes in three traditional types – *las berzas,* with cabbage and either beef or pork; *el puchero,* chicken and bacon broth with turnips and mint; and *los potajes,* with dried beans and chorizo. Dishes that Granada is famous for include *habas con jamón* (broad beans with ham) and the ubiquitous *rabo de toro* (oxtail stew).

Soups

Andalucía's most famous soup – the chilled gazpacho – is eaten around the world. A blended mix of tomatoes, peppers, cucumber, garlic, breadcrumbs, lemon and oil, it's a legacy of the New World, when Columbus brought back tomatoes and peppers from his travels. It is sometimes served in a jug with ice cubes, with side dishes of chopped raw vegetables such as cucumber and onion. The basis for gazpacho developed in Andalucía among the *jornaleros,* agricultural day labourers, who were given rations of oil and bread, which they soaked in water to form the basis of a soup, adding the oil, garlic and whatever fresh vegetables were at hand. All of the ingredients were pounded using a mortar and pestle and a refreshing and nourishing dish was made that would conquer the world.

A thicker version of gazpacho is *salmorejo cordobés,* from Córdoba, served with bits of *jamón* and crumbled egg. *Ajo blanco* is a white

---

ROLL UP YOUR SLEEVES & MAKE YOUR OWN GAZPACHO

It should be piping hot outside for this recipe. It's easy enough to make on the road:

3 garlic cloves
1kg ripe, sweet tomatoes, diced
1 green pepper, seeded and sliced
¾ cucumber, peeled and sliced
1 tablespoon grated onion
2 handfuls of crumbled old-ish white bread, no crusts
1¾ tablespoons red-wine vinegar or sherry vinegar, the best you can get
2 tablespoons olive oil
pinch of sea salt and freshly cracked pepper

Crush the garlic with a pinch of salt in a mortar and pestle until you have a smooth paste. Stick the vegetables and bread into a food processor (or just pound hard) and blend until smooth. Season with the garlic, vinegar, olive oil, salt and pepper. To thin it down, add some ice cubes. Leave the soup in the fridge for a couple of hours and check for seasoning once more when the temperature is right. It should be cold enough to give you a tingle, but not that cold to make you shiver.

Serves 4

gazpacho, a North African legacy, with almonds, garlic and grapes used instead of tomatoes. Another tasty soup is *sopa de ajo* (garlic soup).

DRINKS
Wine

Vino (wine) production in Andalucía was introduced by the Phoenicians, possibly as early as 1100 BC. Nowadays, almost every village throughout Andalucía has its own simple wine, known simply as *mosto*. Eight areas in the region produce distinctive, good, non-DO wines that can be sampled locally: Aljarafe and Los Palacios (Sevilla province); Bailén, Lopera and Torreperogil (Jaén province); Costa Albondón (Granada province); Laujar de Andarax (Almería province); and Villaviciosa (Córdoba province).

The Montilla-Morales DO in southern Córdoba province produces a wine that is similar to sherry but, unlike sherry, is not fortified by the addition of brandy – the *fino* variety is the most acclaimed. Andalucía's other DO is in Málaga province: sweet, velvety Málaga Dulce pleased palates from Virgil to the ladies of Victorian England, until the vines were blighted around the beginning of the 20th century. Today the Málaga DO area is Andalucía's smallest. You can sample Málaga wine straight from the barrel in some of the city's numerous bars.

Wine not only accompanies meals but is also a popular bar drink – and it's cheap: a bottle costing €5 in a supermarket or €12 in a restaurant will be a decent wine. *Vino de mesa* (table wine) may cost less than €1.50 a litre in shops. You can order wine by the *copa* (glass) in bars and restaurants: the *vino de la casa* (house wine) may come from a barrel for about €1.

Sherry

Sherry, Andalucía's celebrated fortified wine, is produced in the towns of Jerez de la Frontera, El Puerto de Santa María and Sanlúcar de Barrameda, which make up the 'sherry triangle' of Cádiz province (see p183). A combination of climate, chalky soils that soak up the sun but retain moisture, and a special maturing process called the *solera* process (see p195) produces these unique wines.

The main distinction in sherry is between *fino* (dry and straw-coloured) and *oloroso* (sweet and dark, with a strong bouquet). An *amontillado* is an amber, moderately dry *fino* with a nutty flavour and a higher alcohol content. An *oloroso* combined with a sweet wine results in a cream sherry. A *manzanilla* – officially not sherry – is a camomile-coloured, unfortified *fino* produced in Sanlúcar de Barrameda; its delicate flavour is reckoned to come from sea breezes wafting into the bodegas (wineries).

Beer

The most common ways to order a *cerveza* (beer) is to ask for a *caña* (a small draught beer; 250mL), or a *tubo* (a larger draught beer; about 300mL), which come in a straight glass. If you just ask for a *cerveza* you may get bottled beer, which tends to be more expensive. A small bottle (250mL) is called a *botellín* or a *quinto*; a bigger one (330mL) is a *tercio*. San Miguel, Cruzcampo and Victoria are all decent Andalucian beers.

Coffee

In Andalucía the coffee is good and strong. A *café con leche* is half-milk, half-coffee (something like café latte), a *cortado* is espresso with a dribble of milk (like an Italian *macchiato*), and *solo* is a straight, black espresso. Ask for a *grande* or *doble* if you want a large cup, *en vaso* if you want it in a glass and *sombra* or *manchado* if you want lots of milk.

Muslim rulers liked their ices to be made with snow from the mountains which was carried down perilous tracks in the panniers of donkeys.

A Traveler's Wine Guide to Spain by Desmond Begg (1998) is an authoritative and well-illustrated guide through the wine country of Spain.

The website www.sherry .org provides a good introduction to the subject of sherry and the firms that make it.

Hot Chocolate (& Churros!)

OK, so it's not the world's healthiest, but there are few sweeter pleasures in life than a breakfast of fresh *churros* (coils of deep-fried doughnuts) dunked into thick, creamy *chocolate hecho* (hot chocolate). *Churros* are a Spanish institution and every town and village in Andalucía has a *churros* stand, where people chat and joke around while waiting in a queue.

Spaniards brought chocolate back from Mexico in the mid-16th century and adopted it enthusiastically. You can even find hot chocolate among *postres* (desserts) on menus.

CELEBRATIONS

The Spanish celebrate better and more than anyone else – the word *fiesta* (party/celebration) has entered the vocabularies of many languages across the world (a bit like *la vida loca*, thanks to Ricky Martin). In fact, celebrating here is a bit like a national art. There are family celebrations with religious overtones, usually honouring a patron saint, or bigger celebrations such as Semana Santa (Holy Week) and Christmas. And that is when the kitchen plays a crucial role.

At Easter you will see *monas de Pascua* (figures made out of chocolate), *torrijas* (French toast) or *torta pascualina* (spinach-and-egg pie). All Saints' Day is when the *huesos de santo* (saints' bones; sweet breads) come out, and at Christmas all children devour a *roscón de Reyes* (spongy doughnut decorated with dried fruit and sugar), hiding a little present inside. But of all seasons, Christmas is the gastronomic timepiece calling for the famous *turrón* (nougat made of almonds, honey and egg whites) and a host of other *pasteles* (pastries or cakes). Christmas Eve and lunch is a wonderful mix of seafood, followed by *asado* (roasted) *cordero* (lamb), *cochinillo* (piglet) or *cabrito* (kid); or sometimes *merluza* (hake), *bacalao* (cod) or *besugo* (red bream).

WHERE TO EAT & DRINK

If you want to live like the locals, you'll spend plenty of time in bars and cafés. Bars come in many guises, such as *bodegas* (traditional wine bars), *cervecerías* (beer bars), *tascas* (bars specialising in tapas), *tabernas* (taverns) and even *pubs* (pubs). In many of them you'll be able to eat tapas at the bar but there will usually be a *comedor* (diner) too, for a sit-down meal (or tapas). You'll often save 10% to 20% by eating at the bar rather than at a table.

The *restaurantes* (restaurants) are usually more formal places, where you sit down to eat. A *mesón* is a simple restaurant attached to a bar with home-style cooking. A *venta* is (or once was) a roadside inn – the food can be delectable and inexpensive. A *marisquería* is a seafood restaurant, while a *chiringuito* is a small open-air bar or kiosk, or sometimes a beachside restaurant.

Log on to www.vegetar ian guides.co.uk to order *The New Spain: Vegan and Vegetarian Restaurants*, a guide to over 100 vegetarian restaurants throughout Spain.

VEGETARIANS & VEGANS

Throughout Andalucía fruit and vegetables are delicious and fresh, and eaten in season, but unfortunately there are only a handful of avowedly vegetarian restaurants. A word of warning: 'vegetable' dishes may contain more than just vegetables (eg beans with bits of ham). Vegetarians will find that salads in most restaurants are a good bet, as are gazpacho and *ajo blanco*. Another reliable dish is *pisto* (ratatouille), especially good when eaten with bread dipped into the sauce; *espárragos trigueros* (thin wild asparagus) grilled or in *revueltos* (scrambled eggs) done with gorgeous slices of fried garlic. Tapas without meat are *pimientos asados* (roasted red peppers), *alcachofas* (artichokes), *garbanzos con espinacas* (chickpeas with spinach) and, of course, cheese.

EATING WITH KIDS

Your kids will probably have the best time ever in Spanish restaurants. Children play all over the shop, running back and forth and hooking up with all the other kids whose parents are happily eating and having a nice evening, being left in peace by the little ones. Few restaurants provide a special children's menu but are happy to downsize their portions to a *medio plato* (half plate) on request. Highchairs are available in many restaurants but it is advisable to ask in advance or even bring one along if you can.

HABITS & CUSTOMS

The Spanish eating timetable is at its most extreme in Andalucía, so it's a good idea to reset your stomach clock unless you want to be left starving when all the bars close for the afternoon. Andalucians, like most Spaniards, often start the day with a light *desayuno* (breakfast), usually consisting of coffee with a *tostada* or *churros con chocolate*. If you're hungry, a *tortilla/revueltos* (omelette/scrambled eggs) is a good option. *Huevos* (eggs) also come *fritos* (fried) or *cocidos* (boiled). A great snack is a *bocadillo*, a sandwich of anything from cheese or *jamón* to *tortilla*, or the equally good *montadito* or *serranito*, a slice of toasted bread with meat, peppers, *jamón* and anything else mounted on top.

Comida or *almuerzo* (lunch) is usually the main meal of the day, eaten between 2pm and 4pm. It can consist of tapas or a several-course meal, starting with a soup or salad, continuing with a main course of meat or fish with vegetables, or a rice dish or bean stew, and ending with dessert. As well as ordering from *la carta* (the main menu), you nearly always have the option of the *menú del día* (set three-course meal). A *plato combinado* is a combination of eggs, chorizo, squid or any other thing you want to add, served on one plate. Note that prices for fish and seafood are sometimes given by weight, which can be misleading. Desserts are a simple, nonfussy affair – *helado* (ice cream), *arroz con leche* (rice pudding) and *flan* (crème caramel) are often the only choices.

La cena (dinner) is usually a combination of tapas and drink, and the Spaniards eat late, sometimes at 10pm or 11pm. Going out for dinner in a restaurant is also popular, but before about 9pm you're unlikely to see anyone but foreigners.

To learn about the food and drink of Andalucía visit www.andalucia.com/gastronomy.

COOKING COURSES

Cookery courses are now as popular as language or flamenco classes, and they are an excellent way to get down with the culture. The top five:

All Ways Spain (☎ 958 22 37 66; www.allwaysspain.com) Perfect for dabblers: a half-day crash course in Spanish traditional cooking, as part of a three-day active weekend.

Andalucian Adventure (www.andalucian-adventures.co.uk) A UK-based company organising well-reputed cookery courses in the wonderful Sierra Nevada.

Finca Buen Vino (☎ 959 12 40 34; www.fincabuenvino.com) A wonderfully warm kitchen and an excellent course in the stunning rural setting of the Parque Natural Sierra de Aracena y Picos de Aroche (see p170).

On the Menu (www.holidayonthemenu.com) Cookery courses in Seville, where you stay at the plush Las Casas de la Judería Hotel (p116) for a week or short break. Lots of wine tasting and eating well, as well as cooking.

Turismo Rural Hidalgo (☎ 954 88 35 81; www.turismoruralhidalgo.com) Want to get to grips with the new Spanish creative cuisine? Try this week-long course in the old-fashioned town of Cazalla de la Sierra (see p141).

THE TAPAS TALE

Tapas are Spain's most popular export and a way of life that can bring much joy to food lovers. The word tapa means 'lid', originating from Cádiz province in the 19th century, when bar owners placed a saucer with a piece of bread on top of a sherry glass either to deter flies or prevent the punter from getting too tipsy. As years went by, the contents of the saucers became more elaborate, so olives, almonds, chorizo or *jamón* started to feature.

Tapas are as varied as can be: you can get little nibbles like olives or cheese, and progress onto a piece of tortilla or *charcutería* (cured meat). Go a bit further and you start getting more serious propositions like *garbanzos con espinacas* (chickpeas with spinach), pork *solomillo* (sirloin) or *lomo* (loin) with garnish, *pinchos morunos* (minikebabs on sticks), *flamenquines* (deep-fried, breaded veal or ham) or *boquerones* (anchovies), which might be marinated in vinegar or fried. Accompany them with a glass of cool beer or a *fino* sherry. Depending on where you are, you can get different twists on the basic tapa formula: in Seville you can sample courgettes (zucchini) with Roquefort cheese, or mushroom-filled artichoke hearts, and in Granada you can have North African tagine tapas, or a tapa of Brazilian *feijoada* (bean and rice stew).

The real luxury is seafood tapas: marinated, fried or fresh. The sherry triangle of Cádiz province (see p183) has some of the best seafood in Andalucía – from Atlantic *conchas finas* (Venus shell, the biggest of the clams) to *cangrejos* (tiny crabs, cooked whole) or *búsanos* (sea snails or whelks). A dish that makes a grown (wo)man weep with joy is *langostinos a la plancha*, grilled sweet, juicy king prawns sprinkled with flakes of sea salt.

Be brave and dip into *sesos* (brains), *callos* (tripe), *criadillas* (bull or sheep testicles), *riñones* (kidneys) and *hígado* (liver) served in small earthenware dishes, simmering in a tomato sauce or gravy. Or if you prefer salad tapas, there is *pipirrana* (based on diced tomatoes and red peppers), *salpicón* (the same with bits of seafood), *ensaladilla rusa* (Russian salad; a salad of cold diced vegetables mixed with Russian dressing) and *aliño* (any salad in a vinegar-and-oil dressing).

Bars sometimes display a range of tapas on the counter or have a menu or a blackboard listing what's available. If you don't see tapas or a menu, just ask what's available – tapas are always around.

EAT YOUR WORDS

Andalucía has such a variety of foods and food names that you could travel for years and still find unfamiliar items on almost every menu. The following guide should help you sort out what's what.

Useful Phrases

Table for ..., please.
Una mesa para ..., por favor.   *oo*·na *me*·sa *pa*·ra ..., por fa·*vor*

Can I see the menu please?
¿Puedo ver el menú, por favor?   *pwe*·do ver el me·*noo*, por fa·*vor*

Do you have a menu in English?
¿Tienen un menú en inglés?   *tye*·nen oon me·*noo* en een·*gles*

I'm a vegetarian.
Soy vegetariano/a.   soy ve·khe·ta·*rya*·no/a

What would you recommend?
¿Qué recomienda?   ke re·ko·*myen*·da

What's the speciality here?
¿Cuál es la especialidad de este restaurante?   kwal es la es·pe·sya·lee·*dad* de *es*·te res·to·*ran*·te

I'd like the set lunch, please.
Quisiera el menú del día, por favor.   kee·*sye*·ra el me·*noo* del *dee*·a, por fa·*vor*

The bill, please.
La cuenta, por favor.   la *kwen*·ta por fa·*vor*

Do you accept credit cards?
¿Aceptan tarjetas de crédito?   a·*thep*·tan tar·*khe*·tas de *kre*·dee·to

Food Glossary
BASICS & STAPLES

arroz	a·ros	rice
bocadillo	bo·ka·dee·jo	filled roll
bollo	bo·jo	small soft roll; also mollete
gazpacho	gas·pa·cho	chilled soup of blended tomatoes, peppers, cucumber, garlic, breadcrumbs, lemon and oil
huevo	we·vo	egg
media-ración	me·dya·ra·syon	half a ración
menú del día	me·noo del dee·a	fixed-price meal
mollete	mo·je·te	small soft roll; also bollo
montadito	mon·ta·dee·to	open sandwich
paella	pa·e·ja	rice dish with shellfish, chicken and vegetables
pan	pan	bread
plato combinado	pla·to kom·bee·na·do	'combined plate'; seafood, omelette, meat with trimmings
queso	ke·so	cheese
ración	ra·syon	meal-sized serving of tapas
revueltos	re·vwel·tos	scrambled eggs
rosquilla	ros·kee·ja	toasted roll
tapas	ta·pas	light snacks, usually eaten with drinks
tortilla	tor·tee·ja	omelette
tostada	tos·ta·da	toasted bread often served with a variety of toppings such as tomatoes and olive oil

CARNE (MEAT)

ato	a·to	duck
cabra	ka·vra	goat
cabrito	ka·vree·to	kid; also choto
carne de monte	kar·ne de mon·te	'meat of the mountain'; local game
carne de vaca	kar·ne de va·ka	beef
caza	ka·sa	game
charcutería	char·koo·te·ree·a	cured meat
choto	cho·to	kid; also cabrito
chorizo	cho·ree·so	spicy pork sausage
codorniz	ko·dor·nees	quail
conejo	ko·ne·kho	rabbit
cordero	kor·de·ro	lamb
hígado	ee·ga·do	liver
jamón	kha·mon	ham
jamón ibérico	kha·mon ee·ve·ree·ko	ham from the black Iberian breed of pig
jamón ibérico de bellota	kha·mon ee·ve·ree·ko de be·jo·ta	ham from Iberian pigs fed on acorns
jamón serrano	kha·mon se·ra·no	mountain-cured ham
jamón York	kha·mon york	uncured ham
liebre	lee·e·vre	hare
pavo	pa·vo	turkey
pollo	po·jo	chicken
riñón, riñones (pl)	ree·nyon, ree·nyo·nes	kidney

solomillo	so·lo·*mee*·jo	sirloin; quality fillet of beef or pork
ternera	ter·*ne*·ra	veal

FRUTAS & VERDURAS (FRUIT & VEGETABLES)

aceituna	a·say·*too*·na	olive
aguacate	a·gwa·*ka*·te	avocado
ajo	*a*·kho	garlic
alcachofa	al·ka·*cho*·fa	artichoke
apio	*a*·pee·o	celery
berenjena	be·ren·*khe*·na	aubergine (eggplant)
calabacín	ka·la·va·*sin*	courgette (zucchini)
calabaza	ka·la·*va*·sa	pumpkin
cebolla	se·*vo*·ja	onion
cereza	se·*re*·sa	cherry
frambuesa	fram·*bwe*·sa	raspberry
fresa	*fre*·sa	strawberry
lima	*lee*·ma	lime
limón	lee·*mon*	lemon
manzana	man·*sa*·na	apple
manzanilla	man·sa·*nee*·ja	camomile
melocotón	me·lo·ko·*ton*	peach
naranja	na·*ran*·kha	orange
piña	*pee*·nya	pineapple
plátano	*pla*·ta·no	banana
sandía	san·*dee*·a	watermelon
uva	*oo*·va	grape

PESCADOS & MARISCOS (FISH & SEAFOOD)

almeja	al·*me*·kha	clam
anochoa	a·no·*cho*·a	anchovy; also *boquerón*
atún	a·*toon*	tuna
bacalao	ba·ka·*low*	cod
bogavante	bo·ga·*van*·te	lobster; also *langosta*
boquerón	bo·ke·*ron*	anchovy; also *anochoa*
caballa	ka·*va*·ja	mackerel
cangrejo	kan·*gre*·kho	crab
chipirón, chipirones (pl)	chee·pee·*ron*, chee·pee·*ro*·nes	baby squid; also *chopito*
chopito	cho·*pee*·to	baby squid; also *chipirón*
gamba	*gam*·ba	prawn
langosta	lan·*gos*·ta	lobster; also *bogavante*
langostino	lan·gos·*tee*·no	king prawn
mejillón, mejillones (pl)	me·khee·*lyon*, me·khee·*lyo*·nes	mussel
merluza	mer·*loo*·sa	hake
ostra	*os*·tra	oyster
sardina	sar·*dee*·na	sardine
trucha	*troo*·cha	trout

TARTAS & POSTRES (CAKES & DESSERTS)

arroz con leche	a·*ros* kon *le*·che	rice pudding
churro	*choo*·ro	long thin doughnut with sugar
flan	flan	crème caramel
helado	e·*la*·do	ice cream
pastel	pas·*tel*	pastry or cake
torta	*tor*·ta	pie or tart
turrón	too·*ron*	nougat

TÉCNICAS (COOKING TECHNIQUES)

a la brasa	a la *bra*·sa	grilled or barbecued
a la parrilla	a la pa·*ree*·ja	grilled or barbecued
a la plancha	a la *plan*·cha	grilled on a hotplate
ahumado/a	a·oo·*ma*·do/a	smoked
al carbón	al kar·*bon*	char-grilled
asado	a·*sa*·do	roast
cocido	ko·*see*·do	cooked or boiled; also hotpot/stew
crudo	*croo*·do	raw
frito/a	*free*·to/a	fried
guiso	*gee*·so	stew
rebozado/a	re·vo·*sa*·do/a	battered and fried
relleno/a	re·*je*·no/a	stuffed
salado/a	sa·*la*·do/a	salted, salty
seco/a	*se*·ko/a	dry, dried

Drinks Glossary
NONALCOHOLIC DRINKS

agua de grifo	*a*·gwa de *gree*·fo	tap water
agua mineral	*a*·gwa mee·ne·*ral*	bottled water
agua potable	*a*·gwa po·*ta*·vle	drinking water
café con leche	ka·*fe* kon *le*·che	50% coffee, 50% hot milk
café cortado	ka·*fe* kor·*ta*·do	short black with a dash of milk
café solo	ka·*fe* so·lo	short black
chocolate hecho	cho·ko·*la*·te *he*·cho	hot chocolate
con gas	kon gas	fizzy (bottled water)
refresco	re·*fres*·ko	soft drink
sin gas	seen gas	still (bottled water)
té	te	tea
zumo	*soo*·mo	fruit juice

CERVEZA (BEER)

botellín	bo·te·*jin*	bottled beer (250mL); also *quinto*
caña	*ka*·nya	draught beer (250mL) served in a small, wide glass
quinto	*keen*·to	bottled beer (250mL); also *botellín*
tercio	*ter*·syo	bottled beer (330mL)
tubo	*too*·bo	draught beer (300mL) served in a straight glass

VINO (WINE)

blanco	*blan*·ko	white wine
rosado	ro·*sa*·do	rosé wine
tinto	*teen*·to	red wine
vino de la casa	*vee*·no de la *ka*·sa	house wine
vino de la mesa	*vee*·no de la *me*·sa	table wine

OTHER ALCOHOLIC DRINKS

aguardiente	a·gwar·*dyen*·te	grape-based spirit (similar to grappa)
anís	a·*nees*	aniseed liqueur
coñac	ko·*nyak*	brandy
sangría	san·*gree*·a	wine and fruit punch

Sevilla Province

Most visits to Andalucía are dominated by the region's capital, Seville (Sevilla in Spanish). It's no wonder: Spain's fourth-biggest city is loaded with romanticism and expectation, and it delivers on many fronts. There's the neck-creaking delights of its architecture, the gluttony-inducing tapas, the palm-aching flamenco clapping, not to mention the adrenaline-pumping bullfighting, and the sleepless *marcha* (nightlife), or the spectacular celebrations of Semana Santa (Holy Week) and Feria de Abril. With a city like this in the centre, who needs anything else? But if you give it a chance, Sevilla the province also has many wonderful things to offer.

With the Río Guadalquivir nourishing the fertile valley, Sevilla the province has provided Andalucía with the fruits of culture and economy since the Tartessos culture grew here, centuries before Christ. The aristocracy of the region enjoyed the rolling agricultural plains of La Campiña, at the east of the province, endowing the area with the three baroque and Spanish Renaissance beauties of Carmona, Écija and Osuna. The fabulous architecture of the three towns offers some of the most stylish hotels in Spain.

But if you really want to get away and hear nothing but birdsong (and an occasional tractor), head for the ever-changing Sierra Morena, a surprise less than two hours away from Seville city. Here you'll be able to indulge in hill walking, bird-watching and flower-smelling, and explore quaint old villages and towns.

HIGHLIGHTS

- Imagine you were part of the Sultan's in-crowd as you walk through the dreamy **Alcázar** (p99)

- Be humbled by the sheer size of Seville's **cathedral** (p97) and see the city from the top of the beautiful **Giralda** (p99)

- Get professional at the art of *tapear* in Seville's countless **tapas bars** (p118)

- Stay up all night chasing the Virgins in Seville's mesmerising **Semana Santa** (p113) and show off your dancing skills at the **Feria de Abril** (p114)

- Clap till you're blue in the palms at Seville's **flamenco haunts** (p127) and its **Bienal de Flamenco** (p114) festival

- Walk, watch birds, wild flowers and the rolling scenery of the **Parque Natural Sierra Norte** (p139)

- See history at your feet at the Roman **Itálica** (p130) and get a taste of La Campiña's Spanish aristocracy at **Carmona** (p132), **Écija** (p135) and **Osuna** (p137)

| POPULATION: 1.78 MILLION | SEVILLE AV DAILY HIGH: JAN/AUG 15°C/36°C | ALTITUDE RANGE: 0M–959M |

SEVILLE

pop 704,000 / elevation 30m

Seville must be one of the most addictive cities in the world. In it, all of Spain's clichés come together, wrapped in a thick scent of orange blossom: this is the home of the glory and the gore of bullfighting, the soul-ripping sound of flamenco, the sombre and spectacular Semana Santa (Holy Week) processions and the jolly relief of Feria de Abril. Traditional men with slicked-back black hair rule here. There are hundreds of tapas bars with swinging *jamones* (hams), served by barmen with pencil-thin moustaches. Seville is where the highly strung Carmen rolled cigars on her thighs and loved a *torero* (bullfighter), where Don Juan worked his mojo in times long gone, and where Cervantes and Columbus drank sherry. Need we go on? Seville is the essence of Andalucía's biggest export – the cringing cliché of *'pasión'*, which in this city suddenly makes sense.

Seville's most flamboyant season is its Semana Santa. It is celebrated with an odd mix of piousness and hedonism and visiting the city at this time is an absolute must. Its annual *feria* (fair) is the most festive in the region. Its heritage of art and architecture – Roman, Islamic, Gothic, Renaissance, baroque – is without rival in southern Spain.

Seville lives on the street and its inhabitants are in love with their city (and with themselves). To the true *sevillano* or *sevillana* there's little need for any other place. Matador Rafael Guerra (1862–1941), after a fight in A Coruña on the far northwestern tip of Spain, wanted to get back to Seville that same evening. 'Maestro', they said to him, 'Seville is very far away.' 'Seville, far?' countered Guerra. 'Here is far. Seville is where it should be.'

But of course, there are a couple of catches. Seville is expensive. You might pay €80 here for a room that would cost €50 elsewhere. And prices soar during Semana Santa and the Feria de Abril (April Fair). Also bear in mind that Seville gets *very* hot in July and August. The ideal season to come, for temperatures and atmosphere, is spring (late March to early June).

HISTORY

Roman Seville, named Hispalis, was a significant port on the Río Guadalquivir –

navigable to the Atlantic Ocean 100km away – but was overshadowed by Córdoba. Later, Hispalis became a Visigothic cultural centre, especially in the time of St Isidoro (AD 565–636), Spain's leading scholar of the Visigothic period.

The Muslim Ishbiliya became the most powerful of the *taifas* (small kingdoms) after the collapse of the Cordoban caliphate in 1031. Its rulers Al-Mutadid (r 1042–69) and Al-Mutamid (r 1069–91) were both poets. Al-Mutamid, one of the first people in history recorded as falling in love with Seville, presided over a languid, hedonistic court in the Alcázar, but in 1085 had to call in help from the Muslim fundamentalist rulers of Morocco, the Almoravids, for support against the growing threat of Christian reconquest. After taking over all Islamic Spain, the Almoravids were replaced by another strict Muslim sect from North Africa, the Almohads, in the 12th century. Caliph Yacub Yusuf, who made Seville capital of the Almohad realm, built a great mosque where Seville cathedral now stands, and his successor, Yusuf Yacub al-Mansur, added the Giralda tower. But as Almohad power dwindled after the disastrous defeat of Las Navas de Tolosa in 1212, Castile's Fernando III (El Santo; the Saint) went on to capture Seville in 1248.

Fernando brought 24,000 settlers to Seville and by the 14th century it was the most important Castilian city. Seville's biggest break was Columbus' discovery of the Americas in 1492. In 1503 the city was awarded an official monopoly on Spanish trade with the new-found continent. It rapidly became one of the biggest, richest and most cosmopolitan cities on earth, a magnet for everyone from beggars and *pícaros* (card and dice tricksters) to Italian merchants, artists of genius and the clergy of more than 100 religious institutions. Seville was labelled the *puerto y puerta de Indias* (port and gateway of the Indies), the Babylon of Spain and even the new Rome. Lavish Renaissance and baroque buildings sprouted and the city's population jumped from about 40,000 in 1500 to 150,000 in 1600.

But it was not to last. A plague in 1649 killed half the city and, as the 17th century wore on, the Río Guadalquivir became more silted up and less navigable for the

SEVILLA PROVINCE

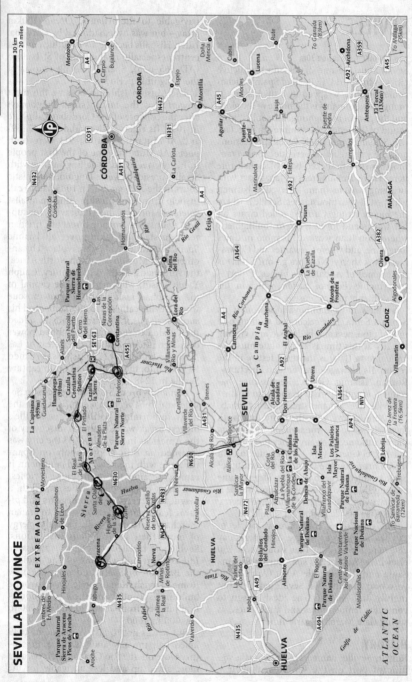

bigger ships of the day; many ships foundered on a sandbar at the river mouth near Sanlúcar de Barrameda. In 1717 the Casa de la Contratación (the government office controlling commerce with the Americas) was transferred to Cádiz. Another Seville plague in 1800 killed 13,000 people. Napoleonic troops occupied the city from 1810 to 1812, stealing, it is said, 999 works of art when they left.

The beginnings of industry in the mid-19th century brought a measure of prosperity for some. The first bridge across the Guadalquivir, the Puente de Triana (or Puente de Isabel II), was built in 1852, and the old Almohad walls were knocked down in 1869 to let the city expand. However, the majority of people in the city and countryside remained impoverished. In 1936 Seville fell very quickly to the Nationalists at the start of the Spanish Civil War, despite resistance in working-class areas (which brought savage reprisals).

Things finally looked up in the 1980s when Seville was named capital of the new autonomous Andalucía within democratic Spain, and the left-of-centre Partido Socialista Obrero Español (PSOE) party, led by Sevillan Felipe González, came to power in Madrid. The Expo '92 international exhibition, marking the 500th anniversary of Columbus' great voyage, brought Seville millions of visitors, eight new bridges across the Guadalquivir, the superfast AVE (Alta Velocidad Española) rail link to Madrid, an opera house and thousands of new hotel rooms. The Expo party had its hangover during the succeeding years of economic recession, but Seville's economy is now steadily improving with a mix of tourism, commerce, technology and industry.

ORIENTATION

Seville straddles the Río Guadalquivir, with most places of interest found on the eastern bank. The central area is mostly a tangle of narrow, twisting old streets and small squares, with the exceptions of Plaza Nueva and broad, straight Avenida de la Constitución. The *avenida* (avenue) runs south from Plaza Nueva to the Puerta de Jerez, which is a busy intersection marking the southern edge of the central area. Just east of Avenida de la Constitución are the city's major monuments: the cathedral,

the Giralda tower and the Alcázar fortress-palace. The Barrio de Santa Cruz, east of the cathedral and the Alcázar, is touristy, and a popular place to sleep and eat. The true centre of Seville, El Centro, is a little further north, around Plaza de San Francisco and Plaza Salvador. The area between Avenida de la Constitución and the river is El Arenal.

The bus and train stations are on the periphery of the central area, all served by city buses that circle the centre (see p128): Prado de San Sebastián bus station is on Plaza San Sebastián, 650m southeast of the cathedral and within walking distance of the Barrio de Santa Cruz; Plaza de Armas bus station is 900m northwest of the cathedral, within walking distance of El Arenal; and Santa Justa train station is 1.5km northeast of the cathedral, on Avenida Kansas City.

INFORMATION
Bookshops

Casa del Libro (Map pp102-3 ; ☎ 954 50 29 50; Calle Velázquez 8; ☼ 9.30am-9.30pm Mon-Sat) A great resource for guidebooks and novels in different languages, as well as maps, dictionaries and Spanish course books.
LTC (Map pp102-3; ☎ 954 42 59 64; Avenida Menéndez y Pelayo 42-44; ☼ Sun-Fri) Andalucía's top map shop.
Vértice International Bookshop (Map pp102-3; ☎ 954 21 16 54; Calle San Fernando 33) Novels in many languages, some guidebooks.

Emergency
Ambulance (☎ 061)
Fire (☎ 085)
Policía Local (Local Police; ☎ 092)
Policía Nacional (National Police; ☎ 091)

Internet Access
Ciber Alcázar (Map pp102-3; ☎ 954 21 04 01; Calle San Fernando 35; per hr €1.80; ☼ 10.15am-10.30pm Mon-Fri, noon-10.30pm Sat & Sun)
First Center (Map pp102-3 ; Avenida de la Constitución 34; per hr €2; ☼ 9am-10pm Mon-Fri, 10am-9.30pm Sat, noon-9pm Sun)
Internetia (Map pp102-3 ; Avenida Menéndez y Pelayo 46; per hr €2; ☼ 10.30am-1.30am Mon-Fri, noon-1.30am Sat & Sun)
Interpublic (Map pp102-3 ; Calle O'Donnell 3; per hr €1.80; ☼ 10am-11pm Mon-Fri, 10am-3pm & 5-11pm Sat, 5-11pm Sun)
Seville Internet Center (Map pp102-3; ☎ 954 50 02 75; Calle Almirantazgo 2; per min €0.05; ☼ 9am-10pm Mon-Fri, 10am-10pm Sat & Sun)

SEVILLE

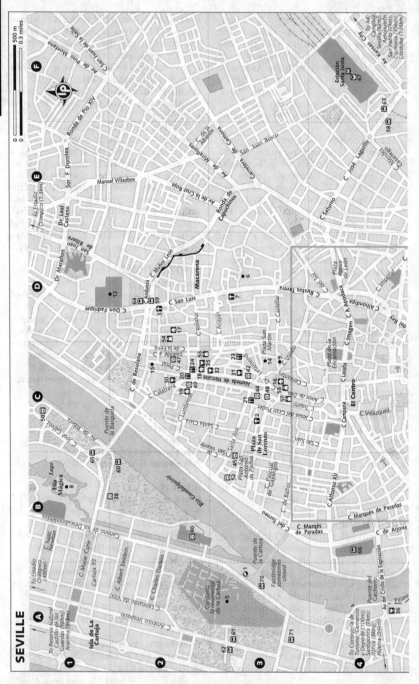

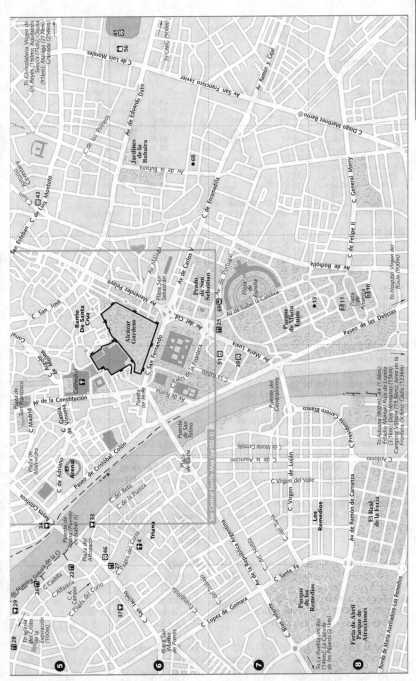

Internet Resources

Discover Sevilla (www.discoversevilla.com) Set up by a group of young Americans and a Sevillian, this site abounds with useful, hip and fun tips.

Explore Seville (www.exploreseville.com) A good, informative site.

Sevilla Online (www.sol.com) Sights, language schools, accommodation, festivals.

Seville Tourism (www.turismo.sevilla.org) The city's useful official tourism site; its 'Accessible Guide' is especially useful for travellers with a disability, with lists of hotels, restaurants, museums etc with wheelchair access.

Turismo de la Provincia (www.turismosevilla.org) Informative official tourist information site for Sevilla province.

Laundry

Laundries here do the job for you (usually in half a day), with washing, drying and folding included in their prices.

Auto-Servicio de Lavandería Sevilla
(Map pp102–3; ☎ 954 21 05 35; Calle Castelar 2C; per load €6; ☯ 9.30am-1.30pm & 5-8.30pm Mon-Fri, 9am-2pm Sat)

La Segunda Vera (Map pp102–3; ☎ 954 54 11 48; Calle Alejo Fernández 3; per load €8; ☯ 9.30am-1.30pm & 5-8pm Mon-Fri, 10am-1.30pm Sat)

Media

El Giraldillo Andalucía-wide what's-on mag with a strong Seville emphasis, available free from tourist offices and some hotels.

Sevilladc The *ayuntamiento*'s (town hall's) free cultural-events magazine.

Tourist Free mag for tourists, with worthwhile information about what to see and do.

Welcome & Olé Ditto.

Medical Services

Centro de Salud El Porvenir (Map pp102–3; ☎ 955 03 78 17; cnr Avenidas Menéndez Pelayo & de Cádiz) Public clinic with emergency service.

Hospital Virgen del Rocío (Map pp94–5; ☎ 955 01 20 00; Avenida de Manuel Siurot s/n) The main general hospital, 1km south of Parque de María Luisa.

Money

There's plenty of banks and ATMs in the central area. Santa Justa train station, the airport and both bus stations have ATMs. You'll find exchange offices on Avenida de la Constitución and at Estación Santa Justa.

American Express (Map pp102–3; ☎ 954 21 16 17; Plaza Nueva 8; ☯ 9.30am-1.30pm & 4.30-7.30pm Mon-Fri, 10am-1pm Sat)

Post

Main post office (Map pp102-3; Avenida de la Constitución 32; ⏰ 8.30am-8.30pm Mon-Fri, 9.30am-2pm Sat)

Telephone

There are many pay phones around the centre of town. The following call centres offer cheap international calls (per minute €0.20 or less to Western Europe, USA, Canada or Australia):

Ciber Alcázar (Map pp102-3; ☎ 954 21 04 01; Calle San Fernando 35; ⏰ 10.15am-10.30pm Mon-Fri, noon-10.30pm Sat & Sun)

First Center (Map pp102-3; Avenida de la Constitución 34; ⏰ 9am-10pm Mon-Fri, 10am-9.30pm Sat, noon-9pm Sun)

Tourist Information

Infhor (Map pp94-5; ☎ 954 54 19 52; Estación Santa Justa; ⏰ 8am-10pm Mon-Fri, 8am-2pm & 4-10pm Sat, 8am-2pm & 6-10pm Sun & holidays) Independent tourist office at the train station.

Municipal tourist office (Map pp102-3; ☎ 954 22 17 14; barranco.turismo@sevilla.org; Calle de Arjona 28; ⏰ 9am-9pm Mon-Fri, 9am-2pm Sat & Sun) Reduced hours during Semana Santa & Feria de Abril.

Regional tourist office Airport (☎ 954 44 91 28; ⏰ 9am-8.30pm Mon-Fri, 10am-6pm Sat, 10am-2pm Sun, closed holidays); Constitución (Map pp102-3; ☎ 954 22 14 04; otsevilla@andalucia.org; Avenida de la Constitución 21; ⏰ 9am-7pm Mon-Fri, 10am-2pm & 3-7pm Sat, 10am-2pm Sun, closed holidays); Estación Santa Justa (Map pp94-5; ☎ 954 53 76 26; Santa Justa; ⏰ 9am-8pm Mon-Fri, 10am-2pm Sat & Sun, closed holidays) The staff at the Constitución office are well informed but often very busy.

Turismo Sevilla (Map pp102-3; ☎ 954 21 00 05; Plaza del Triunfo 1; ⏰ 10.30am-7pm Mon-Fri) Information on all Sevilla province.

DANGERS & ANNOYANCES

Seville has a bit of a reputation for petty crime against tourists – pickpockets, bag snatchers and the like. In reality the risks seem no greater here than in any other large Andalucian city. Stay awake to those around you and make sure you avoid walking alone in empty streets at night and during siesta hours. For general tips on safety in Andalucía see p430.

SIGHTS

The city's major monuments – the cathedral, the Giralda and the Alcázar – are all just east of Avenida de la Constitución and south of the city's true centre (El Centro). But there's plenty to see in El Centro and in the neighbouring El Arenal area too, as well as in the areas to the south, north and west.

Cathedral & Giralda

Seville's immense **cathedral** (Map pp102-3; ☎ 954 21 49 71; www.catedralsevilla.org in Spanish; adult/ child under 12yr/disabled/student/senior €7.50/free/free/ 1.50/1.50, Sun free; ⏰ 11am-6pm Mon-Sat, 2.30-7pm Sun Sep-Jun, 9.30am-4.30pm Mon-Sat, 2.30-7pm Sun Jul & Aug, closed 1 & 6 Jan, Palm Sunday, Corpus Christi, 15 Aug & 8 & 25 Dec), one of the biggest in the world, stands on the site of the great 12th-century Almohad mosque, with the mosque's minaret (the Giralda) still towering beside it. After Seville fell to the Christians in 1248 the mosque was used as a church until 1401. Then, in view of its decaying state, the church authorities decided to knock it down and start again. 'Let us create such a building that future generations will take us for lunatics,' they decided (or so legend has it). They certainly got themselves a big church – 126m long and 83m wide. It was completed by 1507, all in Gothic style, though later work done after its central dome collapsed in 1511 was mostly in Renaissance style.

The enormity of the broad, five-naved cathedral is disguised by a welter of interior structures and decoration that is typical of Spanish cathedrals. This truly is one of the most magnificent churches in Spain.

The entry system and timetable for visiting Seville's cathedral change frequently. Current regulations are usually posted up fairly clearly.

EXTERIOR

From close up, the bulky exterior of the cathedral gives few hints of the treasures within. But have a look at the **Puerta del Perdón** on Calle Alemanes (a legacy of the Islamic mosque) and the two impressive 15th-century Gothic **doorways**, with terracotta reliefs and statues by Lorenzo Mercadante de Bretaña and Pedro Millán, on Avenida de la Constitución.

The **Giralda**, the 90m decorative brick tower on the northeastern side of the cathedral, was the minaret of the mosque, constructed between 1184 and 1198 at the height of Almohad power. Its proportions, its delicate brick-pattern decoration, and its colour, which changes with the light, make it perhaps Spain's most perfect Islamic building. The top-most parts of the Giralda – from the bell level up – were added in the 16th century, when Spanish Christians were busy 'improving on' surviving Islamic buildings. At the very top is **El Giraldillo**, a 16th-century bronze weathervane representing Faith that has become a symbol of Seville. (The entrance to the Giralda is inside the cathedral – see opposite).

SALA DEL PABELLÓN

Selected treasures from the cathedral's art collection are exhibited in this room, the first after the ticket office. Much of what's displayed here, as elsewhere in the cathedral, is the work of masters from Seville's 17th-century artistic golden age.

SOUTHERN & NORTHERN CHAPELS

The chapels along the southern and northern sides of the cathedral hold riches of sculpture and painting. Near the western end of the northern side is the **Capilla de San Antonio**, housing Murillo's large 1666 canvas depicting the vision of St Anthony of Padua; thieves cut out the kneeling saint in 1874 but he was later found in New York and put back.

VAULTING & STAINED GLASS

Don't forget to look up from time to time to admire the cathedral's marvellous Gothic vaulting and rich-hued stained glass. The oldest stained glass, with markedly different colour tones, was done between 1478 and 1483 by a German known as Enrique Alemán. This master artisan takes credit for the glass above the five westernmost chapels on both sides of the nave and the glass in the four westernmost bays on either side of the uppermost storey of the nave.

COLUMBUS' TOMB

Inside the **Puerta de los Príncipes** stands the monumental tomb of Christopher Columbus (Cristóbal Colón in Spanish) – the subject of a continuous riddle – containing what were long believed to be the great explorer's bones, brought here from Cuba in 1899. The monument, dating from 1902, shows four sepulchre bearers representing the four kingdoms of Spain at the time of Columbus' famous 1492 voyage: Castile (carrying Granada on the point of its spear), León, Aragón and Navarra. For more on Columbus' four voyages, see p151.

Columbus died in 1506 in Valladolid, northern Spain – poor and apparently still believing he had reached Asia. His remains lay at La Cartuja monastery in Seville before being moved to Hispaniola in 1536. Even though there were suggestions that the bones kept in Seville's cathedral were possibly those of his son Diego (who was buried with his father in Santo Domingo, Hispaniola), recent DNA tests seemed to finally prove that it's really Cristopher Columbus who was the owner of these mysterious bones. The researchers managed to convince the Dominican Republic – which had claimed the *real* bones were in Santo Domingo – to open the monument where the remains were held, in order to compare samples. To confuse matters further, the researchers say that although they are certain that the bones in Seville are the real bones, the ones in Santo Domingo could also be real, since Columbus' body was moved several times after his death. Seems that even death couldn't dampen the great explorer's urge to travel.

CORO

In the middle of the cathedral you'll find the large **coro** (choir), which has 117 carved Gothic-Mudejar choir stalls. The lower ones have marquetry representations of the Giralda. Vices and sins are depicted on their misericords.

CAPILLA MAYOR

East of the choir is the **Capilla Mayor** (Main Chapel). Its Gothic retable is the jewel of the cathedral and reckoned to be the biggest altarpiece in the world. Begun by Flemish sculptor Pieter Dancart in 1482 and finished by others in 1564, this sea of gilded and polychromed wood holds over 1000 carved biblical figures. At the centre of the lowest level is the tiny 13th-century silver-plated cedar image of the Virgen de la Sede (Virgin of the See), patron of the cathedral.

EASTERN CHAPELS

East of the Capilla Mayor, situated against the eastern wall of the cathedral, are some more chapels. These chapels are normally closed to visitors, which is a shame, because the central one is the **Capilla Real** (Royal Chapel), which contains the tombs of two great Castilian kings – Fernando III and Alfonso X.

SACRISTÍA DE LOS CÁLICES

South of the Capilla Mayor are rooms containing some of the cathedral's main art treasures. The westernmost of these is the Sacristy of the Chalices, where Francisco de Goya's painting of the Seville martyrs, *Santas Justa y Rufina* (1817), hangs above the altar. These two potters, one depicted with a lion licking her feet, died at the hands of the Romans in AD 287.

SACRISTÍA MAYOR

This large room with a finely carved stone dome, east of the Sacristía de los Cálices, is a plateresque (a decorative genre of architecture, with effects resembling those of silverware) creation of 1528–47: the arch over its portal has carvings of 16th-century foods. Pedro de Campaña's 1547 *Descendimiento* (Descent from the Cross) above the central altar at the southern end, and Francisco de Zurbarán's *Santa Teresa*, to its right, are two of the cathedral's most precious paintings. The room's centrepiece is the **Custodia de Juan de Arfe**, a huge 475kg silver monstrance made in the 1580s by Renaissance metalsmith Juan de Arfe. Also here are Pedro Roldán's 1671 statue *San Fernando* (Fernando III) and Alonso Martínez's *La Inmaculada* (Mary, the Immaculate) of 1657, both of which are carried with the Custodia in Seville's Corpus Christi processions. In one of the glass cases are the city keys that were handed over to the conquering Fernando III in 1248.

CABILDO

The beautifully domed chapter house, also called the Sala Capitular, in the southeastern corner, was originally built between 1558 and 1592 as a venue for meetings of the cathedral hierarchy. The Cabildo was designed by Hernán Ruiz, architect of the Giralda belfry. Hanging high above the archbishop's throne at the southern end is a Murillo masterpiece, *La Inmaculada*. Eight Murillo saints adorn the dome at the same level.

GIRALDA

In the northeastern corner of the cathedral you'll find the passage for the climb up to the belfry of the Giralda. The ascent is quite easy, as a series of ramps – built so that the guards could ride up on horseback – goes all the way up. The climb affords great views of the buttresses and pinnacles surrounding the cathedral, as well as of the city beyond.

PATIO DE LOS NARANJOS

Outside the cathedral's northern side, this patio was originally the courtyard of the mosque. It's planted with 66 *naranjos* (orange trees), and a Visigothic fountain remains in the centre. Hanging from the ceiling in the patio's southeastern corner is a replica stuffed crocodile – the original was a gift to Alfonso X from the Sultan of Egypt. On the northern side of the patio is the beautiful Islamic Puerta del Perdón.

Alcázar

This is Seville's Alhambra, on a smaller scale, but just as beautiful. The **Alcázar** (Map pp102-3; ☎ 954 50 23 23; www.patronato-alcazarsevilla .es; adult/child under 16yr/student/senior/disabled €7/free/ free/free/free; ⏱ 9.30am-8pm Tue-Sat, 9.30am-6pm Sun & holidays Apr-Sep, 9.30am-6pm Tue-Sat, 9.30am-2.30pm Sun & holidays Oct-Mar), a World Heritage monument, stands south of the cathedral across Plaza del Triunfo.

Originally founded as a fort for the Cordoban governors of Seville in 913, the Alcázar is intimately associated with the lives and loves of several later rulers. These include the extraordinary Christian King Pedro I of Castile (r 1350–69), who was known either as Pedro el Cruel or as Pedro el Justiciero (the Justice-Dispenser), depending which side of him you were on.

The Alcázar has been expanded or reconstructed many times in its 11 centuries of existence, making it a complicated building to understand, but in the end this only increases its fascination. In the 11th century, Seville's prosperous Muslim *taifa* rulers developed the original fort by building a palace called Al-Muwarak (the Blessed) in what's now the western part of the Alcázar. The 12th-century Almohad rulers added another palace east of this, around what's now the Patio del Crucero. Christian Fernando III moved into the

Alcázar when he captured Seville in 1248, and several later Christian monarchs used it as their main residence. Fernando's son Alfonso X replaced much of the Almohad palace with a Gothic one. Between 1364 and 1366 Pedro I created the Alcázar's crown jewel, the sumptuous **Mudéjar Palacio de Don Pedro**, partly on the site of the old Al-Muwarak palace. The Catholic Monarchs, Fernando and Isabel, set up court here in the 1480s as they prepared for the conquest of Granada. Later rulers created the Alcázar's lovely gardens.

PATIO DEL LEÓN

From the ticket office inside the **Puerta del León** (Lion Gate) you emerge into the Patio del León (Lion Patio), which was the garrison yard of the original Al-Muwarak palace. Off here is the **Sala de la Justicia** (Hall of Justice), with beautiful Mudéjar plasterwork and an *artesonado* (a ceiling of interlaced beams with decorative insertions); this room was built in the 1340s by Christian king Alfonso XI, who disported here with one of his mistresses, Leonor de Guzmán, reputedly the most beautiful woman in Spain. Alfonso's many dalliances left his heir, Pedro I, with five illegitimate half-brothers and a severe case of sibling rivalry. Pedro had a dozen relatives and friends murdered in his efforts to stay on the throne. One of them, Pedro's half-brother Don Fadrique, met his maker right here in the Sala de la Justicia.

The room gives on to the pretty **Patio del Yeso**, part of the 12th-century Almohad palace reconstructed in the 19th century.

PATIO DE LA MONTERÍA

The rooms on the western side of this patio were part of the Casa de la Contratación (Contracting House) founded by the Catholic Monarchs in 1503 to control trade with Spain's American colonies. The **Salón del Almirante** (Admiral's Hall) houses 19th- and 20th-century paintings showing historical events and personages associated with Seville; the room off its northern end has an international collection of elaborate and beautiful fans. The **Sala de Audiencias** (Audience Hall) is hung with tapestry representations of the shields of Spanish admirals and Alejo Fernández' 1530s painting *Virgen de los Mareantes* (Virgin of the Sailors), the earliest known painting about the discov-

ery of the Americas. The Virgin shelters Columbus, Fernando El Católico, Carlos I, Amerigo Vespucci and native Americans beneath her cloak. This room also contains a model of one of Columbus' ships, the *Santa María*.

CUARTO REAL ALTO

The Alcázar is still a royal palace. In 1995 it staged the wedding feast of the Infanta Elena, daughter of King Juan Carlos I, after her marriage in Seville's cathedral. The Cuarto Real Alto (Upper Royal Quarters), the rooms used by the Spanish royal family on their visits to Seville, are open for around 12 half-hour tours (€3), some in Spanish, some in English. The tours are for a maximum of 15 people: if you're keen, it's best to book ahead on ☎ 954 56 00 40. Any unreserved tickets are sold at the main ticket office. The tours start in the southwestern corner of the Patio de la Montería: highlights include the 14th-century Salón de Audiencias, still the monarch's reception room, and Pedro I's bedroom, with marvellous Mudéjar tiles and plasterwork.

PALACIO DE DON PEDRO

Whatever else Pedro I may have done, posterity owes him a big thank you for creating this palace (also called the Palacio Mudéjar), which rivals Granada's Alhambra (p359) in its splendid decoration. The palace, unlike the Alhambra, has retained the vivid colours used to fill in the carvings of the wall decorations. This gives the full idea of the incredible visual richness of the interiors of not only the Alcázar, but also of the Alhambra as it once was.

Though at odds with many of his fellow Christians, Pedro had a long-standing alliance with the Muslim emir of Granada, Mohammed V, the man responsible for much of the Alhambra's finest decoration. So in 1364, when Pedro decided to build a new palace within the Alcázar, Mohammed sent along many of his best artisans. These were joined by others from Seville and Toledo. Their work, drawing on the Islamic traditions of the Almohads and caliphal Córdoba, is a unique synthesis of Iberian Islamic art.

Inscriptions on the palace's **façade**, facing the Patio de la Montería, encapsulate the collaborative nature of the enterprise.

While one announces in Spanish that the building's creator was 'the very high, noble and conquering Don Pedro, by the grace of God king of Castila and León', another proclaims repeatedly in Arabic that 'there is no conqueror but Allah'.

At the heart of the palace is the wonderful **Patio de las Doncellas** (Patio of the Maidens), surrounded by beautiful arches, plasterwork and tiling. The doors at its two ends are among the finest made by Toledo's carpenters. The sunken garden in the centre was uncovered by archaeologists in 2004 from beneath a 16th-century marble covering.

The **Cámara Regia** (King's Quarters), on the northern side of the patio, has stunningly beautiful ceilings and wonderful plaster- and tile-work. Its rear room was probably the monarch's summer bedroom.

From here you can move west into the little **Patio de las Muñecas** (Patio of the Dolls), the heart of the palace's private quarters, featuring delicate Granada-style decoration; indeed, plasterwork was actually brought here from the Alhambra in the 19th century when the mezzanine and top gallery were added for Queen Isabel II. The **Cuarto del Príncipe** (Prince's Room), to its north, has a superb wooden cupola ceiling trying to recreate a starlit night sky. It was probably the queen's bedroom.

The spectacular **Salón de Embajadores** (Hall of Ambassadors), at the western end of the Patio de las Doncellas, was the throne room of Pedro I's palace – as it had been, in earlier form, of Al-Muwarak palace (from which Pedro retained the horseshoe-arched doorways). The room's fabulous wooden dome of multiple star patterns, symbolising the universe, was added in 1427. The dome's shape gives the room its alternative name, Sala de la Media Naranja (Hall of the Half Orange). The coloured plasterwork is magnificent. It was in this room that Pedro laid a trap for the so-called Red King, who had temporarily deposed Pedro's buddy Mohammed V in Granada. During a banquet, armed men suddenly leapt from hiding and seized the Red King and his retinue of 37, all of whom were executed outside Seville a few years later.

On the western side of the Salón de Embajadores the beautiful **Arco de Pavones**, named after its peacock motifs, leads into the **Salón del Techo de Felipe II**, with a Renaissance ceiling (1589–91). The **Capilla** (chapel), located along the southern side of the Patio de las Doncellas, has another fine ceiling (1540s).

SALONES DE CARLOS V
Reached by a staircase from the southeastern corner of the Patio de las Doncellas, these are the much-remodelled rooms of Alfonso X's 13th-century Gothic palace. It was here that Alfonso's intellectual court gathered and, a century later, Pedro I installed the mistress he loved, María de Padilla. The rooms are now named after the 16th-century Spanish king Carlos I, using his title as Holy Roman Emperor, Charles V. His wedding feast was held here on 11 March 1526 and the **Sala de las Bóvedas** (Hall of the Vault) is adorned with beautiful tiles by Cristóbal de Augusta, commissioned in memory of that event by his son, Felipe II, in the 1570s.

PATIO DEL CRUCERO
This patio outside the Salones de Carlos V was originally the upper storey of the patio of the 12th-century Almohad palace. Originally it had consisted only of raised walkways along the four sides and two cross-walkways that met in the middle. Below grew orange trees, whose fruit could be plucked at hand height by the lucky folk strolling along the walkways. The patio's lower level was built over in the 18th century after earthquake damage.

GARDENS & EXIT
From the Salones de Carlos V you can go out into the Alcázar's large and peaceful gardens. The gardens in front of the Salones de Carlos V and Palacio de Don Pedro date in their present form from the 16th and 17th centuries. Immediately in front of the buildings is a series of small linked gardens, some with pools and fountains. From one, the **Jardín de las Danzas** (Garden of the Dances), a passage runs beneath the Salones de Carlos V to the **Baños de Doña María de Padilla** (María de Padilla Baths). These are the vaults beneath the Patio del Crucero – originally that patio's lower level – with a grotto that replaced the patio's original pool.

The gardens to the east, beyond a long wall, are 20th-century creations. The way

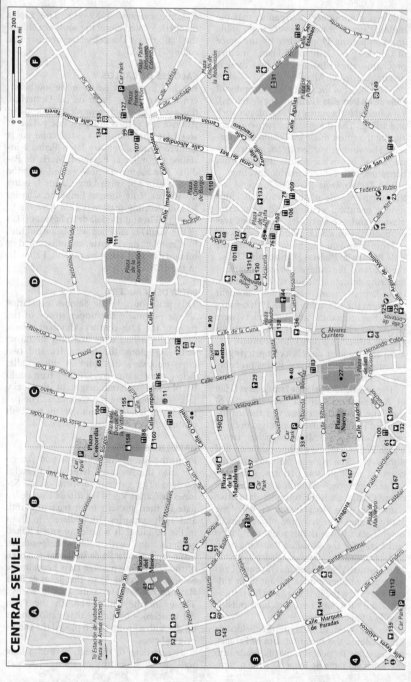

CENTRAL SEVILLE

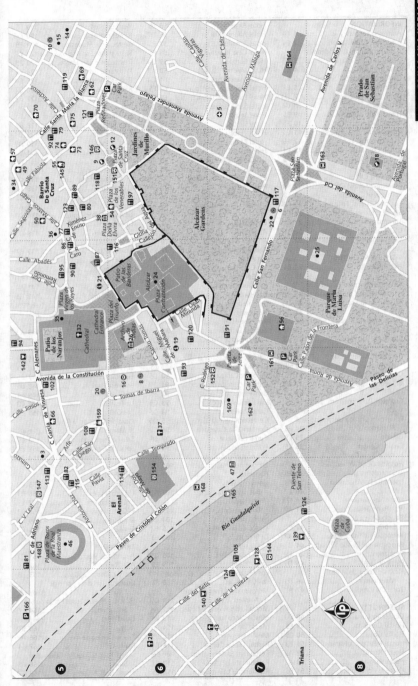

SEVILLA PROVINCE

out is via the **Apeadero**, a 17th-century entrance hall, and the **Patio de las Banderas** (Patio of the Flags).

Archivo de Indias

Found on the western side of Plaza del Triunfo, the World Heritage **Archivo de Indias** (Archive of the Indies; Map pp102–3; ☎ 954 21 12 34; Calle Santo Tomás) has been the main archive on Spain's American empire since 1785. The 16th-century building, designed by Juan de Herrera, was originally Seville's Lonja (Exchange) for commerce with the Americas. Its 8km of shelves hold 80 million pages of documents dating from 1492 through to the end of the empire in the 19th century. Normally, the archive exhibits rotating displays of fascinating maps and documents, including manuscripts written by the likes of Columbus, Cervantes, Cortés or Pizarro. For an update on schedules, check at a tourist office.

Barrio de Santa Cruz

The old *judería* (Jewish quarter), the Barrio de Santa Cruz (Map pp102–3), has dozens of beautiful squares shaded by orange trees that sag with fruit and perfume the streets with their exquisite blossoms. Although this is tourist central, it's still a vital part of the city and one that's remarkably easy and pleasant to wander.

The barrio (district) extends east of the cathedral and the Alcázar in a tangle of narrow, winding streets and lovely squares, with numerous popular places to stay, eat and drink and plenty of souvenir shops. It became the city's *judería* after the Christian reconquest of Seville in 1248, flourishing especially under Pedro I, whose court included many Jewish financiers and tax collectors. Racial jealousies led eventually to a pogrom that emptied the *judería* in 1391.

Squeeze yourself down the narrow lanes from Plaza del Triunfo and breathe the smell of oranges on the barrio's most beautiful square, **Plaza Doña Elvira**, where you can rest on the *azulejo*-covered benches, under the shade of the orange trees. A few steps east is Plaza de los Venerables, where you can visit the 17th-century **Hospital de los Venerables Sacerdotes** (Map pp102–3; ☎ 954 56 26 96; adult/child under 12yr/student/senior €5/free/2.50/2.50, Sun afternoon free; ☖ 10am-2pm & 4-8pm). Used until the 1960s as a residence for aged priests,

this has a lovely central courtyard and several exhibition rooms, one with a collection of prints of Seville. Don't miss the church with murals by Juan de Valdés Leal and fine sculptures by Pedro Roldán.

Carry on down more narrow lanes eastward to the silent **Plaza de Santa Cruz**, whose central cross, made in 1692, gives the barrio its name and ranks as one of the finest examples of Seville wrought-iron work. A short distance north from here is the **Casa de la Memoria de Al-Andalus** (Map pp102–3; ☎ 954 56 06 70; Calle Ximénez de Enciso 28; ☖ 9am-2pm & 6-7.30pm), an 18th-century mansion on the site of a medieval Jewish house, with one of the most wonderful patios in town which doubles as a stage for quality flamenco performances.

El Arenal

A short walk west from Avenida de la Constitución brings you to the Río Guadalquivir, with a pleasant riverside footpath. This district, El Arenal (Map pp102–3), is home to some of Seville's most interesting sights.

TORRE DEL ORO

The Tower of Gold is a 13th-century Almohad watchtower on the riverbank. It once crowned a corner of the city walls that stretched here from the Alcázar, and its dome was, according to legend, covered in golden tiles. Inside is a small **maritime museum** (☎ 954 22 24 19; admission €1; ☖ 10am-2pm Tue-Fri, 11am-2pm Sat & Sun, closed Aug). The collection of models of famous boats merits a visit.

HOSPITAL DE LA CARIDAD

A marvellous sample of Sevillan golden-age art adorns the church in the **Hospital de la Caridad** (Hospice of Charity; Map pp102–3; ☎ 954 22 32 32; Calle Temprado 3; admission €4, free Sun & holidays; ☖ 9am-1.30pm & 3.30-7.30pm Mon-Sat, 9am-1pm Sun & holidays), a block east of the river. The Hospital de la Caridad, basically a hospice for the elderly, was founded by Miguel de Mañara, by legend a notorious libertine who changed his ways after seeing a vision of his own funeral procession. In the 1670s Mañara commissioned a series of works on the theme of death and redemption from Seville's three finest artists of the day, Bartolomé Esteban Murillo, Juan de Valdés Leal and Pedro Roldán, for the church here. The juxtaposition of Murillo's optimistic paintings with the suffering depicted by Roldán and the unforgiving vision of Valdés Leal makes for fascinating contrasts.

Valdés Leal's two masterpieces, chillingly illustrating the futility of worldly glory, are at the western end of the church: *Finis Gloriae Mundi* (The End of Earthly Glory) is above the door by which you enter, and *In Ictu Oculi* (In the Blink of an Eye), hangs on the opposite wall. On this same, northern, side of the church are Murillo's *San Juan de Dios* (St John of God), *Anunciación* (Annunciation) and *Moises Haciendo Brotar el Agua de la Roca* (Moses Drawing Water from the Rock). Beneath this last is a sweet depiction of the infant Christ by Murillo (facing an equally sweet infant St John the Baptist on the opposite wall).

The sculpture on the elaborate baroque high altar illustrates the final act of compassion – the burial of the dead (in this case Christ). The tableau, with its strong sense of movement, is Pedro Roldán's masterpiece. To the left of the high altar, steps descend to the crypt where Miguel de Mañara is buried.

Along the southern side of the church is another fine Roldán sculpture, this time of Christ praying before being crucified. It stands between Murillo's *La Multiplicación de Panes y Peces* (The Miracle of the Loaves and Fishes) and *Santa Isabel de Húngria* (St Isabel of Hungary). The church's four largest Murillos were among eight that he painted for this site on the themes of transcending death by compassion and mercy. Four of the eight paintings were looted by Napoleonic troops in the early 19th century.

PLAZA DE TOROS DE LA REAL MAESTRANZA

Seville's **bullring** (☎ 954 22 45 77; www.realmaestranza.com; Paseo de Cristóbal Colón 12; tour adult/senior €4/3.20; ⏰ half-hourly 9.30am-6.30pm, 9.30am-3pm bullfighting days) is one of the most handsome and important bullrings in Spain, and probably the oldest (building began in 1758). It was in this ring and the one at Ronda that bullfighting on foot began in the 18th century. Interesting guided visits, in English and Spanish, take you into the ring and its museum, with a peep into the minihospital for bullfighters where a worried picture of

the Virgin Mary above the door prays for their wellbeing. For more on bullfights in Seville, see p127; for general information on bullfighting, see p39.

IGLESIA DE LA MAGDALENA

One of Seville's outstanding baroque churches, the **Iglesia de la Magdalena** (Map pp102-3; Calle San Pablo 12; ⏰ Mass times, usually 8-11.30am & 6.30-9pm) was built between 1691 and 1709. Two paintings by Zurbarán hang in the Capilla Sacramental (the first chapel on the right from the entrance), and a fine 1612 Crucifixion sculpture, *El Cristo del Calvario* (The Christ of Calvary) by Francisco de Ocampo, is in the chapel to the right of the main altar.

The church is the home of the Quinta Angustia brotherhood, whose 17th-century *Descendimiento* tableau, showing Jesus being taken down from the cross, is carried through Seville's streets during Semana Santa. This can usually be seen in the chapel on the left as you enter the church: the Christ is attributed to Pedro Roldán.

MUSEO DE BELLAS ARTES

Housed in the beautiful former Convento de la Merced, Seville's **Museo de Bellas Artes** (Fine Arts Museum; Map pp102-3; ☎ 954 22 07 90; Plaza del Museo 9; non-EU citizen €1.50, EU citizen free; ⏰ 2.30-8.30pm Tue, 9am-8.30pm Wed-Sat, 9am-2.30pm Sun; ♿) does full justice to Seville's leading role in Spain's 17th-century artistic Siglo de Oro.

Room I exemplifies the 15th-century beginnings of the Sevillan school: the best exhibits are Pedro Millán's terracotta sculptures, displaying a realism that was then rare in Spanish art.

Room II, the dining hall of the convent, displays Renaissance work from Seville and elsewhere, including sculptures by Pietro Torrigiano, an Italian who came to Seville in 1522 and was the major artistic figure of the early Renaissance here.

Room III exhibits Sevillan Renaissance retables and early 17th-century Sevillan paintings. The penetrating portrait of Don Cristóbal Suárez de Ribera by the young Velázquez grabs the attention, as does Alonso Cano's striking *Las Ánimas del Purgatorio* (Souls in Purgatory), in the corner between rooms III and IV.

In room IV, devoted mainly to Mannerism (the transition from Renaissance to baroque), Alonso Vázquez's large *Sagrada Cena* (Last Supper) is the outstanding canvas. The lovely anonymous statuettes of the child Jesus and child St John the Baptist contrast markedly with the grisly head of St John the Baptist (1591) by Gaspar Núñez Delgado in the centre of the room. From here you move through the beautiful cloister to room V, the convent church, which is hung with paintings by masters of Sevillan baroque, above all Murillo. His *Inmaculada Concepción Grande* at the head of the church, displays all the curving, twisting movement that is so central to baroque art.

Upstairs, highlights of room VI include José de Ribera's very Spanish-looking *Santiago Apóstol* (St James the Apostle) and Zurbarán's deeply sombre *Cristo Crucificado* (Christ Crucified). Room VII is devoted to Murillo and disciples, room VIII to Valdés Leal, and room IX to European baroque art.

Room X has a few carvings by Juan Martínez Montañés and Juan de Mesa but is otherwise all Zurbarán, with a masterly depiction of the contrast between the worldly Pope Urban II and the ascetic St Bruno in *Visita de San Bruno a Urbano II*.

Room XI, the closed-in gallery around the upper storey of the cloister, displays Spanish paintings of the 18th century, a time of little creative verve, though Domingo Martínez's Seville carnival scenes are interesting in their detail. Rooms XII to XIV show 19th- and 20th-century painting, mainly Sevillan but also with Goya's 1824 portrait of Don José Duaso. Among the Sevillan work, don't miss the Romantic portraits of Antonio María Esquivel (1806–57), the early flamenco scenes by Manuel Cabral Bejarano (1827–91), or the eclectic work of impressionist-influenced Gonzalo Bilbao (1860–1938).

El Centro

As the name suggests, this is Seville's centre, and the densely packed zone of narrow streets and squares north of the cathedral is home to excellent bars and restaurants.

PLAZA DE SAN FRANCISCO & CALLE SIERPES

With a lively history as a market square in Muslim times and then the prime spot for Inquisition burnings, Plaza de San Francisco has been Seville's main public square since the 16th century. The **ayuntamiento** (town hall; Map pp102–3), on its western side, is a building of contrasting characters: its southern end is encrusted with lovely Renaissance carving from the 1520s and '30s, while its northern end, a 19th-century extension, is bare.

The pedestrianised Calle Sierpes, which runs north from the square, and the parallel Calle Tetuán/Velázquez are Seville's fanciest shopping streets. Between the two streets, on Calle Jovellanos, look into the **Capilla de San José** (Map pp102-3; 8am-12.30pm & 6.30-8.30pm). This small 18th-century chapel, created by the city's carpenters' guild, is a whole world of breathtakingly intense baroque ornamentation.

The **Palacio de la Condesa de Lebrija** (Map pp102-3; ☎ 954 22 78 02; www.palaciodelebrija.com; Calle de la Cuna 8; admission ground fl only €4, whole bldg €7; 10.30am-1.30pm & 4.30-7pm Mon-Fri, 10am-1pm Sat Oct-Apr, 10.30am-1.30pm & 5-7.30pm Mon-Fri, 10am-1pm Sat May-Sep), a block east of Calle Sierpes, is a 16th-century mansion with a rich collection of art and artisanry, and a beautiful Renaissance-Mudejar courtyard. If you want to see the top floor, you must wait for the guided tour, but it's worth it. The late Countess of Lebrija was an archaeologist, and she remodelled the house in 1914, filling many of the rooms with treasures from her travels. Ancient Rome was the Countess' speciality, so the library is full of books on antiquity and there are plenty of remains from Roman Itálica (p130), including some marvellous mosaics – especially the large one in the main patio. Upstairs are Arabic, baroque and Spanish rooms. The three-flight main staircase is lined with 16th- and 17th-century Sevillan tiles, and has a coffered ceiling imported from a now-demolished palace at Marchena.

PLAZA SALVADOR

A couple of blocks northeast of Plaza de San Francisco, this plaza was once the main forum of Roman Hispalis. It's dominated by the **Parroquia del Divino Salvador**, a major baroque church built between 1674 and 1712 following the demolition of Muslim Ishbiliya's main mosque at this site. Before the mosque, early Christian churches had stood here, and before them, a Roman temple. Archaeologists are digging at the site, hoping to establish the exact age of the mosque and install walkways for the public to view the excavations. Hundreds of 18th-century burials, just beneath the church floor, were among the archaeologists' first discoveries in 2003. On the northern side of the church, the mosque's small **patio** remains, with orange trees, a font and a few half-buried Roman columns. To visit the church you have to first make an appointment by telephone (☎ 954 59 54 05, 10am to 2pm Monday to Friday). The patio can be visited daily from 10am to 2pm and from 5pm to 7pm.

CASA DE PILATOS
Another of Seville's finest noble mansions, the **Casa de Pilatos** (☎ 954 22 52 98; admission ground fl only €5, whole house €8, EU citizen 1-5pm Tue free; ⏰ 9am-7pm Mar-Sep, 9am-6pm Oct-Feb) is still occupied by the ducal Medinaceli family. It's a mixture of Mudejar, Gothic and Renaissance styles, with some beautiful tilework and *artesonado*. The overall effect is similar to that of the Alcázar.

One explanation for the building's name ('Pilate's House') is that its 16th-century creator, Don Fadrique Enríquez de Ribera, was trying to imitate Pontius Pilate's palace in Jerusalem, to which city he had made a pilgrimage. A rival theory is that the house served as the first station of a Via Crucis (Way of the Cross) route, in which penitents symbolically retraced Christ's steps to the Crucifixion. The first station would represent Christ's appearance before Pilate.

The **Patio Principal** has lots of wonderful 16th-century tiles and intricate Mudejar plasterwork. The armless statue of Athene is ancient Greek; the statues in the other corners are Roman. Around the walls are busts of Roman historical and mythical figures, plus King Carlos I of Spain.

The names of the rooms off the Patio Principal recall the supposed Pontius Pilate connection. The **Descanso de los Jueces** (Judges' Retiring Room), **Salón Pretorio** (Palace Hall) and **Gabinete de Pilatos** (Pilate's Study) have *artesonado*. Beyond the Salón Pretorio is the **Zaquizami**, a corridor with Roman sculptures and inscriptions. The Gabinete de Pilatos leads into the **Jardín Grande** (Big Garden), which features Italian-style loggias.

The **staircase** to the upper floor has the most magnificent tiles in the building, and a great golden *artesonado* dome above. Visits to the **upper floor** itself, still partly inhabited by the Medinacelis, are guided. Of interest are the several centuries' worth of Medinaceli portraits and a small Goya bullfighting painting.

South of the Centre
ANTIGUA FÁBRICA DE TABACOS
The agony and love trouble of Bizet's operatic Carmen took place in Seville's massive 250m by 180m former tobacco factory, **Antigua Fábrica de Tabacos** (Map pp102-3; Calle San Fernando; ⏰ 8am-9.30pm Mon-Fri, 8am-2pm Sat). It was built in the 18th century and served its original purpose until the mid-20th century. Long a cornerstone of the city's economy, the factory had its own jail, stables for 400 mules, 21 fountains, 24 patios and even a nursery for the children of its mostly female workers.

It's an impressive if rather gloomy building, in neoclassical style. The main portal sports carvings on the theme of the discovery of the Americas, where tobacco came from: among them are Columbus, Cortés (conqueror of the Aztecs) and two Native Americans, one of them smoking a pipe. At the top of the portal is Fame, blowing a trumpet.

The tobacco factory is now part of the Universidad de Sevilla (Seville University). You're free to wander through and take a look.

PARQUE DE MARÍA LUISA &
PLAZA DE ESPAÑA
Standing in a large area south of the tobacco factory, the **Parque de María Luisa** (Map pp94-5; ⏰ 8am-10pm Sep-Jun, 8am-midnight Jul & Aug) was transformed for Seville's first international fair, the 1929 Exposición Iberoamericana, when architects spattered it with all sorts of excellent and quirky buildings, many of them modelled on the native styles of Spain's former colonies. The park is a beautiful oasis of calm with a maze of paths, flowers, fountains, lawns and 3500 magnificent trees. It provides a place to escape from the traffic and noise of the city and is the prime spot where *sevillanos* (people of Seville) go to relax on the weekends.

Plaza de España, a rather isolated and relaxing spot with its fountains and mini-canals, faces the northeastern side of the park across Avenida de Isabel la Católica. Curving round the plaza is the most grandiose of the 1929 buildings, a brick-and-tile confection featuring Seville tilework at its gaudiest, with a map and historical scene for each Spanish province – all designed by the leading Exposición Iberoamericana architect, Sevillan Aníbal González.

On **Plaza de América** at the southern end of the park is a large flock of white doves (they'll clamber all over you if you buy a €1.50 bag of seed from vendors) and two interesting museums. The big **Museo Arqueológico** (Map pp94-5; ☎ 954 23 24 01; non-EU citizen €1.50, EU citizen free; ☒ 3-8pm Tue, 9am-8pm Wed-Sat, 9am-2pm Sun & holidays) has a room of gold jewellery from the mysterious Tartessos culture, and fine collections of Iberian animal sculptures and beautiful Roman mosaics. Large quantities of Roman sculpture include statues of two emperors from Itálica near Seville – Hadrian (Adriano) and Trajan (Trajano), with the top half of his head missing.

The claim to fame of the **Museo de Artes y Costumbres Populares** (Map pp94-5; ☎ 954 23 25 76; non-EU citizen €1.50, EU citizen free; ☒ 3-8pm Tue, 9am-8pm Wed-Sat, 9am-2pm Sun & holidays) was a walk-on part as an Arabic palace in *Lawrence of Arabia*. It is in the 1929 exhibition's Mudejar pavilion and its collection includes mock workshops of local crafts, and some really beautiful old festival costumes.

Triana

The legendary barrio of Triana, across the Río Guadalquivir from central Seville, used to be the quarter of the city's *gitanos* (Roma) and was one of the birthplaces of flamenco. The neighbourhood's name is often heard in flamenco songs, nostalgically remembered by the singers over many generations. Even though the *gitanos* were moved out to new suburban areas in the 1960s and '70s, Triana's teenagers still sit by the river and sing flamenco – Beyoncé would be jealous.

Triana is also a famed **pottery-and-tile-making area**. A dozen shops and workshops still sell charming and artistic ceramics on the corner of Calles Alfarería and Antillano Campos (Map pp94–5). Triana has several diverse and important churches and chapels. Among the most important are

the **Iglesia del Cristo de la Expiración** (Map pp94-5; ☎ 954 33 33 41; Calle Castilla 182; ☒ 10.30am-1.30pm & 6-9.30pm Tue-Sat, 10.30am-1.30pm Sun) houses a much-loved figure of the dead Christ, dating from 1682, that takes an honoured place in Seville's Semana Santa processions. The image is known as El Cachorro (The Puppy): sculptor Antonio Ruiz Gijón was reputedly inspired by the agonised body of a *gitano* singer of that name who had died in a fight in this street. In the southern part of Triana, the **Capilla del Rocío** (Map pp94-5; Calle Evangelista 23) is home to the Hermandad del Rocío de Triana. The departure of this brotherhood's procession of horses and covered wagons to El Rocío (see the boxed text, p157) on the Thursday before Pentecost is one of the most colourful and emotive events in the Seville calendar.

At the **Capilla de los Marineros** (Map pp102-3; ☎ 954 33 26 45; Calle de la Pureza 53; ☒ 9am-1pm & 5.30-9pm Mon-Sat) you'll find the gorgeously bedecked, much adored image of the Virgen de la Esperanza (Virgin of Hope), patroness of Triana sailors, another who has an honoured role in the Semana Santa processions. The **Parroquia de Santa Ana** (Map pp102-3; Calle de la Pureza 80), dating from 1280, has a wealth of antique religious imagery. A strange tradition has it that every woman who kicks 'El Negro', a 16th-century tomb that has tiles depicting a recumbent knight, will find a husband. Poor El Negro has been protected by benches and other obstacles to prevent damage to this precious artwork, but women still want husbands and keep on kicking.

Isla de la Cartuja

North of Triana, this northern part of an island between two branches of the Guadalquivir was the site of Expo '92. Today it's home to the Isla Mágica theme park (p111), Cartuja 93 technology business park and the historic La Cartuja monastery. Buses C1 and C2 (p130) serve the Isla de la Cartuja.

CONJUNTO MONUMENTAL DE LA CARTUJA

Founded in 1399, the **Conjunto Monumental de la Cartuja** (Cartuja Monastery; Map pp94-5; ☎ 955 03 70 70; admission incl/excl temporary exhibitions €3/1.80, EU citizen free Tue; ☒ 10am-9pm Mon-Fri, 11am-9pm Sat, 10am-3pm Sun, to 8pm Mon-Fri Oct-Mar, last admission 1hr before closing time) became the favourite Sevillan lodging place for Columbus, King Felipe II and other luminaries. Columbus' remains lay here from 1509 to 1536. Over the centuries benefactors endowed the monastery with a rich collection of Sevillan art, but in 1836 the monks were expelled during the Disentailment (when church property was auctioned off by the state). In 1839 the complex was bought by a Liverpudlian, Charles Pickman, who turned it into a porcelain factory, building the tall bottle-shaped kilns that stand incongruously beside the monastery buildings. The porcelain factory functioned until 1982.

The whole complex was restored for Expo '92. The entrance is on the monastery's western side on Calle Américo Vespucio. The monastery features a now rather bare 15th-century **church**; a pretty 15th-century Mudejar **cloister**; and the **Capilla de Santa Ana**, which was built as the Columbus family tomb. It also features the **Capítulo de Monjes** (Chapter House), full of disarmingly realistic 16th-century funerary sculptures of members of the Ribera family, who were among the monastery's chief benefactors. Also here is the **Centro Andaluz de Arte Contemporáneo** (Andalucian Contemporary Art Centre), with a large collection of modern Andalucian art and frequent temporary exhibitions by contemporary artists.

CARTUJA 93

Many of the exotic Expo pavilions are now encompassed within this **technology park**, which is home to nearly 200 companies and organisations employing nearly 9000 people. Many of the pavilions still look futuristic, though the built-in obsolescence of a few is starting to show through. You can wander around the area during daylight hours but you may find that the gates are only open on the western side on Calle Américo Vespucio (Map pp94–5).

Alameda de Hércules & Around

The working-class area of Alameda de Hércules and further north of Calle Alfonso XII and Plaza Ponce de León provides a fascinating contrast to the city centre. There's good nightlife here, and it's the centre of Seville's 'alternative' scene, with intriguing nooks and crannies, boho cafés and one of the city's best street markets (on Calle de la Feria, Thursday morning – see p128).

BASÍLICA DE JESÚS DEL GRAN PODER

Found behind a large baroque portal in the corner of Plaza de San Lorenzo, the **Basílica de Jesús del Gran Poder** (Map pp94-5; ☎ 954 91 56 72; Plaza de San Lorenzo 13; ☼ 8am-1.30pm & 6-9pm Sat-Thu, 7.30am-10pm Fri) dates only from the 1960s but houses a famous and far older sculpture of the cross-bearing Christ (after which it's named). The almost wizened image of Christ, sculpted in 1620 by Juan de Mesa, inspires much Sevillan devotion and takes place of honour in the Semana Santa processions on Good Friday morning. On either side of the altar are a sculpture of St John the Evangelist, also by de Mesa, and an anonymous *Virgen del Mayor Dolor* (Virgin of the Deepest Grief) from the 18th century or earlier.

ALAMEDA DE HÉRCULES

Once a no-go area reserved only for the city's 'painted ladies', pimps and a wide range of shady characters, the dusty 350m-long parklike strip has reinvented itself as Seville's only 'alternative area', with trendy bars, chic shops, a small gay community and the popular **Teatro Alameda** (see p126). Indeed the city's *la marcha* is rife here and people fill the streets all night at weekends, chatting and drinking till the sun comes up over the *álamo* (poplar) trees that gave Alameda its name. Even though the area's straightened up its act, prostitutes still live and work in the area and some of the streets are pretty uninviting, especially after dark, so it's not a good idea for women to walk alone around here at night.

The Alameda was created in the 1570s by draining a marsh, erecting two columns from a ruined Roman temple at its southern end, topped with statues of Hercules and Julius Caesar by Diego de Pesquera. Its avenues became a fashionable meeting place in the 17th century before sinking into anonymity and dereliction until the 1990s, when it emerged as one of the fastest up-and-coming areas.

BASÍLICA DE LA MACARENA

The 1940s **Basílica de la Macarena** (Map pp94-5; ☎ 954 90 18 00; Calle Bécquer 1; ☼ 9am-2pm & 5-9pm), off Calle San Luis, the home of Seville's most revered Virgin, will give you a whiff of the fervour inspired by Semana Santa. The *Virgen de la Esperanza Macarena*

(Macarena Virgin of Hope), a magnificent statue adorned with a golden crown, lavish vestments, and five diamond-and-emerald brooches donated by a famous 20th-century matador, Joselito El Gallo, stands in splendour behind the main altarpiece. Believed to have been sculpted in the mid-17th century by María Luisa Roldán ('La Roldana'), La Macarena, as she is commonly known, is the patron of bullfighters and Seville's supreme representation of the grieving, yet hopeful, mother of Christ. The power of this fragile, beautiful statue is most evident in the wee hours of the *madrugá* (Good Friday) Semana Santa procession. Where she passes, a rain of rose petals falls, and crazed *sevillanos* shout: *¡Macarena, guapa!* (Beautiful Macarena!). To top it all off a *saeta* (sacred Andalucian song) is sung, praising the Virgin's beauty.

A magnificent 1654 statue of *El Cristo de la Sentencia* (Christ of the Sentence) by Felipe Morales is normally positioned in a chapel on the left of the church. Both statues are carried from the church at midnight at the start of every Good Friday. Their journey through the city is the climax of Semana Santa in Seville, and their return to the church around 1.30pm on the Saturday is attended by enormous crowds.

The church's **museum** (adult/student/senior €3/1.50/1.50; [clock] 9.30am-2pm & 5-8pm) displays some of La Macarena's extraordinarily lavish vestments, plus bullfighters' suits donated by famous matadors and the Semana Santa *pasos* (platforms) on which both images are carried. The *paso* of *El Cristo de la Sentencia* is a tableau showing Pontius Pilate washing his hands while the order for Christ's Crucifixion is read out.

Buses C1, C2, C3 and C4 (see p130) stop on Calle Andueza, near the Basílica de la Macarena. Across this street is the **Parlamento de Andalucía**, Andalucía's regional parliament (generally not open to visitors). The longest surviving stretch of Seville's 12th-century **Almohad walls** extends east of the church.

IGLESIA DE SAN LUIS

One of Seville's most impressive churches, **Iglesia de San Luis** (Map pp94-5; [phone] 954 55 02 07; Calle San Luis s/n; admission free; [clock] 9am-2pm Tue-Thu, 9am-2pm & 5-8pm Fri & Sat, closed Aug) stands 500m south of the Basílica de la Macarena. Designed for the Jesuits by Leonardo de

Figueroa in 1731, the baroque San Luis has an unusual equal-armed cross plan, 16 twisting stone pillars and a superb soaring dome. Statues of saints and virtues by Pedro de Mena perch very precariously on pedestals around the lower levels of the dome. *Religio* (Religion) looks as if she's about to topple over and crash to the church floor. Only in use as a church for a few decades, San Luis became a hospice before being abandoned in 1877, but has recently been restored and opened for visits.

ACTIVITIES
Isla Mágica

The theme park **Isla Mágica** (Map pp94-5; [phone] 902 16 17 16; www.islamagica.es; adult high season day/night pass €23.50/16.50, child under 13yr high season day/night pass €16.50/12.50; [clock] 11am-11pm mid-Jun–mid-Sep, 11am-7pm Apr–mid-Jun & mid-Sep–Oct, closed Nov-Mar) attracts a million visitors a year and is a great day's fun for kids and anyone who likes white-knuckle rides. Opening hours vary from year to year and between weekdays and weekends, so it's always best to confirm times before going. Half-day and evening tickets are also available; see the website for more information.

The theme is the 16th-century Spanish colonial adventure. Highlight rides include **El Jaguar**, a roller coaster with high-speed 360-degree turns, and the **Anaconda** water roller coaster with vertiginous drops. At busy times you may have to wait 45 minutes for the big attractions. There are also pirate shows, virtual rides, bird-of-prey displays and lots of entertaining street-theatre-type stuff, plus plenty of places to eat and drink.

Baños Árabes

Rest your weary, sightseeing muscles by taking a soak and a massage at **Aire de Sevilla** (Map pp94-5; [phone] 955 01 00 25; www.airedesevilla.com; Calle Aire 15; bath/bath & massage €18/26; [clock] on the hr every 2hrs from 10am-2am) Arab baths. There are two warm pools and one cold, plus a steam room.

COURSES
Flamenco & Dance

The city has many dance and flamenco schools. Check these out:

Espacio Meteora (Map pp94-5; [phone] 954 90 14 83; www.espaciometeora.com; Calle Duque Cornejo 16A) Innovative arts centre where flamenco and other dance courses are usually ongoing.

Fundación Cristina Heeren de Arte Flamenco (Map pp102–3; ☎ 954 21 70 58; www.flamencoheeren.com; Calle Fabiola 1) Long-term courses in all flamenco arts; also one-month intensive summer courses.

Sevilla Dance Centre (Map pp94–5; ☎ 954 38 39 02; Calle Conde de Torrejón 19) Salsa, flamenco, classical, hip-hop, contemporary.

Taller Flamenco (Map pp94–5; ☎ 954 56 42 34; www .tallerflamenco.com; Calle Peral 49) Flamenco dance and guitar and Spanish-language courses.

Tourist offices and *El Giraldillo* magazine (p96) have further information.

Language

Along with Granada, Seville is one of the two most popular cities in Andalucía for foreigners to study Spanish. The following are among the best schools: all offer short- and long-term courses at a variety of levels, nearly always with a range of excursions and other spare-time and social activities.

Carpe Diem (Map pp102-3; ☎ 954 21 85 15; www.carpediemsevilla.com; Calle de la Cuna 13) Small, friendly school with courses also available in arts, culture, translation and Spanish for business.

CLIC (Map pp102–3; ☎ 954 50 21 31; www.clic.es; Calle Albareda 19) Well-established language centre with good social scene; courses in business Spanish and Hispanic studies available.

Giralda Center (Map pp102–3; ☎ 954 21 31 65; www .giraldacenter.com; Calle Mateos Gago 17) Friendly atmosphere, plenty of excursions, reputation for good teaching.

Lenguaviva (Map pp94–5; ☎ 954 90 51 31; www .lenguaviva.es; Calle Viriato 24) Good on spare-time activities like tapas tours and social drinks; courses in business Spanish available.

LINC (Map pp102–3; ☎ 954 50 04 59; www.linc.tv; Calle General Polavieja 13) Small, popular school, good on cultural activities and excursions.

SEVILLE FOR CHILDREN

The riverbank of the **Guadalquivir** and **Parque de María Luisa** (p108) are good places for younger children to run off some steam, and they'll enjoy feeding the doves in Parque de María Luisa. **Isla Mágica** (p111) gives kids of all ages a great day of fun, though those aged over about 10 will get the most out of the rides. Another likely hit is a **city tour** in an open-topped double-decker bus or horse-drawn carriage (opposite). On

---

IN SARA'S SHOES

After a few painful attempts at flamenco dancing, followed by verbal abuse from the neighbour downstairs, I was ready to give up altogether. But then a friend said to me: 'You need a role model, someone whose success can be a guide. Someone like Sara Baras.' And I decided to seek out this woman whose dancing career started at the age of eight, just to talk to her, see what drove her and what keeps her going.

She's a charming young woman, small off stage, and the severe flamenco expression is replaced by a kind smile. I don't tell her I am attempting to learn flamenco, but ask her what inspired her to dance. 'I owe absolutely everything to my mother, as a person and as an artist. She is the kind of person who falls in love with things in a way that transmits to other people. I was very lucky to have been able to follow her to all the festivals and schools since I was a child. I was always watching people dance.' The mother she talks about is Concha Baras, a woman whose school was famed in Andalucía and where flamenco stars started out. 'I was fortunate as a child to be in contact with flamenco's best: Camarón de la Isla. His older brother, Manuel, sang at my mother's school. When Camarón first showed up, it was really bizarre, because he was so shy. It was as if he had no voice, as if he wasn't born with this magical music box in his throat.' I ask her what her first memory of dancing flamenco is. She's embarrassed: 'It was when my mother started her school. There were lots of boys there and I was too embarrassed to dance in front of them.' I think that's a much better memory than mine, which I shan't go into.

I wonder whether she ever gets bored dancing when she's on tour. Surely it gets a little repetitive? 'When I am dancing, I don't think of anything. I just dance. We have long silences during our shows, but for me, when there is complete silence in the auditorium, it's the same as music. They say it's impossible, but I think I can hear people breathing. It's like a rhythm, a part of the dance.'

Sara is mesmerising, and entertaining, to watch on stage. I decide to stick with it, at least for one more class.

Sunday morning visit the **pet market** in **Plaza de la Alfalfa** (Map pp102–3).

The **Teatro Alameda** (p126) and other venues stage regular theatre for children.

Also recommended:

Aquópolis Sevilla (Map pp94–5; ☎ 954 40 66 22; www.aquopolis.es in Spanish; Avenida del Deporte s/n; adult/child under 11yr €16/10.50; ☼ 11am-7 or 8pm approx late May–early Sep) Waterslides and wave pools, in Barrio Las Delicias on the east of the city (off the A92 towards Málaga).

Reserva Natural Castillo de las Guardas (Map pp94–5; ☎ 955 95 25 68; Finca Herrerías Bajas s/n, Carretera A476 Km 6.82; adult/child under 13yr €15/11; ☼ 10.30am-6pm Tue–Sun, last admission 4.30pm) About 1000 animals from around the planet roam in semi-liberty and can be viewed from your own vehicle or the park's road-train. There are also bird-of-prey demonstrations. It's 58km northwest of Seville in the village of El Castillo de las Guardas, off the N433 towards Aracena.

TOURS

Cruceros Turísticos Torre del Oro (Map pp102-3 ; ☎ 954 56 16 92; child over 14yr/under 14yr €12/free) One-hour sightseeing river cruises every half-hour from 11am from the riverbank by the Torre del Oro, with loudspeaker commentary in Spanish, English and German; last departure can range from 6pm in winter to 10pm in summer. From around May to September, there are also Saturday and Sunday round-trip day cruises to Sanlúcar de Barrameda, 100km downriver (adult/child under 14yr/ senior €27/15/21); it's 4½ hours each way, usually with 4½ hours in Sanlúcar in between.

Discover Sevilla (☎ 954 22 66 42; www.discover sevilla.com) Out-of-town adventure trips, including horse riding on Doñana beaches and whale- and dolphin-watching in the Strait of Gibraltar, with prices from €25 to €75.

Horse-drawn carriages These wait around near the cathedral, Plaza de España and Puerta de Jerez, charging €30 for up to four people for a one-hour trot around the Barrio de Santa Cruz and Parque de María Luisa areas. Prices are posted on boards near their stops.

Sevilla Tour (☎ 902 10 10 81; www.citysightseeing -spain.com) One-hour city tours in open-topped double-decker buses and converted trams make with earphone commentary in a choice of languages. The €11 ticket is valid for 48 hours and you can hop on or off along Paseo de Cristóbal Colón (Map pp102–3; near the Torre del Oro), Avenida de Portugal behind Plaza de España (Map pp94–5), or the Isla de la Cartuja (Map pp94–5). Buses typically leave every 30 minutes from 7am to 8pm.

Sevilla Walking Tours (☎ 902 15 82 26; www.sevilla walkingtours.com) English-language tours of the main monumental area, lasting about 1½ hours, at 9.30am

and 11.30am daily. The same people also offer tours of the cathedral and the Alcázar.

Tour por Sevilla/Guide Friday (☎ 954 56 06 93; sevirama.cjb.net) Same deal as Sevilla Tour but doesn't start until 10am.

Walking in Seville with Carmen A 90-minute combination of walking tour, street theatre and history lesson given in English by a lively and amusing young woman several days a week from March to October (except July). Look for her flyers around the Barrio de Santa Cruz telling where and when to meet. Your donation is up to you.

FESTIVALS & EVENTS
Semana Santa

If you're lucky enough to be in Seville for Semana Santa, prepare yourself for the spectacle of a lifetime. The amount of preparation, witnessed in the streets for weeks in advance, results in a phenomenally intense experience, unmatched by any other city in Spain. It gives a special insight into both Spanish Catholicism and the enormous strength of tradition in Seville.

Every day from Palm Sunday to Easter Sunday, large, richly bedecked images and life-size tableaux of scenes from the Easter story are carried from Seville's churches through the streets to the cathedral. They're accompanied by long processions, which may take more than an hour to pass, and are watched by vast crowds. These rites go back to the 14th century but they took their present form in the 17th, when many of the images – some of them supreme works of art – were created.

Programmes showing each procession's schedule and route are widely available before and during Semana Santa. *El País* newspaper publishes a daily route leaflet and *ABC* newspaper prints maps showing the churches, recommended viewing spots and other details. **Semana-Santa.org** (www .semana-santa.org) is devoted to Semana Santa in Seville. It's not too hard to work out which procession will be where and when. Pick up a procession in its own barrio or as it leaves or re-enters its church – always an emotional moment. Crowds along most of the *carrera oficial* (official route) in the city centre make it hard to get much of a view there, unless you can manage to get yourself a seat. These are sold at nearby ticket windows for anything from about €10 on Plaza Virgen de los Reyes behind the cathedral to €25 or more on Good Friday morning on

Calle Sierpes. But if you arrive early in the evening, you can usually get close enough to the cathedral to see plenty for free.

Feria de Abril

The April Fair, held in the second half of the month (sometimes edging into May), is the jolly counterpart to the sombre Semana Santa. The biggest and most colourful of all Andalucía's *ferias* is less invasive (and also less inclusive) than the Easter celebration – it takes place on El Real de la Feria, in the Los Remedios area west of the Guadalquivir. Much of the site is taken up by private areas for clubs, associations, families and groups of friends. But there are public areas, too, where much the same fun goes on. The ceremonial lighting-up of the fairgrounds on the opening Monday night is the starting gun for six nights of *sevillanos'* favourite

activities: eating, drinking, talking, dressing up and dancing till dawn.

In the afternoons, from about 1pm, those who have horses and carriages parade about the site – and the city at large – in their finery (many of the horses are dressed up too). Seville's major bullfighting season also takes place during the *feria*.

Other Festivals & Events

Other major Seville events:

Bienal de Flamenco (www.bienal-flamenco.org) Most of the big names of the flamenco world participate in this major flamenco festival, with events every night for a month in the Alcázar or the city's theatres. Held in September of even-numbered years.

Corpus Christi An important early-morning procession of the Custodia de Juan de Arfe, along with accompanying images from the cathedral. Held 7 June 2007 and 22 May 2008.

INSIDE SEMANA SANTA

Visit Seville at Easter and you'll be up all week, getting excited about men carrying crosses, following Virgin Marys and Jesuses, alongside all the *sevillanos* who are dressed up to the nines.

There are more than 50 *hermandades* or *cofradías* (brotherhoods, some of which include women). Membership of an *hermandad* is an honour keenly sought, even by some who rarely attend Mass. Each brotherhood normally carries two lavishly decorated *pasos* (platforms) and you can work out which *hermandad* is passing by the emblems and the colours of their capes. The first *paso* bears a statue of Christ, crucified, bearing the cross, or in a tableau from the Passion; the second carries an image of the Virgin. They are carried by teams of about 40 bearers called *costaleros*, who work in relays. The *pasos* are heavy – each *costalero* normally supports about 50kg – and they move with a hypnotic swaying motion to the rhythm of their brass-and-drum bands and the commands of their *capataz* or *patrón* (leader). Watching the *costaleros* stop and then start again, each time lifting the heavy *paso* in unison, and the *capataz* shouting encouraging words, is a magnificent experience. Each pair of *pasos* has up to 2500 costumed followers, known as *nazarenos*. Many *nazarenos* wear tall Ku Klux Klan–like capes, concealing the identity of the person wearing them, so that no one knows who they are, apart from God. The most contrite go barefoot and carry crosses.

Each day from Palm Sunday to Good Friday seven or eight *hermandades* leave their churches around the city in the afternoon or early evening. The *carrera oficial* (official route) goes along Calle Sierpes, through Plaza San Francisco and along Avenida de la Constitución to the cathedral.

The climax of the week is the *madrugá* (night/dawn) of Good Friday, when the most respected and popular *hermandades* file through the city, starting with the oldest, El Silencio, which goes in complete silence. Next comes **Jesús del Gran Poder** (p110), followed by **La Macarena** (p110). Then come El Calvario from the Iglesia de la Magdalena, Esperanza de Triana, and lastly, at dawn, Los Gitanos, the *gitano* (Roma) brotherhood. On the Saturday evening just four *hermandades* make their way to the cathedral, and finally, on Easter Sunday morning, the Hermandad de la Resurrección.

City-centre brotherhoods, such as El Silencio, are traditionally linked with the bourgeoisie. They are austere and wear black tunics, usually without capes. *Hermandades* from the working-class districts outside the centre (such as La Macarena) have bands and more brightly decorated *pasos*. Their *nazarenos* wear coloured, caped tunics, often of satin, velvet or wool. They also have to come from further away, and some are on the streets for more than 12 hours.

SLEEPING

The attractive Barrio de Santa Cruz, which is close to the cathedral, Alcázar and Prado de San Sebastián bus station, has many places to stay in all price brackets. So do El Arenal (west of Santa Cruz towards the river, near Plaza de Armas bus station) and El Centro (the true city centre north of Santa Cruz).

Room rates in this section are for each establishment's high season – typically (but not strictly) from about March to June and again in September and October – and most rates don't include breakfast. Prices go down by at least €10 per room in low season. *Hostales* (budget hotels) may keep the same prices almost year-round. On the other hand, just about every room in Seville costs extra during Semana Santa and the Feria de Abril. The typical increase is between 30% and 60% over normal high-season rates, but a few places even double their prices. Some hotels extend this *temporada extra* (extra-high season) for a whole month from the start of Semana Santa to the end of the *feria*. It's vital to book ahead for rooms in Seville at this time, if you can afford them. Even at normal times, it's always worth ringing ahead. Note that some places ask for credit-card details and charge for the first night in advance.

Barrio de Santa Cruz
BUDGET
Pensión Cruces (Map pp102-3; ☎ 954 22 60 41; Plaza de las Cruces 10; s/d/t €35/50/60; d with shared bathroom €40) This lovely old patio house has sparsely decorated rooms on three floors, painted in turquoise blues and whites; beds are on the uncomfortable side. The rooms look a little worn, despite having been refurbished in 2005.

Huéspedes Dulces Sueños (Map pp102-3; ☎ 954 41 93 93; Calle Santa María La Blanca 21; s/d €40/50, with shared bathroom €20/40; ✱) 'Sweet Dreams' is a friendly little *hostal* with seven spotless rooms. Those overlooking the street are good and bright. Doubles have air-con, singles don't.

Pensión San Pancracio (Map pp102-3; ☎ /fax 954 41 31 04; Plaza de las Cruces 9; s/d €45, s/d with shared bathroom €20/30) The charming furnishings are almost as old as the rambling family house, but it's all sweet and clean. There's a curfew

at 1.30am, when the house closes down for the night (not during Semana Santa and Feria de Abril).

MIDRANGE
Hostal Córdoba (Map pp102-3; ☎ 954 22 74 98; Calle Farnesio 12; s/d €50/70, with shared bathroom €40/60; ✱) Twelve bright, spotless rooms surround a plant-draped three-storey atrium. The Córdoba is run by a friendly older couple and situated on a quiet pedestrian street.

Hostal Goya (Map pp102-3; ☎ 954 21 11 70; hgoya@hostalgoya.e.telefonica.net; Calle Mateos Gago 31; s/d €50/80; ✱) Since the Goya had a facelift in 2005, the gleaming *hostal*'s been more popular than ever. The rooms are elegant and simple, with shining en-suite bathrooms. There's also a lift. Book ahead.

Un Patio en Santa Cruz (Map pp102-3; ☎ 954 53 94 13; www.patiosantacruz.com; Calle Doncellas 15; s/d €58/68; ✱ 💻) An understated hotel defying the elaborate concept of traditional Andalucian décor. The rooms are kept stylish and simple, and the roof terrace has views of the Giralda.

Hotel Alcántara (Map pp102-3; ☎ 954 50 05 95; www.hotelalcantara.net; Calle Ximénez de Enciso 28; s/d €66/84; lift; ✱ ♿) Tucked in next to Casa de la Memoria de Al-Andalus, the Alcántara has a wonderful, bright look. The rooms are in gentle vanilla whites with an autumn-leaves print on the curtains and plenty of light. The bathrooms all have bathtubs and luxurious marble sinks.

Hotel Puerta de Sevilla (Map pp102-3; ☎ 954 98 72 70; www.hotelpuertadesevilla.com; Calle Santa María la Blanca 36; s/d €65/85; 🅿 ✱ 💻) A small shiny hotel in a great location, the Puerta de Sevilla is all flower-pattern textiles, wrought-iron beds and pastel wallpaper. Rooms are comfortable with plasma-screen TVs and writing tables, and there's a lift.

Hostería del Laurel (Map pp102-3; ☎ 954 22 02 95; www.hosteriadellaurel.com in Spanish; Plaza de los Venerables 5; s/d incl breakfast €72/104; ✱) Legend has it that this establishment inspired playwright José Zorrilla (who stayed here in 1844) to write *Don Juan Tenorio*, one of the most popular versions of the Don Juan story. So rather fittingly, each room here is named after a character in the play. The simple, spacious and bright rooms have cool marble floors and good-sized bathrooms. Renovations are planned for some of the rooms.

SEVILLA PROVINCE

THE AUTHOR'S CHOICE

Hotel Amadeus (☎ 954 50 14 43; www.hotel amadeussevilla.com; Calle Farnesio 6; s/d €70/85; P ✖ 🖳) Here is a hotel for music lovers to come and indulge their passion. An entrepreneurial musician family converted their 18th-century mansion into this unique hotel and named each of the 14 elegant, fabulously designed rooms after a different composer. If you want to practise piano or violin, there are instruments on the premises and a couple of soundproof practise rooms. A glass elevator lifts you to your floor or onto the roof terrace, where you can have your breakfast with views of the Giralda. Music for everyone's ears, in exquisitely stylish surroundings.

TOP END

Las Casas de la Judería (Map p102-3; ☎ 954 41 51 50; www.casasypalacios.com; Callejón de Dos Hermanas 7; s/d from €108/167; P ✖) Once an entire block in the *judería*, this is now a charming hotel comprising a series of restored houses and mansions around lovely patios and fountains. Most of the 116 comfortable, traditional-style rooms and suites sport four-poster beds, bath and shower, writing table, cable TV, phone and safe, and an amazing range of art on the walls.

Hotel Alfonso XIII (Map pp102-3; ☎ 954 91 70 00; www.westin.com/hotelalfonso; Calle San Fernando 2; s/d €371/487; P ✖ 🖳 🖳 🛋) The pride and joy of old Seville, with mahogany, marble and tiles, just the sound of 'Alfonso XIII' sends trembles of pleasure down a *sevillano*'s spine. Built to house heads of state visiting the Exposición Iberoamericana of 1929, it has 147 ultra-elegant rooms and suites with every amenity you could imagine, an outdoor pool, a fine restaurant and a sophisticated bar with terrace under lush tropical foliage.

El Arenal
BUDGET

Hostal Residencia Naranjo (Map pp102-3; ☎ 954 22 58 40; fax 954 21 69 43; Calle San Roque 11; s/d €35/50; ✖) Colourful bedspreads and pine furniture add a touch of warmth to this *hostal*, almost opposite Hotel Zaida. The 27 rooms are all equipped with TV and phone.

Hotel Zaida (Map pp102-3; ☎ 954 21 11 38; www .hotelzaida.com; Calle San Roque 26; s/d €37/55; ✖)

A gorgeous Mudejar-style patio is central to this 18th-century town house and is its loveliest feature. The 27 rooms here are plain and decent, with phones and reading lamps. There's a lift to the upper floor, and the street is quiet, but ground-floor rooms open straight onto the foyer.

Hotel Madrid (Map pp102-3; ☎ 954 21 43 07; www .hotelmadridsevilla.com; Calle San Pedro Mártir 22; s/d €40/55; P ✖) At the end of a quiet street, this is a friendly, small, family-run hotel. The 21 pretty rooms have firm beds, nice blue-tiled bathrooms, and little balconies overlooking orange-tree-lined streets.

Hostal Roma (Map pp102-3; ☎ 954 50 13 00; www .hostales-sp.com; Calle Gravina 34; s/d €48/56; P ✖) This attractive *hostal* has 17 rooms and a lift linking its three floors. Rooms all have phone, writing table, prints on the walls and double glazing. The owners have three other *hostales* close by.

Also recommended:

Hostal Romero (Map pp102-3; ☎ 954 21 13 53; Calle Gravina 21; d €40, s/d with shared bathroom €20/30) A friendly low-budget choice; the attic rooms with shared bathrooms are like something out of *La Bohème*.

MIDRANGE

Hotel Simón (Map pp102-3; ☎ 954 22 66 60; www .hotelsimonsevilla.com; Calle García de Vinuesa 19; s €45-60, d €70-95; ✖) The charming Hotel Simón is a small hotel in a fine 18th-century house. It's extremely popular so book well ahead. It's built around a lovely patio with a fountain, and antiques and beautiful Sevillan tilework adorn the passages, sitting areas and broad staircase, as well as some of the 29 good-sized, spotless and comfortable rooms. All have phone and desk.

Hotel Maestranza (Map pp102-3; ☎ 954 56 10 70; www.hotelmaestranza.es; Calle Gamazo 12; s/d €49/87; ✖ 🖳) Dedicated to the Maestranza bullring, and with a large photograph in the reception to prove it. This small and friendly hotel is on a quietish street and has just 18 spotless but plain rooms, all equipped with phone, safe and little chandeliers. The reception has glitzy gilded armchairs and sofas. The singles are small, but have queen-size beds.

Hotel Puerta de Triana (Map pp102-3; ☎ 954 21 54 04; www.hotelpuertadetriana.com; Calle Reyes Católicos 5; s/d €70/96; ✖) The Puerta de Triana is steps away from Triana bridge, and also conveniently close to El Centro and El

Arenal neighbourhoods. The handsome 65-room hotel has traditional fittings and all the modern comforts. The rooms are cosy and medium-sized, with marble floors, desk and telephone, and windows look on to the street or interior patios. Breakfast is included in the price.

Also recommended:

Hotel Europa (Map pp102-3; ☎ 954 21 43 05; www .hoteleuropasevilla.com; Calle Jimios 5; s/d €77/95; (P)(※)) Classic furniture and colonial style; comfortable, marble-floored rooms in a fine 18th-century house.

TOP END

Hotel Vincci La Rábida (Map pp102-3; ☎ 954 50 12 80; www.vinccihoteles.com; Calle Castelar 24; s/d €154/182; (P)(※)(🖳)) A beautiful four-storey, columned atrium-lounge greets you in this converted 18th-century palace, now a classy four-star hotel. There are 81 extremely comfortable rooms, with terracotta and marble floors and attractive prints. The hotel boasts a seasonal rooftop bar-café with magnificent views of the cathedral. Service is professional, friendly and polished.

El Centro

BUDGET

Oasis Backpackers Hostel (Map pp102-3; ☎ 954 29 37 77; www.oasissevilla.com; Calle Don Alonso el Sabio 1A; dm €18 per person, d incl breakfast €40; (※)(🖳)) The sister hostel of the massively popular Oasis in Granada, this stylish, buzzing backpackers is one of a kind in Seville. The neat lounge has 24-hour free internet access, and breakfast is eaten in the top-floor kitchen or the glass-floored roof terrace. Each dorm bed has a personal safe, the atmosphere is good

and the hosts keep you entertained with tapas tours and Spanish classes.

Casa Sol y Luna (Map pp102-3; ☎ 954 21 06 82; www.casasolyluna1.com; Calle Pérez Galdós 1A; d €45, s/d/tr with shared bathroom €22/38/60) This is a first-rate *hostal* set in a large, elegantly floor-creaking and beautifully decorated old town house, with antiques in each room, and white embroidered linen that makes you feel as if you're staying at your grandma's house. The shared bathrooms (none shared by more than two rooms) are the biggest and most beautiful you'll find in any *hostal* in Andalucía. No credit cards are accepted, and pay special attention to the 24-hour booking-confirmation policy.

MIDRANGE

Hotel San Francisco (Map pp102-3; ☎/fax 954 50 15 41; Calle Álvarez Quintero 38; s/d €55/68; (※)) On a pedestrian street linking El Centro with the Barrio de Santa Cruz, the friendly, good-value Hotel San Francisco is a recently converted 18th-century family home. Nearly all the 16 good-sized rooms look on to the street or an interior patio; all have marble floors, TV and heating.

TOP END

Las Casas del Rey de Baeza (Map pp102-3; ☎ 954 56 14 96; www.hospes.es; Plaza Jesús de la Redención 2; s/d €163/189; (P)(※)(🖳)(📶)) This tranquil, expertly run and marvellously designed hotel occupies former communal-housing patios dating from the 18th century, with traditional Andalucian exterior blinds made of esparto grass. The 41 large rooms, in tasteful blue, white, orange and red hues, boast

---

TOURIST APARTMENTS IN SEVILLE

Four people can rent a clean, comfortable, tasteful, well-located and well-equipped apartment in Seville for well under €100 a night. Two people normally pay between €30 and €70. The accommodation will usually compare well with what you get for the same money in a hotel or *hostal* (a simple guesthouse or small place offering hotel-like accommodation).

There are several websites that provide details of a range of apartments in Seville: they don't usually offer immediate online booking, but provide the chance to request availability and await email confirmation. Try the following:

Apartamentos Embrujo de Sevilla (☎ 625 060 937; www.embrujodesevilla.com)

Sevilla5.com (☎ 637 011 091; www.sevilla5.com)

Sol (www.sol.com)

There's further information available at **Explore Seville** (www.exploreseville.com).

attractive modern art, CD player, DVD and wi-fi. The public areas include a super-comfortable lounge and reading room and a gorgeous pool.

Hotel Casa Imperial (Map pp102-3; ☎ 954 50 03 00; www.casaimperial.com; Calle Imperial 29; s/d €235/257; P ✗) One of Seville's most luxurious and atmospheric hotels, the Casa Imperial is a 16th-century palace with three lovely plant-filled patios – one with a fountain and sometimes a guitarist. Decoration is sumptuous; the 24 luxurious suites and junior suites in various bold colours all have a kitchenette and sitting area, though not all are as big as you might hope. The hotel has a good restaurant and a roof terrace with gorgeous views.

Alameda de Hércules
BUDGET
Hotel Sevilla (Map pp102-3; ☎ 954 38 41 61; www.hotel-sevilla.com; Calle Daoíz 5; s/d €35/55; ✗) The recently modernised Hotel Sevilla, on a quiet little plaza, is good value. The 30 medium-sized rooms in pink-and-green colour schemes have good bathrooms, large mirrors, desk, reading lamps and phone. There's a pretty little greenery-filled patio off the broad foyer.

MIDRANGE
Hotel Corregidor (Map pp94-5; ☎ 954 38 51 11, fax 954 38 42 38; Calle Morgado 17; s/d €78/97; P ✗) On a quiet little street up towards the Alameda de Hércules, the 77-room Corregidor is com-

---

THE AUTHOR'S CHOICE

Hacienda Benazuza (☎ 955 70 33 44; www.elbullihotel.com; Sanlúcar la Mayor; r from €350; tasting menu from €110; ✗ 🖵 🛎) This hacienda 22km west of Seville is luxury beyond belief. Opened by Ferrán Adrià, Spain's, and the world's, most famous and inventive chef, this place not only has massive Andalucian gardens, rooms that feel like shrines to luxury, and long, tranquil pools, but also 3 restaurants, one of which, La Alquería, is a 2 Michelin-star sister to Adriàs elBulli (proclaimed the best restaurant in the world). So surrender to Adriàs experimental cuisine in the most luxurious hotel in Andalucía, and don't forget to write!

---

fortable. It has pleasant rooms with phone, TV and a spot of art on the walls. Singles are a decent size. Downstairs are spacious sitting areas and a little open-air patio.

Patio de la Cartuja (Map pp94-5; ☎ 954 90 02 00; www.patiosdesevilla.com; Calle Lumbreras 8-10; s/d €69/98; P ✗) Excellent-value accommodation for those wanting to self-cater, this is an apart-ment hotel in a former *corral* – a three-storey patio community that was once the typical form of Sevillan lower-middle-class hous-ing. Located just off the northern end of Alameda de Hércules, each of the 30 cosy apartments has a double bedroom, kitchen and sitting room with double sofa bed.

Patio de la Alameda (Map pp94-5; ☎ 954 90 49 99; www.patiodelaalameda.com; Alameda de Hércules 56; s/d €69/90; P ✗) Another wonderful former *corral*, recently renovated and under new ownership. The hotel is right on the Alameda nightlife beat, but manages to keep a quiet atmosphere even at the most raucous of times. The large apartments have blush walls and a modern design, kitchens and sitting rooms, and there's plenty of space for a party of four to sleep comfortably.

TOP END
Hotel San Gil (Map pp94-5; ☎ 954 90 68 11; www.fp-hoteles.com; Calle Parras 28; s/d €126/158; P ✗ 🛎) Just around the corner from the Basílica de la Macarena, San Gil is one of the city's hidden gems. The renovated early-20th-century building focuses on a pretty garden-courtyard and combines acclaimed mod-ern design with beautiful antique tiling and other traditional touches. The 61 cosy, tasteful rooms and suites feature marble-tiled bathrooms; the public areas include a restaurant, bar and pool.

EATING
Seville's hundreds of tapas bars are the city's culinary pride, and Spanish and Andalucian cuisine doesn't come more honest than this, with gazpacho, simple grilled sardines, or chickpeas bathing in a tomato and spinach sauce. *Tapear* (feeding yourself on tapas) has been described as the most civilised way to eat, and you'll probably end up a tapas addict by the end of your trip. The art of eating tapas is to be with a few friends, have a good appetite, not mind standing up, and

liberally explore the menu. For decoding your tapas menu, see p86.

Classier modern eateries usually give an *alta cocina* (haute cuisine) edge to their Spanish basics, with impeccable, elegant presentation and complex taste structures, and prices to match.

Barrio de Santa Cruz & Around

CAFÉS

Cervecería Giralda (Map pp102-3; ☎ 954 22 74 35; Calle Mateos Gago 1; breakfast €3-5) Conquer the effects of the night before with one of the recommended breakfasts here. Munch on your *tostada* (toasted bread; €1.50 to €4.50) and imagine the place in its former guise – an Arabic bathhouse. It's also a tapas bar (see below).

Cafe Alianza (Map pp102-3; Plaza de la Alianza; tapas €2-2.50) Old-fashioned street lights, a trickling fountain and colourful wall plants make this small plaza a charming place to relax with a coffee, and Cafe Alianza is positioned perfectly for just that. Its tapas nibbles are also good.

TAPAS

For views and mouthfuls at the same time, go to Calle Mateos Gago – most bars here have good-quality food and wine.

Bodega Santa Cruz (Map pp102-3; ☎ 954 21 32 46; Calle Mateos Gago; tapas €1.50-2) A place that has kept its delicious soul despite being within spitting distance from the Giralda's tourist hordes. There's a wonderful range of tapas to be enjoyed here, especially good when paired up with a glass of cool manzanilla, while you stand outside with the chatty crowd.

Álvaro Peregil (Map pp102-3; 20 Calle Mateos Gago; tapas €1.50-2) Just up the road from Bodega Santa Cruz, this tiny bar has not much more in terms of decoration than garlic bunches hanging overhead and a couple of tall tables outside to rest your tapas on. But the food is so good you'll need nothing more. The *salmorejo* (a thicker version of gazpacho) is particularly good and is served with strips of *jamón* sprinkled over the top; try the orange wine, made from Seville's famous (and ubiquitous) oranges.

Cervecería Giralda (Map pp102-3; ☎ 954 22 74 35; Calle Mateos Gago 1; tapas €1.50-2.50) Exotic variations are merged with traditional dishes, such as *pechuga bechamel* (chicken breast in bechamel sauce), at this central tapas bar.

Café-Bar Campanario (Map pp102-3; ☎ 954 56 41 89; Calle Mateos Gago 8; tapas €2-2.50) A hotchpotch of tapas favourites can be found here, including the cornerstone of Spanish cuisine, the *tortilla de patata* (Spanish omelette), aubergines with cheese and divine croquettes with ham and bechamel. Unlike most of the old bars it has an airy feel.

Café Bar Las Teresas (Map pp102-3; ☎ 954 21 30 69; Calle Santa Teresa 2; tapas €2-4, media-raciones €6-8) This atmospheric bar has *jamones* dangling from the ceiling in tidy rows, lovely Andalucian tiles lining the walls, and a red wooden bar propping up the chatting crowd. A great place to stop and have some good and traditional tapas.

RESTAURANTS

Despite the tourists tirelessly snapping the Giralda, there are authentic, good-quality restaurants in Barrio de Santa Cruz. The interlacing narrow streets and squares just east of the Alcázar are where most restaurants are situated and ordinary Calle Santa María La Blanca has a throng of eateries, whose muddle of outdoor seating is invariably crammed with diners.

Restaurante San Marco (Map pp102-3; ☎ 954 21 43 90; Calle Mesón del Moro 6; mains €6-9; ✟ closed Mon) Once a place with a cult following for its pasta and pizza, nowadays San Marco's produces average Italian food. The setting of this particular branch is wonderful though, in a large refurbished Arabic bath. Try a plate of *penne all'Arrabbiata* and a glass of frosty white wine.

Carmela (Map pp102-3; Calle Santa María La Blanca 6; menú €7) The rustic-looking waiting staff, dressed in headscarves and aprons, give this establishment a rather earthy feel. It cooks up a wholesome quiche Lorraine (€6).

Bar Casa Fernando (Map pp102-3; Calle Santa María La Blanca; menú €7) This place bustles with punters, most of whom are trying out the good-value menu of the day. There is a variety of options but a small dish of paella, followed by fried fish and a dreamy caramel flan will set you up nicely.

Altamira Bar-Café (Map pp102-3; ☎ 954 42 50 30; Calle Santa María La Blanca 4; raciones €7-8) With a pleasant terrace perfect for some al fresco dining or lunching and busy, efficient waiters darting to and fro, Altamira is a decent choice for seafood *raciones* (meal-sized portions).

Restaurante Las Lapas (Map pp102-3; ☎ 954 21 11 04; Calle San Gregorio 6; menú €9; closed Sun) Lying in the path of incessant horse-drawn traffic and, it seems, the whole of Seville's student population, you might find this eatery rather noisy outside and in. But sit back and enjoy the hubbub with a chorizo and potato mixed dish (€7.50).

Restaurant La Cueva (Map pp102-3; ☎ 954 21 31 43; Calle Rodrigo Caro 18; mains €11-24) As you stroll through Plaza Doña Elvira, inhale the whiff of orange blossom and sizzling fish, which wafts from this popular seafood eatery. It cooks up a storming fish casserole (€24 for two people), and a hearty *caldereta* (lamb stew; €11) if something meatier takes your fancy.

Corral del Agua (Map pp102-3; ☎ 954 22 07 14; Callejón del Agua 6; mains €12-18, menú €23; noon-4pm & 8pm-midnight Mon-Sat) If you're hankering after inventive food on a hot day, then book a table at Corral del Agua. Its leafy courtyard makes a pleasant spot to sample traditional stews and Arabic-inspired desserts (such as orange, carrot and cinnamon).

Restaurante La Albahaca (Map pp102-3; ☎ 954 22 07 14; Plaza de Santa Cruz 12; mains €18-22, menú €27) Gastronomic inventions are the mainstay of this swish restaurant. Try the pork trotter with mushroom, young garlic and pea mousse (really, a posh version of mushy peas).

Restaurante Modesto (Map pp102-3; ☎ 954 41 68 11; www.grupomodesto.com; Calle Cano y Cueto 5; mains €7.50-43) Modesto presents a full range of fish dishes, such as Sevillan-style cod (€12.60), served to a classy lot on a persistently busy terrace. Its sister restaurant, **Restaurante La Judería** (Map pp102-3; ☎ 954 41 20 52; Calle Cano y Cueto 13A; menú around €28) gives fans a change of scenery, though the dishes are basically the same.

The dizzily bright lights of the restaurants north of the cathedral function to attract and trap buzzing sightseers, so be prepared. One good option is **Casa Robles** (Map pp102-3; ☎ 954 21 31 50; Calle Álvarez Quintero 58; mains around €20), an upmarket choice that prides itself on its natural food and elegantly styled restaurant. Its dishes, which range from braised bulls' tails to seasonal salads, are beautifully presented.

El Arenal
TAPAS

Bar Pepe-Hillo (Map pp102-3; ☎ 954 21 53 90; Calle Adriano 24; tapas €1.50-2) For no-nonsense, quality tapas head for easy-going Bar Pepe-Hillo.

Mesón de la Infanta (Map pp102-3; Calle Dos de Mayo 26; tapas €2-3) If you like your tapas with a touch of class and a glass of cool sherry, indulge in innovative, well-presented dishes at this Sevillan favourite.

La Tienda de Eva (Map pp102-3; Calle Arfe; tapas around €2) Decked out like a village shop, this place offers an escape from the norm. Settle down with a beer and a few slices of chorizo (€2.50) in front of the well-presented tinned goods and gourmet *jamón*.

Bar Horacio (Map pp102-3; Calle Antonia Díaz; tapas €2, mains €10-14) Friendly, bow-tied waiters serve up a great selection of tapas at this bar, which heaves with chattering locals.

Mesón Cinco Jotas (Map pp102-3; ☎ 954 21 05 21; Calle Castelar 1; tapas €3, media-raciones €7) In the world of *jamón*-making, if you are awarded 'Cinco Jotas' (Five Js) for your *jamón*, it's like you got an Oscar. The owner of this place, Sánchez Romero Carvajal, is the biggest producer of Jabugo ham, and has a great selection on offer. It's best to try a range of different things here, so you can compare and develop your taste for *jamón* to perfection, but know that the prices are high.

RESTAURANTS

Mesón Serranito (Map pp102-3; ☎ 954 21 12 43; Calle Antonia Díaz 11; serranito €3) Specialising in the *serranito*, a Spanish gastronomic institution consisting of a slice of toasted bread heaped with a pork fillet, roasted pepper, a nice bit of *jamón* and garlic, this place is tops for trying this simple but scrumptious bite. The décor is all stuffed bulls' heads and there are photos of Hemingway enjoying a bullfight.

Bar Gloria Bendita (Map pp102-3; Calle de Adriano 24; platos combinados around €8) This place smells of strong coffee and strong cheese, and will happily ply you with both. Share the intimate bar with a few locals or escape with your *bocadillo* (sandwich; €3.50) to the tables outside.

Enrique Becerra (Map pp102-3; ☎ 954 21 30 49; Calle Gamazo 2; mains €15-21; closed Sun) Adding a smart touch to El Arenal, Enrique Becerra cooks up hearty Andalucian dishes to rave about. The lamb drenched in honey sauce and stuffed with spinach and pine nuts (€18) is just one of many delectable offerings.

El Centro
SELF-CATERING

Mercado del Arenal (Map pp102-3; Calle Pastor y Landero) and the **Mercado de la Encarnación** (Map pp102-3; Plaza de la Encarnación) are central Seville's two food markets. The Encarnación, which mainly sells fruit, veg and fish, has been in its current 'temporary' quarters, awaiting construction of a new permanent building, since 1973!

The department store **El Corte Inglés** (Map pp102-3; Plaza del Duque de la Victoria) has a well-stocked supermarket in the basement.

CAFÉS

Confitería La Campana (Map pp102-3; cnr Calles Sierpes & Martín Villa) La Campana has been heaving with sugar addicts since 1885, and workers and the elite alike storm Seville's most popular bakery for a *yema* (a soft, crumbly biscuit cake wrapped like a toffee), a delicious *nata* (custard cake) that quivers under the glass, or a swollen muffin that's great for dipping into a *café con leche* (coffee with milk; €1.50 or €1 standing inside). The service can be on the slow side at the outside seating area.

Bar Laredo (Map pp102-3; cnr Calle Sierpes & Plaza de San Francisco) Watch them slap together a variety of *bocadillos* (€3) for rapid consumption at this popular breakfast stop.

Alfalfa 10 (Map pp102-03; ☎ 954 21 38 41; Plaza de la Alfalfa 10) The health conscious might be tempted by the multivitamin breakfast (€5) or the natural yogurt and runny honey (€1.50) here. Both slip down a treat.

Horno de San Buenaventura (Map pp102-3; Plaza de la Alfalfa 10) The Buenaventura chain is much loved in this city, and the cakes are pretty good. Their offerings are treated like precious jewels and showcased in particularly shiny glass cabinets. You can also have breakfast: a coffee and *jamón serrano* (mountain-cured ham) *tostada* costs €3. There's another branch on the corner of Calles Pagés del Corro and Covadonga.

Café Bar Duque (Map pp102-3; Plaza del Duque de la Victoria; €2) This café is perfect for a breakfast or afternoon delight of *churros con chocolate* (see p84).

TAPAS

Plaza de la Alfalfa is the hub of the tapas scene, with excellent bars.

Hop from sea-themed **La Trastienda** (Map pp102-3; Calle Alfalfa; tapas €1.50-3), off the eastern end of the plaza, to **La Bodega** (Calle Alfalfa; tapas €1.50-2), where you can mix head-spinning quantities of *jamón* and sherry.

El Patio San Eloy (Map pp102-3; Calle San Eloy 9; tapas €1.50-2) *Bocadillo* is the name of the game here, and punters sit on the tiled benches that descend in levels below each other, so you get the full view of the goings-on in the bar, while you balance your plate on your knees. Try the *pringá*, a sandwich made with crushed beans and their yummy juice.

La Giganta (Map pp102-3; ☎ 954 21 09 75; Calle Alhóndiga 6; tapas €2) On the same street as El Rinconcillo (see p122), and rivalling its talent for tapas, despite being a lot newer. While you're here, marvel at the weeds sprouting from the roof of the old church of Santa Catalina nearby.

Bodega Extremeña (Map pp102-3; ☎ 954 41 70 60; Calle San Esteban 17; tapas €1.50-2) Decorated with rustic bits and bobs, Bodega Extremeña flexes its muscles in the meat department and offers mouthwatering *solomillo ibérico* (Iberian pork sirloin).

Robles Placentines (Map pp102-3; ☎ 954 21 31 62; Calle Placentines 2; tapas around €2) Modelled on a Jerez wine cellar, this popular haunt serves up tempting dishes such as white asparagus from the Sierra de Córdoba.

Taberna los Terceros (Map pp102-3; Calle del Sol; tapas €2.50-3) Los Terceros pulls an energetic, young crowd and serves up fine tapas.

Bar Levíes (Map pp102-3; ☎ 954 215 308; Calle San José 15; tapas €1.50-4) The ultimate student tapas bar, Levíes is constantly crowded

---

THE AUTHOR'S CHOICE

Los Coloniales (Map pp102-3; cnr Calle Dormitorio & Plaza Cristo de Burgos; tapas €1.50-3.50) The demand at Los Coloniales is so great that sitting down at one of the terrace tables demands plenty of waiting time. If you're ready to wait, get your name chalked onto the board. If not, get your tapas at the bar or sit down in the back room *comedor* (dining room). But make sure you eat here at least once: the superb tapas are huge (try the *churrasco*) and as cheap as they get.

with youngsters who love the huge tapas and small prices, and who come here when everything else is closed, either during siesta, or for late-night munchies. Indeed, a tapa of *solomillo al whiskey* is as big as a *ración* in some places and a tapa per person is more than enough. Oh, and beer is served in big glasses.

Bar Alfalfa (Map pp102-3; cnr Calles Alfalfa & Candilejo; tapas €2-3) This is one of the most charming tapas bars in town, and it serves excellent *jamón*, in generous cuttings. The bar is so small that 10 is a crowd, but if you get to sit down or perch by a barrel-table, you can enjoy the intimate décor of dark, forest greens and tiled walls, and sip a glass of *fino*.

El Rinconcillo (Map pp102-3; ☎ 954 22 31 83; Calle Gerona 40; tapas €1.50-4) Seville's oldest bar traces its tapas roots back to the dark 1670s, and its popularity just keeps on growing. Decent, simple tapas like chickpeas with spinach or garlic chicken are served until midnight. One of the favourites at El Rinconcillo is the *revueltos* (scrambled eggs) with *jamón* (€4).

RESTAURANTS

Los Alcazares (Map pp102-3; Plaza de la Encarnación; tapas €2-3, raciones from €5) A perfect, old-world haunt for those who need to fill a gap after visiting the nearby market.

Habanita (Map pp102-3; ☎ 606-716456; Calle Golfo 3; raciones €6-9, media-ración €4, tapas from €1.50; 12.30-4.30pm & 8pm-12.30am Mon-Sat, 12.30-4.30pm Sun) A great restaurant with tasty Cuban food. Try the plantain balls in tomato sauce, or tuck into the *plato variado* with its combination of dishes such as the white and black bean dish, crunchy plantain fritters, *ropa vieja* (literally 'old clothes', a pork dish), and tender yucca with garlic.

Horno del Duque (Map pp102-3; ☎ 954 21 77 33; Plaza del Duque de la Victoria; mains around €7-11) The invariably busy Horno del Duque offers standard helpings of paella Valenciana with chicken (€10.50) to bag-laden shoppers.

Alameda de Hércules

TAPAS

Bar-Restaurante Las Columnas (Map pp94-5; Alameda de Hércules; tapas €1.50-2) Beefy men and tasty tapas are brought together at this low-key restaurant, which serves down-to-earth fare such as *albóndigas* (meatballs).

La Ilustre Víctima (Map pp94-5; Calle Doctor Letamendi 35; tapas €2.50, raciones €7) This offbeat place is a popular Alameda hang-out, with some curious wall-paintings. The celebrated vegetarian tapas, including *calabacines al roque* (courgettes with Roquefort cheese; €2.50), are as tasty as ever, followed by a mint tea (€1.50).

RESTAURANTS

La Piola (Map pp94-5; cnr Alameda de Hércules & Calle Relator; mains around €4-7) A pair of trendy media spectacles would blend in splendidly at this comfortably hip Alameda joint. The mixed salad (€4) is best mixed with a freshly squeezed orange juice, for a pick-me-up.

Badaluque (Map pp94-5; cnr Calles Calatrava & Pacheco y Núñez de Prado; breakfast €2-4, pizzas €7-9.50) Argentine-owned and always busy, the Badaluque has a good-value breakfast, or join the evening crowds who come for the pizzas. Coffee with a ham-and-cheese *tostada* costs €2.50.

South of the Centre

Café-Bar Puerta de Jerez (Map pp102-3; Puerta de Jerez; tapas around €1.80) Cars and horses whizz around the fountain at Puerta de Jerez at great speed and it's fun to watch the spectacle at this café-bar; an accompanying coffee costs €1.50.

Restaurant San Fernando (Map pp102-3; ☎ 954 91 70 00; Calle San Fernando 2; mains €14-27; 7-11am, 1-4pm & 8.30-11.30pm) The posh Sevillan crowd comes to eat at Hotel Alfonso XIII's restaurant, so slick your hair back and don your best gown if you want to fit in. Haute cuisine is at its hautest here, and dishes like guinea fowl with grated potatoes and sautéed chanterelle mushrooms (€20) are served with a tidy, self-conscious presentation. Most importantly, they taste good.

Restaurante Egaña Oriza (Map pp102-3; ☎ 954 22 72 11; Calle San Fernando 41; mains €15-40; closed Sat lunch & Sun) Still one of the best restaurants in Seville, Egaña Oriza cooks up a superb mix of Andalucian-Basque cuisine, and big meaty dishes such as steak tartar (€24). While it's an undeniably good restaurant, it's a shame about the fume-choked location.

La Raza (Map pp94-5; ☎ 954 23 20 24, 954 23 38 30; Avenida de Isabel la Católica 2; mains €10-17) Great for taking a break when you're exploring the area around Plaza de España. The tables are shaded by the large trees in cool Parque de

María Luisa, and this is a perfect place for having your morning coffee.

Triana

TAPAS

Sol y Sombra (Map pp94-5; Calle Castilla 151; tapas €2; media-raciones €5) The entire ceiling is hung with *jamones* and every inch of wall space is filled with old posters advertising bullfights, some originals dating back as far as 1933. The barmen wear maroon sweaters and brooding smiles while they serve excellent tapas of green beans with tomatoes, *gambas al ajillo* (prawns with garlic), and other traditional dishes.

Mariscos Emilio (Map pp94-5; ☎ 954 33 25 42; Calle San Jacinto 39; www.mariscos-emilio.com in Spanish; tapas around €2) This seafood supremo steams, grills and fries an assortment of aquatic creatures for your enjoyment. A few other branches dot the city.

RESTAURANTS

Ristorante Cosa Nostra (Map pp102-3; ☎ 954 27 07 52; Calle del Betis 52; pizzas €5.50-7.50; ☽ Tue-Sun) Although there are a few pizzerias and pasta parlours on Calle del Betis, Cosa Nostra has an intimate feel that the others lack. The tortellini with gorgonzola (€6.50) is tasty.

Kiosco de las Flores (Map pp102-3; ☎ 954 27 45 76; Calle del Betis; media-raciones around €5, raciones around €9, mains €15-40; ☽ Tue-Sun afternoon) Still revelling in the transformation from 70-year-old shack to a glam conservatory (just take a look at the photos on display), this eatery doles out great *pescadíto frito* (fried fish).

Casa Cuesta (Map pp94-5; ☎ 954 33 33 37; Calle de Castilla 3-5; mains around €9-10) Something about the carefully buffed wooden bar and gleaming beer pumps gives a sense that the owners are proud of Casa Cuesta. Indeed they should be; it's a real find for food and wine lovers alike.

La Triana (Map pp94-5; ☎ 954 33 38 19; Calle de Castilla 36; menú €10, mains €10-16) The hosts at La Triana are suave and courteous, and while the décor may be minimalist the dishes are not. Menu-of-the-day options include *pisto* (ratatouille) and a meaty main dish. The restaurant also backs out onto a quieter stretch of the river.

Río Grande (Map pp102-3; ☎ 954 27 39 56, 954 27 83 71; Calle del Betis; seafood mains €15-29) This restaurant wins the prize for most desirable location; many diners spend their mealtime gazing at the Torre del Oro. If the menu does manage to catch your eye, try the cuttlefish (€10).

DRINKING

Bars usually open from 6pm to 2am weekdays and 8pm to 4am on the weekend. Drinking and partying get going as late as midnight on Friday and Saturday (daily when it's hot), upping the tempo as the night goes on.

Thirst-quenching *cerveza* (beer) is just as important to Spaniards as tapas, and it's normally served as a *caña* (almost the equivalent of half a pint). Bodegas also serve sherry (p83), which is perfect for sipping with tapas.

In summer, dozens of *terrazas de verano* (summer terraces; temporary, open-air, late-night bars), many of them with live music and plenty of room to dance, spring up along both banks of the river. They change names and ambience from year to year.

Barrio de Santa Cruz & Around

P Flaherty Irish Pub (Map pp102-3; ☎ 954 21 04 15; Calle Alemanes 7) Not really very Andalucía or anything to do with Seville, but Paddy Flaherty's choice of location (right next to the Cathedral) makes this one of the busiest bars around. Guinness and footie are on offer here, and if there's a game on, the atmosphere is fun.

Antigüedades (Map pp102-3; Calle Argote de Molina 40) Blending mellow beats with weird mannequin parts and skewered bread rolls that hang from the ceiling, this is a strange but cool place. Wander past and it'll suck you in.

La Subasta (Calle Argote de Molina 36; ☽ 8pm-3am) A smattering of antique paraphernalia gives this place a chic-classy-conservative feel, which goes down a treat with the more upmarket Sevillanos.

Casa de la Moneda (Map pp102-3; Calle Adolfo Jurado) Part of a group of rambling old buildings, Casa de la Moneda is a fine watering hole that offers old-world charm, tapas (€2 to €2.50) and football on TV.

Bodega Santa Cruz (p119), and **Café Bar Las Teresas** (p119), in the heart of the Barrio de Santa Cruz, are two much-loved beer (and tapas) haunts.

El Arenal

El Capote (Map pp94–5; Calle Arjona) An old-time favourite summer al fresco bar, right next to Puente de Triana, El Capote is a fabulous place for day- and night-time drinking. The music is good, and a young, groovy crowd comes here to drink cocktails, beer or sip on a cappuccino.

Isbiliyya Café (Map pp102–3; ☎ 954 21 04 60; Paseo de Cristóbal Colón 2) Cupid welcomes you to this busy gay music bar, which puts on extravagant drag-queen shows on Thursday and Sunday nights.

Nu Yor Café (Map pp102–3; ☎ 954 212 889; Calle Marqués de Paradas 30) This cocktail lounge gets sweaty with salsa on Thursdays after 10.30pm, when a Cuban band swings its maracas. There are occasional flamenco nights too.

El Centro

Drinking is best done around Plaza Alfalfa and Plaza del Salvador. Both throb with drinkers from midevening to 1am and are great places to experience Cruzcampo (the local beer) al fresco. On Plaza del Salvador, grab a drink from **La Antigua Bodeguita** (Map pp102–3; ☎ 954 56 18 33) or **La Saportales** next door, and sit on the steps of the Parroquia del Salvador.

El Perro Andalúz (Map pp102–3; Calle Bustos Tavera 11) A bar dedicated to the eponymous surrealist film by Buñuel and Dalí, with suitably odd décor, such as stand-up hair dryers as lamps, chairs with a large eye printed across them (but, thankfully, without being sliced by a razor, like in the movie). Live music is on most nights – just ask in advance what they are staging.

Bar Europa (Map pp102–3; ☎ 954 22 13 54; Calle Siete Revueltas 35) With its soothingly colourful tiling, Bar Europa is a pleasant place for a drink and a chat. It also does tea (€0.90) and croissants (€1.10) if you want a break from alcohol and tapas.

Cervecería International (Map pp102–3; ☎ 954 21 17 17; Calle Gamazo 3) There are more varieties of bottled beer here (€1.50 for beer on tap) than you may sample in a lifetime, so it's no surprise people keep on coming back. It's a big foreign crowd here.

Alfalfa's Calle Pérez Galdós has a handful of pulsating bars: **Bare Nostrum** (Map pp102–3; Calle Pérez Galdós 26); **Cabo Loco** (Map pp102–3; Calle Pérez Galdós 26); **Nao** (Map pp102–3; Calle Pérez Galdós

28); and **La Rebótica** (Map pp102–3; Calle Pérez Galdós 11). If you're in a party mood, you should find at least one with a scene that takes your fancy.

Alameda de Hércules

In terms of hipness and trendy places to go out, La Alameda is where it's at. The slightly run-down feeling of the area adds to the exclusivity and repels the more posh *sevillanos*, so the boho lot get to keep the place more or less to themselves.

Café Central (Map pp94–5; ☎ 954 38 73 12; Alameda de Hércules 64) One of the oldest and most popular bars along the street, the Central has yellow bar lights, wooden flea-market chairs and a massive crowd that gathers on weekends and sits outside.

Habanilla (Map pp94–5; ☎ 954 90 27 18; Alameda de Hércules 63) Just opposite Café Central and just as busy, Habanilla's *pièce de résistance* is the lovely handmade bottle-chandelier that dominates the room. Andalucian tiles cover the walls and an impressive collection of coffee-makers decorates the area behind the bar.

Bar Ego (Map pp94–5; Calle Calatrava s/n) A strange hybrid of a DJ bar, restaurant, clothes shop and art gallery, this place strives for something completely different in the still predominantly traditional Seville. It's newly opened, Barcelona-hip, and original, and we are hoping it'll survive.

Bulebar Café (Map pp94–5; ☎ 954 90 19 54; Alameda de Hércules 83; 4pm-late) This place fills up with young sweaty bodies at night, though it still retains a pleasantly chilled atmosphere in the early evening. Lounge around on the old furniture or sit in the courtyard out front.

Triana

For a real treat, prop yourself up with a drink by the banks of the Guadalquivir in Triana; the wall along Calle del Betis forms a fantastic makeshift bar. Carry your drink out from one of the following watering holes: Alambique, Big Ben, Sirocca and Mú d'Aquí. They are all clustered on Calle del Betis 54 (Map pp94–5) and open from 9pm.

Maya Soul (Map pp102-3; Calle del Betis 41-42) Beat-up leather sofas and soulful house music make this a soporific afternoon stop-off. Things get livelier in the evening.

Café de la Prensa (Map pp94-5; Calle del Betis 8) Dedicated and decorated in honour of all things in print (*prensa* is 'press' in Spanish), this café's walls are stuck with yellowed, printed paper and create a warm (and highly flammable) effect. The bar is relaxed and people come to have a beer and a game of cards here.

La Otra Orilla (Map pp94-5; Paseo de Nuestra Señora de la O) A couple of passages lead through to the river bank, where you'll find this buzzing music bar blessed with a great outdoor terrace.

Madigan's (Map pp102-3; ☎ 954 27 49 66; Plaza de Cuba 2; ☺ from noon) This raucous Irish pub is the best on Plaza de Cuba, and is now one of the hip places for mass youth gatherings.

Shiva (Map pp94-5; Calle San Jacinto 68) Handsome barmen aside, you'll be swooning from the candlelight and incense (and maybe the alcohol) before you know it.

North of Calle del Betis, Calle de Castilla has several more good bars, brimming with a mixed local crowd on weekend nights, including **Casa Cuesta** (Map pp94-5; Calle de Castilla 3-5) and **Aníbal Café** (Map pp94-5; Calle de Castilla 98).

ENTERTAINMENT
Nightclubs

Seville's nightlife, or *la marcha*, as it's commonly known, is famed throughout Spain, and it mainly ranges from just hanging out in bars, drinking and talking at the top of your voice, continuing on to late-opening clubs, or going to see experimental theatre and stomping flamenco. You can find a range of live music most days, and some bars have space for grooving. DJs mix a range of beats every night, with soulful house and funk as the most popular choices.

The ever-present *botellón* is big all over Spain, and consists of crowds of young boozers, gathered around bottle-covered cars and scooters, listening to the beats of *reggaeton* – a hybrid of hip hop, Jamaican dancehall (soca and calypso) and Latin music.

Clubs in Seville come and go with amazing rapidity but a few have stood the test of time. The partying starts between 2am and 4am at the weekend, so make the most of your siesta.

If a club flyer is thrust into your hand, keep hold of it – you're more likely to get in for free. Dress smarter (so no sportswear) at the weekend as clubs become much pickier about their punters, and prices are hiked up dramatically if you don't fit the scene.

Get to grips with the latest action by picking up *Welcome & Olé* or *¿Qué Hacer?* (both monthly and free from tourist offices) or by logging onto www.discoversevilla.com, a great resource, or www.exploreseville.com. For flamenco listings and events try www.tallerflamenco.com.

Boss (Map pp102-3; Calle del Betis 67; admission free with flyer; ☺ 8pm-7am Tue-Sun) Make it past the two gruff bouncers wedged in the doorway and you'll find Boss to be a top dance spot. The music is a total mix but mainly appeals to the masses.

Weekend (Map pp94-5; ☎ 954 37 88 73; Calle del Torneo 43; admission around €7; ☺ 11pm-8am Thu-Sat) Just across the road from the Guadalquivir, Weekend is one of Seville's top live-music and DJ spots.

Lisboa Music Club (Map pp94-5; Calle Faustino Álvarez 27; admission €6; ☺ midnight-6am Wed-Sat) LMC, near the Alameda de Hércules, is a fashionable club for house and techno lovers. Stylish, '60s-inspired decor spars with modernity; it's very hip.

Fun Club (Map pp94-5; ☎ 95 825 02 49; Alameda de Hércules 86; admission live-band nights €3-6, other nights free; ☺ around 11.30pm-late Thu-Sun, from 9.30pm live-band nights) When live music isn't taking over the stage, DJs play anything from indie to rock and pop, and sometimes funk, and there's plenty of dancing space.

Antique Teatro (Map pp94-5; ☎ 954 46 22 07; Matemáticos Rey Pastor y Castro s/n; admission varied; ☺ Thu-Sat 11pm-7am) Notorious for turning foreigners away; get your hair slicked back Sevilla-style if you're a man, and look drop-dead gorgeous if you're a woman, and try getting into this top club, located at the Expo '92 Olympic Pavillion. In summer, there's a torch-lit garden and cocktail sipping under the stars.

Apandau (Map pp94-5; Avenida de María Luisa s/n; admission varied ☾ 8pm-late Sat & Sun summer) Looking more like a palatial greenhouse than a disco, Apandau has three separate halls in which to salsa the night away.

Aduana (☎ 954 23 85 82; www.aduana.net; Avenida de la Raza s/n; admission varied ☾ midnight-late Thu, Fri & Sat) Located 1km south of Parque de María Luisa, this huge dance venue plays nonstop grooves for manic party people.

Elefunk (Map pp102-3; Calle de Adriano 10; admission free; ☾ 8pm-late) A super popular club packed with youngsters in search of, well, funk.

Live Music

Tickets for some major events are sold at the music shop **Sevilla Rock** (Map pp102-3; Calle Alfonso XII 1). For information on flamenco in Seville, see the boxed text, opposite.

Fun Club (Map pp94-5; ☎ 95 825 02 49; Alameda de Hércules 86; admission live-band nights €3-6, other nights free; ☾ around 11.30pm-late Thu-Sun, from 9.30pm live-band nights) When it comes to music, this little dance warehouse is deadly serious. With a host of funk, Latino, hip-hop and jazz bands, it's not surprising that it's a music-lovers' favourite. Live bands play Friday and/or Saturday.

Naima Café Jazz (Map pp94-5; ☎ 954 38 24 85; Calle Trajano 47; admission free; ☾ live performances from 10pm) This intimate place sways to the sound of mellow jazz that goes live on weekends. Ask the friendly bar staff for details of who's playing and when.

La Buena Estrella (Map pp94-5; Calle Trajano 51; ☾ live performances from 10pm) Tap along to weekly jazz sessions in the evening or sip tea by day at this chilled café.

Jazz Corner (Map pp94-5; Calle Juan Antonio Cavestany; ☾ 7pm-late Tue-Sat, 5pm-late Sun) A big venue for jazz aficionados.

La Imperdible (Map pp94-5; ☎ 954 38 82 19; sala@imperdible.org; Plaza San Antonio de Padua 9; admission €5-6) A few blocks west of Alameda de Hércules is an epicentre of experimental arts in Seville. Its small theatre stages lots of contemporary dance and a bit of drama and music, usually at 9pm. Its bar, the

Almacén (☎ 954 90 04 34; admission free), stages varied music events from around 11pm Thursday to Saturday – from soul and blues bands to psychedelic punks and DJs mixing everything from soulful house to industrial breakbeat.

Theatre

Seville is big on cultural entertainment, be it classical drama, contemporary dance, flamenco or world music. Catch performances at the following venues:

Auditorio de la Cartuja (Map pp94-5; ☎ 954 50 56 56; Isla de La Cartuja) Huge venue for big-name acts.

Teatro Central (Map pp94-5; ☎ 95 503 72 00; Calle José Gálvez s/n) From top-end flamenco productions to plays and contemporary dance.

Teatro de la Maestranza (Map pp102-3; ☎ 954 22 65 73; Paseo de Cristóbal Colón 22) Opera and classical-music buffs should head here for stirring concerts.

Teatro Lope de Vega (Map pp94-5; ☎ 954 59 08 53/54; Avenida de María Luisa s/n) This theatre will seduce you with its ornate-looking exterior and its wide range of shows.

There are a couple of municipally run but innovative experimental theatres:

Sala La Fundición (Map pp102-3; ☎ 954 22 58 44; Calle Matienzo s/n) Has offbeat offerings.

Teatro Alameda (Map pp94-5; ☎ 954 90 01 64; Calle Crédito 13) Located just off the northern end of Alameda de Hércules.

Cinemas

Avenida 5 Cines (Map pp102-3; ☎ 954 29 30 25; Calle Marqués de Paradas 15 s/n; admission €5) This is the best cinema for *v.o.* (*versión original*; foreign-language) films in Seville, with around 14 film options from which to choose. It has around three showings per day.

Cine Nervión Plaza (Map pp94-5; ☎ 954 42 61 93; Avenida de Luis Morales s/n; tickets €3.90 Mon-Fri, €5 Sat & Sun) This massive 20-screen cinema is within the Nervión Plaza shopping complex. It has between three and six showings per day.

Sport

Seville's modern 60,000-seat Estadio Olímpico (Map pp94–5) is at the northern end of Isla de la Cartuja. It wasn't enough to secure Seville's bid for the 2012 Olympics but there's always 2016.

La Teatral (Map pp102-3; ☎ 954 22 82 29; Calle Velázquez 12) Based in El Centro, this ticket

---

SEVILLE'S TOP FLAMENCO SPOTS

Casa de la Memoria de Al-Andalus (Map pp102-3; ☎ 954 56 06 70; Calle Ximénez de Enciso 28; adult/child/concession €11/5/9; ⊙ 9pm daily) Highly recommended show in a great patio setting.

Sol Café Cantante (Map pp102-3; ☎ 954 22 51 65; Calle Sol 5; adult/concession €18/11) Up-and-coming flamenco performers and guitarists head to this popular café for shows on Wednesday, Thursday, Friday and Saturday nights at 9pm.

Los Gallos (Map pp102-3; ☎ 954 21 69 81; www.tablaolosgallos.com; Plaza de Santa Cruz 11) A *tablao* above average. Some top-notch flamenco artists have trodden Los Gallos' boards in the early stages of their careers. There are two-hour shows at 9pm and 11.30pm nightly for €27, including one drink.

La Carbonería (Map pp102-3; ⊙ 954 21 44 60; Calle Levíes 18; admission free; ⊙ about 8pm-4am) A converted coal yard in the Barrio de Santa Cruz with two large rooms, each with a bar, that has flamenco shows of varying quality.

La Sonanta (Map pp94-5; ☎ 954 34 48 54; Calle San Jacinto 31; admission free; ⊙ 10pm Thu) A Triana bar with flamenco on Thursday.

El Tamboril (Map pp102-3; Plaza de Santa Cruz; admission free; ⊙ from 10pm) Pack in to watch Sevillans flamenco the night away.

---

agency sells tickets for bullfights, football matches and some concerts at a mark-up of a few euros. You need to book well in advance for the most popular events.

BULLFIGHTING

Queues for tickets outside Seville's **Plaza de Toros de la Real Maestranza** (Map pp102-3; Paseo de Cristóbal Colón 12; www.realmaestranza.com) start weeks before the first fights, which take place just before the Feria de Abril. They stretch for hundreds of metres down the road and show the Maestranza's popularity and prestige in the bullfighting world. Even though it's a relatively small ring (it holds 14,000 spectators), it's one of the oldest and most elegant. The fights held here are some of the best in Spain, fought by the top toreros. Seville's crowds are some of the most knowledgeable, and many say, the most demanding and difficult to please. The season runs from Easter Sunday to early October, with fights every Sunday, usually at 7pm, and every day during the Feria de Abril and the week before it.

From the start of the season until late June/early July, nearly all the fights are by fully fledged matadors (every big star in the bullfighting firmament appears at least once a year in the Maestranza). These are the *abono* (subscription) fights, for which locals buy up the best seats on season tickets. Often only *sol* seats (in the sun at the start of proceedings) are available to nonsubscribers attending these fights. The cheapest seats start at €25. The most ex-

pensive tickets, if available, cost a whopping €110. Most of the rest of the season, the fights are *novilladas* (novice bullfights), with young bulls and junior bullfighters, costing from €9 to €42. Tickets are sold in advance at **Empresa Pagés** (Map pp102-3 ; ☎ 954 50 13 82; Calle de Adriano 37), and from 4.30pm on fight days at the *taquillas* (ticket windows) at the bullring itself.

For more on the Plaza de Toros de la Real Maestranza, see p106.

FOOTBALL

It is said that the only thing that divides Seville, apart from the Guadalquivir, is the *sevillanos*' passionate support for its two rival professional clubs, **Real Betis** (www.realbetis balompie.es) and **Sevilla** (www.sevillafc.es). Both teams are currently well established in the Primera Liga and Sevilla won the UEFA Cup in 2006. Players on Betis' books include Spanish international midfield star Joaquín.

Betis plays at the Estadio Manuel Ruiz de Lopera (Map pp94–5), beside Avenida de Jerez (the Cádiz road), 1.5km south of Parque de María Luisa (take bus 34 southbound from opposite the main tourist office). Sevilla's home is the **Estadio Sánchez Pizjuán** (Map pp94-5; Calle de Luis Morales), east of the centre.

Except for the biggest games – against Real Madrid or Barcelona, or when the Seville clubs meet each other – tickets cost between €25 and €60, payable at the gates.

SHOPPING

Shopping in Seville is a major pastime, and shopping for clothes is at the top of any *sevillano*'s list. The lovely cluster of pedestrianised shopping streets is among the prettiest in Europe.

Calles Sierpes, Velázquez/Tetuán and de la Cuna (all on Map pp102–3) have retained their charm with a host of small shops selling everything from polka-dot *trajes de flamenca* (flamenco dresses) and trendy Camper shoes to diamond rings and antique fans. Most shops open between 9am and 9pm but expect ghostly quiet between 2pm and 5pm when they close for siesta.

For a more alternative choice of shops, such as independent and rare-recordings music shops or vintage clothes, head for Calle Amor de Dios and Calle Doctor Letamendi, close to Alameda de Hércules (Map pp94–5).

Tourist-oriented craft shops are dotted all around the Barrio de Santa Cruz (Map pp102–3), east of the Alcázar. Many sell local tiles and ceramics with colourful Al-Andalus designs, scenes of old rural life etc, as well as a lot of gaudy T-shirts.

El Postigo (Map pp102-3; cnr Calles Arfe & Dos de Mayo) This indoor arts-and-crafts market houses a few shops selling a variety of goods ranging from pottery and textiles to silverware.

Green UFOs (Map pp94-5; ☎ 954 37 63 14; Calle Amor de Dios 42) A great independent music shop, with a great collection of electronic, breakbeat, pop and rock CDs by artists worldwide. The shop has its own recording label too, and it sponsors the South Pop music festival.

Record Sevilla (Map pp94-5; Calle Amor de Dios 27) Fancy mixing flamenco with house? Then grab your vinyl here. Staff are knowledgeable about the music scene, too.

Nervión Plaza (Map pp94-5; ☎ 954 98 91 41; Avenida Luis de Morales s/n) This large shopping complex is located about 1.5km east of the Barrio de Santa Cruz, just off Avenida de Eduardo Dato.

El Corte Inglés department store (Map pp102–3) – the best single shop to look for just about anything you might need – occupies four separate buildings in central Seville: two on Plaza de la Magdalena and two on Plaza del Duque de la Victoria.

There is also a large branch located on Calle Montoto.

Markets

The most colourful street market is **El Jueves Market** (Map pp94-5; Calle de la Feria; ⊙ Thu), east of Alameda de Hércules, where you can find everything from hat stands to antiquated household appliances. It's as interesting for those who like people-watching as it is for those with an eye for a bargain. Alternatively, lose yourself among the leather bags and hippy-type necklaces on Plaza del Duque de la Victoria and Plaza de la Magdalena, which both stage **markets** (⊙ Thu-Sat).

GETTING THERE & AWAY

Air

Seville's **Aeropuerto San Pablo** (Map pp94-5; ☎ 954 44 90 00) has a fair range of international and domestic flights (see p441).

Bus

Seville has two bus stations. Buses to/from the north of Sevilla province, Huelva province, Portugal, Madrid, Extremadura and northwest Spain use the **Estación de Autobuses Plaza de Armas** (Map pp94-5; ☎ 954 90 80 40, 954 90 77 37) by the Puente del Cachorro. Other buses use the **Estación de Autobuses Prado de San Sebastián** (Map pp102-3; ☎ 954 41 71 11; Plaza San Sebastián), just southeast of the Barrio de Santa Cruz.

Buses go to various destinations from Plaza de Armas:

Destination	Cost	Duration	Daily Frequency
Aracena	€6	1¼hr	2
Ayamonte	€10.50	2hr	4-6
Cáceres	€15	4hr	6 or more
El Rocío	€5	1½hr	3-5
Huelva	€6.50	1¼hr	18 or more
Isla Cristina	€9	2hr	1-3
Madrid	€16	6hr	14
Matalascañas	€6	2hr	3-5
Mérida	€11	3hr	12
Minas de Riotinto	€4	1hr	3

For information on buses to/from Portugal, see p445. Plaza de Armas is also the station for buses to Santiponce (€0.80, 30 minutes), and Sevilla province's Sierra Norte (p139).

Various buses leave from Prado de San Sebastián:

Destination	Cost	Duration	Daily Frequency
Algeciras	€14-15	3½hr	4
Antequera	€10	2hr	6
Arcos de la Frontera	€7	2hr	2
Cádiz	€10.50	1¾hr	10 or more
Carmona	€2	45min	
Córdoba	€9.50	1¾hr	10 or more
Écija	€5.50	1¼hr	
El Puerto de Santa María	€8	1½hr	5
Granada	€18	3hr	10 or more
Jaén	€16	3hr	3-5
Jerez de la Frontera	€6.50	1¼hr	10 or more
Málaga	€15	2½hr	10 or more
Osuna	€6	1¼hr	
Ronda	€9	2½hr	5 or more
Sanlúcar de Barrameda	€8	1½hr	5 or more
Tarifa	€15	3hr	4
Vejer de la Frontera	€11.50	3hr	5

Other buses travel to destinations along the Mediterranean coast from the Costa del Sol to Barcelona, and there's one bus at 5.30pm Monday to Friday to Conil (€10, two hours), Los Caños de Meca (€13, 2½ hours), Barbate (€13, three hours) and Zahara de los Atunes (€14, 3½ hours).

Car & Motorcycle
Some local car-rental firms are cheaper than the big international companies, though booking before you come (see p451) is usually the cheapest option of all. Several local firms have their offices on Calle Almirante Lobo off the Puerta de Jerez: most of them are open on Sunday morning, plus the typical office hours from Monday to Saturday:

ATA Rent A Car (Map pp102–3; ☎ 954 22 17 77; Calle Almirante Lobo 2)
Good Rent A Car (Map pp102–3; ☎ 954 21 03 44; Calle Almirante Lobo 11)
Triana Rent A Car (Map pp102–3; ☎ 954 56 44 39; Calle Almirante Lobo 7)

You'll find larger companies at the transport terminals:
Atesa (☎ 954 41 26 40; Airport)
Avis Airport (☎ 954 44 91 21); Estación Santa Justa (Map pp94-5; ☎ 954 53 78 61)

Europcar Airport (☎ 954 25 42 98); Estación Santa Justa (☎ 954 53 39 14)
Hertz (☎ 954 51 47 20; Airport)

Train
Seville's **Estación Santa Justa** (Map pp94-5; ☎ 954 41 41 11; Avenida Kansas City) is 1.5km northeast of the centre. There's also a city-centre **Renfe information & ticket office** (Map pp102-3; Calle Zaragoza 29).

Fourteen or more superfast AVEs, reaching speeds of 280km/h, whizz daily to/from Madrid (€64 to €70, 2½ hours). There are cheaper 'Altaria' services (€55, 3½ hours). (For fares and other information see p445.)

Trains go to various destinations:

Destination	Cost	Duration	Daily Frequency
Antequera	€11	1¾hr	3
Barcelona	€53-88	10½-13hr	3
Cádiz	€9-29	1¾hr	9 or more
Córdoba	€7-€24	40min-1½hr	21 or more
El Puerto de Santa María	€7.50-26	1-1½hr	10 or more
Granada	€20	3hr	4
Huelva	€7-16	1½hr	4
Jaén	€16	3hr	1
Jerez de la Frontera	€6-16	1-1¼hr	9 or more
Málaga	€16	2½hr	5
Mérida	€12	3¾hr	1

For Ronda or Algeciras, take a Málaga train and change at Bobadilla. For Lisbon (€51, 2nd-class, 16 hours), you must change in the middle of the night at Madrid.

GETTING AROUND
To/From the Airport
Seville airport is about 7km east of the centre on the A4 Córdoba road. From Monday to Friday, buses of **Amarillos Tour** (☎ 902 21 03 17) make the trip from Puerta de Jerez to the airport (€2.50, 30 to 40 minutes) every 30 minutes from 6.15am to 2.45pm and 4.30pm to 11pm, and from the airport (arrivals terminal) to Puerta de Jerez 30 minutes later. On Saturday, Sunday and holidays, the service is reduced to 15 buses in each direction daily. The buses stop at Santa Justa train station en route.

A taxi costs €15 (€18 from 10pm to 6am and on Saturday, Sunday and holidays).

Bus

Buses C1, C2, C3 and C4 do useful circular routes linking the main transport terminals and the city centre. The C1, going east from in front of Santa Justa train station, follows a clockwise route via Avenida de Carlos V (close to Prado de San Sebastián bus station), Avenida de María Luisa, Triana, the Isla de la Cartuja (including Isla Mágica) and Calle de Resolana. The C2 follows the same route in reverse. Bus 32, from the same stop as bus C2 outside Santa Justa station, runs to/from Plaza de la Encarnación in the northern part of the centre. The clockwise C3 route goes from Avenida Menéndez Pelayo (near Prado de San Sebastián bus station) to the Puerta de Jerez, Triana, Plaza de Armas bus station, Calle del Torneo, Calle de Resolana and Calle de Recaredo. The C4 does the same circuit anticlockwise except that from Plaza de Armas bus station it heads south along Calle de Arjona and Paseo de Cristóbal Colón.

A single bus ride is €1. You can pick up a route map, the *Guía del Transporte Urbano de Sevilla,* from tourist offices or from information booths at major stops, including Plaza Nueva, Plaza de la Encarnación and Avenida de Carlos V.

Car & Motorcycle

Seville's one-way and pedestrianised streets are no fun for drivers. Hotels usually charge €10 to €15 a day for parking. Most underground car parks charge around €16 for 24 hours – see the Seville map (pp94–5) and Central Seville map (pp102–3) for locations. **Parking Paseo de Colón** (Map pp102-3; cnr Paseo de Colón & Calle Adriano; up to 10 hr €1.50 per hr, 10-24 hr €12) is a little cheaper.

Taxi

From 6am to 10pm Monday to Friday, taxis cost €1 plus €0.65 per kilometre. At other times and on public holidays, it's €1 plus €0.80 per kilometre.

AROUND SEVILLE

SANTIPONCE

pop 7560 / elevation 20m

The small town of Santiponce, about 8km northwest of Seville, is the location of Itálica, the most impressive Roman site in Andalucía, and of the historic and artisti-

cally fascinating Monasterio de San Isidoro del Campo. There's a **tourist office** (☎ 955 99 80 28; Calle La Feria s/n; ☺ 9am-4pm Tue-Fri & Sun) next to the Roman theatre.

Itálica (☎ 955 99 65 83; Avenida de Extremadura 2; non-EU citizen €1.50, EU citizen free; ☺ 8.30am-8.30pm Tue-Sat, 9am-3pm Sun & holidays Apr-Sep, 9am-5.30pm Tue-Sat, 10am-4pm Sun & holidays Oct-Mar, closed 1 & 6 Jan, 28 Feb, Good Friday, 1 May, 15 Aug, 1 Nov, 25 Dec) was the first Roman town in Spain, founded in 206 BC for soldiers wounded in the Battle of Ilipa, nearby, in which a Roman army under General Scipio Africanus extinguished Carthaginian ambitions on the Iberian Peninsula. Itálica was the birthplace of the 2nd-century-AD Roman emperor Trajan, and probably of his adopted son and successor Hadrian (he of the wall across northern England).

Most of the Romans' original *vetus urbs* (old town) now lies beneath Santiponce. The main area to visit is the *nova urbs* (new town), added by Hadrian, at the northern end of town. The site includes broad paved streets, one of the biggest of all Roman amphitheatres (able to hold 20,000 spectators), and ruins of houses built around patios with beautiful mosaics. The most notable houses are the **Casa del Planetario** (House of the Planetarium), with a mosaic depicting the gods of the seven days of the week, and the **Casa de los Pájaros** (House of the Birds).

To the south, in the old town, you can also visit a restored **Roman theatre**. In April or May each year this is the setting for a European youth festival of Greco-Latin theatre, with plays by classical playwrights. Itálica has been heavily recycled over the centuries and parts of its buildings have been reused in Santiponce, Seville and elsewhere. You can see statuary and more mosaics from here in Seville's Palacio de la Condesa de Lebrija (p107) and Museo Arqueológico (p108).

The **Monasterio de San Isidoro del Campo** (☎ 955 99 69 20; admission €2; ☺ 10am-2pm & 5.30-8.30pm Fri & Sat Apr-Sep, 10am-2pm & 4-7pm Fri & Sat Oct-Mar, 10am-3pm Sun & holidays) is at the southern end of Santiponce, 1.5km from the Itálica entrance. The monastery was founded in 1301 by Guzmán El Bueno, hero of the defence of Tarifa in 1294 (see p215). In the 15th century its order of hermitic Hieronymite monks decorated the Patio de Evangelistas and central cloister with a rare set of mural paintings of saints and Mudejar geometric and floral designs. By the 16th century the monastery had one of Spain's best libraries, and one monk, Casiodoro de Reina, did the first translation of the Bible into Spanish (published 1559). But Reina and others were too much influenced by Lutheran ideas for the liking of the Inquisition, which dissolved the nascent Protestant community, imprisoning and executing some monks while others managed to escape into exile.

In 1568 the monastery was occupied by a different (nonhermitic) order of Hieronymites, for whom the great 17th-century Sevillan sculptor Juan Martínez Montañés carved one of his masterpieces – the retable in the larger of the monastery's twin churches – as well as the effigies of Guzmán El Bueno and his wife María Alonso Coronel that lie in wall niches either side of the retable, above their tombs.

In the 19th century the monks were again expelled from this monastery. It subsequently served as a women's prison, brewery and tobacco factory. Finally, after a 12-year Junta de Andalucía restoration project, it was recently opened for visits.

Santiponce has several spots for a meal. **Casa Venancio/Gran Venta Itálica** (☎ 955 99 67 06; Avenida Extremadura 9; mains €6-13), opposite the Itálica entrance, has good rabbit or partridge with rice (€17 for two). For seafood or more rice dishes, head to the slightly fancier **La Caseta de Antonio** (☎ 955 99 63 06; Calle Rocío Vega 10; mains €10-18; ✴ closed Sun night, Mon & all Aug), a few steps south of Casa Venancio then a minute's walk along a side street.

Buses run to Santiponce (€1, 30 minutes) from Seville's Plaza de Armas bus station at least twice an hour from 6.30am to 11pm Monday to Friday, a little less often on weekends. In Santiponce they make a stop near the monastery, and terminate at the petrol station outside the Itálica entrance.

DETOUR: BIRDS & PINE FORESTS

A detour through the northeast fringes of the Doñana area (p154) en route to El Rocío (p156), or a day trip into the same territory from Seville, will reward any nature lover. You'll see plenty of large birds – flamingos, storks, eagles, hawks, herons – even before you get out of your car.

Leave Seville southwestward by Avenida de la República Argentina and the A3122 to Coria del Río and La Puebla del Río. For information about the Doñana area, stop for a chat with the friendly, knowledgeable, English-speaking folk at the **Punto de Información Puebla del Río** (☎ 955 77 20 03; www.rutasdedonana.com; Avenida Pozo Concejo s/n; ✴ 9am-2pm & 5-7.30pm), beside the A3122 in La Puebla del Río, 15km from central Seville. Seven kilometres further along the road is **La Cañada de los Pájaros** (☎ 955 77 21 84; www.canadadelospajaros.com; Carretera Puebla del Río-Isla Mayor Km 8; adult/child under 5yr/child under 13yr/student/senior €6/free/€4/5/5; ✴ 10am-dusk), a nature reserve with thousands of easy-to-see birds of 150-plus species, including flamingos and many others that inhabit the Parque Natural de Doñana.

Time for lunch? **Venta El Cruce** (☎ 955 77 01 19; Carretera Puebla del Río-Isla Mayor Km 9.5; raciones €10), 1.75km beyond La Cañada de los Pájaros at the turn-off for Villafranco del Guadalquivir, serves a typical range of meat and fish dishes but the speciality, in this area of rice fields and wildfowl, is *pato con arroz* (duck with rice), served on Saturday and Sunday. If you'd prefer to picnic outdoors, continue past the Villafranco junction and fork right after 600m along the signposted Carril de Cicloturismo Pinares de Aznalcázar-La Puebla. This road running through lovely tall pine woods towards the village of Aznalcázar has been turned into a *vía paisajística* (landscape route), with speed bumps to restrict motor vehicles to 40km/h and special roadside reflectors to warn wildlife of traffic at night. About 6km along is the **Área Recreativa Pozo del Conejo**, with picnic tables beneath the trees.

Return 6km to the main road and turn right (southwest). On the right after 4km is **Dehesa de Abajo**, a 1.5-sq-km nature reserve with walkways to observation points over Europe's largest woodland nesting colony of white storks (400 pairs) and hides overlooking a lake. A variety of raptors also nest here. To continue to El Rocío, carry on southwest from Dehesa de Abajo to the Vado de Don Simón causeway across the shallow Río Guadiamar. At the far end of the causeway turn right (northward) to Villamanrique de la Condesa, from where it's 20km southwest to El Rocío by unpaved road, or 43km on paved roads via Pilas, Hinojos and Almonte.

LA CAMPIÑA

La Campiña – the rolling plains east of Seville and south of the Río Guadalquivir, crossed by the A4 to Córdoba and the A92 towards Granada and Málaga – is still a land of huge agricultural estates belonging to a few landowners, dotted with scattered towns and villages. History goes back a long way here: you'll find traces of Tartessians, Iberians, Carthaginians, Romans, early Christians, Visigoths, Muslims and many others. Three towns of La Campiña region – Carmona and Écija on the A4 and Osuna on the A92 – are especially worth visiting for their architecture, art and fascinating histories.

CARMONA

pop 27,000 / elevation 250m

Carmona is a charming old town, dotted with old palaces and impressive monuments, perched on a low hill overlooking a wonderful *vega* (valley) that sizzles in the summer heat. There's a handful of impressive places to stay, and possibly one of the loveliest hotels in Andalucía.

This strategic site was important as long ago as Carthaginian times. The Romans laid out a street plan that survives to this day: their Via Augusta, running from Rome to Cádiz, entered Carmona by the eastern Puerta de Córdoba and left by the western Puerta de Sevilla. The Muslims built a strong defensive wall around Carmona but it fell in 1247 to Fernando III. The town was later adorned with fine churches, convents and mansions by Mudejar and Christian artisans.

Carmona stands on a low hill just off the A4, 38km east of Seville.

Orientation & Information

Old Carmona stands on the hill at the eastern end of the modern town: the Puerta de Sevilla marks the beginning of the old town. The helpful **tourist office** (☎ 954 19 09 55; www .turismo.carmona.org; ☼ 10am-6pm Mon-Sat, 10am-3pm Sun & holidays) is inside the Puerta de Sevilla. There are banks with ATMs on Paseo del Estatuto and Calle San Pedro, west of the

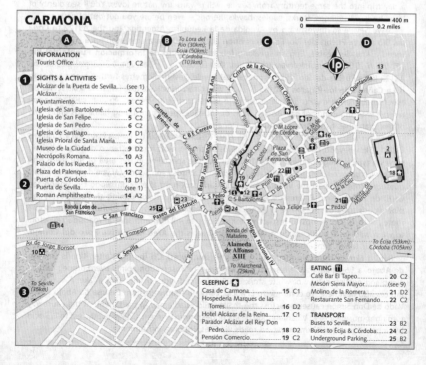

CARMONA

INFORMATION		
Tourist Office	1	C2
SIGHTS & ACTIVITIES		
Alcázar de la Puerta de Sevilla	(see 1)	
Alcázar	2	D2
Ayuntamiento	3	C2
Iglesia de San Bartolomé	4	C2
Iglesia de San Felipe	5	C2
Iglesia de San Pedro	6	C2
Iglesia de Santiago	7	D1
Iglesia Prioral de Santa María	8	C2
Museo de la Ciudad	9	D2
Necrópolis Romana	10	A3
Palacio de los Ruedas	11	C2
Plaza del Palenque	12	C2
Puerta de Córdoba	13	D1
Puerta de Sevilla	(see 1)	
Roman Amphitheatre	14	A2

SLEEPING		
Casa de Carmona	15	C1
Hospedería Marques de las Torres	16	D2
Hotel Alcázar de la Reina	17	C1
Parador Alcázar del Rey Don Pedro	18	D2
Pensión Comercio	19	C2

EATING		
Café Bar El Tapeo	20	C2
Mesón Sierra Mayor	(see 9)	
Molino de la Romera	21	D2
Restaurante San Fernando	22	C2

TRANSPORT		
Buses to Seville	23	B2
Buses to Écija & Córdoba	24	C2
Underground Parking	25	B2

Puerta de Sevilla, and on Plaza de San Fernando, the main square of the old town.

Sights

NECRÓPOLIS ROMANA

Carmona hides a fascinating site just over 1km southwest of the Puerta de Sevilla: the **Necrópolis Romana** (Map p132; Roman cemetery; ☎ 954 14 08 11; Avenida de Jorge Bonsor s/n; admission free; ⌚ 9am-2pm Tue-Sat 15 Jun-14 Sep, 9am-5pm Tue-Fri, 10am-2pm Sat & Sun rest of year, closed holidays). You can climb down into a dozen or more family tombs, hewn from the rock in the 1st and 2nd centuries AD, some of them elaborate and many-chambered (a torch is useful). Most of the dead were cremated, and in the tombs are wall niches for the boxlike stone urns containing the ashes.

Don't miss the **Tumba de Servilia**, as big as a temple (it was the tomb of a family of Hispano-Roman bigwigs), or the **Tumba del Elefante**, with a small elephant statue.

Across the street, you can look down onto a 1st-century-BC **Roman amphitheatre**.

PUERTA DE SEVILLA & AROUND

This impressive main gate of the old town has been fortified for well over 2000 years. Today it also houses the tourist office, which sells tickets for the interesting upper levels of the structure, the **Alcázar de la Puerta de Sevilla** (adult/child/student/senior €2/1/1/1; ⌚ 10am-6pm Mon-Sat, 10am-3pm Sun & holidays), with fine views and an upstairs Almohad patio with traces of a Roman temple. An informative leaflet helps you identify the various Carthaginian, Roman, Islamic and Christian stages of the construction of the Alcázar.

Lengthy sections of Carmona's **walls** extend from the Puerta de Sevilla. The **Iglesia de San Pedro** (☎ 954 14 12 77; Calle San Pedro; admission €1.20; ⌚ 11am-2pm Thu-Mon), west of the Puerta de Sevilla, is worth a look for its richly decorated baroque interior – and if its tower looks familiar, that's because it's an imitation of Seville's Giralda (p99).

OLD TOWN WALKING TOUR

You can go around Carmona in an easy stroll (Map p133), starting from the Puerta de Sevilla. The central Calle Prim leads up to Plaza de San Fernando (or Plaza Mayor), whose 16th-century buildings are painted a pretty variety of colours. Just off this square, the patio of the 17th-century **ayuntamiento**

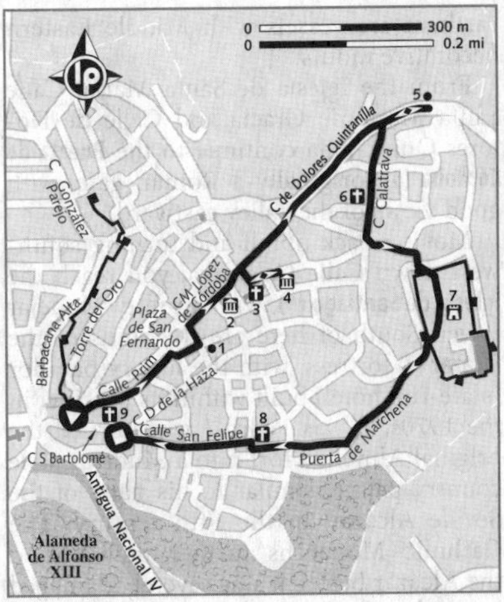

(1) (☎ 954 14 00 11; Calle El Salvador; admission free; ⌚ 8am-3pm Mon-Fri, 4-6pm Tue & Thu) contains a large, very fine Roman mosaic showing the Gorgon Medusa.

Calle Martín López de Córdoba leads northeast off Plaza de San Fernando past the noble **Palacio de los Ruedas (2)** to the splendid **Iglesia Prioral de Santa María (3)** (☎ 954 19 14 82; admission €3; ⌚ 9am-2pm & 5.30-7.30pm Mon-Fri, 9am-2pm Sat 1 Apr-20 Aug, 9am-2pm & 5-7pm Mon-Fri, 9am-2pm Sat 22 Sep-31 Mar, closed 21 Aug-21 Sep). Santa María was built mainly in the 15th and 16th centuries, on the site of the former main mosque in a typical Carmona combination of brick and stone. The Patio de los Naranjos by which you enter (formerly the mosque's ablutions courtyard) has a 6th-century Visigothic calendar carved into one of its pillars. Inside the church, don't miss the fine Gothic pillars and ceiling tracery, and the plateresque main retable.

If Carmona has got under your skin, an extensive background of the town can be explored at the **Museo de la Ciudad (4)** (City History Museum; ☎ 954 14 01 28; www.museociudad.carmona.org; Calle San Ildefonso 1; adult/child/student/senior €2/1/1/1, free Tue; ⌚ 10am-2pm & 4.30-9.30pm Wed-Mon, 10am-2pm Tue 16 Jun-31 Aug, 11am-7pm Wed-Mon, 11am-2pm Tue rest of year), behind Santa María. There are archaeological and historical displays here, housed in a 16th- to 18th-century mansion. Most impressive are the Roman and Tartessos sections, the latter including a unique collection of large earthenware vessels with Middle Eastern decorative motifs.

From the Iglesia de Santa María, Calle Santa María de Gracia and Calle de Dolores Quintanilla continue to the **Puerta de Córdoba (5)**, originally a Roman gate, with good views of the valley eastward.

Moving back uphill and turning southwest down Calle Calatrava, you reach the **Iglesia de Santiago (6)**, with a pretty Mudejar tower. South of here are the ruins of the **Alcázar (7)** fortress, with the luxury parador (state-run hotel) built within its precinct in the 1970s. It was Pedro I who turned the original Almohad fort into a Mudejar-style country palace, similar to his parts of the Seville Alcázar, in the 14th century. The Catholic Monarchs further embellished the Alcázar before it was severely damaged by earthquakes in 1504 and 1755. Join the Spanish families who come to have a drink or a meal at the parador's lovely patio, and enjoy the views.

Start back along Puerta de Marchena, on the southern rim of the town, then head into the tangle of streets to see the 14th-century **Iglesia de San Felipe (8)**, notable for its pretty brick Mudejar tower and Renaissance façade, and the 15th- to 18th-century **Iglesia de San Bartolomé (9)**.

Sleeping

At all the following except the parador expect to pay one-third or 50% more during Semana Santa and Seville's Feria de Abril, and less in the low season (which includes July).

Hospedería Marques de las Torres (☎ 954 19 62 48; www.hospederiamarquesdelastorres.com; Calle Fermin Molpeceres 2; dm €23; r €60; 🔊) An almost unreal combination of dorm beds and hotel rooms in a converted *palacio* (palace), with a fabulous turquoise pool that explodes between terracotta walls in the sunny garden. The dorms are clean and small, and sleep two or four per cabin, with shared bathrooms. The cabins look a bit like train compartments and are separated by a fixed screen which doesn't go all the way up to the ceiling. The comfortable rooms have plush wide beds.

Pensión Comercio (☎ /fax 954 14 00 18; Calle Torre del Oro 56; s/d €32/45; 🔊) A lovely tiled old building with a Mudejar-style arch and patio, surrounded by 14 cosy, clean rooms.

Hotel Alcázar de la Reina (☎ 954 19 62 00; www.alcazar-reina.es; Plaza de Lasso 2; s/d incl breakfast €100/126; 🅿 🔊 🖥 🔊) Luxurious and modern, but essentially soulless, this 68-room hotel is built in what was a monastery garden in the old town. One of its two patios holds a pool and there's a good restaurant.

Parador Alcázar del Rey Don Pedro (☎ 954 14 10 10; www.parador.es; Alcázar s/n; s/d €100/128; 🅿 🔊 🖥 🔊) Built amid the remains of the Alcázar of Pedro I, in a medieval fortress-palace style that mixes Islamic and Christian influences, Carmona's parador exudes historic atmosphere. The 63 spacious rooms and the public spaces are luxuriously equipped with antique and antique-style furnishings, the restaurant is excellent, and few Andalucian swimming pools are more spectacularly sited.

Eating

Several bars and cafés on and around Plaza de San Fernando do *raciones* and tapas; **Café Bar El Tapeo** (☎ 954 14 43 21; Calle Prim 9; tapas/raciones €1.50/5, menú €9) is friendly, down-to-earth and popular.

THE AUTHOR'S CHOICE

Casa de Carmona (☎ 954 14 41 51; www.casadecarmona.com; Plaza de Lasso 1; r incl breakfast from €160; 🅿 🔊 🔊) The concept of luxury is taken to a whole new level in Casa de Carmona. This beautiful 16th-century palace once belonged to an aristocratic family and it feels as if they still live here: the rooms are furnished in an antique country manor style, the wooden beds are laid with soft white-lace pillows, the bathrooms have old-fashioned taps and stand alone baths and there isn't a lifeless room in the building to make you realise you're in a hotel. The reading area that comes with the suite has rugged carpets and slightly torn sofas. Heavy drapes let in rays of light from the tall bright windows. Everything exudes a sense of comfort and lazy learning, and the elegant library is stacked with books and magazines. The almost tropical-looking swimming pool has a matching sense of decadent beauty.

Mesón Sierra Mayor (☎ 954 14 44 04; Calle San Ildefonso 1; tapas €1.30-2.30) It's all about ham and piggies in this place where excellent tapas and *raciones* are served in a little patio inside the Museo de la Ciudad building. Ham and cheese from the hills of Huelva province are the specialities.

Restaurante San Fernando (☎ 954 14 35 56; Calle Sacramento 3; mains €12-15, menú €25; ⏱ 1.30-4pm Tue-Sun, 9pm-midnight Tue-Sat) The *menú* (set menu) at this classy restaurant overlooking Plaza de San Fernando offers a taste of five or so different dishes, perhaps beginning with cream of green apple soup followed by stuffed salmon pastries, then pears in red wine to finish. One or two other morsels are fitted in along the way.

Casa de Carmona (☎ 954 14 41 51; www.casadecarmona.com; Plaza de Lasso 1; mains €16-22, menú €24-48) This elegant hotel restaurant is famed for its quality haute cuisine with an Andalucian touch and its fine wine list.

Molino de la Romera (☎ 954 14 20 00; Calle Sor Ángela de la Cruz 8; 4-course menú incl 2 drinks €18; ⏱ closed Sun evening) Serves hearty, well-prepared Andalucian meals in an interesting 15th-century oil-mill building. It has a bar and café if you fancy something light and a lovely terrace overlooking the valley.

Parador Alcázar del Rey Don Pedro (☎ 954 14 10 10; www.parador.es; Alcázar s/n; menú €27) This parador's refectory-style dining room is one of the best in town. Try the speciality *espinacas de Carmona* (spicy spinach) or *cartuja de perdiz* (partridge and vegetables).

Getting There & Away

Casal (☎ 954 41 06 58) runs buses to Carmona from Seville's Prado de San Sebastián bus station (€2, 45 minutes, 20 a day Monday to Friday, 10 Saturday, seven Sunday). The stop in Carmona is on Paseo del Estatuto, 300m west of the Puerta de Sevilla. **Alsina Graells** (☎ 954 41 86 11) runs buses to Écija (€3.70, 45 minutes) and Córdoba (€7.50, two hours) at 8am and 2.30pm, from an empty lot outside Puerta de Sevilla.

There's around-the-clock underground parking on Paseo del Estatuto (three/six/10/24 hours for €2/4.50/7.50/12).

ÉCIJA

pop 38,900 / elevation 110m

Of the towns of La Campiña, Écija (*ess-i-ha*) is perhaps the most understated. An increase in visitors over recent years has resulted in a growing number of monuments and museums to visit, and a spruce-up campaign aimed at making the town centre progressively more attractive. The town's (sometimes still crumbling) Gothic-Mudéjar churches and imposing, baroque palaces are a treat for the eyes and a retreat from the sun. Écija is known both as *la ciudad de las torres* (the city of towers), for its many baroque church towers whose colourful tiles glitter in the sun, and as *la sartén de Andalucía* (the frying pan of Andalucía), for that same sun which beats cruelly down on the town, sometimes topping 50°C.

The town's reconstruction involves renovating one of the town's most beautiful buildings, Palacio de Peñaflor, and the main town square, Plaza de España, which, although a fascinating archaeological excavation site originally dug up for an underground car park, is a bit of a mess to look at. Écija owes most of its architectural splendours to the 18th century, when the local gentry, rich from wheat and oil production, splashed out on large mansions. The church towers were rebuilt after an earthquake in 1757. Écija's long and fascinating earlier history is still being dug up.

Écija lies 53km east along the A4 from Carmona.

Information

The helpful **tourist office** (☎ 955 90 29 33; www.ecija.es; Plaza de España 1; ⏱ 9.30am-3pm Mon-Fri, to 2pm Jul & Aug, 10.30am-1.30pm Sat, Sun & holidays) is in the front of the *ayuntamiento* on the central plaza. Its good tourist map will guide you around the sights.

Sights

Recent excavations in the central **Plaza de España** (also called El Salón) have yielded spectacular finds. When the plaza was dug up for an intended underground car park, its western half (nearest the *ayuntamiento*) turned out to be the site of a 9th- to 12th-century *makbara*, a Muslim cemetery with 4000 burials. At the eastern end were Roman baths with a swimming pool and a gymnasium stuffed with pieces of sculpture hidden there since the 3rd century AD. At the time of research, both the Roman baths and the Muslim cemetery were being further explored, before the area is eventually replaced by the car park.

The **ayuntamiento** (Plaza de España 1; ☉ 9.30am-3pm Mon-Fri Sep-Jun, 9.30am-2pm Jul & Aug, 10.30am-1.30pm Sat, Sun & holidays) boasts a fine Roman mosaic depicting the punishment of Queen Dirce, tied to the horns of a bull. To see it, ask at the tourist office: a staff member will accompany you and, when possible, show you the art treasures in the building's 19th-century Sala Capitular (Chapter House). Tourist office staff also run a **cámara oscura** (camera obscura; admission €2.50; ☉ 10.30am-1.30pm), which projects live, moving images of the town onto a screen – a uniquely complete panorama of Écija's wonderful spires, belfries and palaces and the main square below.

The famed **Iglesia de Santa María** (Plaza Santa María), just off Plaza de España, has one of Écija's finest church towers. A block south from Plaza de España along Calle Cintería, the handsome 18th-century Palacio de Benamejís houses the fascinating **Museo Histórico Municipal** (☎ 955 90 29 19; Plaza de la Constitución; admission free; ☉ 9am-2pm Tue-Sun Jun-Sep; 9.30am-1.30pm & 4.30-6.30pm Tue-Fri, 9am-2pm Sat, Sun & holidays Oct-May). Pride of place goes to the best finds of Roman sculpture from Plaza de España, including a full-sized sculpture of an Amazon (legendary female warrior), an athlete's torso and a white marble male head (possibly the god Mars). The rest of the museum has absorbing displays covering the full spectrum of Écija's history, including Iberian sculptures and Roman mosaics.

A couple of blocks east, Écija's most ubiquitous image is that of the huge 18th-century **Palacio de Peñaflor** (Calle Emilio Castelar 26; admission free; ☉ 9am-1.30pm Mon-Fri Jun-Sep, 10am-1pm & 4.30-7.30pm Mon-Fri, 11am-1pm Sat & Sun Oct-May) or 'the palace of the long balconies', which is thankfully up for a facelift. Its attractive, curved façade is lined with frescoes, and the balconies stretch above them. Enter to see the grand staircase and the pretty two-storey patio, which houses the town library and two exhibition rooms.

Across the street corner, the **Palacio de Valhermoso** has a lovely Renaissance façade. Turn down Calle Cadenas opposite the Palacio de Valhermoso and head for the elegant tower of the **Iglesia de San Gil** (Calle San Antonio). Just past this church, on the right, is the **Plaza de Armas**, where Écija's 12th-century Islamic Alcazaba (fortress), and,

below that, Roman and Tartessos levels, are being excavated. Fine Phoenician ceramics and the only known mosaic depicting the Roman god of the year, Annus, have been found here, and the site is projected to become an *in situ* museum.

Head back past the Palacio de Valhermoso to check out the towers of the **Iglesia de San Juan** (Plaza San Juan) and the **Convento de San Pablo y Santo Domingo** (Plazuela de Santo Domingo) – the latter hung with a gigantic set of rosary beads – en route to the **Parroquia Mayor de Santa Cruz** (Plazuela de Nuestra Señora del Valle; admission free; ☉ 9am-1pm & 6-9pm Mon-Sat, 10am-1pm & 6-9.30pm Sun Jun-Sep, 9am-1pm & 5-9pm Mon-Sat, 10am-1pm & 6-8pm Sun Oct-May). Santa Cruz is Écija's parish church but was once the town's principal mosque and still has traces of Islamic features and some Arabic inscriptions. Arches, fountains and patios from now-roofless parts of the building surround three sides with romantic effect. The main altar is a lovely 5th-century early Christian stone sarcophagus, carved with Greek script and the images of Abraham, Isaac, Christ the Good Shepherd and Daniel. Across the street is the 16th- to 18th-century **Palacio de los Palma** (☎ 955 90 20 82; Calle Espíritu Santo 10; admission €3; ☉ 10am-2pm), with a porticoed patio and richly decorated halls with Mudejar *artesonados*. From here it's just four blocks south back to Plaza de España.

Sleeping & Eating

Hostal Santiago (☎ 954 831 626; Av Del Genil 18; s/d €17/32) This was the only budget place in town during research, and is for budget emergencies only. Above a petrol station and a 15-minute walk from the centre, the Santiago is not as bad as it looks from the outside. The rooms are decent enough for a night's kip: clean, but plain and slightly depressing. As we said, budget emergencies only.

Hotel Platería (☎ 955 90 27 54; www.hotelplateria.net; Calle Platería 4; s/d €38/64; ❄) Just a block east of Plaza de España, this hotel offers excellent value. The 18 decent-sized vanilla-coloured rooms have spacious beds, and most look on to a pleasant central courtyard. The restaurant, open for all meals, does terrific food at good prices (menu of the day €7).

Hotel Palacio de los Granados (☎ 955 90 10 50; www.palaciogranados.com; Calle Emilio Castelar 42; r/ste

THE AMAZON OF ÉCIJA

Écija's superb marble figure of an Amazon (legendary female warrior) stands 2.11m high, still bearing traces of her original decorative red paint. Looking surprisingly unwarlike and carved with great delicacy, she is thought to have once stood in Rome with a handful of other Roman copies of the same 5th-century-BC Greek original. The original, by sculptor Policletus, adorned the Temple of Artemis at Ephesus (Turkey), one of the seven wonders of the ancient world. One of the Roman copies was, for some reason, brought to Colonia Augusta Firma Astigi (as Écija was then known) in the 1st century AD and then hidden, along with other prized sculptures, in the swimming pool of the town's forum baths in the 3rd century AD when early Christians were on a pagan-idol-smashing rampage. The pool turned out to be such a secure hiding place that the Écija Amazon did not see the light of day again until excited archaeologists scraped away the earth from the pool on 7 February 2002.

    Other copies of Policletus' original, unearthed in Rome in the 17th and 19th centuries, are in museums in Berlin, Copenhagen and New York.

incl breakfast €120/160; ☒ ☐ ☒) Écija's best choice is found along a lovely mansion-rich street. This 18th-century converted mansion is set around two patios and provides 11 palatial-style rooms and suites, all unique and designed by one of the hotel's owners with a fantastic mix of traditional and modern elements. Contemporary art decks many walls. Dinner is available on request, and the hotel can organise visits to Écija's archaeological digs, churches and horse-breeding centres.

    Las Ninfas (☎ 955 90 45 92; Calle Elvira; 3-course menú €9; ☒ closed Mon; ☒) Around the corner from the Museo Histórico Municipal and decorated with local art treasures, this welcoming restaurant offers excellent Andalucian and local specialities.

    Bisturí (☎ 954 83 10 66; Plaza de España 23; menú €10 & €15; ☒) Right on the central square, Bisturí has something for everyone, at reasonable prices. Eat out on the *terraza* (terrace) or in the air-conditioned interior restaurant.

    Bodegón del Gallego (☎ 954 83 26 18; Calle Arcipreste Juan Aparicio 3; mains €10-13) This busy, wood-beamed restaurant is the place for fine seafood.

Getting There & Away

Linesur (☎ 954 83 02 39) operates up to 11 buses daily to/from Seville (Prado de San Sebastián; €6, 1¼ hours). Alsina Graells has three or more buses to Córdoba (€4, 1¼ hours), and one to Carmona (€4, 45 minutes). The bus stop is by the football ground on Avenida de Andalucía, six blocks south of Plaza de España.

OSUNA

pop 17,430 / elevation 330m

Osuna is the loveliest of La Campiña's towns, with beautifully preserved baroque mansions and an impressive Spanish Renaissance monastery. Several of the town's most impressive mansions were created by the ducal family of Osuna, one of Spain's richest since the 16th century, and the family whose name the town now carries.

    It is 91km southeast of Seville, along the Granada–Seville A92.

Information

On the central Plaza Mayor, the **Oficina Municipal de Turismo** (☎ 954 81 57 32; www.ayto-osuna.es; ☒ 9am-2pm Mon-Sat) and the **Asociación Turístico Cultural Ossuna** (☎ 954 81 28 52; ☒ 10am-2pm & 5-8pm Mon-Fri, 10am-2pm Sat & Sun) provide tourist information and hand out useful guides detailing the town's monuments in various languages. The Asociación Turístico can also provide English-, French- or Spanish-speaking guides costing €50/100 per half-/full day.

Sights

Calle Carrera, north from the central Plaza Mayor, is the street where most of the hotels are situated. The museum, monastery, church and university are all in a cluster just east off Plaza Mayor, up a steep hill. The area west of Plaza Mayor, which is a triangle of Calle Carrera, Alfonso XII and Carretería Antequera, is sprinkled with mansions and churches and cut up by lovely little streets and passages, and divided by Calle Sevilla, which leads west off Plaza Mayor. The bus station is southeast of the main square, on Avenida de la Constitución.

PLAZA MAYOR

The leafy square has the partly modernised 16th-century **ayuntamiento** on one side, a large **market building** on the other, and the 16th-century church of the **Convento de la Concepción** at the end. Sit down and eat *pipas* (seeds) with the Osunans, on one of the square's benches.

BAROQUE MANSIONS

You can't go inside most of Osuna's mansions, but their façades are still mesmerising. One is the **Palacio de los Cepeda** (Calle de la Huerta), behind the town hall, with rows of Churrigueresque columns topped by stone halberdiers holding the Cepeda family coat of arms. It now serves as a courthouse. The 1737 portal of the **Palacio de Puente Hermoso** (Palacio de Govantes y Herdara; Calle Sevilla 44), a couple of blocks west of Plaza Mayor, has twisted pillars encrusted with grapes and vine leaves.

Moving north from Plaza Mayor up Calle Carrera, you pass the **Iglesia de Santo Domingo** (1531) before you reach the corner of Calle San Pedro. The **Cilla del Cabildo Colegial** (Calle San Pedro 16) bears a sculpted representation of Seville's Giralda, flanked by the Sevillan martyrs Santa Justa and Santa Rufina. Further down, the **Palacio del Marqués de La Gomera** (Calle San Pedro 20) has elaborate clustered pillars, with the family shield at the top of the façade. This is now a hotel (see opposite) – step inside for a drink.

MUSEO ARQUEOLÓGICO

The Torre del Agua, a 12th-century Almohad tower, just east and uphill from Plaza Mayor, houses Osuna's **Museo Arqueológico** (Archaeological Museum; ☎ 954 81 12 07; Plaza de la Duquesa; admission €1.50; 11.30am-1.30pm & 4.30-6.30pm Tue-Sun Oct-Apr, 11.30am-1.30pm & 5-7pm Tue-Sun May-Sep, closed Sun afternoon Jul & Aug). The collection of mainly Iberian and Roman artefacts found in the vicinity is well worth seeing: it includes copies of the celebrated Iberian Toro de Osuna (Osuna bull) and the Roman Osuna bronzes, whose originals are housed in the Louvre in Paris and Spain's national archaeological museum in Madrid.

COLEGIATA & AROUND

Osuna's most impressive monuments overlook the centre from the hill above the Museo Arqueológico. The **Colegiata de Santa María de la Asunción** (☎ 954 81 04 44; Plaza de la Encarnación; admission by guided tour only €2; 10am-1.30pm & 3.30-6.30pm Tue-Sun Oct-Apr, 10am-1.30pm & 4-7pm Tue-Sun May-Sep, closed Sun afternoon Jul & Aug), a large 16th-century former collegiate church, contains a wealth of fine art collected by the Duques de Osuna, descendants of its founder, Juan Téllez Girón, the Conde de Ureña.

In the main body of the church are José de Ribera's *Cristo de la Expiración,* a marvellous example of this 17th-century painter's use of contrast; an elaborate baroque main retable; a contrasting 14th-century retable in the Capilla de la Virgen de los Reyes; and, in the Capilla de la Inmaculada, a Crucifixion sculpture of 1623 by Juan de Mesa. The church's sacristy contains four more Riberas. The tour also includes the lugubrious underground Sepulcro Ducal, created in 1548 with its own chapel as the family vault of the Osunas, who are entombed in wall niches.

Opposite the Colegiata is the **Monasterio de la Encarnación** (☎ 954 81 11 21; Plaza de la Encarnación; admission €2; same as Colegiata), now Osuna's museum of religious art and well worth a visit. The 18th-century tiles in the cloister, representing the five senses, the seasons, the Alameda de Hércules in Seville and diverse biblical, hunting, bullfighting and monastic scenes, are among the most beautiful of all Sevillan tilework, and the monastery church is richly decked with baroque sculpture and art. One upstairs room has a cute collection of 18th-century child Christs.

On the hill top just above the Colegiata is the **Universidad de Osuna**, a square building with pointed towers and a stately Renaissance patio, founded in 1548 by the Conde de Ureña to help combat Protestantism. It's now an outpost of Seville University, providing courses in nursing and business studies. Down behind the Monasterio de la Encarnación, the 17th-century **Iglesia de la Merced** (Cuesta Marruecos) has a lovely baroque tower and portal.

Sleeping & Eating

Hostal 5 Puertas (☎ 954 81 12 43; Calle Carrera 79; s/d €25/40;) The 14 smallish but decent rooms here have TV, phone and heating. Some are let to university students.

Hostal Esmeralda (☎ 955 82 10 73; www.hostal -esmeralda.com; Calle Tesorero 7; s/d 25.50/42; ✖ 🖵) Clean, friendly and family-run, the Esme- ralda is about 200m south of Plaza Mayor. Rooms are simple and reasonably sized, with TV, and open on to tiled passageways off a small sky-lit patio.

Hostal Caballo Blanco (☎ 954 81 01 84; Calle Gra- nada 1; s/d €30/50; 🅿 ✖) An old coaching inn on the corner of Calle Carrera, 350m north of Plaza Mayor, the friendly 'White Horse Inn' has courtyard parking and 13 comfy rooms in deep red or blue, with reading lamps and tasteful prints. There's a restau- rant here too (open Monday to Saturday).

Hotel Palacio Marqués de la Gomera (☎ 954 81 22 23; www.hotelpalaciodelmarques.com; Calle San Pedro 20; s/d €77/96; 🅿 ✖ 🖵) An excellent oppor- tunity to stay in one of Osuna's finest ba- roque mansions. The gorgeous *casa palacio* has its own chapel, so you can get down to praising the Lord before breakfast, and the religious imagery is hauntingly present throughout the building. There are 20 large, lovely and varied rooms and suites around a beautiful, arcaded, two-storey central patio. Its elegant restaurant, **La Casa del Marqués** (mains €9-18), provides a tempting Andalucian and Spanish menu, while its **Asador de Osuna** grill specialises in charcoal-grilled meats.

Restaurante Doña Guadalupe (☎ 954 81 05 58; Plaza Guadalupe 6; 4-course menú €12.30, mains €11-16; ⏲ closed Tue & 1-15 Aug; ✖) On a small square between Calles Quijada and Gordillo (both off Calle Carrera), Doña Guadalupe serves up quality Andalucian fare from partridge with rice to wild asparagus casserole. There's a good list of Spanish wines too.

El Mesón del Duque (☎ 954 81 28 45; Plaza de la Duquesa 2; raciones €8-11) Enjoy well-prepared Andalucian dishes on the quiet terrace op- posite the Museo Arqueológico, with views up to the Colegiata.

Getting There & Away

The **bus station** (☎ 954 81 01 46; Avenida de la Con- stitución) is 500m southeast of Plaza Mayor. Up to 11 daily buses run to/from Seville (Prado de San Sebastián; €6.50, 1¼ hours). Four daily buses go to Fuente de Piedra (€4.50, 45 minutes) and Antequera (€5, 1¼ hours), and two each to Málaga (€8, 2½ hours) and Granada (€11.50, 3¼ hours).

Six trains a day run to/from Seville (€6 to €6.50, one hour) and three each to/from Antequera (€5.50, one hour), Granada (€12, 2½ hours) and Málaga (€8, 1½ hours): the **train station** (Avenida de la Estación) is 1km south- west of the centre.

PARQUE NATURAL SIERRA NORTE

This 1648-sq-km natural park, stretching across the north of Sevilla province, is beautiful, rolling, often wild Sierra Morena country. It's an ever-changing landscape of green valleys and hills, woodlands, rivers and atmospheric old towns and villages with Islamic-era forts or castles, part-Mudejar churches and narrow, zig-zagging white streets. It's a nature lover's delight that, so far, has been discovered by few foreigners. The spring wildflowers are among the most beautiful you'll see in Andalucía and you'll have a chance to spot bulls grazing, as well as the cute dark *cerdo ibérico* pigs that end up as all that delicious *jamón*.

At least 14 walks of a few hours each are signposted in various areas. The routes are shown on the IGN/Junta de Andalucía 1:100,000 map *Parque Natural Sierra Norte*, and described in Spanish in the booklet *Cuaderno de Senderos*, available at the Cen- tro de Interpretación El Robledo visitors centre (p142).

The two main towns, Cazalla de la Sierra and Constantina, lie 20km apart at the cen- tre of the park.

GETTING THERE & AROUND
Bus
Linesur (☎ 954 98 82 20) runs buses from Se- ville's Plaza de Armas three times daily (twice on Saturday and Sunday) to Cazalla de la Sierra (€6, 1¾ to 2¼ hours) and Gua- dalcanal (€7.50, 2¾ hours), and three to six times daily to El Pedroso (€5, 1¼ hours) and Constantina (€5, 1¾ hours).

Train
Cazalla y Constantina station is on the A455 Cazalla–Constantina road, 7km from Ca- zalla, 12km from Constantina. Three trains daily rattle to/from Seville (€5, 1¾ hours). All stop at El Pedroso en route and continue

to/from Guadalcanal, and one goes to/from Zafra, Mérida and Cáceres in Extremadura. The 4.30pm train from Seville arrives at Cazalla y Constantina station at 6.22pm – in time to catch the Constantina–Cazalla bus that passes the station at about 7.30pm Monday to Friday – but you should confirm current schedules.

EL PEDROSO

pop 2290 / elevation 415m

A pleasant village of broad cobbled streets, El Pedroso lies 16km south of Cazalla de la Sierra on the A432 from Seville. The 15th-century **Iglesia de Nuestra Señora de la Consolación** in the village centre contains a 1608 *Inmaculada* by the great sculptor Juan Martínez Montañés (in the chapel to the right in front of the main altar). The **Sendero del Arroyo de las Cañas**, a 10km marked walking route around the flattish country west of El Pedroso, beginning opposite Bar Triana on the western side of town, is one of the prettiest walks in the park. It goes through a landscape strewn with boulders and, in spring, gorgeous wild flowers.

The eight-room **Hotel Casa Montehuéznar** (☎ 954 88 90 00; www.montehueznar.com; Avenida de la Estación 15; s/d incl breakfast €35/55; 🖭) provides comfortable rooms with attractive wooden furnishings, around the upper floor of a pretty patio. The hotel is in the street leading up towards the village centre (500m away) opposite the train station. Its good restaurant is normally only open Friday to Sunday; at other times **Bar-Restaurante Serranía** (☎ 954 88 96 03; Avenida de la Estación 30; platos combinados €5-8), at the bottom of the street, is a reasonable fallback.

Restaurante Los Álamos (☎ 954 88 96 11; Carretera Cantillana Km 29.5; meat raciones €6), on the A432 just south of El Pedroso, makes a good lunch stop. You can dine al fresco on a large veranda looking out over a garden with lots of birds. Meats are a speciality and the *queso Manchego* (Manchego cheese) is superb.

CAZALLA DE LA SIERRA

pop 5000 / elevation 600m

This attractive little white town, spread around a hill top 85km northeast of Seville, has a great little selection of places to stay and pleasant walks in the woods. The

site of an Islamic castle, it was conquered by Fernando III in 1247. In the 16th and 17th centuries Cazalla was celebrated for its wines and brandies, which were exported to the Americas.

Information

The new **tourist office** (☎ 954 883 562; 🕑 8am-5pm) is on Plaza Mayor, next to the Iglesia de la Consolación. Tourist information is also available at the **ayuntamiento** (☎ 954 88 42 36; Plaza Doctor Nosea s/n; 🕑 8am-3pm Mon-Fri). There are plenty of banks with ATMs on the central pedestrianised street, Calle La Plazuela, and nearby on Calle Llana, the main road passing through town.

Sights

The outstanding building in Cazalla's tangle of old-fashioned streets is the fortresslike **Iglesia de Nuestra Señora de la Consolación** (Plaza Mayor; 🕑 Mass 7.30pm Tue-Sat, noon Sun), a mainly 14th- and 15th-century construction in the region's typical red brick and yellow stone. Badly damaged in the civil war, it's actually more impressive outside than inside.

La Cartuja de Cazalla (☎ 954 88 45 16; adult/child €3/1; 🕑 9am-2pm & 4-8pm) is a large 15th-century monastery in a beautiful, secluded nook of the Sierra Morena, 4km from Cazalla (take the signposted turn-off from the A455 Constantina road, 2.5km from Cazalla). Built on the site of an Islamic mill and mosque, the monastery fell into ruin in the 19th century. In 1977 it was bought by art lover Carmen Ladrón de Guevara, who is devotedly restoring it, in part as an arts centre (it has a ceramics' workshop and art gallery) and the restored church functions as a concert hall. A good guesthouse is part of the project.

Activities

WALKING

Two tracks lead from Cazalla down to the Huéznar Valley and by combining them you can enjoy a round trip of 9km. They pass through typical Sierra Norte evergreen oak woodlands, olive groves and small cultivated plots, plus the odd chestnut wood and vineyard.

One track is the **Sendero de las Laderas**, which starts at El Chorrillo fountain on the eastern edge of Cazalla at the foot of

Calle Parras. A 'Sendero Las Laderas 900m' sign on Paseo El Moro, just down from the Posada del Moro, directs you to this starting point. The path leads down to the Puente de los Tres Ojos bridge on the Río Huéznar, from where you go up the western bank of the river a short way, then head west under the Puente del Castillejo railway bridge (first take a break at the picnic area on the far bank, if you like) and return to Cazalla by the **Camino Viejo de la Estación** (Old Station Track). You can also join this walk from Cazalla y Constantina station by following the 'Molino del Corcho' track down the Huéznar for 1km to the Puente del Castillejo.

HORSE RIDING

Experienced local horseman Ángel Conde runs the recommended stables **Cuadras Al Paso** (☎ 689-944451; Plaza JM López-Cepero 3; per hr/day/week €18/100/600) with home-bred mounts that are a mix of Andalucian, Arab and English thoroughbreds.

Courses

Turismo Rural Hidalgo (☎/fax 954 88 35 81; www .turismoruralhidalgo.com; Calle Virgen del Monte 19; courses incl hostal accommodation per week €260-310), run by a Dutch couple resident in Cazalla, organises an almost year-round programme of one to three week workshop courses in flamenco dance and guitar, *sevillana* dance, painting, ceramics, Andalucian cooking and Spanish language, including some courses for kids.

Sleeping & Eating

Posada del Moro (☎/fax 954 88 48 58; www.laposada delmoro.com; Paseo El Moro s/n; s/d incl breakfast €40/60; 🖫 🕿) Decorated as an improvised tribute to Andalucía's Islamic past with a Moroccan-style interior. A long and narrow fountain in the large garden has a cool swimming pool, and plays host to Moroccan-themed parties. The rooms are spacious, large and comfortable, with red marble floors, pretty cork-topped furnishings, and views of the garden. The restaurant (mains €10 to €15) cooks up local specialities such as wild asparagus and assorted game.

Hospedería de la Cartuja (☎ 954 88 45 16; www .cartujadecazalla.com; s/d incl breakfast €60/95, dinner €22; 🅿 🖫 🕿) The guesthouse at the beautiful Cartuja de Cazalla (opposite) has eight modern rooms hung with work by former resident artists, plus suites and a small house for families. There are two inviting pools, and riding stables on site (ride/class per hour €20/15). Much of the fare at the excellent dinner table, in the monastery's old pilgrims' hostel, is home-grown. Room rates go down if you stay longer than one night.

Palacio de San Benito (☎ 954 88 33 36; www.pala ciodesanbenito.com; Paseo El Moro; r €139-235; 🅿 🖫) This luxurious, antique-filled boutique hotel occupies what was a 15th-century hermitage and pilgrims' hostel and still includes a Mudejar church. All 10 ultra-comfortable rooms are completely different. The restaurant (mains €14 to €20), open to all, serves all meals, with an emphasis on country specialities such as venison, partridge and salmon.

Other options:

Hostal Castro Martínez (☎ 954 88 40 39; Calle Virgen del Monte 36; r €29-35; 🖫) Gloomy budget accommodation in the town centre; it can be noisy.

THE AUTHOR'S CHOICE

Las Navezuelas (☎ 954 88 47 64; www.lasnavezuelas.com; s/d incl breakfast €46/64, 4-person apt €118; 🕑 closed early Jan-late Feb; 🅿 🕿) In the 16th century, this *cortijo* (farm) housed tired workers who'd spent all day toiling at the olive-oil mill. Now, this gorgeous farmhouse, sitting on a hill that overlooks meadows and trees, accommodates tired tourists who've spent all day walking the surrounding hills. The Italian host, Luca, turned the old *cortijo* into this simple, stylish place to stay over 20 years. The rooms and apartments are tasteful and rustic, there are several common areas with open fireplaces for the winter and a large pool for scorching summer days. Excellent meals are based on home-grown produce. Good walks start right here and your friendly host can set up great bird-watching, horse riding and other activities. Altogether this is one of the best places to stay in Andalucía. From Cazalla, go 2km south towards Seville, then 1km east down a dirt road (signposted).

Shopping

Buy Cazalla's celebrated *anisados* (aniseed-based liqueurs), at the handicrafts shop **La Artesa** (Calle La Plazuela 1) or **La Destilería** (Calle Llana 1). The *guinda* (wild cherry) variety is a rich, heart-warming concoction.

HUÉZNAR VALLEY

The Río Huéznar (or Huesna) runs north–south through the countryside about halfway between Cazalla de la Sierra and Constantina. The A455 Cazalla–Constantina road crosses the river just east of the Cazalla y Constantina train station. A 1km drivable track leads downstream from here to the Puente del Castillejo railway bridge and the Área Recreativa Molino del Corcho (p140). Upstream, the river is paralleled by the SE168 road, which runs 13km to the village of San Nicolás del Puerto. The **Isla Margarita picnic area** is about 1km up the river from the station. From Isla Margarita a walking path leads up the eastern side of the river all the way to San Nicolás del Puerto: after about 4km it meets the course of a disused railway running to San Nicolás and the old mines of Cerro del Hierro – you can walk along this instead of the path, if you like. Two kilometres before San Nicolás are the **Cascadas del Huesna**, a series of powerful waterfalls on the river.

There are three camping grounds along this stretch of the river:

Camping Batán de las Monjas (☎ 955 88 65 48; Carretera SE168 Km 7; camping per person/tent/car €3/3/2.50; P) A 20-tent farm site east of the river; access by 1km vehicle track from the SE168, fording the river.

Área de Acampada El Martinete (☎ 955 88 65 83; Carretera SE168 Km 12; camping per person/tent/car €3/3.50/free; P) Shady site 2km from San Nicolás; short paths lead to the Cascadas del Huesna and the good Restaurante El Martinete (*raciones* €7).

Camping La Fundición (☎ 955 95 41 17; Carretera SE168 Km 2; camping per person/tent/car €3.50/2.50/1.50; P 🛇) Large, shady site on the river's western bank, 1km up from Isla Margarita, with a restaurant, pool and bar.

CONSTANTINA

pop 7000 / elevation 555m

Constantina is the 'capital' of the Sierra Norte and really feels like a mountain town, where, unless you're a nature lover, there isn't much to see or do. The Parque Natural Sierra Norte's visitors centre, the **Centro de Interpretación El Robledo** (☎ 955 88 15 97; Carretera Constantina-El Pedroso Km 1; 🕑 10am-2pm Tue-Thu & Sun, 6-8pm Fri, 10am-2pm & 6-8pm Sat Oct-Jun, 11am-1pm Tue & Thu, 6-8pm Fri, 10am-2pm & 6-8pm Sat & Sun Jul-Sep, closed 1 & 6 Jan, extra hr some holidays) is located 1km west along the A452 El Pedroso road from the southern end of Constantina. It has interesting displays on the park's flora, fauna and history, and a clearly labelled

---

DETOUR: LA CAPITANA

If you're heading north into Extremadura, or just fancy a day out from Cazalla or Constantina, don't miss the magnificent vistas from the highest point in Sevilla province, La Capitana (959m).

Head north on the A432 from Cazalla or the SE163 from Constantina, pass Alanís and continue 11km along the A432 to Guadalcanal. At a junction as you enter this village, follow the 'Sendero de la Capitana' sign pointing to the right up a bypass road. After 1.5km, above the village, turn left down a minor road, then almost immediately right up an unpaved road with another 'Sendero de la Capitana' sign. Though signposted as a *sendero* (footpath) this is perfectly drivable, with a little care, in a car of normal clearance. Follow the track as it climbs in a general northwest direction along the Sierra del Viento (Windy Range), taking the major track at all forks. Expansive views open out as you pass an observatory on the left after 1.6km and TV towers up on the right after 2.1km and 4.3km. Keep your eyes open for vultures and birds of prey roaming the updraughts along this very breezy ridge. Some 500m after passing below the second TV tower, you pass through a gate: just beyond it, park and follow the 'Mirador de la Sierra del Viento 300m' sign to the hilltop ahead of you. This is the summit of La Capitana, where the views in every direction are limited only by atmospheric conditions. To the south extend the many ranges of the Sierra Norte, to the north the endless plains of Extremadura. If you're lucky you'll have the entire hill to yourself and the only sounds you'll hear will be wind, birds and the bleating of sheep.

Return the way you came.

botanical garden of Andalucian plants that is a picture in spring and well worth a 20- to 30-minute wander. Also in the garden are a few enclosures with birds of prey that are unfit to be returned to the wild.

Buses stop at **Bar Gregorio** (☎ 955 88 10 43; Calle El Peso 9) in the town centre. There are several banks with ATMs on the pedestrianised main street, Calle Mesones.

Sights & Activities

The western side of Constantina is topped by a ruined Almoravid-era **Islamic fort** – worth the climb for the views alone. Below are the medieval streets and 18th-century mansions of the **Barrio de la Morería** district. The **Iglesia de Santa María de la Encarnación** (Plaza Llano del Sol), in the centre, is a Mudejar church with a 16th-century plateresque portal and a belfry (popular with nesting storks) that was added in 1567 by Hernán Ruiz, who also did the one atop the Giralda in Seville.

The **Sendero Los Castañares**, a 7km marked walk, starts from the north end of Paseo de la Alameda in the north of town. It takes you up through thick chestnut woods to a hilltop viewpoint, then back into Constantina below the fort (about two hours, total).

Sleeping & Eating

Hotel San Blas (☎ 955 88 00 77; www.fp-hoteles.com; Calle Miraflores 4; s/d €46/64 Aug, Semana Santa & Sat all year, €33/48 other times; ❄ ☒) Though pale and uninteresting, the large, decent rooms at this friendly hotel have big bathrooms and either look out towards the castle or to the pool area. It's 200m off the main road from Cazalla and is clearly signposted.

Hotel Casa Rural Las Erillas (☎ 955 88 17 90; http://laserillas.com; s/d incl breakfast €60/80; P ☒) A small family venture about 500m along the Sendero Los Castañares, this is a collection of comfortable farmhouse lodgings in lovely gardens, with a pool. Good meals are available and made with plenty of local produce.

Bodeguita Tomás (Calle El Peso 1; tapas/media-raciones €2/3.50) Come here, next to the bus stop, for tempting tapas of venison or fried potatoes and Roquefort.

Mesón de la Abuela Carmen (☎ 955 88 00 95; Paseo de la Alameda 39; raciones €7-11; ⏰ 9.30am-late Tue-Sun) Locals flock to this large, barnlike eating hall near the northern end of town for its succulent grilled meats; salads and some seafood dishes provide options for noncarnivores.

Huelva Province

Out on a limb at Andalucía's far western extremity, Huelva draws few travellers who are not en route to or from Portugal, except for those drawn to the famous Doñana national park with its vast wetlands and celebrated wildlife. But turn off the Algarve-bound motorway and you will find a land of many and surprising pleasures.

Huelva's coast – the western end of the Costa de la Luz (Coast of Light) – is an almost unbroken 110km stretch of broad, Atlantic sand, interrupted here and there by estuaries and coastal wetlands, Doñana's pre-eminent among them, that provide endless fascination for nature lovers. The coast's human settlements range from appealing ports-cum-local-resorts such as Isla Cristina and Punta Umbría to unabashedly industrial Huelva itself – interspersed with, it has to be said, an amount of uninspired, throw-it-up-quick touristic development.

North of the coastal strip, you move into a thinly populated rural zone of sleepy villages and occasionally bustling market towns. The millennia-old, moonlike mining zone around Minas de Riotinto boasts a set of excellent visitor attractions that really bring its past to life, from Phoenician times to the enormous British-run enterprise of the 19th and 20th centuries.

Far northern Huelva is beautiful, verdant, rolling Sierra Morena country and is the province's most glittering secret. Dozens of timeless stone villages are connected by ancient paths winding along river valleys and through emerald woodlands – a walker's and rider's dreamland that's only beginning to be discovered.

HIGHLIGHTS

- Wind your way along the woodland paths among the ageless villages of the **Sierra de Aracena** (p167), west of Aracena

- Discover the wildlife and vast wetlands of the **Parque Nacional de Doñana** (p154)

- Walk in Columbus' footsteps at the **Lugares Colombinos** (p149)

- Expose yourself to the elements and down plates of fresh seafood along the great Atlantic beaches of the **Costa de la Luz** (p152 and p158)

- Live millennia of unique mining history at **Minas de Riotinto** (p162)

| POPULATION: 484, 000 | HUELVA AV DAILY HIGH: JAN/AUG 12°C/24°C | ALTITUDE RANGE: 0M–960M |

HUELVA

pop 145,000

The capital of Huelva is a modern, unsentimental, industrial port city set between the Odiel and Tinto estuaries. Despite its unpromising approaches, central Huelva is a likable, lively place and the city's people are noted for their warmth. Though there's little evidence of it today, Huelva's history dates back an impressive 3000 years to the Phoenician town of Onuba, whose river-mouth location made it a natural base for the export of inland minerals to the Mediterranean. Onuba is one of several locations postulated for the legendary Tartessos (see p24), and was later developed by the Romans. Huelva was devastated by the 1755 Lisbon earthquake, but later grew rapidly as a port and commercial and administrative centre after the British Rio Tinto Company developed the mines in the province's interior in the 1870s. Today Huelva has a sizable fishing fleet, and a heavy dose of petrochemical industry, unignorable on the southeastern approaches.

ORIENTATION

Huelva's central area is about 1km square, with the main bus station on Calle Doctor Rubio at its western edge, and the train station on Avenida de Italia at its southern edge. The main street is Avenida Martín Alonso Pinzón (also called Gran Vía). Parallel to Avenida Pinzón, one block south, is a long, narrow, pedestrianised shopping street that runs through several names, from Calle Concepción to Calle Berdigón.

INFORMATION

There are banks and ATMs all over the town centre. The bus and train stations have ATMs, too.

Ciber@lameda (Calle Luis Braille s/n; Internet per hr €1.30; ☒ 10am-2pm & 5-9pm Mon-Sat, 5-9pm Sun)

English Bookshop (☎ 959 28 10 94; Calle San Cristóbal 11; ☒ 10am-1.30pm & 5.15-8.15pm Mon-Fri, 10am-1.30pm Sat) Sells bestselling fiction, guides and children's books.

Hospital Juan Ramón Jiménez (☎ 959 01 60 00; Ronda Exterior Norte) The main general hospital, 4km north of the centre.

Medical emergency (☎ 959 49 40 09)

Municipal Tourist Information Kiosk (☎ 959 25 12 18; Plaza de las Monjas; ☒ 10am-2.30pm & 3.30-8.30pm Mon-Fri, 10am-2pm & 4.30-6.30pm Sat)

Policía Local (Local Police; ☎ 959 21 02 21; Plaza de la Constitución 1) In the *ayuntamiento* (city hall).

Post office (Avenida Tomás Domínguez 1; ☒ 8.30am-8.30pm Mon-Fri, 9.30am-2pm Sat)

Regional Tourist Office (☎ 959 65 02 00/02; othuelva@andalucia.org; Plaza Alcalde Coto Mora 2; ☒ 9am-7.30pm Mon-Fri, 10am-2pm Sat & Sun) Well informed and helpful.

DANGERS & ANNOYANCES

Like most port cities Huelva can seem rough and ready at times, but most people are open and very friendly. There are a few dodgy characters around, however, so take care of belongings wherever you go and leave nothing in parked cars.

SIGHTS

Despite its historical importance, Huelva's sights today are few. The well-displayed main museum, the **Museo Provincial** (☎ 959 25 93 00; Alameda Sundheim 13; admission free; ☒ 2.30-8.30pm Tue, 9am-8.30pm Wed-Sat, 9am-2.30pm Sun), concentrates on the province's archaeological pedigree, especially its mining history (see p162). Pride of place goes to a huge Roman water wheel that was used to extract water from mines near Minas de Riotinto. You'll also see a reconstructed gold-and-wood Phoenician funeral cart. Labelling is in Spanish.

An odd legacy of the area's mining history is the **Muelle Río Tinto**, an impressive iron pier curving out into the Odiel estuary about 500m south of the port. It was built for the Rio Tinto Company in the 1870s by George Barclay Bruce, a British disciple of tower specialist Gustave Eiffel.

Two kilometres north of the city centre, off Avenida de Manuel Siurot, is the **Santuario de Nuestra Señora de la Cinta** (☎ 959 15 51 22; admission free; ☒ 9am-1pm & 4-7pm), a chapel where Columbus is believed to have prayed after returning from his momentous 1492 voyage. The event is portrayed in tiles by artist Daniel Zuloaga and the chapel's hilltop position affords good views over the Odiel estuary and the wetlands to the west. City bus 6 (€0.80) goes there from outside the main bus station.

FESTIVALS & EVENTS

From 29 July to 3 August each year, Huelva celebrates Columbus' departure for the Americas (3 August 1492) with its **Fiestas Colombinas**, six days of music, dancing, funfairs, cultural events and bullfighting.

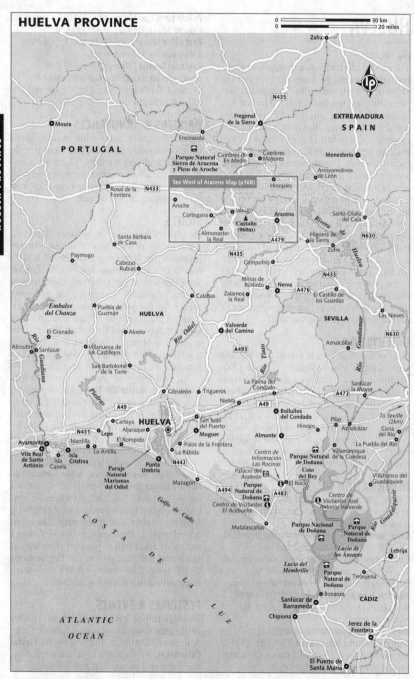

HUELVA PROVINCE

| 0 | 30 km |
| 0 | 20 miles |

See West of Aracena Map (p168)

HUELVA PROVINCE

SLEEPING

Huelva has a limited range of accommodation and a lot of it caters for the business crowd.

Instalación Juvenil de Huelva (☎ 959 65 00 10; www.inturjoven.com; Avenida Marchena Colombo 14; per person incl breakfast under 26yr €13-15, over 26yr €17-19; ☒) A modern youth hostel with a good standard of accommodation: rooms hold two to four and all have a bathroom. It's 2km north of the bus station: city bus 6 (€0.80) from outside the main bus station stops just around the corner, on Calle JS Elcano.

Hotel Costa de la Luz (☎ /fax 959 25 64 22; Calle José María Amo 8; s/d €28/50; ☒) Despite its proximity to the fish market, the Costa de la Luz is reasonable and comfortable. Obviously decorated in the '70s, the hotel remains locked in a furnishings time warp.

Hotel Los Condes (☎ 959 28 24 00; www.hotel loscondes.com in Spanish; Alameda Sundheim 14; s/d incl breakfast €40/59; ☒ ☒ ☒) Almost next door to the luxury NH Luz Huelva, Los Condes has 54 air-conditioned rooms at about half the price. They're large, bright and modern, with big gleaming bathrooms. Together with the friendly reception, free internet and a reasonable restaurant, this makes the best value in town.

NH Luz Huelva (☎ 959 25 00 11; www.nh-hotels .com; Alameda Sundheim 26; s/d €100/105; ☒ ☒ ☒) This is the best hotel Huelva has to offer, with attractive, very comfy rooms in an ugly building with concrete, scallop-shaped balconies. Breakfast (only) is available. It's worth checking the website for discount offers, and ring ahead to book a parking spot.

Hotel Tartessos (☎ 959 28 27 11; www.hotel-tart essos.com in Spanish; Avenida Martín Alonso Pinzón 13; s/d €106/116; ☒ ☒ ☒) This large, modern hotel has 100 rooms with all the comforts a business traveller expects, plus two restaurants and a piano bar. Rates drop to €63/74 from October to June.

EATING

Restaurants and tapas bars cluster along and near Avenida Martín Alonso Pinzón, Avenida Pablo Rada and the streets south of the cathedral.

Taberna El Condado (☎ 959 26 11 23; Calle Sor Ángela de la Cruz 3; tapas €1.50, raciones €10-15; ☒ closed Sun) An atmospheric tapas bar of just two small rooms dominated by a ham-heavy bar, specialising in tasty local meats. Directors' chairs and tables out on the pedestrianised street are great for a quiet evening beer watching the world go by.

Diez Barriles (Calle Jesús de la Pasión s/n; tapas €2; ☒ 1pm-11pm or midnight) This popular uptown tapas bar is large, shiny and modernistically minimalist in design, but traditional meats and seafood remain the stocks in trade.

Pastelería Dioni (☎ 959 24 06 32; Calle Palacios 3; drink & snack €2-3; ☒ 9am-9pm Mon-Sat, 10am-9pm Sun) A glittering bakery with an English-style tearoom upstairs, Dioni is great to drop into for tea or coffee and a mouthwatering array of cakes, pastries and sandwiches from its laden counters.

Trattoria Fuentevieja (Avenida Martín Alonso Pinzón s/n; mains €6-11; ☒ closed Sun evening) This slightly refined and very popular Italian spot serves a good range of salads as well as pizza, pasta and meat dishes, with touches of vaguely classical art amid the tasteful sky-blue-and-lemon decor.

Las Candelas (☎ 959 31 84 33; Avenida Huelva s/n, Aljaraque; mains €10-15; ☒ closed Sun) Huelva's most renowned restaurant is 7km west of the city in Aljaraque. It specialises in delicious fresh fish and *carnes a la brasa* (chargrilled meats), in a traditional inn setting. Turn off the A497 Punta Umbría road at the Aljaraque sign and you'll see the restaurant as you enter the town.

Also recommended:

La Casa de la Patata (☎ 959 28 25 75; Calle Ginés Martín s/n; baked potatoes €1.30-3.50; ☒ closed Sun) Neat uptown diner serving up steaming and satisfying baked potatoes.

Don Camillo e Peppone Aragón (☎ 959 28 01 59; Calle Aragón 43; pasta & pizza €5-7; ☒ closed Tue); Peral (☎ 959 28 18 06; Calle Isaac Peral 3; pasta & pizza €5-7; ☒ closed Wed) Prepares authentic and tasty pizzas and pasta. Both branches get very busy at weekends.

Restaurante La Caña (☎ 959 54 16 75; Calle Garcí Fernández 5; mains €10-18; ☒ closed Sun evening & Mon) A classy place that's particularly good on fish, but there's plenty of meat choice too.

DRINKING

After 9pm tapas bars such as Taberna El Condado and Diez Barriles (see left) get quite lively. Later, crowds flock to the bars and terraces lining Avenida Pablo Rada and the student bars south of Plaza de la

Merced, which get going around 11pm or midnight and include **Moe's** (Calle Aragón), a shrine to the Simpsons, the publike **Donington Bar** (Calle Aragón), **Pub Tumi** (Calle Jacobo del Barco 4), good for a game of pool, the spookily decorated **Templo** (Calle Jacobo del Barco) and the bare, white-tile-clad **Bar Prokope** (Calle Vázquez Limón 8).

ENTERTAINMENT

The **Teatro Huelva** (☎ 959 21 02 57; www.huelva cultura.com in Spanish; Calle Vázquez López 13; ☒ ticket office 11am-1pm & 7-9pm) stages a broad programme of theatre and music. **Recreativo de Huelva** (☎ 959 27 02 08; www.recreativohuelva.com; Estadio Nuevo Colombino, Avenida del Decano) is Spain's oldest officially recognised football club,

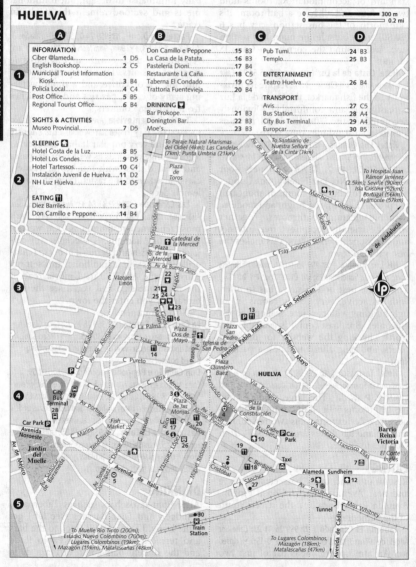

HUELVA

0 ——— 300 m
0 ——— 0.2 mi

INFORMATION
Ciber @lameda....................1 D5
English Bookshop................2 C5
Municipal Tourist Information
Kiosk...................................3 B4
Policía Local.......................4 C4
Post Office..........................5 B5
Regional Tourist Office........6 B4

SIGHTS & ACTIVITIES
Museo Provincial.................7 D5

SLEEPING
Hotel Costa de la Luz..........8 B5
Hotel Los Condes................9 D5
Hotel Tartessos...................10 C4
Instalación Juvenil de Huelva..11 D2
NH Luz Huelva....................12 D5

EATING
Diez Barriles.......................13 C3
Don Camillo e Peppone.......14 B4

Don Camillo e Peppone.......15 B3
La Casa de la Patata............16 B3
Pastelería Dioni...................17 B4
Restaurante La Caña............18 C5
Taberna El Condado............19 C5
Trattoria Fuenteveja............20 B4

DRINKING
Bar Prokope........................21 B3
Donington Bar.....................22 B3
Moe's..................................23 B3

Pub Tumi.............................24 B3
Templo................................25 B3

ENTERTAINMENT
Teatro Huelva......................26 B4

TRANSPORT
Avis.....................................27 C5
Bus Station..........................28 A4
City Bus Terminal.................29 A4
Europcar..............................30 B5

To Paraje Natural Marismas del Odiel (4km); Las Candelas (7km); Punta Umbría (21km)

To Santuario de Nuestra Señora de la Cinta (1km)

To Hospital Juan Ramón Jiménez (2.5km); Seville (90km); Isla Cristina (52km); Portugal (56km); Ayamonte (57km)

Plaza de Toros

Av de Manuel Siurot

Av Marchena Colombo

Catedral de la Merced

C Fray Junípero Serra

Av de Andalucía

Plaza de la Merced

Av de Buenos Aires

C Vázquez Limón

C San Sebastián

Av de Federico Mayo

C La Palma

Plaza Dos de Mayo

Plaza San Pedro

Iglesia de San Pedro

Avenida Pablo Rada

C Isaac Peral

C Pureto

Plaza Quintero Báez

HUELVA

Via Paisajista

C Doctor Rubio

Av de Alemania

Plaza de la Construcción

C Gravina

Av Portugal

Fish Market

Car Park

Avenida Noroeste

Jardín del Muelle

Marina

Av de Méjico

Av de Cánovas de Barranca

Av Tomás Domínguez

Avenida de Italia

C Miguel Redondo

C Berdigón

Alameda Sundheim

Barrio Reina Victoria

El Corte Inglés

Taxi

San Cristóbal

C Sánchez

Av Escultora

Tunnel

Miss Whitney

City Bus Terminal

Car Park

To Muelle Río Tinto (200m); Estadio Nuevo Colombino (700m); Lugares Colombinos (19km); Mazagón (19km); Matalascañas (48km)

Train Station

To Lugares Colombinos, Mazagón (18km); Matalascañas (47km)

Avenida de Cádiz

founded in 1889 by British employees of the Rio Tinto Company (a similar club at Minas de Riotinto predated the Huelva club but was never officially registered). 'Recre' are currently enjoying their best years ever, with an appearance in the Spanish cup final in 2003 and promotion to the national First Division in 2006. Match tickets usually cost between €20 and €50.

GETTING THERE & AROUND
Bus

Most buses from the **bus station** (Calle Doctor Rubio s/n) are operated by **Damas** (☎ 959 25 69 00; www.damas-sa.es), which runs all over Huelva province as well as to Seville and along the Algarve to Faro and Lagos in Portugal. Frequency to most destinations in Huelva province is reduced on Saturday, Sunday and holidays. Damas destinations include the following:

Aracena (€6, 2¼ hours) One or two daily.
Ayamonte (€4.50, one hour) Up to 10 daily.
Isla Cristina (€3.80, one hour) Fourteen daily Monday to Friday, five daily Saturday and Sunday.
Lagos (€13, four hours) Two daily except Saturday, Sunday and holidays from October to May.
Matalascañas (€3.90, 50 minutes) Two daily Monday to Friday.
Mazagón (€1.80, 35 minutes) Thirteen daily Monday to Friday, three daily Saturday and Sunday.
Minas de Riotinto (€5.50, 1¼ hours) Up to six daily.
Niebla (€2.40, 30 minutes) Up to nine daily.
Punta Umbría (€1.90, 30 minutes) Fourteen daily.
Seville (€7, 1¼ hours) Eighteen or more daily.

Socibus (☎ 902 22 92 92) runs to Madrid (€21, seven hours, four daily). For more information on buses to Portugal see p445.

Car & Motorcycle

Poor signage and a user-unfriendly one-way system can make driving in Huelva a frustrating experience. There's streetside parking around the bus station and on Avenida Escultora Miss Whitney (parallel to Alameda Sundheim), and multistorey or underground car parks on Calle Doctor Rubio near the bus station, Calle Padre Marchena off Avenida Martín Alonso Pinzón, and Calle Jesús de la Pasión.

For car hire there's **Avis** (☎ 959 28 38 36; Avenida de Italia 107) or **National/Atesa** (☎ 959 28 17 12) or **Europcar** (☎ 959 28 53 35), both in the train station concourse.

Train

From the **train station** (☎ 959 24 56 14, 902 24 02 02; www.renfe.com; Avenida de Italia) four daily services run to Seville (€7 to €17, 1½ hours), an afternoon Altaria train goes to Córdoba (€31, 2½ hours) and Madrid (€59, five hours), and two daily trains run north to Almonaster–Cortegana (€5.50, 2½ hours) and Jabugo–Galaroza (€6, 2¾ hours) en route to Extremadura.

AROUND HUELVA

PARAJE NATURAL MARISMAS DEL ODIEL

This 72-sq-km wetland reserve, across the Odiel estuary from Huelva, harbours a large, varied bird population, including up to 1000 greater flamingos in winter. There are also about 4000 pairs of spoonbills, plus ospreys, grey and purple herons and many other waterfowl. Some of these birds are easily viewed from a 20km road that runs the length of the marshes.

The marshes can be reached by car along the A497 Punta Umbría road west from Huelva. Cross either of the parallel bridges over Río Odiel, then follow 'PN Marismas del Odiel' signs to reach the **Centro de Visitantes Anastasio Senra** (☎ 959 50 90 11; ☼ 10am-2pm & 6-8pm Tue-Sun Apr-Sep, 10am-2pm & 4-6pm Tue-Sun Oct-Mar). South of here, several paths to good birdwatching spots strike off the road through the reserve, but some are only opened to guided groups: check at the visitors centre.

LUGARES COLOMBINOS

The Lugares Colombinos (Columbus Sites) are the three townships of La Rábida, Palos de la Frontera and Moguer, along the eastern bank of the Tinto estuary. All three played key roles in the discovery of the Americas and can be visited in an enjoyable 40km return trip from Huelva. The nearest and most important of the sites is the monastery at La Rábida, where Columbus retreated after his grand plans had been rejected by Portugal's King João II. Here Columbus met Abbot Juan Pérez (former confessor to Queen Isabel la Católica), who took up his cause and helped him find support for his far-fetched plans not only from the Spanish royal court but also from the sailors of Palos and Moguer.

HUELVA PROVINCE

Getting There & Around

Monday to Friday, 28 buses a day leave Huelva for La Rábida (€1, 20 minutes), with half of them continuing to Palos de la Frontera (€1, 25 minutes) and Moguer (€1.10, 30 minutes). The others go on to Mazagón. On Saturdays, Sundays and holidays, service is reduced by more than half.

La Rábida
pop 400

Critical to Columbus' success was the role of the Franciscan monks in the **Monasterio de la Rábida** (☎ 959 35 04 11; admission incl English, French, German, Portuguese or Spanish audioguide €3; ☽ 10am-1pm & 4-7pm Tue-Sat Apr-Jul & Sep, 10am-1pm & 4-6.15pm Tue-Sat Oct-Mar, 10am-1pm & 4.45-8pm Tue-Sat Aug, 10.45am-1pm Sun year-round). Here Columbus found support for his far-fetched ideas, and much of the planning of his voyage was discussed and agreed upon inside these walls.

Set amid pine trees, this 14th-century Mudejar monastery is a haven of tranquillity and is now devoted to the Columbus myth. Highlights include a series of 1930s murals on the Columbus theme by Huelvan artist Daniel Vázquez Díaz; the church, where Martín Alonso Pinzón, captain of the *Pinta*, is buried; a chapel with a 13th-century alabaster Virgin before which Columbus prayed; and the peaceful 15th-century cloister. Upstairs, the **Sala Capitular** (Chapter House) is where the final plans for the voyage were drawn up by Columbus, Fray Pérez (the abbot of La Rábida) and Columbus' two fellow captains, the Pinzón brothers from Palos de la Frontera.

No Columbus tour would be complete without a walk down to the waterfront to the **Muelle de las Carabelas** (Wharf of the Caravels; ☎ 959 53 05 97; admission €3.20; ☽ 10am-2pm & 5-9pm Tue-Fri, 11am-9pm Sat, Sun & holidays Jun-Sep, 10am-7pm Tue-Sun Oct-May), with life-size replicas of Columbus' faithful three-vessel fleet set against a pseudo-15th-century quayside. The *Niña*, *Pinta* and *Santa María* can all be boarded. Their size (none is more than 30m long) and the evidently ghastly living conditions give you some idea of the huge achievement of the voyage. But the comical mannequins, including some sorry naked natives, are impossible to take seriously.

A couple of cafés around the monastery/ Muelle de las Carabelas area serve drinks and snacks.

Palos de la Frontera
pop 7000

The small town of Palos de la Frontera, 4km northeast of La Rábida, was the port from which Columbus set sail, and which provided two of his ships and their captains (the Pinzón brothers: Martín Alonso Pinzón and Vicente Yañez Pinzón) and more than half his crew. Palos is justifiably proud of its role in the European discovery of the Americas but its access to the Tinto estuary is now silted up and today it's chiefly significant as a centre of Huelva province's big-time strawberry industry. All over the surrounding countryside in winter and spring you'll see huge expanses of plastic sheeting with the red fruit ripening beneath, especially along the road to Mazagón, and you'll notice some of the thousands of temporary strawberry-pickers from eastern Europe and Africa.

Moving northeast up Calle Cristóbal Colón from the central square, you soon reach the **Casa Museo Martín Alonso Pinzón** (☎ 618 570983; Calle Cristóbal Colón 24; admission free; ☽ 10am-2pm & 5-7pm Tue-Sun), the home of the captain of the *Pinta* and leader of the Palos maritime community who organised the local men and ships that sailed with Columbus. Inside are changing exhibitions on Palos-and-Columbus themes.

Further along and downhill is the 15th-century **Iglesia de San Jorge** (Calle Cristóbal Colón; ☽ 10am-noon & 7-8pm Tue-Sun). Before setting sail on 3 August 1492, Columbus and his men took communion in this church and left by the Mudejar portal facing the small square. A monument in the square lists 35 Palos men who sailed with Columbus.

A little further down the street, within a small park, is **La Fontanilla**, a brick well where Columbus' crews drew water for their voyage. A viewing platform above has a plaque marking the site of the jetty from which the three ships sailed.

A short distance down the main street from the main square, **Hotel La Pinta** (☎ 959 35 05 11; www.hotellapinta.com in Spanish; Calle Rábida 79; s/d €42/68; ⌘) has neat, well-kept, marble-floored rooms (a touch overpriced), and a good, traditional-style restaurant serving plenty of local fish, seafood and meat (mains €14 to €22). **El Bodegón** (☎ 959 53 11 05; Calle Rábida 46; mains €8-20; ☽ closed Tue), a busy, atmospheric, noisy cavern of a restaurant, cooks up fish and meat on wood-fire grills and doles out

---

THE FOUR VOYAGES OF CHRISTOPHER COLUMBUS

In April 1492 Christopher Columbus (Cristóbal Colón to Spaniards) finally won Spanish royal support for his proposed westward voyage of exploration to the spice-rich Orient; a proposal that was to result in no fewer than four voyages by the great navigator and a fabulous golden age for Spain.

On 3 August 1492, Columbus embarked from Palos de la Frontera with 100 men and three ships. The flagship, the *Santa María*, was piloted by its owner, Juan de la Cosa from El Puerto de Santa María (Cádiz province), while the *Niña* and *Pinta* were captained by the Pinzón brothers from Palos de la Frontera. After a near mutiny as the crew despaired of finding land, they finally made landfall on the Bahamian island of Guanahaní on 12 October, naming it San Salvador. The expedition went on to discover Cuba and Hispaniola, where the *Santa María* sank. Its timbers were used to build a fort, Fuerte Navidad, which 33 Spaniards were left to hold. The *Niña* and the *Pinta* got back to Palos on 15 March. Columbus, with animals, plants, gold ornaments and six Caribbean Indians (so ludicrously represented at the Muelle de las Carabelas, opposite), received a hero's welcome, as all were convinced that he had reached the fabled East Indies (in fact, his calculations were some 16,000km out).

Columbus made further voyages in 1493 and 1498, discovering Jamaica, Trinidad and the mouth of the Orinoco River. But he proved a disastrous colonial administrator, enslaving the indigenous people and alienating the Spanish settlers. Eventually his mishandling led to a revolt by settlers on Hispaniola and before he could suppress the uprising he was arrested by a royal emissary from Spain and sent home in chains. In a final attempt to redeem himself and find a strait to Asia, Columbus embarked on his fourth and final voyage in April 1502. This time he reached Honduras and Panama, but then became stranded for a year in Jamaica, having lost his ships to sea worms.

Columbus died in 1506 in Valladolid, northern Spain – impoverished and apparently still believing he had reached Asia. His remains were eventually returned to the Caribbean, as he had wished, before being brought back to Seville cathedral in 1899. Or were they? The story of Columbus' posthumous voyages has recently become quite a saga itself – see p98.

---

plates of good cheese and *jamón serrano* (mountain-cured ham).

Moguer
pop 13,000

Like Palos, Moguer is an attractive, small, whitewashed town. The *Niña* was built here and up to one-third of Columbus' crew came from Moguer, including Juan Niño, owner of the *Niña*. Moguer also has its own charming flavour of Andalucian baroque and its sunny beauty was fulsomely expressed by local poet laureate, Juan Ramón Jiménez (1881–1958), who won the Nobel prize for literature in 1956. The streets are dotted with plaques bearing quotes from Jiménez' *Platero y Yo* (Platero and I), which tells of his childhood wanderings around Moguer with his donkey and confidant, Platero, and his old home is now a museum.

ORIENTATION & INFORMATION

Driving into town, 'Centro' and 'Oficina de Turismo' signs will lead you to a car

park outside the castle on Calle Castillo, from which the central Plaza del Cabildo is 1½ blocks away. The helpful **tourist office** (☎ 959 37 18 98; www.aytomoguer.es in Spanish; Calle Castillo s/n; ⏰ 9am-2pm & 4.30-7pm Mon-Sat, 10am-3pm Sun & holidays) is inside the castle.

SIGHTS

The **Castillo** (Castle; admission free; ⏰ 9am-2pm & 4.30-7pm Mon-Sat, 10am-3pm Sun & holidays) is a bare walled enclosure of Almohad origin, expanded in the 14th century. The tourist office, which occupies an old storage building inside the castle, has exhibits on local wine and Moguer's connections with the Americas.

Simply taking a stroll round Moguer's busy morning streets is a pleasure. There are fine buildings everywhere, one of the best being the 18th-century Italianate **ayuntamiento** (town hall; Plaza del Cabildo; ⏰ 10am-2pm Mon-Fri), with its arcaded, two-storey, neo-classical façade. Pop your head inside to see the beautiful patio.

Close by is the 14th-century **Monasterio de Santa Clara** (☎ 959 37 01 07; Plaza de las Monjas; guided tour €2; 11am-1pm & 5-7pm Tue-Sat), where Columbus spent a night of vigil and prayer the night after returning from his first voyage. He had vowed to do so if he survived a terrible storm off the Azores. You'll see a lovely Mudejar cloister, some of the nuns' old quarters and dormitories, and an impressive collection of Renaissance religious art.

Five minutes' walk from Plaza del Cabildo is the **Casa Museo Zenobia y Juan Ramón Jiménez** (☎ 959 37 21 48; www.fundacion-jrj.es in Spanish; Calle Juan Ramón Jiménez 10; admission €2.50; 10.15am-1.15pm & 5.15-7.15pm Tue-Sat, 10.15am-1.15pm Sun), the old home of Juan Ramón Jiménez and his wife, Zenobia Camprubí, normally decked with memorabilia and open for one-hour guided visits. At the time of writing the house was under restoration and the exhibits had been temporarily moved to Jiménez' birthplace at Calle Ribera 2, with the same visiting arrangements.

The 18th-century, baroque **Iglesia de Nuestra Señora de la Granada**, two blocks southeast of Plaza del Cabildo, has a tower that Jiménez immortalised as resembling Seville's Giralda tower from the hazy distance.

SLEEPING & EATING

Hostal Pedro Alonso Niño (☎ 959 37 23 92; Calle Pedro Alonso Niño 13; s/d €15/25;) Close to the Convento de Santa Clara at the end of Calle Monjas, this friendly *hostal* (small, low-budget, hotel-like accommodation) has a pretty patio with paintings, pottery and plants, and comfortable rooms with small baths.

Hostal Platero (☎ 959 37 21 59; Calle Aceña 4; s/d €18/30;) Just around the corner from Hostal Pedro Alonso Niño is another small *hostal* – plain, old-fashioned, simple and very clean.

Mesón El Lobito (☎ 959 37 06 60; Calle Rábida 31; raciones €7-10; closed Wed) This fun restaurant occupies an old winery a couple of blocks west of Plaza del Cabildo and is an experience even without the food. Stacks of wine barrels and curious artefacts adorn the walls and locals occasionally sell fruit and vegetables. The fish and meat *a la brasa* are good and the house wine is cheap.

Mesón La Parrala (☎ 959 37 04 52; Plaza de las Monjas 22; raciones €6.50-9; mains €10-16; 10am-11pm Tue-Sun) Family-run La Parrala, opposite

the Santa Clara convent, serves good grills and fresh fish in two rooms – one in wine-cellar style, the other a bit more formal with classical art.

Bodeguita Los Raposo (☎ 959 37 12 81; Calle Fuente 60; tapas €1-3) Another cracking place, where you order by plate size from a choice of more than 40 fish, meat and salad dishes. There's lots of local wine, too. Try the 'Licor de Viagra', prepared from local sweet wine; it works wonders, according to the ever-smiling host.

SOUTHEASTERN HUELVA

A wide, sandy beach runs along the Costa de la Luz 60km southeast from the outskirts of Huelva to the mouth of the Río Guadalquivir. The beach enjoys good weather for much of the year (although it can be windy) and shares many of the characteristics of the better known beaches of Cádiz province: fine white sand, windswept dunes and a thick, protective barrier of pines. Frequented mainly by Spanish holidaymakers, the resort towns of Mazagón and Matalascañas are unpretentious if unremarkable places to stay. East of Mazagón the beach comes within the territory of Doñana national park, which is the major reason to come to this region – a huge wetland and vital refuge for millions of birds and many mammals, which will fascinate any nature lover.

MAZAGÓN
pop 3000

The low-rise development at Mazagón, just 18km out of Huelva, is inoffensive and in summer the town develops a holiday buzz of its own. Avenida Conquistadores runs 1km down from the A494 to the beach then continues 3km east to the beachfront road of residential Mazagón. There's a **tourist office** (☎ 959 37 63 00; Edificio Mancomunidad, Avenida Conquistadores; 10am-2pm Mon-Fri) halfway down to the beach: look for the flags. This is in the centre of town as far as services are concerned. A large marina spreads out from the west end of the beach and on summer evenings the seafront bristles with life.

The glorious broad, sandy **beach** is backed by low sandstone cliffs for some distance east from Mazagón. You can reach it easily beside the Parador de Mazagón, 3km from town. At **Cuesta de Maneli**, 9km beyond, a 1.2km boardwalk leads across 100m-high dunes from a car park to the beach through glorious pines and junipers. The Cuesta de Maneli beach has a nudist section.

Sleeping

Camping Mazagón (☎ 959 37 62 08; Cuesta de la Barca s/n; adult/tent/car €5.50/5.50/5.50; **P** 🕮) A huge year-round camping ground a couple of minutes' walk from the east end of the beach. The site is well wooded, though much space is taken up by permanent caravans and tents.

Hostal Hilaria (☎ /fax 959 37 62 06; Calle Hilaria 20; r €60; 🕮 closed mid-Dec–early Jan; 🕮) This bright and cheerful *hostal* is just north of the tourist office. All rooms have a terrace or balcony but some are set above a bar, which can be a little noisy in summer. Rates fall 25% to 50% outside July and August.

Hotel Albaida (☎ 959 37 60 29; www.hotelalbaida .com; Carretera Huelva-Matalascañas; s €44-65, d €67-102; **P** 🕮) The elegant Albaida is housed in a classic-looking villa and offers comfortable, airy rooms tastefully kitted out in primary tones with a touch of colourful art. All room prices include breakfast. Staff are welcoming and helpful. It's 600m east of the town centre, amid pine trees just off the highway.

Parador de Mazagón (☎ 959 53 63 00; www.para dor.es; Playa de Mazagón; s/d €120/150; **P** 🕮 🕮 🕮 🕮) Three kilometres east of Mazagón, the creeper-clad Parador is a low-lying '70s classic – a cross between a ranch-house and a Californian beach bungalow, with broad verandas, marble-floored bathrooms, tasteful modern art and neatly manicured hedges and lawns. The luxurious rooms all have sea views and there's easy access to the beach below the cliff-top gardens.

Eating

Las Dunas (☎ 959 37 62 59; Avenida Conquistadores 178; mains €8-15) Right up at the western end of the seafront, big, bright Las Dunas cooks up lovely fresh fish, and the view of the ocean and marina puts you right in the mood.

El Remo (☎ 959 53 61 38; Avenida Conquistadores 123; mains €10-20; 🕮 1-6pm & 8-11pm, closed Sun

evening) This well-run seafood restaurant has a wide terrace overlooking the sands. The simply grilled or fried fish, such as *merluza* (hake) or succulent *dorada* (bream), are always a good choice but the *carnes a la brasa* are fine too.

For tapas and seafood *raciones* (meal-sized servings of tapas) take your pick from four or five bars along Avenida Fuentepiña, running off the inland stretch of Avenida Conquistadores.

Getting There & Away

Buses run from Huelva to Mazagón (€1.80, 35 minutes, 13 daily Monday to Friday, three daily Saturday and Sunday) via La Rábida and Palos de la Frontera.

MATALASCAÑAS

pop 1100

This custom-built resort of uninspired villas, plain ugly apartment blocks and several large hotels, mostly in shades of muddy brown, is a sad contrast to the wilderness of the adjoining Doñana national and natural parks. But despite its aesthetic and environmental negatives, Matalascañas is a favourite of holidaying families from Seville, for its very proximity to Doñana, its terrific beach and plenty of summertime facilities.

Orientation & Information

Matalascañas stretches 4km southeast, parallel to the beach, from the junction of the A494 from Mazagón with the A483 from El Rocío. From here Avenida de las Adelfas heads south straight to the beach, passing the **tourist office** (☎ 959 43 00 86; Edificio Parque Dunar, Avenida de las Adelfas s/n; 🕮 10am-2pm). Buses stop just past the tourist office. The east side of Avenida de las Adelfas is a wall of shops, restaurants and bars a couple of blocks deep.

Sights & Activities

Apart from the attractions of golf, the beach and water-based activities, Matalascañas boasts the **Parque Dunar** (☎ 959 44 80 86; www .parquedunar.com; Avenida de las Adelfas; 🕮 9.30am-6.30pm), a 1.3-sq-km expanse of high, pine-covered dunes at the west end of town laced with cycling routes and a maze of sandy pathways. Within this dune park is the very interesting **Museo del Mundo Marítimo** (Museum of the Maritime World; ☎ 959 43 00 19; adult/under 15yr €5/3;

⏲ 11am-2.30pm & 6-9.30pm Tue-Sat, 11am-2.30pm Sun mid-Jun–mid-Sep, 10am-2pm & 3.30-6pm Tue-Sat, 10am-2pm Sun mid-Sep–mid-Jun) with five themed rooms devoted to the coasts and seas of the Doñana area, the whales and other cetaceans of the Strait of Gibraltar (including skeletons and full-size replicas up to 20m long), and the fishing and boat-building industries.

The best section of beach is at the eastern end of town, where there's also a 1.5km-round-trip **walking trail** through the dunes of Doñana National Park.

Sleeping

Hotel Doñana Blues (☎ 959 44 98 17; www.donana blues.com; Sector I, Parcela 129; r €102-134; 🏊 🖳 🖢) The only place in town with real character, Doñana Blues is a small hotel in comfortable yet appealingly rustic style. Each room sports different art and furnishings but all have terrace or balcony. It also has a pool, a café serving breakfast, and bicycles to rent for €6 a day. Outside the high seasons, rates come down about 30%. Book ahead.

Hotel Tierra Mar Golf (☎ 959 44 03 00; www .vimehoteles.com; s €81-117, d €102-146; 🅿 🏊 🖳 🖢) Well-equipped, modern, seafront hotel with an inviting pool just above the beach. There's a 25% supplement for stays of less than seven days from 10 July to 10 September, but rates can fall as much as 50% from October to Easter. All room prices include breakfast.

Other acceptable options:

Casa Miguel (☎ 959 44 84 72; Avenida Las Adelfas; r €50) Small, pleasant *hostal* with restaurant, conveniently placed just north of the tourist office.

Hotel Flamero (☎ 902 50 52 00, 959 02 64 00; Ronda Maestro Alonso; www.hotelflamero.com; d €56-92; 🅿 🏊 🖢) Large beachfront hotel; half-board (€115 for two) obligatory from mid-July to mid-September.

Eating & Drinking

Restaurante Bajo Guía (☎ 959 44 00 37; Paseo Marítimo, Sector N; mains €9-15) This specialist in seafood and rice dishes, with picture windows overlooking the ocean, sits on the seafront east of Hotel Tierra Mar Golf.

Taberna Tío Paco (☎ 959 44 81 94; Plaza de las Begonias; tapas/raciones €2/8.50, mains €10-20; ⏲ closed Wed) 'Uncle Paco's' is an excellent spot for tapas, *raciones* and grilled meats, in the precinct off the east side of Avenida de las Adelfas. Its *terraza* (terrace) has large sherry barrels for tables.

Getting There & Away

Buses from Huelva (€3.90, 50 minutes, two daily), via Mazagón, generally run Monday to Friday only. Extra services may run in summer. Buses also link Matalascañas with El Rocío and Seville (see p158).

PARQUE NACIONAL DE DOÑANA

Spain's most celebrated and in many ways most important wildlife refuge, the Parque Nacional de Doñana (Doñana National Park) is one of Europe's last remaining great wetlands and a place of haunting natural beauty and romantic myth. It was owned by the dukes of Medina Sidonia in the 16th century, and is named after the wife of the seventh duke, Dona Aña, who retreated from life at court to a specially built mansion here. Dona Aña's spirit, legend has it, still wanders these marshes and forests of the Guadalquivir Delta. There are even claims that the area was the site of the fabled Tartessos (see p24). Today the park is intimately associated with a fervently adored incarnation of the Virgin Mary, Nuestra Señora del Rocío (see p157), who every year draws hundreds of thousands of celebratory pilgrims to the village of El Rocío on the park's northwestern fringe.

The 542-sq-km national park extends 32km along or close to the Atlantic coast and up to 25km inland, bounded by the Río Guadalquivir and various tributaries in the southeast and by the A483 Matalascañas–El Rocío road in the west. El Rocío (p156) and the town of Matalascañas (p153) are the most convenient bases for visiting the park. Much of the national park's perimeter is bordered by the separate Parque Natural de Doñana (Doñana Natural Park), under less strict protection, which comprises four distinct zones totalling 540 sq km and forming a buffer for the national park. The two parks together provide a refuge for endangered species such as the Iberian lynx (with a population estimated at between 30 and 50) and Spanish imperial eagle (about eight breeding pairs), and a crucial habitat for millions of migrating birds. About six million birds spend at least part of each year in the national park and some 350 species have been recorded here.

Ever since its inception in 1969 the national park has been under pressure from tourism, agriculture, hunters, developers and constructors. Many locals believe the park's interests take unfair priority over their own concerns about much-needed jobs. Ecologists argue that Doñana is increasingly hemmed in by tourism and agricultural schemes, roads and other infrastructure that threaten to deplete its water supplies and cut it off from other undeveloped areas. Some 30 lynxes have been run over on roads around the national park's fringes in the past decade. In 1998 the uneasy balance between industry and conservation collapsed when a dam broke at Los Frailes heavy-metals mine at Aznalcóllar, 50km north of the national park. Hastily erected dikes prevented the poisonous tide from entering all but a small corner of the national park, but up to 100 sq km of wetlands to the park's northeast were contaminated. Today, the latest threats to Doñana range from the activities of deer poachers and landings of drug smugglers on the beaches to a barmy proposal for a road along the beach from Matalascañas to Sanlúcar de Barrameda.

Information

The national park's main visitors centre is the **Centro de Visitantes El Acebuche** (☎ 959 44 87 11; Carretera A483 Km 26; ☼ 8am-9pm May-Sep, 8am-7pm Oct-Apr), off the A483 Matalascañas-El Rocío road. To find it, head 4km north from Matalascañas, or 12km south from El Rocío, then go 1.6km west along an ap-

proach road. The centre has an interactive exhibit on the park, a café, and a shop with a large screen showing film (live or recorded) of Iberian lynxes in the El Acebuche captive-breeding programme. (The programme itself – see p64 – is not open to visitors). Also here are paths (1.5km and 3.5km round-trip) leading to bird-watching hides overlooking nearby lagoons.

The national park has two other visitors centres on its western fringes, both also with paths to nearby lagoons: the **Centro de Información Las Rocinas** (☎ 959 44 23 40; ☼ 9am-3pm & 4-7pm, to 8 or 9pm Apr-Aug), with an exhibition on the history of the El Rocío pilgrimage, beside the A483 1km south of El Rocío; and the **Palacio del Acebrón** (☼ 9am-3pm & 4-7pm, to 8 or 9pm Apr-Aug), 6km along a paved road west from Las Rocinas, housing an ethnographic exhibition of the park.

The Junta de Andalucía's *Doñana* map (1:75,000), published in 2004, covers both the national and natural parks. It's sold at the Acebuche centre for €8.

Activities

Keen bird-watchers should find something to keep them happy along the trails near the three western visitors centres, though you won't generally find the numbers or variety of birds seen on tours into the park. The **Charco de la Boca path** at the Las Rocinas centre, a 3.5km round-trip with four hides, is usually best, especially in the evening.

DOÑANA LIFE CYCLES

The many interwoven ecosystems that make up Doñana National Park give rise to fantastic diversity. Nearly half the park is occupied by marshes. These are almost dry from July to October but in autumn they start to fill with water, eventually leaving only a few islets of dry land. Hundreds of thousands of water birds arrive from the north to winter here, including an estimated 80% of Western Europe's wild ducks. As the waters sink in spring, greater flamingoes, spoonbills, storks, herons, avocets, hoopoes, bee-eaters, stilts and other birds arrive for the summer, many of them to nest. Fledglings flock around the ponds known as *lucios* and as these dry up in July, herons, storks and kites move in to feast on trapped perch.

Between the marshlands and the park's 28km-long beach is a band of sand dunes, pushed inland by the wind at a rate of up to 6m per year. The shallow valleys between the dunes, called *corrales*, host pines and other trees favoured as nesting sites by raptors. When dune sand eventually reaches the marshlands, rivers carry it back down to the sea, which washes it up on the beach – and the cycle begins all over again.

Elsewhere in the park, stable sands support 144 sq km of *coto*, the name given here to areas of woodland and scrub. *Coto* is the favoured habitat of many nesting birds and the park's abundant mammal population – 33 species including red and fallow deer, wild boar, mongoose and genets.

The more remote **Centro de Visitantes José Antonio Valverde** (☺ 10am-7pm, to 8pm or 9pm Apr-Aug), on the northern edge of the park, is generally an excellent bird-watching spot as it overlooks a year-round *lucio* (pond). The Caño de Rosalimán waterway just west of here is also a fine site. The easiest way to reach the Valverde centre is an authorised tour from El Rocío (see opposite); the alternative is to drive yourself on rough roads from Villamanrique de la Condesa or La Puebla del Río to the northeast.

The March–May and September–November migration seasons are overall the most exciting for birders.

Tours

Access to the interior of the national park is restricted. Anyone may walk along the 28km Atlantic beach between Matalascañas and the mouth of the Río Guadalquivir (which can be crossed by boats from Sanlúcar de Barrameda in Cádiz province), as long they do not stray inland. But to visit the interior of the national park, you must book a guided tour leaving either from El Acebuche visitors centre or from Sanlúcar de Barrameda (see p190). The tours from El Acebuche, in all-terrain vehicles holding 20 people each, are run by **Cooperativa Marismas del Rocío** (☎ 959 43 04 32/51; per person €23; ☺ 8.30am Tue-Sun year-round, 3pm Oct-Apr, 5pm May-Sep). You need to book ahead by telephone – the tours can be full more than a month before spring, summer and all holiday times. Bring binoculars, if you can, plus mosquito repellent (except in winter) and drinking water (in summer). The tour lasts four hours and most guides speak Spanish only. The route of 70km to 80km normally begins with a drive along the beach to the mouth of the Río Guadalquivir, then loops back through the south of the park, taking in moving dunes, marshlands and woods, where you can be pretty certain of seeing a good number of deer and boar and huge numbers of birds, though ornithologists may be disappointed with the limited opportunities for serious bird-watching.

Keen birders, beginner or expert, will, however, almost certainly be happy with tours along the northern fringe of the national park from El Rocío to the Centro de Visitantes José Antonio Valverde. These trips normally spend part of their time in

the national park and part in the natural park, and range through pine and oak forests and across marshlands, with a great diversity of birds and high chances of seeing deer and boar. The following operators use smallish vehicles carrying a maximum of eight or nine people:

Discovering Doñana (☎ 959 44 24 66, 620 964369; www.discoveringdonana.com; Calle Águila Imperial 150, El Rocío; 6hr trip 1-3 people €110, each extra person €28, 12hr trip 1-3 people €160, each extra person €45) Expert English-speaking guides; most trips are of broad interest but personalised tours also available; binoculars, telescopes, reference books available at no extra cost.

Doñana Bird Tours (☎ 95 575 5460, 637 922688; www.donanabirdtours.com; 9hr trip 1-3 people €110, each extra person €30) Top-class bird tours led by resident British bird expert and author John Butler; also offers longer birding holidays.

Doñana Nature (☎ 959 44 21 60, 630 978216; www.donana-nature.com; Calle Las Carretas 10, El Rocío; 3½hr trip per person €23) Half-day trips, at 8am and 3.30pm daily, are general interest and may not go as far as the Valverde centre, but specialised ornithological and photographic trips are also offered; English- and French-speaking guides available.

Getting There & Away

Buses between El Rocío and Matalascañas (see p158) will stop at the El Acebuche turn-off on the A483. The first bus south from El Rocío, at 7am (7.45am Saturday and Sunday), should get you to El Acebuche (€1, 15 minutes) in time for the 8.30am national park tour. From Matalascañas the northward 7.45am bus Monday to Friday should enable you to make the tour. Check current schedules before you start out.

EL ROCÍO

pop 1200

Overlooking picturesque *marismas* (wetlands) at the northwest corner of the Parque Nacional de Doñana stands the extraordinary village of El Rocío. As you drive into town the tarmac road gives way to wide sandy avenues, cutting between eerily quiet ranch-style houses. Hoof-prints, hitching posts and hat-clad honchos do nothing to dissipate the bizarre guns-at-noon atmosphere that pervades. But despite appearances the town is not a film set, but a bona fide piece of Andalucía's own 'Wild West'. The quiet houses, with their sweeping verandas, are no show homes but are the well-tended properties of over 90 *hermandades* (brotherhoods) whose pilgrims converge on the town every Pentecost (Whitsuntide) for the Romería del Rocío (see below).

Information

The **tourist office** (☎ 959 44 38 08; www.turismode donana.com; Avenida de la Canaliega s/n; ☻ 9.30am-1.30pm & 3-5pm Mon-Fri) is beside the main road (A483) at the western end of the village. It supplies local information and can make reservations for tours in the Doñana national and natural parks. Several ATMs are dotted around town.

Sights & Activities

In the heart of the village, dominating a wide sandy square, stands the **Ermita del Rocío** (☎ 959 44 24 25; admission free; ☻ 8am-9pm), built in its present form in 1964. This is the home of the celebrated **Nuestra Señora del Rocío** (Our Lady of El Rocío), a small wooden image of the Virgin dressed in long, jewelled robes, which normally stands above the main altar. People arrive to see the Virgin every day of the year and especially on weekends, when El Rocío brotherhoods often gather here for colourful celebrations.

The **marshlands** in front of El Rocío have water all year, thanks to the Río Madre de las Marismas which flows through here, so this is nearly always a good place to spot birds and animals. Deer and horses graze in the shallows and you may be lucky enough to see a flock of flamingos wheeling through the sky in a big pink cloud. The bridge over the river 1km south of the village on the A483 is another good viewing spot, and just past the bridge is the Centro de Información Las Rocinas (see p155), with paths to bird-watching hides.

For a longer walk from El Rocío, cross the Puente del Ajolí, at the northeastern edge of the village, and follow the track into the woodland. This is the **Raya Real**, one of the most important routes used by Romería pilgrims on their journeys to and from El Rocío. The track crosses the **Coto del Rey**, a large woodland zone where you may spot deer or boar in early morning or late evening.

Since El Rocío is such a horsey place, it would be a pity not to have a ride yourself. **Doñana Ecuestre** (☎ 959 44 24 74; Avenida de la Canaliega s/n; per 1hr/2hr/half-day €17/23/41; ☻ office 8am-8pm), on the west side of the A483, offers enjoyable guided rides through the woodlands west of El Rocío.

THE ROMERÍA DEL ROCÍO

The Romería del Rocío, Spain's biggest religious pilgrimage, draws hundreds of thousands of festive pilgrims to El Rocío every Pentecost to commemorate the miracle story of the sacred effigy of Nuestra Señora del Rocío (Our Lady of El Rocío).

Like most of Spain's holiest images, this one – known as La Blanca Paloma (The White Dove) – has legendary origins. Back in the 13th century, a hunter from Almonte village found the effigy in a marshland tree and started to carry her home. But when he stopped for a rest, the Virgin magically returned to the tree. Before long, a chapel was built on the site of the tree (El Rocío) and it became a place of pilgrimage. By the 17th century, *hermandades* (brotherhoods) were forming in nearby towns to make pilgrimages to El Rocío at Pentecost, the seventh weekend after Easter. Today, the **Romería del Rocío** (Pilgrimage of El Rocío) is a vast festive cult that draws people from all over Spain. There are over 90 *hermandades,* some with several thousand members, both men and women, who still travel to El Rocío on foot, on horseback and in gaily decorated covered wagons.

Solemn is the last word you'd apply to this quintessentially Andalucian event. In an atmosphere similar to Seville's Feria de Abril (p114), participants dress in fine Andalucian costume and sing, dance, drink, laugh and romance their way to El Rocío. The total number of people in the village on this special weekend can reach about a million.

The weekend reaches an ecstatic climax in the very early hours of Monday. Members of the Almonte *hermandad,* which claims the Virgin as its own, barge into the church and bear her out on a float. Violent struggles ensue as others battle for the honour of carrying La Blanca Paloma. The crush and chaos are immense, but somehow the Virgin is carried round to each of the *hermandad* buildings before finally being returned to the church in the afternoon.

Sleeping & Eating

Accommodation during the Romería is often booked at least a year in advance, at sky-high prices.

Camping La Aldea (☎ 959 44 26 77; www.camping laaldea.com; Carretera El Rocío Km 25; adult/tent/car €5.50/5.50/5.50, cabin or bungalow for 2/4-5 €62/100-134; ☿ closed 25 Dec-5 Jan; P ☒ 🖳 ☒) A well-equipped, modern camping ground at the north end of the village, La Aldea has a range of cosy wood or brick-and-thatch cabins and bungalows, with air-con, private bathrooms and TV, as well as over 250 camping spaces. Rates fall by up to one-third outside August.

Pensión Cristina (☎ 959 44 24 13; Calle El Real 58; s/d €30/36) Just east of the Ermita, the Cristina is one of El Rocío's few budget *hostales*. Rooms are reasonably comfortable and there's a decent and popular restaurant serving paella, venison, seafood and more (mains €6 to €9).

Pensión Isidro (☎ 959 44 22 42; Avenida de los Ánsares 59; s/d €24/48; ☒) This slightly more comfortable *hostal*, with air-con, heating and bathtubs, is 400m north of the Ermita. External rooms have little balconies and it's generally a more tranquil locale than the Cristina.

Hotel & Restaurante Toruño (☎ 959 44 23 23; fax 959 44 23 38; Plaza Acebuchal 22; s/d incl breakfast €57/81; P ☒) An attractive villa overlooking the *marismas*, only 200m from the church, the Toruño has 30 well-appointed rooms. Odd-numbered rooms from 101 to 115 and 207 to 225 have views over the marshland. The restaurant, across the sandy plaza outside, is one of the better options in town, serving up sizeable portions of well-prepared country and coastal fare – lamb, venison and beef from the national park, fish, seafood, cheeses, wild spinach. Mains are €12 to €22.

El Cortijo de los Mimbrales (☎ 959 42 22 37; www .cortijomimbrales.com; Carretera A483 Km 30; r €134-156, 2/4-person cottage €311/364; P ☒ ☒) Four kilometres south of El Rocío on the road towards Matalascañas you'll find this delightful hacienda-style property. Accommodation is in double rooms or cottages (all room prices include breakfast) with bold, vibrant colour washes and curious antiques combined in a uniquely contemporary fashion. The excellent restaurant is worth the trip even if you aren't a guest –

mains are from €9 to €18. There's a beautiful Arabic-style pool, and horse-riding and mountain biking are available on the 10-sq-km estate. Only snag: the seven-night minimum stay from 1 July to 15 September and during major festivals. From March to June and 15 September to 31 October (for which the above prices apply) the minimum is three nights.

Hotel La Malvasía (☎ 959 44 38 70; www.lamalva siahotel.com; Calle Sanlúcar 38; s/d incl breakfast €129/204; ☒ ☒) This new 18-room hotel is the most luxurious option in town with individually and beautifully designed rooms, a distinguished air and a fine *'nuevo andaluz'* restaurant (open from Tuesday through to Sunday afternoon, mains €15 to €20)with a 160-strong wine list. It's almost on the waterfront, though most rooms don't actually overlook the *marismas*.

Aires de Doñana (☎ 959 44 27 19; Avenida de la Canaliega 1; mains €15-19; ☿ Sat-Sun) Most El Rocío eateries focus more on feeding the hungry punters than on culinary niceties. Aires de Doñana, despite its rustic barnlike exterior, makes a great alternative with its picture windows overlooking the *marismas*, polished service and successfully imaginative menu.

Getting There & Away

Damas buses run from Seville to El Rocío (€5.50, 1½ hours, three to five daily) and on to Matalascañas (€6, 1¾ hours). One or two further services along the A483 just between Almonte and Matalascañas also stop at El Rocío. All these buses will stop outside El Acebuche visitors centre (you may have to request this).

From Huelva to El Rocío, take a Damas bus to Almonte (€3.90, 45 minutes, six daily Monday to Friday, fewer services on weekends), then another from Almonte to El Rocío (€1.20, 20 minutes, four to seven daily). You need to leave Huelva by 6pm to make the connection.

WEST OF HUELVA

The Costa de la Luz between Huelva and the Portuguese border, 53km to the west, is lined all the way (apart from a couple of breaks for estuaries and wetlands) by a broad, sandy beach backed for long

DETOUR: NIEBLA

Twenty-five kilometres east of Huelva on the old A472 from Seville, and 4km north of the modern A49, stands the ancient town of Niebla (population: 4000), encircled by 2km-long, red-ochre, Muslim-era walls. Complete with 50 towers and five gates, it has some of the most perfectly preserved medieval remains in Andalucía. Entering Niebla from the east you cross the Río Tinto on a beautiful Roman bridge that was destroyed in the Civil War but has since been carefully restored.

Inside the walls the warren of streets is a pleasure to explore. The major monument is the enormous, 15th-century **Castillo de los Guzmán** (☎ 959 36 22 70; www.castillodeniebla.com; admission €4; 🕑 10am-6pm, to 10pm 1 Jul–mid-Sep, to 8pm Sat & Sun mid-Mar–30 Jun), built around two large patios. You'll need a strong stomach for the gruesome display of torture instruments in the dungeon. Niebla's **tourist office** (☎ 959 36 22 70; 🕑 10am-6pm, to 10pm 1 Jul–mid-Sep, to 8pm Sat & Sun mid-Mar–30 Jun) is in the castle entrance. For a romantic evening take in one of the dance or drama productions staged here on Saturday nights in July and August.

In the heart of the old town the quaint **Iglesia de Nuestra Señora de la Granada** (Plaza Santa María) combines the features of a 9th-century mosque with those of the Gothic-Mudejar church into which it was transformed in the 15th century. Ask at the Casa de la Cultura on the same square for Señor Juan de Dios who will open the church for you. Don't miss the Islamic horseshoe and multi-lobed arches in the entrance patio, the original mihrab (prayer niche) in the south wall, the church tower which was originally a minaret, the Gothic tracery on the east-end roof, and the Visigothic stone bishop's throne behind the altar.

stretches by dunes and trees. The coastal settlements emphasise tourism but also retain river- or sea-port character, especially Isla Cristina with its large fishing fleet. The beach is certainly superb – especially outside the main July–August season, when the crowds disappear and prices fall.

PUNTA UMBRÍA

pop 13,000

Established as a holiday resort in 1880 by the Rio Tinto Company (whose holidaying engineers used to travel from Huelva in a paddle steamer), Punta Umbría is now a favourite summer destination for people from Huelva and becomes very busy in July and August.

Despite the uninspiring development, Punta Umbría has a friendly atmosphere and an attractive location between the Atlantic coast and the peninsular wetlands of the Paraje Natural Marismas del Odiel (see p149). The town has a helpful **tourist office** (☎ 959 49 51 60; www.puntaumbria.es; Avenida Ciudad de Huelva; 8am-3pm & 4.30-7.30pm Mon-Fri, 10am-1pm Sat & Sun Jun-Sep, 8am-3pm Mon-Fri, 10am-1pm Sat Oct-May).

Thirteen kilometres of sandy **beaches** stretch all along the ocean side of town and off to the west. Windsurfing and kitesurfing are popular, especially off the town beach near the estuary mouth.

Sleeping & Eating

Punta Umbría has a big range of accommodation, although even this gets booked up in July and August.

Camping Playa La Bota (☎ 959 31 45 37; www.playalabota.com; Carretera Huelva-Punta Umbría Km 11; adult/tent/car €5.50/5/4.50; P ♿) Set between the roads to Huelva and El Rompido, 6km out of town, this well-kept camping ground is convenient for the beaches and also has pine bungalows sleeping four.

Hotel Real (☎ 959 31 04 56; hotelrealpuntaumbria@hotmail.com; Calle Falucho 2; s €36-60, d €50-85; ❄) The best of several budget places near the east end of Calle Ancha, the pedestrianised main street on the estuary side of town. All rooms are sizeable and comfy but the renovated ones are positively stylish, in cool blues and greens with flat-screen TVs set flush to the wall. Rates dip by 25% to 50% outside July and August.

Hotel Barceló Punta Umbría (☎ 959 49 54 00; www.barcelo.com; Avenida Océano s/n; s/d incl breakfast €132/165; P ❄ 💻 🏊 ♿) This large modern complex in Alhambra-influenced style sits right on the Atlantic seaboard overlooking the beach. It offers all the expected top-end facilities including a large kidney-shaped pool.

Chiringuito Camarón (☎ 959 65 90 38; Avenida Océano; mains €9-15; 🕑 Mon-Sun afternoon) By far the best places to eat in Punta Umbría are the restaurants and *chiringuitos* (open-air eateries) dotted along the ocean beach. The Camarón, almost in front of the Hotel Barceló, serves up terrific fish from the Huelva coasts *a la plancha* (hotplate-grilled) or fried, plus good paella. Efficient waiters, big ocean-view windows and an ample *terraza* make dining here a pleasure – and it's open all year.

Also recommended:

Hotel Ayamontino (☎ 959 31 14 50; hotelayamontino@hotmail.com; Avenida Andalucía 35; s/d €52/81; ☒) Solid midrange place with restaurant and café, centrally placed opposite the tourist office.

Restaurant Miramar (☎ 959 31 12 43; Calle Miramar 1; mains €8-16; ☒ closed Mon) Another top year-round beach restaurant.

Getting There & Away

From Huelva, buses run to Punta Umbría (€1.90, 30 minutes) every hour from 7.15am to 8.15pm and at 9pm. In summer, hourly ferries (€2) sail from the Muelle de Levante at Huelva's port.

ISLA CRISTINA

pop 19,000

Thirty kilometres west of Punta Umbría along the same fabulous beach (broken only by the estuary of the Río Piedras at El Rompido), Isla Cristina is not only a developing beach resort, packed in August (when prices skyrocket), but also a bustling fishing port with a 250-strong fleet. East along the beach, which is backed by attractive dunes and pine woods outside the town, are the custom-built resorts of Islantilla and La Antilla, low-rise and tasteful enough but near-deserted out of season.

Orientation & Information

Isla Cristina stands at the west end of a low promontory between the Carreras estuary along its north side and the Atlantic beach on the south. The town centre, bus station and fishing port are all in the northwest corner of the promontory. From the centre, Gran Vía Román Pérez heads 1km south to the western end of Isla Cristina's blue-flagged beach, while hotels are dotted around the beach side of town, up to 2km east of the centre. The helpful, modern **tourist office** (☎ 959 33 26 94; Calle San Francisco 12; ☒ 10am-2pm daily, plus 5.30-7.30pm Mon-Fri Mar-Oct)

is among the narrow older streets behind the fishing port.

Sights & Activities

Upstairs in the tourist office building is the **Museo de Carnaval** (Carnival Museum; ☎ 959 33 26 94; admission free; ☒ 10am-2pm daily, plus 5.30-7.30pm Mon-Fri Mar-Oct) with a gorgeously colourful display of costumes, crowns and posters from Isla Cristina's annual carnival, which is among the biggest in Andalucía.

The **Puerto Pesquero** (Fishing Port; Muelle Martínez Catena; ☒ auctions about 11am & 4pm Mon-Fri) is a lively scene in the morning and evening as boats sail in with their catches and the fish are auctioned off before being whisked away to the markets of Seville, Córdoba and Madrid.

As you can imagine Isla Cristina and Islantilla enjoy excellent conditions for watersports. The **Estación Naútica Isla Cristina** (☎ 902 07 64 77; www.en-islacristina.com) is a unified information source for local windsurfing, canoeing, sailing, waterskiing and diving operators.

Sleeping & Eating

Camping Giralda (☎ 959 34 33 18; www.campinggiralda.com; Carretera Isla Cristina-La Antilla Km 1.5; adult/tent/car €5.50/5/4.50, bungalow for 4 €49-91; ⓟ ☒) Set among pines at the eastern edge of town, the Giralda has room for over 2000 people. The dune-backed Playa Central is close and you can arrange a host of water-based and other activities at the site.

Hotel El Paraíso Playa (☎ 959 33 02 35; www.hotelparaisoplaya.com; Avenida de la Playa; s/d €65/129; ⓟ ☒ ☒ ☒) A friendly and attractively remodelled two-storey hotel, with restaurant and bar, just a stone's throw from Playa Central, this is the best deal in town – especially outside peak season: prices drop to €49/97 in June and September and €33/59 from October to May.

Hotel Oasis Isla Cristina (☎ 959 48 64 22; www.hotelesoasis.com; Avenida Parque 62; r incl breakfast €161-225; ⓟ ☒ ☒ ☒) If you fancy the comforts of a large, top-end, Spanish holiday hotel, Isla Cristina has three virtually brand-new ones, though you may not find any open in the depths of winter. The luxurious Oasis is set among pine woods a stone's throw from the beach and has a lovely large pool and a kids' club with its own smaller pool. Room rates dip sharply outside July and August.

Casa Rufino (☎ 959 33 08 10; Avenida de la Playa; mains €13-26; 🕑 lunch & dinner 15 Jul-31 Oct, lunch 16 Feb-14 Jul & 1 Nov-21 Dec, closed 22 Dec-15 Feb) You can't miss the gaudy yellow-and-green tilework of Isla Cristina's most celebrated restaurant, just off Playa Central. Its speciality is the *tonteo*, an eight-fish, eight-sauce sampler of local favourites (€24 per person; minimum two people).

Also excellent for fresh seafood are the restaurants on the plaza outside the fishing port. The unassuming upstairs dining room at **Restaurante Hermanos Moreno** (☎ 959 34 35 71; Avenida Padre Mirabent 39; mains & raciones €8-20; 🕑 lunch) and the larger **Restaurante El Pescador** (☎ 959 34 36 35; Avenida Padre Mirabent 19; mains & raciones €7-13; 🕑 6.30am-9pm or later) both serve up tasty fried and *plancha* fare.

Drinking

Some bars in the older streets near the central Plaza Flores stay open late and get lively with a youngish crowd. **Pipirigaña** (Calle Pérez Pascual 12) is an inviting one, with an open courtyard where live music is sometimes staged.

Getting There & Away

Damas (☎ 959 33 16 52; Calle Manuel Siurot) runs buses to Huelva (€3.80, one hour, 14 daily Monday to Friday, five daily Saturday and Sunday), Ayamonte (€1.40, 25 minutes, three to five daily) and Seville (€10, two hours, one to three daily).

AYAMONTE

pop 17,000

Ayamonte has a cheerful borderland buzz about it, although you can now speed straight past it into Portugal on the splendid Puente del Guadiana over the wide Río Guadiana north of town. Romantics can still enjoy the pace of times past, however, by taking the ferry across the Guadiana between Ayamonte and Vila Real de Santo António.

Orientation & Information

Ayamonte's hub is Plaza de la Coronación and its seamless neighbour Paseo de la Ribera, fronting Avenida Vila Real de Santo Antonio, opposite the marina. The *muelle transbordador* (ferry dock) is 300m west of here, on Avenida Muelle de Portugal, beside the Guadiana. The bus station is 700m east of Plaza de la Coronación.

Ayamonte's **tourist office** (☎ 959 32 07 37; Calle Huelva 27; 🕑 10am-2pm & 5-7pm Mon-Fri Oct-Jun, 10am-2pm & 6-9pm Mon-Fri Jul-Sep, 11am-1.30pm Sat), a couple of blocks behind Plaza de la Coronación, is very keen to help you make the most of your time here.

Sights & Activities

The old town between Paseo de la Ribera and the ferry dock, with its narrow, mainly pedestrianised streets, is dotted with attractive plazas and old churches and riddled with bars, cafés, shops and restaurants, making for a pleasant wander. The **Casa Grande** (Calle Huelva 37; admission free; 🕑 10am-1pm & 5-8.30pm Mon-Fri), a fine 18th-century mansion with a carved pinkstone façade and columned interior patio, is now Ayamonte's Casa de la Cultura, staging art exhibitions and other events.

If you'd like to get to know more of the Río Guadiana, one of Spain's longest and biggest rivers, **Cruceros del Guadiana** (☎ 959 64 10 02; www.crucerosdelguadiana.com) runs daily cruises around the estuary (€8, 70 minutes) and some 35km upstream to the Portuguese village of Alcoutim (€42 including lunch, 7½ hours). Check departure times and get tickets at their kiosk on the ferry dock.

Sleeping & Eating

Hotel Marqués de Ayamonte (☎ 959 32 01 26; Calle Trajano 14; s/d €28/45) The Marqués provides plain but good-sized rooms with TV, phone and winter heating. The best thing is its central location just off Paseo de la Ribera.

Hotel Luz del Guadiana (☎ 959 32 20 02; Avenida de Andalucía 119; s/d incl breakfast €45/70; 🔀 🛗) In a bland modern block just west of the bus station, this hotel has pleasant enough rooms with TV and air-con. Ask at neighbouring Bar Los Robles if no-one answers the door.

Hotel Don Diego (☎ 959 47 02 50; www.hoteldon diegoayamonte.com; Avenida Ramón y Cajal 2; r incl breakfast without/with air-con €76/89; 🕑 closed mid-Oct–Semana Santa; P 🔀 🛗) The seasonally open pink confection of the Don Diego is southeast of the marina. Rooms come with TV and bright red bathrooms.

Parador de Ayamonte (☎ 959 32 07 00; www.para dor.es; Avenida de la Constitución; s/d €103/129; P 🔀 🛗 🛗) The modern Parador looks out over the broad Guadiana from a spectacular hilltop perch 1.5km north of the town centre. Decked out in chichi peaches and mint greens, it's well appointed if a bit soulless.

Casa Luciano (Calle Palma del Condado 1; mains €10-17; ⊙ closed Sun) Great fish and a great atmosphere make the unassuming Luciano the place for a slap-up meal. Everything on your plate is freshly cooked and only minutes out of the water – and there's lamb or wild asparagus *revuelto* (scrambled-egg dish) if you fancy something more land-based.

Casa Barberi (☎ 959 47 01 37; Paseo de la Ribera 12; mains €7-16) and **Mesón La Casona** (☎ 959 32 10 25; Calle Lusitania 2; mains & raciones €6-15) are both popular and busy, serving a range of seafood and meat.

Getting There & Around

There are no customs or immigration checks heading in either direction by road or ferry.

BOAT

The ferries of **Transportes Fluvial del Guadiana** (☎ 959 47 06 17) cross the Guadiana to/from Vila Real de Santo António every 40 minutes from 9.40am to 8pm, Monday to Saturday, and hourly from 10.30am to 6.30pm on Sundays and holidays shared by Spain and Portugal. From July to September they go every half-hour, 9.30am to 9pm. One-way fares are €4 for a car and driver and €1.30 for adult passengers. Fairly frequent buses and trains run along the Algarve from Vila Real de Santo António.

BUS

Damas (☎ 959 32 11 71; Avenida de Andalucía) runs to Huelva (€4.50, one hour, six to 10 daily), Seville (€10.50, two hours, four or five daily) and Isla Cristina (€1.40, 25 minutes, three to five daily). Damas also has a twice daily service (except Saturday, Sunday and holidays from October to May) along Portugal's Algarve to Faro (€5.50, 1¾ hours) and Lagos (€10, 3½ hours). Buses to Isla Canela (€0.90, 15 minutes) run every half-hour, 9am to 8pm, from June to September, but just four times a day, Monday to Friday only, the rest of the year.

THE NORTH

As you travel north from Huelva's southern plains, straight highways are replaced by winding byways and you enter a more temperate zone, up to 960m higher than the coast, with a benevolent climate that's relatively rainy by Andalucian standards and a little cooler than most of the region in summer. The rolling hills of Huelva's portion of the Sierra Morena are covered with a thick pelt of cork oaks, chestnuts and pines and punctuated by winding river valleys, dramatic cliffs, age-old, enchanting villages of stone and tile, and bustling market towns such as the area's 'capital', Aracena. This is a wonderful and still little-discovered rural world, threaded with beautiful walking and riding trails and blessed with a rich hill-country cuisine that abounds in game, local cheeses and fresh vegetables but is famous above all for the best *jamón serrano* in Spain. Most of the hill country lies within the 1840-sq-km **Parque Natural Sierra de Aracena y Picos de Aroche**, Andalucía's second-largest protected area.

MINAS DE RIOTINTO

pop 4500 / elevation 420m

Tucked away on the southern fringe of the sierra is one of the world's oldest mining districts – no longer producing the metals it's famed for but still fascinating for its unearthly, sculpted and scarred landscape, its absorbing history, its A1 museum and the opportunity to visit old mines and ride the mine railway. The area's hub is the town of Minas de Riotinto. The Río Tinto itself rises a few kilometres northeast of the town, its name ('Coloured River') coming from the deep red-brown hue produced by the reaction of its acidic waters with the abundant iron and copper ores.

Legend tells us the mines here were the mines of King Solomon. Archaeology has yielded evidence of copper mining as early as the 3rd millennium BC. By the 4th century AD the Romans were going at it hammer and tongs, mining what was described as a veritable mountain of silver by Avienus, who saw the 'slopes glint and shine in the light'. The lodes were then largely neglected until a group of mainly British investors founded the Rio Tinto Company to buy the mines from the Spanish government in 1873. The company turned the area into one of the world's great copper-mining centres, diverting rivers, digging away an entire metal-rich hill (Cerro Colorado), founding Minas de

Riotinto town to replace a village it had demolished, and setting up an enclave of British colonial society which among other things formed Spain's first football club. By 1913 the Rio Tinto Company employed over 14,000 workers, but in the mid-20th century it sold the mines to Spanish interests. The company has since become one of the planet's biggest mining companies, with operations worldwide, but mining in its birthplace went into a steady decline and finally ceased in 2001.

Orientation

Minas de Riotinto is 6km east along the A461 off the N435 Huelva–Jabugo road. Entering the town, turn right at the first roundabout to reach the Museo Minero, about 400m uphill. Buses stop on Plaza de El Minero, a little beyond the same roundabout.

Sights

The attractions are administered by the **Parque Minero de Riotinto** (☎ 959 59 00 25; http://parquemineroderiotinto.sigadel.com; Plaza Ernest Lluch; ⊗ 10.30am-3pm & 4-7pm), headquartered at the well-signposted Museo Minero. Here you can buy tickets for the museum, the Victorian house, the Peña de Hierro and the Ferrocarril Turístico-Minero, with small discounts if you opt for combined tickets. It's worth ringing ahead to confirm timetables, especially for the train and the Peña de Hierro.

The fascinating **Museo Minero** (Plaza Ernest Lluch; adult/child under 13yr €4/3; ⊗ 10.30am-3pm & 4-7pm) is a figurative gold mine for devotees of industrial archaeology, taking you right through the Riotinto area's unique history from the megalithic tombs of the 3rd millennium BC to the Roman and British colonial eras and finally the closure of the mines in 2001, with some information in English as well as Spanish. One of the best features is the 200m-long re-creation of a Roman mine which includes a reconstruction of one of the Roman water wheels built to drain water out of the mines. The tunnels might feel claustrophobic to some, but the displays along the way tell a vivid story of a nightmarish world where slaves worked in galleries only 1m wide by the light of tiny oil lamps, many of them dying within weeks from the wretched conditions. The

museum also features a big display on the railways that served the mines. At one time, 143 steam engines, mostly British-built, were puffing up and down these tracks. Pride of place goes to the **Vagón del Maharajah**, a luxurious carriage built in 1892 for a tour of India by Britain's Queen Victoria and later used by Spain's Alfonso XIII for a visit to the mines.

The museum ticket also gives entry to a **Victorian house** in the **Barrio de Bella Vista**, a 19th-century suburb where British staff of the Rio Tinto Company were housed, complete with Protestant church and colonial-style 'English Club'. The house (Bella Vista 21) is accurately kitted out with British colonial furniture and trappings. The suburb, now inhabited by Spaniards, is beside the A461 opposite the turn-off into the town centre, and anyone can wander round even if not visiting No 21. The English Club is still in existence and remains exclusive though now with a largely Spanish membership, to which women were finally admitted in 2001.

An easy and fun way to see the mining area (especially with children) is to ride the **Ferrocarril Turístico-Minero** (adult/child €10/9; ⊗ 1.30pm 1 Jun-15 Jul, 1.30 & 5pm 16 Jul-30 Sep, 4pm Sat, Sun & holidays Oct-Feb, 1pm Mon-Fri, 4pm Sat, Sun & holidays Mar-May), taking visitors 22km (roundtrip) through the surreal landscape in restored early-20th-century railway carriages. Trips start at Talleres Minas, the old railway repair workshops 2.5km east of Minas de Riotinto, off the road to the nearby town of Nerva. The train is pulled by a diesel locomotive except when a steam engine takes over a few Sundays a year. It's essential to book ahead for the train, and schedules may change, especially in winter. You have to make your own way to the station: ask at the museum about taxis.

The other trip organised by the Parque Minero is to the old copper and sulphur mines of **Peña de Hierro** (adult/child €8/7), in an impressive hilly and forested landscape 4km north of Nerva and 9km from Minas de Riotinto. Here you see the source of the Río Tinto, an 85m-deep opencast mine, and are taken into a 200m-long underground mine gallery and to the site of the fascinating Marte project (see the boxed text, p164). These trips are available daily but times vary and it's essential to book.

HUELVA PROVINCE

The Parque Minero is currently not running trips to the **Corta Atalaya**, one of the world's biggest opencast mines, 1km west of the town. But you can still get a peep at this awesome hole in the ground, 1.2km long and 335m deep and reminiscent of a vast amphitheatre, if you follow the 'Corta Atalaya' sign to the left as you enter Minas de Riotinto from the southwest.

The most recent mining activity took place about 1km north of Minas de Riotinto at another opencast mine, the **Corta Cerro Colorado**. There's a viewing platform on the road towards Aracena, the Mirador Cerro Colorado, where you can ponder the fact that as recently as 1968 Cerro Colorado was a hill.

Sleeping & Eating

Minas de Riotinto itself only has one place to stay, but there are good options in Nerva, another ex-mining town 5km east.

La Estación (☎ 959 58 00 34; www.cnlaestacion.com; Carretera Nerva-Riotinto s/n, Nerva; dm incl breakfast under/over 26yr €12/15; **P**) Offers friendly and sparkling clean hostel-type accommodation in Nerva's renovated 19th-century railway station. It has lots of local information.

Hostal Galán (☎ 959 59 08 40; www.hostalrestaurantegalan.com; Avenida La Esquila 10; s/d €27/39; **※**) Just round the corner from the Museo Minero, the Galán has plain but acceptable rooms and a handy restaurant with a lunch or dinner *menú* (set menu) for €8.50.

THE MARTE PROJECT

On trips to Peña de Hierro you'll be shown the area where, since 2003, scientists from NASA of the US and Spain's Centro de Astrobiología in Madrid have been conducting a research programme known as Marte (Mars Analog Research & Technology Experiment) in preparation for seeking life on Mars. It's thought that the high acid levels that give the Río Tinto its colour (by the action of acid on iron) are a product of underground micro-organisms comparable with those that scientists believe may exist below the surface of Mars. Experiments in locating these microbes up to 150m below ground level are being used to help develop techniques and instruments for looking for similar subterranean life on the red planet.

Hotel Vázquez Díaz (☎ /fax 959 58 09 27; personal.telefonica.terra.es/web/hotelvazquezdiaz; Calle Cañadilla 51, Nerva; s/d €26/43; **※**) A welcoming, well-run hotel in Nerva, which offers decent rooms and has its own good restaurant (*menú* €10).

Cafetería Época (☎ 959 59 20 76; Paseo de los Caracoles 6; mains €7/20; ⏰ 8am-11pm) On the way into Minas de Riotinto from the A461, this bright, modern establishment has a handy café section with a good selection of tapas and *raciones,* and a rear restaurant walled with historical photos.

Getting There & Away

Damas buses run daily from Huelva to Minas de Riotinto (€5.50, 1½ hours, up to six daily) and on to Nerva (€6, 1¾ hours, up to five daily), and vice-versa. **Casal** (☎ 954 99 92 62 in Seville) has three daily buses from Seville (Plaza de Armas) to Nerva (€4, 1½ hours) and Minas de Riotinto (€4.50, 1¾ hours).

Damas departs Minas de Riotinto for Aracena (€2.30, one hour) at 4.35pm (11.05am on Sunday) and at 3.05pm Monday to Friday. This last goes via Nerva. A Casal bus leaves Nerva for Aracena via Minas de Riotinto at 5.45am Monday to Saturday. Returning, the Casal bus leaves Aracena at 5.15pm, while Damas buses depart Aracena for Minas de Riotinto (but not Nerva) at 7.45am (6pm Sunday) and 7am Monday to Friday.

ARACENA

pop 7000 / elevation 730m

In the heart of the sierra lies the old and thriving market town of Aracena, an appealingly lively place spreading around the skirts of a hill crowned by a medieval church and ruined castle. It makes an ideal base from which to explore this lovely area.

Orientation

The town lies between the castle hill, Cerro del Castillo, in the south, and the N433 Seville–Portugal road skirting it to the north and east. The main square is Plaza del Marqués de Aracena, from which the main street, Avenida de los Infantes Don Carlos y Doña Luisa (more simply known as Gran Vía), runs west. The bus station is towards the southeast edge of town, on Avenida de Sevilla.

Information

Centro de Salud (☎ 959 12 62 56; Calle Zulema s/n)
Health centre almost opposite the bus station.

Centro de Visitantes Cabildo Viejo (☎ 959 12 88 25;
Plaza Alta 5; ◷ 10am-2pm & 4-6pm Tue-Sun Sep-Jun,
10am-2pm & 6-8pm Tue-Sun Jul-Aug) The main information centre of the Parque Natural Sierra de Aracena y Picos
de Aroche.

Municipal Tourist Office (☎ 959 12 82 06; Calle
Pozo de la Nieve; ◷ 10am-2pm & 4-6.30pm) Facing the
entrance to the Gruta de las Maravillas; sells some maps
of the area.

P&C (☎ 959 12 63 96; Calle Constitución 9; internet
per hr €2; ◷ 10am-2pm & 5-8.30pm Mon-Fri, 11am-
2pm Sat)

Post office (☎ 959 12 81 52; Calle Juan del Cid 6;
◷ 8.30am-8.30pm Mon-Fri, 9.30am-1pm Sat)

Sights

Dramatically dominating the town are the
tumbling, hilltop ruins of the **castillo**, an atmospheric fort built by the Portuguese in
the 13th century and rebuilt, probably by
the Knights of Santiago, around 1300. Next
door is the **Iglesia Prioral de Nuestra Señora del
Mayor Dolor** (admission free; ◷ 10.30m-6pm), also
built around 1300 – a Gothic-Mudejar hybrid that combines an interior of ribbed
vaults with attractive brick tracery on the
tower. The castle is reached up a steep
road from Plaza Alta, a handsome, cobbled square that was originally the centre
of the town that initially grew up on the
slopes below the castle. The 15th-century
Cabildo Viejo (Old Town Hall) here houses

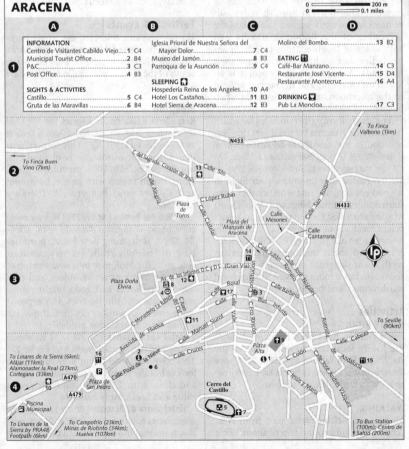

ARACENA

0 ————— 200 m
0 ————— 0.1 miles

INFORMATION
Centro de Visitantes Cabildo Viejo.....**1** C4
Municipal Tourist Office..................**2** B4
P&C...**3** C3
Post Office.....................................**4** B3

SIGHTS & ACTIVITIES
Castillo..**5** C4
Gruta de las Maravillas **6** B4

Iglesia Prioral de Nuestra Señora del
Mayor Dolor...............................**7** C4
Museo del Jamón..........................**8** B3
Parroquia de la Asunción...............**9** C4

SLEEPING 🛏
Hospedería Reina de los Ángeles......**10** A4
Hotel Los Castaños........................**11** B3
Hotel Sierra de Aracena.................**12** B3

Molino del Bombo...........................**13** B2

EATING 🍴
Café-Bar Manzano.........................**14** C3
Restaurante José Vicente...............**15** D4
Restaurante Montecruz..................**16** A4

DRINKING 🍷
Pub La Moncloa.............................**17** C3

the natural park's visitor centre (see p165). Opposite is a huge, unfinished Renaissance church, the **Parroquia de la Asunción** (7.30am-8.30pm Mon-Sat, noon-1pm Sun).

Beneath the castle hill lies a maze of caves and tunnels full of stalagmites and stalactites. Attracting some 150,000 visitors a year, these form Aracena's premier tourist site, the **Gruta de las Maravillas** (Cave of Marvels; ☎ 959 12 83 55; Calle Pozo de la Nieve; tour adult/under 19yr €8/5.50; 10.30am-1.30pm & 3-6pm tours every hr Mon-Fri, every half-hr Sat, Sun & holidays). The 1km route features 12 chambers and six lakes, with all sorts of weird and wonderful rock formations that provided the backdrop for the filming of *Journey to the Centre of the Earth*. Coloured lighting and piped music make you feel that this is still a lurid film set but the cave nevertheless manages to impress. The tour (in Spanish only) culminates at the aptly named **Sala de los Culos** (Chamber of the Bottoms), usually met with roars of laughter from elderly Spanish ladies and bashful silence from their husbands. A maximum of 35 people is allowed on each tour and tickets can sell out in the afternoons and on weekends when busloads of visitors arrive.

The *jamón ibérico* (Iberian ham) for which the Sierra de Aracena is famed gets due recognition in the new **Museo del Jamón** (Museum of Ham; ☎ 959 12 79 95; Gran Vía; tour adult/under 19yr €3/2; tour every 40 min 11.10am-5.10pm;). Visits are by guided tour so unless your Spanish is good enough, ask first whether they have started tours in other languages. You'll learn why the acorn-fed Iberian pig gives such succulent meat, about the importance of the *dehesas* (native oak pastures) in which they are reared, and about traditional and modern methods of slaughter and curing. The museum also has a room devoted to *setas* (wild mushrooms), another local delicacy.

Activities
HORSE RIDING
For a ride on horseback through some of the lovely local countryside, head to the stables at **Finca Valbono** (☎ 959 12 77 11; www .fincavalbono.com; Carretera Carboneras Km 1; guided ride per hr €10), 1km northeast of town.

WALKING
Many good **walking routes** start from Aracena. A beautiful round trip of about 12km

can be made by leaving Aracena between the Piscina Municipal (municipal swimming pool) and the A470 road at the western end of town. This path (see Map p168), the PRA48, rollercoasters down a verdant valley to Linares de la Sierra (p169). To return by a different (and less steep) route, the PRA39, find a small stone bridge over the river below Linares, beyond which the path goes round Cerro de la Molinilla, passing old iron mines for a stony ascent to Aracena, coming out on the A479 in the southwest of town.

You could extend the walk 4km west from Linares to Alájar on the PRA38, via the hamlet of Los Madroñeros. There are great views on this stretch. From Alájar you can catch the afternoon bus, daily except Sunday, back to Aracena (see p168).

Festivals & Events
Ham lovers can celebrate the whole piggy scene at the **Feria del Jamón y del Cerdo Ibérico** (Iberian Ham & Pig Fair), held on a site south of the Cerro del Castillo for four days around 20 October.

Sleeping
Hospedería Reina de los Ángeles (☎ 959 12 83 67; www.hospederiareinadelosangeles; Avenida Reina de los Ángeles s/n; s/d €23/38;) This former residence for out-of-town school students, opened as a hotel in 2005, provides 90 good, clean, bright rooms with phone, bathroom and TV – a good budget deal. There's a café too.

Molino del Bombo (☎ 959 12 84 78; www.molino delbombo.com in Spanish; Calle Ancha 4; s/d €23/45;) A welcoming new *hostal*, purpose-built in tastefully rustic yet very comfortable style, the Molino stands near the top of the town. With attractive indoor and outdoor sitting areas and good bright rooms making use of little frescoes and exposed stone and brick work as design features, it's a great find. Breakfast is available.

Hotel Los Castaños (☎ 959 12 63 00; www.lo scastanoshotel.com; Avenida de Huelva 5; s/d €39/58;) This 33-room hotel is not very exciting to look at but the rooms are good-sized, comfy and clean, with TV and bathtub. It's solid value and breakfast is available.

Hotel Sierra de Aracena (☎ 959 12 61 75; www .hsierraaracena.es; Gran Vía 21; s/d €43/59;) A reliable hotel that has recently had the overhaul it was due for. The style is chintz, classic art and floral prints. Rooms are good-sized: eight enjoy good castle views and the newer, wood-roofed attic rooms, costing €10 to €15 extra, are particularly cosy.

Finca Valbono (☎ 959 12 77 11; www.fincavalbono .com; Carretera Carboneras Km 1; s/d €73/89, 4-person apt €150; P 🏊 ⬛ 🐎 ᚫ) A converted farmhouse 1km northeast of town, this is Aracena's most charming accommodation, all in tasteful rustic style including fireplaces in the apartments. Facilities include a bar, a pool, riding stables and a good, medium-priced restaurant (mains €8 to €15) with local mushroom and meat specialities as well as vegetarian and pasta dishes.

Eating

Café-Bar Manzano (☎ 959 12 63 37; Plaza del Marqués de Aracena; tapas €1.80-3.50, raciones €9-18; ⏱ 8am-8pm or later Wed-Sat & Mon, 10am-8pm Sun) This terrace café on the plaza is a fine spot to watch the world go by and enjoy varied tapas and *raciones*, including many types of wild mushroom, some of which seem to be in season almost year-round here.

Restaurante José Vicente (☎ 959 12 84 55; Avenida de Andalucía 53; 3-course menú €18; ⏱ 1-4pm & 9-11pm, closed Sun evening, last week Jun & 1st week Jul) Aracena's best restaurant and a good place to enjoy the area's famous specialities – *jamón ibérico*, mushrooms and even snails. The proprietor is an expert on sierra cuisine and even the fixed-price *menú* (which includes a drink) is excellent. It's a small place so it's advisable to book.

Restaurante Montecruz (☎ 959 12 60 13; Plaza de San Pedro; raciones €9-15, menú €15) Several tourist-oriented restaurants and bars line Plaza de San Pedro and Calle Pozo de la Nieve near the Gruta de las Maravillas. The Montecruz, adorned with assorted stags' heads and bunches of garlic, takes pride in its Aracena cuisine but don't let the waiters steer you too rapidly to the most expensive dishes.

For further tapas bars, take a wander along Gran Vía or Avenida de Andalucía.

Drinking

A small cluster of late bars starts to unlock their doors around 10.30pm along Calle Rosal, a dark side street between Gran Vía and Avenida de Huelva. For cool company try Pub La Moncloa, with a deep 16th-century well preserved in one corner. Most

nights in summer it stays open till around 4am but off-season it may close at 1am or not even open at all.

Getting There & Away

Casal (☎ 954 99 92 62 in Seville) runs two daily buses to/from Seville's Plaza de Armas bus station (€6, 1¼ hours). **Damas** (☎ 959 25 69 00 in Huelva) travels to/from Huelva (€6, 2¼ hours, one or two daily). There are also buses from Aracena to Minas de Riotinto (see p164), to villages around northern Huelva province (p168) and a daily Casal bus at 10.30am to the Portuguese border just beyond Rosal de la Frontera, where you can change to onward Portuguese buses (Aracena–Lisbon takes nearly nine hours for €16).

WEST OF ARACENA

Stretching west of Aracena is one of Andalucía's most unexpectedly beautiful landscapes, a sometimes lush, sometimes severe hill-country region dotted with old stone villages where time seems to have stood still for a good long while. Many of the valleys are full of woodlands, while elsewhere are expanses of *dehesa* – evergreen oak pastures where the region's famed black pigs forage for acorns. The area is threaded by an extensive network of well maintained walking trails, with ever-changing vistas and mostly gentle ascents and descents, making for some of the most delightful rambling in Andalucía. Most of the villages are served by buses and many of them have accommodation and decent restaurants, so you can make day hikes or string together a route of several days. It's advisable to book ahead for rooms.

Good walking routes extend over all parts of the **Parque Natural Sierra de Aracena y Picos de Aroche**, but they're particularly thick in the area between Aracena and Cortegana, making attractive villages such as Alájar, Castaño del Robledo, Galaroza and Almonaster la Real good bases.

Maps & Guides

Trail marking is erratic so you need the best possible map and preferably a good walking guide. The best of both in any language are Discovery Walking Guides' *Sierra de Aracena* and accompanying *Sierra de Aracena Tour & Trail Map*. These are sold locally at La Posada in Alájar and the Posada del Castaño in Castaño del Robledo, but it makes sense to buy them before you come if possible. Other reasonable maps are *Parque Natural Sierra de Aracena y Picos de Aroche* (1:75,000), published by the Junta de Andalucía, and the IGN 1:25,000 sheets 917-I *Galaroza*, 917-II *Cortelazor*, 917-III *Cortegana* and 917-IV *Aracena*. Also worth having is the Spanish-language *Mapa Guía Sierra de Aracena y Picos de Aroche*.

Getting There & Around
BUS
Casal (☎ 954 99 92 62 in Seville) runs buses from Seville (Plaza de Armas), via Aracena, to many of the villages. Two a day follow the N433 to Galaroza (€1.40, 25 minutes from Aracena), Jabugo (€2, 35 minutes), Cortegana (€2.60, 50 minutes) and Aroche (€3.50, 1¼ hours), and one (Monday to Saturday only) takes the southerly A470 route to Cortegana through Linares de la Sierra (€0.90, 15 minutes), Alájar (€1, 30 minutes) and Almonaster la Real (€1.90, 50 minutes). In addition, two buses a day (one on Sunday) run just from Aracena to Cortegana by the N433 (one continuing to Aroche except on Saturday), and one (Monday to Saturday only) from Aracena to Cortegana and Aroche by the southern route. All these services run in the reverse direction too, making it possible to travel west and east morning and late afternoon every day on the northern route. On the southern route you can go westbound at lunchtime and late afternoon, and eastbound early morning and mid-afternoon (except Sunday in all cases).

Damas (☎ 959 25 69 00 in Huelva) runs one bus each way Monday to Friday between Huelva and Aroche (€7.50, three hours) via Almonaster la Real (€6.50, 2½ hours) and Cortegana (€7, 2¾ hours), and another between Huelva and Jabugo (€7, 2¾ hours) and Galaroza (€7, 2¾ hours). The latter service also runs north (but not south) on Sunday.

CAR & MOTORCYCLE
The N433 from Aracena to Portugal passes through Galaroza and Cortegana and near Jabugo. A more scenic and slower route is the narrower, more winding A470 through Santa Ana la Real and Almonaster la Real (passing close to Linares de la Sierra and Alájar). Several roads and paths cut across the hills to link these two roads.

TRAIN
There are two daily trains running each way between Huelva and the stations of Almonaster-Cortegana (€5.50, 2½ hours) and Jabugo-Galaroza (€6, 2¾ hours). Both trains terminate further north in Extremadura. Almonaster-Cortegana station is 1km off the Almonaster–Cortegana road, about halfway between the two villages. Jabugo-Galaroza station is in El Repilado, on the N433, 4km west of Jabugo.

WEST OF ARACENA

Linares de la Sierra
pop 300 / elevation 500m

Sunk in a river valley 7km west of Aracena on the A470, Linares appears to exist in another era. Cobbled streets, a minute unpaved bullring plaza, black-clad villagers, blind corners and thick silence pervade the tiny streets that are surrounded on all sides by a verdant river valley. There's no accommodation here but there is the famously good **Restaurant Los Arrieros** (☎ 959 46 37 17; Calle Arrieros 2; mains €9-15; ☺ lunch, closed Mon & mid-Jun–mid-Jul), with its summer terrace overlooking the valley, enticing fire in winter and innovative approach to the area's pork products and wild mushrooms, such as the latter caramelised in sweet sherry. It's a great place to break the walk from Aracena to Alájar (see p166), but be sure to reserve a table.

Alájar
pop 750 / elevation 570m

Five kilometres west of Linares de la Sierra is the region's most picturesque village, Alájar. Bigger than Linares, it still retains its tiny cobbled streets and cubist stone houses as well as a fine baroque church. Above the village a rocky spur, the **Peña de Arias Montano**, provides magical views over the village and is reached 1km up the road towards Fuenteheridos. The *peña*'s 16th-century chapel, the **Ermita de Nuestra Señora Reina de los Ángeles** (☺ 11am-sunset), contains a small 13th-century carving of the Virgin that is considered the patron of the whole Sierra de Aracena. The chapel is the focus of the area's biggest annual religious event, the Romería de la Reina de los Ángeles (8 September), when people from all around the sierra and beyond converge here to honour their Virgin.

The Peña de Arias Montano takes its name from Benito Arias Montano, a remarkable 16th-century polymath and humanist who produced one of the first maps of the world, learned 11 languages and was confessor, adviser and librarian to the powerful Spanish king Felipe II. Late in life Montano became parish priest of nearby Castaño del Robledo and made many visits to this spot for retreat and meditation, inspired no doubt by the magnificent views. Felipe II is said to have visited him here and prayed in the cave just below the car park.

THE AUTHOR'S CHOICE

Casa Padrino (☎ 959 12 56 01; Plaza Miguel Moya 2; mains €8-12; ☺ lunch Sat & Sun, dinner Fri & Sat) Formerly a farmhouse belonging to Arias Montano, Casa Padrino, just behind Alájar's church, serves superb fare loosely based on old village recipes in what used to be the building's chapel. Try the *revuelto de hiervas del campo* (scrambled eggs with wild herbs) or the *solomillo al romero* (pork sirloin with rosemary) – and don't miss out on the fabulous list of Spanish wines. You can also enjoy tapas in the front bar.

Outside the chapel are stalls selling local cheeses, and also the 6th- or 7th-century **Arco de los Novios**: by legend any couple who walk together through this 'Arch of the Fiancés' will marry.

There's a very cosy inn, **La Posada** (☎ 959 12 57 12; laposadadealajar.com; Calle Médico Emilio González 2; s/d incl breakfast €45/55), a couple of doors off the central Plaza de España, which has just eight rooms, a good little travellers' library and a small restaurant for guests. The friendly Spanish-British couple who run it are keen walkers and full of information on the area, and can arrange guided walks and horse rides.

Down in a beautiful valley about 1.5km west from the village, the excellent, Dutch-run **Molino Río Alájar** (☎ 959 13 13 08; www.molinorioalajar.com; Finca Cabeza del Molino; cottage for 2/4 from €88/118; ℗ ☺)comprises a set of comfy, warm-feeling, stone, brick and tile holiday cottages, with a spacious communal room, pool, donkeys for hire and plenty of walking information. Minimum stay is two nights, rising to seven at peak seasons.

Alájar's former cinema has been converted into **Mesón El Corcho** (☎ 959 12 57 79; Plaza de España 3; mains €12-15), an authentic temple to the products of the sierra, especially local cheeses and roast leg of lamb. The design is utterly unique, from the stone floor mosaics to the amazing cork sculptures on the bar ceiling.

Castaño del Robledo
pop 200 / elevation 740m

North of Alájar on a minor road between Fuenteheridos and Jabugo, the small village of Castaño del Robledo is enjoying a late

THE AUTHOR'S CHOICE

Off the N433 just west of the small village of Los Marines and 7km from Aracena, **Finca Buen Vino** (☎ 959 12 40 34; www.fincabuenvino.com; Carretera N433 Km 95; per person incl breakfast Oct-Apr €60, May-Sep €70, cottage per week low/high season €500/1000; P 🖳 🐾) is a cross between a working farm and a delightfully comfortable, convivial English country house. It's a great base for walking trips and for enjoying first-class food and wine, and would-be gourmets will be particularly interested in the week-long cookery courses run by cordon bleu–trained owner Jeannie Chesterton, who will take you through a repertoire of Andalucian, Mediterranean and Moroccan dishes. Cooking days are interspersed with trips to local cheese and ham factories, food shops, sherry bodegas and restaurants. Courses run between October and April and cost €1,200 for six nights, all inclusive.

renaissance these days thanks mainly to weekenders from Seville who have bought up houses here. But it still retains an almost medieval charm, with a jigsaw of tiled roofs overlooked by two large churches either of which could easily accommodate the entire village population. The name of the iron-domed **Iglesia Inacabada** (Unfinished Church) speaks for itself (funds ran out in 1793), while the towered **Iglesia de Santiago El Mayor**, favoured by the local storks, was founded by Arias Montano (see p169) back in the 16th century, then rebuilt with baroque additions after the 1755 Lisbon Earthquake.

Castaño is perfectly situated amid some of the Sierra de Aracena's best walking country (see the detour boxed text, opposite), so it's great to find the **Posada del Castaño** (☎ 959 46 55 02; www.posadadelcastano.com; Calle José Sánchez Calvo 33; s/d incl breakfast €35/49) here. This characterful converted old village house has walkers foremost in mind and the young British owners (highly experienced international travellers) are full of information and tips. They offer self-guided walking holidays and horse-riding holidays (bookable through their website).

You'll find a couple of bars serving food on shady Plaza del Álamo, behind the Iglesia de Santiago El Mayor.

Galaroza
pop 1600 / elevation 550m

On the N433, just over 1km cross-country northeast of Jabugo, Galaroza is a pretty village gathered around its 17th-century church, the **Iglesia de la Purísima Concepción**. It's known for its many springs, fountains and water channels, and villagers celebrate their abundance of H2O by chucking buckets of it at each other and all comers on 6 September, in the **Fiesta del Jarrito**.

Hostal Restaurante Toribio (☎ 959 12 30 73; www.hostaltoribio.com; Calle Iglesia 1; r €42; 🆇 🖳), just behind the church, is recently renovated with bright, welcoming rooms sporting pretty little floral murals – and its own cosy restaurant (mains €6 to €15). **Finca La Suerte** (☎ 959 12 30 10; www.fincalasuerte.com; Carril Cuesta Palero) will take you riding on fine Arab horses with British Horse Society-accredited guides along the beautiful trails around here for anything from one hour to several days.

Jabugo
pop 2500 / elevation 650m

Jabugo's mouthwateringly tender *jamón ibérico* is considered the best of the best, even in a ham wonderland like the Sierra de Aracena. Jabugo even has its own system of classification, grading hams from one to five *jotas* (Js), with five Js representing hams from pigs that have only ever gorged themselves on the sierra's acorns. The village itself is not much to look at and has some ugly ham-producing factories around the outskirts, but then you come here for the taste-bud trail, not for the sightseeing.

A line of bars and restaurants along Carretera San Juan del Puerto on the eastern side of the village wait for you to sample Spain's best *jamón*. At **Mesón Cinco Jotas** (☎ 959 12 10 71; Carretera San Juan del Puerto; 🕙 9am-9pm Tue-Sat, 9am-4pm Sun & Mon), run by the biggest producer, Sánchez Romero Carvajal, a tapa of *cinco jotas* (five Js), will set you back €2.50, while a *ración* is €16, or you could 'pig out' on *cinco jotas* and fried eggs for €10. At shops such as **de Jabugo la Cañada** (☎ 959 12 12 07; Carretera San Juan del Puerto 2) you can purchase almost every part of the pig in some form or other. Slices of high-quality *jamón* cost about €5 per 100g, and for a whole 7kg ham you would pay between €150 and €250.

DETOUR: ALÁJAR–CASTAÑO DEL ROBLEDO–GALAROZA FIGURE OF EIGHT

This beautiful day-hike is a superb introduction to walking in the Sierra de Aracena and connects three of the area's most attractive villages in a figure of eight, allowing you to vary the route by starting from any of the three or walking only part of it. Most of the way is through varied woodlands but you'll also enjoy long-distance panoramas, wonderful wildflowers in spring, and the spectacular Peña de Arias Montano. The whole route takes about 5½ hours at an average walking pace, not counting stops. The steeper bits are done downhill and there's nothing any modestly fit walker couldn't cope with.

Leave Alájar (p169) by the track to El Calabacino, signposted from the A470 at the western end of the village. El Calabacino is an international artist/hippy colony and a few creative signs from its inhabitants help you along your way. Your route crosses a stream on a wooden bridge, and a small, square, stone-and-brick church on your right, then ascends through a cork-oak forest, where you'll probably hear the grunts of Iberian pigs rooting around for some acorns. Ten minutes past the small church, fork directly right at an 'El Castaño' sign. Another 10 minutes and you will cross a small stream bed to follow a path marked by a yellow paint dot. Within a further 10 minutes the path becomes a vehicle track. Fifteen minutes along this, carry straight on at a crossroads, and in three minutes more you crest a rise and Castaño del Robledo comes into view. Some 200m past the crest, take the shadier path diverging to the left, indicated again by dots of yellow paint. After 10 to 15 minutes this track starts to veer down to the left, passing between tall cork oaks and gradually wending into Castaño del Robledo (p169).

After refreshments and whatever exploring you're inclined to do, leave Castaño by the path through the shady Área Recreativa Capilla del Cristo, on the north side of the HV5211 road passing the north side of the village. To the left you'll soon be able to see Cortegana and Jabugo, before you fork right at a tree with yellow and white paint stripes, 15 minutes from the *área recreativa* (recreational area). Your path starts winding downhill. Go straight on at a crossing of tracks after 10 minutes, and right at a fork one minute after that (a ruined stone building is up the left-hand path here). In 10 minutes Galaroza comes into view as you pass between its outlying *fincas* (rural properties). Cross a small river on a footbridge and emerge on the N433 road three minutes later. Walk left to Galaroza (opposite). The path by which you will leave (after any explorations and refreshments) is 700m west along the N433, marked by a 'Sendero Ribera del Jabugo' route sign.

Leaving Galaroza, fork right one minute out from the mentioned sign, then turn left four or five minutes later down to a footbridge that stretches over a small river. The path soon starts winding up the valley of the Río Jabugo, a particularly lovely stretch. Half an hour from the footbridge you will reach a vehicle track marked 'Camino de Jabugo a Galaroza'. Head right, passing a couple of *cortijos* (rural properties), to cross the river on a low bridge. Turn left 50m past the bridge, then left at a fork 30m further on. You re-cross the river, then gradually wind up and away from it. Ten minutes from the river, turn left at a red-tile-roofed house (Monte Blanco) and in 15 minutes (mostly upward) you're re-entering Castaño del Robledo, this time from the west.

To leave again, start retracing the route by which you arrived from Alájar earlier – up Calle Arias Montano from Plaza del Álamo, right along the first cobbled lane, up through the cork oaks to the crest then down to the crossing of tracks (30 minutes out of Castaño del Robledo). From here turn left, across the southwestern flank of Castaño (960m, the highest hill in the Sierra de Aracena). The track curves sharply to the left after 12 to 15 minutes. Some 300m further, turn right along a path beside a stone wall, which is marked by yellow paint. At a fork 10 minutes walk down from here, take the lesser path down to the right, and within another 20 minutes you will reach the Peña de Arias Montano (p169). Leaving here, start along the paved road down the hill, but after 50m diverge right down on to a cobbled track. Within 10 minutes this track re-emerges on the road: follow the road down for 25m then turn right down a track through a gap in the wall. Cross the A470 a minute or two later to carry on down into the middle of Alájar.

Almonaster la Real

pop 1800 / elevation 610m

Almonaster la Real is a picturesque little place harbouring the most beautiful gem of Islamic architecture. The little **mezquita** (mosque; admission free; ⊗ approx 8.30am-7pm) stands on a hilltop five minutes' walk up from the main square. Almost perfectly preserved, it was built in the 10th century and is like a miniature version of the great mosque at Córdoba. Despite being Christianised in the 13th century, the building retains nearly all its original features: the horseshoe arches, the semicircular mihrab, an ablutions fountain and various Arabic inscriptions. The Christians added a Romanesque apse on the northern side, where parts of a broken Visigothic altar carved with a dove and angels' wings, from the church that stood here before the mosque, have been reassembled. Even older are the capitals of the columns nearest the mihrab, which are Roman. The original minaret, a square tower, adjoins the building. You can climb to the upper chamber and look down on the Almonaster's 19th-century **bullring** (where a bullfight is held each August), but take care near the open, unprotected windows.

In the village, the Mudejar **Iglesia de San Martín** (Placeta de San Cristóbal) has a 16th-century portal in the Portuguese Manueline style, unique in the region.

The top of **Cerro de San Cristóbal** (915m), a 4km uphill drive from Almonaster, affords fabulous views in almost all directions. It's a magnificent place to be at sunset.

On the first weekend in May the village hosts the **Cruz de Mayo** festival, an excuse to show off the local fandango dancing and some fabulous traditional costumes.

Hotel Casa García (☎ 959 14 31 09; www.hotel casagarcia.com; Avenida San Martín 2; s/d €37/53; Ⓟ ⊠) is a stylish, small hotel with a large, shady *terraza* at the entrance to the village. Rooms have a *Country Living* feel and some have balconies. The restaurant is also highly regarded (mains €8 to €14) and specialises in local meat dishes (but also has vegetarian options).

Pensión La Cruz (☎ 959 14 31 35; Plaza El Llano 8; s/d €20/30), on a pleasant small plaza, has six clean, simple rooms with bathtub, plus an economical bar-restaurant (*raciones* are €5 to €7).

Other Villages

Cortegana, 6km northwest of Almonaster, supplies much of the local *anís* (aniseed liqueur) for Almonaster's fiesta. It's overlooked by a 13th-century **castillo** (admission €1.30; ⊗ 11am-2pm & 6-8pm Tue-Sun) with a local museum inside. The best time to visit Cortegana is during the **Jornadas Medievales**, a huge mid-August fiesta where everyone dresses up in medieval costume and indulges in plenty of eating, drinking and merrymaking, a medieval market, tournaments, falconry displays and archery competitions.

Aroche, 15km west of Cortegana, is only 30km short of the Portuguese border. It's a cheerful, friendly place of narrow, pebbled streets, with a 12th-century **castillo** (admission free; ⊗ 10am-7pm Fri-Sun), remodelled in the 19th century as an unusual bullring. Just below the castle is the large **Iglesia de la Asunción** which, surprisingly, houses some first-class sculpture by La Roldana, the daughter of the famous Pedro Roldán, and Alonso Cano. The town's other main attraction – if you can call it that – is the **Museo del Santo Rosario** (Paseo Ordóñez Valdéz) – a collection of more than 1000 rosaries from around the world, some donated by celebrities such as Mother Teresa, Richard Nixon and General Franco. For visits to the rosary museum and church and to the castle outside its regular opening days, ask at the **Casa Consistorial** (Town Hall; ☎ 959 14 02 01; Plaza Juan Carlos I; ⊗ 9.30am-1pm Mon-Fri). Aroche's **Centro Cultural Las Peñas** (Calle Real; tapas €1.20-1.60, raciones €8-11), full of men swigging the local *anís*, has a great local atmosphere and serves up tasty tapas and *raciones*.

Cádiz Province

As you travel these southernmost reaches of the Spanish (and European) mainland, you may have to remind yourself that you haven't been whisked off to some completely distinct and distant region. It's hard to fathom how an area little more than 100km from north to south or east to west can encompass such variety. Take the three main cities – cosmopolitan, cultured, fun-loving Cádiz can seem a world away from nearby Jerez de la Frontera, where aristocratic, sherry-quaffing, equestrian elegance rubs shoulders with poor quarters that have nurtured some of the great flamenco artists; and neither seems to have anything in common with the unromantic industrial port of Algeciras.

This rich diversity continues as the colourful, bustling towns of the 'sherry triangle' give way to the long, sandy beaches of the Atlantic coast and the hip international surf scene of Tarifa. Inland, the majestic cork forests of Los Alcornocales yield to the rugged peaks and pristine white villages of the Sierra de Grazalema. Active travellers in Cádiz can enjoy Europe's best windsurfing, hike dramatic mountains, trek the countryside on horseback or train their binoculars on some of Spain's most spectacular birds. Meanwhile, the province's fascinatingly diverse history is ever-present in the shape of thrillingly sited hilltop castles, beautiful churches, medieval mosques and much more. This is a place that never lets the senses doze.

CÁDIZ PROVINCE

HIGHLIGHTS

- Savour the windsurfing, kitesurfing beach scene at **Tarifa** (p215)
- Enjoy the festive but cultured and historic port city of **Cádiz** (p174), scene of Spain's wildest **Carnaval** (p179)
- Visit multifaceted **Jerez de la Frontera** (p191), home of sherry, horses, flamenco and festivals
- Explore the white villages, craggy mountains and vulture-inhabited gorges of the **Parque Natural Sierra de Grazalema** (p203)
- Unwind on the **Costa de la Luz** (p208) – long sandy beaches and laid-back coastal villages
- Discover the winding streets and Renaissance palaces of **Arcos de la Frontera** (p200), with its thrilling clifftop setting

Jerez de la Frontera ★
Parque Natural Sierra de Grazalema ★
Arcos de la Frontera ★
Cádiz ★
★
Costa de la Luz
Tarifa ★
★

■ POPULATION: 1.18 MILLION	■ CÁDIZ AV DAILY HIGH: JAN/AUG 15°/30°C	■ ALTITUDE RANGE: 0M–1654M

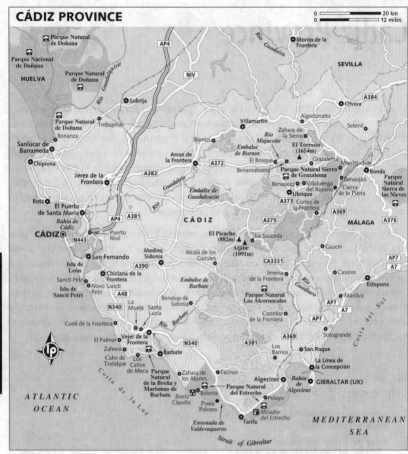

CÁDIZ PROVINCE

CÁDIZ

pop 132,000

Spain's most densely populated city, Cádiz (pronounced *cad*-i) is crammed onto the head of a long promontory like some huge, crowded, ocean-going ship, where the tang of salty air and open ocean vistas are never far away. Once past the coastal marshes and industrial sprawl, you emerge into an elegant, civilised port city of largely 18th- and 19th-century construction. Cádiz has a long and fascinating history, plenty of absorbing monuments and museums, a limitless supply of great bars, some memorable restaurants and a lively nightlife – yet it's the

gaditanos (people of Cádiz) themselves who make their city truly special. Warm, open, cultured and independently minded, most *gaditanos* are above all concerned with making the most of life – whether simply enjoying good company over a drink, staying out late to soak up the cool in the sweltering summer months, or indulging in Spain's most riotous carnival in late winter.

HISTORY

Cádiz may be the oldest city in Europe. It was founded under the name Gadir, at least as early as the 8th century BC, by the Phoenicians, who came here to trade Baltic amber and British tin for Spanish silver. Later, it became a naval base for the Romans, who heaped praise on its culinary, sexual and musical delights.

Cádiz began to boom again with the discovery of the Americas in 1492. Columbus sailed from here on his second and fourth voyages of exploration, returning with vast quantities of precious metals and treasure. Cádiz attracted Spain's enemies too: in 1587 England's Sir Francis Drake 'singed the king of Spain's beard' with a raid on the harbour, delaying the imminent Spanish Armada. In 1596 Anglo-Dutch attackers burnt almost the entire city.

Cádiz's golden age was the 18th century, when it enjoyed 75% of Spanish trade with the Americas. It grew into the richest and most cosmopolitan city in Spain and gave birth to the country's first progressive, liberal middle class.

During the Spanish War of Independence (part of the Napoleonic Wars) Cádiz underwent a two-year French siege during which the Cortes de Cádiz (the Spanish national parliament) convened here. In 1812 this lopsidedly liberal gathering adopted Spain's first constitution (known as La Pepa), proclaiming sovereignty of the people.

But Spain's loss of its American colonies in the 19th century plunged Cádiz into a slump from which it is still emerging. The city's population has actually shrunk by 25,000 since 1991, partly because of unemployment resulting from a decline in shipbuilding and fishing, and partly because there is no new land left to build on. Tourism is a key to recovery, with more monuments being opened to the public and an admirable renovation programme restoring the old city's splendour.

ORIENTATION

Breathing space between the old city's huddled streets is provided by numerous attractive squares. The four key ones for initial orientation are Plaza San Juan de Dios, Plaza de la Catedral and Plaza de Topete in an arc in the southeast, and Plaza de Mina in the north. Pedestrianised Calle San Francisco runs most of the way between Plaza San Juan de Dios and Plaza de Mina.

The train station is just east of the old city, off Plaza de Sevilla, with the main bus station (of the Comes line) 900m to its north on Plaza de la Hispanidad. The main harbour lies between the two.

The 18th-century Puerta de Tierra (Land Gate) marks the eastern boundary of the old city. Modern Cádiz extends back along the peninsula towards the town of San Fernando.

INFORMATION

You'll find plenty of banks and ATMs along Calle San Francisco and the parallel Avenida Ramón de Carranza.

Bookstores

QiQ (☎ 956 20 57 66; Calle San Francisco 31; ⊙ 9.30am-2.30pm & 5.30-9pm Mon-Fri, 10am-2pm & 5.30-9pm Sat) Sells guidebooks in several languages, and local-interest books.

Emergency

Hospital Puerta del Mar (☎ 956 00 21 00; Avenida Ana de Viya 21) Cádiz's large, modern, main general hospital, 2.25km southeast of the Puerta de Tierra.

Medical Emergency (☎ 061)

Policía Nacional (National Police; ☎ 091, 956 28 61 11; Avenida de Andalucía 28) Located 500m southeast of the Puerta de Tierra.

Internet Access

Enred@2 (cnr Calles Isabel La Católica & Antonio López; internet per hr €1.50; ⊙ 11am-2pm, 5-10pm)

Lu@r (☎ 956 21 42 05; Plaza de Mina 4; internet per hr €1.50; ⊙ 10am-11.30pm) Also has inexpensive telephone booths.

Post

Post office (Plaza de Topete; ⊙ 8.30am-8.30pm Mon-Fri, 9.30am-2pm Sat)

Tourist Information

Municipal tourist office main office (☎ 956 24 10 01; Plaza San Juan de Dios 11; ⊙ 9am-2pm & 4-7pm Mon-Fri mid-Sep—mid-Jun, 9am-2pm & 5-8pm Mon-Fri mid-Jun—mid-Sep); information kiosk (Plaza San Juan de Dios; ⊙ 10am-1.30pm & 4-6.30pm Sat, Sun & holidays mid-Sep—mid-Jun, 10am-2pm & 5-7.30pm Sat, Sun & holidays mid-Jun—mid-Sep)

Regional tourist office (☎ 956 25 86 46; Avenida Ramón de Carranza s/n; ⊙ 9am-7.30pm Mon-Fri, 10am-2pm Sat, Sun & holidays)

SIGHTS

Cádiz's sights are scattered around the old city but four main squares – Plaza San Juan de Dios, Plaza de la Catedral, Plaza de Topete and Plaza de Mina – provide focal points for your explorations.

CÁDIZ

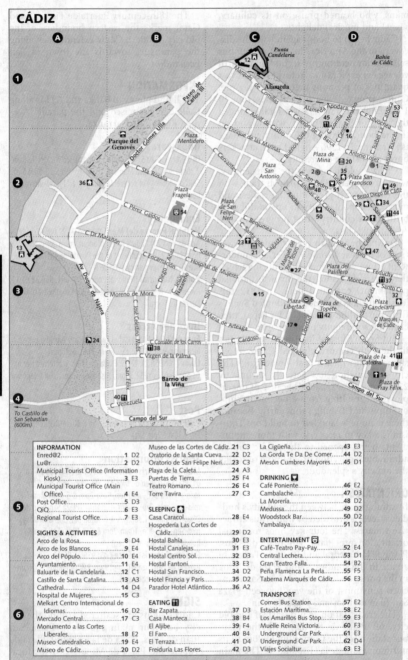

CÁDIZ PROVINCE

CÁDIZ PROVINCE

Plaza San Juan de Dios & Barrio del Pópulo

The broad Plaza San Juan de Dios is surrounded by cafés and dominated by the imposing neoclassical **ayuntamiento** (city hall), built around 1800. Behind the *ayuntamiento*, the Barrio del Pópulo neighbourhood was once the kernel of medieval Cádiz, a fortified enclosure wrecked by the Anglo-Dutch raiders in 1596. Its boundaries are still marked by three 13th-century gate arches, the **Arco de los Blancos**, **Arco de la Rosa** and **Arco del Pópulo**. The once-shabby Barrio del Pópulo has been a focus of the city's restoration programme and its now clean, attractive and pedestrianised streets sport several craft shops, galleries and tapas bars.

On the seaward edge of the Barrio del Pópulo, drop into the excavated **Teatro Romano** (Roman Theatre; ☎ 956 21 22 81; Campo del Sur s/n; admission free; ☽ 10am-2pm), where you can walk along the gallery beneath the tiers of seating. The remains of the ancient stage are still buried beneath the adjacent buildings.

Cathedral & Around

Cádiz's yellow-domed **cathedral** (☎ 956 28 61 54; Plaza de la Catedral; adult/child €4/2.50; ☽ 10am-1.30pm & 4.30-6.30pm Tue-Fri, 10am-1pm Sat) fronts a handsome, broad, palm-lined plaza. The decision to construct a large and imposing cathedral here was taken in 1716 on the strength of the imminent transfer from Seville to Cádiz of the Casa de la Contratación, which controlled Spanish trade with the Americas. But the cathedral wasn't actually finished till 1838, by which time the funds had run short, forcing cutbacks in size and quality, and neoclassical elements (including the dome, towers and main façade) had diluted architect Vicente Acero's original baroque plan. But the cathedral is nonetheless a magnificent construction, seen to best effect when floodlit at night. Inside, don't miss the large, circular underground crypt, built of stone excavated from the sea bed. Cádiz-born composer Manuel de Falla is among those buried here.

From a separate entrance on Plaza de la Catedral you can climb up inside the cathedral's **Torre de Poniente** (☎ Western Tower; 956 25 17 88; adult/child/senior €3.50/2.50/2.50;

CÁDIZ COASTAL WALK

This circuit takes you right around the Cádiz seaboard from Plaza de Mina to the cathedral – a breezy 4.5km walk that could last anything from 1¼ hours upward. Go one block north from Plaza de Mina to the city's northern seafront, with views across the Bahía de Cádiz to El Puerto de Santa María, then head northwest along the jungly **Alameda** (with two truly gigantic rubber trees) to the **Baluarte de la Candelaria** bastion (occasionally housing art exhibitions). Here turn southwest to the **Parque del Genovés**, with its quirkily clipped trees. You might stop for refreshments at the Parador Hotel Atlántico (p180) at the southwest end of the park. Continue to the star-shaped **Castillo de Santa Catalina** (☎ 956 22 63 33; admission free; ☽ 10.30am-6pm, approx to 8pm May-Aug), built to defend the city after the Anglo-Dutch sacking of 1596: inside are an historical exhibit on Cádiz and the sea, and a gallery for temporary exhibitions. Sandy **Playa de la Caleta** (very crowded in summer) separates Santa Catalina from another fort, the 18th-century **Castillo de San Sebastián**. You can't enter San Sebastián but do walk along the airy 750m causeway to its gate. At low tide you can poke around the rock pools along the way. You might like to turn inland here to the Barrio de la Viña, the old fishermen's district, for tapas at El Faro (p181) or Casa Manteca (p181) before finally following the broad promenade east along **Campo del Sur** to the yellow-domed cathedral.

☽ 10am-6pm, to 8pm 15 Jun-15 Sep) for marvellous views over the old city. From here you will see the many watchtowers built in the 18th century so citizens could keep an eye on shipping movements without stepping outside their front doors. Back then, Cádiz had no less than 160 of these watchtowers: 127 still stand and many are now desirable properties, popular with weekenders from Seville.

The cathedral ticket also admits you to the nearby **Museo Catedralicio** (Cathedral Museum; ☎ 956 25 98 12; Plaza Fray Félix; ☽ 10am-1.30pm & 4.30-7pm Tue-Fri, 10am-1pm Sat), with an excavated medieval street and material on the Anglo-Dutch sacking of 1596 alongside cathedral treasures and assorted art.

Plaza de Topete & Around

A short walk northwest from the cathedral, this square is one of Cádiz's liveliest, bright with flower stalls and still widely known by its old name, Plaza de las Flores (Square of the Flowers). It adjoins the large, animated **Mercado Central** (Central Market; ☽ 9.30am-2pm Mon-Sat), built in 1837, the oldest covered market in Spain. A few blocks further northwest, the **Torre Tavira** (☎ 956 21 29 10; www.torretavira .com; Calle Marqués del Real Tesoro 10; admission €3.50; ☽ 10am-6pm, to 8pm mid-Jun–mid-Sep) is the highest of the city's old watchtowers, with a dramatic panorama of Cádiz. It has a camera obscura that projects live, moving images of the city onto a screen (sessions start every half-hour).

The nearby **Hospital de Mujeres** (☎ 956 22 36 47; Calle Hospital de Mujeres 26; admission €0.80; ☽ 10am-1.30pm Mon-Sat) is an 18th-century women's hospital whose chapel is one of the most profusely decorated churches from Cádiz's golden century and contains El Greco's *Extasis de San Francisco* (Ecstasy of St Francis).

A little further northwest you'll find the **Museo de las Cortes de Cádiz** (☎ 956 22 17 88; Calle Santa Inés 9; admission free; ☽ 9am-1pm & 4-7pm Tue-Fri Oct-May, 9am-1pm & 5-7pm Tue-Fri Jun-Sep, 9am-1pm Sat & Sun), full of memorabilia of the 1812 Cádiz parliament, with pride of place belonging to a large, marvellously detailed model of 18th-century Cádiz, made in mahogany and ivory in the 1770s for Carlos III. Within the museum and open during the same hours is **Cádiz Virtual Siglo XVIII** (Virtual Cádiz 18th Century; ☎ 956 27 20 62; www.cadiz-virtual.com; admission €6) where you don a '3D stereoscopic' helmet to take interactive tours of 18th-century Cádiz – gimmicky but quite fun. Along the street is the baroque church where the parliament actually met, the **Oratorio de San Felipe Neri** (☎ 956 21 16 12; Plaza de San Felipe Neri; admission €2; ☽ 10am-1.30pm Mon-Sat). This has an unusual and beautiful oval dome, and a masterly Murillo *Inmaculada* of 1680 in its main retable.

Plaza de Mina & Around

Plaza de Mina, one of Cádiz's largest and leafiest squares, is home to the city's excellent major museum, the **Museo de Cádiz** (☎ 956 21 22 81; EU/non-EU citizen free/€1.50; ⓧ 2.30-8.30pm Tue, 9am-8.30pm Wed-Sat, 9.30am-2.30pm Sun). Information here is in Spanish only, but they do have explanatory leaflets in other languages. The stars of the ground-floor archaeology section are two Phoenician marble sarcophagi carved in human likeness. There's also some beautiful Phoenician jewellery and Roman glassware, and lots of headless Roman statues, plus Emperor Trajan, with head, from the ruins of Baelo Claudia (see p214). The fine arts collection, upstairs, features a group of 18 superb canvases of saints, angels and monks by Francisco de Zurbarán, mostly painted in 1638–39 for La Cartuja of Jerez. Also here is the painting that cost Murillo his life, the beautifully composed altarpiece from the chapel of Cádiz's Convento de Capuchinas: the artist died in 1682 from injuries received in a fall from the scaffolding.

The **Oratorio de la Santa Cueva** (☎ 956 22 22 62; Calle Rosario 10; admission €2.50; ⓧ 10am-1pm & 4.30-7.30pm Tue-Fri mid-Sep–mid-Jun, 10am-1pm & 5-8pm Tue-Fri mid-Jun–mid-Sep, 10am-1pm Sat & Sun), just a short distance southeast of Plaza de Mina, is a 1780s neoclassical church whose richly decorated oval-shaped Capilla Alta (Upper Chapel) contains three impressive paintings by the inimitable Francisco de Goya.

Beaches

Old Cádiz has one short curve of beach, Playa de la Caleta (see Cádiz Coastal Walk, opposite), but the newer part of the city is fronted by a superb, wide ocean beach of fine Atlantic sand, **Playa de la Victoria**, beginning about 1.5km beyond the Puerta de Tierra and stretching about 4km back along the peninsula. The beach earns a blue flag for its water quality and facilities, and on summer weekends almost the whole city seems to be out here. Where the city ends, the beach continues under the name **Playa de la Cortadura**, also blue-flagged. Bus 1 'Plaza España-Cortadura' from Plaza de España will get you to both beaches (€0.90).

COURSES

Cádiz's attractions are making it an increasingly popular place to study Spanish language and culture. Recommended schools offering these types of courses include the following:
Gadir Escuela Internacional de Español (☎ /fax 956 26 05 57; www.gadir.net; Calle Pérgolas 5) Well-established school a couple of blocks southeast of the Puerta de Tierra.
Melkart Centro Internacional de Idiomas (☎ /fax 956 22 22 13; www.centromelkart.com; Calle General Menacho 7) In the old city.
SIC (☎ 956 25 27 24; www.spanishincadiz.com; Calle Condesa Villafuente Bermeja 7) About 1km southeast of the Puerta de Tierra, near the beach.

FESTIVALS & EVENTS

No other Spanish city celebrates **Carnaval** (www.carnavaldecadiz.com in Spanish) with the verve, dedication and humour of Cádiz, where it turns into a 10-day singing, dancing and drinking fancy-dress party spanning two weekends (15 to 25 February 2007, 31 January to 10 February 2008). The fun, abetted by huge quantities of alcohol, is irresistible. Costumed groups called *murgas* tour the city on foot or on floats, dancing, singing satirical ditties or performing sketches (unfortunately most of their famed verbal wit will be lost on all but fluent Spanish speakers). In addition to the 300 or so officially recognised *murgas*, who are judged by a panel in the Gran Teatro Falla, there are also the *ilegales* – any group that fancies taking to the streets and trying to play or sing.

Some of the liveliest and most drunken scenes are in the working-class Barrio de la Viña, between the Mercado Central and Playa de la Caleta, and along Calle Ancha and around Plaza de Topete, where *ilegales* tend to congregate. Wear strong footwear as the streets will be carpeted with discarded bottles.

Rooms in Cádiz are all booked months in advance for Carnaval. If you haven't managed to snatch a room, you can still, like many other people, just go to Cádiz for the night from anywhere within striking distance.

SLEEPING

Room rates given here can almost double during the festivities of Carnaval. They also rise in some places in August, but often go down about 20% to 25% outside the summer season.

Budget

A reasonable number of budget places can be found in the old city.

Casa Caracol (☎ 956 26 11 66; www.caracolcasa .com; Calle Suárez de Salazar 4; dm/d incl breakfast €15/28; 🖳) Friendly and crowded, Casa Caracol is a true backpacker hostel and easily the best option if you're on a budget. It has bunk dorms for four and eight, a sociable communal kitchen, free internet, and a roof terrace with a few hammocks where you can sleep the night under the stars (€10). There's no sign outside: look for the blue door.

Hostal San Francisco (☎ 956 22 18 42; Calle San Francisco 12; d €49, s/d with shared bathroom €24/38) Well situated in the old city, the San Francisco has well kept but moderately sized rooms with pine-veneer furnishings. Some have little natural light. Bicycles can be rented for €10 a day.

Hostal Centro Sol (☎ /fax 956 28 31 03; www.hostal centrosolcadiz.com; Calle Manzanares 7; s/d €45/54) This efficient, well-kept *hostal*, in an attractive 19th-century house, has plain and smallish rooms, with TV and wooden furniture of assorted vintage. Breakfast is available, and the owners speak French.

Hostal Fantoni (☎ 956 28 27 04; www.hostalfantoni .net; Calle Flamenco 5; s/d €45/60, with shared bathroom €35/40; 🔀) The recently renovated, friendly Fantoni is in an 18th-century house with a dozen attractive, spotless rooms in cool blue-and-white tones. The roof terrace has fantastic views and catches a breeze in summer.

Midrange

Hostal Canalejas (☎ /fax 956 26 41 13; Calle Cristóbal Colón 5; s/d €48/66; 🔀) An excellent new *hostal* in the old city with neat, comfortable rooms each with pine furniture, a small bathtub, and one or two single beds.

Hostal Bahía (☎ 956 25 90 61; hostalbahia@terra .es; Calle Plocia 5; s/d €56/70; 🔀) Handily placed just off Plaza San Juan de Dios, the Hostal Bahía's 21 rooms, all with an exterior outlook, are neat and spotless, with phone and TV. This is the best value you'll find for this sort of price – so book ahead to ensure a room.

Hotel Francia y París (☎ 956 21 23 19; www.hotel francia.com in Spanish; Plaza San Francisco 6; s/d €66/82; 🔀 🖳) Well placed on an old-city plaza, this bigger hotel (57 rooms) has perfectly comfortable rooms but little atmosphere. Breakfast is available.

Hotel Regio (☎ 956 27 93 31; www.hotelregiocadiz .com in Spanish; Avenida Ana de Viya 11; s/d incl breakfast €59/97; 🅿 🔀 🖳) A short stroll from Playa de la Victoria, the Regio has comfy and inviting rooms with balconies, and a decent café.

Hospedería Las Cortes de Cádiz (☎ 956 21 26 68; www.hotellascortes.com in Spanish; Calle San Francisco 9; s/d incl breakfast €70/102; 🅿 🔀 🖳 ♿) This excellent old-city hotel occupies a remodelled 1850s mansion centred on an elegant four-storey atrium. The 36 stylish rooms, each dedicated to a figure or place associated with the Cortes de Cádiz, have attractive period-style furnishings and plenty of modern comforts. Three singles are adapted for travellers with disabilities and the hotel also has a roof terrace, gym and Jacuzzi.

Top End

Parador Hotel Atlántico (☎ 956 22 69 05; www.para dor.es; Avenida Duque de Nájera 9; s/d €103/129; 🅿 🔀 🖳 🌊 ♿) Cádiz's Parador is an ugly mud-brown concrete building but inside it's as comfortable, spacious and attractive as you'd expect from this luxury chain. All rooms have a private terrace with sea view of some sort (best at the front), and the pool, encircled by lawn, overlooks the ocean.

Hotel Tryp La Caleta (☎ 956 27 94 11; www.sol melia.com; Avenida Amílcar Barca 47; r €144; 🅿 🔀 🖳) Half the 143 luxurious rooms face Playa de la Victoria, 2.2km from the Puerta de Tierra. Check for weekend deals.

Hotel Playa Victoria (☎ 956 20 51 00; www.pala foxhoteles.com; Glorieta Ingeniero La Cierva 4; s/d from €125/156, with ocean views from €145/176; 🅿 🔀 🖳 🌊) The stylish Playa Victoria is the best of Cádiz's beach hotels, fronting directly onto the sands 2.6km from the Puerta de Tierra. The 188 elegant rooms have balconies shaped like ocean waves. If you're paying this much, go for an oceanfront room (one-third of the rooms face inland). Outside peak seasons there are sometimes good weekend discounts.

EATING

Old Cádiz may have Spain's densest concentration of tapas bars: there seem to be a couple on almost every block. There's also an increasing number of good restaurants for more sedate dining.

Around Plaza San Juan de Dios

La Cigüeña (☎ 956 25 01 79; Calle Plocia 2; mains €13-16; ☒ closed Sun) A few steps off the plaza, 'The Stork' has a Dutch chef who prepares adventurous and delicious food, and friendly and relaxed service.

Around Plaza de Mina & Plaza San Antonio

La Gorda Te Da De Comer (Calle General Luque 1; tapas €1.60, raciones €5; ☒ 9-11.30pm Mon, 1.30-4pm & 9-11.30pm Tue-Sat) Incredibly tasty food at incredibly low prices amid cool pop-art design. No wonder competition for the half-dozen tables is fierce: get there at least 10 minutes before opening to avoid a long wait. Try the curried chicken strips with Marie-Rose sauce, the deep-fried aubergines with honey or a dozen other mouthwatering concoctions.

Mesón Cumbres Mayores (☎ 956 21 32 70; Calle Zorrilla 4; tapas €1.50-2, mains €7-17) This ever-busy place, dangling with hams and garlic, has an excellent tapas bar in the front and a small restaurant in the back, both serving delicious fare at reasonable prices. In the bar it's hard to beat the ham and cheese *montaditos* (open sandwiches). In the restaurant, there are great salads, seafood, barbecued meats and *guisos* (stews).

Around Plaza de Topete & Plaza de la Catedral

Freiduría Las Flores (☎ 956 22 61 12; Plaza de Topete 4; seafood per 250g €2.50-8) Cádiz is addicted to fried fish, and Las Flores, a kind of self-respecting fish and chip shop, is one of the best places to sample it. You order by weight. To try an assortment of things together, have a *surtido* (a mixed fry-up).

Bar Zapata (Plaza Candelaria; montaditos €1.50-2, raciones €6-10) The crowd often spills out of the door at this highly popular but very narrow street-corner tapas joint. The scrumptious *montaditos* are the house speciality, and the jazz/rock/blues soundtrack adds to the enjoyment.

El Terraza (Bar Pelayo; ☎ 956 28 26 05; Plaza de la Catedral 3; raciones €8-18) Easily the most long-standing and best spot on the cathedral square, this place serves up top fresh seafood and meat from the Andalucian hills.

Barrio de la Viña

Casa Manteca (☎ 956 21 36 03; Calle Corralón de los Carros 66; tapas €1.20-1.60; ☒ closed Sun evening & Mon) Set on the corner that is the hub of La Viña's carnival fun, and with almost every inch of wall covered in colourful flamenco, bullfighting and carnival memorabilia, Casa Manteca is inevitably one of the barrio's (neighbourhood) liveliest bars. Ask the amiable bar staff for a tapa of *chicharrones* – pressed pork dressed with a squeeze of lemon, served on a paper napkin and amazingly delicious.

El Faro (☎ 956 22 99 16; Calle San Félix 15; raciones & mains €6-22) Over in the old La Viña fishermen's district near Playa de la Caleta, El Faro is Cádiz's most famous seafood eatery. Sit in the restaurant decorated with pretty ceramics, or squeeze up to the adjoining tapas bar among the locals. The fare is great in both parts but the bar offerings are less pricey.

Playa de la Victoria

There's heaps of choice along the beachfront of Paseo Marítimo. Both the following top choices are between the hotels Playa Victoria and Tryp La Caleta, with *terrazas* (terraces) out front.

Arana Restaurante (☎ 956 20 50 90; Paseo Marítimo 1; mains €9-16) Arana serves quality Andalucian meat and seafood (entrecôte in sweet Pedro Ximénez wine, monkfish in white-wine sauce) in stylish, modern surroundings.

Arte Serrano (☎ 956 27 72 58; Paseo Marítimo 2; mains €9-18) Specialises in meat from the Andalucian hill country.

THE AUTHOR'S CHOICE

El Aljibe (☎ 956 26 66 56; www.pablogrosso .com; Calle Plocia 25; tapas €2.50-4, mains €10-15) Refined restaurant upstairs and civilised tapas bar downstairs, El Aljibe is one of the best bets in town for either mode of eating. The cuisine developed by *gaditano* chef Pablo Grosso is a delicious combination of the traditional and the adventurous – *solomillo ibérico* (Iberian pork sirloin) stuffed with Emmental cheese, ham and piquant peppers; couscous with raisins and wine; seafood-stuffed halibut in puff pastry...

DRINKING

Cádiz has intriguing bars round every corner. They range from old tile-walled joints with a few locals chinwagging over a *vino tinto* (red wine) to chic music bars with a cool young clientele. The area around Plazas San Francisco, España and Mina is the hub of the old city's late-night bar scene. Things get going around 11pm or midnight at these places but can be quiet in the first half of the week.

Medussa (cnr Calles Manuel Rancés & Beato Diego de Cádiz) Number-one nocturnal magnet for an alternative/studenty crowd, with red walls and banks of lime-green fluorescent lighting to set the tone. Varied DJs and occasional live music – from garage and rock-groove to punk, ska and reggae – get the bodies moving.

Cambalache (Calle José del Toro 20; ✆ closed Sun) This long, dim, jazz and blues bar often hosts live music on Thursdays around 10.30pm.

Woodstock Bar (☎ 956 21 21 63; cnr Calles Sagasta & Cánovas del Castillo) This bar has a good range of on-tap and bottled international beers and plenty of rock music on the TVs.

Café Poniente (☎ 956 21 26 97; Calle Beato Diego de Cádiz 18; ✆ closed Sun & Mon) A popular bar that draws a mixed/gay crowd with its line up of house-music, waiters in vest tops (or no tops), and drag shows on Thursdays.

Yambalaya (Calle Sagasta 3; ✆ 8am-midnight Mon-Fri, 4pm-midnight Sat & Sun) A high-ceilinged café-bar with assorted ethnic artefacts, Yambalaya is a nice spot for any kind of drink any time of day. It has internet facilities for €1 per 25 minutes.

La Morería (Calle San Pedro 5; ✆ 4pm-midnight Sun-Thu, 4pm-3am Fri & Sat) If your preferred beverage is tea, drop into this cool Moroccan tearoom serving all manner of infusions in silver pots.

The second hot spot is down by the beach around the Hotel Playa Victoria, with lively music bars along Paseo Marítimo and nearby Calle General Muñoz Arenillas. This area comes into its own in summer. The hippest bars include **Barabass** (☎ 856 07 90 26; www.barabasscadiz.com; Calle General Muñoz Arenillas 4-6; admission incl 1 drink €8; ✆ 4pm-6am), with a shiny chillout lounge and different DJs nightly, and **Yunque** (Calle General Muñoz Arenillas 5; ✆ 10pm-late), a gathering ground of '*gente guapa*' (beautiful people). A taxi from the old city costs about €5.

ENTERTAINMENT

Cádiz has a lively entertainment scene: pick up one of the several what's-on mags from a tourist office.

Peña Flamenca La Perla (☎ 956 25 91 01; Calle Carlos Ollero s/n; admission free) Cádiz is one of the true homes of flamenco. This atmospheric, cavernlike den of a club hosts flamenco nights at 10pm many Fridays in spring and summer.

Gran Teatro Falla (☎ 956 22 08 34; Plaza de Falla) The city's main theatre, a fine neo-Islamic building in pink brick, stages a busy, varied and impressive programme of theatre, dance and music.

Central Lechera (☎ 956 22 06 28; Plaza de Argüelles) A smaller venue playing host to more adventurous and experimental music, dance and theatre.

Café-Teatro Pay-Pay (☎ 956 25 25 43; Calle Silencio 1; admission free; ✆ 10.30 or 11pm Wed-Sat) This café/bar in the Barrio del Pópulo hosts flamenco, singer-songwriters, storytellers and other performers.

Taberna Marqués de Cádiz (☎ 956 25 42 88; Calle Marqués de Cádiz 3; admission free) Stone-walled grotto with flamenco nights starting at 10pm every Friday.

Dance till dawn? Head out towards Punta de San Felipe (also known as La Punta) on the northern side of the harbour. A long line of disco bars here rocks from around 3am to 6am Thursday to Saturday (well, Friday to Sunday, to be pedantic). To try out your salsa turns, head to **El Malecón** (☎ 956 22 45 51; www.elmalecon.net; Paseo Pascual Pery; ✆ midnight-6am Thu-Sat), at the far end of the line of disco bars – but don't leave it too late on Saturday night, when the music switches to more commercial stuff around 3am.

GETTING THERE & AWAY
Boat

The catamaran ferry to El Puerto de Santa María leaves from the Muelle (Jetty) Reina Victoria near the train station; the less frequent *El Vapor* sails from the Estación Marítima near the Comes bus station. See p188 for schedules and fares.

Bus

Most buses are run by **Comes** (☎ 956 80 70 59, 902 19 92 08; Plaza de la Hispanidad). Destinations include the following:

Destination	Cost	Duration	Daily Frequency
Algeciras	€10	2¼hr	10
Arcos de la Frontera	€5.50	1¼hr	6
Barbate	€5.50	1½-2hr	14
Córdoba	€20	4hr	1-2
El Puerto de Santa María	€1.70	30-40min	23
Granada	€28	5hr	4
Jerez de la Frontera	€2.70	40min	20
Los Caños de Meca via El Palmar	€5	1¼hr	2 daily Mon-Fri
Málaga via Marbella	€20	4hr	6
Ronda	€13	3hr	3
Seville	€10.50	1¾hr	12
Tarifa	€8	2hr	5
Vejer de la Frontera	€4.50	1hr	8
Zahara de los Atunes	€6.50	2hr	2-3

Frequency of some services is reduced on Saturday and Sunday.

Los Amarillos also runs buses from its stop by the southern end of Avenida Ramón de Carranza. Tickets and information are available at **Viajes Socialtur** (☎ 956 28 58 52; Avenida Ramón de Carranza 31). Buses run to the following destinations:

Arcos de la Frontera (€4.50, 1¼ hours) Four daily Monday to Friday, two daily on Saturday and Sunday.
El Bosque (€7, two hours) Four daily Monday to Friday, two daily on Saturday and Sunday.
El Puerto de Santa María (€1.70, 40 minutes) Eleven daily Monday to Friday, five daily Saturday and Sunday.
Sanlúcar de Barrameda (€3, 1¼ hours) Eleven daily Monday to Friday, five daily Saturday and Sunday.
Ubrique (€8, 2½ hours) Four daily Monday to Friday, two daily Saturday and Sunday.

Buses M050 and M051, run by the **Consorcio de Transportes Bahía de Cádiz** (☎ 956 01 21 00; www.cmtbc.com), travel from Jerez de la Frontera airport to Cádiz's Comes bus station (€2.60, one to 1¼ hours), via Jerez city and El Puerto de Santa María, 12 times a day Monday to Friday and six times on Saturday, Sunday and holidays.

Car & Motorcycle

The AP4 motorway from Seville to Puerto Real, on the eastern side of the Bahía de Cádiz, carries a toll of €5.50. From Puerto Real, a bridge crosses the neck of the bay to join the A48/N340 entering Cádiz from the south.

Train

From the **train station** (☎ 956 25 43 01; Plaza de Sevilla), up to 37 trains run daily to/from El Puerto de Santa María (from €2.70, 30 to 35 minutes) and Jerez de la Frontera (from €3.40, 35 to 50 minutes), 11 or more to/from Seville (€9 to €30, two hours), and two or three to/from Córdoba (€33 to €52, three hours).

GETTING AROUND

The old city is best explored on foot, and its narrow, winding streets are no fun to drive around anyway, so if you have a vehicle it's best to leave it in a car park. Twenty-four-hour car parks in the old city include the following:

Underground car park (Campo del Sur; per 24hr €12)
Underground car park (Paseo de Canalejas; per 24hr €8)

THE SHERRY TRIANGLE

North of Cádiz, the towns of Jerez de la Frontera, Sanlúcar de Barrameda and El Puerto de Santa María are best known as the homes of that unique, smooth Andalucian wine, sherry. But the 'sherry triangle' also offers a rich mixture of additional attractions: beaches, music, horses, trips into the Parque Nacional de Doñana, and a fascinating history.

EL PUERTO DE SANTA MARÍA

pop 82,000

El Puerto, 10km northeast of Cádiz across the Bahía de Cádiz (22km by road), is easily and enjoyably reached by ferry – a fitting way to arrive at a town with such a rich seagoing history. Christopher Columbus was a guest of the knights of El Puerto from 1483 to 1486: it was here that he met Juan de la Cosa, the owner of his 1492 flagship, the *Santa María*. From the 16th to 18th centuries El Puerto was the base of the Spanish royal galleys. Its heyday came in the 18th century, when it flourished on American trade and earned the name Ciudad de los Cien Palacios (City of the Hundred Palaces). Today its fabulous beaches, sherry bodegas, restaurants, tapas bars and vibrant nightlife make it a favourite outing for *gaditanos, jerezanos* and others looking for a change of scenery. In summer, El Puerto comes alive.

Orientation & Information

The heart of the town is on the northwest bank of the Río Guadalete, just upstream from its mouth, though development spreads along the beaches to the east and west. The ferry *El Vapor* arrives dead centre at the Muelle del Vapor on Plaza de las Galeras Reales. Calle Luna, one of the main streets, runs straight inland from Plaza de las Galeras Reales. The train station is a 10-minute walk northeast of the centre, beside the Jerez road. Some buses stop at the train station, others at the Plaza de Toros (Bullring), five blocks south of Calle Luna.

Ciberbahía (Avenida Aramburu de Mora 21; internet per hr €2; 🕑 11am-11pm Mon-Fri, 3-10pm Sat & Sun) Also a *locutorio* (telephone call centre) for cheap calls worldwide.

Post office (Avenida Aramburu de Mora)

Tourist office (☎ 956 54 24 13; www.turismoelpuerto .com; Calle Luna 22; 🕑 10am-2pm & 6-8pm May-Sep, 10am-2pm & 5.30-7.30pm Oct-Apr) Excellent, with plenty of information about water sports, bodega visits and flamenco events.

Sights & Activities

The historic, four-spouted **Fuente de las Galeras Reales** (Fountain of the Royal Galleys; Plaza de las Galeras Reales), by the riverfront, is a good place to start your explorations. America-bound ships drew their water here.

Two blocks southwest, then a block inland, stands the **Castillo San Marcos** (☎ 627 56 93 35; Plaza Alfonso El Sabio 3; admission €2; 🕑 10am-2pm Tue). Heavily restored in the 20th century, the fine castle was built over a Muslim mosque by Alfonso X of Castile after he took the town in 1260. The castle's decorated battlements are beautiful but the old mosque inside, now converted to a church, is the highlight. The building was closed at the time of writing; visits are normally by half-hour guided tour.

Three blocks further inland, the **Fundación Rafael Alberti** (☎ 956 85 07 11; Calle Santo Domingo 25; admission €3; 🕑 11am-4pm Tue-Sun) displays interesting exhibits on one of El Puerto's most famous sons, Rafael Alberti (1902–99). A poet, painter and communist politician of the Generation of '27 (see p47), Alberti lived in this house as a child.

Nearby, the little **Museo Municipal** (☎ 956 54 27 05; Calle Pagador 1; admission free; 🕑 10am-2pm Tue-Fri, 10.45am-2pm Sat & Sun) has an elegant patio and interesting archaeological and fine art sections, including paintings by Rafael

Alberti. Just across from the museum, the impressive sandstone **Iglesia Mayor Prioral** (☎ 956 85 17 16; 🕑 8.30am-12.45pm Mon-Fri, 8.30am-noon Sat & Sun) dominates Plaza de España. Built between the 15th and 18th centuries, it boasts a lavish plateresque/baroque portal, the Puerta del Sol, facing the plaza, and a huge 17th-century Mexican-made silver retable in the Capilla del Sagrario (to the right of the main altar).

Four blocks southwest from Plaza de España is El Puerto's grand 19th-century **Plaza de Toros** (Plaza Elías Ahuja; admission free; 🕑 11am-1.30pm & 6-7.30pm Tue-Sun May-Sep, 11am-1.30pm & 5.30-7pm Tue-Sun Oct-Apr), one of Andalucía's most beautiful and important bullrings, with room for 15,000 spectators. It's closed on days before and after bullfights. Entry to the bullring is on the Calle Valdes side of Plaza de España.

A short walk northeast from Plaza de España is the **Casa de los Leones** (House of the Lions; ☎ 956 87 52 77; Calle La Placilla 2; admission free; 🕑 10am-2pm & 6-8pm), one of the finest of the many baroque mansions that were built in El Puerto's 18th-century heyday. Most impressive is its façade but there are also interesting information panels in the interior patio. You can stay in its holiday apartments.

SHERRY BODEGAS

Several of the sherry wineries are in the breezy area between the Plaza de Toros and the riverfront. They boast extensive gardens and tall palm trees. Tours are in Spanish with English translations if necessary (or all in English if only English-speakers are present). Phone ahead to visit **Bodegas Osborne** (☎ 956 86 91 00; Calle los Moros 7; €5; 🕑 tours 10.30am & 1pm Mon-Fri). You can visit three other sherry houses without booking:

Bodegas 501 (☎ 956 85 55 11; Calle Valdés 9; admission €4; 🕑 tours noon Mon-Fri)

Bodegas Gutiérrez Colosía (☎ 956 85 28 52; Avenida de la Bajamar; admission €3; 🕑 tours 1.30pm Sat)

Bodegas Terry (☎ 956 85 77 00; Calle Toneleros s/n; tour €6.50; 🕑 10am & noon Mon-Fri). Hosts shows in the summer, including horse spectaculars and more (see p188).

BEACHES

When you've finished sightseeing, sample El Puerto's fabulous white, sandy beaches. You can canoe, windsurf and more (pick up the tourist office's activities leaflet for

CÁDIZ PROVINCE

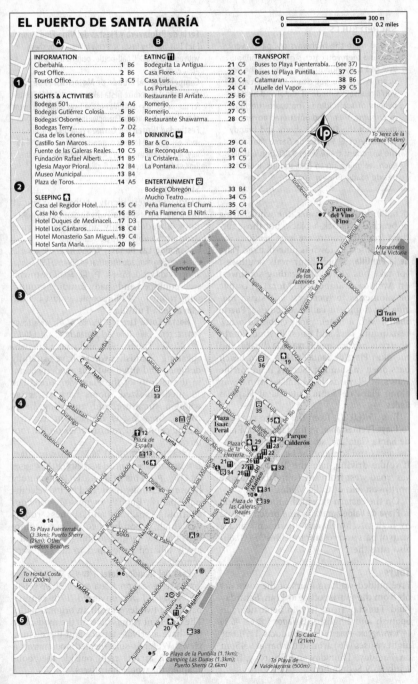

EL PUERTO DE SANTA MARÍA

0 _____ 300 m
0 _____ 0.2 miles

INFORMATION
Ciberbahía.............................1 B6
Post Office.............................2 B6
Tourist Office........................3 C5

SIGHTS & ACTIVITIES
Bodegas 501...........................4 A6
Bodegas Gutiérrez Colosia....5 B6
Bodegas Osborne.................6 B6
Bodegas Terry........................7 D2
Casa de los Leones...............8 B4
Castillo San Marcos..............9 B5
Fuente de las Galeras Reales..10 C5
Fundación Rafael Alberti......11 B5
Iglesia Mayor Prioral...........12 B4
Museo Municipal..................13 B4
Plaza de Toros......................14 A5

SLEEPING
Casa del Regidor Hotel.........15 C4
Casa No 6..............................16 B5
Hotel Duques de Medinaceli..17 D3
Hotel Los Cántaros...............18 C4
Hotel Monasterio San Miguel..19 C4
Hotel Santa María................20 B6

EATING
Bodeguita La Antigua...........21 C5
Casa Flores...........................22 C4
Casa Luis..............................23 C4
Los Portales..........................24 C4
Restaurante El Arriate..........25 B6
Romerijo................................26 C5
Romerijo................................27 C5
Restaurante Shawarma.........28 C5

DRINKING
Bar & Co...............................29 C4
Bar Reconquista....................30 C4
La Cristalera..........................31 C5
La Pontana............................32 C5

ENTERTAINMENT
Bodega Obregón...................33 B4
Mucho Teatro........................34 C4
Peña Flamenca El Chumi......35 C4
Peña Flamenca El Nitri..........36 C4

TRANSPORT
Buses to Playa Fuenterrabía....(see 37)
Buses to Playa Puntilla...........37 C5
Catamaran.............................38 B6
Muelle del Vapor....................39 C5

CÁDIZ PROVINCE

SACRED BULLS

As you roam the highways of Spain, every now and then you catch sight of the silhouette of a truly gigantic black bull on the horizon. When you get closer to the creature you'll realise it's made of metal and held up by bits of scaffolding. These are the *toros de Osborne*, silent and unlettered advertisements for the Osborne sherry and brandy company of El Puerto de Santa María. At the last count there were 92 Osborne bulls, each weighing up to four tonnes, looming beside roads all over Spain.

---

details). In high summer, the whole string of beaches is chock-a-block, but those furthest from the centre are least hectic.

The closest to town is pine-flanked **Playa de la Puntilla**, a half-hour walk southwest (or take bus 26, €0.80, heading southwest on Avenida Aramburu de Mora). A couple of kilometres further west is a swish marina development called, of course, **Puerto Sherry**, with a hotel, yacht club and a few restaurants, bars and cafés. Beyond Puerto Sherry is picturesque **Playa de la Muralla**, and the 3km **Playa de Santa Catalina**, with beach bars open in summer. Surfers head for the waves at Playa de la Muralla and halfway along Playa de Santa Catalina at **Playa las Redes**.

Bus 35 (€0.80) from the centre runs out to **Playa Fuenterrabía**, at the far end of Playa de Santa Catalina, stopping at the residential areas and some of the beaches en route. If you're driving, take the 'Rota' and 'Playas' road west from the roundabout at the northwest end of Calle Valdés.

On the eastern side of the Río Guadelete is **Playa de Valdelagrana**, a fine beach backed by high-rise hotels and apartments and a strip of bars and restaurants. Bus 35 (€0.80) also runs there.

Tours

Free guided walking tours of the town set off from the tourist office at 11am Saturday (and Tuesday from July to September; in Spanish and English). **El Vapor** (☎ 629 46 80 14; www.vapordeelpuerto.com) conducts 1½-hour night cruises (€6) around the bay at 9.45pm on Tuesday, Thursday and Saturday, from 1 July to 9 September.

Festivals & Events

Feria de Primavera y Fiestas del Vino Fino (Spring Fair) This four-day fiesta is deeply influenced by sherry, with around 200,000 half-bottles being drunk; late April/early May.

Campeonato del Mundo de Motociclismo de Jerez An unofficial motorbike fiesta takes over central El Puerto for the weekend in early May of the Jerez Grand Prix event of the World Motorcycle Championship (see p199).

Festividad Virgen del Carmen Fisherfolk Andalucía-wide pay homage to their patroness on the evening of 16 July; in El Puerto the virgin's image is paraded along the Río Guadalete followed by a flotilla.

Sleeping

El Puerto offers plenty of choice to suit all pockets, but especially in the upper bracket. Book ahead for July and August. Prices drop noticeably out of season.

Camping Las Dunas (☎ 956 87 22 10; www.las dunascamping.com; adult/tent/car €4.50/4.50/3.90, bungalow for 2 incl 1 vehicle €55-84; **P** ☁ ☒) The town's well-equipped and shady camping ground, with room for 1200 people, is just behind Playa de la Puntilla.

Hostal Costa Luz (☎ 956 05 47 01; www.hostal costaluz.com; Calle Niño del Matadero 2; s/d €40/63; **P** ☒ ☁) The friendly and young English-speaking Spanish owners have carefully designed and fitted out this modern *hostal* in the vicinity of the Plaza de Toros. The 11 medium-sized rooms have attractive wooden furniture and appealing bathrooms. Breakfast is available in the cosy dining room and you can relax on the roof terrace.

Casa No 6 (☎ 956 87 70 84; www.casano6.com; Calle San Bartolomé 14; r/f incl breakfast €70/120, 4-person apt €130; **P**) This is an early-19th-century house beautifully renovated by its welcoming Spanish-English owners. It provides charming, spacious and spotless rooms with high, wood-beamed ceilings, comfy beds and old-fashioned tiling, all around a lovely pillared patio open to the sky. Very central!

Casa del Regidor Hotel (☎ 956 87 73 33; www .hotelcasadelregidor.com; Ribera del Río 30; s/d €64/91; **P** ☒ ☁ ☒) A converted 17th-century palace on two levels with an original patio. The excellent rooms have all the mod cons: two have a private terrace and three enjoy views. Water is solar-heated and there's a lift which arrives right outside the room adapted for wheelchair users.

CÁDIZ PROVINCE

Hotel Santa María (☎ 956 87 32 11; www.hotel santamaria.es; Avenida de la Bajamar s/n; s/d €87/106; P 🏊 🛈) The very comfortable, 100-room Santa María has a commanding position overlooking the Río Guadalete and expansive views from its rooftop pool area – probably the best reason to stay here.

Hotel Los Cántaros (☎ 956 54 02 40; www.hotellos cantaros.com; Calle Curva 6; s/d €98/115; P 🏊 🖳 🛈) A classy hotel (named after the 17th-century water jugs found by archaeologists beneath it) with 39 comfortable, well-equipped rooms, all with new furniture and some with balconies. Its restaurant looks out to a small garden.

Hotel Monasterio San Miguel (☎ 956 54 04 40; www.jale.com/monasterio; Calle Virgen de los Milagros 27; s/d from €140/184; P 🏊 🛈 🛈) This stylish and luxurious hotel occupies a converted 18th-century monastery, now home to a tropical garden, pool, valuable artworks and a gourmet restaurant.

Hotel Duques de Medinaceli (☎ 956 86 07 77; www.jale.com/dmedinaceli; Plaza de los Jazmines 2; s/d €165/206; P 🏊 🛈) Converted from an 18th-century mansion, this elegant hotel dripping with antiques provides 28 gorgeous rooms equipped with every comfort, including four-poster beds in some. This is the former home of the Terry Irish sherry family; beautiful manicured gardens separate it from the Terry winery.

For hotels and apartments out at the beaches, consult the tourist office website.

Eating

El Puerto is justly known for its outstanding seafood, fine restaurants and terrific tapas bars. Try the local speciality *urta roteña* (sea bream cooked in white wine, tomatoes, peppers and thyme), and don't forget the local wines!

Romerijo (☎ 956 54 12 54; Ribera del Marisco s/n; seafood per 250g from €4) This is a huge El Puerto institution, with crowds flocking to its two facing buildings. One building boils the seafood, the other fries it, and you buy portions in paper cones to take away or eat at the many tables. Everything's on display (boggle at the 18 types of fresh seafood) and you just take your pick and buy by the quarter-kilogram: for example, €4 for chunks of fried *cazón* (dogfish), €12 for a mixed fish/seafood fry-up, or €6 to €13 for various types of boiled prawns.

Restaurante Shawarma (☎ 956 87 64 23; Ribera del Marisco 11; falafel roll €3.50, mains €9; V) Vegetarians will just love this small, simple restaurant next to the large Romerijo. The food, authentic Lebanese-Greek, provides a welcome change. The falafel is unbeatable, as are the little spinach-and-feta filo pastries. Meat options include kebabs and moussaka.

Bodeguita La Antigua (☎ 956 67 68 56; Calle Misericordia 8; tapas €3, media-raciones from €4) Calle Misericordia sports half-a-dozen tapas bars dishing up some of the tastiest morsels in the region. La Antigua helpfully provides tapas menus in English and French as well as in Spanish. The *serranito*, a bread roll with pork, fried green pepper and a few chips (€3), makes people happy.

Casa Luis (☎ 956 87 20 09; Ribera del Marisco s/n; tapas/raciones €3/8; 🕑 1.30-4pm & 9-11pm Tue-Sat, 1.30-4pm Sun) This is a tightly packed little den with just a few tables inside and out, and a bar you can only elbow towards. They come for amiable Luis' innovative tapas, such as *paté de cabracho* (scorpion fish pâté) or *hojaldres* (puff pastries) with prawn, or cheese and anchovy filling.

Restaurante El Arriate (☎ 956 85 28 33; Calle los Moros 4; mains €9-15; 🕑 closed Mon) German-Spanish owned, this local favourite serves up a broad Mediterranean cuisine. Unusual dishes (for Spain) are salmon lasagne, sole in an orange sauce, and potatoes *au gratin*.

Los Portales (☎ 956 54 21 16; Ribera del Río 13; mains €15-18) It's hard to go wrong with the grilled fish and seafood here. Specialities include *lenguado al crema de langosto*, sole in a creamy sauce with prawns, and *parrillada de pescado y mariscos*, a two-person platter of grilled fish and seafood.

Casa Flores (☎ 956 54 35 12; Ribera del Río 9; raciones €7.50-12, mains €13-34) A favourite of both locals and visitors, this restaurant offers an enticing array of appetisers including a tasty shellfish cocktail. The fish mains come with various sauces such as hake with mushrooms, and bream with seafood and ham. Meat eaters might like to choose the roast lamb (€26).

Drinking

Youthful music bars cluster around the centre and on the eastern side of town at Playa de Valdelagrana.

La Pontana (Parque Calderón; ☾ from 3.30pm) Get the real maritime feel at this bar floating on the river just north of Plaza de las Galeras Reales. Best late.

La Cristalera (Plaza de las Galeras s/n; ☾ from 4.30pm) Big glass windows capture the river views and light. You can sip a tea, or something stronger, inside or out.

Bar Reconquista (Calle Javier de Burgos 2) The quirky medieval décor here is inspired by a mix of Islamic and Christian themes.

Bar & Co (Plaza de la Herrería; ☾ from 9.30pm) A local favourite, based in the 16th-century building where seafarers once paid their taxes.

Entertainment

El Puerto has a pulsating night scene with some funky themed clubs. One of the best is **Mucho Teatro** (www.muchoteatro.com; Calle Misericordia 12; ☾ closed Mon), a glitzy recreation of an old-style movie house, with a dance floor and often live music.

Flamenco happens (at least) every Friday at 9.30pm at **Peña Flamenca El Nitri** (☎ 956 54 32 37; Calle Diego Niño 1) and **Peña Flamenca El Chumi** (☎ 956 54 00 03; Calle Luja 15). **Bodega Obregón** (Calle Zarza 51), the oldest bar in town, has flamenco on Sunday from 12.30pm to 3.30pm. There are more flamenco performances in July and August.

Top matadors fight every Sunday in July and August at El Puerto's **Plaza de Toros** (☎ 956 54 15 78; www.justo-ojeda.com; Plaza Elías Ahuja; sun €15-25, shade €21-60). Tickets can be purchased at the bullring.

Bodegas Terry (see p184) puts on horse spectaculars, flamenco shows and tapas tastings during the summer.

Getting There & Away
BOAT

The small passenger ferry *Adriano III*, better known as *El Vapor* or **El Vaporcito** (The Little Steamship; ☎ 956 85 59 06; www.vapordelpuerto .com in Spanish) sets sail for El Puerto (€3, 40 minutes) from Cádiz's Estación Marítima at 10.15am, 12.15pm, 2.15pm, 4.45pm and 6.45pm daily from 3 February to 9 December (except nonholiday Mondays from 1 October to 30 May), with an extra trip at 8.45pm from 1 June to 30 September. Trips from El Puerto to Cádiz leave one hour earlier than the above times from the Muelle del Vapor. The *Adriano III* and its predecessors *Adriano I* and *Adriano II* have

provided this vital link between the two cities since 1929.

The faster catamaran (€1.80, 25 minutes), run by the public **Línea Metropolitana/Consorcio de Transportes Bahía de Cádiz** (☎ 956 01 21 00; www.cmtbc.com), sails between Cádiz and El Puerto 13 times a day Monday to Friday, six times on Saturday and three on Sunday. The boat docks on the river in front of the Hotel Santa María.

BUS

There are regular bus services connecting El Puerto de Santa María to the following destinations:

Cádiz (€1.70, 30 to 40 minutes) Buses depart Monday to Friday between 6.45am to 10pm about half-hourly from the Plaza de Toros, and at least seven times from the train station. Weekend services are about half as frequent.

Chipiona (€2.30, 30 minutes) Five to 11 buses go daily from the Plaza de Toros.

Jerez de la Frontera (€1, 20 minutes) Nine to 16 buses depart daily from the train station and 11 from the Plaza de Toros Monday to Friday (but only two on Saturday and Sunday).

Sanlúcar de Barrameda (€1.60, 30 minutes) Five to 11 buses go daily from the Plaza de Toros.

Seville (€8.50, 1½ hours) Three buses go daily from the train station.

TRAIN

Up to 37 trains travel daily to/from Jerez de la Frontera (from €1.30, 12 minutes) and Cádiz (from €2.20, 30 to 35 minutes), and 10 or more daily to/from Seville (€6 to €18, one to 1½ hours).

Getting Around

Traffic is thick in the centre. There's plenty of parking along the riverfront, especially south of Plaza de las Galeras Reales. Most of it is free, but the supervised area next to the plaza costs €1.60 for 24 hours. You can park for free outside the Plaza de Toros.

SANLÚCAR DE BARRAMEDA
pop 63,000

The northern tip of the sherry triangle and a thriving summer resort, Sanlúcar is 23km northwest of El Puerto de Santa María. It has a likable, mellow atmosphere and a sublime location on the Guadalquivir estuary looking across to the Parque Nacional de Doñana. The Atlantic waters here provide the freshest of succulent seafood – Sanlúcar prawns carry a high price tag – and the town's bodegas produce a distinctive sherry-like wine, manzanilla, the perfect complement to the ocean's offerings. Sanlúcar also lays on the fabulous and unusual spectacle of its unique August horse races when sleek horses, bearing colourfully clad jockeys, thunder along the sands beside the estuary.

Sanlúcar's nautical history is proud. Columbus sailed from Sanlúcar in 1498 on his third voyage to the Caribbean, as did the Portuguese Ferdinand Magellan in 1519, seeking – like Columbus – a westerly route to the Asian Spice Islands. Magellan succeeded by making the first known voyage around the bottom of South America but was killed in a battle in the Philippines. His Basque pilot Juan Sebastián Elcano completed the first circumnavigation of the globe by returning to Sanlúcar with just one of the expedition's five ships, the *Victoria*.

Orientation & Information

Sanlúcar stretches along the southeast side of the Guadalquivir estuary. Calzada del Ejército (often just called La Calzada), running 600m inland from the seafront Paseo Marítimo, is the main avenue and it has underground parking. A block beyond its inland end is Plaza del Cabildo, the central square. The old town spreads around and uphill from here. The bus station is on Avenida de la Estación, 100m southwest of the middle of La Calzada.

The old fishing quarter, Bajo de Guía, site of Sanlúcar's best restaurants and boat departures to Doñana, is 750m northeast along the riverfront from La Calzada. There are banks on Calle San Juan, which runs southwest off Plaza del Cabildo.

Centro de Visitantes Bajo de Guía (☎ 956 38 09 22; Bajo de Guía s/n; ☾ 10am-2pm Tue-Sun & 4-6pm holidays & Oct-May, 10am-2pm & 6-8pm Tue-Sun Jun-Sep) Run by the Junta de Andalucía, this visitors centre has info on the Parque Natural de Doñana (distinct from the Parque Nacional – for the difference, see p154) and other natural spaces in Andalucía.

Centro de Visitantes Fábrica de Hielo (☎ 956 38 16 35; www.parquenacionaldonana.es; Bajo de Guía s/n; ☾ 9am-7pm or 8pm) This, the original visitors centre, is run by the national parks folk, with interesting displays and information on the Parque Nacional de Doñana and related topics.

CyberGuadalquivir (Calle Infanta Beatriz 11; internet per hr €2; ☾ 10am-11.30pm Mon-Sat, noon-11.30pm Sun)

Tourist office (☎ 956 36 61 10; www.turismosanlucar .com; Calzada del Ejército s/n; ☾ 10am-2pm & 4-6pm Mon-Sat Nov-Mar, 10am-2pm & 5-7pm Mon-Sat April-May & Oct, 10am-2pm & 6-8pm Mon-Sat Jun-Sep) Helpful staff with plenty of printed info.

Sights & Activities

The old town's sights are clustered on the hill above Plaza del Cabildo. On your way up, admire the elaborate Gothic façade of **Las Covachas** (Cuesta de Belén), a set of 15th-century wine cellars in an outer wall of the Palacio de los Duques de Medina Sidonia (see below). The brightly painted **Palacio de Orleans y Borbon** (cnr Cuesta de Belén & Calle Caballero; admission free; ☾ 10am-1.30pm Mon-Fri) is a beautiful neo-Mudejar palace built as a summer home for the aristocratic Montpensier family in the 19th century. Its creation stimulated Sanlúcar's growth as a resort. Today the palace is Sanlúcar's *ayuntamiento* (town hall). It has a ritzy restored patio with glass roof.

Beyond the town hall along Calle Caballero is the 15th-century **Iglesia de Nuestra Señora de la O** (Plaza de la Paz; ☾ mass 7.30pm Mon-Fri & Sun, 9am & noon Sun), with a Mudejar façade and ceiling. Next door is the **Palacio de los Duques de Medina Sidonia** (☎ 956 36 01 61; www .fcmedinasidonia.com; Plaza Condes de Niebla 1; admission €3; ☾ tours 11am & noon Sun by appointment), a rambling stately home that dates all the way back to Guzmán El Bueno, the 13th-century ancestor of the Duques de Medina Sidonia (see p216 for more on Guzmán). This powerful aristocratic family once owned more of Spain than anyone else. The current incumbent, Luisa Isabel Álvarez de Toledo, has fought long and hard to keep the priceless Medina Sidonia archive in Sanlúcar. The house is bursting with antique furniture, paintings by famous Spanish artists, even Goya and Zurbarán, and other wonderful decorations. To really soak up the olde worlde vibe, you might treat yourself to afternoon tea at the café (p191), or, better still, enjoy a night of luxury (p190).

Along the street is the 15th-century **Castillo de Santiago** (Plaza del Castillo), amid the buildings of Sanlúcar's biggest sherry company, Barbadillo. After many years of restoration, the castle was set to open to the public in summer 2006. By June, it still had not. You can expect to enjoy stunning views from its towers. A cultural centre, concert space, restaurant and shops are planned.

BEACH

Sanlúcar's good sandy beach runs all along the riverfront and for several kilometres beyond to the southwest.

BODEGAS

Of the town's six or so bodegas, at least three give tours for which you don't need to book ahead. Tours are principally in Spanish, but they can be adapted for the group.

Barbadillo (☎ 956 38 55 00; Calle Luis de Eguilaz 11; tour €3, museum free; ☽ tours noon & 1pm Mon-Sat, in English 11am Tue-Sat, Museo de Manzanilla 11am-3pm Mon-Sat) The museum, in a 19th-century building, traces the 200-year history of Sanlúcar's unique manzanilla wine and the history of the Barbadillo family, the first to bottle manzanilla. It also outlines the production process from start to finish.

Bodegas Hidalgo-La Gitana (☎ 956 38 53 04; Calle Banda Playa; tour €5; ☽ tours noon Wed, Fri & Sat)

La Cigarrera (☎ 956 38 12 85; Plaza Madre de Dios; tour €2.50; ☽ 10am-2pm Mon-Sat)

Tours

Both these outings to the Parque Nacional de Doñana start from Bajo de Guía. You will need mosquito protection, except in winter.

Real Fernando (Centro de Visitantes Fábrica de Hielo; ☎ 956 36 38 13; www.visitasdonana.com; 3½-hr trips adult/under 15yr/under 13yr €15.50/11.20/7.80; ☽ 10am Nov-Feb, 10am & 4pm Mar-May & Oct, 10am & 5pm Jun-Sep) Despite stops in the national park and Parque Natural de Doñana, these Guadalquivir boat trips offer a leisurely tour of the park's fringes but are not designed for serious nature enthusiasts. Book two or three days ahead, and a week or more ahead in summer and during holiday periods.

Viajes Doñana (☎ 956 36 25 40; Calle San Juan 20; 3½-hr tour per person €36; ☽ 8.30am & 4.30pm Tue & Fri May–mid-Sep, 8.30am & 2.30pm Tue & Fri mid-Sep–Apr) These fun tours in 4WD vehicles holding about 20 people go deep into the national park: after the river crossing, they visit much the same spots as the tours from El Acebuche (see p155). Great for kids! Book well in advance.

Festivals & Events

Feria de la Manzanilla The Sanlúcar summer begins with a big fair devoted to Sanlúcar's unique wine, manzanilla; held late May/early June.

Romería del Rocío (Pentecost) Though this festival centres on El Rocío on the far side of the Parque Nacional de Doñana (see p157), Sanlúcar is inextricably involved as many pilgrims and covered wagons set out for El Rocío from here; 7th weekend after Easter.

Music Festivals Summer revs up in July and August with jazz, flamenco and classical music festivals, and one-off concerts by top Spanish bands. Check out www.turismo sanlucar.com to find out the latest information on upcoming festivals.

Carreras de Caballos (www.carrerassanlucar.com) Two horse-race meetings of three or four days every August: exciting thoroughbred races on the sands beside the Guadalquivir estuary, held almost every year since 1845.

Sleeping

Book well ahead for a room at holiday times. Budget accommodation is scarce.

Hostal Blanca Paloma (☎ 956 36 36 44; hostal blancapaloma@msn.co; Plaza San Roque 15; s/d/tr €18/30/45) This *hostal* maintains the same prices all year and is a good warm-weather option. The best of the 10 simple, clean rooms is a triple with French doors to a little balcony.

Hostal La Bohemia (☎ 956 36 95 99; Calle Don Claudio 5; s/d €25/40) Pretty, folksy-painted chairs dot the corridors of this little *hostal* in a tranquil street off Calle Ancha, 300m northeast of Plaza del Cabildo. Rooms are neat and clean and the service is friendly.

Hotel Los Helechos (956 36 13 49; www.hotelos helechos.com; Plaza Madre de Dios 9; s/d €47/62; **P** ☒) Los Helechos, off Calle San Juan in the lower section of the old town, is an attractive former mansion with brightly decorated rooms mainly set around two plant-filled patios with fountains.

Hospedería Duques de Medina Sidonia (☎ 956 36 01 61; www.ruralduquemedinasidonia.com; Plaza Condes de Niebla 1; r €65-105; **P** ☒) Enjoy top-end luxury and views in an aristocrat's palace (see p189) in the upper part of the old town. Olde-worlde Spain unfolds before your eyes – the place has 800 years of history and is brimming with swish furnishings and decorations.

Hotel Guadalquivir (☎ 956 36 07 42; www.hotel guadalquivir.com in Spanish; Calzada del Ejército 20; s/d incl breakfast €82/103; **P** ☒) Opposite the tourist office, the modern, 12-storey Guadalquivir is freshly refurbished and has plenty of spacious communal areas, including a 12th-floor bar with panoramic views. Rates halve in winter.

Hotel Posada de Palacio (☎ 956 36 48 40; www.posadadepalacio.com; Calle Caballeros 11; s/d/q €85/105/149; **P** ☒) Nestled in the upper part of the old town, this 18th-century mansion is one of Sanlúcar's most charming lodgings. It has 27 rooms, a couple of pretty patios and a roof terrace and is adorned with heavy, old-style furniture. The hotel is quite sumptuous (not appropriate for kids).

Hotel Tartaneros (☎ 956 36 20 44; hoteltartaneros@ telefonica.net; Calle Tartaneros 8; s/d €104/128, ste €300-360; P ✿) At the inland end of Calzada del Ejército you'll find this century-old industrialist's mansion with 22 solidly comfortable but slightly over-priced rooms.

Eating

The line of seafood restaurants overlooking the river at Bajo de Guía are reason enough for visiting Sanlúcar. It's idyllic watching the sun go down over the Guadalquivir while tucking into the succulent fresh fare and washing it down with a drop of manzanilla. Lunchtime is great here too! Just wander along and pick a restaurant that suits your pocket. Lots of cafés, bars, and restaurants, many serving manzanilla from the barrel, also surround bustling Plaza del Cabildo.

Casa Balbino (Plaza del Cabildo 11; tapas/raciones €1.50/9) Sit out at a table here to enjoy an array of wonderful snacks such as *tortillas de camarones* (crisp shrimp fritters) or the local favourite *coctel de bogavante* (giant-prawn cocktail, €6).

Palacio de los Duques de Medina Sidonia (☎ 956 36 01 61; www.ruralduquemedinasidonia.com; Plaza Condes de Niebla 1; ☒ 9am-2pm & 3.30-10pm, closed Sat am) Feel like an aristocrat at the café of Sanlúcar's Palacio de los Duques de Medina Sidonia, where you'll find sumptuous décor, classical music, coffee, tea and cakes.

Casa Bigote (☎ 956 36 26 96; Bajo de Guía; fish mains €7-14; ☒ closed Sun) This place gets excellent reviews from everyone and is usually packed, even in the downstairs dining room without views. Find the entrance down a little lane towards the end of the Bajo de Guía strip. Try the house speciality – *hamburguesas de bacalao con salsa*, codburgers with sauce (€8.50).

Restaurante Virgen del Carmen (☎ 956 38 22 72; Bajo de Guía; fish €9-36, menú €15) This restaurant with a large terrace is good but not too expensive. Decide whether you want your fish *plancha* (grilled) or *frito* (fried), and don't skip the starters: *langostinos* (king prawns) and the juicy *coquines al ajillo* (clams in garlic), both €9, are specialities. A half-bottle of manzanilla costs €6.

Bar Joselito Huertas (☎ 956 36 26 94; Bajo de Guía; fried fish €10, fresh wholefish €13-36) At the far end of the strip. Dine outside here, drinking in the pure air and watching the returning fishing fleet, with Doñana as backdrop. Waiters helpfully decide whether or not you'll need a *ración* or *media-ración* of your chosen dish.

Drinking

Two excellent places to relax from sightseeing over a tea or coffee are the Hotel Tartaneros (see opposite) and the Palacio de los Duques de Medina Sidonia (left).

Entertainment

There are some lively music bars on and around Calzada del Ejército and Plaza del Cabildo. Many concerts are held here during the summer. The tourist office's website www.turismosanlucar.com regularly updates events.

Bodegón de Arte (☎ 653 07 10 99; Calle San Miguel 5) Flamenco and flamenco/jazz fusion performances happen at 11.30pm Friday and Saturday year-round. Admission is from €6 to €12 depending on the performance.

Getting There & Away
BOAT

Though you can visit Sanlúcar on day-trip boats from Seville (see p113), you can't take a one-way ride upriver from Sanlúcar to Seville.

BUS

Buses leave from the bus station on Avenida de la Estación. **Los Amarillos** (☎ 956 38 50 60) runs five to 10 buses daily to/from El Puerto de Santa María (€1.60, 30 minutes) and Cádiz (€3, 1¼ hours) and six to 12 to/from Seville (€7, 1½ hours). **Linesur** (☎ 956 34 10 63) has seven to 15 buses daily to/from Jerez de la Frontera (€1.60, 30 minutes). Change in Jerez for buses to Arcos de la Frontera and El Bosque.

JEREZ DE LA FRONTERA
pop 196,000 / elevation 55m

Jerez beguiles with its eclectic mix of sherry, horses and flamenco. Spread over a low rise in the rolling countryside 36km northeast of Cádiz, Jerez (heh-*reth* or, in the Andalucian accent, just heh-*reh*) is world-famous for its wine – sherry – made from grapes grown on the chalky soil surrounding the town. Many people come here to visit its bodegas, but Jerez is also Andalucía's horse capital and, alongside its affluent upper-crust society, is home to a *gitano* (Roma) community that is a hotbed of flamenco.

The Muslims originally called the town 'Scheris', from which the words 'Jerez' and 'sherry' are both derived. 'De la Frontera', a commonly used suffix in Cádiz province, dates back to the days of the Reconquista (Christian reconquest) when this whole region was a *frontera* (frontier) of Christian territory.

Sherry was already famed in England in Shakespeare's time, and British money

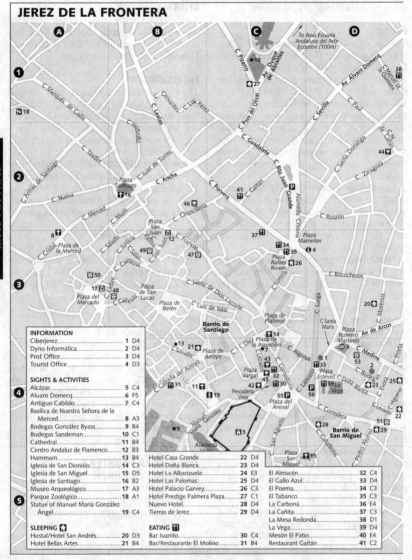

JEREZ DE LA FRONTERA

To Real Escuela Andaluza del Arte Ecuestre (100m)

INFORMATION	
Ciberjerez	1 D4
Dyno Informática	2 D4
Post Office	3 D4
Tourist Office	4 D3

SIGHTS & ACTIVITIES	
Alcázar	5 C4
Aluaro Domecq	6 F5
Antiguo Cabildo	7 C4
Basílica de Nuestra Señora de la Merced	8 A3
Bodegas González Byass	9 B4
Bodegas Sandeman	10 C1
Cathedral	11 B4
Centro Andaluz de Flamenco	12 B3
Hammam	13 C4
Iglesia de San Dionisio	14 C3
Iglesia de San Miguel	15 D5
Iglesia de Santiago	16 B2
Museo Arqueológico	17 A3
Parque Zoológico	18 A1
Statue of Manuel María González Ángel	19 C4

SLEEPING	
Hostal/Hotel San Andrés	20 D3
Hotel Bellas Artes	21 B4
Hotel Casa Grande	22 D4
Hotel Doña Blanca	23 D4
Hotel La Albarizuela	24 E3
Hotel Las Palomas	25 D4
Hotel Palacio Garvey	26 C3
Hotel Prestige Palmera Plaza	27 C1
Nuevo Hotel	28 D4
Tierras de Jerez	29 D4

EATING	
Bar Juanito	30 C4
Bar/Restaurante El Molino	31 B4
El Almacén	32 C4
El Gallo Azul	33 D4
El Poema	34 C3
El Tabanco	35 C3
La Carboná	36 E4
La Cañita	37 C3
La Mesa Redonda	38 D1
La Vega	39 D4
Mesón El Patio	40 E4
Restaurant Gaitán	41 C2

developed the wineries from the 1830s. Today, Jerez high society is a mixture of Andalucian and British, as the families of wine traders have intermarried over the past 150 years. Since the 1980s most of the wineries, previously owned by about 15 families, have been bought out by multinational companies.

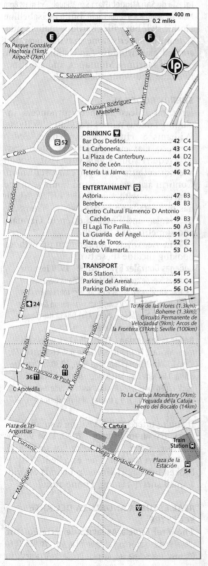

DRINKING 🍺	
Bar Dos Deditos	42 C4
La Carbonería	43 C4
La Plaza de Canterbury	44 D2
Reino de León	45 C4
Tetería La Jaima	46 B2

ENTERTAINMENT 🎭	
Astoria	47 B3
Bereber	48 B3
Centro Cultural Flamenco D Antonio Cachón	49 B3
El Lagá Tio Parilla	50 A3
La Guarida del Ángel	51 D4
Plaza de Toros	52 E2
Teatro Villamarta	53 D4

TRANSPORT	
Bus Station	54 F5
Parking del Arenal	55 C4
Parking Doña Blanca	56 D4

Jerez is dripping with money, with fancy shops, well-heeled residents, and old mansions and beautiful churches in its old quarter, now the subject of ambitious revitalisation projects. The city stages fantastic fiestas with sleek horses, beautiful people and flamenco.

Orientation & Information

The centre of Jerez is between the Alameda Cristina and the revamped Plaza del Arenal, which are connected by the north–south Calle Larga and Calle Lancería (both pedestrianised). The old quarter extends west and southeast of Calle Larga.

There are plenty of banks and ATMs on and around Calle Larga.

Ciberjerez (Calle Santa María 3, internet per hr €2; ⏰ 10am-11pm Mon-Sat, noon-11pm Sun) Also offers cheap phone rates worldwide.

Dyno Informática (Calle Bodegas s/n; internet per hr €1.75; ⏰ 10am-2pm & 5-9pm Mon-Thu, 10am-10pm Fri & Sat, 3-10pm Sun)

Post office (☎ 902 19 71 97; cnr Calles Cerrón & Medina)

Tourist office (☎ 956 32 47 47; www.turismojerez .com; Alameda Cristina; ⏰ 10am-3pm & 5-7pm Mon-Fri, 10am-2.30pm Sat & Sun mid-Jun—mid-Sep, 9.30am-3pm & 4.30-6.30pm Mon-Fri, 9.30am-2.30pm Sat & Sun mid-Sep—mid-Jun) Expert multilingual staff have mountains of information on offer.

Sights & Activities
OLD QUARTER

The obvious place to start a tour of the old town, parts of whose walls survive, is the impressive 11th- and 12th-century Islamic fortress southwest of Plaza del Arenal, the **Alcázar** (☎ 956 32 69 23; Alameda Vieja; admission incl/excl camera obscura €5.40/3; ⏰ 10am-8pm Mon-Sat, 10am-3pm Sun May—mid-Sep, 10am-6pm Mon-Sat, 10am-2.30pm Sun mid-Sep—Apr). Inside the Alcázar are a beautiful **mezquita** (mosque), converted to a chapel by Alfonso X in 1264, an impressive set of **Baños Árabes** (Arab Baths) and the 18th-century **Palacio Villavicencio**, built over the ruins of the old Islamic palace. Don't miss the gardens, which recreate the ambience of Islamic times with their geometrical plant beds and tinkling fountains. You'll want to linger here! Top off your visit with a bird's-eye view of Jerez: a **camera obscura** in the palace's tower provides a picturesque live panorama of Jerez accompanied by an interesting 15-minute commentary in Spanish, English, French and German. Sessions begin every half-hour until 30 minutes before closing time.

In the foreground of the Alcázar's westward vista stands a large **statue of Manuel María González Ángel** (1812–87), the founder of Bodegas González Byass (right). It was this man's uncle, José Ángel, who gave his name to González Byass' famous dry sherry Tío Pepe (*tío* meaning uncle and Pepe being a nickname for José). Behind Señor González is Jerez's mainly 18th-century **cathedral** (admission free; ☾ 11am-1pm Mon-Fri, mass 7.30pm daily), which has Gothic, baroque and neoclassical features, and was built on the site of the Islamic town's main mosque. The 15th-century Mudejar-Gothic belfry is set slightly apart.

A couple of blocks northeast of the cathedral is Plaza de la Asunción, with the handsome 16th-century **Antiguo Cabildo** (Old Town Hall) and the lovely 15th-century Mudejar **Iglesia de San Dionisio**, named after the town's patron saint – Jerez fell to the Christians on 9 October 1264, San Dionisio's feast day.

North and west of here is the **Barrio de Santiago**, a quarter with a sizable *gitano* population and one of the centres of flamenco. Here you'll also find the excellent **Museo Arqueológico** (Archaeological Museum; ☎ 956 32 63 36; www.museoarqueologico.webjerez.com; Plaza del Mercado; admission €3; ☾ 10am-2.30pm Tue-Sun mid-Jun–Aug, 10am-2pm & 4-7pm Tue-Fri, 10am-2.30pm Sat, Sun & holidays Sep–mid-Jun). The pride of the museum's collection is a 7th-century-BC Greek helmet found in the Río Guadalete. Also noteworthy are two cylindrical idols with big circular eyes and facial tattoo lines, possibly associated with worship of the Copper Age earth goddess. The museum was closed for refurbishing in 2006.

Also in this area is the **Centro Andaluz de Flamenco** (Andalucian Flamenco Centre; ☎ 956 34 92 65; http://caf.cica.es; Plaza de San Juan 1; ☾ 9am-2pm Mon-Fri). Jerez is at the heart of the Seville–Cádiz axis where flamenco began and where its heartland remains today. This centre is a museum and school dedicated to the flamenco arts, with print and music libraries holding thousands of works. Flamenco videos are screened every morning.

Jerez's ambitious Ciudad de Flamenco (Flamenco City) project, intended to revitalise the old quarter and to celebrate and promote flamenco, is well underway. The site, Plaza de Belén, between the flamenco districts – Barrio de Santiago and Barrio de San Miguel – was the heart of Islamic Jerez. The 'city' will have an auditorium, a library, a flamenco school and a museum.

Southeast of Plaza del Arenal is one of Jerez's loveliest churches, the 16th-century **Iglesia de San Miguel** (Plaza San Miguel; ☾ mass 8pm Mon-Sat, 9am, noon & 8pm Sun), built in Isabelline Gothic style but with a baroque main façade. It features superb stone carving, beautiful stained-glass windows, an elaborate retable by Juan Martínez Montañés, and a distinctive blue-and-white-tiled steeple.

SHERRY BODEGAS

Jerez has at least 20 sherry producers, including famous names like González Byass, Williams & Humbert, Sandeman, Pedro Domecq, Garvey and Harveys. Most bodegas require you to book your visit, though a few offer tours where you can just turn up. Confirm arrangements and hours with the wineries or with the tourist office, which has full details on bodega visits. Tours are in Spanish and English, often in German, and sometimes in French.

Wineries where you can turn up without booking include these two:

Bodegas González Byass (☎ 956 35 70 16; www.bodegastiopepe.com; Calle Manuel María González 12; tour €8.50, with tapas €13.50; ☾ tours in English 11.30am, 12.30am, 1.30pm, 2pm year-round & 3.30pm, 4.30pm & 5.30pm Mon-Sat Oct-Apr) One of the biggest sherry houses, just west of the Alcázar.

Bodegas Sandeman (☎ 956 15 17 11; www.sandeman.com; Calle Pizarro 10; tour in English €6, tapas €5.50; ☾ 11.30am-1.30pm Mon, Wed & Fri, 10.30am-2pm Tue & Thu, 11.30am-2pm Sat) Sandeman sherries carry the black-caped 'Don' logo. Regular visits include an audiovisual presentation and a tasting of three sherries.

If you're interested in visiting a smaller bodega, try **Álvaro Domecq** (☎ 956 33 96 34; www.alvarodomecq.com; Calle Madre de Dios s/n; tour €6; ☾ 10am-2pm Mon-Fri). The excellent tour is broken by a short video and winds up with a small sherry tasting. Phone ahead.

REAL ESCUELA ANDALUZA DEL ARTE ECUESTRE

The **Real Escuela Andaluza del Arte Ecuestre** (Royal Andalucian School of Equestrian Art; ☎ 956 31 80 08; www.realescuela.org; Avenida Duque de Abrantes), in

---

THE SOLERA PROCESS

How you get your bottle of sherry is intriguing. Once sherry grapes have been harvested, they are pressed and the resulting must is left to ferment. Within a few months a frothy veil of *flor* (yeast) appears on the surface. The wine is then transferred to the bodegas (wineries) in big barrels of American oak.

Wine enters the *solera* process when it is a year old. The barrels, about five-sixths full, are lined up in rows at least three barrels high. The barrels on the bottom layer, called the *solera* (from *suelo*, meaning floor), contain the oldest wine. From these, around three times a year, 10% of the wine is drawn off. This is replaced with the same amount from the barrels in the layer above, which is in turn replaced from the next layer. The wines age for between three and seven years. A small amount of brandy is added to stabilise the wine before bottling, bringing the alcohol content to 16% to 18%, which stops fermentation.

A sherry tour will take you through the cellars where the wine is stored and aged, inform you about the process and the history of the sherry producers, and give you a tasting. You can buy sherry at the bodegas too – or in any supermarket.

See p83 for an explanation of the various types of sherry. Jerez *coñac* (brandy), widely drunk in Spain, is also a profitable, locally made product – 63 million bottles are produced annually.

---

the north of town, is a top Jerez attraction. This famous school trains horses and riders in dressage and you can watch them being put through their paces in **training sessions** (adult/child €8/5; 11am-2pm Mon, Wed & Fri Sep-Jul, 11am-2pm Mon & Wed Aug). There's an official **espectáculo** (show; adult/child €23/14; noon Tue & Thu Sep-Jul, noon Tue, Thu & Fri Aug), where the handsome white horses show off their tricks to classical music. Tickets entitle you to tour the grounds, facilities and two museums.

PARQUE ZOOLÓGICO

A couple of kilometres west of the centre, the **Parque Zoológico** (Jerez Zoo; ☎ 956 15 31 64; www.zoobotanicojerez.com in Spanish; Calle Taxdirt s/n; adult/child €6.50/4.50; 10am-8pm Jun-Sep, 10am-6pm Tue-Sun Oct-May) has over 1300 animals, well-established gardens, a recuperation centre for wild animals and a breeding programme for the Iberian lynx.

Festivals & Events

Festival de Jerez (www.festivaldejerez.com) This two-week event in late February/early March is dedicated to music and dance, particularly flamenco; a good opportunity to see big flamenco names in action. The Teatro Villamarta (p198) is the main venue.

Feria del Caballo One week in the first half of May, Jerez's Horse Fair is one of Andalucía's biggest festivals, with music, dancing and bullfights, as well as all kinds of horse competitions. Colourful parades of horses pass through the Parque González Hontoria fairgrounds in the north of town, the aristocratic-looking male riders decked out in flat-topped hats, frilly white shirts, black trousers

and leather chaps, their female *crupera* (sideways pillion) partners in long, frilly, spotted dresses. Jerez's motorcycle Grand Prix race of the World Motorcycle Championship (see p199) sometimes coincides with the Feria del Caballo.

Fiestas de Otoño The 'Autumn Fiestas', celebrating the grape harvest for two weeks or so in September, range from flamenco and horse events to the traditional treading of the first grapes on Plaza de la Asunción. The fiestas conclude with a massive parade of horses, riders and horse-drawn carriages.

Sleeping

Jerez has plenty of accommodation but prices go sky-high during the Feria del Caballo, for which you need to book well ahead.

Most budget and midrange accommodation clusters around the eastern part of the centre. Jerez's top hotels are in the north of town along Avenida Álvaro Domecq and the parallel Avenida Duque de Abrantes, good locations for the horse fair. Some sleek options are cropping up in the centre.

Hostal/Hotel San Andrés (☎ 956 34 09 83; www .hotelsanandres.org; Calle Morenos 12; s/d €24/38, with shared bathroom €20/28;) The friendly San Andrés' plant-filled and tiled entrance patio is one of the prettiest and most traditional that you'll see in Jerez. The clean and fairly comfy hotel rooms have TV and winter heating. The 18 *hostal* rooms are more basic, though with heaters in winter.

Hostal Las Palomas (☎ 956 34 37 73; www.hostal -las-palomas.com; Calle Higueras 17; s/d €30/45, with shared bathroom €25/40) New youthful management

JEREZ'S HAMMAM

Live like a sultan or Muslim princess and pamper yourself at Jerez's new **hammam** (Arabic baths; ☎ 956 34 90 66; www.hammamandalusi.com; Calle Salvador 6; baths €15, plus 15 min massage €25, plus full-body massage €40) or *baños Árabes*. You can loll about in one of three pools – hot, tepid, or cold – moving from one to the other as your body dictates, or add a massage and/or a variety of beauty treatments (2½ hours, €70-80). Whichever package you opt for, the sensuous hammam experience is a perfect complement to travelling. Numbers per session are limited to 15 people, so be sure to reserve beforehand.

The hammam's design and décor aim to recreate the ambience of Al-Andalus (medieval Muslim Spain). This begins from the minute you step through the wooden front door into the entrance foyer where you are greeted by an intoxicating aroma, a blend of essential oils and incense. Staff explain the routine, and hand over a soft towel, thin rubber slippers (for hygiene purposes), and a bikini or swimming trunks if you don't have these with you.

You move on to the changing rooms and shower. Moroccan grapefruit body gel and natural shampoos are provided, even more welcome at the end of the experience if you've had a massage where Moroccan argane oil (similar to olive oil) is used. The changing rooms have power showers, lockers and hairdryers.

From here, you pass into a dimly-lit area where to your right is a square-shaped pool with fairly shallow, tepid water. Straight ahead is a rectangular hot pool, while to the left is the cold pool, small but deep like a plunge pool, only for the very fit or very crazy in mid-winter.

With one hour and 15 minutes to luxuriate in the pools, you can unwind to the sound of classical Arabic music drifting through the Arabic arches and decoratively tiled walls, as lights under the water and on the high ceiling move slowly through the colour spectrum.

When your time is almost up, you are brought a pot of sweetened herbal tea. Then, if you're having a massage or beauty treatment, you are guided into another room. The 15-minute massage is for the shoulders, back and legs. For the front, face, arms and feet, you need to take the half-hour option. Exfoliation, mud bath or aloe vera bath are additional options.

Now, completely rejuvenated, you head back to the changing rooms and prepare to face the world. A radiant smile comes easily.

---

and lots of mood-enhancing yellow paint, new floor tiles throughout, and colourful, decorative Andalucian tiles have transformed a plain *hostal* into an appealing budget option. Many rooms are set around a glass-roofed patio and you'll like the sweeping views from the roof terrace.

Hotel La Albarizuela (☎ 956 34 68 62; www.hotel albarizuela.com; Calle Honsario 6; r €66; P ✖) An ultra-modern place, an easy walk east of the centre. A celeste-with-grey-trim colour scheme complements clean-cut lines. Five of the 17 good-sized rooms have a private patio – no views though. There's a cafeteria with buffet breakfast (€7). The youthful desk staff have the low-down on the local nightlife.

Nuevo Hotel (☎ 956 33 16 00; www.nuevohotel .com; Calle Caballeros 23; s/d €45/74; ✖ ♿) In a modernised 19th-century mansion, this popular, family-run hotel provides 27 rooms (nine singles and 18 spacious doubles) all with TV and winter heating. Rates halve outside peak periods. A buffet breakfast (€6) is served in the bright dining room. Reservations are essential.

Tierras de Jerez (☎ 956 34 64 00; www.intergroup hoteles.com; Calle Corredera 58; s/d €62/96; P ✖ 🖵) This is a first-rate, though somewhat bland, midrange choice with all you need, right on the spot for shopping, restaurants and nightlife. The 30 rooms are reasonably attractive, though singles are typically small. The hotel has on-site parking (€12 per day) via a quirkily steep entrance.

Hotel Casa Grande (☎ 956 34 50 70; www.casa grande.com.es; Plaza de las Angustias 3; s/d €70/91, ste €164; P ✖ 🖵 ♿) This brilliant hotel occupies a carefully restored and strikingly decorated 1920s mansion. Rooms are on three floors and set around a patio, or beside the roof terrace, which has views of Jerez's attractive roofline and tall palm trees out front. All is overseen by the congenial Monika Schroeder who is a mine of information about Jerez.

Hotel Doña Blanca (☎ 956 34 87 61; www.hotel donablanca.com in Spanish; Calle Bodegas 11; s/d €77/96; P ⊠ ▣) On a quiet side street, this is an excellent 30-room hotel with parquet floors, soothing light-blue paintwork, decent bathrooms with funky tiling, satellite TV and safety boxes. Staff are friendly and efficient.

Hotel Bellas Artes (☎ 956 34 84 30; www.hotel bellasartes.com; Plaza de Arroyo 45; s/d €107/128, ste from €160; P ⊠ ▣) A top-notch palace conversion, the Bellas Artes overlooks the Jerez cathedral from its main terrace and suites. An exquisite carved stone corner pillar graces the sand-coloured neoclassical exterior. Strong interior colours contrast with white marble floors. Free-standing bath tubs contribute to an olde-worlde ambience, though the rooms are decked out with all the mod cons.

Hotel Prestige Palmera Plaza (☎ 956 03 15 00; www.palmeraplaza.com; Calle Pizarro 1; s/d from €215/246; P ⊠ ▣ ⛱) This top luxury option incorporates the buildings and extensive grounds of a 19th-century bodega. There's plenty of space and light, and elegant, modern furnishings complement stylish design features throughout. The suites, with Jacuzzi, are sumptuous, and the restaurant highly praised. Fitness enthusiasts will enjoy the facilities.

Hotel Palacio Garvey (☎ 956 32 67 00; www .sferahoteles-net; Calle Tornería 24; s/d €226/292; P ⊠ ▣ ⛱) The Garvey is a sensational 19th-century neoclassical palace conversion, with part of the ancient city wall visible from the lift and more of it in the gardens. The public areas sport animal prints, large, colourful paintings and Japanese-inspired bowls on low-slung tables, while subtle colours and luxurious leather furniture feature in the 16 individually decorated rooms. The restaurant's lacquered red chairs and excellent food are all talking points.

Eating

Jerez food combines an Islamic heritage and maritime influences with English and French touches. Not surprisingly, sherry flavours many local dishes such as *riñones al jerez* (kidneys braised in sherry) and *rabo de toro* (oxtail stew). Don't miss Jerez's central market, which has a fantastic selection of meats, fish and seafood, fruits, vegetables and fresh herbs.

RESTAURANTS & CAFÉS

Bar/Restaurante El Molino (☎ 956 33 71 86; Plaza Domecq 16; mains €7-10, menú €7; ☾ closed Sun night) A neighbourhood kind of place preparing local dishes, with tables outside on the street below the cathedral as well as a dining room. The stuffed eggplants with béchamel sauce are a good choice, or try the house speciality, *revueltos* (scrambled eggs) with salmon and prawns.

La Vega (Plaza Estévez s/n; mains €7.50-12) Get a good glimpse of local life at this bustling café beside the market, a fine though noisy spot for breakfast, or a break at any time of day. There's something to please everyone including *churros* (long thin doughnuts with sugar) to be eaten with a coffee or hot chocolate, all the usual meat and fish dishes, and a selection of pastries and cakes.

Mesón El Patio (☎ 956 34 07 36; Calle San Francisco de Paula 7; fish raciones €6-10, meats €5-18; ☾ closed Sun evening & Mon) This place combines a touch of refinement with local conviviality. It has lofty ceilings, warm tones, carved wooden chairs, Islamic-style tilework and a collection of old radios. Above all, the food is terrific and there's a huge choice.

Restaurant Gaitán (☎ 956 34 58 59; Calle Gaitán 3; starters €10-21, mains €14-17; ☾ closed Sun evening) With a fancy décor of antlers and photos of past clients, Gaitán tempts with dishes like *rape mozárabe con pasas de corinto* (Mozarabic-style monkfish prepared in a sauce, with currants) and *cordero con miel y coñac* (lamb in a honey and brandy sauce). The *menú turístico* (tourist menu) at €16 is easier on the pocket.

La Mesa Redonda (☎ 956 34 00 69; Calle Manuel de la Quintana 3; mains €12-19) An intimate restaurant at the bottom of a Soviet-style block of flats. Décor and waitstaff attire are old-fashioned, soft music plays and excellent food prepared in an adventurous manner arrives at the tables. Wild duck, ox tail, wild boar and rabbit all appear on the menu, though portions are small.

La Carboná (☎ 956 34 74 75; Calle San Francisco de Paula 2; mains €9-28; ☾ closed Tue; Ⓥ) This popular, cavernous restaurant with an eccentric menu occupies an old bodega. Sit next to the hanging fireplace in winter! Specialities include grilled meats and fresh fish and the quirky quail with foie gras and rose petals! Cantabrian anchovies make the *ensalada de siempre* (everyday salad) rock.

CÁDIZ PROVINCE

TAPAS BARS

El Gallo Azul (Calle Larga 2; tapas €1.80) This beautiful, circular, historic building has a bar downstairs and restaurant upstairs. Street level is the perfect place for people watching, quaffing a fino and sampling innovative tapas of local ingredients. The *timbal de huevo relleno con langostino* (eggs stuffed with prawns in a mould) is a work of art.

Bar Juanito (☎ 956 33 48 38; www.bar-juanito .com; Pescadería Vieja 8-10; tapas €2, media-raciones €4-6) Superb place to sample tasty tapas with a sherry. You can sit or stand at the bar, sit at the tables outside, or take to the folksy dining room out back and eat larger portions. Pescadería Vieja, which runs off Plaza del Arenal, catches a refreshing breeze on a hot day.

El Almacén (Calle Ferros 8; tapas €2-3.50) Get a table in El Almacén's *bodega*-like back room, put together a *tabla* (selection of tapas) of pâtés and cheeses or hams and sausages, and soak up the atmosphere. The *patatas bravas* (spicy fried potatoes) are a must.

La Cañita (Calle Porvera 11; tapas €1-2) The best of another string of tapas spots just a short walk from Plaza Rafael Rivero – if you've still got room! The *montaditos* (small open sandwiches) are small but delicious: try brie and anchovies.

Further brilliant tapas bars surround quiet little Plaza Rafael Rivero, about 500m north of Plaza del Arenal, with tables out under the sky. Head here after 9.30pm or late Sunday morning and don't miss the inspired *montaditos* or *panes* (larger open sandwiches; €1.80 to €5) at El Poema. Then move a couple of tables away for a bite of ham at El Tabanco.

Drinking

Tetería La Jaima (Calle Chancillería 10; tea €2-3; ⏰ 4.30pm-10.30pm Mon-Fri, 4.30pm-2am Sat & Sun) This youthful tea drinker's haven has Moroccan décor, including carpets and cushions on the floor and tiled tables of various heights. Sip from an extensive list of teas.

A small cluster of bars in the narrow streets north of Plaza del Arenal can get lively with a 20-ish crowd late in the evening: try **Bar Dos Deditos** (Plaza Vargas 1), **Reino de León** (Calle Ferros) or **La Carbonería** (Calle Letrados 7). Northeast of the centre, **La Plaza**

de Canterbury (Calle N de Cañas), with lots of bars around a central courtyard, attracts a similar crowd.

For music bars and dancing, head a little further northeast to Avenida de Méjico. The crowd is young but not as young as the hundreds of teenagers who hang out and drink on the street after midnight around here.

A new leisure zone is emerging a couple of kilometres east of the centre around Avenida de las Flores (€4 by taxi). **Boheme** (Avenida de las Flores 13) is one of several café/bars, which also has a dance floor upstairs.

Entertainment

To find out what's on in Jerez check www .turismojerez.com, watch for posters and look in the newspapers *Diario de Jerez* and *Jerez Información*.

THEATRE

The busy **Teatro Villamarta** (☎ 956 32 71 00; www .villamarta.com; Plaza Romero Martínez) puts out a seasonal programme.

LIVE MUSIC

A hip venue for live music (Latin and other) is **La Guarida del Ángel** (☎ 956 34 96 98; Calle Porvenir 1; ⏰ 8pm-late). Varied music happens at **Astoria** (Calle Francos), an outdoor concert area, and concerts are sometimes held in the Plaza de Toros.

CLUBS

Bereber (☎ 956 34 00 16; Calle Cabezas 10; ⏰ from 4.30pm-late), an amazing reformed palace in the Barrio de Santiago, is – as its name (Berber) suggests – more like something out of Morocco than Spain, with exotic foliage planted in front of the old city walls that remain here. Roman-style murals recall another epoch. Much of the premises are open-air and cater for a mixed-age crowd but the soundproofed disco in the middle is where the young ones head to dance away the night.

FLAMENCO

There are several active *peñas flamencas* (flamenco clubs) in the Barrio de Santiago and elsewhere. They usually welcome genuinely interested visitors: ask at the tourist office about upcoming events (it has a list of 16 *peñas flamencas*).

Centro Cultural Flamenco D Antonio Cachón (☎ 956 34 74 72; Calle Salas 12) The Centro hosts authentic flamenco nights. It's often open on weekends, when you might be lucky enough to experience some impromptu flamenco.

El Lagá Tio Parrilla (☎ 956 33 83 34; Plaza del Mercado; admission €18) The flamenco performances here, held at 10.30pm and 12.30am Monday to Saturday, are more tourist-oriented but can still be pretty gutsy.

The Viernes Flamencos season sees open-air flamenco performances on August Friday nights at the Astoria (opposite): the season culminates in the Fiesta de la Bulería, a festival of flamenco song and dance held in the Plaza de Toros, one Saturday in September.

SPORT

Jerez's **Circuito Permanente de Velocidad** (☎ 956 15 11 00; www.circuitodejerez.com; Carretera de Arcos Km 10), on the A382 10km east of town, hosts several motorcycle and car racing events through the year including – in March, April or May – one of the Grand Prix races of the **World Motorcycle Championship**. Held in Jerez since 1987, this is one of Spain's biggest sporting events, with around 150,000 spectators, and Jerez and other nearby towns are swamped by fans and their bikes.

Getting There & Away

AIR

Jerez **airport** (☎ 956 15 00 00; www.aena.es), the only one serving Cádiz province, is 7km northeast of town on the NIV. Budget airline **Ryanair** (☎ 956 15 01 52; www.ryanair.com) flies here from London Stansted at least twice daily. **Thomas Cook Airlines Belgium** (www.thomascookairlines.com) flies from Brussels, and several airlines fly from major German airports including **Hapagfly** (☎ 902 48 05 00; www.hapagfly.com) and **Air-Berlin** (☎ 956 15 01 20; www.airberlin.com) – for more details see p443. **Iberia** (☎ 956 15 00 10; www.iberia.com) has at least two direct flights daily to/from Madrid and one daily to/from Barcelona.

BUS

The **bus station** (☎ 956 33 96 66; Plaza de la Estación) is 1.3km southeast of the centre. **Comes** (☎ 956 34 21 74) runs buses to the following destinations:

Destination	Cost	Duration	Frequency
Algeciras	€8.50	2½hr	1 daily
Arcos de la Frontera	€2.30	45min	n/a
Barbate	€7	2hr	1 daily Mon-Fri
Cádiz	€2.60	40min	11-21 daily
El Puerto de Santa María	€1	20min	Up to 25 daily
Los Caños de Meca	€7	1¾hr	Jun-Sep only
Ronda	€10	3hr	Up to 7 daily
Seville	€7	1¼hr	Up to 9 daily
Tarifa	€8.50	2hr	1 daily

Linesur (☎ 956 34 10 63) runs plenty of buses to Seville (€7, 1¼ hours), as well as to both Sanlúcar de Barrameda (€1.60-2.20, 30 minutes) and Algeciras (€8.50, 2½ hours) at least seven times daily. For Málaga (€16; four hours) there are two buses daily.

Los Amarillos (☎ 956 32 93 47) has more frequent buses to Arcos and also runs two to six times daily to El Bosque (€5.50, 1½ hours) and Ubrique (€7.50, 1¾ hours).

TRAIN

The **train station** (☎ 956 34 23 19; Plaza de la Estación) is beside the bus station (€3 by taxi from the centre). Jerez is on the Cádiz–El Puerto de Santa María–Seville line with trains to Seville (€6.50 to €21, one to 1¼ hours, up to 15 daily), El Puerto de Santa María (€1.50 to €15, 12 minutes, up to 37 daily) and Cádiz (from €3.40, 40 to 50 minutes, up to 37 daily).

Getting Around

TO/FROM THE AIRPORT

A taxi costs €12.50, more late at night and on weekends. The local airport buses M050 and M051 (€0.90, 30 minutes) also run 12 times daily Monday to Friday and six times daily on weekends, roughly between 6am and 10pm (to 8 or 9pm on weekends). From Jerez this service continues to El Puerto de Santa María and Cádiz.

CAR

Jerez is not too difficult to get around by car but, to avoid city centre congestion, you're best off parking and walking, or taking buses to the slightly more distant sights.

The two most central underground car parks are **Parking Doña Blanca** (cnr Plaza Estévez & Calle Doña Blanca; per 24hr €13), and Parking Plaza del Arenal, beneath Plaza del Arenal.

CÁDIZ PROVINCE

AROUND JEREZ DE LA FRONTERA

The much-prized Spanish thoroughbred horse, also called the Cartujano or Andaluz, is particularly admired for its grace, strength, and gentle temperament. This horse features in Jerez's major festivals and is as much a symbol of the town as are sherry and flamenco. It dates back at least to Carthaginian times. Two places inextricably linked with this wonderful animal and worth visiting are southeast of Jerez on and near the A381 towards Medina Sidonia.

La Cartuja monastery (☎ 956 15 64 65; Carretera Jerez-Algeciras; ۞ gardens 9.30-11.15am & 12.45-6.30pm Mon-Sat, mass 8am Tue & Sat, 5.30pm Mon) is an architectural gem founded in the 15th century, set amid lovely gardens beside the A381, 9km from central Jerez. The early Carthusian monks here are credited with breeding the Cartujano at a time when the horse's popularity had declined. You can look around the gardens and admire the church's impressive baroque façade but you can only peep inside during mass.

Yeguada de la Cartuja – Hierro del Bocado (☎ 956 16 28 09; www.yeguadacartuja.com; Finca Fuente del Suero; adult/child €15/9; ۞ 11am-1pm Sat) is a stud farm dedicated to improving the Cartujano stock, on land that once belonged to La Cartuja monastery. You can take a look around, followed by a spectacular show consisting of free-running colts, demonstrations by a string of mares, and dressage. Book ahead. To get here, turn off the A381 at the 'La Yeguada' sign 5km after La Cartuja, and follow the side road for 1.6km to the entrance.

ARCOS & THE SIERRA DE GRAZALEMA

The Sierra de Grazalema in northeastern Cádiz province is one of Andalucía's most beautiful and greenest mountain areas, great for active pursuits like canyoning and caving as well as more sedate strolling. En route to the mountains from the coast stands the spectacular clifftop town, Arcos de la Frontera.

ARCOS DE LA FRONTERA

pop 29,000 / elevation 185m

Thirty kilometres east of Jerez past rolling wheat and sunflower fields, vineyards and orchards, Arcos' old town could not be more thrillingly sited: it perches on a high, unassailable ridge with sheer precipices plummeting away on both sides. This strategic location has been prized since time immemorial. During the 11th century Arcos was an independent Berber-ruled kingdom before being absorbed by Seville, then taken over by Christian Alfonso X in 1255. When the last Duque de Arcos died heirless in 1780, his cousin, the Duquesa de Benavente, took over his estates. With her help, agriculture around Arcos diversified and more-profitable cereals, olives, vines and horse breeding replaced sheep farming.

Arcos' charm today lies in exploring the old, mazelike, upper town with its Renaissance palaces, beautiful Gothic churches, whitewashed houses and uniquely spectacular setting. The best places to stay have fantastic clifftop locations.

Orientation & Information

The newer, lower parts of town extend west, northwest and southeast from the high, sheer-sided ridge where the old town sits. From the bus station on Calle Corregidores, it's 1.5km eastward and uphill to the old town, via leafy Paseo de Andalucía from which Paseo de los Boliches and Calle Debajo del Corral (becoming Calle Corredera) both head up towards the old town's main square, Plaza del Cabildo. You'll find several banks and ATMs on these two streets.

Post office (Paseo de los Boliches 24; ۞ 8.30am-2.30pm Mon-Fri, 9.30am-1pm Sat)

Tourist information kiosk (Paseo de Andalucía; ۞ 10.30am-1.30pm & 5-7pm Mon-Fri, 10am-2pm Sat)

Tourist office (☎ 956 70 22 64; Plaza del Cabildo; ۞ 10am-2pm & 4-8pm Mon-Sat mid-Mar–mid-Oct, 10am-2pm & 3.30-7.30pm Mon-Sat mid-Oct–mid-Mar) Helpful office on the main square.

Sights & Activities

Plaza del Cabildo is surrounded by fine old buildings and has a wonderful but vertiginous **mirador** (lookout) with panoramic views of the river and countryside. On the plaza's west side the large, strongly fortified **Castillo de los Duques**, dating from at least the 11th century, is a private residence of the Marqués de Tamarón and firmly closed to the public. On the northern side of the plaza, the **Basílica-Parroquia de Santa María** (admission

€1.50; ☉ 10am-1pm & 3.30-6.30pm Mon-Fri, 10am-2pm Sat) was begun on the site of a mosque in the 13th century but not completed until the 18th century. Its western façade is in Gothic style but the landmark tower, built later, is baroque. Inside are beautiful 1731 choir stalls carved in stone and exotic woods, and lovely Isabelline ceiling tracery. On the eastern side of the square, the **Parador Casa del Corregidor** is a 1960s reconstruction of a 16th-century magistrate's residence. Drop in for a drink to enjoy the superb vistas from the terrace or spend the night here in luxury (p202).

Heading east, you'll pass by lovely buildings such as the early-16th-century **Convento de la Encarnación** (Calle Marqués de Torresoto), with its Gothic façade, and the **Iglesia de San Pedro** (Calle Núñez de Prado; admission €1; ☉ 10am-1pm & 4-7pm Mon-Sat, 10am-1.30pm Sun), in 15th-century Gothic style but with an impressive 18th-century baroque façade and bell tower. Nearby, the 17th-century **Palacio Mayorazgo** (Calle Núñez de Prado; admission free; ☉ 10am-2pm & 5-8pm Mon-Sat, 11am-2pm Sun), with a Renaissance façade and pretty

patios, is now a community building. Its rear patio, which is entered independently, has been transformed into a soothing little medieval-Islamic-style garden, the **Jardín Andalusí** (Calle Tallista Morales; admission free; ☉ 10am-2pm daily, plus 5-8pm Mon-Fri mid-Sep–mid-Jun, 8-11pm mid-Jun–mid-Sep).

Hípica El Granero (☎ 607 374160; www.caballosandaluces.net; Cortijo Barranco; rides per 1/2/4hr €20/35/60, classes per hr €35) offers horse rides through lovely countryside, riding classes and even courses of up to a week. It's 8km from Arcos on a farm, which also has excellent guest accommodation – see Cortijo Barranco (p202).

Tours

Guided walking tours (€5, one hour) of the old town's monuments start from the tourist office at 10.30am Monday to Friday. Tours of Arcos' pretty patios, which you wouldn't otherwise get to see, go at noon Monday to Friday. Early evening and Saturday morning tours also happen but you need to book ahead for these. The tours are in Spanish and English.

ARCOS DE LA FRONTERA

Festivals & Events

Semana Santa (Holy Week) These dramatic Easter processions held in March or April weave through the town's narrow streets; on Easter Sunday there's a hair-raising running of the bulls.

Feria de San Miguel Arcos celebrates its patron saint with a four-day fair; held around 29 September.

Sleeping

Arcos has some charming midrange and top-end places to stay but there's very limited budget accommodation up in the old town.

Hotel Real de Veas (☎ 956 71 73 70; www.hotelreal deveas.com; Calle Corredera 12; s €45, d €55-65; 🅿 💷) Friendly folk run this converted traditional home on the edge of the old town. It has a glass-covered patio and a roof terrace with 360-degree views. Rustic wooden furniture, wrought-iron fittings and gentle colours make for agreeable rooms, and breakfast is available.

Hotel Los Olivos (☎ 956 70 08 11; http://los olivos.profesionales.org; Paseo de los Boliches 30; s/d incl breakfast €45/70; 🅿 💷 🖥) With helpful staff, neat and cosy rooms, and plenty of space to sit around including a pretty patio, this friendly, small hotel is one of the best deals in town.

Hotel El Convento (☎ 956 70 23 33; www.web dearcos.com/elconvento; Calle Maldonado 2; s/d €55/70, d with terrace €85; 🕒 closed 7-21 Jan; 🖥) Set in a beautiful 17th-century convent just east of Plaza del Cabildo, welcoming El Convento has 13 tasteful, varied rooms with marble floors and period prints and sculptures. All but one of the rooms enjoy great views, six have their own terraces, and there's a large communal terrace on the cliff edge.

THE AUTHOR'S CHOICE

La Casa Grande (☎ 956 70 39 30; www .lacasagrande.net; Calle Maldonado 10; r €75-95, ste €88-135; 🕒 closed 7 Jan-6 Feb; 🖥) A gorgeous, rambling, cliffside mansion, the Casa Grande once belonged to the great flamenco dancer Antonio Ruiz Soler. With each of the seven rooms done in different but always tasteful styles, it feels more like a home-cum-artist's retreat than a hotel. Great breakfasts are served (€8.50), there's a good library to browse, and the roof terrace feels like it's in the sky. Massage and yoga available too.

Cortijo Barranco (☎ 956 23 14 02; www.cortijo barranco.com; Carretera Arcos-El Bosque Km 5.7; s/d €57/75, apt or casita €95-140; 🅿 💷 🖥) Set amid unspoiled countryside 8km from Arcos, Cortijo Barranco is also a working 4.5-sq-km agricultural estate. The rooms are in appealing rustic style, set around a lovely arcaded courtyard, with an atmospheric dining room and salon in an 18th-century olive mill along one side. There's a beautiful big swimming pool in the gardens. Five apartments and *casitas* (small houses) sleep up to six. Breakfast (€4.50), lunch and dinner (€27) are available. Also here is Hípica El Granero (p201) for horse-riding adventures. To find Cortijo Barranco, take the A372 El Bosque road from Arcos as far as Km 5.7, where a sign indicates the start of the 3km driveway.

Parador Casa del Corregidor (☎ 956 70 05 00; www.parador.es; Plaza del Cabildo; s/d €116/145; 💷 🖥) This rebuilt 16th-century magistrate's residence combines typical parador luxury with another magnificent cliffside setting. Eight of the 24 rooms have balconies with cliff views.

Also recommended:

Hostal San Marcos (☎ 956 70 07 21; Calle Marqués de Torresoto 6; s/d/tr €25/35/45; 🖥) Simple old-town *hostal* with four pretty little rooms and a roof terrace.

Eating & Drinking

Recommendable restaurants are fairly thin on the ground, but tapas bars compensate.

Bar San Marcos (☎ 956 70 07 21; Calle Marqués de Torresoto 6; tapas & montaditos €1.50-2.50, platos combinados €3.50-6) San Marcos is a friendly and reliable little old-town place. The dressed-carrot tapas are original and the *platos combinados* (mixed plates) are good value. The owner enjoys flamenco music.

Bar La Cárcel (☎ 956 70 04 10; Calle Deán Espinosa 18; tapas & montaditos €2, raciones €7-12; 🕒 8am-noon Mon, 8am-late Tue-Sun) A fine snacking spot up in the old town, with sensational *pinchitos de langostino con béicon* (prawns wrapped in bacon)!

Taberna José de la Viuda (☎ 956 70 12 09; Plaza Rafael Pérez del Álamo 13; tapas/raciones €2/8; 🕒 11.30am-late) Venture into the new town to find this temple of all that's *típico andaluz*, hung with hams and sausages, stacked with wines and cheeses and swaying to flamenco rhythms. Whatever you select from the lengthy tapas menu, amiable owner

Alfonso will probably suggest you choose something else, maybe the local goat cheese or his spicy *pincho moruno* (small lamb kebab). Take his advice.

El Convento (☎ 956 70 32 22; Calle Marqués de Torresoto 7; mains €8-15, menú €24; ⊙ closed 7-21 Jan) In the pillared patio of a 17th-century palace, Arcos's finest restaurant turns out country specialities such as herbed lamb and partridge in almond sauce.

Mesón Don Fernando (☎ 956 71 73 26; Calle Botica 5; raciones €6-15, mains €9-20; ⊙ closed Mon) The best of several bars-cum-eateries along the old town's Calle Botica, Don Fernando has a lively Spanish atmosphere and flamenco soundtrack. Good *montaditos* and *raciones* are served in the vaulted bar while the small restaurant focuses on meaty main dishes and tempting desserts.

There are plenty more places to get a snack and drink around lively Paseo de Andalucía.

Entertainment
Arcos bursts into song in July and August. The Jueves Flamencos are a series of weekly flamenco nights on Thursday at 10.30pm throughout the two months, at various old-town locations including the small, atmospheric Plaza del Cananeo. Also in July and August, free world music and jazz gigs are staged in Parque La Verbena, west of the bus station, and live pop, salsa, rock and the like can be heard on Friday nights at the Carpas de Verano, an open-air entertainment area on Avenida Duque de Arcos.

Getting There & Away
Departures from the **bus station** (☎ 956 70 49 77), by Los Amarillos and/or Comes, include the following buses:

Destination	Cost	Duration	Daily Frequency
Cádiz	€4.50-5.50	1¼hr	15
El Bosque	€2.50	1hr	11
Jerez	€2.30	45min	18
Málaga	€14	4hr	1
Ronda	€7.50	2hr	4
Seville	€7	2hr	2

Frequency on some routes is reduced at weekends.

Getting Around
You can park on Plaza del Cabildo in the old town and under Paseo de Andalucía in the subterranean car park. A local minibus (€0.90) runs up from the bus station to Paseo de Andalucía and Plaza del Cabildo every half-hour from 7.45am to 9.45pm Monday to Friday and 9.15am to 9.15pm Saturday.

PARQUE NATURAL SIERRA DE GRAZALEMA
The Cordillera Bética – the band of rugged mountain ranges that stretches across much of Andalucía – has beautiful beginnings in the Sierra de Grazalema in northeastern Cádiz province. This is one of the greenest parts of Andalucía (Grazalema village has the highest rainfall in Spain at an average 2153mm a year) and yields some of its most stunning landscapes, from pastoral river valleys and white villages to precipitous gorges and rocky summits. Much of the area is covered in beautiful Mediterranean woodland, and snow is common on the mountains in late winter.

This is excellent walking country (see the boxed text, p205) and it's also great for many other adrenaline-pumping adventure activities from canyoning, caving and climbing to paragliding, kayaking and bungee jumping. Experienced adventure tourism outfits are based in Grazalema village and Zahara de la Sierra.

The 517-sq-km Parque Natural Sierra de Grazalema protects the area, also extending into northwestern Málaga province, where it includes the Cueva de la Pileta (p284). The whole park is within easy reach of Ronda (p277).

Getting There & Around
Los Amarillos (☎ 902 21 03 17) runs buses to El Bosque, in the west of the park, from Jerez (€5.50, two hours, six daily), Cádiz (€7, two hours, four daily), Arcos de la Frontera (€2.50, one hour, 11 daily) and Seville (Prado de San Sebastián bus station; €7, 2¼ hours, two daily). On Saturday and Sunday some frequencies are reduced. From El Bosque, buses leave for Grazalema (€2, 30 minutes) at 3.30pm Monday to Saturday. Grazalema–El Bosque buses depart at 5.30am Monday to Friday and 7pm Friday.

CÁDIZ PROVINCE

Los Amarillos also runs twice daily from Málaga to Ronda, Grazalema, Villaluenga del Rosario, Benaocaz and Ubrique, and vice-versa. Grazalema is 45 minutes from Ronda (€2.10) and 2¾ hours from Málaga (€10). There are connections in Ronda for Seville, Jerez and Cádiz.

Comes (☎ 902 19 92 08) operates two buses each way Monday to Friday between Ronda and Zahara de la Sierra (€3.50, one hour), via Algodonales. Departures from Ronda are at 7am and 1pm. There's no bus service between Zahara and Grazalema.

El Bosque

pop 2000 / elevation 385m

El Bosque, 33km east of Arcos across rolling countryside, is prettily situated below the wooded Sierra de Albarracín. Grazalema park's main information office and a selection of decent-value places to stay can be found here.

INFORMATION

The natural park's **Centro de Visitantes El Bosque** (☎ 956 72 70 29; Avenida de la Diputación s/n; ☾ 10am-2pm & 6-8pm Mon-Fri, 9am-2pm & 6-8pm Sat, 9am-2pm Sun Apr-Sep, 10am-2pm & 4-6pm Mon-Fri, 9am-2pm & 4-6pm Sat, 9am-2pm Sun Oct-Mar), with limited displays and information on the park, is off the A372 at the western end of town (turn opposite Hotel Las Truchas).

SIGHTS & ACTIVITIES

The **Jardín Botánico El Castillejo** (☎ 956 71 61 34; Avenida El Castillejo s/n; admission free; ☾ 10am-2pm & 6-9pm Jun-Aug, 10am-2pm & 5-8pm Apr, May, Sep & Oct, 10am-2pm & 3.30-6.30pm Nov-Mar) contains a pretty good selection of the region's trees, shrubs, herbs and wildflowers – including a mini-*pinsapar* (forest of Spanish fir). It takes around half an hour to stroll round the garden.

A nice walk from El Bosque follows the Río Majaceite (also called the Río El Bosque) upstream for 4km to Benamahoma (see opposite), starting by the bridge outside the El Bosque youth hostel.

SLEEPING & EATING

Instalación Juvenil El Bosque (☎ 956 71 62 12; Molino de Enmedio s/n; per person incl breakfast under 26yr €9.50-15, over 26yr €13-19; ☒ ☒) El Bosque's modernised 131-capacity youth hostel is pleasantly sited in a wooded area by the Río Majaceite. Accommodation is in double,

triple and quadruple rooms, nearly all with private bathroom.

Hotel Enrique Calvillo (☎ 956 71 61 05; Avenida Diputación 5; s/d €25/45; ☒ ☒) The 19 attractive rooms here, near the park information office, have wood-beam ceilings, stained-wood furniture and nicely tiled bathrooms, and there's a comfy lounge with internet.

Hotel El Tabanco (☎ 956 71 60 81; Calle La Fuente 3; s/d incl breakfast €30/50; ☾ closed 7-12 Jan & 2nd half Jun; ☒) Up in the village centre, this almost-new hotel provides spotless rooms with tasteful wooden furniture, comfy beds, tile floors and bathtubs. And it adjoins the Mesón El Tabanco, the best eatery in town.

Hotel Las Truchas (☎ 956 71 60 61; www.tugasa.com/index2.htm; Avenida Diputación s/n; s/d €36/59; ☒ ☒ ☒) El Bosque's largest hotel (27 rooms) has been going since 1970 and though a mite stodgy in style, it still offers comfortable, well-equipped rooms, spacious public areas and an outdoor pool. Meals are also available (€8 to €15).

Mesón El Tabanco (☎ 956 71 60 81; Calle Huelva 1; mains €9-15; ☾ 9.30am-1.30am Mon-Fri, 10.30am-1.30am Sat, Sun & holidays, closed 7-12 Jan & 2nd half Jun) El Tabanco serves excellent meat and *revueltos* in two sky-lit dining rooms. Don't pass up the *queso fresco* salad, with superb local soft goat cheese. Good tapas are available in the popular adjoining bar.

Grazalema

pop 2200 / elevation 825m

The most popular travellers' base in the sierra, Grazalema is a picture-postcard, red-tile-roofed village tucked into a corner of beautiful mountain country beneath the rock-climbers' crag Peñón Grande. It has a broad selection of places to stay and some good country-style eateries. Local products include pure wool blankets and rugs, whose production follows centuries-old traditions.

INFORMATION

The village centre is the pretty Plaza de España, where you'll find the **tourist office** (☎ 956 13 20 73; ☾ 10am-2pm & 4-9pm), with an upstairs shop selling local wool products and other crafts (blankets and rugs start around €55). Two banks on Plaza de España have ATMs.

GRAZALEMA WALKS

The Sierra de Grazalema's beautiful scenery makes for great walking, especially in May, June, September and October, when climatic conditions are best. Equip yourself with a good walking guide such as *Walking in Andalucía* by Guy Hunter-Watts or *Eight Walks from Grazalema* by RE Bradshaw, and the best map you can get: Editorial Alpina's *Sierra de Grazalema* (1:25,000), with a walking-guide booklet in English and Spanish, is the pick. Some of these are sold locally, but also look for them before you come.

The natural park's three major highlight walks – El Torreón, the Pinsapar and the Garganta Verde – are all within its 38-sq-km reserve area, and for these you need a free permit from the visitors centre in El Bosque (opposite). You can telephone or visit the visitors centre up to 15 days in advance for this, and they can fax permits to be collected at the Zahara de la Sierra information office or Grazalema tourist office. Staff at any of these offices may or may not speak languages other than Spanish. It's advisable to book 10 to 15 days ahead for weekends or public holidays; otherwise, it's usually OK to make arrangements the same day or day before. For the Pinsapar walk in July, August and September, when fire risk is high, it's obligatory to go with a guide from an authorised local company such as Horizon (p206), Al-qutun (p207) or Zahara Catur (p207). The Torreón route is closed in these months.

El Torreón

El Torreón (1654m) is the highest peak in Cádiz province and from the summit on a clear day you can see Gibraltar, the Sierra Nevada and the Rif Mountains of Morocco. The usual route starts 100m east of the Km 40 marker on the Grazalema–Benamahoma road, about 8km from Grazalema. It takes about 2½ hours of walking to reach the summit and 1½ hours back down.

The Pinsapar

The dark green Spanish fir (*pinsapo* in Spanish) is a rare and beautiful relic of the great Mediterranean fir forests of the Tertiary period. Today it survives in significant numbers only in pockets of southwest Andalucía and northern Morocco, and the largest pocket in Andalucía (about 3 sq km) is the Pinsapar on the northern slopes of Sierra del Pinar between Grazalema and Benamahoma. The 14km walk between the two villages via the Pinsapar takes around six hours: you start by walking about 40 minutes up from Grazalema to a point on the Zahara road where a footpath heads off westward. After an ascent of 300m, this path sticks close to the 1300m contour.

Garganta Verde

The path into this lushly vegetated ravine, more than 100m deep, starts 3.5km from Zahara de la Sierra on the Grazalema road. It passes a large colony of enormous griffon vultures before the 300m descent to the bottom of the gorge. Then you come back up! It's a beautiful walk. Allow three to four hours' walking if you drive to the start.

Other Walks

These excellent walks are outside the reserve area and require no permit. You'll need a guide (human or printed) for the Salto del Cabrero and Casa del Dornajo routes, which can be combined in one full day's circuit starting from Grazalema.

Casa del Dornajo This ruined farmstead in a beautiful high-level valley is about two hours' walk southwest from Grazalema, or 1½ hours north from Benaocaz. There are good chances of seeing ibex on the walk.

Llanos del Republicano This 4km (each way) route starts from the A374 at Villaluenga del Rosario. The track leads through native oak woods and down to the lonesome Llanos del Republicano plains where the entrance to the Sima del Republicano, one of Andalucía's deepest caves, is found.

Salto del Cabrero About two hours' walk southwest from Grazalema, or 1¼ hours north from Benaocaz, the 'Goatherd's Leap' is a dramatic fissure in the earth, 100m deep and 500m long.

DETOUR: ALCALÁ DE LOS GAZULES TO UBRIQUE

This alternative route to the Sierra de Grazalema takes you across the beautiful northern wood-lands of the Parque Natural Los Alcornocales, the Grazalema park's southern neighbour. In early summer the roadside wild flowers are unbelievable. You also have the opportunity (bureaucracy permitting) to stop off and climb one of Los Alcornocales' most prominent peaks, El Picacho (882m) or Aljibe (1091m).

Make first for Alcalá de los Gazules, just off the A381 in the centre of Cádiz province. On Plaza San Jorge at the top of the town is the office of the **Consejería de Medio Ambiente** (☎ 956 41 33 07; fax 956 42 05 11; ☻ 8am-2.30pm Mon-Fri), which issues the permit needed for climbing Aljibe or El Picacho. Regulations on permits change from time to time and you should ring the office at least 10 days in advance to find out the current situation.

Leave Alcalá northeast along the A375. After about 8km, the rocky sandstone El Picacho ap-pears ahead of you, and 11km from Alcalá is the joint start of the trails up **El Picacho** and **Aljibe**, opposite the entrance to the Área Recreativa El Picacho picnic area. The Picacho walk (about 3km each way; 500m ascent) takes approximately five hours there and back. Aljibe (6km each way; 700m ascent) is about seven hours there and back.

Continuing the drive, head on along the A375 towards Ubrique, ignoring turn-offs to other places. The road winds up and down through thick woodlands of cork oak, wild olive and other native trees, with some wonderful long-distance panoramas. After 30km, at the Puerto de Mogón de la Víbora pass, turn left down the A373 for the 9km to **Ubrique**, a white splash against the dramatic backdrop of the Sierra de Grazalema. If you need a smart leather bag, briefcase, wallet, jacket or belt, in any colour you fancy, take a stroll along Ubrique's main street, Avenida Solís Pascual, which is lined with shops selling these goods, all made locally.

From Ubrique it's a further 26km to Grazalema village via Benaocaz and Villaluenga del Ro-sario (p208).

SIGHTS & ACTIVITIES

A chief pleasure of Grazalema is simply en-joying the mountain vistas and exploring the cobbled, sloping streets lined by their sturdy white houses with black grilles, flow-ery window boxes and carved stone por-tals around solid, nail-studded doors. The **Salto del Cabrero** and **Casa del Dornajo walks** (see p205) can both be done from here, and RE Bradshaw's *Eight Walks from Grazalema* details more options.

Horizon (☎ /fax 956 13 23 63; www.horizonaventura .com; Calle Corrales Terceros 29), a block off Plaza de España, is a highly experienced adventure firm that will take you climbing, bungee jumping, canyoning, caving, paragliding or walking, with English-speaking guides. Prices per person range from around €14 for a half-day walk to over €60 for the 4km underground wetsuit adventure from the Cueva del Hundidero near Montejaque to the Cueva del Gato near Benaoján. Min-imum group sizes apply for some activities.

FESTIVALS & EVENTS

The **Fiestas del Carmen** take over Grazalema for several days and nights in mid-July,

with lots of late-night music and dancing, and a bull-running through the streets on the final Monday.

SLEEPING

Camping Tajo Rodillo (☎ 956 13 24 18, 651 91 09 72; www.campingtajorodillo.com in Spanish; Carretera El Bosque-Grazalema Km 47; adult/tent €4.50/4.50, 4-person cabin €95; ☻ closed Dec & Jan; P ☒ ☒) Though small, this camping ground at the top of the village is well equipped with restaurant, pool and comfy cabins with kitchen, bath-room and TV.

Casa de las Piedras (☎ /fax 956 13 20 14; www .casadelaspiedras.net; Calle Las Piedras 32; s/d €37/45, with shared bathroom €10/20; ☒ ☒) Casa de las Piedras is a friendly, good-value *hostal* occupying a fine old village house with a couple of pleasant patios and a log fire in winter. The 32 rooms are of assorted sizes and facilities, but all with winter heating. The restaurant serves hearty meals (€6 to €11), and the *hostal* also runs some comfy apartments nearby.

Hotel Peñón Grande (☎ 956 13 24 34; www.hotel grazalema.com; Plaza Pequeña 7; s/d €36/53; ☒) This small, friendly hotel just off Plaza de España has an attractively rustic style, with comfortable, well-equipped, good-sized rooms. One of the best bets in town.

La Mejorana (☎ 956 13 23 27, 649 61 32 72; www .lamejorana.net; Calle Santa Clara 6; r incl breakfast €50; ☒) A lovely house towards the upper end of the village, hospitable La Mejorana has just five rooms with beautiful wrought-iron bedsteads, plus a large lounge and kitchen, all in fetching country styles – and a leafy garden that even manages to fit in a pool. A great find!

Hotel Puerta de la Villa (☎ 956 13 23 76; www .grazalemahotel.com in Spanish; Plaza Pequeña 8; s/d €103/129; P ☒ ☒) A centrally located top-end hotel with tasteful, good-sized rooms plus a gym, crafts shop, and classy restaurant (mains €10 to €16). Prices drop significantly outside the high seasons (mid-July to mid-September and early December to early January).

EATING
Mesón El Simancón (☎ 956 13 24 21; Plaza Asoma-deros; mains €7-12, menú €13; ☒ closed Tue) Set by the main car park, this is one of the best places to eat. Well-prepared local dishes – ham, beef, quail, venison, wild boar, *revueltos* – are served at tables outside or in a dining room adorned with deer heads.

There are several places to eat and drink on pedestrian Calle Agua, between Plaza de España and the main car park:

Bar La Posadilla (☎ 956 13 20 51; Calle Agua 19; platos combinados €2-6; ☒ closed Thu) Excellent-value budget eating.

Restaurant El Torreón (☎ 956 13 23 13; Calle Agua 44; mains €7-11; ☒ closed Wed) Reliable upstairs restaurant with a long menu.

Zahara de la Sierra
pop 1500 / elevation 550m

Clinging to the sides of a crag topped by a ruined castle, Zahara is the most dramatically sited of the Grazalema villages – impossibly picturesque when seen from the north across the Embalse de Zahara reservoir. The 18km drive from Grazalema via the vertiginous 1331m Puerto de los Palomas (Doves' Pass, but with more vultures than doves) is even more spectacular, and quite otherworldly if there's heavy mist along the way. Zahara is a lovely place to stay a night or two and a convenient base for the Garganta Verde walk.

ORIENTATION & INFORMATION
The village centres on Calle San Juan, with a church at each end. Near one end is the natural park's helpful **Punto de Información Zahara de la Sierra** (☎ /fax 956 12 31 14; Plaza del Rey 3; ☒ 9am-2pm & 4-7pm), with displays on the park, and local cheese, honey and other products on sale. There's a car park 150m uphill from here.

SIGHTS & ACTIVITIES
Zahara's steep, winding streets invite investigation, with vistas framed by tall palms, hot-pink bougainvillea or fruited orange trees. To climb up to the remains of the 13th-century Muslim-built **castle**, take the path almost opposite the Hotel Arco de la Villa – a steady 10- to 15-minute climb. The castle fell to the Christians in 1407: its brief recapture by Abu al-Hasan of Granada in a daring night raid in 1481 provoked the Catholic Monarchs to launch the last phase of the Reconquista of Andalucía, leading to the fall of Granada in 1492.

Adventure-tourism firm **Al-qutun** (☎ 956 13 78 82; www.al-qutun.com), in Algodonales, 7km north of Zahara, organises canyoning in the Garganta Verde, guided walks in the natural park's reserve area, kayaking on Zahara's reservoir, paragliding, caving, climbing and bungee jumping, with beginners welcome. Get in touch for the schedule. **Zahara Catur** (☎ 956 12 31 14; www.zaharacatur.com; Plaza del Rey 3), at the Zahara information office, rents two-person canoes for €10/18 per one/two hours, and offers guided walks, canyoning and caving for groups of six to 10.

FESTIVALS & EVENTS
For **Corpus Christi** (7 June 2007, 22 May 2008), Zahara de la Sierra dresses its main streets in a mantle of green vegetation and aromatic flowers and herbs for a festive religious procession that dates back to Reconquista times.

SLEEPING & EATING
Hostal Marqués de Zahara (☎ /fax 956 12 30 61; www.marquesdezahara.com; Calle San Juan 3; s/d €32/42; ☒) This converted mansion right in the village centre has 10 cosy rooms with winter heating, friendly service, plus a restaurant and a bookcase full of good local reference material. Rooms with balcony cost a few euros extra.

Hotel Arco de la Villa (☎ 956 12 32 30; www
.tugasa.com/index2.htm; Paseo Nazarí s/n; s/d €36/59;
P 🐾) The Arco de la Villa is a sparkling-
clean, modern hotel with a spectacular cliff-
top setting opposite the foot of the castle
path. All 17 rooms and the restaurant are
endowed with jaw-dropping views.

Restaurante Los Naranjos (☎ 956 12 33 14; Calle
San Juan 15; mains €7-12; 🕙 9am-11pm) Calle San
Juan is strung with bars, most serving food
of some kind, but the best eats are at Los
Naranjos, serving hearty hill-country plate-
fuls both indoors and outside under the
orange trees.

Villaluenga del Rosario
pop 450 / elevation 900m
Villaluenga huddles at the foot of the cliffs
of the Sierra del Caillo, 13km south of
Grazalema. The village is a popular destination for cavers thanks to the proximity of several of Andalucía's deepest and
longest cave systems. Noncavers can easily walk to the entrance of the 250m-long
Sima de Villaluenga by a balustraded walkway across the fields at the bottom of the
village. An enjoyable longer hike starting
beside the abandoned Hostal Villaluenga
on the A374 takes you to the entrance of
the 222m-deep **Sima del Republicano** cave –
see p205.

The excellent little **Hotel La Posada** (☎ 956
12 61 19; www.tugasa.com/index2.htm; Calle Torre 1; s/d
€36/59; 🐾), in a thick-stone-walled 18th-cen-
tury building, features wrought-iron bedsteads and bathrooms with bathtubs, and
a quality restaurant serving hill-country
meat, game and egg dishes (mains €6 to
€12). Also good for similar fare is the surprisingly elegant **La Cancela** (☎ 956 46 37 79;
Calle Doctor Vázquez 24; mains €7-12), with a balcony
overlooking the valley.

COSTA DE LA LUZ

The 90km coast between Cádiz and Tarifa
can be windy, and its Atlantic waters are
a shade cooler than those of the Mediterranean. But these are small prices to pay for
an unspoiled, often wild shore, strung with
long, clean, white-sand beaches and just a
few small towns and villages. (It has been
christened the Costa de la Luz – Coast of
Light – due to the brightness that results

from many hours of sunlight hitting the
white sandy beaches.) Andalucians are well
aware of its attractions and they flock down
here in their thousands during July and August, bringing a vibrant fiesta atmosphere
to the normally quiet coastal settlements.
Be sure to book ahead for rooms in these
months.

From before Roman times until the ad-
vent of 20th-century tourism, this coast was
mainly devoted to tuna fishing. Shoals of
big tuna, some weighing 300kg, are still intercepted by mazes of *almadraba* (net) several kilometres long as the fish head in from
the Atlantic towards their Mediterranean
spawning grounds in spring, and again as
they head out in July and August. Barbate
has the main tuna fleet today.

VEJER DE LA FRONTERA
pop 12,000 / elevation 190m
This old-fashioned white town looms mys-
teriously atop a rocky hill above the busy
A48, 50km southeast from Cádiz. It's well
worth investigating. Like much of the Costa
de la Luz, Vejer is experiencing a foreign
influx. Hip boutiques and charming places
to stay are proliferating. Vejer has long been
popular with Spanish artists and alternative
types so, not surprisingly, there's a vital art-
and-crafts scene here. Vejer is a good base
for activities too.

Orientation
The oldest area of town, still partly walled
and lined with narrow winding streets
clearly signifying its Islamic origins,
spreads over the highest part of the hill.
Just below is the small Plazuela, more or
less the heart of town, with the Hotel Convento de San Francisco. About 800m east
of the Plazuela (a 10-minute stroll along
Calle Marqués de Tamarón) is Plaza de
España, around which are several places
to stay and eat.

Information
Bookend English Bookshop (☎ 625 870255; Avenida
Juan Relinque 45) New and secondhand books in English;
some secondhand books in German.
Post office (Calle Juan Bueno 10)
Tourist office (☎ 956 45 17 36; www.turismovejer
.com; Avenida de los Remedios; 🕙 10am-2pm Mon-Sat
mid-Sep–May, 10am-2pm & 6-9pm Mon-Sat, 11am-2pm
Sun Jun–mid-Sep) You can arrange local tours here.

Sights & Activities

Vejer's walls date from the 15th century. Four gateways and three towers survive. Within the 40,000-sq-metre walled area, seek out the **Iglesia del Divino Salvador** (☎ 956 45 00 56; 11am-1pm daily, plus 5-7pm Mon, Wed, Fri & Sat), whose interior is Mudejar at the altar end and Gothic at the other. The much-reworked **castle** (10am-2pm & 5.30-8.30pm Jul & Aug), with great views from its battlements, has a small museum that preserves one of the black cloaks that Vejer women wore, covering everything but the eyes, until just a couple of decades ago. Don't miss pretty palm-filled **Plaza de España** with its attractive Seville-tiled fountain and the town hall on its south side.

You can rent good mountain bikes (€12 per day) at **Nature Explorer** (☎ 956 45 14 19; www.naturexplorer.com; Avenida de los Remedios 43), opposite the bus stop. They also run walking, mountain biking and diving trips (€25 to €55 per person) for four people or more in the beautiful surrounding area.

Festivals & Events

Easter Sunday There's a Toro Embolao (running of the bull, with bandaged horns) at noon and 4pm.
Feria Music and dancing nightly in Plaza de España, with one night devoted entirely to flamenco; 10 to 24 August.

Sleeping

Camping Los Molinos (☎ 956 45 09 88; www.campinglosmolinosvejer.com; Pago de Santa Lucía; adult/tent/car €5.50/5/4;) This wooded camp site with a supermarket and good facilities is a few kilometres north of Vejer.

Hostal La Janda (☎ 956 45 01 42; Calle Machado s/n; s/d €25/50;) A friendly place across town from the old walled area. The 36 rooms sprawl over a large property; some have interior patio views, others town vistas. Décor is simple but pretty.

Hotel Convento de San Francisco (☎ 956 45 10 01; www.tugasa.com/index2/htm; Plazuela s/n; s/d €48/70;) This restored 17th-century convent has 25 simple but charming rooms, and helpful reception staff. Its café is a central meeting place.

CÁDIZ PROVINCE

DETOUR: SANCTI PETRI & MEDINA SIDONIA

If you're driving up or down the A48 between Cádiz and Vejer de la Frontera with half a day to spare, two contrasting but equally attractive detours can be made from the Chiclana de la Frontera junction where the A48 meets the A390, 22km southeast of Cádiz.

Sancti Petri

Head west towards the coast from the A48/A390 junction: the road skirts the southern edge of Chiclana. Follow 'Puerto Deportivo' signs, which will lead you to Sancti Petri, a small, historically intriguing fishing village, no longer inhabited but still with fishing boats and a marina. The village has a nautical and water-sports centre and is a fine windsurfing spot. An offshore island, Isla de Sancti Petri, has a ruined, mainly 19th-century **castle**, beneath which are the remains of a Roman temple dedicated to Hercules. You can visit the island daily from 1 July to 15 September with **Cruceros Sancti Petri** (☎ 617 378894; Playa de Sancti Petri; 1hr trip per person €10).

Medina Sidonia

If you head east along the A390, a 19km drive brings you to the interesting hill-top town of Medina Sidonia, whose long and turbulent history goes at least as far back as Phoenician times. Later it fell into the hands of invaders as diverse as the Byzantines and the Normans. After the Christians reconquered the town from the Muslims in 1264, it became a bone of contention between the Castilian monarchy and the powerful Guzmán family (see p215), changing hands repeatedly until 1445 when King Juan II ceded it to Juan Alfonso Guzmán III. Guzmán thus became the Duque de Medina Sidonia, the first of a long and very powerful aristocratic line.

On arrival head up to the top of the hill to the helpful **tourist office** (☎ 956 41 24 04; Plaza de la Iglesia Mayor; 10am-2pm & 5-6pm Sep-Jul, 10am-2pm & 5-9pm Jul-Sep), then make for the main monuments nearby – the remains of the 12th- to 15th-century **castle**, the 16th-century **Iglesia de Santa María La Coronada** and the **Conjunto Romano** (well-preserved sections of Roman streets and Roman drains).

Hostal la Botica (☎ 902 07 51 30; www.laboticade vejer.com; Calle Canalejas 15; s/d incl breakfast from €55/65; 🅿) A former pharmacy, Hostal la Botica offers appealing rooms set around a patio where breakfast is served. There's a roof terrace with rural views.

Hotel La Casa del Califa (☎ 956 44 77 30; www .grupocalifa.com; Plaza de España 16; s incl breakfast €63-94, d incl breakfast €69-112; 🅿) This great place fronting Plaza de España rambles over several floors of what were previously five houses. Twisting corridors and little staircases lead to peaceful, comfortable rooms, each with individual proportions and décor, though an Islamic theme predominates. There's a sun terrace.

No 1 Tripería (☎ 956 44 77 30; www.grupocalifa .com; Calle Tripería 1; r €99-150; 🅿 🛋) This charming luxury hotel with Islamic features occupies a large townhouse near Plaza de España. It's the only place in Vejer with a swimming pool, and the underfloor heating makes it cosy in winter. Most rooms enjoy views across town and to the countryside.

Eating & Drinking

You're spoilt for choice when it comes to eating out in Vejer, not only in the town but also in the villages that dot the surrounding region, known as La Janda – head to Santa Lucía and La Muela, both north of the A48, or wander further into the hinterland and seek out the *ventas* (roadside inns).

Pastelería Galvin (Calle Altozano 1; cake €2) This is a terrific tea, coffee and cakes haunt just around the corner from the Plazuela.

La Bodeguita (☎ 956 45 15 82; Calle Marqués de Tamarón 9; tapas & montaditos €1; ⏲ from 4.30pm) A plain but tastefully decked-out bar, La Bodeguita has good vibes, breakfast (in summer), excellent tapas and snacks, and an extensive music collection. It's just beside the Arco de la Segur arch.

Bar Joplin (Calle Marqués de Tamarón; beer €2.50) Opposite La Bodeguita, this laid-back drinking haunt lives up to its namesake. It's best late on the weekends.

Restaurante Trafalgar (☎ 956 44 76 38; Plaza de España 31; mains €10-19) The Trafalgar offers semiformal dining on the town's happening plaza. Typical Cádiz province fish, seafood and meat are prepared with a flourish.

El Jardín del Califa (☎ 956 44 77 30; Plaza de España 16; mains €7.50-18; ⏲ closed Tue morning Nov-Easter; Ⓥ) Hotel La Casa del Califa's restaurant,

extending out into the garden, is Vejer's coolest eatery. Food and décor are Arabic: Moroccan-tiled tables under tall trees, the scent of jasmine, and walls with ancient brickwork set the mood. Choose from vegetable or meat couscous and tagine dishes or, in the evenings, barbecued meats and fish.

Getting There & Away

The small office of **Comes** (☎ 902 19 92 08; Plazuela) has bus information; tickets can be purchased here or on the bus. Buses to/ from Cádiz (€4.50, 50 minutes) and Barbate (€1.10, 10 minutes) stop on Avenida de los Remedios, the road up from the A48, about 500m below the Plazuela up to 10 times a day. More buses for the same places, plus Tarifa (€3.80, 50 minutes, about 10 daily), La Línea de la Concepción (€7, 1½ to two hours, seven daily), Málaga (€16, 2¾ hours, two daily) and Seville (€14, three hours, five daily), stop at La Barca de Vejer, on the A48 at the bottom of the hill. By road it's 4km uphill from La Barca to the town; on foot, there's an obvious 15-minute short cut.

EL PALMAR
pop 850

Sleepy El Palmar, 10km southwest of Vejer de la Frontera, has a lovely 4.8km sweep of white sandy beach, which is good for body surfing, and for board surfing from October to May. Green fields with crops or grazing cows surround the hamlet, but 'sleepy' probably won't describe it for much longer as development plans include two new hotels, at the Conil end of the beach.

El Palmar has at least two surf schools and private individuals giving surf lessons. **El Palmar Surf School** (☎ 956 23 21 37; www .elpalmarsurf.com; Dehesa El Palmar 43; board rental per hr/half-day/full day €10/25/30, 5hr beginner course €100) is a popular choice, offering board hire and instruction in Spanish or English.

Camping El Palmar (☎ 956 23 21 61; www .pogoland.com/elpalmar; adult/tent/car €5.50/4.50/3.80; 🛋) is a well-equipped camp site 900m from the beach down a dirt track.

There are several *hostales* right in front of the beach but most close in winter. **Hostal Casa Francisco** (☎ 956 23 22 49; d incl breakfast €90, with sea view €120) has reasonable, if bare, rooms and a good restaurant (*menú* €20). Prices dip by more than a third outside peak periods.

La Chanca (☎ 659 977420; mains €14-20; ⊙ closed Feb–mid-Mar) occupies an old tuna preparation factory at the southeastern end of the beach. It has a garden dining area overlooking the ocean and is popular for its tasty meat and fresh fish dishes.

Cortijo El Cartero (☎ 956 23 26 24) is a distinctive purple-and-orange bar-restaurant with a thatched roof, which is firmly fixed on the Cádiz gig circuit. Expect live music on weekend nights year-round.

Two buses run to/from Cádiz Monday to Friday (€4.50, one hour).

LOS CAÑOS DE MECA
pop 300
Los Caños, once a hippy hideaway, straggles along a series of gorgeous sandy coves beneath a pine-clad hill about 7km southeast of El Palmar and 12km west of Barbate. It maintains its laid-back, off-beat air even during the height of summer when it gets very busy. The informal architecture around here is an eclectic mix of Moroccan, Andalucian, beachside and alternative.

Orientation & Information
Coming from El Palmar or Vejer, you pass through the separate settlement of Zahora, a couple of kilometres short of Los Caños. The road from Barbate comes out on Los Caños' main street, Avenida Trafalgar, towards the eastern end of town. The Barbate tourist office (p213) can provide information for the whole area. There's an ATM on the main road in front of the camp site at Zahora.

Sights & Activities
At the western end of Los Caños, a side road leads out to a lighthouse on a low spit of land, the famous **Cabo de Trafalgar**. It was off this cape that Spanish naval power was terminated in a few hours one day in 1805 by a British fleet under Admiral Nelson. A plaque commemorating those who died in the battle was erected at Trafalgar on the bicentennial in October 2005.

Wonderful **beaches** stretch either side of Cabo de Trafalgar. A marine wind park is planned 18km out to sea from Cabo de Trafalgar, but opposition is significant.

The main beach is straight in front of Avenida Trafalgar's junction with the Barbate road. Nudist beachgoers head to the small headland at its eastern end where there are more secluded beaches, including Playa de las Cortinas. The western end is the best windsurfing zone and has surfable waves in winter.

The coast between Los Caños and Barbate is mostly cliffs up to 100m high. The road between the two places runs inland through captivating umbrella pine forest. These cliffs and forest, along with wetlands east and north of Barbate, form the **Parque Natural de la Breña y Marismas de Barbate**. A walking path leads from the road to the **Torre del Tajo**, a 16th-century cliff-top lookout tower. Another tower, the 18th-century **Torre de Meca** on the hill behind Los Caños, can be reached from this road, and you can also walk up to it from Los Caños.

Activities in and around Los Caños such as horse riding, surfing and mountain biking can be organised through the Hostal Madreselva.

Sleeping
Prices at most places dip significantly outside the high season.

Camping Camaleón (☎ 956 43 71 54; Avenida Trafalgar s/n; adult/tent/car €5.50/5.50/5.50; ⊙ Apr-Sep) Los Caños has three medium-sized camping grounds, which tend to get pretty crowded and rowdy in high summer. The Camaleón has shady sites and is nearest the centre, 1km west from the Barbate road corner.

Hostal Minigolf (☎ 956 43 70 83; Avenida de Trafalgar 251; s/d €45/50; ℗ ✗) This good little budget place opposite the Cabo de Trafalgar turning has fresh, clean rooms, with TV and winter heating, around a simple, very Spanish patio. Hearty breakfasts are served in the restaurant next door.

Hostal Mar de Frente (☎ 956 43 70 25; www.hotel mardefrente.com; Avenida Trafalgar 3; s/d incl breakfast €48/77, r with sea view €102; ⊙ closed Dec-Feb; ℗ ✗) The charming Mar de Frente, on several levels right on the cliff edge above the eastern end of the main beach, has a youthful management and bright, comfy rooms with satellite TV and terrace.

Sajoramibeach (☎ 956 43 74 24; www.sajora mibeach.com; r €80) For plum beach location and unique architecture, try this place at Playa Zahora.

Hostal Madreselva (☎ 956 43 72 55; www.mad reselvahotel.com/canos; Avenida Trafalgar 102; s/d incl breakfast €68/84, ste €155; ⊙ 27 Mar-30 Sep; ℗ ✗)

THE AUTHOR'S CHOICE

Casas Karen (☎ 956 43 70 67, last-minute bookings 649 780834; www.casaskaren.com; Fuente del Madroño 6; r €92-99, q €118-132, 2-person traditional hut per week €555; **P**) This eccentric gem is owned by warm, vibrant Karen Abrahams, who settled here around 20 years ago. Her large, pretty, mimosa-covered plot has seven or so eclectic buildings, all with kitchen, bathroom, lounge and outdoor sitting areas: they range from a converted farmhouse to exotic, thatched *chozas* (traditional huts) built of local materials. Décor is casual Andalucian-Moroccan with a sensitive use of colour. Massage is available. Casas Karen is accessed from the main road 500m east of the Cabo de Trafalgar turning. Turn off at the wall with 'Apartamentos y Bungalows' tiled into it and go 500m. Turn right at the 'Fuente de Madroño' sign and you'll see Casas Karen's wooden ranch-style fence.

This place was artistically transformed a few years back by the owner of the Hurricane Hotel near Tarifa. The 18 rooms, run by a friendly management, are set around a plant-filled patio and have small gardens at the rear and exotic design features. Mountain biking, horse riding and surfing can be arranged.

Casa Meca (☎ 639 613402; www.casameca.com; Avenida Trafalgar s/n; studio d per week €475, 2-bedroom apt per week €660; **P**) An attractive house with pretty garden and grounds, Casa Meca is 100m east of the Cabo de Trafalgar turning. It comprises three bright apartments with kitchen, lounge, views and outdoor sitting areas. Double-glazed windows and central heating make it a good year-round choice.

Eating

Bar Saboy (Carril de Mangueta, Zahora; tagines €9, menú €10) Sit under a yucca palm and watch bulls grazing in fields opposite while birds twitter in nearby trees. The Saboy, 200m from the main road with a thatched roof and fireplace, offers good snacks and meals, including a delicious gently spiced Moroccan lentil soup.

Bar-Restaurante El Caña (☎ 956 43 73 98; Avenida Trafalgar s/n; mains €13; Apr-Sep) Super position atop the small cliff above the beach a short distance east of the Barbate road corner. Very hectic in summer.

Restaurante Trafalgar (☎ 956 43 71 21; Avenida Trafalgar 86; www.eltrafalgar.com; mains €12-17.50; menú €12; Apr-Sep) This excellent restaurant, with a summer patio, serves up creative Mediterranean cuisine. You can expect a few unusual flavours and the freshest of food here. *Arroz marinero* (seafood rice) is recommended. Internet out back.

More good eateries:

Sajorami (☎ 956 43 70 72; Playa Zahora; mains €10-16; **V**) Unbeatable sea views, stylish building and excellent Spanish cuisine with international, vegetarian and Moroccan additions.

El Jazmín (Avenida Trafalgar s/n; mains €9-20; **V**) Fish, seafood and Moroccan and Mexican dishes.

Drinking & Entertainment

Las Dunas (Carril El Faro; 10.30am-late) An attractive stone building with *choza*-style (traditional hut) roofing and impressive stone fireplace. You can come here for snacks, fresh fruit juices and late breakfasts but it's really a late-night place with a pool table.

La Pequeña Lulu (www.lapequenalulu.com; Avenida Trafalgar s/n; open daily year-round) At the far eastern end of the village backing on to the natural park, this cosy French-run café/bar with funky décor often has live music, even some jammin'.

Bar Saboy (Carril de Mangueta, Zahora) Also has regular live music (see left).

In the main tourist season, good bars include the cool Los Castillejos at the eastern end of the village, and Café-Bar Ketama across the street from El Pirata.

Getting There & Away

From Monday to Friday, three buses run to/from Barbate (€1, 15 minutes) and two to/from Cádiz (€5, 1¼ hours). Extra buses may run from Seville or Cádiz from mid-June to early September.

BARBATE
pop 22,000

A fishing and canning town with a long sandy beach and a big harbour, Barbate is mostly a drab place though it becomes a fairly lively resort in summer, and there are signs that it may just be slowly moving a little upmarket. The town rocks from 12 to 16 July during its annual fair, which culminates in the maritime procession in honour of the Virgen del Carmen.

Orientation & Information

The Comes bus station is more than 1km back from the beach at the northern end of the long main street, Avenida del Generalísimo, where it intersects with Avenida José Antonio. Barbate's **tourist office** (☎ 956 43 39 62; www.barbate.es; Avenida José Antonio 23; 8am-2.30pm & 4.30-7.30pm Mon-Fri, 10am-2pm Sat), the only one in the Los Caños–Barbate–Zahara area, is 1.5km along Avenida José Antonio from the bus station in the direction of the beach. Banks are on Avenida del Generalísimo.

Sleeping

Hotel Nuro (☎ 956 43 02 54; Avenida José Antonio s/n; d €35-55; P ✿ ✿) This is a simple but comfy hotel with winter heating and TV in the rooms, 100m from the bus station. Improvements include new beds and a cafeteria.

Hotel Galia (☎ 956 43 33 76; Calle Doctor Valencia 5; s/d €45/70; Apr-Sep; P ✿) A few blocks towards the sea from the bus station, the Galia is friendly and the rooms are fine.

Hotel Chili (☎ 956 45 40 33, 696 281760; www.elchilihotel.com; cnr Calle Real & Avenida José Antonio; s incl breakfast €69, d incl breakfast €80-95; P ✿) Set up by the owners of Tarifa's Hurricane Hotel, the Chili then passed into the hands of an Austrian who's lived in Cuba. Rooms are stylishly simple and decorated in subdued colours. It's 1km from the bus station.

Eating & Drinking

Stop by the excellent market on Avenida de Andalucía and the port to goggle at the day's fish catch. There are plenty of seafood eateries preparing local specialities on Paseo Marítimo.

Café-Bar Estrella Polar (Avenida del Generalísimo 106; salads from €4.50, mains €9-14) About 50m back from the beach, this café-bar offers good portions at fair prices. Try the swordfish or the excellent *chocos* (cuttlefish) or *calamares* (squid).

El Capitán (Puerto de la Albufera; tapas €1.30-2, raciones & mains €7-17) This appealing, two-storey,

wooden construction with wide verandahs looks down over the port. On the ground floor is a café-bar with tables surrounding a huge crustacean-filled tank. More formal dining is available upstairs. Cuisine is regional with some creative touches.

El Campero (☎ 956 43 23 00; Avenida de la Constitución 5C; mains €14-21) Head to ever-popular El Campero if you feel like a splurge. Fish is the house speciality: try the *urta a la roteña* (bream cooked in white wine with tomatoes, peppers and thyme) or the tasty local speciality *atún encebollado* (tuna stewed with onions and tomatoes).

Getting There & Away

From the **Comes bus station** (☎ 956 43 05 94; Avenida del Generalísimo) buses run to/from the following destinations:

Algeciras (€6, 1¼ hours) One daily.
Cádiz (€5.50, 1 hour) Up to 13 daily.
La Barca de Vejer (€1.10, 10 minutes) Near Vejer de la Frontera; see p210.
Tarifa (€4.50, 50 minutes) One daily.
Vejer de la Frontera (€1.10, 10 minutes) Up to 10 daily.
Zahara de los Atunes (€1, 15 minutes) Two to three times daily.

ZAHARA DE LOS ATUNES

pop 1000

Plonked in the middle of nothing except a broad, 12km-long, west-facing sandy beach, Zahara is elemental. At the heart of the village stand the crumbling walls of the old Almadraba, once a depot and refuge for the local tuna fishers, who were an infamously rugged lot. Miguel de Cervantes, in *La Ilustre Fregona*, wrote that no-one deserved the name *pícaro* (low-life scoundrel) unless they had spent two seasons at Zahara fishing for tuna. Records state that in 1541 no fewer than 140,000 tuna were brought into Zahara's Almadraba. Today the tuna industry has disappeared but Zahara is an increasingly popular and fashionable Spanish summer resort. With a little old-fashioned core of narrow streets, it's a super spot to let the sun, sea, wind and, in summer, a lively nightlife batter your senses.

Nature lovers will be delighted by the pristine beaches and walking trails of the Sierra de la Plata between Zahara and Bolonia. Head past Zahara's southern extension, Atlanterra, to get there.

Information

A tourist information kiosk opens for July and August on the sands near the Almadraba. ATMs are on Calle María Luisa, opposite Plaza de Tamarón.

Sleeping

Camping Bahía de la Plata (☎ 956 43 90 40; Avenida de las Palmeras; adult/tent/car €6.50/5.50/4, 4-person bungalow €95) This is a good treed camping ground fronting the beach at the southern end of Zahara.

Hostal Monte Mar (☎ 956 43 90 47; Calle Bullón 17; s/d €33/53; P) A congenial place right on the sands at the northern tip of the village. It may not have the best beds in town but at least it may have a room when everywhere else is full in July and August.

Hotel Almadraba (☎ 956 43 92 74; www.hotelesalmadraba.com; Calle María Luisa 13; s/d €45/73; closed Nov; P) This friendly hotel has just 11 simple but attractive rooms with TV, bathroom, winter heating and a popular restaurant.

Hotel Gran Sol (☎ 956 43 93 09; www.gransolhotel.com; Avenida de la Playa s/n; s/d incl breakfast €102/116, d with sea view incl breakfast €121; P) The Gran Sol occupies the prime beach spot right by the sands, facing the old Almadraba walls on one side and the ocean on the other. The large, comfortable rooms have all the trims, and the terrace restaurant enjoys stupendous views.

Hotel Doña Lola (☎ 956 43 90 09; Plaza Thompson 1; s €100, d €130-150; P) Near the entrance to Zahara, but only two minutes from the beach, this is a modern place in lovely large grounds, with good rooms in attractive old-fashioned style.

Eating

Restaurants can be found on the seafront or near Plaza de Tamarón behind Hotel Doña Lola. While many offer similar lists of fish, seafood, salads, meats and sometimes pizzas, new possibilities are starting to appear.

Casa Juanita (Calle Sagasta; fish dishes €9.50-11; closed Jan) Off the main drag on a little pedestrian street facing Plaza de Tamarón, this good place has a long tapas list with lots of fishy things. Garlic prawns and monkfish brochette are heartier choices.

Restaurante Ropiti (☎ 956 43 94 01; Calle María Luisa 6; mains from €12; closed Dec-Feb) The Ropiti impresses the locals with its range of well-prepared fish and seafood.

Restaurante La Jabega (☎ 956 43 04 92; Calle Tomollo 7; raciones €7-8, mains €12-25) Fronting the sands, the Jabega is acclaimed for its fishballs and its rice dish with giant *carabineros* prawns. It also does fancier fish and seafood dishes.

Hotel Gran Sol (Avenida de la Playa s/n; mains €10-36) From the terrace restaurant, gaze out to sea or check out the old Almadraba on the sands while you sample an exotic seafood or fresh vegetable starter. To follow, share a paella (€25 for two) or try a whole baked fish encrusted with salt.

Drinking & Entertainment

In July and August a line of tents and makeshift shacks along the beach south of the Almadraba serves as bars, discos and *teterías* (Arabian-style tearooms). They rock after midnight, especially those with music.

Getting There & Away

Comes runs up to five buses daily to/from Barbate (€1, 15 minutes), up to four to/from Cádiz (€6.50, two hours) via Barbate, and one daily Monday to Friday to/from Tarifa (€3.50, 45 minutes). These bus services run more frequently from mid-June to September.

BOLONIA

pop 125

This tiny village, 10km down the coast from Zahara de los Atunes and about 20km northwest of Tarifa, has a gorgeous white-sand beach (good for windsurfing), several restaurants and small *hostales*, lots of cockerels, and the impressive ruins of Roman **Baelo Claudia** (☎ 956 68 85 30; EU/non-EU citizen free/€1.50; 10am-7pm Tue-Sat Mar-May & Oct, 10am-8pm Tue-Sat Jun-Sep, 10am-6pm Tue-Sat Nov-Feb, 10am-2pm Sun year-round). The ruins include the substantial remains of a theatre, a paved forum surrounded by the remains of temples and other buildings, and the remains of the workshops that turned out the products that made Baelo Claudia famous in the Roman world: salted fish and *garum* paste (a spicy seasoning derived from fish). The place particularly flourished in the time of Emperor Claudius (AD 41 to 54) but declined after an earthquake in the 2nd century.

West beyond the ruins is a big dune that you can climb and there are other good walks here (see right). The sandstone crag San Bartolo (or San Bartolomé) looming just east of Bolonia is the biggest magnet for rock climbers in the area.

A couple of years back Bolonia began to show minor signs of growing prosperity – part of the main street was paved, street lights were erected and a few palms were planted. Things haven't moved on much since.

Sleeping

The following places are open year-round. There are 13 places in total, some are only seasonal.

Hostal Lola (☎ 956 68 85 36; www.hostallola.com; El Lentiscal 26; r with shared/private bathroom €45/55; **P**) The amiable Lola keeps 16 simple but attractive and well-kept rooms. There's cheerful paintwork throughout and a Moroccan-inspired sitting area and a pretty flower-filled garden to enjoy. The shared-bathroom area has designer washbasins. Follow the signs on giant surfboards beyond Hostal Miramar.

Apartamentos Ana (☎ 956 68 85 50; 2–6-person apt €60-70; **P**) Ana's provides new, well-fitted, good-value one- or two-bedroom apartments, though they're not oriented towards the ocean. Look for a little cul-de-sac just beyond the Hostal Lola turning.

Apartamentos Isabel (☎ 956 68 85 69; El Lentiscal 5; apt €75; **P**) These apartments are similar to the Apartamentos Ana, but are positioned right on the beach.

La Hormiga Voladora (☎ 956 68 85 62; El Lentiscal 15; d €57-69, 2-/3-/4-person apt €85/95/105; **P**) Extending back from the seafront, the 'Flying Ant' is a warren of carefully decorated and comfortable rooms and apartments set around various courtyards.

Eating

In summer there are five or so open-air restaurants on the beach, mainly at the eastern end, and more by the ruins. **Los Caracoles** (☎ 654 096251; El Lentiscal 1; paella €8, grilled fish & seafood platter €18) at the far eastern end is excellent and opens year-round at least for lunch, weather permitting. Live music in summer and paella cooked on a fireplace make it well worth a visit. On the main drag in the village, try the seafood at **Restaurante**

Marisma (mains €6-12; ☯ daily Semana Santa-Oct, weekends year-round), with tables outside, or at the slightly more upmarket **Bar Restaurante Las Rejas** (salad €6, paella €11; ☯ year-round), where the ever-helpful waitstaff will suggest the day's tastiest options.

Getting There & Away

The only road to Bolonia heads west off the N340, 15km north of Tarifa. In July and August there's usually some sort of bus service between Tarifa and Bolonia (see p223 for details). Otherwise, without wheels, it's a 7km hilly walk from the main road. You can walk 8km along the coast from Ensenada de Valdevaqueros (p218) via Punta Paloma, and there's a path west from Bolonia through the woods of the lower Sierra de la Plata to Torre de Cabo de Gracia, from where you can walk along the beach to Atlanterra, the southern end of Zahara de los Atunes.

TARIFA

pop 17,000

Tarifa is an attractive, laid-back town even during the summer frenzy, although this could change as glitzy shop fronts proliferate and steady development continues. Relatively unknown a couple of decades ago, Tarifa is now a mecca for windsurfers and kitesurfers, and a hip international scene. An eclectic bunch of restaurants, bars, lodgings and shops has grown up around the surf crowd. The town has a thriving art scene stimulated by the natural beauty and the crazy population mix.

Tarifa may be as old as Phoenician Cádiz and was definitely a Roman settlement, but it takes its name from Tarif ibn Malik, who led a Muslim raid in AD 710, the year before the main Islamic invasion of the peninsula. The town's attractive old centre has narrow streets, a striking castle, whitewashed houses and flowers cascading from balconies with fancy ironwork and window boxes. The Tarifa beaches have clean, white sand and good waves, and the country inland is green and rolling (though it can be chilly and wet in winter).

A big negative – though not for surfers or the hundreds of modern windmills on the hilltops inland – is the wind on which Tarifa's new-found prosperity is based. For much of the year, either the *levante* (easterly) or *poniente* (westerly) is blowing, which is ruinous for relaxing on the beach – even if Tarifa's famous winds do seem to have moderated some over the last couple of years. The windmill operation, originally a mainly EU-funded experiment feeding power into Spain's national grid, has expanded into a huge private business.

A major factor affecting the area's immediate future is the imminent construction of the local section of the new A48 *autovía*, which as yet runs from just north of Chiclana de la Frontera to Vejer de la Frontera.

Orientation

Two roads lead into Tarifa from the N340. The one from the northwest becomes Calle Batalla del Salado, which ends at east–west Avenida de Andalucía, where the Puerta de Jerez leads through the walls into the old town. The one from the east becomes Calle Amador de los Ríos, which also meets Avenida de Andalucía at the Puerta de Jerez.

The main street of the old town is Calle Sancho IV El Bravo, with the Iglesia de San Mateo at its eastern end.

To the southwest of the town protrudes the Isla de las Palomas, a military-occupied promontory that is the southernmost point of continental Europe, with the Strait of Gibraltar to the south and east and the Atlantic Ocean to the west. Africa is only 14km across the strait.

Information

Banks and ATMs are on Calle Sancho IV El Bravo and Calle Batalla del Salado, the main shopping street. Useful information for visitors can be found at www.tarifa .net and www.tarifacostasur.com. The glossy magazine *Vida* has interesting local articles.

Al Sur (Calle Batalla del Salado) International newspapers and a good range of surfing and snowboarding mags in Spanish and English.

Centro de Salud (Health Centre; ☎ 956 68 15 15/35; Calle Amador de los Ríos)

El Navegante (Calle General Copons 1; internet per hr €2) Also cheap phone calls.

Lavandería Acuario (Laundrette; Calle Colón 14; 4kg wash €4, 4kg wash, dry & fold €7-8; ⏰ 10.30-2pm & 6-8pm Mon-Fri, 9.30am-3pm Sat)

Pandora's Papelería (Calle Sancho IV El Bravo; internet per hr €3; ⏰ 10am-2pm & 5-9pm)

Policía Local (Local Police; ☎ 956 61 41 86; Plaza de Santa María)

Post office (☎ 956 68 42 37; Calle Coronel Moscardó 9)

Tourist office (☎ 956 68 09 93; www.tarifaweb.com in Spanish; ⏰ 10.30am-2pm & 4-6pm mid-Sep–May, 10.30am-2pm & 6-8pm Jun–mid-Sep) Near the top end of the palm-lined Paseo de la Alameda.

Sights & Activities

Tarifa is easy to enjoy. Stroll through the tangled streets of the old town to the castle walls, check out the castle, stop in at the busy port and sample the beaches.

The Mudejar **Puerta de Jerez** was built after the Reconquista. Look in at the bustling, neo-Mudejar **market** (Calle Colón) before winding your way to the heart of the old town and the mainly 15th-century **Iglesia de San Mateo**. The streets south of the church are little-changed since Islamic times. Climb the stairs at the end of Calle Coronel Moscardó and go left on Calle Aljaranda to reach the **Mirador El Estrecho** atop part of the castle walls, with spectacular views across to Africa.

The **Castillo de Guzmán** (Calle Guzmán) extends west from here with an entrance at its far end on Calle Guzmán. At the time of writing, the castle was closed for refurbishment until June 2007 (so check with the tourist office for opening hours thereafter), but until then it's still worth walking about the exterior of this imposing fortress. The Castillo was originally built in AD 960 under the orders of the Cordoban caliph, Abd ar-Rahman III, as fortification against Norse and African raids. Christian forces took Tarifa in 1292 but it was not secure until Algeciras was won in 1344. But the castle is named after the Reconquista hero Guzmán El Bueno: in 1294 Merenid attackers from Morocco kidnapped Guzmán's son and threatened to kill him unless Guzmán relinquished the castle. Refusing to comply, Guzmán threw down his own dagger for his son to be killed, a supreme gesture of defiance and sacrifice. Guzmán's descendants became the Duques de Medina Sidonia, who ran much of Cádiz province as a private fiefdom for a long period.

You can walk along the castle's parapets and stand atop the 13th-century Torre de Guzmán El Bueno (which houses the town museum) for 360-degree views.

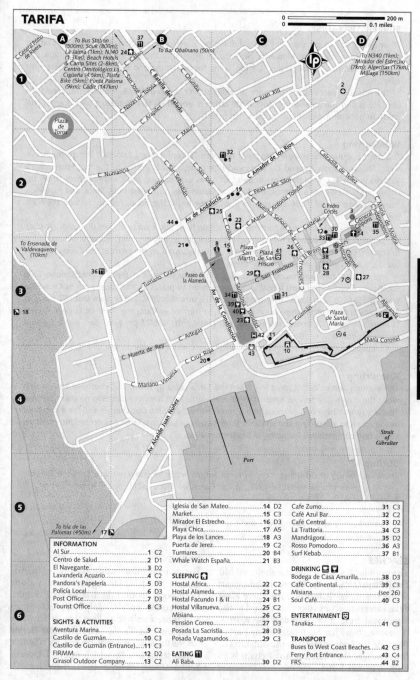

TARIFA

0 _____ 200 m
0 _____ 0.1 miles

CÁDIZ PROVINCE

Map labels: To Bus Station (500m); Souk (800m); La Jaima (1km); N340 (1.3km); Beach Hotels & Camp Sites (2-8km); Centro Ornitológico La Cigüeña (4-5km); Tarifa Bike (5km); Punta Paloma (9km); Cádiz (147km); To Bar Obaínano (50m); To N340 (1km); Mirador del Estrecho (7km); Algeciras (17km); Málaga (150km)

Plaza de Toros; C Cánovas del Castillo; C General Primo de Rivera; Batalla del Salado; C Olumba; C Juan XIII; Calzadilla de Tellez; C Navas de Tolosa; C San José; C Arapiles; C Maura; C San José; C San Sebastián; C Numancia; C Bailén; Av de Andalucía; C Amador de los Ríos; C Peso Calle Silos; C Nuestra Señora de la Luz; Calzada de la Villa; C Pedro Cortés; C General Copons; Mirador de Molina; C Independencia; C Colón; C María Señora de la Luz; C Castelar; C Coronel Moscardó; Plaza San Martín de San Hiscio; Plaza Francisco; Paseo de la Alameda; C San Francisco; Av de la Constitución; C Turriano Gracil; C Santísima Trinidad; C Guzmán; Plaza de Santa María; C Artegas; C Huerta de Rey; C Cruz Roja; C Mariano Vinuesa; Av Alcalde Juan Núñez; María Coronel; C Alameda

To Ensenada de Valdevaqueros (10km); To Isla de las Palomas (450m); Strait of Gibraltar; Port; Paseo de la Alameda

SURFERS' PARADISE

What better way to start the day than slipping on a wet suit, grabbing your board and hitting the waves for a day in the elements. No need for alternative therapies. This is the therapy. Age is really no barrier, although this is a big scene for the young and beautiful. Then there's the après-surf…

The Atlantic coast of Cádiz province provides Spain's, and arguably Europe's, finest conditions for windsurfing and kitesurfing. Most of the action is around Tarifa, which has a cool international scene to go with it, but there are other spots too.

Windsurfing

The most popular strip is along the coast between Tarifa and Punta Paloma, 10km to the north-west. The best spots depend on wind and tide conditions. El Porro, on the bay Ensenada de Valdevaqueros, is one of the most popular, as it has easy parking and plenty of space to set up. Other popular take-off points are the Río Jara, about 3km northwest from Tarifa, and Arte-Vida, Hurricane, and Hostal Valdevaqueros, in front of the respective hotels out of town on the N340 (see p220).

Slalom is the more common form of sailboarding here, but wave riders get their chance when the *poniente* (west wind from the Atlantic) is blowing, especially in spring and autumn and during full moon. The best waves for wave-riding are actually found up the coast at Los Caños de Meca (p211), though winds are less reliable there.

You can buy new and secondhand windsurfing gear in Tarifa at the surf shops along Calle Batalla del Salado. For board rental and classes, head to places up the coast such as **Club Mistral** (☎ 956 68 90 90, at Hostal Valdevaqueros 619 340913; www.clubmistral.com) or **Spin Out** (☎ 956 23 63 52; www.tarifaspinout.com), which is on the beach in front of ex-Camping Torre de la Peña II, near El Porro. At Spin Out, board, sail and wetsuit rental costs €35/73 per hour/day, and a six-hour beginner's course is €150.

Competitions are held year-round; for other spots with good winds, see p74.

Kitesurfing

This exciting and colourful sport has taken the Tarifa coast by storm, but kites give way to sails when the wind really gets up. Kitesurf rental is available from the same places as windsurfing gear. This is a sport where beginners definitely need instruction: Spin Out charges €50 for a two-hour introduction to kitesurfing and €150 for three two-hour sessions. Tarifa has hosted international kitesurfing competitions including in September 2006.

Surfing

There's a low-key board-riding scene in Tarifa but it's better for bodyboarding. Between October and May there can be surfable waves at Los Caños de Meca (p211) and – usually better – El Palmar (p210).

For introductory information about these sports, see p73.

BEACHES

The popular town beach is the sheltered but small **Playa Chica**, on the isthmus leading out to the Isla de las Palomas. From here **Playa de los Lances** stretches 10km northwest to the huge sand dune at **Ensenada de Valdevaqueros**. A new walkway has been built along part of Playa de los Lances towards the outskirts of town, where the Marriott hotel chain is to build a luxury hotel.

DIVING

For general information on diving in Andalucía, see p74. Diving is generally done from boats around the Isla de las Palomas. Shipwrecks, corals, dolphins, octopuses and more await you. There are a few dive companies in Tarifa – try **Aventura Marina** (☎ 956 05 46 26; www.aventuramarina.com in Spanish; Avenida de Andalucía 1), which offers Discover Scuba Diving courses (€72, three hours).

One-tank dives with equipment rental and guide cost €50.

HORSE RIDING

Both these stables, based out of town at hotels on Playa de los Lances, rent horses with excellent English-speaking guides. An hour's ride along the beach costs €30. Three-hour beach or inland rides cost around €70.

Aventura Ecuestre (☎ 956 23 66 32; www.aventura ecuestre.com) At Hotel Dos Mares (p221).

Club Hípica (☎ 956 68 90 92) At Hurricane Hotel (p221).

WHALE-WATCHING

This is great fun! At least three groups run two- to three-hour biologist-led boat trips to track and watch dolphins and whales. Most trips cost around €30/20/10 for an adult/child under 14/child under six. In all but the Turmares boat, expect to get wet if the sea is rough.

FIRMM (Foundation for Information & Research on Marine Mammals; ☎ 956 62 70 08, 619 459441; www.firmm.org; Calle Pedro Cortés 4) Uses every trip to record data.

Turmares (☎ 956 68 07 41, 696 448349; www.tur mares.com; Avenida Alcalde Juan Núñez 3; dolphin- & whale-watching adult/under 14yr €27/14, killer whale–watching €40/20) Has the largest boat (with a glass bottom).

Whale Watch España (☎ 956 62 70 18, 639 476544; www.whalewatchtarifa.org in Spanish; Avenida de la Constitución 6)

ROCK CLIMBING, TREKKING & MOUNTAIN BIKING

Girasol Outdoor Company (☎ 615 456506; www .girasol-adventure.com; Calle Colón 12; orientation rock climb €29, 6hr trek €38, bike trips €25-42) Orientation, courses at all levels and climbs on San Bartolo, near Bolonia.

Tarifa Bike (☎ 696 973656; Apartamentos Las Flores, Carretera N340 Km 77.1; 2hr/day €9/18) Good mountain-bike rental and guided tours (in English).

Festivals & Events

Reggae Festival International and Spanish reggae acts delight the crowds in Tarifa's humble bullring, one night in August.

Feria de la Virgen de la Luz The town fair in honour of its patroness mixes religious processions, featuring the area's beautiful horses, with all the usual singing, dancing, eating and fair rides. Held during the first week in September.

Sleeping

You can stay in the old town or on and around Calle Batalla del Salado. Plenty more places to stay are dotted along the beach and the inland side of the N340 within 10km northwest of Tarifa, but none are particulary cheap. Rooms are tight on long weekends, at Easter, from May to September, and when there are windsurfing and kitesurfing competitions. The prices listed here are for August: expect reductions of 25% to 40% at most places for much of the rest of the year. For a range of self-catering apartments and villas, try www.tarifadirect.com.

IN TOWN

Pensión Correo (☎ 956 68 02 06; Calle Coronel Moscardó 8; per person €20) This good budget choice in the old post office has amiable Italian-Spanish owners and a bright new foyer. The cheerfully painted rooms, some with bathroom, remain much the same – they're not flash, but comfy enough. The top-floor double room sports gorgeous views and its own little terrace.

Hostal Villanueva (☎ 956 68 41 49; Avenida de Andalucía 11; s/d €28/45) Built into the old city walls a few doors west of the Puerta de Jerez, this *hostal* has no-nonsense rooms, some with TV and some with views of the castle. There's a terrace and the genial owner speaks French.

Hostal Africa (☎ 956 68 02 20, 606 914294; hostal_africa@hotmail.com; Calle María Antonia Toledo 12; s/d €40/60, with shared bathroom €30/40) This revamped old house close to the market is conveniently located and run by hospitable, well-travelled owners who know what travellers need. Rooms are bright and attractive and an expansive roof terrace with an exotic cabana and views of Africa can be enjoyed. Storage for boards and bicycles is available.

Hostal Facundo I & II (☎ 956 68 42 98; hotel facundo@terra.es; Calle Batalla del Salado 47; dm €10, r with private/shared bathroom €70/58; P) The Facundo is gradually getting a makeover. It's long been geared to windsurfers with a storage place for boards, and is popular for its prices, which nose-dive out of peak season. The 52 rooms vary: the best open right on to the street. There's also a communal kitchen and lounge with TV. Dormitories contain eight beds.

CÁDIZ PROVINCE

Hostal Alameda (☎ 956 68 11 81; www.hostal alameda.com; Paseo de la Alameda 4; s/d €60/70; 🔀) This good-value place is on the edge of the old town in front of the port. Rooms are cosy, with winter heating and satellite TV; beds could be more comfy. Some rooms have sea views, while others look out over the Alameda or Tarifa's undulating roof line.

Posada Vagamundos (☎ 956 68 13 13; www.posada vagamundos.com; Calle San Francisco 18; s/d incl breakfast €60/80, ste €85; 🖳) A new enterprise right in the centre occupying a carefully restored old building. The eleven double rooms are oriented towards the light and have attractive bathrooms and double-glazed windows. Old local floor tiles mix with furniture and decorations from Morocco, Indonesia and Mexico. There's an attached cafeteria.

Misiana (☎ 956 62 70 83; www.misiana.com in Spanish; Calle Sancho IV El Bravo; s/d incl breakfast €97/112) This place has seen a few incarnations. The current comfortable hotel is mod, almost futuristic, in its design, colours and funky details. Rooms on one floor are painted lilac and silver, while others are red and turquoise; rooms with big views are available too. All have fan and satellite TV.

Posada La Sacristía (☎ 956 68 17 59; www.la sacristia.net; San Donato 8; r incl breakfast €115-135) Tarifa's most elegant central accommodation is in a beautifully renovated 17th-century town house with rooftop views. Attention to detail is impeccable. The eight rooms, on several levels around a central courtyard, are painted a fresh white and furnishings are mainly neutral. Beds are large.

ALONG THE COAST

There are five year-round **camping grounds** (www.campingsdetarifa.com) with room for more than 4000 campers, on or near the beach between Tarifa and Punta Paloma, 10km northwest from Tarifa along the N340. They charge around €20 for two people with a tent and car. Four of the sites also have bungalows. Camping Tarifa and Camping Torre de la Peña I are the more modern.

All the following places are on, or just off, the N340, northwest of Tarifa. The owners of the Hurricane Hotel are the creative energy behind the refitting of several hotels along this road.

OTB (☎ 661 030446; www.otb-tarifa.com; N340 Km 81; dm €12, r per person €15; 🕙 Mar-Nov; 🅿 🖳 🖳) This Italian-run place, geared to backpackers, offers dorm accommodation, doubles and quads, along with kitchen use, TV, and laundry facilities. It's 2km out of town towards Cádiz.

Hostal Oasis (☎ 956 68 50 65; s/d €35/40, 2-/4-person bungalow €60/€100; 🅿) The Oasis is in substantial grounds about 8km out of Tarifa, and its 11 clean bungalows, set around the large lawn, have equipped kitchens. They're better than the rooms in the main block.

Molino El Mastral (☎ 679 193503; www.mastral .com; Carretera Sanctuario de la Luz; apt d/q €70/90, small house q €120; 🅿 🖳) Fancy something far from the madding crowd and yet still within easy reach of the beach and Tarifa? Then this rural retreat is for you. It's a working stud and cattle farm but the farm buildings have been converted into cheerfully decorated apartments. There's plenty of space and

---

HIGH-FLIERS OVER THE STRAIT OF GIBRALTAR

Keen bird-watchers mustn't miss the Strait of Gibraltar, a key point of passage for migrating birds between Africa and Europe. In general, northward migrations occur between mid-February and early June, and southbound flights between late July and early November. When a westerly wind is blowing, Gibraltar itself is usually a good spot for seeing the birds. When the wind is calm or easterly, the Tarifa area (including the Mirador del Estrecho lookout 7km east of the town) is usually better. Also, you can visit the **Centro Ornitológico Cigüeña** (☎ 639 859350; http://cocn .tarifainfo.com; N340 Km 78.5; 🕙 5-7pm Tue-Sat, 10am-2pm Sun), 4km out of Tarifa, a bird-watching station staffed by volunteers who collect data and produce information leaflets.

Soaring birds such as raptors, black-and-white storks and vultures cross at the Strait of Gibraltar because they rely on thermals and updraughts, which don't happen over wider expanses of water. White storks sometimes congregate in flocks of up to 5000 to cross the strait (January and February northbound, July and August southbound). There are just two places where the seas are narrow enough for the stork to get into Europe by this method. One is the Bosphorus (the strait between the Black Sea and the Sea of Marmara); the other is right here at the Strait of Gibraltar.

shade in the grounds and pool area, and horse riding is available

Hotel Tres Mares (☎ 956 68 06 65; www.tresmares hotel.com in Spanish; N340 Km 76; d incl breakfast €107; ☺ Mar-Nov; 🅿 🄐) This has the same owners as the Hotel Dos Mares but it's a few kilometres further out of Tarifa. The designer rooms have sea views and are on two levels of a plain '70s-style brown-painted block. What's really distinctive here is the extensive grounds with wooden oriental furniture, a wooden elephant, a Moroccan tent, hammocks and a bar-restaurant. There is certainly room to chill.

Hotel Arte-Vida (☎ 956 68 52 46; www.artevida hotel.com; N340 Km 79.3; s/d incl breakfast €110/130; 🅿) The Arte-Vida, 5km from the town centre, has a garden with lawn opening onto the beach, an excellent restaurant with stunning views, and attractive, medium-sized rooms. Décor is oriental minimalist (lots of white, cane and bamboo) with a later addition of blue, black and red paintings by a Russian artist.

Hotel Dos Mares (☎ 956 68 40 35; www.dosmares hotel.com in Spanish; d incl breakfast from €141, 2-person -bungalow incl breakfast from €135; 🅿 🄐 🄐 🄐) This excellent choice is right on the beach about 4.5km from Tarifa. Its eclectic architecture has a mainly Islamic theme. You can stay in the main building (seven rooms), or go for one of 29 bungalows in the gardens or on the beachfront. The bar, with tremendous views out to Africa, is a popular hang-out. The hotel has its own well-run stables, too (see p219).

Hotel Punta Sur (☎ 956 68 43 26; www.punta surhotel.com; N340 Km 77; s/d €117/166; 🅿 🄐 🄐) With a logo of a surfer riding a wave, the Punta Sur, near the pharmacy on the N340, is another Hurricane Hotel project: here the team has waved its magic wand and worked miracles on what was an ordinary roadside hotel. A restaurant, the reception and a billiard table are in a huge open space that has been decorated with flights of fantasy combining modern, futuristic, Gaudiesque and Moroccan influences. The comfortable, eccentrically decorated rooms are set in big gardens with a tennis court. Most recently, the gardens and the front of the hotel have been totally remodelled.

Hurricane Hotel (☎ 956 68 49 19; www.hotelhur ricane.com; r incl breakfast land/ocean side €149/166; 🅿 🄐 🄐) Six kilometres out of Tarifa, this

> ### THE AUTHOR'S CHOICE
>
> **Hostal Valdevaqueros** (☎ 956 23 67 05; www .hotelhurricane.com; N340, Km 75; r incl breakfast €107, 3-/4-person apt incl breakfast €134; ☺ Mar-Nov; 🅿) This attractive old farmhouse, 20m from the beach at Valdevaqueros, is owned by the Hurricane Hotel folk. It has a few trademark features such as careful and creative renovation and decoration using natural and ethnic materials, plus a beautiful garden. The bar area, featuring mosaic work, extends outside to covered areas with loads of plants and Moroccan lamps. To find it, look for the metallic sign with a horse and a cow head that arches over the beginning of the longish track to the hostal from the N340, opposite 100% Fun.

hip Moroccan-style hotel is the place to go if you're feeling flush. Set in semitropical beachside gardens, it has around 30 large, comfy, refurbished rooms, two pools, two restaurants and a health club. It also has the famous Club Mistral windsurfing and kitesurfing school with board rental next door, and Club Hípica, a horse-riding school (see p219). The scrumptious buffet breakfast has all manner of homemade goodies.

Eating

Tarifa brims with eateries. International residents and visitors guarantee plenty of variety.

IN TOWN

Calle Sancho IV El Bravo is good for takeaways, and the streets around it for tapas.

Ali Baba (Calle Sancho IV El Bravo; falafel €3, kebab €3.50) The popular Ali Baba, with benches and stand-up tables outside, serves cheap, filling and tasty Arabic food made with lovely fresh ingredients. Vegetarians can enjoy excellent falafel while carnivores might like to tuck into the tasty kebabs.

Surf Kebab (Calle Batalla de Salado 40; falafel €3, kebab €3.50) This place prepares similar fare to Ali Baba, though with less salad, and is convenient if you're shopping.

Café Central (Calle Sancho IV El Bravo 8; breakfast €2.80-4.50) This café is the prime location for people-watching, delicious *churros con chocolate* (fingers of doughnut dipped into a cup of hot chocolate) and a large range of breakfasts and teas.

CÁDIZ PROVINCE

THE AUTHOR'S CHOICE

Café Azul Bar (Calle Batalla del Salado; breakfast €3.50-5; ☺ 9am-9pm, closed Wed in winter) This eccentric place with eye-catching décor has been energised by its new Italian owners who prepare the best breakfasts in town. Don't miss the large muesli, fruit salad and yoghurt. There's good coffee, excellent juices, *bocadillos* (sandwiches), healthy cakes, and sometimes Thai or Italian fare in the evening.

Cafe Zumo (Calle Sancho IV El Bravo; sandwiches €2.50-5; ☺ 9am-9pm) This convivial little place near the castle is popular for its juices, light meals, and soups. Magazines and books add to the attraction.

La Trattoria (☎ 956 68 22 25; Paseo de la Alameda; pasta & pizza €6.50-10, mains €10.50-15) Italian restaurants are proliferating in Tarifa. A good location, generally great food and always top-rate service make this one of the best.

Rosso Pomodoro (☎ 956 68 20 30; Avenida de Andalucía 24; pizza & pasta €6-7, fish mains €10-15) Another local Italian favourite, this place serves up authentic Italian cuisine.

Souk (☎ 956 62 70 65; Calle Mar Tirreno 46; entrées €4-6, mains €10-14; **V**) In a new location on Tarifa's outskirts, the expanded Souk still drips with Moroccan decorations and serves terrific Moroccan- and Asian-inspired food. *Thai amarillor de verduras* (Thai vegetables in coconut) goes down well after the *hojaldre de espinacas* (spicy spinach and feta pastry). There are tagines and couscous too.

Mandrágora (☎ 956 68 12 91; Calle Independencia 3; mains €9-16; ☺ dinner only, closed Sun & 2 weeks in Feb; **V**) Behind Iglesia San Mateo, this intimate place serves Andalucian-Arabic food. Delicious options include lamb with plums and almonds, and prawns with *nora* (Andalucian sweet pepper) sauce.

ALONG THE COAST

Most of the hotels and *hostales* up here have restaurants.

Chiringuito Tangana (mains €4-7.50; ☺ 10.30am-9.30pm) Next to Spin Out on the beach, this place serves up pies, lasagne, savoury pastries and *bocadillos* (sandwiches). Chill to the beat on the grass or relax on the Moroccan carpets on the floor of the glassed-in patio.

Terrace Restaurant (☎ 956 68 49 19; www.hotel hurricane.com; lunch mains €8; fresh juices €2.50) This

casual beachfront restaurant at the Hurricane Hotel is good for an economical lunch (various salads, hamburgers, chicken, local fish, steaks). In the evenings the hotel's interior restaurant, with candle-lit tables by the pool in summer, prepares creative meals, including very good salads (€6 to €8; try the Italian salad), and main dishes such as lamb chops with garlic and rosemary (€12).

Hostal Valdevaqueros (☎ 956 23 67 05; www .hurricanehotel.com; mains €8-11; ☺ Mar-Nov) The Hotel Hurricane's relative, this place fills windsurfer stomachs with large plates of chicken, hamburgers, exotic salads, bread and condiments.

Miramar (☎ 956 68 52 46; www.artevidahotel.com; N340 Km 79.3; mains €8-17) Hotel Arte-Vida's restaurant lives up to its name with expansive ocean views looking out to Africa. The chefs here whip up a range of pastas and some international meat dishes plus fresh local seafood. Try the pasta Miramar – with seafood, parsley and chilli.

Drinking

Soul Café (Calle Santísima Trinidad 9) This hip, popular bar is run by travel-loving Italians. You may hear guest DJs from Milan spin their favourites. Stop by after 11pm, but not in winter when the owners are travelling.

Bodega de Casa Amarilla (Calle Sancho IV El Bravo 9) A convivial *típico* bar-restaurant run by the Café Central.

Bar Obaïnano (Calle Braille 27) No longer in the old town, this place still serves up fresh juices and exotic cocktails to a cheerful background beat. It's popular with French travellers.

Misiana (☎ 956 62 70 83; Calle Sancho IV El Bravo; 9pm-2am) This cool, loungy place at the Misiana hotel is one of *the* places to be seen in Tarifa. Its décor is always eye-catching – now orange, black and gold in the bar and swirling pink in the lounge area. Come for juices, cocktails and shakes, and creative tapas.

Café Continental (Paseo de la Alameda) This good tapas, drinks and coffee stop is popular for its central position on the Paseo de Alameda.

Entertainment

Tanakas (Plaza de San Hiscio) A central disco that keeps the neighbours awake all night. An upstairs bar with tapas draws an older crowd.

La Jaima (Playa de los Lances) In summer, this Moroccan tent arrangement pops up on the beach near the edge of town. From 7pm to 10pm it's an Islamic-style tearoom but, come midnight, disco sounds take over.

Getting There & Away
BOAT
FRS (☎ 956 68 18 30; www.frs.es; Avenida de Andalucía) runs a fast ferry between Tarifa and Tangier in Morocco (€27/75/25 per passenger/car/motorcycle, 35 minutes one-way) up to five times daily, with possibly more sailings in July and August. There are sailings from Tarifa at 9am, noon, 3pm, 4pm and 9pm (Spanish time) and from Tangier at 9.30am, 12.30pm, 3.30pm, 6.30pm and 9.30pm (Moroccan time). Get details of the service at the port, or FRS. All passengers need a passport.

BUS
From its base near the petrol station at the north end of Calle Batalla del Salado. **Comes** (☎ 902 19 92 08, 956 68 40 38; Calle Batalla del Salado) runs five or more buses daily to the following destinations:

Destination	Cost	Duration	Daily Frequency
Algeciras	€1.70	30min	7-13
Barbate	€4	50min	1
Cádiz	€8	1¾hr	up to 7
Jerez de la Frontera	€8.50	2½hr	1
La Línea de la Concepción	€3.50	45min	8
Málaga	€12.50	2hr	2
Seville	€15	3hr	3
Zahara de los Atunes	€3.50	45min	1 (Mon-Fri)

CAR & MOTORCYCLE
Stop at the Mirador del Estrecho, about 7km out of Tarifa on the N340 towards Algeciras, to take in magnificent views of the Strait of Gibraltar, the Mediterranean, the Atlantic and two continents. Beware of the frequent police speed trap in the 50km/h zone at Pelayo, a few kilometres further east.

Getting Around
In July and August buses run every 90 minutes from Tarifa up the west coast to Punta Paloma. Some go on to Bolonia. There's a stop at the bottom of the Paseo de la Alameda. The main stop is at the bus station where a

timetable and prices should be posted. Taxis line up on Avenida de Andalucía near the Puerta de Jerez. For bicycle hire see p219.

THE SOUTHEAST

PARQUE NATURAL LOS ALCORNOCALES
This large (1700 sq km) and beautiful natural park stretches 75km north almost from the Strait of Gibraltar to the border of the Parque Natural Sierra de Grazalema. It's a spectacular jumble of sometimes rolling, sometimes rugged hills of medium height, much of it covered in Spain's most extensive *alcornocales* (cork-oak woodlands).

Los Alcornocales is rich in archaeological, historical and natural interest, but it's well off the beaten track and sparsely populated. There are plenty of walks and opportunities for other activities in the park, but you need your own wheels to make the most of it (see the boxed text, p206, for a driving detour). The park has several visitors centres and information offices, including the following:
Centro de Visitantes Cortes de la Frontera (☎ 952 15 45 99; Avenida de la Democracia s/n, Cortes de la Frontera; ☑ 10am-2pm Thu year-round, 10am-2pm & 6-8pm Fri-Sun Apr-Sep, 10am-2pm & 4-6pm Fri-Sun Oct-Mar)
Centro de Visitantes Huerta Grande (☎ 956 67 91 61; N340 Km 96, Pelayo; ☑ 10am-2pm Thu year-round, 10am-2pm & 6-8pm Fri-Sun Apr-Sep, 10am-2pm & 4-6pm Fri-Sun Oct-Mar) On the Tarifa–Algeciras road.
Punto de Información Castillo de Castellar (☎ 956 23 66 24; Taraguilla, Castellar de la Frontera; ☑ 11.30am-2pm & 5-7.30pm Wed-Sun May-Sep, 10am-2pm & 3-5pm Wed-Sun Oct-Apr)
Punto de Información Jimena de la Frontera (☎ 956 23 68 82; Calle Misericordia s/n, Jimena de la Frontera; ☑ 10am-2pm & 4-8pm Mon-Fri, 10am-2pm Sat & Sun)

One good base is **Jimena de la Frontera**, a small town on the A369 Algeciras–Ronda road on the park's eastern boundary. It's crowned by a fine Islamic castle, has a handful of *hostales* and hotels and many *casas rurales* (country properties for rent) and is served by train and bus from Algeciras and Ronda.

The CA3331 heading northwest leads to **La Sauceda**, an abandoned village that's now the site of a recreational area and field education centre. The La Sauceda area is beautiful country that was once a den of bandits and smugglers, and even guerrillas during the Spanish Civil War (when the village was bombed by Francisco Franco's planes). It's the starting point for an alternative route up Aljibe, the park's highest peak (see p206).

ALGECIRAS

pop 111,000

Algeciras, the major port linking Spain with Africa, is also an industrial town, a big fishing port and a drug smuggling centre. Though it's unattractive and polluted, it's not without interest. Proximity to Africa gives the port an air of excitement and the continuing gentrification of the town centre makes it quite pleasant to walk around. A few pretty old buildings with wrought-iron balconies remain and there are some good restaurants and shops. In summer the port is hectic with hundreds of thousands of Moroccans who have been working in Europe and are on the way home for summer holidays.

Algeciras was an important Roman port. Alfonso XI of Castilla wrested it from the Merenids of Morocco in 1344 but later Mohammed V of Granada razed it to the ground. In 1704 Algeciras was repopulated by the many who left Gibraltar after it was overtaken by the British. During the Franco era, the town's extensive industry was developed.

Orientation

Algeciras is on the western side of the Bahía de Algeciras, opposite Gibraltar. Avenida Virgen del Carmen runs north to south along the seafront, becoming Avenida de la Marina around the entrance to the port. From here Calle Juan de la Cierva (becoming Calle San Bernardo) runs inland beside a disused rail track to the bus station (350m) and the train station (400m). The central square, Plaza Alta, is a couple of blocks inland from Avenida Virgen del Carmen. Plaza Palma, with a bustling daily market (except Sunday), is one block west of Avenida de la Marina.

Information

Exchange rates for buying dirham (the Moroccan currency) are better at the banks than at travel agencies. There are banks and ATMs on Avenida Virgen del Carmen and around Plaza Alta, plus a couple of ATMs inside the port.

In the port, luggage storage (€3) is available from 7am to 9.30pm. If you have valuables there are lockers nearby (€3). The bus station also has luggage storage.

Hospital Punta de Europa (☎ 956 02 50 50; Carretera de Getares s/n) Three kilometres west of the centre.

Policía Nacional (☎ 956 66 04 00; Avenida de las Fuerzas Armadas 6) Next to Parque de María Cristina, northwest of the town centre.

Post office (☎ 956 58 74 05; Calle José Antonio) Just south of Plaza Alta.

Tourist office (☎ 956 57 26 36; Calle Juan de la Cierva s/n; ⏰ 10am-2pm Mon-Sat, plus 3.30-7pm Tue-Fri) A block inland from Avenida de la Marina. Friendly English-speaking staff.

Dangers & Annoyances

Be alert in the port, bus terminal and market in the evening. If you want to leave your vehicle in Algeciras, your most secure bet is the multistorey car park inside the port (€15 per 24 hours).

Sights & Activities

Wander up to the palm-fringed Plaza Alta, which is home to a lovely tiled fountain. On the plaza's western side sits the 18th-century **Iglesia Nuestra Señora de la Palma** and on its eastern side the 17th-century **Santuario Nuestra Señora Virgen de Europa**, both worth a look. A few houses dotted along the streets around the plaza are fetchingly tumbledown.

Leafy **Parque de María Cristina**, a few blocks to the north, provides a change from the hustle and bustle of the port. The **Museo Municipal** (☎ 956 57 06 72; Calle Nicaragua; admission free; ⏰ 9am-2pm Mon-Fri Jul-Sep, 9am-3pm & 5-7pm Oct-Jun), just south of the main tourist office, is reasonably interesting. If you've got your own wheels, check out the town's two beaches – **Playa Getares** (to the south) and **Playa del Rinconcillo** (to the north), which are kept quite clean.

Festivals & Events

Feria The town's nine-day fair, complete with bull fights, held 17 to 25 June.

Fiesta del Virgen de la Palma The town honours its patroness with a maritime pilgrimage on 15 August.

Sleeping

There's loads of budget accommodation in the streets behind Avenida de la Marina, but some of it's grim and market traffic in the small hours makes sleep difficult.

Hostal Marrakech (☎ 956 57 34 74; Calle Juan de la Cierva 5; s/d €20/30) This clean, secure place is run by a helpful Moroccan family. It has thoughtfully decorated rooms and an exotic communal lounge with TV.

Hostal Nuestra Señora de la Palma (☎ 956 63 24 81; Plaza Palma 12; s/d €25/35; ✗) Fronting the market, this friendly *hostal* has 26 comfortable rooms with TV. It's in earplug zone, though.

Hotel Marina Victoria (☎ 956 63 28 65; Avenida de la Marina 7; s/d €32/50; ✗) A solid choice with good rooms in a high-rise with excellent views over the port.

Hotel Al-Mar (☎ 956 65 46 61; Avenida de la Marina 2-3; s/d €51/100; P ✗) Two oversized Moroccan lamps decorate the foyer of this comfortable midrange place, which is handy for the port. There are 192 rooms, some with sea views and a good restaurant.

Hotel Reina Cristina (☎ 956 60 26 22; www.reina cristina.com in Spanish; Paseo de la Conferencia s/n; s/d €72/107; P ✗ 😊) This colonial-style hotel, just south of the port, has 188 olde-worlde rooms, and swimming pools set amid tropical gardens. Tales of it being a spy haunt in WWII intrigue: apparently they observed sea traffic in the Strait of Gibraltar from here.

Hotel Octavio (☎ 956 65 27 00; www.husa.es; Calle San Bernardo 1; s/d incl breakfast €107/123; P ✗)

Public spaces at the Octavio are a little shabby. But the 74 spacious rooms, with carpets, bright floral bedspreads, satellite TV and hairdryer, are a huge step up from most other places to stay in town.

Eating

Restaurante Montes (☎ 956 65 42 07; Calle Juan Morrison 27; menú €8, mains €8-18) Several blocks northwest of the tourist office, the slightly flashy Montes has a hugely popular lunch *menú* and a long list of delicious dishes such as *rape a la cazuela* (monkfish baked in a clay pot). Bar Montes on pedestrianised Calle Emilio Castelar is excellent for tapas.

Restaurante Casa María (☎ 956 65 47 02; Calle Emilio Castelar 53; menú €8, mains €10-18) Diagonally opposite Bar Montes, this is another popular lunch place. À la carte fish dishes come with various sauces and there are steaks. The *menú* looks especially good.

Restaurante Hotel Al-Mar (☎ 956 65 46 61; Avenida de la Marina 2-3; breakfast/lunch buffets €6/11, mains €14-22) Top-floor hotel restaurant with big glass windows and sweeping views of the port. This slightly refined restaurant offers

CÁDIZ PROVINCE

ALGECIRAS

0 — 200 m
0 — 0.1 miles

INFORMATION	
Moroccan Consulate	1 B2
Post Office	2 B1
Tourist Office	3 C2

SIGHTS & ACTIVITIES	
Iglesia Nuestra Señora de la Palma	4 B1
Santuario Nuestra Señora Virgen de Europa	5 B1

SLEEPING 🛏	
Hostal Marrakech	6 C2
Hostal Nuestra Señora de la Palma	7 B2
Hotel Al-Mar	8 C2
Hotel Marina Victoria	9 C2
Hotel Octavio	10 B3

EATING 🍴	
Bar Montes	11 B2
Café Mercedes	12 B1
Market	13 B2

Pastelería-Cafe La Dificultosa	14 B2
Restaurante Casa María	15 B2
Restaurante Hotel Al-Mar	(see 8)
Restaurante Montes	16 B2

TRANSPORT	
Bus Station	17 B3
Bus Stop Bacoma/Alsa/Enatcar	18 D2
Estación Marítima (Port)	19 D2
Information Puerto Algeciras	(see 19)
Multistorey Car Park	20 D2

daily specials as well as regional dishes. Good for coffee and pastries too.

The city **market** (Plaza Palma) has a wonderful array of fresh fruit, vegetables, hams and cheese, and a cheerful ambience. Nearby, **Pastelería-Cafe La Dificultosa** (Calle José Santacana; breakfast €8) is good for breakfast. Plaza Alta also has a couple of sidewalk cafés and restaurants. Try **Café Mercedes** (Plaza Alta; tapas €1.20) on the north side.

Entertainment

In the summer, flamenco, rock and classical music concerts are held at Parque de María Cristina and the Plaza de Toros. The tourist office has a list of events.

Getting There & Away

The daily paper *Europa Sur* has up-to-date transport arrival and departure details.

BOAT

The little office of **Information Puerto Algeciras** (☎ 956 58 54 63) in the port has all sailings information.

Trasmediterránea (☎ 956 58 75 06, 902 45 46 45; www.trasmediterranea.es), **EuroFerrys** (☎ 956 65 23 24; www.euroferrys.com) and other companies operate frequent passenger and vehicle ferries to/from Tangier and Ceuta, the Spanish enclave on the Moroccan coast. Usually at least 14 daily sailings go to each place. From mid-June to September ferries operate almost around the clock to cater for the Moroccan migration – you may have to queue for up to three hours. Buy your ticket in the port or at the agencies on Avenida de la Marina; prices are the same everywhere.

To Tangier, on a ferry taking 2½ hours, one-way fares for passenger/car/motorcycle over 500cc are €27/91/34. On a fast ferry (1¼ hours) one-way fares for passenger/car/motorcycle are €32/89/31.

To Ceuta, a fast ferry takes 35 minutes. One-way fares for passenger/car/motorcycle over 500cc are €25/81/19. **Buquebus** (☎ 902 41 42 42) also does Algeciras–Ceuta in 35 minutes for almost the same price, a little more for motorcycles.

BUS

Most buses leave from the bus station on Calle San Bernardo. **Comes** (☎ 956 65 34 56) buses go to La Línea (€1.80, 30 minutes) every half-hour (every 45 minutes on week-

ends) from 8.45am to 11.15pm. Other daily buses include the following:

Cádiz (€9.80, 2½ hours) Up to 10 daily.
Barbate (€5.50, 1¼ hours) One daily Monday to Friday.
Jimena de la Frontera (€3.60, 30 minutes) Three daily Monday to Friday, one daily Saturday.
Ronda (€9, 1½ hours) One daily Monday to Friday.
Seville (€15, 3½ hours) Up to four daily.
Tarifa (€1.70, 30 minutes) Up to 13 daily.
Zahara de los Atunes (€5, 1 hour) One daily Monday to Friday.

Daibus (☎ 956 65 34 56; www.daibus.es in Spanish) runs four daily buses to Madrid (€26, eight to nine hours) starting at the port then stopping at the Comes station.

Portillo (☎ 902 14 31 44; www.ctsa.portillo.com) operates at least 11 direct buses daily to Málaga (€10, 1¾ hours), four to Granada (€19, 3½ hours) and two to Jaén (€25, five hours). Several more services to Málaga (€10.50, three hours) stop at towns en route.

Bacoma/Alsa/Enatcar (☎ 902 42 22 42; www.alsa.es), inside the port, runs five services daily to Murcia, Alicante, Valencia and Barcelona. This company also runs daily buses to Portugal and thrice-weekly buses to France, Germany and Holland.

TRAIN

From the **station** (☎ 956 63 02 02), adjacent to Calle San Bernardo, two direct trains run daily to/from Madrid (€38 to €57, six or 11 hours) and three to/from Granada (€17, 4½ hours). All trains pass through Ronda (€6.50 to €17, 1¾ hours) and Bobadilla (€10.50 to €21, 2¾ hours) taking in some spectacular scenery en route. At Bobadilla you can change for Málaga, Córdoba and Seville plus more trains to Granada and Madrid.

GETTING AROUND

If driving in Algeciras, you're best to follow signs to the port, park and then walk as most places of interest are in the old centre or near the port.

LA LÍNEA DE LA CONCEPCIÓN
pop 63,000

La Línea, 20km east of Algeciras around the bay, is the unavoidable stepping stone to Gibraltar. The city was built in 1870 in response to the British expansion around the rock of Gibraltar. The increasing pedestrianisation of the centre is a huge improvement.

Orientation & Information

A left turn as you exit La Línea's bus station will bring you out on Avenida 20 de Abril, which runs the 300m between the town's main square, Plaza de la Constitución, and the Gibraltar border.

Municipal tourist office (☎ 956 17 19 98; Avenida Príncipe Felipe s/n; ☺ 8am-8pm Mon-Fri, 9am-2pm Sat) Facing the frontier.

Regional tourist office (☎ 956 76 99 50; ☺ 9am-3pm & 4-7.30pm Mon-Fri, 10am-2pm Sat & Sun) On the corner of Plaza de la Constitución.

Sights & Activities

La Línea's city centre has a couple of museums worth visiting. The **Museo del Istmo** (Plaza de la Constitución; admission free; ☺ 10am-2pm Tue-Sat plus 5-9pm Tue-Fri) has archaeological finds, paintings, sculptures and changing exhibitions. **Museo Cruz Herrera** (Calle Doctor Villar; admission free; ☺ 10am-2pm Tue-Sat, 5-9pm Tue-Fri), on palm-lined Plaza Fariñas, exhibits the work of José Cruz Herrera, a successful early-20th-century painter from La Línea. His subjects were often beautiful Andalucian women and he lived and worked for a time in Morocco, which is reflected in his paintings.

You can also visit **WWII bunkers** opposite Gibraltar, which face the frontier to the east and south of the Plaza de la Constitución; the tourist office has leaflets detailing the routes.

Sleeping & Eating

La Línea has around four midrange to top-end options. Cheaper rooms are around Plaza de la Constitución.

Hostal La Campana (☎ 956 17 30 59; Calle Carboneros 3; s/d €42/48) This super-friendly *hostal* just off the western side of Plaza de la Constitución has decent rooms with fan and TV. Its restaurant does a three-course *menú* (€7.50).

Hostal Carlos II (☎ 956 76 13 03; Calle Méndez Núñez 12; s/d €42/48; ✷) Another *hostal* with decent rooms, and this time with satellite TV. From the main plaza, walk to the end of pedestrianised Calle Real, which meets Plaza La Iglesia. Calle Méndez Núñez is off the southwest corner of this plaza.

AC La Linea (☎ 956 17 55 66; www.ac-hoteles.com; Calle Los Cairoles 2; r with pool view €77; Ⓟ ✷ 🖵 ⬛) For more luxury, stop at this stylish hotel a block back from the seafront and the main

drag, just a kilometre or so before the town centre.

La Pesquera (☎ 956 69 21 20; Avenida 20 de Abril; salads €4.50, mains around €9) You can sit here and look at Gibraltar, with the restaurant's palms and fountains in the foreground. A fabulous choice from a creative menu is the grilled salmon which is served on a stack of delicious vegetables. This place is best on a quiet weeknight.

Bar La Parada (☎ 956 12 16 69; Calle Duque 2; raciones €10) Head here for some excellent fried fish tapas and *raciones*. In fine weather you can sit outside under the dappled shade of the mature oak trees.

In the evening, check out Plaza del Pintor Cruz Herrera, with a pretty tiled fountain, orange trees, and places to drink.

Getting There & Away

BUS

Comes (☎ 956 17 00 93) runs buses about every 30 minutes (every 45 minutes on weekends) from 7.45am to 11.15pm to/from Algeciras (€1.80, 30 minutes). Buses also run to the following destinations:

Destination	Cost	Duration	Daily Frequency
Cádiz	€12	2½hr	4
Granada	€19	5hr	2
Seville	€19	4hr	4
Tarifa	€3.50	45min	8

Portillo also runs a bus service to Málaga (€10.50, 2½ hours, three to five daily) and Estepona (€3.50, one hour 20 minutes, eight daily).

CAR & MOTORCYCLE

Owing to the usually long vehicle queues at the Gibraltar border, many visitors to Gibraltar opt to park in La Línea and then walk across the border. Parking meters in La Línea cost €1 for one hour or €5 for six hours and are free from 8pm until 9am Monday to Friday and from 2pm Saturday until 9am Monday. Meters are plentiful on Avenida Príncipe Felipe opposite the frontier. The underground Parking Fo Cona, just off Avenida 20 de Abril, charges €1.90/14 per hour/day. Parking on the street in La Línea is fine but do not leave any items visible.

Gibraltar

When travelling by road to the British colony of Gibraltar, you can see this geological giant from afar but there are no road signs until the last minute. Seems bizarre, but this is a reminder that Spain still wants the 'Rock'. Gibraltar has been sought after since time immemorial for its strategic position guarding the entrance to the Mediterranean. It is one of the two Pillars of Hercules, split from the other, Jebel Musa in Morocco, that marked the edge of the ancient world of the Greeks and Romans.

This vast limestone ridge, 5km long and up to 1.6km wide, rises to 426m, with sheer cliffs on its northern and eastern sides. Along its lower western reaches clings a town of 30,000 inhabitants who are a mesmerising cultural melange of British, Jewish, Genoese, North African, Portuguese, Spanish, Maltese and Indian. Together these engaging people have created a thriving economy.

Gibraltar offers the visitor a terrific agenda. Get into its natural world and discover its animals, plants and caves, and the sea around them, which is home to dolphins and is visited by other creatures of the deep. Visit the military installations and mull over their old-fashioned names. Seek out the hidden nooks of quaint Gibraltar Town with its red letter boxes and phone booths. A pint at one of its quirky pubs is a fitting finale.

HIGHLIGHTS

- Enjoy refreshments and a Mediterranean ambience in a quasi-English setting at one of the cafés on Grand Casemates Sq in **Gibraltar Town** (p237)

- Whizz up to the top of the Rock in the **cable car** (p233) for smashing views of the Strait of Gibraltar, Morocco and the Bahía de Algeciras

- Get acquainted with Gibraltar's most unusual inhabitants at the **Apes' Den** (p233)

- Marvel at British ingenuity as you explore one of the best defence systems in the world in the **Upper Rock Nature Reserve** (p233)

- Seek out **dolphins** (p236) and whales in the Bahía de Algeciras

- **Dive** (p236) to the depths and discover the Rock's shipwrecks and fascinating marine life

| ■ POPULATION: 29,000 | ■ GIBRALTAR AV DAILY HIGH: JAN/AUG 15°C/24°C | ■ ALTITUDE RANGE: 0M–426M |

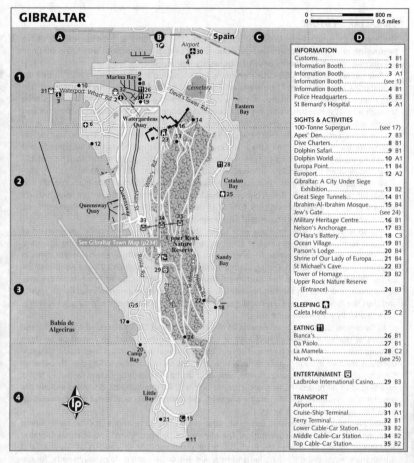

GIBRALTAR

0 ————— 800 m
0 ————— 0.5 miles

INFORMATION	
Customs...................................**1** B1
Information Booth.....................**2** B1
Information Booth.....................**3** A1
Information Booth..................(see 1)
Information Booth.....................**4** B1
Police Headquarters.................**5** B3
St Bernard's Hospital................**6** A1

SIGHTS & ACTIVITIES	
100-Tonne Supergun..............(see 17)
Apes' Den.................................**7** B3
Dive Charters...........................**8** B1
Dolphin Safari..........................**9** B1
Dolphin World.........................**10** A1
Europa Point...........................**11** B4
Europort..................................**12** A2
Gibraltar: A City Under Siege
Exhibition............................**13** B2
Great Siege Tunnels.................**14** B1
Ibrahim-Al-Ibrahim Mosque......**15** B4
Jew's Gate.............................(see 24)
Military Heritage Centre...........**16** B1
Nelson's Anchorage.................**17** B3
O'Hara's Battery.......................**18** C3
Ocean Village..........................**19** B1
Parson's Lodge.........................**20** B4
Shrine of Our Lady of Europa....**21** B4
St Michael's Cave.....................**22** B3
Tower of Homage.....................**23** B2
Upper Rock Nature Reserve
(Entrance)...........................**24** B3

SLEEPING 🛏	
Caleta Hotel............................**25** C2

EATING 🍴	
Bianca's...................................**26** B1
Da Paolo.................................**27** B1
La Mamela...............................**28** C2
Nuno's..................................(see 25)

ENTERTAINMENT 🎭	
Ladbroke International Casino...**29** B3

TRANSPORT	
Airport....................................**30** B1
Cruise-Ship Terminal................**31** A1
Ferry Terminal.........................**32** B1
Lower Cable-Car Station...........**33** B2
Middle Cable-Car Station..........**34** B2
Top Cable-Car Station..............**35** B2

HISTORY

Almost every square metre of Gibraltar can tell a tale as far back as the days of the last Neanderthals, as skulls discovered in 1848 and 1928 testify. The skull discovered in 1848 was that of a female; a find that predated the discovery of a male skull in Germany's Neander Valley by eight years. (The latter discovery inspired the anthropological term 'Neanderthal man', although 'Gibraltar woman' surely had the fairer claim.)

In historic times, Gibraltar's strategic position has made it an irresistible proposition to everyone from the Phoenicians on. Both the Phoenicians and the ancient Greeks left traces here, but Gibraltar really entered the history books in AD 711 when Tariq ibn Ziyad, the Muslim governor of Tangier, made it the initial bridgehead for the Islamic invasion of the Iberian Peninsula, landing with an army of some 10,000 men. The name Gibraltar is derived from Jebel Tariq (Tariq's Mountain).

The Almohad Muslims founded a town here in 1159 and were usurped by the Castilians in 1462. Then in 1704 an Anglo-Dutch fleet captured Gibraltar during the War of the Spanish Succession. Spain ceded the Rock of Gibraltar to Britain by the Treaty of Utrecht in 1713, but didn't give up military attempts to regain it until the failure of the Great Siege of 1779–83. In the aftermath of the capture of the Rock, most of the resident Spanish population fled and

GIBRALTAR'S FUTURE

The immediate future looks fairly rosy on the Rock. The economy is thriving, new talks have begun with Britain over modernising the colonial relationship, and relations with Spain continue to improve, though the thorny issue of sovereignty lies unresolved.

Over the last two years, Gibraltar's economy has continued to perform well, with around 8% annual growth in real terms. There are now 16,000 jobs in Gibraltar's economy mainly concerned with shipping, tourism and financial services. It is a real working port with over 9000 ships passing through annually. Investment on the Rock continues apace with a huge luxury, residential and commercial waterfront development on the western side of the Rock, Ocean Village, well under way, and a recently sealed deal with the same company to take over Marina Bay and update and regenerate the whole area. The idea is to create a world-class marina to rival Sotogrande and Puerto Banús (along the coast in Spain), to improve the visual appeal of the Rock, to provide luxury housing and to stimulate economic growth. A new Monaco in the making!

With regards to Old Blighty, discussions are taking place to modernise Gibraltar's constitution so that Gibraltar will remain British but in a noncolonial relationship. On a practical level, Britain's Ministry of Defence has handed over 40% of its land on Gibraltar to the Gibraltar government, thus releasing land for new homes and businesses.

And so to the big issue, relations with Spain. Shortly after the new Socialist government of José Luis Rodríguez Zapatero came to power in Spain in early 2004, Spain and Britain agreed to put Gibraltar on the back burner for a while. But the August 2004 tricentennial celebrations in Gibraltar upset the apple cart. During the celebrations, Gibraltar was given a 21-gun warship salute by the British HMAS *Grafton*, and both the British defence minister, Geoff Hoon (representative of a government backing the Iraq invasion), and Princess Anne (representative of British royalty and thus the 'occupier') were guests, all seen by the Spanish government as provocative. Things have thankfully moved on since then.

In December 2005, the governments of the UK, Spain and Gibraltar set up a new, trilateral process of dialogue where all decisions or agreements reached must be agreed by all three participants. The three sides have met several times, and real progress has been made. Valuable decisions reached include Spain's removal of restrictions on cruise ships sailing directly between Gibraltar and Spanish ports, and also the removal of the ban on Gibraltar-bound civilian air flights diverting, if at all necessary, to nearby Spanish airports. Further subjects discussed include the possibility of expanded use of Gibraltar's airfield, and a normalisation of telephonic communications between Gibraltar and Spain.

However, tricky topics remain. Britain has strategic military installations on Gibraltar including radar systems and a submarine station. The Ministry of Defence 'owns' and operates Gibraltar airport and more land around the Rock. Spain still wants outright sovereignty of Gibraltar, and Gibraltarians want self-determination and to retain British citizenship. Joint sovereignty, for the moment, doesn't seem to be the way ahead.

Few foresee a change in the status quo. However, the tripartite talks are thrashing out some of the practical problems that have hitherto created huge tensions between the three parties involved.

---

settled in what is now called the Campo de Gibraltar, the area around the Bahía de Algeciras (or the Bay of Gibraltar), incorporating towns such as San Roque, Algeciras and La Línea de la Concepción.

The British brought in Genoese ship repairers in the 18th century. Subsequently, Britain developed Gibraltar into an important naval base, and during WWII it became a base for allied landings in North Africa. The British garrison

was withdrawn in the early 1990s but the British navy continues to use Gibraltar's facilities. The constant shipping services and the free-port status only strengthened the relationship between the local population and Britain and continues to attract investment today.

In 1969 Francisco Franco closed the Spain–Gibraltar border (infuriated by a referendum in which the Gibraltarians voted by 12,138 to 44 to remain under British sovereignty). The result was the complete severing of cross-border relationships and the seemingly irrevocable polarisation of attitudes and sentiments in Gibraltar and Spain. The same year a new constitution committed Britain to respecting Gibraltarians' wishes over sovereignty, and gave Gibraltar domestic self-government and its own parliament, the House of Assembly. In 1985, just prior to Spain joining the EC (now the EU) in 1986, the border was opened after 16 long years, bringing a breath of fresh air to the Rock.

Today, tourism, the port and financial services are the mainstays of Gibraltar's economy. Of Gibraltar's civilian population, about 77% are classed as Gibraltarians, 14% as British and 9% as other nationalities. A substantial percentage of those of other nationalities are Moroccans, many of whom are on short-term work contracts.

GOVERNMENT & POLITICS

For six years, Gibraltar has been governed by the centre-right Gibraltar Social Democrat Party, led by Peter Caruana. The main opposition is the Gibraltar Socialist Labour Party, led by Joe Bossano. Caruana willingly talks with Spain about Gibraltar's future, but fiercely opposes any concessions over sovereignty.

Over the years, when Spain has wanted to exert pressure on Gibraltar, it has employed methods such as extra-thorough customs and immigration procedures, which cause hours-long delays at the border. Spain has proposed a period of joint British-Spanish sovereignty leading to Gibraltar eventually becoming the 18th Spanish region, with greater autonomy than any of the others.

Successive British governments have refused to give way over Gibraltar's sovereignty, but in March 2002 Spain and Britain came to a broad agreement about sharing sovereignty. The agreement was backed by the 15 member states of the EU but Gibraltar was not represented – and the Rock reacted angrily to this Europewide support for a deal over Gibraltar, allegedly set up by Britain's prime minister Tony Blair and his Spanish counterpart José María Aznar, who were great chums at the time.

In response, an estimated 20,000 Gibraltarians took to the streets on 18 March 2002 in a peaceful but passionate demonstration of their commitment to retaining British nationality. On 7 November 2002, the Gibraltar government held a referendum asking its people whether Britain should share sovereignty with Spain over Gibraltar. Gibraltarians rejected the idea resoundingly. Both Britain and Spain said they would not recognise the referendum, but the British government reiterated its position that it would not relinquish Gibraltar's status against local wishes.

As Gibraltar celebrated 300 years of British rule in 2004 it was obvious that most Gibraltarians no longer viewed Britain as the mother country. Although they still adore British traditions, they also adore their own particular way of life.

LANGUAGE

Gibraltarians speak English, Spanish and a curiously accented, singsong mix of the two, slipping back and forth from one to the other, often in midsentence. Signs are in English.

ORIENTATION

To reach Gibraltar by land you must pass through the Spanish frontier town of La Línea de la Concepción (p226). Just south of the border, the road crosses the runway of Gibraltar airport, which stretches east to west across the neck of the peninsula. The town and harbours of Gibraltar lie along the Rock's less-steep western side, facing the Bahía

---

VISAS & DOCUMENTS

To enter Gibraltar you need a passport or, for those EU nationalities that possess them, an identity card. Passport holders from Australia, Canada, the EU, Israel, New Zealand, Singapore, South Africa and the USA are among those who do not need visas for Gibraltar. For further information contact Gibraltar's **Immigration Department** (Map p234; ☎ 51725; Joshua Hassan House, Secretary's Lane). There is another office in the **Police Headquarters** (Map p229; ☎ 46411; rgpimm@gibgibtelecom.net; New Mole House, Rosia Rd).

Those who have a UK Multiple Visa (valid for one year or more) are eligible to enter Gibraltar without needing a second visa. For those intending to return or travel to Spain after visiting Gibraltar, a valid Schengen visa is essential to ensure re-entry to Spain.

GIBRALTAR

PUBLIC HOLIDAYS

New Year's Day 1 January
Commonwealth Day March (second Monday)
Good Friday 6 April 2007, 21 March 2008
Easter Monday 9 April 2007, 24 March 2008
May Day 1 May
Spring Bank Holiday May (last Monday)
Queen's Birthday June (Monday after the second Saturday)
Late Summer Bank Holiday August (last Monday)
Gibraltar National Day 10 September
Christmas Day 25 December
Boxing Day 26 December

---

de Algeciras. From Grand Casemates Sq, just inside Grand Casemates Gate, Main St with all the shops runs south for about 1km.

INFORMATION
Bookshops
Good places to stock up on English-language reading material include the following:
Bell Books (Map p234; ☎ 76707; 11 Bell Lane)
Gibraltar Bookshop (Map p234; ☎ 71894; 300 Main St)

Electricity
Electric current is the same as in Britain, 220V or 240V, with plugs of three flat pins.

Emergency
The police wear British uniforms.
Emergency (☎ 199) For the police or an ambulance.
Police Headquarters (Map p229; ☎ 72500; Rosia Rd) In the south of the town at New Mole House.
Police Station (Map p234; ☎ 72500; 120 Irish Town)

Foreign Consulates
Fourteen countries, mostly European, have consulates in Gibraltar. Tourist offices can provide you with lists of these.

Internet Access
PC Clinic & Computer Centre (Map p234; ☎ 49991; cnr Convent Pl & Governor's St; per hr £3; ☺ 9.30am-6.30pm Mon-Fri)

Internet Resources
For useful Gibraltar-specific websites try the following:
www.gibraltar.gi
www.gibraltar.gov.uk Maintained by the government of Gibraltar.

Medical Services
Primary Care Centre (Map p234; ☎ 72355; ICI Bldg, Grand Casemates Sq)
St Bernard's Hospital (Map p229; ☎ 79700; Europort) Offers 24-hour emergency facilities.

Money
The currencies in Gibraltar are the Gibraltar pound and the pound sterling, which are interchangeable. You can use euros (except in payphones and post offices) but you'll get a better value if you convert them into pounds. Exchange rates for buying euros are a bit better here than in Spain. You can't use Gibraltar money outside Gibraltar, so it's worth requesting change in British coins and changing any unspent Gibraltar pounds before you leave.

Banks are open between 9am and 3.30pm Monday to Friday. There are several (with ATMs) on Main St. There are also exchange offices, which are usually open longer hours.

Post
Main post office (Map p234; 104 Main St; ☺ 9am-2.15pm Mon-Fri & 10am-1pm Sat mid-Jun–mid-Sep, 9am-4.30pm Mon-Fri & 10am-1pm Sat mid-Sep–mid-Jun)

Telephone
To phone Gibraltar from Spain, precede the five-digit local number with the code ☎ 9567; from other countries dial the international access code, then ☎ 350 (Gibraltar's country code) and the local number. It costs €0.11 plus €0.12 per minute to phone Gibraltar from a private line anywhere in Spain. Calls from a phone box cost 50% more. Mobile-phone numbers are all eight-digit numbers beginning with a ☎ 5.

In Gibraltar you can make international as well as local calls from street payphones. To make a call to Spain, just dial the nine-digit number. Calls to Spain from a private line cost 15p per minute from 8am to 8pm, 11p per minute from 8pm to 8am and on weekends and public holidays. Calls to Spain from a phone booth cost 25p per minute.

To make a call to any other country, dial the international access code (☎ 00), followed by the country code, area code and number.

Tourist Information

Gibraltar Tourist Board (Map p234; ☎ 45000, 74950; www.gibraltar.gov.gi; Duke of Kent House, Cathedral Sq; ⏱ 9am-5.30pm Mon-Fri) Very helpful with plenty of free information sheets and brochures.

Information booths airport (Map p229; ☎ 73026; ⏱ Mon-Fri, mornings only); coach park (Map p229; ☎ 78198; Waterport Wharf Rd; ⏱ 9am-4.30pm Mon-Fri, 10am-1pm Sat); cruise-ship terminal (Map p229; ☎ 47670; ⏱ only when a cruise liner is in port); customs (Map p229; ☎ 50762; Frontier; ⏱ 9am-4.30pm Mon-Fri & 10am-1pm Sat)

Tourist office (Map p234; ☎ 74982; Grand Casemates Sq; ⏱ 9am-5.30pm Mon-Fri, 10am-3pm Sat, 10am-1pm Sun & public holidays)

SIGHTS

Most of the interesting things to see are on the upper parts of the Rock or in Gibraltar Town on the Rock's western shore.

Upper Rock

Naturally, the most impressive feature of Gibraltar is the Rock itself, a huge pinnacle of limestone, with sheer sides rising some 426m. Most of the upper parts of the Rock are a nature reserve with spectacular views. Tickets for the **Upper Rock Nature Reserve** (adult/child/vehicle £8/4/1.50, pedestrians excl attractions £1; ⏱ 9.30am-7pm, last visit 6.45pm) include entry to St Michael's Cave, the Apes' Den, the Great Siege Tunnels, the Military Heritage Centre, the Tower of Homage and the 'Gibraltar: A City Under Siege' exhibition. The upper Rock is home to 600 plant species and is ideal for observing the migrations of birds between Europe and Africa (see the boxed text, p220).

The Rock's most famous inhabitants are the tailless Barbary Macaques, the only free-living primates in Europe. Some of the 240 apes hang around the **Apes' Den** near the middle cable-car station; the others can often be seen at the top cable-car station and the Great Siege Tunnels. Legend has it that when the apes (which may have been introduced from North Africa in the 18th century) disappear from Gibraltar, so will the British. When numbers were at a low ebb during WWII, the British brought in simian reinforcements from Africa. Recently, however, their numbers have been increasing rapidly and a range of control measures from contraceptive implants to 'translocation' to European zoos have been implemented. Summer is the ideal time to see newborn apes, but keep a safe distance to avoid their sharp teeth and short tempers for which they are well known. For those who are nervous around animals or who are with very small children it may be worth considering a guided tour as the official guides know the moods and habits of the apes. Gibraltar's **Ornithological & Natural History Society** (☎ 72639) is happy to provide details about the apes.

To reach the Apes' Den and the upper Rock take the **cable car** (see p239). At the top station there are breathtaking views over the Bahía de Algeciras and across the Strait of Gibraltar to Morocco if the weather is clear. You can also look down the sheer precipices of the Rock's eastern side to the biggest of the old water catchments, which channelled rain into underground reservoirs.

About 15 minutes' walk south down St Michael's Rd from the top cable-car station, O'Hara's Rd leads up to the left to **O'Hara's Battery**, an emplacement of big guns on the Rock's summit. A few minutes further down (or 20 minutes up from the Apes' Den) is the extraordinary **St Michael's Cave** (St Michael's Rd; admission £2; ⏱ 9.30am-7pm), a huge natural grotto full of stalagmites and stalactites. In the past, people thought the cave was a possible subterranean link with Africa and, needless to say, its size is impressive. Today, apart from attracting tourists in droves, it's used for concerts, plays and even fashion shows. For a more extensive look at the cave system the **Lower St Michael's Cave Tour** (£5; ⏱ Wed after 6pm, Sat after 2.30pm) is a three-hour guided adventure into the lower cave area, which ends at an underground lake. This tour involves scrambling and minor climbing with ropes, so a reasonable degree of physical fitness and appropriate footwear are essential. The cave is in its original state but is fully lit. Children must be over 10 years old. Contact the tourist office (left) to arrange your guide.

About 30 minutes' walk north (downhill) from the top cable-car station is Princess Caroline's Battery, housing the **Military Heritage Centre**. From here one road leads down to the Princess Royal Battery – more gun emplacements – while another leads up to the **Great Siege Tunnels** (or Upper Galleries), a complex defence system hewn out of the Rock by the British during the siege of 1779–83 to provide gun emplacements. They constitute only a tiny proportion of more than 70km of tunnels and galleries in the Rock, most of which are off limits to the public.

GIBRALTAR

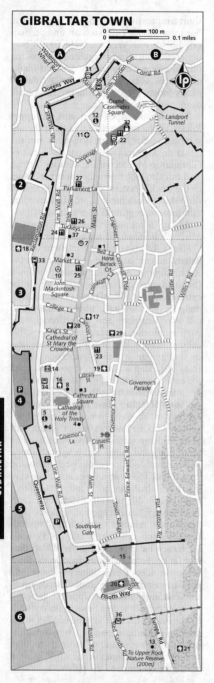

GIBRALTAR TOWN

0   100 m
0   0.1 miles

However, new Ministry of Defence Tunnel Tours can now take you through the WWII caves (tours £2) where the Allied invasion of North Africa was planned. Contact the tourist office for details.

On Willis' Rd, the way down to the town from Princess Caroline's Battery, you'll find the **'Gibraltar: A City Under Siege' exhibition**, in the first British building on the Rock (originally an ammunition store), and the **Tower of Homage**, the remains of Gibraltar's Islamic castle built in 1333. The tower has been undergoing extensive renovations for a couple of

GIBRALTAR

years and at the time of writing there was no date set for its opening (check with the tourist office for up-to-date information).

Gibraltar Town

Gibraltar's town centre generates an engaging midmorning Mediterranean buzz, although there is an emphatically British flavour about the shops, pubs and restaurants that line either side of the pedestrianised Main St. A Spanish lilt in the air and the fairly regular sight of Moroccans in traditional dress are reminders that this little slice of Blighty is still part of Mediterranean Europe and was a Muslim stronghold for over seven centuries and a Spanish one for 240 years.

Nowadays, the entire Rock reflects 300 years of British military and bureaucratic administration, literally bristling with the often antique remnants of British fortifications, gates and gun emplacements. The *Guided Tour of Gibraltar* booklet by TJ Finlayson is rewarding if you want to delve into details of the British heritage. It's available from the Gibraltar Museum for £2.

To get acquainted with Gibraltar's cultural melange and volatile history visit the **Gibraltar Museum** (Map p234; ☎ 74289; Bomb House Lane; adult/child under 12yr £2/1; 🕑 10am-6pm Mon-Fri, 10am-2pm Sat) which contains an extensive, if in some cases odd, assortment of historical, architectural and military displays dating back to prehistoric times. Highlights include a well-preserved 14th-century Arab bathhouse and a cast of the 100,000-year-old female skull discovered in Forbes Quarry on the Rock's northern face in 1848 (the original is now in the Natural History Museum in London).

A more poignant lesson in history can be found in the atmospherically overgrown **Trafalgar Cemetery** (Map p234; Prince Edward's Rd; 🕑 9am-7pm), just south of Southport Gate. The graves are those of British sailors who died at Gibraltar after the Battle of Trafalgar (1805). Further south, **Nelson's Anchorage** (Map p229; Rosia Rd; admission £1; 🕑 9.30am-6.15pm Mon-Sat) pinpoints the site where Nelson's body was brought ashore from HMS *Victory* – preserved in a rum barrel, so legend says. A **100-tonne Victorian supergun**, made in Britain in 1870, commemorates the spot. A little further south is **Parson's Lodge** (Map p229; Rosia Rd; adult/child £2/1; 🕑 10am-5pm Tue-Sun), a gun battery atop a 40m cliff. Beneath the gun emplacements is a labyrinth of tunnels with former ammunition stores and living quarters.

SMUGGLERS' COVE

Once a den of smugglers who supplied the mountain bandits of Ronda with contraband, Gibraltar in the 21st century has continued to receive complaints from the Spanish authorities about the smuggling of physical goods and also about the alleged laundering of illicit funds that end up invested in construction or property in Spain.

Thanks to Gibraltar's VAT-free status, goods such as electronics, chocolates and cigarettes cost less than in Spain, but the much greater availability of electronics and chocolate in Spain in recent years has greatly reduced the demand for smuggled goods. Gibraltar has also dealt tobacco smugglers a major blow by banning from its waters the superfast motor launches used by the smugglers. But to combat smuggling of cigarettes across the land border, customs checks can still be very lengthy and customs police are constantly rotated in an attempt to thwart underhand deals.

Spain continues to complain from time to time – such as during the Ballena Blanca (White Whale) case, which in 2005 brought the arrests of over 40 people allegedly connected with a Marbella-centred network laundering the proceeds of international organised crime – that Gibraltar fails to assist in efforts to combat this kind of thing. The Gibraltar authorities maintain that despite the tax advantages enjoyed by offshore companies registered on the Rock, its financial regulatory system is rigorous enough to prevent money laundering. In 2002 Gibraltar committed itself to make its regulatory system more transparent, and although Gibraltar is recognised as a tax haven, it is not on the list of 'uncooperative' tax havens produced by the Organisation for Economic Cooperation & Development (OECD). Gibraltar's tax-haven status is in any case due to come to an end by 2010.

History aside, take some time to meander through the **Alameda Botanical Gardens** (Map p234; Europa Rd; admission free; ☺ 8am-sunset), the lushly overgrown scene of Molly Bloom's famous deflowering in James Joyce's *Ulysses*.

Europa Point

The southern tip of Gibraltar is known as **Europa Point**, the location of Gibraltar's first lighthouse, sacked by the infamous corsair (pirate) Barbarossa. It is also the site of the Christian **Shrine of Our Lady of Europe** (Map p229; ☎ 71230; ☺ 10am-1pm & 2-7pm Mon-Fri, 11am-1pm & 2-7pm Sat & Sun), whose 15th-century statue of the Virgin and Child was miraculously unscathed during the pirate's devastating attack. Nearby, a symbol of the racial and religious symbiosis of Gibraltar's past and, to some degree its present, is the **Ibrahim-Al-Ibrahim Mosque**, opened in 1997. It was built at the behest of King Fahd of Saudi Arabia to cater for all the Moroccans working on the Rock and is said to be the largest mosque in a non-Islamic country.

ACTIVITIES
Dolphin Watching

The Bahía de Algeciras has a sizable year-round population of dolphins and visiting dolphins. At least three companies run dolphin-watching trips that are really fun. From about April to September most outfits make two or more daily trips; at other times of the year they make at least one trip daily, depending on the weather and numbers. Most of the boats go from Watergardens Quay or the adjacent Marina Bay, north-west of the town centre. Trips last 1½ to 2½ hours and the cost per adult is around £20. Children go for around half price. You'll be unlucky if you don't get plenty of close-up dolphin contact, and you may even come across whales. Two possibilities for trips are **Dolphin World** (Map p229; ☎ 54481000; www.dolphin safari.gi; Ferry Terminal, Waterport; adult/child under 12yr £20/10) and **Dolphin Safari** (Map p229; ☎ 71914; Marina Bay; adult/child under 12yr £20/15) – you need to book.

Diving

Around the Rock there is also some surprisingly good (and reasonably priced) diving. The Rock has its own unique sea life and underwater landscape, with many wrecks.

There are at least three dive companies. **Dive Charters** (Map p229; ☎ 45649; www.divegib.gi; 4 Admiral's Walk, Marina Bay) runs a variety of dives from £30 to £50, plus £10 for equipment, including an exciting night dive.

Beaches

To escape from the town for a spot of sunbathing take bus 4 from Line Wall Rd (every 15 minutes) to **Catalan Bay**, a tiny fishing village on the eastern side of the Rock. Its early inhabitants were Genoese and reputedly had red hair.

TOURS

Taxi drivers will take you on a 1½-hour 'Official Rock Tour' of Gibraltar's main sights for £16 per person (minimum four people) plus the cost of admission to the Upper Rock Nature Reserve. Most drivers are knowledgeable. Many travel agents run tours of the same sights for £12.50.

Bland Travel (Map p234; ☎ 77012; 81 Irish Town), **Parodytur** (Map p234; ☎ 76070; Cathedral Sq) and **Exchange Travel** (Map p234; ☎ 76151; 241 Main St) offer guided day trips to Tangier for £45 including lunch.

SLEEPING

Cannon Hotel (Map p234; ☎ 51711; www.cannonhotel .gi; 9 Cannon Lane; s/d with shared bathroom incl breakfast £25.50/37.50, d incl breakfast £46) An attractive small hotel with 18 rooms right in the main shopping centre of Gibraltar Town. Rooms are modestly kitted out with pine furnishings and some overlook an appealing patio. A great location within walking distance of all the major sights and good value for money.

Herald Travel Lettings (Map p234; ☎ 712350; www.gibraltar.gi/herald; Suite No 1E Ocean Heights; apt £40-75; 🏊) Good apartments from studios to two bedroom in a block just a minute or two from Grand Casemates Sq. There are cheaper prices by the week and month; weekly cleaning and use of a communal swimming pool are extra bonuses. Free street parking is plentiful nearby.

Queen's Hotel (Map p234; ☎ 74000; www.queens hotel.gi; 1 Boyd St; s/d incl breakfast £50/65; Ⓟ 🏊) A large, pink, modern monstrosity, Queen's Hotel is not the most attractive sight. However, rooms have recently been spruced up and it does offer good discounts of 20% to students and travellers under the age of 25.

Bristol Hotel (Map p234; ☎ 76800; www.gibraltar.gi
/bristolhotel; 10 Cathedral Sq; s/d without sea views
£49/64, s/d with sea views £62/79; P ☒ ☒) This
hotel, with its pretty walled garden and
swimming pool, is centrally located. Many
of the 60 recently refurbished rooms have
lovely sea views. Parking is available but
you must request it when booking your
room.

Caleta Hotel (Map p229; ☎ 76501; www.caletahotel
.gi; Sir Herbert Miles Rd; d with/without sea view £140/125;
P ☒ ☐ ☒) Gibraltar's best four-star
hotel in a wonderful location overlooking
Catalan Bay (five minutes from town). On
the edge of a rocky outcrop the cascading
terraces have panoramic sea views, and a
host of gym and spa facilities make this a
truly posh option. It does special deals.

Rock Hotel (Map p234; ☎ 73000; www.rockhotel
gibraltar.com; 3 Europa Rd; d with/without balcony £180/175;
P ☒ ☐ ☒) Built by the Marquis of Bute
in 1932 this institution has hosted the likes
of Winston Churchill and Noel Coward.
The Rock Hotel was recently modernised
and the lavish service includes bathrobes,
CD players and free parking.

O'Callaghan Eliott Hotel (Map p234; ☎ 70500;
www.ocallaghanhotels.com; 2 Governor's Parade; d £230-
260, ste £300-600; P ☒ ☐ ☒) Located in
a leafy square the O'Callaghan Eliott has
sumptuous rooms, fittings and furnishings
and a range of facilities such as a gym and
rooftop pool plus a gorgeous rooftop restaurant. Its new Hollywood-style entrance,
balconies and restaurant come courtesy of
recent Irish investment.

If you feel daunted by Gibraltar's prices,
there are economical options in the Spanish frontier town of La Línea de la Concepción (p226).

EATING

Most of the many pubs in Gibraltar do
typical British pub meals. However, there's
plenty more scintillating food to be had
around town. Start with the cafés and restaurants on the lower levels of the former
barracks surrounding the main square,
Grand Casemates.

Clipper (Map p234; ☎ 79791; 78B Irish Town; mains
£3.50-6, roast £4) One of the best and busiest
pubs, all varnished wood with full-on football and a cracking Sunday roast. Vegetarians should go for the tasty Greek salad wrap.
Friendly service.

Figaro (Map p234; 9 Market Lane; mains £4-8) More
commonly referred to as the 'Tea Room',
this neat café-cum-restaurant serves up traditional scones, jam and cream and it does
some good lunchtime specials too.

Café Solo (Map p234; ☎ 44449; Grand Casemates Sq 3;
pastas £6-9) With tables inside, and out on the
square where there is always a buzz, this is a
good place to stop for coffees and a variety of
pastas with tantalising fillings and sauces.

Cannon Bar (Map p234; ☎ 77288; 27 Cannon Lane;
mains £5.50-9.50, fish & chips £5.50) Justifiably famous for some of the best fish and chips
in town, and in big portions. It also does
steak-and-kidney pie and salads.

Star Bar (Map p234; ☎ 75924; 12 Parliament Lane;
breakfast £3.50-5, mains £5-11; ☼ 24hr) Gibraltar's
oldest bar, if the house advertising is to be
believed, the Star Bar is still one of its best
having won the Golden Egg Award at least
five years in a row. Hearty main dishes include lamb chops, Irish fillet, and hake in a
Spanish-style green sauce.

House of Sacarello (Map p234; ☎ 70625; 57 Irish
Town; daily specials £7-11.50; ☼ closed Sun; V) A
chic place in a converted coffee warehouse
that has a good range of vegetarian options
and some tasty homemade soups. You can
linger over afternoon tea (£3.50) between
3pm and 7.30pm. It also hosts regular art
exhibitions.

La Mamela (Map p229; ☎ 72373; Catalan Bay; mains
£5.50-13.50) An excellent and atmospheric
fish eatery located right on Catalan Bay at
the southern end of the beach. Dust the
sand off your feet and sit down to a range
of hearty paellas and fish stews. Meat fans
can enjoy a peppercorn steak.

Nuno's (Map p229; ☎ 76501; Caleta Hotel, Sir Herbert Miles Rd; mains £11-15) A top-class, formal
Italian restaurant in the Caleta Hotel with
fabulous terrace views. Delicious home-
made pastas and risottos, or tender leg of
lamb roasted for seven hours, are accompanied by an extensive wine list. Come
here for a stylish and romantic evening
meal.

At Marina Bay, a little out of the centre,
there's a line of pleasant waterside cafés
and restaurants including **Bianca's** (Map p229;
☎ 73379; 6-7 Admiral's Walk, Marina Bay; mains £9-12),
which has fairly exotic flavours and is a
huge local favourite for an early-evening
drink. Nearby **Da Paolo** (Map p229; ☎ 76799;
Unit B, The Tower, Admiral's Walk; mains £12; ☼ closed

GIBRALTAR

Sun) is slightly more formal and serves international cuisine with flair: choose from the likes of lobster bisque, veg tartlets and seafood crepes.

There are more restaurants on the waterfront at Queensway Quay.

DRINKING

There are drinking dives, haunts and respectable places all over the lower Rock but here are a couple of special ones.

Get Joost Smoothie Bar (Map p234; 240 Main St; £3.50) Australian-run bar serving fresh juice and energising drinks with fantastic fruit and veg combos. All Australians know what a smoothie is and the objective here is to let Europe know too.

Three Roses Bar (Map p234; ☎ 51614; 60 Governor's St; ☼ 11am-late) This is Gibraltar's unofficial 'Scottish Embassy', with Scottish drinks a speciality.

ENTERTAINMENT

Several of Gibraltar's pubs put on live music from pop to rock, jazz to folk. Grand Casemates Sq is really the centre of the action with many of its daytime bistro-cafés becoming bars at night. **Lord Nelson's** (Map p234; ☎ 50009; Grand Casemates Sq 10) kicks on until later than most with live music starting as late as 2am. Just outside the square by the town walls, the **UnderGround** (Map p234; ☎ 40651; 8 West Place of Arms) has two dance floors and an open-air terrace.

Concerts and other performances are staged in the atmospheric venue of St **Michael's Cave** (Map p229; St Michael's Rd); check with the tourist offices for details. The **Ladbroke International Casino** (Map p229; ☎ 76666; 7 Europa Rd) offers casino gaming and slot machines, and also has live entertainment, a disco and restaurant. No membership or passport is needed and smart casual wear is accepted.

SHOPPING

Gibraltar has lots of British high-street chain stores, and Morrisons supermarket (in the Europort development at the northern end of the main harbour). **Gibraltar Crystal** (Map p234; ☎ 50136; Grand Casemates Sq) produces elegant glassware on its premises and gives free demonstrations. Shops are normally open 9am to 7.30pm Monday to Friday and until 1pm Saturday.

GETTING THERE & AWAY

The border is open 24 hours daily. Give yourself ample time if you are heading out of Gibraltar to catch a bus from La Línea. Vehicles and pedestrians are delayed from crossing the airport runway for a minimum of five minutes when flights are landing or taking off – there are two to three flights a day. You may also be delayed passing through Spanish customs, where bag searches are usually perfunctory, but may be time-consuming.

Air

At the time of writing, the only flights serving Gibraltar Airport (☎ 73026) were to/from the UK. **GB Airways** (☎ 79300; www .gbairways.com; Gibraltar Airport) flies daily to/from London Gatwick and Heathrow airports. **Monarch Airlines** (☎ 47477; www.flymonarch.com; Gibraltar Airport) flies daily to/from London Luton and Manchester.

Boat

There is only one ferry (adult one-way/return £23/41, child one-way/return £11.50/20, car one-way/return £46/92, 70 minutes) a week between Gibraltar and Tangier (Morocco) departing Gibraltar at 6pm on Friday. The ferry leaves from the terminal in front of the coach park. In Gibraltar, you can buy tickets for the ferry at **Turner & Co** (Map p234; ☎ 78305; turner@gibnynex.gi; 67 Irish Town). Booking ahead is advised. Ferries to and from Tangier are more frequent from Algeciras (p226).

For information on the Gibraltar–Tangier and Algeciras–Tangier ferries, see www .frs.es.

Bus

Buses from Spain do not terminate within Gibraltar itself, but the bus station in La Línea de la Concepción (p227) is only a short walk from the border, from where there are frequent buses into Gibraltar's town centre (see Map p234).

GETTING AROUND

The 1.5km walk from the border to the town centre is entertaining, not least because it crosses the airport runway. A left turn (south) off Corral Rd will take you through the pedestrian-only Landport Tunnel (once the only land entry through

Gibraltar's walls) into Grand Casemates Sq and on to Main St.

All of Gibraltar can be covered on foot and much of it (including the upper Rock) by car or motorcycle, but there are other options worth considering. The late 18th-century 'Mediterranean Steps' that link paths up to O'Hara's Battery, the highest point of the Rock, are closed as they're considered to be dangerous. The route started at Jew's Gate, the entrance to the Upper Rock Nature Reserve.

Bus

Buses 3, 9 and 10 go from the border into town about every 15 minutes on weekdays, and every 30 minutes on Saturday and Sunday. Bus 9 goes to Market Place (Grand Casemates Gate). It runs between 7am and 9pm Monday to Saturday and from 9am to 9pm on Sunday. Bus 3 goes to Cathedral Sq and the lower cable-car station and then on to Europa Point. It runs between 6.25am and 9pm Monday to Saturday and from 8am to 9pm on Sunday. Bus 10 goes from the border to Europort (with a stop at Morrisons supermarket), then via Queens Way to Reclamation Rd near the town centre. Bus 4 connects Catalan Bay on the Rock's eastern side with the centre and Europort. All buses cost adult/child/senior 60/40/30p per trip.

Cable Car

An obvious way to explore Gibraltar is via the **cable car** (Map p229; ☎ 77826; Red Sands Rd; adult one-way/return £6.50/8, child one-way/return £4/4.50; ⏰ 9.30am-5pm Mon-Sat). Tickets at the prices shown do not include admission to the attractions on the upper Rock (see p233). For the Apes' Den, disembark at the middle station. You can get back on to go up to the top station. The operation of the cable car may be halted during periods of bad weather, especially if wind speeds are very high. The cable car runs every few minutes, with the last cable car going down at 4.45pm.

Car & Motorcycle

Gibraltar's streets are congested and parking can be difficult. Vehicle queues at the border often make it less time-consuming to park in La Línea, then walk across the border. To take a car into Gibraltar you need an insurance certificate, registration document, nationality plate and a valid driving licence. You do not have to pay any fee: some people driving into Gibraltar have been cheated of a dozen or so euros by con artists claiming you need to pay to take a vehicle across the border. In Gibraltar, driving is on the right, as in Spain. There are car parks on Line Wall Rd and Reclamation Rd (Map p229), and at the Airport Car Park on Winston Churchill Ave; the hourly charge at these car parks is 80p.

Málaga Province

Though best known for the urban excitements of the Costa del Sol resorts and Málaga city, this province is also endowed with tremendous natural beauty. It has rugged mountains and a gorgeous coastline in the east where cliffs drop to pretty coves and bays. Inland in winter almonds show their white blossoms and plump olives glisten with the morning dew. This wonderful landscape offers a range of activities from hiking and canoeing to abseiling and horse riding. It also has a stunning architectural heritage in the elegant old towns of Ronda and Antequera, and the picturesque white villages of the interior.

Bustling Málaga city, the second-biggest metropolis in Andalucía, has a rich cultural scene, recently much enhanced by the opening of its state-of-the-art Picasso Museum, and is also a great place to go out and have fun. It has many characterful late-night bars dotted around its atmospheric old centre.

Along the coasts stretch what can seem nothing more than an endless purgatory of concrete and noise. Yet if you want to party and have fun on the beach, or let your hair down at a theme park, the Costa del Sol is perhaps the best place in Andalucía to do it – and the same party spirit infuses the many colourful local fiestas throughout the province.

HIGHLIGHTS

- Soak up the vibrant street life of Málaga and catch the coast's most ebullient festivals, the **Feria de Málaga** (p257), Marbella's **Feria de San Bernabé** (p273) and **Día de la Virgen del Carmen** (p268) in Fuengirola

- Get up close with the stunning Picasso collection at Málaga's **Museo Picasso** (p245) or step back in time at its **Castillo de Gibralfaro** (p245)

- Come to grips with the history of bullfighting, brought to life in the **Feria de Pedro Romero** (p281) at stunningly located Ronda

- Scale the spectacular limestone walls of **El Chorro gorge** (p287)

- Explore the spectacular back country around Ronda, especially the **Parque Natural Sierra de las Nieves** (p285)

- POPULATION: 1.45 MILLION
- MÁLAGA AV DAILY HIGH: JAN/AUG 13°C/26°C
- ALTITUDE RANGE: 0M–2069M

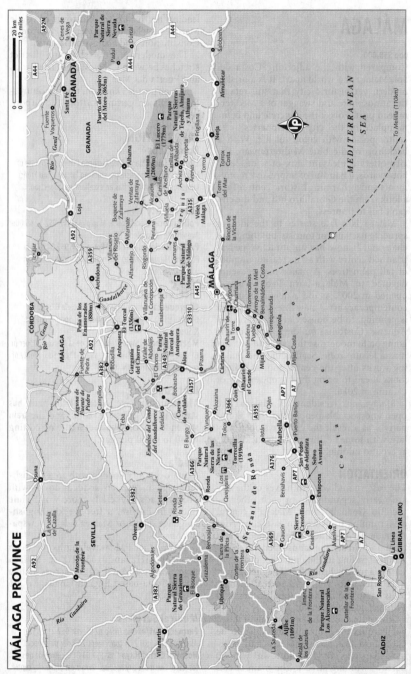

MÁLAGA

pop 558,000

Compared with the adjoining Costa del Sol, Málaga is a world apart. It is a briskly modern yet historic city that still retains the atmosphere and swagger of a Mediterranean port. Forget the concrete and commonplace of the city's peripheries – its centre pulses with colourful life. With a backdrop of the blue Mediterranean, the city offers a pleasant mix of wide, leafy boulevards, a handful of impressive monuments and a charming historic centre. Take a look from the Gibralfaro hill and the city can't fail to impress.

Málaga is a late starter to the idea of sprucing itself up for tourists, but things are changing. It now has an attractive pedestrianised centre with an increasing number of tall palm trees. A major new museum devoted to Málaga-born Pablo Picasso opened in 2003, as did a new museum of contemporary art. A new fine-arts museum is pending, to be housed in the impressive Aduana (Customs) building, and work is going on to modernise the port and develop it as a leisure zone. Scaffolding and building works litter the centre, too, as Málaga looks ahead to being the European City of Culture in 2016.

Malagueños (residents of Málaga) are open and sociable people and they like to party – as a result the city stays open very late, with some healthy nightlife kicking off at around midnight.

ORIENTATION

The eastern and western halves of the city are neatly separated from each other by the Río Guadalmedina. Málaga's central axis, running from west to east, comprises Avenida de Andalucía, the Alameda Principal and finally the landscaped Paseo del Parque (ending in the upmarket district of La Malagueta). From La Malagueta, Avenida Pries takes you, with several changes to its name, out to the eastern beaches of El Pedregalejo and El Palo.

Rising up above the eastern half of Paseo del Parque, the Alcazaba and Castillo de Gibralfaro dominate the city and overlook the *casco antiguo* (old town) with its narrow, winding streets. The main streets leading north into the old town are Calle Marqués de Larios, ending at Plaza de la Constitución, and Calle Molina Lario.

The modern central shopping district stretches between Calles Marqués de Larios and Puerta del Mar.

The airport is 9km from the city centre – for details on getting to/from the airport, see p263.

INFORMATION
Bookshops

Librería Luce (Map p246; Alameda Principal 16) One of Málaga's largest bookshops, stocking English- and French-language titles. It also has an excellent travel section.

Emergency

Policía Local (Local Police; Map p243; ☎ 952 12 65 00; Avenida de la Rosaleda 19)
Policía Nacional (National Police; ☎ 952 04 62 00; Plaza de Manuel Azaña) The main police station is 3km west of the centre.

Internet Access

Ciberquetzal (Map p246; Calle Carretería 67; per hr €1.20; ⏰ 10.30am-10.30pm Mon-Fri, 5pm-10pm Sat & Sun)
Meeting Point (Map p246; Plaza de la Merced 20; per hr €1-2; ⏰ 10am-1am Mon-Sat, 11am-11pm Sun) Plenty of computers, and friendly staff.

Left Luggage

There are baggage lockers at the main **bus station** (Map p243; Paseo de los Tilos) and the **train station** (Map p243; Explanada de la Estación), costing €2.40 to €4.50 per day.

Media

Costa del Sol is flooded with free English-language magazines loaded down with property ads. Generally more worthwhile is *Sur in English,* a free weekly English-language digest of Málaga's daily newspaper *Sur.*

Roam the FM wavelengths between about 97MHz and 105MHz in Málaga province and you'll come across half a dozen Costa-based English-language radio stations.

Medical Services

Farmacia Caffarena (Map p246; ☎ 952 21 28 58; Alameda Principal 2) A convenient 24-hour pharmacy.
Hospital Carlos Haya (☎ 951 03 01 00; Avenida de Carlos Haya) The main city hospital, 2km west of the centre.

MÁLAGA

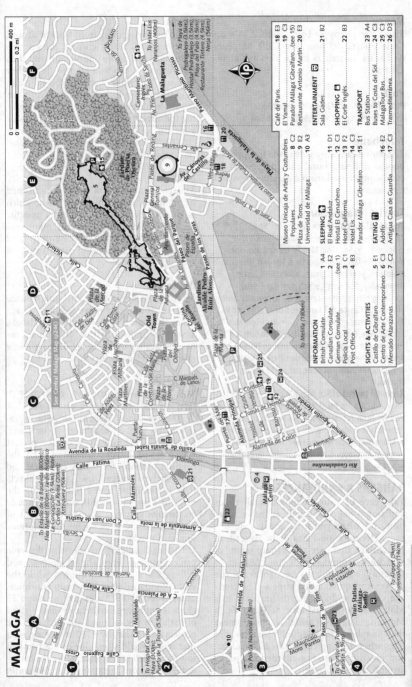

INFORMATION
British Consulate...............................1 A4
Canadian Consulate...........................2 E2
German Consulate............................(see 1)
Policía Local....................................3 C1
Post Office......................................4 B3

SIGHTS & ACTIVITIES
Castillo de Gibralfaro.........................5 E1
Centro de Arte Contemporáneo...........6 C2
Mercado Atarazanas..........................7 C2
Museo Unicaja de Artes y Costumbres
  Populares.....................................8 C2
Plaza de Toros..................................9 C3
Universidad de Málaga......................10 A3

SLEEPING
El Riad Andaluz...............................11 D1
Hostal El Cenachero.........................12 C3
Hotel California...............................13 F2
Hotel Lis..14 C3
Parador Málaga Gibralfaro................15 E1

EATING
Adolfo..16 E2
Antigua Casa de Guardia...................17 C3

Café de París.................................18 E3
El Yamal.......................................19 C3
Parador Málaga Gibralfaro..............(see 15)
Restaurante Antonio Martín..............20 E3

ENTERTAINMENT
Sala Gades....................................21 B2

SHOPPING
El Corte Inglés...............................22 B3

TRANSPORT
Bus Station....................................23 A4
Buses to Costa del Sol......................24 C3
MálagaTour Bus..............................25 C3
Trasmediterránea............................26 D3

Money

There are plenty of banks with ATMs on Calle Puerta del Mar and Calle Marqués de Larios, as well as in the airport's arrivals' hall.

Post

Post office (Map p243; Avenida de Andalucía 1; ☼ 8.30am-8.30pm Mon-Fri, 9.30am-2pm Sat)

Telephone

Telephone calls are easily made from phone booths dotted around the city, and cards can be purchased from cigarette shops and newsagents.

Tourist Information

Municipal tourist office (Map p246; ☎ 952 12 20 20; Plaza de la Marina; www.malagaturismo.com in Spanish; ☼ 9am-7pm Mon-Fri Apr-Oct, 9am-6pm Mon-Fri Nov-Mar, 10am-6pm Sat & Sun year-round) Offers a range of city maps and booklets, including the monthly ¿Qué Hacer?, which gives day-by-day upcoming events in the province. It also operates another office in the **Casita del Jardinero** (Map p243; ☎ 952 13 47 31; Avenida de Cervantes 1; ☼ 9am-7pm Mon-Fri Apr-Oct, 9am-6pm Mon-Fri Nov-Mar, 10am-6pm Sat & Sun year-round) and information kiosks on Plaza de la Aduana, at the main bus station, on Plaza de la Merced, in front of the main post office and on the eastern beaches.

Regional tourist office (Map p246; ☎ 951 30 89 11; www.andalucia.org; Pasaje de Chinitas 4; ☼ 9am-7.30pm Mon-Fri, 10am-7pm Sat, 10am-2pm Sun) On an alley off Plaza de la Constitución. Provides a range of information including maps of the regional cities. The staff speak numerous languages. It operates a second office at the airport.

DANGERS & ANNOYANCES

Take care of your valuables at all times and watch bags, especially at the bus station and when you're seated at café *terrazas* (terraces; on Plaza de la Merced, in particular); there are some sharp teams of snatchers around. Night-time Málaga is generally safe, but it's best to avoid the darker and quieter side streets. The teenage craze for drinking in the plaza hits Málaga in locations such as Plaza de la Merced. The downside is more mess than mayhem. Remove all valuables and bags when leaving cars parked overnight, and be sure to use the guarded car parks around the city centre.

Scams

If you're driving away from Málaga airport, be aware of a scam whereby thieves surreptitiously puncture one of your tyres then follow you. When you stop to fix it, they stop too and while 'helping' you they also help themselves to contents from your car. If you should get a puncture soon after leaving the airport, you're advised to stay inside your car and call the emergency number ☎ 112. If you don't have a mobile phone, try to flag down a police car.

SIGHTS

Málaga's major cultural sights are clustered in or near the charming old town, which is situated beneath the Alcazaba and the Castillo de Gibralfaro. However, many visitors take an additional day or two to head out to the beaches on the eastern edge of the city.

Old Town

Essentially a Renaissance city with its wide boulevards and decorative façades, Málaga bears the stamp of Fernando and Isabel's ambitious transformation of Islamic Andalucía as they united Spain under a single rule in the 15th century.

CATHEDRAL

Málaga's **cathedral** (Map p246; ☎ 952 21 59 17; Calle Molino Lario; cathedral & museum admission €3.50; ☼ 10am-6pm Mon-Sat, closed holidays) was begun in the 16th century and building continued for 200 years. From the start, the project was plagued by over-ambition, and the original proposal for a new cathedral had to be shelved. Instead, a series of architects (five in total) set about transforming the original mosque – of this, only the **Patio de los Naranjos** survives: a small courtyard of fragrant orange trees where the ablutions fountain used to be.

Inside, it is easy to see why the epic project took so long. The fabulous domed ceiling soars 40m into the air, while the vast colonnaded nave houses an enormous cedar-wood choir. Aisles give access to 15 chapels with gorgeous retables and a stash of 18th-century religious art. Such was the project's cost that by 1782 it was decided that work would stop. One of the two bell towers was left incomplete, hence the cathedral's well-worn nickname, *La Manquita* (the one-armed lady). The cathedral entrance is on Calle Císter. The cathedral's museum displays a collection of religious items covering a period of 500 years. These include sacred paintings and sculptures, liturgical ornaments, and valuable pieces made of gold, silver and ivory.

PALACIO EPISCOPAL

In front of the cathedral spreads the sumptuous Plaza del Obispo, where the blood-red Bishop's Palace, the **Palacio Episcopal** (Map p246; admission free; 10am-2pm & 6-9pm Tue-Sun), now forms an exhibition space. The square provided an atmospheric set for Inquisition burnings in the filming of *The Bridge of San Luis Rey*, starring Robert de Niro.

HOMAGE TO PICASSO

From the cathedral a short walk up Calle San Agustín brings you to the new holy grail of Málaga's tourist scene, the **Museo Picasso** (Map p246; ☎ 902 44 33 77; www.museopicasso malaga.org; Palacio de Buenavista, Calle San Agustín 8; permanent collection €6, temporary exhibition €4.50, combined ticket €8, 50% concession for youths 11-16yr with an adult, students under 26yr & senior citizens; 10am-8pm Tue-Thu & Sun, 10am-9pm Fri & Sat). It has an enviable collection of 204 works, 155 donated and 49 loaned to the museum by Christine Ruiz-Picasso (wife of Paul, Picasso's eldest son)

and Bernard Ruiz-Picasso (his grandson). Fascinating temporary exhibitions on Picasso themes fill out the collection.

The regional government of Andalucía invested €66 million in the restoration of the 16th-century Palacio de los Condes de Buenavista to house the museum, with fabulous results. Be sure not to miss the atmospherically preserved Phoenician, Roman, Islamic and Renaissance archaeological remains in the museum's basement, or the fantastic Café Museo Picasso (see p259). As expected, the museum seems to be fuelling a Málaga cultural and economic revival.

For a more intimate insight into the painter's childhood, head to the **Casa Natal de Picasso** (Map p246; ☎ 952 06 02 15; Plaza de la Merced 15; admission free; 10am-8pm Mon-Sat, 10am-2pm Sun, closed holidays), the house where Picasso was born in 1881, which now acts as a study foundation. The house has a replica 19th-century artist's studio. Personal memorabilia of Picasso and his family make up part of the display. Ironically, the Picasso family had to move from this house, which was too expensive, to the cheaper number 17.

Castle Complex
CASTILLO DE GIBRALFARO

One remnant of Málaga's Islamic past is the craggy ramparts of the **Castillo de Gibralfaro**

RETURN OF THE NATIVE

Perhaps it is the luminosity of Málaga's light or the severe, angular shapes of the region's dozens of *pueblos* (villages), but Picasso believed that 'to be a cubist one has to have been born in Málaga'. Banned from Spain by General Franco for his 'degenerate' art, Picasso lived much of his life in France, claiming he would never return to Spain as long as Franco was in power. But his passion for Málaga never faded. When the idea for a Picasso museum was first mooted in 1954, the town council asked him to send a few paintings from Paris. He declared: 'I will not send one or two examples. I will send lorry-loads of paintings.' And so some 50 years later with the spectacular opening of the Museo Picasso, some 200 paintings, drawings, sculptures, ceramics and engravings have finally been exhibited. They chart practically every phase of his career from cubism to modernism.

Picasso was surrounded and influenced by women all his life, from his mother, sisters, grandmother and aunts to a string of beautiful muses – most famously Olga Kokhlova, Dora Maar, Françoise Gilot and Jacqueline Roque – and women create the most obvious theme in the new museum. There are famous works such as *Olga Kokhlova with Mantilla* (1917), *Woman with Raised Arms* (1939) and *Jacqueline Sitting* (1954), with each woman evoking a different stylistic response from the artist.

As ever, there are also doves in the paintings. It is said that doves and pigeons reminded him of his early childhood, when they scratched on the windowsill of the house in the Plaza de la Merced in Málaga. For a wonderful account of Picasso's life, get hold of John Richardson's two-volume *A Life of Picasso*, which won the Whitbread Book of the Year award in 1991.

CENTRAL MÁLAGA

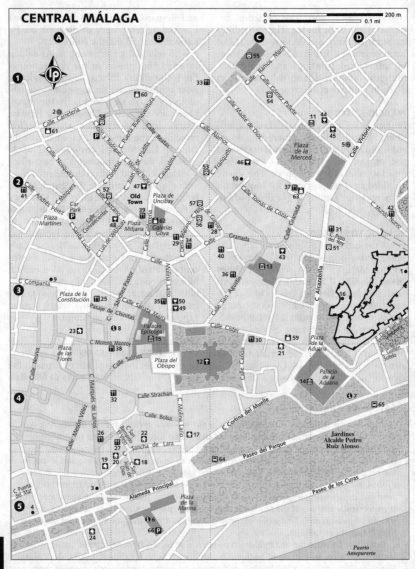

(Map p243; ☎ 952 22 72 30; admission €2, Alcazaba & Castillo de Gibralfaro €3.20; ☺ 9am-8pm Apr-Sep, 9am-6pm Oct-Mar), spectacularly located high on the hill overlooking the city. Built by Abd ar-Rahman I, the 8th-century Cordoban emir, and later rebuilt in the 14th century when Málaga was the main port for the Emirate of Granada, the castle originally acted as a

lighthouse (its name means Beacon Hill) and a military barracks.

Nothing much remains of the interior of the castle, but the airy walkway around the ramparts affords the best views over Málaga. There is also a **military museum**, which includes a small-scale model of the entire castle complex and the lower residence, the Alcazaba. The model clearly shows the 14th-century curtain wall that connected the two sites and that is currently being restored. As the walk up to the castle and around the ramparts takes a full morning, lunch or a drink on the panoramic terrace of the nearby Parador Málaga Gibralfaro (p260) is recommended.

The best way to reach the castle is walking via the scenic Paseo Don Juan de Temboury, to the south of the Alcazaba. From there a path winds pleasantly (and steeply) through lushly gardened terraces with viewpoints over the city. Alternatively you can drive up the Camino de Gibralfaro or take bus 35 from Avenida de Cervantes.

ALCAZABA
In the shadow of the Gibralfaro, the 11th-century **Alcazaba** (Map p246; ☎ 952 22 51 06; Calle Alcazabilla; admission €2, Alcazaba & Castillo de Gibralfaro €3.20; ☯ 9.30am-8pm Tue-Sun Apr-Sep, 8.30am-7pm Tue-Sun Oct-Mar; &) was the sumptuous palace-fortress of the Muslim governors. Its multifaceted construction, meandering waterways and leafy terraces, with their rising sequence of viewpoints, are a pleasure to visit, especially in the summer heat. Just below the palace is a small **Roman theatre** (Map p246), which is perfect for outdoor performances.

For immediate access to the Alcazaba from Calle Guillén Sotelo (behind the mu-

nicipal tourist office), take the lift, which brings you out in the heart of the palace.

Around the Alameda Principal
The Alameda Principal, now a busy thoroughfare, was created in the late 18th century as a boulevard on what were then the sands of the Guadalmedina estuary. It's adorned with old trees from the Americas and lined with 18th- and 19th-century buildings.

The **Paseo del Parque** (Map p243), a palm-lined extension of the Alameda, was created in the 1890s on land reclaimed from the sea. The garden along its southern side, **Paseo de España** (Map p246), is full of exotic tropical plants, making a pleasant refuge from the bustle of the city. The whole park was closed in 2006 for a complete overhaul. On the northern side is the grand **Palacio de la Aduana** (Map p246; Paseo del Parque; admission free; ☯ 3-8pm Tue, 9am-8pm Wed-Fri, 9am-3pm Sat & Sun), which has temporary exhibitions of works from the former **Museo de Málaga** (originally housed in the Picasso Museum). The Aduana building is due to be converted to the permanent home of the city museum. The collection includes fine works by great artists such as Francisco de Zurbarán, Bartolomé Esteban Murillo, José de Ribera and Pedro de Mena.

North of the Alameda, in what's now the commercial district, you will find the

MÁLAGA PROVINCE

neo-Islamic **Mercado Atarazanas** (Map p243; Calle Atarazanas), entered through its huge horse-shoe-shaped arch. The daily market in here is pleasantly noisy and animated and there is a whole host of food on sale. You can choose from swaying legs of ham and rolls of sausages or cheese, fruit, fish and sweets. Nearby are plenty of cafés on pedestrian-ised Calle Herredería del Rey.

If you strike out south of the Alameda you will find the funky **Centro de Arte Contemporáneo** (Map p243; ☎ 952 12 00 55; Calle Alemania; admission free; ☼ 10am-8pm 25 Sep-19 Jun, 10am-2pm & 5-9pm 20 Jun-24 Sep, Tue-Sun), which is housed in a skilfully converted 1930s wholesale market on the river estuary. The bizarre triangular floor plan of the building has been retained, with its cubist lines and shapes displaying the modern art brilliantly. Painted entirely white, windows and all, the museum exhibits works from well-known 20th-century artists and collectors such as Roy Lichtenstein, Gerhard Richter and Miquel Barceló. For a good introduction to the museum, ask about the free half-hour guided tours.

La Malagueta & the Beaches
At the end of the Paseo del Parque lies the exclusive residential district of La Malagueta. Situated on a spit of land protruding into the sea, apartments here have frontline sea views, and some of Málaga's best restaurants are found near the local **Playa de la Malagueta** (the beach closest to the city centre). Take a walk along the beach before settling down to a full-on fish lunch at Adolfo (p260) or visiting the museum of the **Plaza de Toros** (bullring; Map p243; Paseo de Reding; admission €1.80; ☼ 10am-1pm & 5-8pm Mon-Fri), the busiest bullring on the coast (see p263). The museum is fine if you want to see some stuff on bullfighting, but the museum in Ronda (p280) is much better.

East of Playa de la Malagueta, sandy beaches continue to line most of the waterfront for several kilometres. Next along from Playa de la Malagueta are two man-made beaches, **Playa de Pedregalejo** and **Playa del Palo**, El Palo being the city's original, salt-of-the-earth fishing neighbourhood. This is a great place to bring children and an even better place to while away an afternoon with a cold beer and a plate of fantastic, sizzling

seafood. To top it off, the efforts of the city council have resulted in a huge clean-up of the beach and water. To reach either beach take bus 11 from Paseo del Parque.

Jardín Botánico La Concepción
Four kilometres north of the city centre is the large, tropical **Jardín Botánico La Concepción** (☎ 952 25 21 48; adult/child €3.10/1.60; ☼ 9.30am-8.30pm Apr-Sep, 9.30am-5.30pm Oct-Mar, closed Mon, 25 Dec & 1 Jan). Dating from the mid-19th century, the gardens are the brainchild of a local aristocratic couple, Amalia Heredia Livermore and Jorge Loring Oyarzabal. They decided to re-create a tropical forest near the shores of the Mediterranean. It is famous for its purple wisteria blooms in spring.

You can visit by 90-minute guided tour or solo, wending your way through some of the 5000 tropical plants, ponds, waterfalls and lakes.

By car, take the A45 Antequera road north from the Málaga ring road (A7) to Km 166 and follow the signs for the 'Jardín Botánico'. Alternatively, the MalagaTour bus (p257) makes a stop here.

ACTIVITIES
A most welcome activity in Málaga is the **Baños Árabes** (Arab Baths; Map p246; ☎ 952 21 23 27; www.elhammam.com; Calle Tomás de Cózar 13; bath with/without Turkish wash €32/23, massages €34-80; ☼ 10am-10pm), a perfect place to sit back and sweat it out amid the steamy semidarkness to the sound of soothing music. Unlike some Arabic baths in Andalucía, there are no pools to bathe in here. Book your visit in advance. Specialist massages, including Ayurvedic and aromatherapy treatments, are by appointment only.

COURSES
The **Universidad de Málaga** (Map p243; ☎ 952 27 82 11; www.uma.es/estudios/extranj/extranjeros.htm; Avenida de Andalucía 24, 29007 Málaga) runs very popular language courses for foreigners. Four-week intensive Spanish-language courses cost from €442. Check out the website then contact the Directorá de Cursos de Español para Extranjeros.

There are at least 16 private language schools in Málaga; the main tourist offices have contact lists.

(Continued on page 257)

MÁLAGA PROVINCE

Plaza de España (p108), Seville

Flamenco haunt (p127), Seville

Andalucía's high-quality olive oil (p81)

ESBIN ANDERSON PHOTOG

White-washed houses, Grazalema (p204), Cádiz province

BETHUNE CARMICHAEL

Seville's World Heritage Alcázar (p99)

Dusk sets across Seville's Cathedral (p97)

PAUL BERNHARDT

OLIVER STREWE

Andalucía's world-famous sherry, Cádiz province (p183)

Flamenco (p182), Cádiz

PAUL BERNHARDT

Rock of Gibraltar (p233), viewed from La Línea de la Concepción (p227)

PHILIP GAME

252

MARTIN LLADO
The way to Museo Picasso (p245), Málaga

Puente Nuevo, Ronda (p277),
Málaga province
DAVID TOMLINSON

ROBIN CHAPMAN
Festival-goers, Feria de Málaga (p257), Málaga

Marina, Benalmádena Costa (p264), Costa del Sol, Málaga province
DAVID TOMI

The ancient, winding streets of Córdoba (p300)

The Mezquita (p301) by night, Córdoba

Semana Santa celebrations (p310), Córdoba

Stained-glass windows of the Mezquita (p301), Córdoba

Generalife gardens (p364), the Alhambra (p359), Granada

Green olives of Jaén province
(p330)

Hills of olive groves, Baeza (p334), Jaén province

Las Alpujarras (p386), Granada province

Views from Torre de la Vela, Alcazaba (p362), Granada

Feria de Corpus Cristi (p372), Granada

WITOLD SKRYPC

Almería city seen from the Alcazaba (p401)

Bank raids and shoot 'em ups: movie set of Almería's Wild West (p407)

JON DAV

(Continued from page 248)

MÁLAGA FOR CHILDREN

Málaga for kids is not so different from Málaga for adults, but that is not to say that the city isn't child-friendly. It has an easily navigable, compact centre, lots of child-friendly eateries and kilometres of popular beaches.

Of the sights, children will particularly like the craggy ramparts of the Castillo de Gibralfaro (p245) – a good morning's entertainment.

The most suitable museum is the **Museo Unicaja de Artes y Costumbres Populares** (Map p243; ☎ 952 21 71 37; www.museoartespopulares.com; Pasillo de Santa Isabel 10; adult/child €2/free; ⏱ 10am-1.30pm & 4-7pm Mon-Fri, 10am-1.30pm Sat), which focuses on everyday rural life with all the requisite farming and fishing regalia. Note the glass cabinets containing painted *barros* (clay figures) of characters from local folklore.

Cheaper than the Costa del Sol, Málaga is also a great base from which to enjoy many of the treats of the *costa* without the expense. A frequent and efficient bus service (see p263) links the city with the towns of the Costa del Sol enabling easy day trips to all the large adventure parks and aquariums (see p268).

TOURS

To pick up the child-friendly, open-topped **MalagaTour** (Map p243; ☎ 902 10 10 81; www.malaga-tour.com; adult/child €15/7.50; ⏱ half-hourly 9.30am-7pm) bus ride, head for Avenida Manuel Agustín Heredia or the easternmost end of the Paseo del Parque. This hop-on-hop-off tour does a complete circuit of the city with stops at all the major points of interest. It is a great way to see the city – especially with small children – and tickets (valid for 24 hours) include an informative multilingual audio guide.

FESTIVALS & EVENTS

There are a whole host of festivals taking place throughout the year in Málaga province, and the booklet *¿Qué Hacer?*, available each month from the municipal tourist office, will give you a blow-by-blow account. The following are the city's main events:

Semana Santa (Holy Week) Each night from Palm Sunday to Good Friday, six or seven *cofradías* (brotherhoods) bear their holy images for several hours through the city, watched by big crowds. A good place to watch is the Alameda Principal.

Feria de Málaga Málaga's nine-day *feria* (fair), launched by a huge fireworks display on the opening Friday in mid-August, is the most ebullient of Andalucía's summer *ferias*. During the day the city jumps with music and dancing: head for Plaza Uncibay, Plaza de la Constitución, Plaza Mitjana or Calle Marqués de Larios to be in the thick of it. At night the fun switches to large fairgrounds and nightly rock and flamenco shows at Cortijo de Torres, 4km southwest of the city centre. Special buses run from all over the city.

Fiesta Mayor de Verdiales Thousands congregate for a grand gathering of *verdiales* folk groups at Puerto de la Torre on 28 December. They perform an exhilarating brand of music and dance unique to the Málaga area. Bus 21 from the Alameda Principal goes to Puerto de la Torre.

SLEEPING

There are some new options on the Málaga accommodation scene but little of interest in the budget range. Most top-end places have offers of some sort and some have considerably cheaper weekend rates.

Budget

Hotel Lis (Map p243; ☎ 952 22 73 00; www.costadelsol .spa.es/hotel/hotelis; Calle Córdoba 7; s/d €34/43; 🐕 P) If you don't mind the south side of the Alameda, this is a smart choice as the Lis offers very good value. The rooms are a steal for the facilities they offer, though standard doubles are not big. Décor throughout is upbeat and there's a bar-café. Apartments are also available.

Hostal El Cenachero (Map p243; ☎ 952 22 40 88; 3rd fl, Calle Barroso 5; s €32, d €47-55) This modest family-run *hostal* (simple guesthouse) is close to the harbour. It's named after Málaga's folkloric fishmonger character. Cheerful and friendly, the *hostal* has 14 pleasant rooms that are simply furnished and carpeted and come with showers.

Hostal Derby (Map p246; ☎ 952 22 13 01; 4th fl, Calle San Juan de Dios 1; s/d €36/48) This good-value *hostal* has spacious rooms and big windows, some of which overlook the harbour. Décor is quaint but the bathrooms have been modernised. The *hostal* shares a high-rise building with various offices.

Hostal Larios (Map p246; ☎ 952 22 54 90; www .hostallarios.com; Calle Marqués de Larios 9; s/d €40/50, with shared bathroom €32/42; 🐕) This central *hostal* outclasses all others in the budget range. The 12 rooms are newly fitted out and sport cheerful apricot and blue paintwork. Only four rooms have private bathroom, and these rooms have windows onto the main street.

Hostal Pedregalejo (☎ 952 29 32 18; www.hotel eshijano.com; Calle Conde de las Navas 9; s/d €41/61; ☒) Near the beach, about 4km east of the city centre, this *hostal* is family-run and has attractive rooms and a little coffee shop where you can buy breakfast. The only drawback is the hike into town.

Midrange

Hotel Carlos V (Map p246; ☎ 952 21 51 20; carlosv@spa .es; Calle Císter 10; s €32-50, d €67; ☒) Hotel Carlos V has a steady trail of guests due to being tucked behind the cathedral in an atmospheric old street, and offering good prices. The wear and tear shows; however, the basic rooms are clean and functional and have good shower pressure. The place grows on you.

Hostal Victoria (Map p246; ☎ 952 22 42 24; hostal victoria@hostalvictoria.net; Calle Sancha de Lara 3; s/d €52/75; ☒) The Victoria is enduringly popular, due to its central location and friendly staff. The clean and comfortable rooms are a cut above most other *hostales* and have satellite TV, and a bath in the bathrooms. Book well in advance.

Hotel California (Map p243; ☎ 952 21 51 65; www .costadelsolspa.es/hotelcalifornia; Paseo de Sancha 17; s/d €53/80; ☒) One kilometre east of the city centre, this place is close to the beach. A lovely flowery entrance is a good start to the 28 good-sized rooms. Breakfast is available.

El Riad Andaluz (Map p243 ☎ 952 21 36 40; www .elriadandaluz.com; Calle Hinestrosa 24; s/d 70/90; ☒) At last, a characterful, slightly exotic place to stay in Málaga. This French-run guesthouse, near the Teatro Cervantes, has eight rooms set around the kind of atmospheric patio that's known as a *riad* in Morocco. The decoration is Moroccan but each room is different, including colourful tiled bathrooms. Breakfast is available.

Hotel Venecia (Map p246; ☎ 952 21 36 36; www.hotelveneciamalaga.com; Alameda Principal 9; s/d €70/90; ☒ ☒ ☒) On the southern side of the Alameda, Hotel Venecia has 40 very comfortable, renovated rooms and helpful English-speaking staff. Décor combines old and new; there are funky turquoise lounge chairs at reception and attractive metalwork bed heads in the rooms.

Hotel Don Curro (Map p246; ☎ 952 22 72 00; www .hoteldoncurro.com; Calle Sancha de Lara 7; s/d €74/104;

☒ ☒) The busy Don Curro is a favourite with businessmen and although it has a corporate air about it, the hotel is efficient, comfortable and centrally located. It's also conveniently positioned for getting in and out of town. The rooms are well appointed and spacious with speckled marble bathrooms.

Hotel Los Naranjos (☎ 952 22 43 16 17; www .hotel-losnaranjos.com; Paseo de Sancha 35; s/d €75/118; ☒ ☒) East of the bullring on the way to the beaches and a little beyond Hotel California, this hotel has a garish orange exterior but modern rooms decorated, in contrast, in neutral tones. Front-facing rooms have small balconies, some of which catch glimpses of the sea.

Top End

AC Málaga Palacio (Map p246; ☎ 952 21 51 85; www.ac-hotels.com; Calle Cortina del Muelle 1; d €137; ☒ ☒ ☒) This 15-storey, sleek hotel has sensational views over the busy seafront. Smart, modern design and excellent facilities also make it the best of Málaga's luxury options. It has a rooftop pool and fully fitted-out gym.

Hotel Cortijo La Reina (☎ 951 01 40 00; www .hotelcortijolareina.com; Carretera Málaga-Colmenar; s/d €116/150; ☒ ☒ ☒ ☒) This Andalucian-style *cortijo* (country property) is 30 minutes' drive north of Málaga. At 800m it enjoys beautiful views over the valleys, and rooms are sumptuously decorated with four-poster beds and lots of swishy fabrics. A great base for exploring the Parque Natural Montes de Málaga.

Parador Málaga Gibralfaro (Map p243; ☎ 952 22 19 02; www.parador.es; s/d €128/162; ☒ ☒ ☒) With an unbeatable location perched on the pine-forested Gibralfaro, Málaga's stone-built Parador is a real winner. Most rooms have spectacular views from their terraces, and you can dine at the excellent terrace restaurant (p260) even if you are not a guest at the hotel.

Hotel Larios (Map p246; ☎ 952 22 22 00; www .hotel-larios.com; Calle Marqués de Larios 2; d €192; ☒ ☒) This quaint, boutique Art Deco hotel occupies a huge corner of Plaza de la Constitución. With all the deep purple, dark reds and browns the hotel certainly has a faded verve, but sometimes the service is rather high-handed. Check its website for offers.

EATING

A Málaga speciality is fish fried quickly in olive oil. *Fritura malagueño* consists of fried fish, anchovies and squid. Cold soups are popular in summer: as well as gazpacho (a chilled soup of blended tomatoes, peppers, cucumber, garlic, breadcrumbs, lemon and oil) and *sopa de ajo* (garlic soup), try *sopa de almendra con uvas* (almond soup with grapes). Ham is a requisite in most tapas combinations. Málaga's restaurants are well priced and maintain a good standard due to the largely local clientele.

Budget

Café Moka (Map p246; ☎ 952 21 40 02; Calle San Bernardo El Viejo 2; breakfast €3.50) Just off the main drag, tucked behind Hotel Don Curro, this busy little retro café caters to a mainly Spanish crowd. It is a great place for breakfast, but fills up quickly both for breakfast (around 10am) and late lunch (3pm).

La Tetería (Map p246; Calle San Agustín 9; speciality tea €2.50, breakfast €2.30-5; ⏰ 9am-midnight) This place serves heaps of aromatic and classic teas, herbal infusions, coffees and juices, with teas ranging from peppermint to '*antidepresivo*'. You can breakfast on fresh juices and *bocadillos* (filled rolls); there are only crepes from around 2pm. Sit outside and marvel at the beautiful church opposite or stay inside to enjoy the wafting incense and background music.

Café Lepanto (Map p246; Calle Marqués de Larios 7; ice cream €3.70-4.20) A noisy local favourite right on pedestrianised Calle Marqués de Larios, the Regent St of Málaga. As Málaga's poshest *confitería* (sweet shop), Lepanto serves up a whole host of delicious *pasteles* (pastries and cakes), ice creams, sweets, chocolates, coffees, teas and other drinks to manicured *malagueños*.

Comoloco (Map p246; Calle Denis Belgrano 17; salads & pittas €4.50-5; ⏰ 1pm-1am) This place with huge windows onto the little street is packed out at lunch time. Good healthy food at a good price in a laid-back setting is the reason. You choose your own sauces and salad dressings.

Restaurante Tintero (☎ 607 607586; Carretera Almería 99, El Palo; plates €7; ⏰ 12.30pm-1am) A longstanding, fun, seafront eatery where plates of seafood are brought out by the waiters and you call out for what you want. Shout if you want it sizzling hot.

Café Central (Map p246; Plaza de la Constitución; mains €5-11.50) This extremely popular café is located on the main pedestrianised square. A cold beer and plate of *rosada frita* (fried hake) is a lunch-time must. Choose your table carefully (somewhere in the middle) or you may well be plagued by various musical impresarios determined to serenade you, a feature of outdoor eating in the centre.

Midrange

El Vegetariano de la Alcazabilla (Map p246; ☎ 952 21 48 58; Calle Pozo del Rey 5; mains €9-10.50; ⏰ 1.30-4pm & 9-11pm Mon-Sat; Ⓥ) Manages to juggle friendly service and good food, while keeping a laid-back vibe. Lacto-vegetarian and vegan meals are served in good-sized portions. Leave your mark: add to the graffiti on the yellow walls.

Café Museo Picasso (Map p246; ☎ 952 22 50 43; Palacio de Buenavista, Calle San Agustín 8; coffee €1.50, cakes €6, glass of wine €3-5, light meals €12) Simply excellent, serving the best rich, dark coffee in town. It was established by Málaga's most dynamic young chef, José Carlos García (of Café de Paris), though he no longer runs it. The beautiful, secluded little patio at the back of the museum is alone worth a trip here.

El Jardín (Map p246; ☎ 952 22 04 19; Calle Cañón 1; mains €12.50; ⏰ 9am-midnight Mon-Thu, 9am-2pm & 5pm-midnight Fri & Sat, 5pm-midnight Sun) Next to the palm-filled gardens of the cathedral, this busy Viennese-style café fills up quickly on the weekends (due to live music acts). It features lots of mock-gold leaf and fancy furniture. The food is nothing special but the ambience inside and the cathedral and garden views outside are just great.

Clandestino (Map p246; ☎ 952 21 93 90; Calle Niño de Guevara 3; mains €9-17; ⏰ 1pm-1am) This trendy backstreet joint serves up top meals (fusing northern European and Latin cuisines: crunchy salads, pastas, lasagne, meat dishes) to hip house beats. Hedonistic diners can choose from a long list of mouthwatering desserts.

Rojo (Map p246; ☎ 952 22 74 86; Calle Granada 44; mains €10-17, menú €13; ⏰ 2-4pm Tue-Fri, 8.30pm-12.30am Tue-Sat) A relatively new contender on the Málaga restaurant scene, Rojo is slap bang in the middle of the old town. Red banquettes line the walls, contrasting sharply with white tablecloths. Rojo attracts a youngish professional crowd with its simple but excellent menu.

El Yamal (Map p243; ☎ 952 21 20 46; Calle Blasco de Garay 7; mains €11-16; ⏰ 1-5pm & 6pm-midnight, closed Sun) This restaurant serves tasty Moroccan food in traditional tagines (earthenware dishes with pointed lids). Choose from fish, chicken or couscous with vegetables and soak up the relaxed atmosphere. Finish with a mint tea with a drop of orange-flower essence (*azahar*).

Mesón El Chinitas (Map p246; ☎ 952 21 09 72; Calle Moreno Monroy 4-6; mains €7-17.50; ⏰ 1-4pm & 8pm-midnight) This place appeals to diners who don't mind being eyeballed by cheesy portraits. Cuisine is *malagueño* and specialities are rice dishes and whole fish baked with salt.

Zenart (Map p246; ☎ 952 06 00 79; Calle Mundo Nuevo 4; salads & tempura €8-9, sushi €19; ⏰ 9pm-midnight) Come here like the locals to enjoy the sensational views of the Alcazaba and the different flavours of Japanese cuisine. The food presentation lives up to the restaurant's name and the tempura is especially good.

Top End

Adolfo (Map p243; ☎ 952 60 19 14; Paseo Marítimo Picasso 12; starters €7-8, seafood extra, mains €12-22; ⏰ 1.30-5pm & 8.30pm-1am Mon-Sat) A classy place in the well-heeled La Malagueta area, Adolfo does a range of imaginative Mediterranean dishes including vegetarian starters with goat's cheese, lobster salad, and kid with rosemary honey.

Restaurante Antonio Martín (Map p243; ☎ 952 22 73 98; Playa de la Malagueta; mains €13-24; ⏰ 1-5pm & 9pm-12.30am, closed Sun Nov-Apr) Right on the beach with a large sea-view terrace, this place is one of Málaga's oldest restaurants. Antonio Martín rustles up some of the best fish in town and also does excellent desserts. Celebrities and matadors are rumoured to hang out here. Reservations are recommended.

Parador Málaga Gibralfaro (Map p243; ☎ 952 22 19 02; www.parador.es; menú €28) Nestled among pine trees and overlooking the Alcazaba and port, the terrace restaurant of the Parador is a fantastic dining experience and very romantic in the evenings. The menu is a tour-de-force of Andalucian gastronomy,

---

THE TAPAS TRAIL

The pleasures of Málaga are essentially undemanding, easy to arrange and cheap. One of the best is a slow crawl around the city's numerous tapas bars and old bodegas (traditional wine bars). In summer these bars are open from late-morning to midnight, and beyond.

Antigua Casa de Guardia (Map p243; ☎ 952 21 46 80; Alameda Principal 18; raciones €4.50, wine by the glass €1) This venerable old tavern has been serving Málaga's sweet dessert wines since 1840. Try the dark-brown, sherry-like *seco* (dry) or the romantically named Lágrima Trasañejo (Very Old Tear), complemented by a plate of monster prawns, oysters or mussels.

Gorki (Map p246; ☎ 952 22 14 66; Calle Strachan 6; dishes €6-16) A popular upmarket tapas bar with pavement tables and an interior full of wine-barrel tables and stools. It serves an extensive list of Spanish wines, and tangy cheeses. Try the belly-warming *alubias con cordoniz* (white-bean stew with partridge).

La Rebana (Map p246; Calle Molina Lario 5; tapas €3, raciones €5-8.50) A great, noisy and central tapas bar. The dark wooden interior (with its wrought-iron gallery) creates an inviting ambience. Goat's cheese with cherries, foies and cured meats are among the offerings.

La Posada Antonio (Map p246; Calle Granada 33; tapas €1.80, mains €10-17) A very popular place with locals where you will be hard pressed to find a table after 11pm, despite its barnlike proportions. Great for greasy meat in tremendous proportions; the filling *paletilla cordero* (shoulder of lamb) will set you back €17.

Pepa y Pepe (Map p246; Calle Calderería; tapas €1.30-1.50, raciones €3.60-5.50) A snug tapas bar that brims with young diners chomping their way through *calamares fritos* (battered squid) and fried green peppers.

Lechuga (Map p246; Plaza de la Merced 1; tapas €2.50-3.60, raciones €8; **V**) Here vegetables reign supreme and the chef does wonderful things with them. The street is noisy outside but inside is a calm ambience created by warm orange walls, a row of Japanese lanterns, and studded rustic furniture. Choose from a plate of dips, a taco, enchilada, canapés and more.

specialising in the popular *fritura de pes-
caítos a la malagueña* (small, fried fish of
Málaga). The inside dining room is a formal affair of beamed ceilings, high-backed
chairs and heavy tablecloths.

La Casa del Ángel (Map p246; ☎ 952 60 87 50; Calle
Madre de Dios 29; starters €9-10, mains €14-23; ☼ 1.30-4pm
& 8pm-late; closed Mon) An extraordinary restaurant filled with the owners' considerable art
collection. The brainchild of Ángel Garó, the
interior is a series of unusual features: Renaissance arches, beamed and frescoed ceilings, antique tiled floors and heart-warming
orange and ochre paint washes. The cuisine
is equally sumptuous: a combination of Andalucian, Arab and international tastes. The
restaurant's intimate Salón Cervantes, with
its heavy red curtains and double French
windows overlooking the Teatro Cervantes,
is the place to eat. Reservations necessary.

DRINKING

The best areas to look for bars are from
Plaza de la Merced in the northeast to Calle
Carretería in the northwest, plus Plaza Mit-
jana (officially called Plaza del Marqués
Vado Maestre) and Plaza de Uncibay. Plaza
Mitjana heaves after midnight on Friday
and Saturday.

Tetería El Harén (Map p243; Calle Andrés Pérez 3; fresh
juice €2.70; ☼ 4.30-late) A larger, newly established tea house that rambles over several
floors with lots of private nooks and crannies. Come here for mint tea, a fresh juice
or a *mojito*. Thursday to Saturday, there is
often live music.

Bodegas El Pimpi (Map p246; ☎ 952 22 89 90; Calle
Granada 62; ☼ 7pm-2am) A Málaga institution

with a warren of rooms and mini-patios.
The huge wine casks are signed by stars
(even Tony Blair!) and walls are lined with
celebrity pictures and bullfighting posters.
It attracts a fun-loving crowd with its sweet
wine and thumping music.

Puerto Oscura (Map p246; Calle Molina Lario 5; cocktails €4; ☼ 6pm-late) An elegant and intimate
cocktail lounge with plush velvet seats and
secret alcoves, Puerto Oscura is a great way
to start an evening. It stays open until 5am
on busy summer nights and sometimes puts
on live music. Relatively smart clothes are
the order of the day. Nonsmokers beware!

Calle de Bruselas (Map p246; ☎ 952 60 39 48; Plaza
de la Merced 16; ☼ 9am-2am) A retro, Belgian bar
appealing to a bohemian crowd. During the
day it caters to the coffee scene with pavement tables out in the plaza, then at night
the dark little bar comes to life.

O'Neill's (Map p246; ☎ 952 60 14 60; Calle Luis de
Velázquez 3; ☼ noon-late) A spit-and-sawdust
bar that likes to prove how Irish it is by
playing nonstop U2. Very busy with a noisy
mixed crowd of Spaniards, expats and tourists, and friendly bar staff.

Sala Tantra Buddha Bar (Map p246; Calle Molino
Lario 7; ☼ 9pm-late) This place is worth taking
a peep at even if you don't hang about. It's
decorated with all the little details associated with Buddha – statues, silk screens etc.
This type of décor replicates the Parisian
prototype and is a fad in Spain at present –
an odd theme for a drinking den! There's a
small dance floor too.

La Botellita (Map p246; Calle Álamos 36; ☼ 11pm-
4am Thu-Sat) Just off Plaza de la Merced, Botellita is chock-a-block with miniature bottles
of spirits. Spanish music attracts a young
and invariably tipsy crowd.

ENTERTAINMENT

Party-seeking holidaymakers tend to ignore
Málaga and head along the coast, which
means the bars and clubs in Málaga are
left for discerning locals. The back pages
of *Sur* newspaper, and its Friday entertainment section, are useful for what's-on information, as is monthly *¿Qué Hacer?* (free
from tourist offices). Bi-monthly *Youthing*
reveals what's on at the trendiest places.

Nightclubs

On nonfreezing weekends, the web of narrow old streets that lie north of Plaza de

COSTA GAY *Joy Lucas*

The laid-back lifestyle combined with the constant coming and going of international visitors make the Costa del Sol an ideal meeting point for gay and 'gay-friendly' people. The idea of exclusively gay restaurants, nightlife or accommodation is fast becoming an anachronism.

Whether you want to 'chill and chat' or 'drink and dance', there are plenty of places to choose from in the centre of Málaga and around Plaza de la Merced that build up a fairly mixed crowd. Calle de Bruselas (p261) and **Flor de Lis** (Map p243; Plaza de la Merced; 11am-late) are ideal for tapas, afternoon coffee or the first drink of the evening. Late loafers can club crawl to Warhol (below) or unwind to the soothing sounds of lounge in **Mondo Tiki** (Map p246; Calle Méndez Núñez 3).

If it's a louder ambience you're looking for, you'll find the pink party at the mega clubs and gay bars in Torremolinos (p267). That's right, the 'in crowd' goes to Torremolinos for fun!! What had turned into a decayed symbol of a better past is now making a comeback. New bars, restaurants and clubs are opening and the area is becoming one of the major gay holiday destinations in Spain. La Nogalera (close to Torremolinos train station) is the centre of BLGT – bi, lesbian, gay and transgendered – tourism in the province. Here, the variety of bars, pubs, clubs and discos guarantees a good time. Check out the new and trendy **El Gato Lounge** (La Nogalera; 4pm-late), where cool cats chill over a beer and a bite, or **Ánfora** (La Nogalera 522; 6pm-dawn), primarily a girls' bar with local clientele and loud pop music.

The weekend is for partying at **Passion** (Avenida Palma de Mallorca 18; admission & 1 drink €16; 11pm-6am) and/or **Palladium** (Avenida Palma de Mallorca 36; admission & 1 drink €16; 11pm-6am), two of Torremolinos' hottest clubs which both boast of having two floors, three different atmospheres (depending on your mood), international DJs, live performances, swimming pool, go-go dancers and singers...

In early August, don't miss the Costa del Sol's Freedom Festival, considered the most important gay festival in southern Europe. Check out the programme of electronic music, dance and performances at www.freedom-spain.com.

If none of the above sounds glamorous, or pricey, enough, you could flock with the fashionistas to Dreamers (p276) at Puerto Banús, the *costa*'s cathedral of house music with top international DJs like Roger Sánchez to get you giddy! Or catch the celebrities at Glam (p276), also in Puerto Banús.

la Constitución comes alive; midweek, the place is dead.

Asúcar (Map p246; cnr Calle Convalecientes & Calle Lazcano; 9pm-late) Salsa fans need go no further. You can even join the lines of folk learning salsa steps from 11pm Wednesdays to Saturdays. Salsa, merengue etc are sweeping the nation.

Liceo (Map p246; Calle Beatas 21; 7pm-3am Thu-Sat) A grand old mansion turned young music bar, Liceo buzzes with a student crowd after midnight. Go up the winding staircase and you'll find more rooms to duck into.

Warhol (Map p246; Calle Niño de Guevara; 11pm-late Thu-Sat) A stylish haunt for choosy gay clubbers who want funky house beats mixed by dreadlocked DJs.

White (Map p246; Niño de Guevara; 11.30pm-late) This place is a favourite dance haunt (hip-hop, funk) of northern European language students.

Onda Pasadena (Map p246; Calle Gómez Pallete 5), with jazz on Tuesday and flamenco on Thursday, and **ZZ-Pub** (Map p246; Calle Tejón y Rodríguez 6), with rock on Thursday, are two central places which have regular live music, mainly rock, but not exclusively.

Theatre

Teatro Cervantes (Map p246; ☎ 952 22 41 00; www .teatrocervantes.com; Calle Ramos Marín s/n) Housed in a palatial building, the beautiful Cervantes has a good programme of music, dance and theatre. Several other theatres have busy schedules, including the dance conservatory's Sala Gades (Map p243), on Calle Cerrojo.

Cinemas

Posters and the *Sur* newspaper list the current movies at Málaga's cinemas.

Albéniz Multicines (Map p246; ☎ 952 21 58 98; Calle Alcazabilla 4) The home of the large Cinemateca Municipal (Municipal Cinema), showing international films with Spanish subtitles at 10pm most nights.

Bullfights

The main season at Málaga's bullring (p248) takes place during the Feria de Málaga in August. The festival has an 11-day programme of fights, the longest of its kind in the province. Tickets for the fights, depending on where you sit, can cost from €14 to €112.

SHOPPING

Central Calle Marqués de Larios and nearby streets have glitzy boutiques and shoe shops in handsomely restored old buildings.

El Corte Inglés (Map p243; Avenida de Andalucía) Málaga's branch of this department store is chock-full of goodies ranging from chocolate spread to tailored suits.

For hand-crafted Andalucian ceramics try **Alfajar** (Map p246; Calle Císter 3), and for some tasty *malagueño* treats (and late-night desperation shopping) look no further than the deli **Ultramarinos Zoillo** (Map p246; Calle Granada 65). There is a Sunday morning **flea market** (Map p243; Paseo de los Martiricos) near the Estadio de la Rosaleda. **Flamenka** (p246; 952 22 59 65; www.flamenka.com; Galerías Goya, Calle Calderería 6) is a one-stop shop for flamenco-related goods and music.

For camping essentials, **El Yeti** (Map p246; Calle Carretería 66) and **Deportes La Trucha** (Map p246; Calle Carretería 100) have a wide range of general and specialist camping and climbing equipment.

GETTING THERE & AWAY
Air

Málaga's busy **airport** (952 04 88 38), the main international gateway to Andalucía, is 9km southwest of the city centre and host to a rash of budget airlines. Most airline offices are at the airport.

See p441 for information on flights.

Boat

Trasmediterránea (Map p243; 952 06 12 18, 902 45 46 45; www.trasmediterranea.com; Estación Marítima, Local E1) operates a fast ferry (€55, four hours) and a slower ferry (€36, 7½ hours) daily year-round to/from Melilla (€139 per car on both boats).

Bus

The **bus station** (Map p243; 952 35 00 61; Paseo de los Tilos) is 1km southwest of the city centre. Destinations include the following:

Destination	Cost	Duration	Daily Frequency
Antequera	€5	50min	9 or more
Cádiz	€20	4hr	3
Córdoba	€12	2½hr	5
Granada	€9	1½hr	17
Ronda	€7.50-9.50	2½hr	9 or more
Seville	€14.50	2½hr	10-12

Destinations beyond Andalucía include Madrid (€20, six hours, nine daily), Barcelona, France, Germany, Portugal and Morocco. The station has a rather spartan café, and an internet cabin.

For the Costa del Sol, regular buses leave Avenida Manuel Agustín Heredia (Map p243) for Torremolinos (€1.20, 30 minutes), Benalmádena Costa (€1.60) and Fuengirola (€2.50, one hour).

Car

Numerous international (including Avis and Hertz) and local agencies have desks at the airport. You'll find them down a ramp in the luggage-carousel hall, and beside the arrivals hall.

Train

The **Málaga-Renfe train station** (Map p243; 952 36 02 02; www.renfe.es; Explanada de la Estación) is around the corner from the bus station. Regular trains run daily to/from Córdoba (€16 to €21, 2¼ hours, 10 daily) and Seville (€16, 2½ hours, five daily). For Granada (€19, 2½ hours) there are no direct trains, but you can get there with a change at Bobadilla. For Ronda (€8.20, 1½ to two hours), too, you usually change at Bobadilla.

Fast Talgo 200s go to/from Madrid (€52 to €87, 4½ hours, six daily), and there's also a slower, cheaper Intercity train leaving in the late morning (€35, 6½ hours). There are also trains for Valencia (€48, 8½ to 9½ hours, two daily) and Barcelona (€54 to €141, 13 hours, two daily).

GETTING AROUND
To/From the Airport

A taxi from the airport to the city centre costs €15 to €16.

Bus 19 to the city centre (€1.10, 20 minutes) leaves from the 'City Bus' stop outside the arrivals hall, every 20 or 30 minutes from 6.35am to 11.45pm, stopping at Málaga's main train and bus stations en route. Going out to the airport, you can catch the bus at the western end of Paseo del Parque, and from outside the stations, about every half-hour from 6.30am to 11.30pm.

The Aeropuerto train station, located on the Málaga-Fuengirola line, is a five-minute walk from the airport terminal: follow signs from the departures hall. Trains run about every half-hour from 7am to 11.45pm to the Málaga-Renfe station (€1.20, 11 minutes) and the Málaga-Centro station beside the Río Guadalmedina. Departures from the city to the airport and beyond are about every half-hour from 5.45am to 10.30pm.

Bus

Useful buses around town (€1.10 for all trips around the centre) include bus 11 to El Palo, bus 34 to El Pedregalejo and El Palo and bus 35 to Castillo de Gibralfaro, all departing from Avenida de Cervantes (see Map p246). The MalagaTour (p257) bus is also a useful option.

Car

Convenient car parks such as on Plaza de la Marina (Map p243) tend to be expensive (per hour/24 hours €1.50/24). Side-street parking, off the south side of Alameda Principal, for example, is metered (€1.60 per 90 minutes). Vacant lots are much cheaper (pay €1 to the attendant).

Taxi

Taxi fares typically cost around €3 to €4 per 2km to 3km. Fares within the city centre, including to the train and bus stations and the Castillo de Gibralfaro, usually cost around €6.

COSTA DEL SOL

The Costa del Sol stretches along the Málaga seaboard like a wall of wedding cakes several kilometres thick. Its recipe for success is the certainty (more or less) of sunshine, convenient beaches, warm sea, cheap package deals and plenty of nightlife and entertainment.

Until the 1950s the resorts were fishing villages but there's little to show for that now. Launched as a Francoist development drive for impoverished Andalucía, the Costa del Sol is an eye-stinging example of how to fill all open spaces with concrete buildings and paying customers. And with over 40 golf clubs, several busy marinas, numerous riding schools, a host of beaches offering every imaginable water sport, and a riotous international nightlife, the *costa* attracts an ever-increasing following of pleasure seekers who continue to swell the boom year in, year out.

Getting There & Around

A convenient train service links Málaga and its airport with Torremolinos, Arroyo de la Miel and Fuengirola, and plenty of buses run to the coastal towns from Málaga.

The AP7 Autopista del Sol, bypassing Fuengirola, Marbella, San Pedro de Alcántara and Estepona, makes moving along the Costa del Sol a lot easier for those willing to pay its tolls (Málaga–Marbella June to September costs €5.50 October to May €3.40; Marbella–Estepona June to September €6.50, October to May €3.90).

The toll-free alternative, running parallel to the AP7, is the A7/N340, which runs nearer the coast and almost entirely through built-up areas. Many places along this road use Km numbers to pinpoint their location. These numbers rise from west to east: Estepona is at Km 155 and central Marbella at Km 181. Km markers aside, undoubtedly the most useful sign on the A7/N340 is 'Cambio de Sentido', indicating that you can change direction to get back to a turning you might have missed. Don't let impatient drivers behind push you into going too fast for comfort on this road – and watch out for footloose drunks!

Bargain rental cars (€130 to €150 a week, all-inclusive) are available from local firms in all the resorts.

TORREMOLINOS & BENALMÁDENA

Britain's Blackpool would kill for what the *costa* capitals have, as far as sunshine goes. This concrete high-rise jungle, beginning 5km southwest of Málaga airport, is designed to squeeze as many paying customers as possible into the smallest available space. Even in winter, pedestrian traffic blocks the narrow lanes behind the main beaches, with holidaymakers scouring endless souvenir shops and real-estate agents.

After leading the Costa del Sol's mass tourist boom of the 1950s and '60s, Torremolinos (Torrie) lost ground to other resorts but is trying hard to spruce itself up. A pleasant seafront walk, the Paseo Marítimo, extends for nearly 7km and gives a degree of cohesion and character to the resort.

Adjoining Torremolinos to its southwest is the tamer Benalmádena, split into three distinctive areas: Benalmádena Costa at sea level, Benalmádena Pueblo up the hill, and Arroyo de la Miel, a lively suburb of restaurants and shops.

A clear few grades above Torremolinos, Benalmádena Pueblo still retains an attractive historic centre of cobbled alleys and flower-filled balconies around its central square, Plaza de España. It affords great views and is usually a touch cooler in summer. Down in Benalmádena Costa, the Puerto Deportivo, with some classy restaurants and bars, is one of the liveliest nightspots in the area.

Orientation

The main road through Torremolinos from the northeast (the direction of the airport and Málaga) is called Calle Hoyo, becoming Avenida Palma de Mallorca after it passes through Plaza Costa del Sol. Calle San Miguel is the main pedestrian artery, running most of the 500m from Plaza Costa del Sol down to Playa del Bajondillo. The bus station is on Calle Hoyo and the train station is on Avenida Jesús Santos Rein, a pedestrianised street intersecting Calle San Miguel 200m down from Plaza Costa del Sol. Southwest of Playa del Bajondillo, around a small point, is Playa de la Carihuela, once the fishing quarter, backed by generally lower-rise buildings.

The southwestern end of Torremolinos merges with Benalmádena Costa, the seafront area of Benalmádena. About 2km uphill from here is the part of Benalmádena called Arroyo de la Miel, with Benalmádena Pueblo some 4km to its west.

Information

BOOKSHOPS

Secondhand Bookshop (Calle San Miguel 26, Torremolinos) Plenty of used paperbacks – great if you're not working off that hangover on the beach.

EMERGENCY

Policía Local (☎ 952 38 14 22; Calle Rafael Quintana 28, Torremolinos)

Policía Nacional (☎ 952 38 99 95; Calle Skal 12, Torremolinos) The main police station.

INTERNET ACCESS

Cyber Café (Avenida Los Manantiales 4, Torremolinos; per hr €2; 🕑 9am-10pm)

Miramar (☎ 952 57 75 75; Avenida del Puerto, Benalmádena Costa; per hr €2; 🕑 11am-11pm)

MEDICAL SERVICES

Red Cross Emergencies (☎ 952 37 37 27; Calle María Barrabino 16, Torremolinos)

Sanatorio Marítimo (☎ 951 03 20 00; Calle del Sanatorio 5, Torremolinos) The main hospital.

MONEY

All the resorts have plenty of banks with ATMs, concentrated on the main pedestrianised shopping streets.

POST

Post office Benalmádena (Avenida Antonio Machado 20; 🕑 8.30am-8.30pm Mon-Fri, 8.30am-2pm Sat); Torremolinos (Avenida Palma de Mallorca 23; 🕑 8.30am-8.30pm Mon-Fri, 9.30am-1pm Sat)

TOURIST INFORMATION

Benalmádena tourist office (☎ 952 44 24 94; www .benalmadena.com in Spanish; Avenida Antonio Machado 10, Torremolinos; 🕑 9am-8.30pm Mon-Fri, 10am-4.30pm Sat) On the main road from Torremolinos. There are branches on the seafront in Benalmádena Costa, and on the Benalmádena exit road from the AP7.

Torremolinos tourist office (☎ 952 37 95 12; www .ayto-torremolinos.org; Plaza Pablo Picasso; 🕑 9am-1.30pm Mon-Fri) In the town hall. There are also offices on Playa Bajondillo (☎ 952 37 19 09) and Playa Carihuela (☎ 952 37 29 56) with the same hours as the town hall. Pick up information leaflets on the surrounding amusement parks and news of monthly events.

Sights & Activities

Bars and beaches – that says it all. 'Torrie' is still a good-time resort where people come to party hard on the neon-lit **Calle San Miguel** and soak up the sun on the wide, sandy beaches. With the exception of the lonely **Torre de los Molinos** (Tower of the Mills), a 14th-century Arab watchtower, there is precious little to see. Torrie is a 'doing', not a 'seeing', place, and along with the rest of the Costa del Sol specialises in **theme**

MÁLAGA PROVINCE

parks (see p268), water sports and a host of largely free music and dance festivals that run throughout the summer months (the tourist offices have details).

However, people never seem to tire of the good old seafront promenade, which in the case of Torremolinos runs several kilometres west from Playa de Bajondillo. It extends to the more-upmarket La Carihuela, the original fishing village that used to serve Málaga and that preserves something of its humble past, not least in a good selection of fish restaurants. Drivers note: there is no road along the seafront connecting the two beaches.

Further west and uphill, the prettier and less garish Benalmádena Pueblo, with its geranium-filled balconies and narrow streets, is a welcome relief from the unrelenting party atmosphere along the coast. A municipal museum, the Museo Benalmádena (☎ 952 44 85 93; Avenida Juan Peralta 49; admission free; ☯ 10am-2pm & 4-7pm Mon-Fri), has two sections, one exhibiting local archaeological finds, the other, curiously, exhibiting a fantastic collection of Mexican and Central and South American artefacts. There is a magnificent view of the coast from the tiny church at the top of the village.

At Benalmádena Costa there is a cable car (☎ 952 19 04 82; www.teleferico.com in Spanish; Esplanade Tívoli s/n; adult/child return-trip €12/8.50; ☯ 10.30am-late Apr-Oct) that transports you up into the hills from where you can walk down two marked pathways. The cable car belongs to the Selwo organisation, which has organised activities once you're up the top. You can ride a donkey, watch bird-of-prey exhibitions and horse-riding displays or ramble along the walking trails up there. Boat cruises to Fuengirola (€12, three or four daily, two hours return) leave from the Puerto Deportivo at Benalmádena. To reserve a ticket contact Costasol Cruceros (☎ 952 44 48 81; www.costasolcruceros.com), which also does dolphin-spotting trips (adult/child €20/10, four daily, two hours return).

Festivals & Events

Torremolinos hosts an exhaustive list of festivals, including the Championship Ballroom Dance Contest, Carnival, the Verdiales (folk-dancing) festival, Holy Week, Crosses of May and the Day of the Tourist (!). But the most important event is the Romería de San Miguel

(29 September), when a colourful parade of *gitano* (Roma) caravans, Andalucian horses and flamenco dancers wends its way through the streets of Torremolinos to the forest behind the town for a night of barbecues, drinking and dancing.

Sleeping

There are huge numbers of rooms at almost every price. However, to avoid a weary trudge from one *completo* (full) sign to another, you are strongly advised to book ahead during July, August and, in some places, September. Outside these peak months, room rates often drop sharply. The area has several camping grounds (ask at the tourist offices for details).

Hostal Flor Blanco (☎ 952 38 20 71; Pasaje de la Carihuela 4, Torremolinos; d €44) Just metres from Playa de la Carihuela (about 1.5km southwest of central Torremolinos), the small and friendly Flor Blanco has sea-view rooms with little balconies. As it has only 12 rooms you should book in advance.

Hotel Miami (☎ 952 38 52 55; www.residencia -miami.com; Calle Aladino 14, Torremolinos; s/d €38/59; ☒ ☯) A lovely Andalucian-style villa built in the 1950s by Manolo Blascos (Picasso's cousin) for flamenco dancer Lola Medina. Only 100m from La Carihuela beach, this small hotel has tastefully decorated rooms and is set in the midst of a tropical garden with a wonderful pool.

Hotel El Pozo (☎ 952 38 06 22; www.world-traveler .com/spain/pozo/htm; Calle Casablanca 2, Torremolinos; s/d €34/65; ☒) Made famous in a 2002 edition of the TV show *Eastenders*, Hotel El Pozo has 28 spacious rooms and is just off pedestrianised Calle San Miguel in the thick of the action in Torremolinos.

Red Parrot (☎ 952 37 54 45; www.theredparrot .net; Avenida Los Manantiales 4, Torremolinos; s/d €60/65; ☒ ☯) Refurbished a couple of years back and centrally located, the Red Parrot offers comfortable balconied rooms around an internal patio. The pool area is inviting.

Hotel Tarik (☎ 952 38 23 00; www.hoteltarik.com; Paseo Marítimo 49, Torremolinos; s/d €60/91; P ☒ ☯) This large, Andalucian-style hotel is located right on the seafront behind a swath of sandy beach. Communal areas are attractively decorated with Moroccan *zellij* tilework and there is a large secluded pool. Bedrooms have less character but are extremely comfortable, with all modern facilities.

La Fonda Benalmádena (☎ /fax 952 56 82 73; www.123casa.com/hotels/benalmadendahotellafonda .htm; Calle Santo Domingo 7, Benalmádena Pueblo; s/d incl breakfast €60/86; P 🅿 💻 🌐) La Fonda is a charming place with large rooms built around Islamic-style patios (which feature fountains). The owners have another hotel and many apartments in the village.

Eating

British pit stops pop up everywhere, but plenty of seafood eateries are strewn along palm-lined Playa del Bajondillo in Torremolinos. The best fish restaurants and beach cocktail bars are on Playa de la Carihuela and in Benalmádena Costa.

Bodega Quitapeñas (Cuesta del Tajo, Torremolinos; raciones €4.50-9) Tucked away at the top of the steps down from Calle San Miguel to the beach, this busy tapas bar has a small terrace, and is popular with Spaniards for its delicious range of seafood tapas and *raciones* (meal-sized servings of tapas).

Bar Mesón Pepe (☎ 952 56 86 14; Calle Santo Domingo 2, Benalmádena Pueblo; mains €7-8) With outdoor tables by the church on the plaza, this place is full to bursting most nights, mainly with locals. No wonder, with good, filling meals at such a good price. Stick with the fish dishes – the *brocheta de pescado* (fish kebab) is just great!

La Paella (☎ 952 37 50 55; Paseo Marítimo, Torremolinos; paella for 2 €16, whole fish for 2 per kg €29) This excellent seafood eatery on Playa Bajondillo has many varieties of fish and seafood but also serves meat dishes.

Casa Juan (☎ 952 38 41 06; Calle San Gine's 20, Torremolinos; mains €8-18, whole fish & fancy seafood extra) One of a string of first-rate seafood eateries in La Carihuela, this place does fantastic fish and seafood, *malagueño*-style. Share an avocado and prawn salad then crack apart a plump lobster. Casa Juan doesn't have sea views and it extends over several premises.

Restaurant La Fonda (☎ /fax 952 56 82 73; www.123casa.com/hotels/benalmadendahotellafonda .htm; Calle Santo Domingo 7, Benalmádena Pueblo; mains €10-17) The excellent restaurant at La Fonda has a fantastic terrace for barbecues and summer dining. At other times you can choose from the streetfront restaurant or an interior room draped with fabric and full of Moroccan lamps. The baked-fish dishes are splendid.

Restaurant El Roqueo (☎ 952 38 49 46; Calle Carmen 35, Torremolinos; mains €13-20) With its wide terrace, El Roqueo has the atmosphere of a beachside diner, but it's much classier than that. It's bustling and friendly and you can't beat the simple but delicious *dorada a la plancha* (grilled bream).

Drinking & Entertainment

Torremolinos' clubs are back in vogue, despite stiff competition from Benalmádena Costa's Puerto Deportivo area, where there are some classy (and touristy) bars. Torrie has some big venues as well as a thriving gay scene (see p262).

Playa Miguel (www.playa-miguel.com; Playa de la Carihuela) This substantial beach bar has good music and cocktails. Sit on a comfy cane chair and join in the fun.

Atrévete (Avenida Salvador Allende, La Carihuela; 🕐 8pm-5am) A sexy salsa club with two cosy dance floors on which the clientele can strut their stuff.

Fun Beach (☎ 952 05 23 97; Avenida Palma de Mallorca 7, Torremolinos; 🕐 8pm-6am) Reputedly the largest club in Europe, Fun Beach has several huge, packed dance floors in which to lose yourself. Expect to hear pop, house and garage.

Palladium (☎ 952 38 42 89; Avenida Palma de Mallorca 36, Torremolinos; admission €8; 🕐 10pm-7am mid-Mar–mid-Oct) A huge, frenetic club with a fancy swimming pool and two dance floors spinning out some thumping tunes.

Disco Kiu (Plaza Sol y Mar, Benalmádena Costa; 🕐 11pm-4am Thu-Sat) Another popular giant, which has foam parties for added excitement. Dress codes aren't strict but men generally wear collared shirts.

Getting There & Away

From the Torremolinos **bus station** (☎ 952 38 24 19; Calle Hoyo), Portillo buses run to Benalmádena Costa (€1.10, 15 minutes, every 15 minutes), Málaga (€1.20, 30 minutes, every 15 minutes), Benalmádena Pueblo (€1.10, 40 minutes, every 30 minutes) and Fuengirola (€1.20, 30 minutes, every 30 minutes). Buses to Ronda, Estepona, Algeciras, Tarifa, Cádiz and Granada also leave from the bus station. Buses for Marbella (€3.60, one hour, 14 daily) go from a stop on Avenida Palma de Mallorca, near the post office.

Trains run to Torremolinos about every half-hour from 5.30am to 10.30pm from

KIDS' COSTA

A growing number of attractions along the coast cater for children of all ages. The oldest and biggest amusement park is **Tivoli World** (☎ 952 57 70 16; www.tivolicostadelsol.com; Avenida de Tivoli, Arroyo de la Miel; admission €6; ☺ noon-8pm Sun Oct-Apr, 1-9pm May, 4-11pm Jun, 6pm-2am Jul-Sep). As well as various rides and slides (for which you pay extra to the admission price), it stages daily dance, musical and children's events. It's five minutes' walk from Benalmádena-Arroyo de la Miel train station. For children, consider the good-value 'Supertivolino' ticket for €10, which covers admission and unlimited use on more than 30 rides.

Alternatively, just off the A7 in Torremolinos is the ever-popular **Aquapark** (☎ 952 38 88 88; Calle Cuba 10; adult/child €19/14; ☺ 10am-6pm May, Jun & Sep, 10am-7pm Jul & Aug), with its chutes and slides, and the similar but cheaper **Parque Acuático Mijas** (☎ 952 46 04 04; www.aquamijas.com; adult/child €15/10; ☺ 10.30am-5.30pm May, 10am-6pm Jun & Sep, 10am-7pm Jul & Aug), beside the A7 Fuengirola bypass, which also has a separate minipark for toddlers.

Another watery hit is Benalmádena's well-organised **SeaLife** (☎ 952 56 01 50; www.sealifeeurope .com in Spanish; Puerto Deportivo; adult/child €10.85/9.25; ☺ 10am-10pm Jun, 10am-midnight Jul-Sep, 10am-6pm May), with minigolf, organised games and shark-feeding of Europe's largest shark collection. There's a new Amazon section and a display of sea snakes. Giving SeaLife stiff competition is the newer **Selwo Marina** (☎ 902 19 04 82; www.selwomarina.com; Parque de la Paloma, Benalmádena; ☺ 10am-6pm, or 8pm, 9pm or midnight, depending on its own peculiar timetable, closed for most of Nov-Feb; adult/child €15/11, swim with sea lions €49), a relative of Selwo Aventura in Estepona. It has a dolphinarium and ice-penguinarium, an Amazonian aviary and the awesome option of swimming with sea lions. Selwo offers discounted packages for visits to the two Selwos and the Benalmádena cable car.

A good cloudy-day option is the **Crocodile Park** (☎ 952 05 17 82; www.crocodile-park.com; Calle Cuba 14, Torremolinos; ☺ 10am-6pm; adult/child €9/6.50), where experienced guides handle and give details about various types of crocodile.

Málaga city (€1.30, 20 minutes) and the airport (€1.10, 10 minutes). These continue on to Benalmádena–Arroyo de la Miel and Fuengirola (€1.30, 20 minutes).

FUENGIROLA
pop 63,000

Fuengirola, a beach resort 18km down the coast from Torremolinos, the two separated by Benalmádena Costa and Torrequebrada, has more of a family-holiday scene but is even more densely packed than Torremolinos. Its somewhat drab buildings rather overpower the waterfront and beaches, though the beaches are surprisingly pleasant.

Orientation & Information

The narrow streets in the few blocks between the beach and Avenida Matías Sáenz de Tejada (the street on which the bus station is located) constitute what's left of the old town, with Plaza de la Constitución at its heart. The train station is a block inland from the bus station, on Avenida Jesús Santos Rein.

The **tourist office** (☎ 952 46 74 57; Avenida Jesús Santos Rein 6; ☺ 9.30am-2pm & 5-7pm Mon-Fri, 10am-1pm Sat) is just along from the train station.

Sights & Activities

One great evening to be had is at the **Hipódromo Costa del Sol** (☎ 952 59 27 00; www .carreraentertainment.com; admission race days €7, otherwise free; ☺ 10pm-2am Sat Jul-Sep, 11.30am-4pm Sun Oct-Jun), which is Andalucía's leading horse-race track. You'll find it at Urbanización El Chaparral, off the A7 at the southwestern end of Fuengirola. Another worthwhile day out is at Fuengirola's **street market** (Avenida Jesús Santos Rein), held in the fairground. It takes place every Tuesday and is the biggest on the Costa. There's a *rastro* (flea market) in the same place on Saturday, and a Sunday market in the port.

Festivals & Events

The biggest festival in Fuengirola is the **Día de la Virgen del Carmen** (16 July), in which 120 bearers carry a heavy platform (which supports a lavish effigy of the Virgin) in a two-hour procession from Los Boliches church into the sea. From July to September music and dance performances are held in the Arabic **Castillo Sohail**, which is also the venue for a medieval market in August.

Sleeping

While there are simply dozens of hotels in Fuengirola, the following are a few of the most appealing.

Hostal Italia (☎ 952 47 41 93; fax 952 46 19 09; Calle de la Cruz 1; s/d €40/64; 🔀) A good, friendly economical option in the heart of things, a couple of blocks from the beach. Calle de la Cruz is a pedestrianised street. The rooms are all clean and comfortable.

Las Islas (☎ 952 47 55 98; Calle Canela 12, Torreblanca del Sol; d incl breakfast €67; 🔀 🖭) Just east of Fuengirola, Las Islas is a haven of taste and calm run by the exceptionally friendly Ghislaine and Hardy Honig. Twelve comfortable guest rooms are spread throughout lush tropical gardens and there is an excellent restaurant serving international and vegetarian food.

Hotel El Puerto (☎ 952 47 01 00; www.hotel-elpuerto.com; s incl breakfast €75-104, d incl breakfast €88-134; Calle Marbella 34; 🔀 🖭) A towering three-star hotel on Fuengirola's beach. Balconies have great sea views and there's an amazing oval-shaped rooftop pool.

Eating

Calle Moncayo and Calle de la Cruz, a block back from the Paseo Marítimo, are awash with mediocre international eateries. The Paseo Marítimo itself and the Puerto Deportivo have further strings of bargain eateries.

Cafetería Costa del Sol (☎ 952 47 17 09; Calle Marbella 3; rosquillas €3.60) Cheerful breakfast spot with a bright, striped awning. It turns out hot, tasty ham-and-cheese *rosquillas* (toasted bagels) and lovely fresh juices (€2.60).

Lizzaran (☎ 952 47 38 29; Avenida Jesús Santos Rein 1; raciones €4.50-11.50, lunch mains €6) A welcome Spanish relief from the overwhelming number of Chinese and Italian eateries in Fuengirola. Tuck into salty sardine or ham *pinxos* (bread with toppings).

Mo Mo (☎ 952 19 73 21; Calle Marbella 8; mains €8-9.50; 🕒 closed Sun & dinner Mon; 🔽) Mo Mo is an art gallery–cum–vegetarian restaurant offering yummy dishes like moussaka, tofu brochettes and spinach pastries.

Restaurante Portofino (☎ 952 47 06 43; Paseo Marítimo 29; mains €12-17; 🕒 closed Mon) One of Fuengirola's better offerings, this restaurant has an international menu featuring a host of classic fish dishes. Specialities include all manner of fried fish, sole with a wine and cream sauce and some excellent shellfish.

Taberna del Pintxo (Calle Hermsnos Pinzón 2; pintxos €2) This is a glossy new place specialising in *pintxos* (Basque for tapas).

Drinking & Entertainment

Plenty of tacky disco-pubs line Paseo Marítimo, and a cluster of music bars and discos can be found opposite the Puerto Deportivo. A few hip bars also dot the town.

Habana Club (Avenida Condes San Isidro 9) A Spanish and *Latino* music bar. Salsa dance classes happen at 10pm Sunday and Friday.

Irish Times (🕒 noon-midnight) and **Cafetería La Plaza** (9am-midnight) are bars at opposite ends of Plaza de la Constitución. Both fill up with lively, mainly Spanish crowds in the evening. The Irish Times' patio is great on a hot night. Rock fans can head for **Sal's Paradise** (Paseo Marítimo, Parque Doña Sofía) for live music on at least Saturday night.

Getting There & Away

From the **bus station** (☎ 902 14 31 44), frequent bus services travel to Torremolinos (€1.50, 30 minutes), Málaga (€2.50, one hour), Marbella (€2.44, one hour) and Mijas (€1, 25 minutes).

Fuengirola is served by the same trains as Torremolinos, costing €2.30 from Málaga and the airport.

MIJAS

pop 57,000 / elevation 428m

The story of Mijas encapsulates the story of the Costa del Sol. Originally a humble pueblo, it is now the richest town in the province. Since finding favour with discerning bohemian artists and writers in the 1950s and '60s, Mijas has sprawled across the surrounding hills and down to the coast yet managed to retain the original pueblo's picturesque charm. Much like Capri, the effect is somewhat spoiled by the hordes of day-tripping package tourists that pile into the town in summer, but in winter it is blissfully quiet. Actually, wander the back streets at any time and you'll appreciate its charm. Mijas has a foreign population of at least 40% and the municipality includes Mijas Costa, on the coast west of Fuengirola. Golf courses abound.

Information

For information on sights, activities and events in and around Mijas, stop by the helpful **tourist office** (☎ 958 58 90 34; www.mijas.es; Plaza Virgen de la Peña s/n; 🕑 9am-7pm Mon-Fri Oct-Mar, 9am-8pm Mon-Fri Apr-Sep, 10am-3pm Sat year-round).

Sights & Activities

Mijas is home to the most interesting 'folk' museum on the *costa*, the **Casa Museo de Mijas** (☎ 952 59 03 80; Calle Málaga; admission free; 🕑 10am-2pm & 4-7pm Sep-Mar, 10am-2pm & 5-8pm Apr-Jun, 10am-2pm & 6-9pm Jul-Aug). It was created and is still run by Carmen Escalona, who specialises in crafting folk-themed models. The small models are dotted around the museum, and in light of the explanations and artefacts, show perfectly the style and mode of living of some 40 years ago. There are no explanations in English. It is a great place for children, who will particularly like the donkey made from esparto grass. The museum is just uphill from Plaza de la Constitución, Mijas' second main plaza.

Mijas has an unusual square-shaped **Plaza de Toros** (☎ 952 48 52 48; fights €45-85; 🕑 10am-8pm). It also has an interesting grotto of the **Virgen de la Peña**, where the Virgin is said to have appeared to two shepherds in 1586. On the cliff edge in an ornamental garden, the spot has wonderful views and is the start of a **panoramic pathway** that wends its way around the vertical edges of the town. During the annual village procession, 8 September, the effigy of the Virgin is carried 2km up to the **Ermita del Calvario**, a tiny chapel built by Carmelite brothers. Black-iron crosses mark a short walking trail that leads through the forest up to the hermitage. Alternatively, you can take one of the donkey taxis from the town centre for €8.

Mijas is a noted area for **rock climbing** (particularly in winter), with around 100 grade V-7 climbs.

Sleeping

Hostal La Posada (☎ 952 48 53 10; Calle Coin 47; s/d €25/35, apt d €45; 🔀) Budget travellers should try this friendly place with tidy and spacious rooms and apartments set around a flower-filled garden-patio.

Casa El Escudo de Mijas (☎ 952 59 11 00; www.el-escudo.com; Calle Trocha de los Pescadores 7; s/d €70/80) A tidy midrange option with pretty colour-

washes, wrought-iron furnishings and tiled bathrooms.

TRH Mijas/Hotel Mijas (☎ 952 48 58 00; www.trhhoteles.com; Plaza de la Constitución; s/d €102/25; P 🔀 🖭) This sumptuous, Andalucian-style hotel has excellent facilities including horse riding, tennis and hydromassage.

There are two excellent B&Bs, **Casa Kay** (☎ /fax 952 48 57 91; www.anit.es/casa kay; Urbanización Las Lomas de Mijas; s/d €35/70; P 🖭) and **Finca Blake** (☎ /fax 952 59 04 01; www.fincablake.com; Carretera de Mijas Km 2; d €78-90). For details of how to reach them, see the websites. Another quality top-end hotel is the slick **Beach House** (☎ /fax 952 49 45 40; www.beachhouse.nu; Urbanización El Chaparral, Mijas Costa; s/d €125/140, d with sea view €175; P 🖵 🖭).

Eating

El Mirlo Blanco (☎ 952 48 57 00; Paseo Marítimo 29, Mijas Costa; mains €16-35; 🕑 closed Tue Sep-Jun) The Basque-style El Mirlo Blanco is one Mijas' best restaurants. The menu varies seasonally but roast lamb and hake in a green sauce are good choices. Finish with a Grand Marnier soufflé.

El Padrastro (☎ 952 48 50 00; Paseo del Compás; mains €12-27; 🔥) The *haute*-Med Padastro is perched on a cliff above the Plaza Virgen de la Peña, with suitably spectacular views. You don't have to climb the stairs as there is a lift. Delicious fare includes a leek-filled pastry, rice with seafood, and plenty of fish dishes.

For tapas and local specialities, find the lively **El Alarcón** (☎ 952 48 52 45; Calle Lasta 1). **The Lemon Tree** (☎ 952 48 64 74; Plaza Virgen de la Peña; lunches €4.50; 🕑 closed Sat), an English café decked out fully in yellow, serves tasty food.

Getting There & Away

Frequent buses run from Fuengirola (€1, 25 minutes).

MARBELLA

pop 124,000

Marbella is justly renowned both as the *costa*'s honey pot of glamour and wealth and as its capital of corruption and crime, and its two reputations of course go hand in hand. With so much *dinero* sloshing around here, it would be a surprise if some people *didn't* break rules to get their hands on it. See p34 for some of the dirt on Marbella, which fortunately won't interfere with the fun of ordinary innocent travellers who are just here to enjoy themselves.

Even though Marbella's most celebrated holiday-home owner, King Fahd of Saudi Arabia, died in 2005 and won't be making any more multimillion-euro visits to his private palace here, the money in Marbella is still very real. Just witness the parade of very expensive cars rolling down to the marina at nearby Puerto Banús of an evening.

Marbella is not just crowded Marbella town with its mix of glamorous boutiques, pretty plazas, down-to-earth bars, good and bad restaurants and moderate beaches. It's also the Milla de Oro (Golden Mile; actually about 5km long), west of town between Marbella and Puerto Banús, which is lined with luxury hotels and turn-offs towards the tree-girt mansions inhabited by the really rich. And it's a baffling sprawl of outlying concrete urbanisations sporting names like Costa Azalea and Brisa del Golf, full of the villas and apartments thrown up by the runaway construction juggernaut that has made the Costa del Sol what it is.

All of which actually adds up to a recipe for a lot of fun, and that's what Marbella's huge crowd of international visitors are here for. Though prices here are among the highest in Andalucía, moderate budgets can still make for good times, on the beaches and in the bars, restaurants, shops and clubs. As for the Marbella 'glamour', most of the celebrities here are B-list at best, but everyone enjoys playing the game of ostentation. If you can forget the dirty deeds in the background, come and join the party.

Orientation

The A7/N340 through town goes by the names Avenida Ramón y Cajal and, further west, Avenida Ricardo Soriano. The old town, with its narrow, crooked lanes, is centred on Plaza de los Naranjos, north of Avenida Ramón y Cajal. The bus station is on the northern side of the Marbella bypass, 1.2km north of Plaza de los Naranjos.

Information

There are plenty of banks with ATMs in the central area.

Centro de Salud Leganitos (☎ 952 77 21 84; Plaza Leganitos 5; ☯ 8am-5pm Mon-Fri, 9am-5pm Sat) For emergency medical attention.

Cibercafé (☎ 952 86 42 62; Travesía Carlos Mackintosh; internet per hr €3.50; ☯ 9am-10pm Mon-Fri, 9am-8pm Sat, 10am-10pm Sun) A real internet café, between the centre and the beach.

Farmacia Mingorance (☎ 952 77 50 86; Avenida Ricardo Soriano 44) Large, 24-hour pharmacy.

Hospital Costa del Sol (☎ 952 82 82 50; Carretera N340 Km 187) Big public hospital 6km east of the centre.

Municipal tourist office (www.marbella.es; ☯ 9.30am-9pm Mon-Fri, 10am-2pm Sat) Fontanilla (☎ 952 77 14 42; Glorieta de la Fontanilla) Naranjos (☎ 952 82 35 50; Plaza de los Naranjos 1) The Fontanilla branch is the main information office.

Policía Nacional (National Police; ☎ 952 76 26 00; Avenida Arias de Velasco) The main police station, in the north of town.

Post office (Calle de Jacinto Benavente 14)

Sights & Activities

The picturesque **Casco Antiguo** (Old Town) is chocolate-box perfect, with pristine white houses, narrow, mostly traffic-free streets and geranium-filled balconies. You can easily spend an enjoyable morning or evening exploring these delightful alleyways crammed with cafés, restaurants, bars, designer boutiques and antique and crafts shops. At the heart of its pleasant web is pretty **Plaza de los Naranjos**, the focal point of the old town, dating back to 1485. The 16th-century **ayuntamiento** (town hall), scene of so many political shenanigans, is on the plaza's northern side and the **fountain** opposite was put in place in 1504 by Marbella's first Christian mayor. Nearby is the stout **Iglesia de la Encarnación** (Plaza de la Iglesia; ☯ hours of service 8.30am, 8pm & 9pm Mon-Sat, 8am, 10am, 11am, 12.30pm, 8.30pm & 10pm Sun), begun in the 16th century and later remodelled in baroque style. On the north side of Plaza de la Iglesia, and along streets such as Calle Arte and Calle Portada, are stretches of Marbella's old **Islamic walls**.

A little east of the church, the **Museo del Grabado Español Contemporáneo** (Museum of Contemporary Spanish Prints; ☎ 952 76 57 41; Calle Hospital Bazán s/n; admission €2.50; ☯ 10am-2pm & 5.30-8.30pm Tue-Sat mid-Sep–mid-Jun, 10am-2pm & 7-9pm Tue-Sat mid-Jun–mid-Sep) exhibits works by Picasso, Joan Miró and Salvador Dalí, among other artists.

Cross Avenida Ramón y Cajal to the Plaza de la Alameda and a marble walkway, **Avenida del Mar**, strung with crazed sculptures by Dalí, leads you down to the

MÁLAGA PROVINCE

MARBELLA

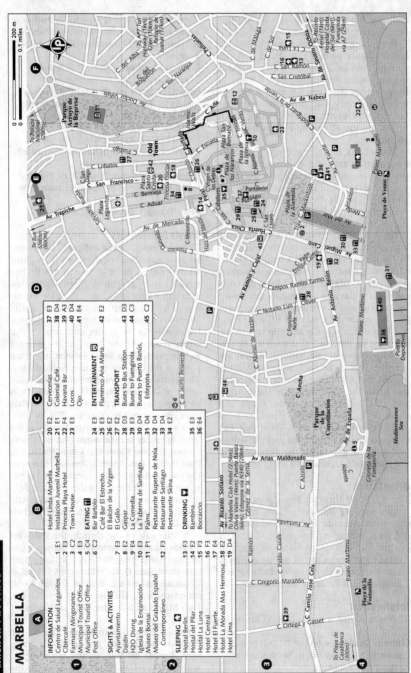

INFORMATION
Centro de Salud Leganitos......1 E1
Cibercafé.................................2 E3
Farmacia Mingorance..............3 C2
Municipal Tourist Office...........4 F3
Municipal Tourist Office...........5 C4
Post Office...............................6 C2

SIGHTS & ACTIVITIES
Ayuntamiento..........................7 E3
Daidín.....................................8 E2
H2O Diving..............................9 E4
Iglesia de la Encarnación........10 E3
Museo Bonsái.........................11 F1
Museo del Grabado Español
   Contemporáneo...................12 F3

SLEEPING
Hostal Berlín...........................13 F3
Hostal del Pilar.......................14 E2
Hostal La Luna........................15 F3
Hotel Central..........................16 F3
Hotel El Fuerte........................17 E4
Hotel La Morada Mas Hermosa.18 D4
Hotel Lima..............................19 D4
Hotel Linda Marbella..............20 E2
Instalación Juvenil Marbella....21 E1
Princesa Playa Hotel...............22 F4
Town House............................23 E3

EATING
Bar Bartolo.............................24 E3
Café Bar El Estrecho...............25 E3
El Balcón de la Virgen.............26 E2
El Gallo..................................27 E2
Gaspar...................................28 D3
La Comedia.............................29 E4
La Taberna de Santiago...........30 D4
Palms.....................................31 F1
Restaurante Ruperto de Nola..32 D4
Restaurante Santiago..............33 D4
Restaurante Skina...................34 E2
Cevecerías..............................37 E3
Colonial Café..........................38 D4
Havana Bar.............................39 A3
Locos.....................................40 D4
Ojo..41 E4

ENTERTAINMENT
Flamenco Ana María................42 E2

TRANSPORT
Buses to Bus Station................43 D3
Buses to Fuengirola.................44 C3
Buses to Puerto Banús,
   Estepona.............................45 C2

DRINKING
Bambina..................................35 E3
Boccaccio................................36 E4

beaches, backed by the long, pedestrian Paseo Marítimo. The central **Playa de Venus**, immediately below Avenida del Mar, is a fairly standard *costa* beach. For a longer, broader stretch of sand, walk west to the 800m-long **Playa de la Fontanilla** or the 2km **Playa de Casablanca** beyond it.

The watery **Parque Arroyo de la Represa**, just northeast of the old town, has a nice play area for young children. It also has the charming **Museo Bonsai** (☎ 952 86 29 26; adult/child €3/1.50; ☼ 10am-1.30pm & 4-7pm Sep-Jun, ☼ 10.30am-1.30pm & 5-8pm Jul & Aug), devoted to the Japanese miniature-tree art.

For maritime activities, head to **H2O Diving** (☎ 952 77 82 49; Paseo Marítimo) which offers two- to three-hour fun dives (€28) for all levels, as well as four- to six-day PADI diving courses, water skiing and (if the wind's right) some exhilarating kitesurfing. Call ahead to arrange activities out of the April-to-September season. Or take a catamaran cruise looking for dolphins with **Fly Blue** (☎ 952 92 36 33; www.fly-blue.com; adult/child per day €65/35, 3hr trip €35/20).

On land, the expert guides of **Daidín** (☎ 952 82 05 79; www.daidin.com; Calle Ancha 17) will take you horse riding, mountain biking, hiking, bird-watching or on 4WD tours in the inland hills and natural parks.

Festivals & Events

The **Feria de San Bernabé**, commemorating Marbella's patron saint (in the week leading up to 11 June), is one of the biggest festivities on the Andalucian coast, with a party atmosphere taking over the old centre by day, and a big fairground and concerts, plus more partying and dancing, at the Recinto Ferial (Fairgrounds) on Avenida Arroyo Primero in the east of town by night.

Sleeping

Marbella's old town has a smattering of charming small hotels and a larger number of basic *hostales*. The luxury places (there are 28 four- and five-star hotels in and around Marbella) are dotted along the seafront and the A7/N340 for several kilometres in both directions (but chiefly west) from the centre.

BUDGET

Instalación Juvenil Marbella (☎ 952 27 03 01; www .inturjoven.com; Avenida Trapiche 2; per person incl break-fast under 26yr €9.50-14.50, 26 or over €13-19; 🖨 👍) Marbella's bright, modern youth hostel has 158 beds in rooms for one to four people (half have private bathroom). It's by far the cheapest place to stay in town and is fairly central.

Hostal del Pilar (☎ 952 82 99 36; www.hostal -marbella.com; Calle Mesoncillo 4; s/d/tr with shared bathroom €25/35/50) This popular backpacker-friendly British-run place off Calle Peral has a bar with a pool table and a roof terrace for sunbathing, and breakfasts are also available.

Hostal La Luna (☎ 952 82 57 78; Calle La Luna 7; r €55; 🖨) Calle La Luna is one of four quiet pedestrian lanes just east of the centre and close to the beach, where at least half a dozen *hostales* provide suitable budget accommodation. Delightful Hostal La Luna has balconied rooms overlooking an internal patio.

Hostal Berlin (☎ 952 82 13 10; www.hostalberlin .com; Calle San Ramón 21; s/d/tr €40/60/70; 🅿 🖨 🖳) This very friendly *hostal* with good facilities on a quiet street parallel to Calle La Luna serves breakfast for €2.50, and discounts are negotiable if you stay several days.

MIDRANGE

Hotel Lima (☎ 952 77 05 00; www.hotellimamarbella .com; Avenida Antonio Belón 2; s/d €56/70, Aug €72/90; 🖨 🖳) Without huge character but providing a good central base near the beach, the Lima is an eight-floor corner building and most of its ample rooms have balconies over the leafy streets.

Hotel Linda Marbella (☎ 952 85 71 71; www.hotel lindamarbella.com; Calle Ancha 21; s/d €55/75; 🖨 🖳) This is a reliable, central, small hotel with plain rooms; a few have balconies overlooking the attractive old-town street.

Hotel Central (☎ 952 90 24 42; www.hotelcentral marbella.com; Calle San Ramón 15; r €78; 🖨 🖳) A cut above the neighbouring *hostales*, the Central enjoys the same quiet location but has 15 large, tasteful rooms with bathtubs and chessboard-tile floors. Breakfast is available.

Hotel La Morada Mas Hermosa (☎ 952 92 44 67; www.lamoradamashermosa.com; Calle Montenebros 16A; s/d €73/92; 🖨 🖳) A small, warm and character-filled hotel on a tranquil, flowery, old-town street. Quaintly decorated with wrought-iron beds and white linen, the five rooms and one suite (all nonsmoking) are in major demand, so advance bookings are highly recommended.

TOP END

Town House (☎ 952 90 17 91; www.townhouse.nu; Calle Alderete 7; s/d incl breakfast €115/130; ☒) A superb, intimate, small hotel in a traditional town house, with its nine all-nonsmoking rooms arranged over four floors. Design is chic and uncluttered, and there's a fabulous roof terrace to chill out on. Book early, for style at what for Marbella is a pretty good price.

Princesa Playa Hotel (☎ 952 82 09 44; www.prin cesaplaya.com; Avenida Duque de Ahumada s/n; s €113-129, d €132-150; ☐ ☒ ☒) With great sea views, this modern apartment hotel represents great value for money on the seafront.

Hotel El Fuerte (☎ 952 86 15 00; www.hotel -elfuerte.es; Avenida El Fuerte s/n; s/d from €136/198; ☐ ☒ ☐ ☒) A huge 263-room complex right on the Paseo Marítimo with a host of facilities including gym, heated pool, gardens and spa. Many of the rooms have sea views, for which you will pay a premium price.

Marbella Club Hotel (☎ 952 82 22 11; www .marbellaclub.com; Carretera de Cádiz 178; s/d €425/450; ☐ ☒ ☐ ☒ ☒) Created in the 1950s by Austrian-Mexican aristocrat Alfonso von Hohenlohe, this was the original super-deluxe, super-discreet hotel that launched Marbella as a luxury tourism venue. Set in its own gorgeous, semitropical, beachfront gardens 2km along the 'Golden Mile', the hotel has every conceivable luxe facility, plus its own beautifully landscaped golf course a 20-minute drive away.

Eating

Dining in Marbella doesn't necessarily mean chichi interiors and bikini-size portions at whale-sized prices. There are some authentic tapas bars and a few trendy restaurants that do delicious, good-value cuisine. The seafront Paseo Marítimo is lined with restaurants and bars. Playa de Venus also has a clutch of eateries on the sand.

El Gallo (☎ 952 82 79 98; Calle Lobatos 44; mains €4.50-9; ☒ closed Thu) In the upper part of the old town, neat and economical El Gallo serves well-prepared, home-style Andalucian food. Fish dishes are delicious.

La Taberna de Santiago (☎ 952 77 00 78; Avenida del Mar 20; tapas €1.50-2, raciones €5-14; ☒ closed Nov) Blue tiles adorn this refined tapas bar, and

---

THE AUTHOR'S CHOICE

La Comedia (☎ 952 77 64 78; Calle San Lázaro; mains €15-25; ☒ 7pm-1am Tue-Sun) This creative upstairs restaurant is run by a dedicated Swedish duo who put together some terrific international taste combinations – hope the mussels in white-wine sauce are on the menu, and follow them with duck breast in fruit compote, sweet chicken curry or a vegetarian couscous crepe. It's candlelit yet animated, with interesting art on the walls and some tables on a balcony overlooking little Plaza Victoria.

---

the blue sea is in view from its *terraza*, as are the curious sculptures on pedestrianised Avenida del Mar. Go for cockles, fried sardines, *jamón serrano* (mountain-cured ham) or even snails in thyme sauce.

El Balcón de la Virgen (☎ 952 77 60 52; Calle Virgen de los Dolores; mains €8-16; ☒ closed Sun) One of the nicest restaurants in the Plaza de los Naranjos vicinity, this place has a lovely summer *terraza* overlooked by a 300-year-old grieving Virgin and the biggest bougainvillea you've ever set eyes on. The fare is a respectable combination of meat, seafood and salads.

Gaspar (☎ 952 77 00 78; Calle Notario Luis Oliver 19; mains €20; ☒ closed dinner Sun) This good-value, family-run restaurant is just off the seafront. Food ranges from *raciones* to full-blown meals. The restaurant also has a quaint small library and a comprehensive wine list.

Restaurante Santiago (☎ 952 77 00 78; Paseo Marítimo 5; mains €18-25; ☒ closed Nov) One of Marbella's finest restaurants, Santiago is right on the seafront, offering top-class seafood in elegant surrounds. Sit on the terrace and survey the palms on Playa de Venus.

Restaurante Skina (☎ 952 76 52 77; Calle Aduar 12; mains €20-27; ☒ 7-11.30pm Mon-Sat) A good bet for an imaginative meal, tiny Skina is great for outdoor dining on summer evenings. Try sole with lime and ginger or suckling pig with caramelised tomatoes.

Restaurante Ruperto de Nola (☎ 952 76 55 50; Avenida Antonio Belón 3; mains €24-30; ☒ closed mid-Jan–mid-Feb) This classy establishment serves up gourmet meat and seafood with a creative touch in classical surroundings.

If you can cope with its skinny bronzed bodies then head for **Palms** (Playa de Venus; salads, fish & seafood €6-12; ☺ lunch). **Café Bar El Estrecho** (☎ 952 77 00 04; Calle San Lázaro; tapas €1.20) and **Bar Bartolo** (☎ 952 82 69 50; Calle San Lázaro; tapas €1.80) are good old-town spots for varied tapas and strong coffee. If they're busy, just elbow your way in.

Drinking

Marbella's once-notorious Puerto Deportivo has been cleaned up, renovated and reopened and now provides an entertaining after-dark scene without the sleaze.

Colonial Café (☎ 649 08 41 72; ☺ 6pm-3am or later) A hip disco-pub playing funky-house or reggae-dub, with a *terraza* facing the harbour.

Locos (☺ 1.30pm-4am or later) This alternative place at the back of the Puerto Deportivo has a wild atmosphere, and diverse live bands some nights.

Bambina (Calle Pasaje 5) In the old town, there are cocktails and more house at this stylishly designed bar.

Calle Pantaleón has a string of popular *cervecerías* (beer bars). Posier drinkers head west to Calle Camilo José Cela and nearby streets, where you'll find the fashionable, lounge-style **Havana Bar** (☎ 952 86 36 41; Calle Pablo Casals 17), with live Latin music some nights. Gay male drinkers can head to neighbours **Boccaccio** (Calle Puerto del Mar 7) and **Ojo** (Calle Puerto del Mar 9), both open from 10 or 11pm to around 6am.

Entertainment

The serious big-name clubs cluster around the Golden Mile and the vanity fair of Puerto Banús.

Flamenco Ana María (☎ 952 77 11 17; Plaza Santo Cristo 5; admission incl 1 drink €20; ☺ shows 11.30pm Wed-Sat) As far as flamenco goes on the Costa del Sol, Ana María's is a relatively good-value, authentic show. Reservations are essential.

Shopping

The winding streets of the old town are full of glittering, designer-label boutiques, enticing craft shops and fancy antique showrooms. There's another area with many upmarket boutiques south of Avenida Ramón y Cajal and west of Avenida Miguel Cano. A lively street market takes place on Monday mornings in the **Recinto Ferial** (Avenida Albarizas), east of the old town.

Getting There & Away

Buses to Fuengirola (€2.50, one hour), Puerto Banús (€1, 20 minutes) and Estepona (€2.40, one hour) leave about every 30 minutes from Avenida Ricardo Soriano. Services to and from the **bus station** (☎ 952 76 44 00; Avenida Trapiche) include the following destinations:

Destination	Cost	Duration	Daily Frequency
Algeciras	€6	1½hr	20
Cádiz	€16	2½hr	3
Córdoba	€16	5hr	1 or 2
Granada	€14	2¾hr	7
Málaga	€4.70	1¼hr	up to 27
Málaga airport	€4	1hr	10 or more
Ojén	€1	30min	9 (Mon-Sat)
Ronda	€4.70	1½hr	7
Seville	€15	3¾hr	2 or 3

Getting Around

From the bus station, bus 7 (€1) runs every 20 minutes (6.30am to 11.10pm) to the Fuengirola/Estepona bus stop on Avenida Ricardo Soriano, near the town centre. Returning from the centre to the bus station, take bus 2 from Avenida Ramón y Cajal (at the corner of Calle Huerta Chica). To walk from the bus station to the centre, cross the bridge over the bypass and carry straight on down Avenida Trapiche.

Marbella's streets are notoriously traffic-clogged and the one-way system may add to drivers' frustrations. Fortunately there's a reasonable number of pay car parks located throughout the town where you can hole up on arrival; they typically charge €1 to €1.20 per hour, with a daily maximum of €10 to €12.

AROUND MARBELLA
Ojén & Around

The hills of the Sierra Blanca towering behind Marbella provide an escape from the coastal mayhem, and the village of Ojén, among eucalyptus and citrus groves 9km north of town, is a good place to start exploring. At Ojén's **Museo del Vino Málaga** (☎ 952 88 14 53; Calle Carrera 39; admission free; ☺ 11am-3pm & 6-10pm Jul-Oct, 11am-8pm Nov-Jun), you can taste and buy some of Málaga's finest wine in its oldest distillery. Ojén's **Castillo de Cante** flamenco festival, on the night of the first or second Saturday of

August, always features some of the big flamenco names.

Ojén has a couple of straightforward village restaurants, and a further 7km up the hill is the smarter country-house hotel **Refugio de Juanar** (☎ 952 88 10 00; www.juanar.com; Sierra Blanca s/n; s/d €79/102; P ✄ ▣), with a restaurant specialising in game. The Refugio de Juanar is the starting point of some good, well-marked walking trails, for which the hotel can provide you with a map. A gentle 2km hike will take you to the **mirador**, a lookout point with views over the coast and, on a clear day, as far as Africa. Even better views are to be had from the Cruz de Juanar, a hilltop cross a half-kilometre up to the west of the *mirador*. Keen hikers can follow trails back down to Ojén or Marbella, or west to the village of Istán.

Puerto Banús
pop 15,000

Six kilometres along the coast west of Marbella you'll find Puerto Banús, Spain's original village-style port development and today the flashiest marina on the Costa del Sol. Some truly enormous floating palaces are tied up near the control tower at the western end of the harbour. Marbella's 'spend, be seen, have fun' ethos is at its purest here, with the constant parade of the glamorous, the would-be glamorous and the normal in front of the luscious boutiques and bustling restaurants strung along the waterfront. A couple of narrow lanes immediately behind here contain the busiest nightlife zone in the whole Marbella area, and further back are a couple of enormous shopping malls. Either side of the marina, good broad sandy beaches stretch east and west.

It's definitely a fun place to visit, and a fun way to arrive is with **Cruceros Turísticos Marbella** (☎ 676 000099), whose boats leave Marbella's Puerto Deportivo hourly from 10am to 6pm for the half-hour sail to Banús (one-way/return €5/8).

Time to refuel? Choose from the Greek **Red Pepper** (☎ 952 81 21 48; mains €17-25), Italian **Don Leone** (☎ 952 81 17 16; pizza & pasta €9-12) and **Picasso** (☎ 952 81 36 69; pizza & pasta €9-10), or American **Jacks** (☎ 952 81 36 25; burgers €10-16), all along the waterfront Calle de Ribera.

Popular meeting-place bars include **Salduba Pub** (☎ 952 81 10 92; ❧ noon-2am) and Sinatra Bar, both towards the west end

---

DANCING QUEEN

Olivia Valere (☎ 952 82 88 61; www.oliviava lere.com; Carretera de Istán Km 0.8; admission Sep-Jul €20-30, Aug €50; ❧ midnight-6am Thu-Sat, nightly in Aug) If there's one nightclub that epitomises the extravagant image of Marbella, it's Olivia Valere, less than 1km up the Istán road off the Golden Mile. Modelled on Granada's Alhambra, the interior is an *Arabian Nights* fantasy of interlinking courtyard dance floors, splashing fountains, gold columns and darkly beautiful bars. Its exclusive restaurant Babilonia (open 8.30pm to 3am) serves an exquisite international menu (mains €18 to €30). It is hard to overrate the extravagant experience and it should be on everyone's Marbella itinerary.

---

of Calle de Ribera. **Taco Loco** (☎ 952 81 14 38; ❧ noon-2am), to their east, develops quite a party atmosphere. Many other busy bars, including several Irish pubs, are found along the parallel street behind here, generally known as the *segunda línea* (second line).

Come 1am or later, it's time to dance. Top spots along the *segunda línea*:
Comedia (❧ 11pm-dawn) Fashionable spot with mainstream dance music.
Heaven Café (☎ 952 90 85 29; ❧ 9pm-4am) Resident house DJs.
Terra Blues (☎ 686 908016; ❧ 11pm-dawn Wed-Sat) Depending on the night, DJs spin almost everything from funk and acid jazz to hip-hop and rock, and there are even reggae nights.

Over by the roundabout at the western entrance to the marina, you might spot a celebrity at glamorous **Glam** (☎ 952 81 78 20; Edificio Gray d'Albion; ❧ from midnight Fri & Sat), while **Dreamer's** (☎ 952 81 20 80; www.dreamers-disco .com; N340 Km 175, Río Verde; admission incl 1 drink €20; ❧ 12.30am-6am Mon-Sat), on the eastern outskirts of Puerto Banús, brings house and garage music lovers a taste of paradise. With an ever-changing menu of DJs, a calendar of parties and room for 1400 clubbers you'll be pushed to find somewhere better to let your hair down.

Estepona
pop 55,000

Lower-key and lower-rise than the resorts to its east, Estepona remains a pleasant town with a long seafront promenade overlooking the wide, sandy **Playa de la Rada**. The huge, safe beach, clean water and relaxed atmosphere make this an excellent base for families and there is a great play area on the beach almost opposite the end of Avenida San Lorenzo, where the **tourist office** (☎ 952 80 20 02; www.estepona.es; Avenida San Lorenzo 1; 9am-8pm Mon-Fri, 10am-1.30pm Sat) is to be found. The beaches around Estepona are also popular surf spots for beginners.

SIGHTS & ACTIVITIES

The popular safari park, **Selwo Aventura** (☎ 902 19 04 82; www.selwo.es; Carretera A7 Km 162.5; adult/under 8yr €22/€15; 10am-6pm Sep-Jun, 10am-8pm Jul & Aug, closed early Dec-early Feb), located 6km east of Estepona, has over 200 exotic animal species. You can tour the park by 4WD or on foot and enjoy various adventure activities. A direct bus runs to Selwo from Málaga via Torremolinos, Fuengirola and Marbella (phone Selwo for information), but to get there from Estepona, a taxi (€10) is best.

For adult adventure, the **Happy Divers Club** (☎ 952 88 90 00; www.happy-divers-marbella.com; Atalaya Park Hotel, Carretera de Cádiz Km 168.5), based 11km east of Estepona, organises a wide range of diving courses and trips.

Away from the beach, Estepona's focal point is **Plaza de las Flores**, a pretty square at the heart of a small area of narrow old streets reminiscent of Marbella's *casco antiguo*.

A sizable fishing fleet and a large marina share the port beyond the lighthouse at the western end of town, and a lively **fish market** takes place every morning, although it's pretty much over by 7am.

SLEEPING & EATING

Accommodation in Estepona town is limited, and all in the budget or midrange, but a dozen four- and five-star hotels are dotted along the coast to the east.

Hostal La Malagueña (☎ 952 80 00 11; www.hlmestepona.com; Calle Castillo 1; s/d €25/49; P) Just off the central Plaza de las Flores, La Malagueña offers plain but adequately comfortable rooms, with fans.

Hostal El Pilar (☎ 952 80 00 18; www.telefonica.net/web2/hostalelpilar; Plaza de las Flores 10; s/d €28/50;) An old-fashioned but well-kept and friendly *hostal*, in a 250-year-old house nicely positioned on leafy Plaza de las Flores.

Hotel Aguamarina (☎ 952 80 61 55; www.hotelaguamarina.com; Avenida San Lorenzo 32, s/d incl breakfast €58/82;) The Aguamarina has comfortable, up-to-date rooms, some with balconies from which you can see the sea, and a handy ground-floor café-restaurant.

Plaza de las Flores is a student hang-out that's home to a few tapas bars and restaurants. Eating out focuses on the Puerto Deportivo: try the well-patronised **Maharajah's** (☎ 952 80 14 52; dishes €7-10; 7-11.30pm) for biryani, Punjabi or Goan dishes, or you can enjoy an excellent candlelit Italian meal at **Ristorante Rosatti** (☎ 952 79 66 06; mains €12-20, menú €26; 7pm-midnight). Also here is a flush of popular late-night bars.

GETTING THERE & AWAY

The **bus station** (☎ 952 80 02 49; Avenida de España) is 400m west of the tourist office along the seafront. Buses run every half-hour, from 6.40am to 10.40pm, to Marbella (€2.40, one hour), and 10 times daily to Málaga (€7, two hours). There are also services to La Línea de la Concepción (€3.50, one hour, eight daily), Algeciras (€3.60, one hour, nine daily) and Cádiz (€13, 3½ hours, two daily).

THE INTERIOR

The mountainous interior of Málaga province is an area of raw beauty and romantic *pueblos blancos* (white villages) sprinkled across craggy landscapes. Beyond the mountains, the verdant countryside opens out into a wide chequerboard of floodplains. It's all a far cry from the tourist-clogged coast.

RONDA

pop 36,000 / elevation 744m

Perched on an inland plateau riven by the 100m fissure of El Tajo gorge, Ronda has the most dramatic location of all the *pueblos blancos*. It owes its name, which means 'surrounded by mountains', to the encircling Serranía de Ronda. Established in the 9th century BC, Ronda is also one of Spain's oldest towns. Its existing old town, La Ciudad (the City), largely dates back to Islamic times, when it was an important cultural centre filled with mosques and palaces. Its wealth as a trading depot made it an attractive prospect for bandits and profiteers and the town has a colourful and romantic past in Spanish folklore.

Ronda was a favourite with the Romantics of the late 19th century, and has attracted an array of international artists and writers, such as David Wilkie, Alexandre Dumas, Rainer Maria Rilke, Ernest Hemingway and Orson Welles, who flocked to admire it. Nowadays, Ronda has a lot to live up to, and at just an hour inland from the Costa del Sol it attracts a weight of daytrippers, who nearly double its population in summer. The best time to enjoy the town with some ease is in the honeyed light of evening, or in the early spring and late autumn when the tourist season has lost its sting.

Orientation

La Ciudad stands on the southern side of El Tajo gorge. Following the Reconquista (Christian reconquest) in 1485, new taxes imposed on La Ciudad forced the residents to set up the newer town, El Mercadillo (the Market), to the north. Three bridges cross the gorge, the main one being the Puente Nuevo linking Plaza de España with Calle de Armiñán. Both parts of town come to an abrupt end on their western sides with cliffs plunging away to the valley of the Río Guadalevín far below. Places of interest are mainly concentrated in La Ciudad while most places to stay and eat, along with the bus and train stations, are in El Mercadillo.

Information

BOOKSHOPS
Comansur (☎ 952 87 86 67; www.comansur.com; Calle Lauria 33) Sells 1:50,000 SGE maps.

EMERGENCY
Policía Local (☎ 952 87 13 69; Plaza Duquesa de Parcent s/n) In the *ayuntamiento*.
Policía Nacional (☎ 952 87 10 01; Avenida de Madrid s/n)

INTERNET ACCESS
Central Corner Cibercafé (☎ 952 87 98 39; Calle Los Remedios 26; per hr €2.70; ☉ 4pm-late) A popular drinking bar and internet café with fast computers.

MEDICAL SERVICES
Hospital General Básico (☎ 952 87 15 41; El Burgo Rd) One kilometre from the town centre.

MONEY
Banks and ATMs are mainly on Calle Virgen de la Paz (opposite the bullring) and Plaza Carmen Abela.

POST
Post office (Calle Virgen de la Paz 18-20; ☉ 9am-8pm Mon-Fri, 9am-2pm Sat)

TOURIST INFORMATION
Municipal tourist office (☎ 952 18 71 19; www.turismoderonda.es; Paseo de Blas Infante; ☉ 10am-7.30pm Mon-Fri, 10.15am-2pm & 3.30-6.30pm Sat, Sun & holidays) Helpful and friendly staff with a wealth of information on the town and region.
Regional tourist office (☎ 952 87 12 72; www.andalucia.org; Plaza de España 1; ☉ 9am-7.30pm Mon-Fri, 10am-2pm Sat)

Sights
LA CIUDAD
Straddling the dramatic gorge and the Río Guadalevín (Deep River) is Ronda's most recognisable sight, the towering Puente Nuevo, best viewed from the Camino de los Molinos, which runs along the bottom of the gorge. The bridge separates the old and new towns. The former is surrounded by massive fortress walls pierced by two ancient gates: the Islamic Puerta de Almocábar, which in the 13th century was the main gateway to the castle; and the 16th-century Puerta de Carlos V. Inside, the Islamic layout remains intact, and its maze of narrow streets now takes its character from the Renaissance mansions of powerful families whose predecessors accompanied Fernando el Católico in the taking of the city in 1485.

Nearly all of the mansions still bear the crest of each family, including the Palacio de Mondragón (☎ 952 87 84 50; Plaza Mondragón; adult/concession €2/1; ☉ 10am-6pm Mon-Fri, 10am-3pm Sat, Sun & holidays) Built for Abomelic, ruler of Ronda in 1314, the palace retains its internal courtyards and fountains, the most impressive of these being the Patio Mudéjar, from which a horseshoe arch leads into a cliff-top garden with splendid views. It houses the city museum, which has artefacts and information especially related to both Roman and Islamic funerary systems.

A minute's walk southeast from the Palacio de Mondragón is the city's original mosque, now the ornate Iglesia de Santa María La Mayor (☎ 952 87 22 46; Plaza Duquesa de

RONDA

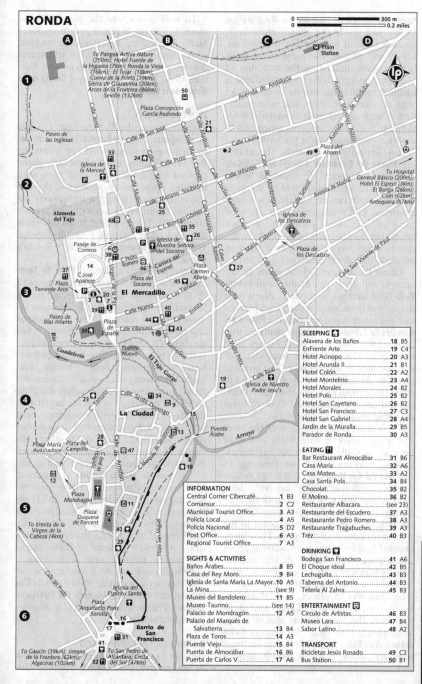

0 300 m
0 0.2 miles

To Pangea Active Nature
(250m); Hotel Fuente de
la Higuera (7km); Ronda la Vieja
(16km); El Tejar (18km);
Cueva de la Pileta (19km);
Sierra de Grazalema (20km);
Arcos de la Frontera (86km);
Seville (132km)

Train
Station

Avenida de Andalucía

Plaza Concepción
García Redondo

Paseo de
las Inglesas

Calle Jerez

Calle de San José

Calle Lauria

Plaza del
Ahorro

Iglesia de
la Merced

Calle de Sevilla

Calle Pozo

Calle de Molino

Calle Infantes

Calle de Monterejas

To Hospital
General Básico (200m);
Hotel El Espejo (3km);
El Burgo (26km);
Coin (62km);
Antequera (87km)

Alameda
del Tajo

Calle Mariano Soubirón

C.L. Borrego Gómez

Iglesia de
Nuestra Señora
del Socorro

Iglesia de
los Descalzos

Plaza de
los Descalzos

Pasaje de
Correos

Calle María Cabrera

Calle San Vicente de Paúl

Plaza
Teniente Arce

Plaza del
Socorro

Plaza
Carmen
Abela

Paseo de
Blas Infante

El Mercadillo

Calle Nueva

Calle Ermita

Plaza
de
España

Calle Villanueva

Río

Guadalevín

Puente
Nuevo

El Tajo Gorge

Calle de Remedios

Calle Madre Petra

Iglesia de Nuestro
Padre Jesú's

Calle Real

La Ciudad

Puente
Árabe

Arroyo

Plaza María
Auxiliadora

Plaza del
Campillo

Plaza
Mondragón

Plaza
Duquesa
de Parcent

To Ermita de la
Virgen de la
Cabeza (4km)

Hoyo San Miguel

Iglesia del
Espíritu Santo

Plaza
Arquitecto Pons
Sorolla

Barrio de
San
Francisco

To Gaucín (39km); Jimena
de la Frontera (62km);
Algeciras (102km)

To San Pedro de
Alcántara; Costa
del Sol (47km)

INFORMATION

Central Corner Cibercafé....................1	B3
Comansur..2	C2
Municipal Tourist Office.....................3	A3
Policía Local.......................................4	A5
Policía Nacional.................................5	D2
Post Office..6	A3
Regional Tourist Office......................7	A3

SIGHTS & ACTIVITIES

Baños Árabes......................................8	B5
Casa del Rey Moro.............................9	B4
Iglesia de Santa María La Mayor.......10	A5
La Mina.......................................(see 9)	
Museo del Bandolero........................11	B5
Museo Taurino...........................(see 14)	
Palacio de Mondragón......................12	A5
Palacio del Marqués de	
Salvatierra....................................13	B4
Plaza de Toros..................................14	A3
Puente Viejo.....................................15	B4
Puerta de Almocábar.........................16	B6
Puerta de Carlos V............................17	A6

SLEEPING

Alavera de los Baños.........................18	B5
EnFrente Arte.....................................19	C4
Hotel Acinopo...................................20	A3
Hotel Arunda II..................................21	B1
Hotel Colón.......................................22	A2
Hotel Montelirio................................23	A4
Hotel Morales....................................24	B2
Hotel Polo...25	B2
Hotel San Cayetano...........................26	B2
Hotel San Francisco...........................27	C3
Hotel San Gabriel..............................28	A4
Jardín de la Muralla...........................29	B5
Parador de Ronda..............................30	A3

EATING

Bar Restaurant Almocábar.................31	B6
Casa María...32	A6
Casa Mateo..33	A2
Casa Santa Pola.................................34	B4
Chocolat..35	B2
El Molino...36	B2
Restaurante Albacara..................(see 23)	
Restaurante del Escudero..................37	A3
Restaurante Pedro Romero................38	A3
Restaurante Tragabuches...................39	A3
Tréz...40	B3

DRINKING

Bodega San Francisco........................41	A6
El Choque Ideal.................................42	B5
Lechuguita...43	B3
Taberna del Antonio..........................44	B3
Tetería Al Zahra.................................45	B3

ENTERTAINMENT

Círculo de Artistas.............................46	B3
Museo Lara.......................................47	B4
Sabor Latino......................................48	A2

TRANSPORT

Bicicletas Jesús Rosado......................49	C2
Bus Station..50	B1

Parcent; admission €3; ☾ 10am-6pm Nov-Mar, 10am-7pm Apr-Oct). Just inside the church entrance is an arch covered with Arabic inscriptions, which was part of the mosque's mihrab (prayer niche indicating the direction of Mecca). The church has been declared a national monument, and its interior is an orgy of decorative styles and ornamentation. A huge central cedar choirstall divides the church into two sections: aristocrats to the front, everyone else at the back.

Just opposite the church, the amusing **Museo del Bandolero** (☎ 952 87 77 85; Calle de Arminán 65; admission €3; ☾ 10.30am-6pm Oct-Mar, 10.30am-7pm Apr-Sep) is dedicated to the banditry for which central Andalucía was once renowned. Old prints reflect that when the youthful *bandoleros* (bandits) were not being shot, hanged or garrotted by the authorities they were stabbing each other in the back, literally as much as figuratively.

Taking the narrow Calle Marqués de Salvatierra will bring you to the small **Puente Viejo** (Old Bridge), with views down onto the river as it rushes into the gorge. Just before you reach it you will pass the **Palacio del Marqués de Salvatierra**, a huge mansion that required the demolition of 42 houses for it to be built. Owned by the descendants of the Marqués de Moctezuma, the Governor of South America, the palace is decorated on its portal with carvings of native American Indians. The palace and all its antiques are sometimes open to the public.

For a more dramatic view of the river and gorge, leave Puente Viejo and head back along Calle Marqués de Salvatierra, turning right up Calle Santo Domingo to the **Casa del Rey Moro** (☎ 952 18 72 00; Calle Santo Domingo 17; adult/child €4/2; ☾ 10am-7pm). Here, terraced gardens give access to **La Mina**, an Islamic stairway of over 300 steps that are cut into the rock all the way down to the river at the bottom of the gorge. These steps enabled Ronda to maintain water supplies when it was under attack. It was also the point where Christian troops forced entry in 1485. The steps are not well lit and are steep and wet in places. Care should be taken, even by the fit and able. Also backing on to the river are the almost intact, atmospheric 13th- and 14th-century **Baños Árabes** (Arab Baths; ☎ 656 950937; Hoyo San Miguel; admission €2, Sun free; ☾ 10am-7pm Mon-Fri, 10am-3pm Sat & Sun).

To walk down into the gorge (a good morning's walk), take the path from Plaza María Auxiliadora. It is steep and long but is well worth the effort, and in springtime the valley below is carpeted in flowers. Further afield is the lovely chapel **Ermita de la Virgen de la Cabeza**.

EL MERCADILLO
Directly across the Puente Nuevo is the main square, **Plaza de España**, made famous by Hemingway in his novel *For Whom the Bell Tolls*. Chapter 10 tells how early in the civil war the 'fascists' of a small town were rounded up in the *ayuntamiento*, clubbed and made to walk the gauntlet between two lines of townspeople before being thrown off the cliff. The episode is based on events that took place here in Plaza de España. What was the *ayuntamiento* is now Ronda's parador.

Nearby, Ronda's elegant **Plaza de Toros** (☎ 952 87 41 32; Calle Virgen de la Paz s/n; admission €5; ☾ 10am-6pm Oct-Mar, 10am-8pm Apr-Sep) is a mecca for bullfighting aficionados. In existence for more than 200 years, it is one of the oldest and most revered bullrings in Spain. It has also been the site of some of the most important events in bullfighting history (see the boxed text, opposite). Built by Martín Aldehuela, the bullring is universally admired for its soft sandstone hues and galleried arches. At 66m in diameter it is also the largest and, therefore, most dangerous bullring, yet it only seats 5000 spectators – a tiny number compared with the huge 50,000-seater bullring in Mexico City. In July the ring is used for a series of fabulous concerts, and opera.

The on-site **Museo Taurino** is crammed with memorabilia such as blood-spattered costumes worn by Pedro Romero and 1990s star Jesulín de Ubrique. It also includes photos of famous fans such as Orson Welles and Ernest Hemingway, whose novel *Death in the Afternoon* provides in-depth insight into the fear and tension of the bullring.

Behind the Plaza de Toros, spectacular cliff-top views open out from **Paseo de Blas Infante** and the leafy **Alameda del Tajo** park nearby. The park has a good play area for younger children.

BARRIO DE SAN FRANCISCO
Outside La Ciudad's city walls is the **Barrio de San Francisco**, the original Muslim cem-

etery of the city. A small market was established here in the 15th century, when traders refused to enter the city in order to avoid paying hefty taxes. Some inns and taverns were built and thus began a new quarter. The barrio still has a reputation for down-to-earth tapas bars.

Activities

Ronda is a hub for outdoor activities, and many villa rentals offer a host of on-site activities (see the boxed text, p285). In Ronda itself, the activity company **Pangea Active Nature** (☎ 952 87 34 96; www.pangeacentral.com; Calle Dolores Ibarruri 4) offers a range of activities from one-day caving (per person €69) to longer hiking or biking trips.

For guided horse treks contact **Hotel El Espejo** (☎ 952 11 40 11; www.serraniaderonda.org in Spanish; Camino del Cuco), located off the Arriate road, about 3km from Ronda. Cost is €15 per hour with a minimum price of €60, ie one person for four hours or two people for two hours.

Ronda has traditionally been a haven for artists and that is no less true today than it was in the past. Check out www.artgaucin.com for information about the local art scene.

Tours

For a lively and engaging guided tour of Ronda, contact the bubbly **Teresa Montero Verdú** (☎ 952 87 21 02, 609 879406), locally born and full of enthusiastically delivered information.

Festivals & Events

Corpus Cristi On the Thursday after Trinity there are bullfights and festivities after the 900kg Station of the Cross is carried 6km through the town.

Feria de Pedro Romero An orgy of partying during the first two weeks of September, including the important flamenco Festival de Cante Grande. Culminates in the Corridas Goyesca (bullfights in honour of legendary bullfighter Pedro Romero – see below).

Sleeping

Ronda's accommodation can be tight, even on weekends outside of the summer high season. In the first half of May and from July to September, you definitely need to book ahead.

BUDGET

Ronda has some of the best character-filled and best-value accommodation in Málaga province.

RONDA'S FIGHTING ROMEROS

Ronda can bullishly claim to be the home of bullfighting – and it does. It proudly boasts the Real Maestranza de Ronda equestrian school, founded in 1572 for the Spanish aristocracy to learn to ride and fight. They did this by challenging bulls in an arena, and thus was born the first bullfight.

Legend has it that one of these fights went awry when a nobleman fell from his horse and risked being gored to death. Without hesitation local hero Francisco Romero (b 1698) leapt into the ring and distracted the bull by waving his hat. By the next generation Francisco's son, Juan, had added the *cuadrilla* (the matador's supporting team), consisting of two to three banderilleros (who work on foot) and two to three picadors (men on horseback with pike poles). This married both the habits of the aristocracy (who previously conducted fights on horseback) and the common, dangerous bullfights which took place during fiestas in the main square of each town.

Juan's son Pedro Romero (1754–1839), whose distinguished career saw the death of over 5000 bulls, invented the rules and graceful balletlike movements of the modern bullfight, introducing the *muleta* (a variation on his grandfather's hat), a red cape used to attract the bull's attention.

In 1932 Ronda also gave birth to one of Spain's greatest 20th-century bullfighters, the charismatic Antonio Ordóñez, who was immortalised by Hemingway in *The Dangerous Summer*.

It was the Ordóñez family that inaugurated Ronda's *Corridas Goyesca*, held each year in early September in honour of Pedro Romero, and which attracts Spain's best matadors. During the bullfights the matadors wear the stiff, ornate 19th-century costume that Goya depicted in his paintings of Romero. Out of the three days of fights the most popular is on Saturday, for which you will need to book tickets at least two months in advance. Tickets cost from around €65 in the *sol* (sun) to €110 in *sombra* (shadow). Buy tickets at the bullring in Ronda from 1 July, or phone **Tazdevil** (☎ 954 50 37 94, 607 909345).

Hotel Morales (☎ 952 87 15 38; fax 952 18 70 24; Calle de Sevilla 51; s/d €25/42; ✗) A friendly, small hotel with 18 pleasant rooms. Its walls are decked with maps of the area, it has a room for bicycles, and the staff are full of information on the town and nearby natural parks.

Hotel Arunda II (☎ 952 87 25 19; www.hotel esarunda.com; Calle José María Castelló Madrid 10; s/d incl breakfast €27/44; P ✗) Convenient for both the bus and the train station, the Arunda offers good rooms and the bonus of parking in its own garage.

Hotel Colón (☎ 952 87 02 18; hotelcolon@ronda.net; Calle Pozo; s/d €27/44; ✗) A good budget option with 10 spick-and-span rooms. Ask for a room with a roof terrace – these overlook the 16th-century Iglesia de la Merced.

Hotel San Francisco (☎ 952 87 32 99; www.hotel sanfranciscoronda.com; Calle María Cabrera 18; s/d incl breakfast €38/59; ✗ 🖋) Possibly the best budget option in Ronda, this hotel offers a warm welcome. The *hostal* has recently been refurbished and upgraded to a hotel with facilities to match. Eye-catching floral fabrics and yellow paintwork are cheering.

MIDRANGE
Hotel San Cayetano (☎ 952 16 16 72; www.hotel sancayetano.com; Calle de Sevilla 16; s€35, d 55-80) Run by an astute, young businesswoman who has completely reformed and decorated an old town house. Rooms are attractive and comfortable and there's a communal lounge room with TV.

Alavera de los Baños (☎ 952 87 91 43; www.anda lucia.com/alavera; Hoyo San Miguel s/n; s/d incl breakfast €50/85; ✗ 🖋) Taking its cue from the Arab baths next door, the Alavera de los Baños

---

THE AUTHOR'S CHOICE

EnFrente Arte (☎ 952 87 90 88; www.en frentearte.com; Calle Real 40; r incl breakfast & drinks €82-106; ✗ 🖋 🖋) On a historic cobble-stoned street, Belgian-owned EnFrente offers a huge range of facilities and funky modern/oriental décor. It has a bar, recreation room, pool, flowery patio with black bamboo, sauna, film room and fantastic views out to the Sierra de la Nieves. What's more, the room price includes all drinks, to which you help yourself, and a sumptuous buffet breakfast, overseen by two cooks.

---

continues the Hispano-Islamic theme throughout, with oriental décor and tasty North African–inspired cuisine (much of it excellent vegetarian food). Ask for a room on the terrace, as they open out onto a small, lush garden.

Jardín de la Muralla (☎ 952 87 27 64; www .jardindelamuralla.com; Calle Espíritu Santo 13; d incl breakfast €87; ✗ 🖋 🖋) This newish Ronda hotel has stepped gardens which merge into the countryside yet it is only five minutes' walk from the centre and is in a zone chock-full of historic buildings. Such is Ronda! Décor is elegant, olde-worlde with fancy mirrors and vases of fresh flowers.

Hotel Polo (☎ 952 87 24 47; www.hotelpolo.net; Calle Mariano Soubirón 8; s/d incl breakfast 74/92; P ✗ 🖋) This is a charming hotel in a graceful 19th-century building. Inside all is light and airy, with elegant, high-ceilinged rooms, many with balconied French windows, and attractively furnished communal areas such as the colonial-style lounge. The parking is a bonus.

Hotel San Gabriel (☎ 952 19 03 92; www.hotel sangabriel.com; Calle José M Holgado 19; s/d 73/96; ✗) This charming, historic hotel is filled with antiques and photographs that offer an insight into Ronda's history – bullfighting, celebrities and all. Ferns hang down the huge mahogany staircase, there is a billiard room, a cosy living room stacked with books and a super cinema with 10 velvet-covered seats rescued from Ronda's theatre.

TOP END
Hotel Montelirio (☎ 952 87 38 55; www.hotelmonte lirio.com; Calle Tenorio 8; s/d €100/150; ✗ 🖋) Hugging El Tajo gorge, the new Montelirio has magical views. The converted *palacio* has been sensitively refurbished, with sumptuous suites. The lounge retains its gorgeous Mudejar ceiling and opens out onto a terrace complete with plunge pool. There is also a fantastic restaurant (see opposite).

Parador de Ronda (☎ 952 87 75 00; www.parador .es; Plaza de España s/n; s/d €129/161; P ✗ 🖋 🖋) Also on the gorge, although set back behind a wide terrace, the Ronda Parador is another luxurious option with well-appointed rooms and excellent services.

If you like ultra-modern places, try the new **Hotel Acinopo** (☎ 952 16 10 02; www.acinopo .com; Calle José Aparicio 7; r from €104).

Eating

Typical Ronda food is hearty mountain fare, with an emphasis on stews (called *cocido*, *estofado* or *cazuela*), *trucha* (trout), and game such as *conejo* (rabbit), *perdiz* (partridge), *codorniz* (quail) and *toro* (oxtail). But, as elsewhere, inspired chefs are trying out new ideas.

Chocolat (Calle de Sevilla 18; breakfast from €2.20) A sophisticated café next door to Hotel San Cayetano. Choose from a long list of teas, coffees and breakfasts and a boggling array of cakes and pastries. The mellow background music is easy to take.

El Molino (☎ 952 87 52 49; Calle Molino 6; pizza €7, menú €9) Popular for its pizzas, good prices, and its position on Plaza del Soccorro, the food here is a little perfunctory but perfectly adequate. A dinner of pizza and salad will keep you happy for hours.

Casa Mateo (☎ 952 87 46 42; Calle Jerez 6; raciones €10) Recognise this new, slick place, near Iglesia de la Merced, by its Arab-style brickwork. It has good meat and fish *raciones* and interesting salads using local products.

Tréz (☎ 952 87 72 07; Calle Los Remedios 27; mains €6-10.50; ☀ 1-4pm & 7pm-midnight Tue-Sat; Ⓥ) Previously called Relax, this place is now run by a young Dutch couple who are continuing with many of the vegetarian dishes and the general café theme of the place while putting their own stamp on it. While there are a couple of meat and fish options, vegetarians will find favourites like spinach and feta pies, mushroom pies and vegetarian lasagne.

Bar Restaurant Almocábar (☎ 952 87 59 77; Calle Ruedo Alameda 5; tapas €1.50, mains €10-14; ☀ 1.30-5pm & 8pm-1am Wed-Mon) In the Barrio San Francisco, Almocábar is an excellent authentic tapas bar, little touched by the tourist hordes at the top of town. In the evening you'll be hard pressed to get into the tapas bar, so delicious are its tapas. At least you can reserve for the restaurant section.

Restaurante Pedro Romero (☎ 952 87 11 10; Calle Virgen de la Paz 18; menú €16, mains €15-18) Opposite the bullring, this celebrated eatery dedicated to bullfighting turns out classic *rondeño* dishes (dishes from Ronda). This is a good place to try the *rabo de toro* (oxtail stew). Vegetarians will enjoy the fried goat's cheese starter served with apple sauce.

Restaurante Albacara (☎ 952 16 11 84; Calle Tenorio 8; mains €14.50-19) One of Ronda's best restaurants, the Albacara is in the old stables of the Montelirio palace and teeters on the edge of the gorge. It serves up creative meals and has an extensive wine list. Try the codfish with a spicy leek sauce.

Restaurante del Escudero (☎ 952 87 13 67; Paseo de Blas Infante 1; menú €17, mains €17-21; ☀ 1.30-3.30pm Tue-Sun, 8-10.30pm Tue-Sat) This is a sister restaurant to Tragabuches, situated in an attractive garden near the Plaza de Toros, with a good set menu and more reasonable prices than Tragabuches. The garden makes it popular in the summer.

Casa Santa Pola (☎ 952 87 92 08; Calle Santo Domingo 3; starters €10-12, mains €17-22) This is an atmospheric restaurant spread over three floors of an old aristocratic house. At night each of the small dining rooms is intimate and candlelit and during the day there are good views over El Tajo. The roast lamb cutlets or the roast pork are a must.

Casa María (☎ 952 87 62 12; Calle Ruedo Alameda 27; 2-course meal €20-25; ☀ 1-5pm & 7.30pm-1am Thu-Mon) Although it doesn't draw the crowds in quite the same way as the nearby Almocábar, Casa María is still worth the trip to the Barrio de San Francisco. The fresh seafood is great value and when things get going there is a wonderfully unpretentious atmosphere. The owner-chef has an impressive wine stash and orders good cuts of meat from around the country.

Restaurante Tragabuches (☎ 952 19 02 91; Calle José Aparicio 1; mains €26-29; ☀ 1.30-3.30pm & 8-10.30pm Tue-Sat) A complete change from the ubiquitous 'rustic' restaurant, Tragabuches is modern and sleek with an innovative menu to match. Michelin-starred in 1998, chef Daniel García continues to send out *cocina creativa*.

Drinking

Tetería Al Zahra (Calle Las Tiendas 17; ☀ 4.30pm-midnight) Come here and try a pot of herbal, Moroccan, Pakistani or a host of other teas, all served in pretty Moroccan ceramic teapots and cups and saucers.

El Choque Ideal (☎ 952 16 19 18; www.elchoqueideal.com; Espíritu Santo 9; ☀ 9.30am-3am Feb-Oct, 1pm-1am Nov-Jan) A great café with fantastic views, lots of mosaic work and a basement recording studio. It puts on a host of events from films out on the terrace to live bands.

A modest nightlife zone centres on Calle Los Remedios, with the ever-popular tapas bars of **Taberna del Antonio** (Calle Los Remedios 22; 🕒 11am-midnight), serving more than 60 kinds of tapas, and **Lechuguita** (Calle Los Remedios 25; 🕒 11am-midnight). Down in the Barrio San Francisco try the heaving **Bodega San Francisco** (Calle Ruedo Alameda; 🕒 11am-midnight) – if you can squeeze in the door.

Entertainment

For flamenco performances seek out the **Círculo de Artistas** (Plaza del Socorro; 🕒 Mon-Wed) and **Museo Lara** (Calle de Armiñán 29; 🕒 Thu-Sat), both from 10pm and costing €23. Salsa and merengue fans can dance at **Sabor Latino** (Calle Mariano Soubirón; 🕒 from 9pm).

Getting There & Away

BUS

The bus station is at Plaza Concepción García Redondo 2. **Comes** (☎ 952 87 19 92) has buses to Arcos de la Frontera (€7.50, two hours), Jerez de la Frontera (€10, three hours) and Cádiz (€13, two hours) up to four times daily; and Gaucín, Jimena de la Frontera and Algeciras (€8, 1½ hours, one daily Monday to Friday). **Los Amarillos** (☎ 952 18 70 61) goes to Seville (€10, 2½ hours, three to six daily) via Algodonales; Grazalema (€2.30, 35 minutes, two daily); and Málaga (€8.50, two hours, four to 10 daily) via Ardales. **Portillo** (☎ 952 87 22 62) runs to Málaga (€9.50, 1½ hours, at least three daily) via San Pedro de Alcántara and Marbella.

TRAIN

Ronda's **train station** (☎ 952 87 16 73; Avenida de Andalucía) is on the scenic line between Bobadilla and Algeciras. Trains run to Algeciras (€6.50 to €16, 1¾ hours, six daily) via Gaucín and Jimena de la Frontera. This train ride is incredibly scenic and worth taking just for the views. Other trains depart for Granada (€11.50, 2½ hours, three daily) via Antequera; Málaga (€5.50, 1½ to two hours, one daily Monday to Saturday); Córdoba (€18 to €22, 2½ hours, two daily); and Madrid (by day €53, 4½ hours; overnight €34, nine hours). For Seville change at Bobadilla or Antequera.

Getting Around

BICYCLE

Bicicletas Jesús Rosado (☎ /fax 95 287 02 21, 637 457756; jrosado@ronda.net; 87 Plaza del Ahorro 1; 1 day €10) rents out well-equipped mountain bikes.

BUS

It's less than 1km from the train station to most accommodation. Supposedly every 30 minutes, town minibuses run to Plaza de España from Avenida Martínez Astein (across the road from the train station), but they're not very reliable. It's not too far to walk to the town centre but, with luggage, you'll need a taxi (€4).

CAR & MOTORCYCLE

Parking in Ronda is, inevitably, difficult. There are a number of underground car parks and some hotels have parking deals for guests. Parking charges are about €2.50 per hour, €14 for 14 to 24 hours. Taxis are found in Plaza Carmen Abela.

AROUND RONDA
Serranía de Ronda

Curving around the south and southeast of the town, the **Serranía de Ronda** may not be the highest or most dramatic mountain range in Andalucía, but it's certainly among the prettiest. Any of the roads through it between Ronda and southern Cádiz province, Gibraltar or the Costa del Sol, makes a picturesque route. **Cortés de la Frontera**, overlooking the Guadiaro Valley, and **Gaucín**, looking across the Genal Valley to the Sierra Crestellina, are among the most beautiful spots to stop.

To the west and southwest of Ronda stretch the wilder Sierra de Grazalema (p203) and Los Alcornocales (p223) natural parks. There are plenty of walking and cycling possibilities and Ronda's tourist office can provide details of these as well as maps.

Ronda la Vieja

To the north of Ronda, off the A376, is the relatively undisturbed Roman site of **Acinipo** at **Ronda la Vieja** (☎ 630 429949; admission free; 🕒 9am-3pm Tue-Sat, 8am-2pm Sun), with its partially reconstructed theatre. Although completely ruinous, with the exception of the theatre, it is a wonderfully wild site with fantastic views of the surrounding countryside and you can happily while away a few hours wandering through the fallen stones trying to guess the location of various baths and forums.

Cueva de la Pileta

Twenty kilometres southwest of Ronda la Vieja are some of Andalucía's most ancient

RURAL RONDA

The beautiful countryside surrounding Ronda has attracted a large number of enterprising individuals who have converted traditional houses into gorgeous rural accommodation. If you have your own car it is most certainly worth staying in one of these *cortijos* (country properties) that often offer a host of extras such as guided walks and both traditional fare and *haute cuisine*. For information on rural accommodation, try Ronda's municipal tourist office, the regional website www.serraniaronda.org, or www.rusticblue.com. We recommend the following places:

First up, the *Condé Nast Traveller* favourite, **Hotel Fuente de la Higuera** (☎ 952 11 43 55; www .hotellafuente.com; Partido de los Frontones, Ronda; d/deluxe ste €135/260; P ✗ ⊠ ⚿), a chic colonial villa, with a contemporary interior, that overlooks vast olive groves.

Walking enthusiasts can't do any better than **El Tejar** (☎ 952 18 40 53; eltejar@mercuryin.es; Calle Nacimiento 38, Montecorto; Oct–mid-May d €65, mid-May–Sep whole house per week €1000; P ✗ ⊠). Here, experienced walker Guy Hunter-Watts, author of *Walking in Andalucía*, can expertly guide you through the surrounding countryside. During summer you have to book the whole place.

For sheer indulgence, cosmopolitan atmosphere and out-of-this-world views, opt for **El Nobo** (☎ 952 15 13 03; www.elnobo.co.uk; Apartado 46, Gaucín; d €125, 4-person villa per week €1150-1700; P ✗ ⊠) or **Hotel Casablanca** (☎ 952 15 10 19; fax 952 15 14 05; Calle Llana 12, Gaucín; r incl breakfast €140-200; ⚿ closed Nov–Mar; P ✗ ⊠).

A truly gourmet indulgence can be found at the welcoming and convivial **La Almuña Cottage** (☎ 952 15 12 00; www.i-escape.com; Apartado 20, Gaucín; d €91, cottage for 4 per week €710; P ✗ ⊠), which serves up local, home-grown produce (dinner €44).

caves, the **Cueva de la Pileta** (☎ 952 16 73 43; adult/child/student €6.50/2.50/3; ⚿ hourly tours 10am-1pm & 4-6pm, call for details). The guided tour by candlelight into the dark belly of the cave reveals Palaeolithic paintings of horses, goats and fish from 20,000 to 25,000 years ago. Beautiful stalactites and stalagmites add to the effect. The guided tour is given by a member of the Bullón family, who discovered the paintings in 1905 and who speak some English. The maximum group size is 25, so if you come on a busy day you may have to wait for a place.

Benaoján village is the nearest that you can get to the Cueva de la Pileta by public transport. Here you can stay at the beautiful converted water mill of **Molino del Santo** (☎ 952 16 71 51; www.molinodelsanto.com; Barriada Estación s/n; d B&B/half-board €67/90; ⚿ mid-Feb–mid-Nov), which also puts on a fantastic lunch menu.

The caves are 4km south of Benaoján, about 250m off the Benaoján–Cortes de la Frontera road – there is no transport to the caves, only a bus to Benaoján, so you will need your own car to get here. The turn-off is signposted. Benaoján is served by two Los Amarillos buses (from Monday to Friday) and up to four daily trains to/from Ronda. Walking trails link Benaoján with Ronda and villages in the Guadiaro Valley.

Parque Natural Sierra de las Nieves

Southeast of Ronda lies the 180-sq-km **Parque Natural Sierra de las Nieves**, noted for its rare Spanish fir, the *pinsapo*, and fauna including some 1000 ibex and various species of eagle. The *nieve* (snow) after which the mountains are named usually falls between January and March. **El Burgo**, a remote but attractive village 10km north of **Yunquera** on the A366, makes a good base for visiting the east and northeast of the park. Information is available from Yunquera's **tourist office** (☎ 952 48 28 01; Calle del Pozo 17; ⚿ 8am-3pm Tue-Fri), or the **ayuntamiento** (☎ 952 16 00 02) in El Burgo.

Camping Conejeras (☎ 619 180012; bungalow €48, camping per adult/tent/car €2.50/2.50/2.40; ⚿ Oct-Jun), 800m off the A376 on the road to Los Quejigales, and **Camping Pinsapo Azul** (☎ 952 48 27 54; Yunquera; adult/tent/car €4/4/3.50; ⚿ daily 15 May-15 Oct, weekends only 16 Oct-14 May) at Yunquera are both pleasant sites. In El Burgo, the charming **Hotel La Casa Grande** (☎ 952 16 02 32; www .hotel-lacasagrande.com; Calle Mesones 1; d €66; ✗ ⊑) has spacious, well-furnished rooms, a cosy sitting room, and a restaurant.

To tap into the new wave of spiritual tourism in beautiful surroundings, check into the extraordinary converted mill of **Molino del Rey** (☎ 952 48 00 09; www.molinodelrey .com; Valle de Jorox, Alozaina; 1-week course per person

---

DETOUR: TORRECILLA

The most rewarding walk in the Sierra de las Nieves is the ascent of **Torrecilla** (1919m), the highest peak in western Andalucía. Start at the Área Recreativa Los Quejigales, which is 10km east by unpaved road from the A376 Ronda–San Pedro de Alcántara road. The turn-off, 12km from Ronda, is marked by 'Parque Natural Sierra de las Nieves' signs. From Los Quejigales you have a steepish 470m ascent by the **Cañada de los Cuernos gully**, with its tranquil Spanish-fir woods, to the high pass of **Puerto de los Pilones**. After a fairly level section, the final steep 230m to the summit rewards you with marvellous views. The walk takes five to six hours round-trip. The IGN/Junta de Andalucía *Parque Natural Sierra de las Nieves* map (1:50,000) shows the relevant path and other hikes.

---

from €710; P ⊠), with teachers including one of the owners and from abroad. London's popular Triyoga centre brings their groups for hatha and ashtanga yoga. The mill overlooks the Sierra de las Nieves and features a yoga room, meditation caves and a good vegetarian restaurant.

Buses between Málaga and Ronda (€8.50, 2½ hours, two daily) through Yunquera and El Burgo are run by **Sierra de las Nieves** (☎ 952 87 54 35).

ARDALES & EL CHORRO

Fifty kilometres northwest of Málaga, the Río Guadalhorce carves its way through the awesome Garganta del Chorro (El Chorro gorge). Also called the Desfiladero de los Gaitanes, the gorge is about 4km long, as much as 400m deep, and sometimes just 10m wide. Its sometimes sheer walls, and other rock faces nearby, are the biggest magnet for rock climbers in Andalucía, with hundreds of bolted climbs snaking their way up the limestone cliffs.

Along the gorge runs the main railway into Málaga (with the aid of 12 tunnels and six bridges) and a path called the Camino (or Caminito) del Rey (King's Path), so named because Alfonso XIII walked on it when he opened the Guadalhorce hydro-electric dam in 1921. For long stretches the path becomes a concrete catwalk 100m above the river, clinging to the gorge walls. It has been officially closed since 1992 and has gaping holes in its concrete floor, making it impassable for all but skilled rock climbers. You *can* view much of the gorge and the path by walking along the railway.

The pleasant, quiet town of Ardales is the main centre of the area and is a good base for exploring further afield. However, most people aim for the climbing mecca of El Chorro, a tiny settlement in the midst of a spectacular and surreal landscape of soaring limestone crags.

Sights & Activities

At the entrance to Ardales is the **Museo de Ardales** (☎ 952 45 80 46; Avenida de Málaga 1; admission €1; ⊠ 10am-2pm & 4-6pm Mon-Sat, 10am-2pm Sun mid-Jun–mid-Sep, 9am-2pm & 4-6pm Tue-Sat, 9am-2pm Sun mid-Sep-mid Jun), a new ethnographic and archaeological museum largely concerned with the **Cueva de Ardales**, a Palaeolithic cave complex similar to the Cueva de la Pileta. For two-hour guided visits to the Cueva de Ardales itself (4km from the museum; Tuesday, Thursday, Saturday and Sunday year-round; €5), contact the museum two to three weeks in advance. The caves contain 60 Palaeolithic paintings and carvings of animals, done between about 18,000 and 14,000 BC, and traces of later occupation and burials from about 8000 BC to after 3000 BC. The museum has copies of the prehistoric rock paintings and carvings and an exhibit of Roman and Islamic artefacts and more.

Six kilometres from Ardales is the picturesque **Embalse del Conde del Guadalhorce** – a huge reservoir that dominates the landscape and is noted for its carp fishing.

Most of the activity in the area centres on the thriving hamlet of El Chorro, amid spectacular scenery. **Tienda Aventura El Chorro** (☎ 649 249444), near the train station, can organise guided activities – hiking, climbing, cycling (bring your own bike) – at all levels of difficulty. The best place for organised activities, and great company, is the **Finca La Campana** (see the boxed text, opposite).

Nine kilometres east of El Chorro is Valle de Abdalajís, Andalucía's paragliding capital. Tuition is offered by the **Club-Escuela de**

Parapente (☎ 952 48 91 80; Calle Sevilla 4, Valle de Abdalajís).

Sleeping & Eating

Albergue-Camping El Chorro (☎ /fax 952 49 52 44; www.alberguecampingelchorro.com; camping per adult/tent/car €4/4/free, hostel per person €10, bungalow for 2/4/6 €42/58/70; **P** **ⓧ**) Set among eucalyptus trees 350m towards the gorge from El Chorro village, the camp site has room for 150 people and there are also bungalows – you need to bring sleeping bags and towels. The *albergue* (hostel) has clean and smart rooms with beds for 60 people. A bar and supermarket are on-site.

Pensión Estación (☎ 952 49 50 04; r with shared bath €25) Found at El Chorro station, this guesthouse has great novelty value and two simple clean rooms. Its Bar Isabel, a renowned climbers' gathering spot, serves *platos combinados* (combined plates) for around €5.

Hostal El Cruce (☎ 952 45 90 12; www.elcruceardales.com; Carretera Alora-Campillos, Ardales; s/d €20/38) At the foot of Ardales, this *hostal* has adequate rooms and a lunch *menú* for €15.

La Posada del Conde (☎ 952 11 24 11; Pantano del Chorro 16-18; s/d €45/68, superior d €78, ste €118) Across the dam from Ardales, La Posada has lovely rooms overlooking the reservoir. It also has a very good restaurant offering delicious grilled meats for €15. Specialities are shoulder of lamb and suckling pig.

Apartamentos La Garganta (☎ 952 49 50 00; www.lagarganta.com; 2-/4-person apt €60/90; **P** **ⓧ** **ⓡ** **ⓖ**) The best option actually in El Chorro, this converted flour mill has small beautifully decorated apartments and an excellent restaurant (mains €10).

El Refugio Alamut Hotel (☎ 952 48 94 00; Carretera Antequera-Valle de Abdalajís Km 26.9; s/d €30/40; **ⓡ**) Outdoor enthusiasts, including paragliders, head for this place just off the A343 Antequera road just north of Valle de Abdalajís, at the foot of one of the main paragliding take-off points. This hotel has appealing rooms and a huge hexagonal-shaped restaurant (closed Monday October to May) with a central fireplace and gigantic windows. The restaurant has a *menú* for €7.

For food in Ardales there are bars on the main plaza and Hostal El Cruce. Out at the reservoir are some very popular weekend restaurants and La Posada del Conde.

In El Chorro, you can eat at the places to stay and at **El Pilar** (mains €5-12), just before the village on the road from Ardales reservoir. This new Argentine-run place has a little verandah looking out over a clutch of banana palms. It serves typical Andalucian fare as well as some traditional Argentine dishes.

Getting There & Away

Los Amarillos buses between Ronda and Málaga (€8.50, two hours, four to 10 daily)

THRILLS & SPILLS

Finca La Campana (☎ /fax 952 11 20 19; www.el-chorro.com; dm €10, d €24, 2–8-person apt €38-88; **ⓧ** **ⓡ**) above El Chorro is more than a great place to stay, it is a club for like-minded adrenaline junkies. It has a cultlike following and is run by experienced climbers Jean-Bernard and Christine Hofer.

The Finca offers a huge range of activities and supervised climbing courses for all levels from beginners through to push-the-grade courses (€90 per person in groups of four). Its group-led climb along the Camino del Rey is a real adrenaline rush. The crumbling walkway can only be accessed by a thrilling abseil and the climb then follows the river to El Chorro, with spectacular views all the way. The climb takes about five hours and is worth every centimo of the €90 (for one to three people).

Just outside El Chorro, the underground Águilas cave system provides another opportunity to test nerve and verve. A 70m abseil brings you to a beautiful system of tunnels full of amazing rock formations. The demanding, full-day trip includes diving through two siphons (per person €80).

If your nerves are frayed by this point, rent a mountain bike for €12 to €18 (including helmet, repair kit and map) and explore some of the delightful countryside. Or, you could just relax by the pool!

To reach the Finca follow the signs from behind Apartamentos La Garganta in El Chorro. During the climbing season (October to March) the Finca is very busy, so book ahead.

MÁLAGA PROVINCE

DETOUR: BOBASTRO

Back in the 9th century, the rugged El Chorro area was the redoubt of a kind of Andalucian Robin Hood, Omar ibn Hafsun, who resisted the armies of Córdoba for nearly 40 years from the hill fortress of **Bobastro**. At one stage he controlled territory all the way from Cartagena to the Strait of Gibraltar.

Legend has it that Ibn Hafsun converted to Christianity (thus becoming a Mozarab) and built Bobastro's **Iglesia Mozárabe**, where he was then buried in AD 917. When Bobastro was finally conquered by Córdoba in 927, Ibn Hafsun's remains were taken away for posthumous crucifixion outside Córdoba's *mezquita* (mosque).

Although the small church is now only a ruin, the drive and walk to get to it are delightful. From El Chorro follow the road up the valley from the western side of the dam, and after 3km take the signposted Bobastro turn-off. Nearly 3km up, an 'Iglesia Mozárabe' sign indicates the 500m footpath to the remains of the church. The views are magnificent.

---

stop at Ardales but there's no bus service to El Chorro.

Trains run to El Chorro from Málaga (€3.40, 45 minutes, two daily), except on Sundays and holidays. You can also reach El Chorro from Ronda (€5.50, 70 minutes, one daily except Sundays and holidays) or Seville (€13.50, two hours, one daily).

To reach El Chorro, drivers from Málaga can branch off the A357 Málaga–Ardales road onto the A343 Antequera road near Pizarra. About 4km north of Pizarra, turn left for Álora and El Chorro. The road passes narrowly between houses, and you eventually hit a potholed road to El Chorro. Another approach from Málaga is to continue on the A357 to the Ardales junction. Turn right here along the MA444 with the reservoir on your left, then in about 5km turn off right, signed to El Chorro. Also from Ardales, a partly unpaved road leads 20km southwest along the remote Turón Valley to El Burgo.

ANTEQUERA

pop 43,000 / elevation 577m

The sleepy provincial town of Antequera, a mass of red-tiled roofs punctuated by some 30 church spires, hides one of the richest historical legacies in Andalucía. In addition to the tall churches, there are numerous chapels dotted around the town.

The area's Neolithic and Bronze Age inhabitants erected some of Europe's largest and oldest dolmens (burial chambers built with huge slabs of rock) around 2500 BC to 1800 BC. Since then, Antequera has had a long and illustrious history spanning the three major influences in the region – Roman, Islamic and Spanish – due to its

strategic location. The scattered remains of each of these civilisations are dotted around the town in a rich tapestry of architectural gems, whose highlight is the opulent Spanish baroque style that gives the town its character. The commercial momentum that contributed to Antequera's importance also led to the town's cultural 'golden age' during the 16th and 17th centuries, when it became a centre for the Spanish humanist movement. Nowadays the civic authorities are working hard to restore and maintain the town's unique historic character.

Orientation

The substantial remains of a hilltop Muslim-built castle, the Alcazaba, dominate Antequera's centre. Down to the northwest is Plaza de San Sebastián, from which the main street, Calle Infante Don Fernando, runs northwest.

Information

There are plenty of banks and ATMs along Calle Infante Don Fernando.

Cyber-Locutorio Las Americas (Calle Encarnación 15; per hr €2; 10.30am-2pm & 4.30pm-11pm Mon-Fri, 11am-3pm & 4.30-11pm Sat, 4.30-11pm Sun) Internet access and cheap phone calls.

Hospital Comarcal de Antequera (☎ 952 84 62 63)

Municipal tourist office (☎ 952 70 25 05; www .antequera.es; Plaza de San Sebastián 7; 11am-2pm & 5-8pm Mon-Sat Jun-15 Oct, 10.30am-1.30pm & 4-7pm Mon-Sat 16 Oct-May, 11am-2pm Sun year-round) Friendly staff with plenty of information.

Policía Local (☎ 952 70 81 04; Avenida la Legión s/n)

Policía Nacional (☎ 952 84 34 94; Calle Carrera 14)

Post office (Calle Nájera 26; 9am-8pm Mon-Fri, 9am-2pm Sat)

Sights

Favoured by the Granada emirs of Islamic times, Antequera's hilltop **Alcazaba** gives the best views of the town. The main approach to the hilltop is from Plaza de San Sebastián, up the stepped Cuesta de San Judas and then through an impressive archway, the **Arco de los Gigantes**, built in 1585 and incorporating stones with Roman inscriptions. Not a huge amount remains of the Alcazaba itself, but it has been turned into a pine-scented, terraced garden and you can normally visit its **Torre del Homenaje** (Keep; admission free), though this was closed at the time of writing, so ask the tourist office for details of reopening. There are great views from this high ground, especially towards the northeast and the **Peña de los Enamorados** (Rock of the Lovers), about which there are many legends.

Just below the Alcazaba is the large 16th-century **Colegiata de Santa María la Mayor** (Plaza Santa María; admission free; 10am-2pm & 4.30-8pm Tue-Fri, 10.30am-2pm Sat, 11.30am-2pm & 4.30-6.30pm Sun Sep–mid-Jun, 10.30am-2pm Tue, Wed, Fri & Sat plus 8-10.30pm Wed & Fri, 11.30am-2pm Sun mid-Jun–Sep). This church-cum-college played an important part in Andalucía's 16th-century humanist movement, and boasts a beautiful Renaissance façade, lovely fluted stone columns inside, and a Mudejar *artesonado* (a ceiling of interlaced beams with decorative insertions). It also plays host to some excellent musical events and exhibitions.

In the town below, the pride of the **Museo Municipal** (Plaza del Coso Viejo; hourly tours €3; 10am-1.30pm & 4.30-6.30pm Tue-Fri, 10am-1.30pm Sat, 11am-1.30pm Sun Oct–mid-Jun, 8-10.30pm Wed & Fri mid-Jun–Sep) is the elegant and athletic 1.4m bronze statue of a boy, *Efebo*. Discovered on a local farm in the 1950s, it is possibly the finest example of Roman sculpture found in Spain. The museum also displays some pieces from a Roman villa in Antequera, where a superb group of mosaics was discovered in 1998. There's also a treasure-trove of religious items, containing so much silver that you can only visit by guided tour on the half-hour.

The **Museo Conventual de las Descalzas** (Plaza de las Descalzas; compulsory guided tour €3; 10.30am-1.30pm & 5-6.30pm Tue-Fri, 10am-noon & 5-6.30pm Sat, 10am-noon Sun), in the 17th-century convent of the Carmelitas Descalzas (Barefoot Carmelites), approximately 150m east of the Museo Municipal, displays highlights of Antequera's rich religious-art heritage. Outstanding works include a painting by Lucas Giordano of St Teresa of Ávila (the 16th-century founder of the Carmelitas Descalzas), a bust of the Dolorosa by Pedro de Mena and a *Virgen de Belén* sculpture by La Roldana.

Only the most jaded would fail to be impressed by the **Iglesia del Carmen** (Plaza del Carmen; admission €1.50; 10am-2pm) and its marvellous 18th-century Churrigueresque retable. Carved in red pine (unpainted) by Antequera's own Antonio Primo, it's spangled with statues of angels by Diego Márquez y Vega, and saints, popes and bishops by José de Medina.

The **Dolmen de Menga** and **Dolmen de Viera** (Avenida Málaga 1; admission free; 9am-6pm Tue-Sat, 9.30am-2.30pm Sun), both dating from around 2500 BC, are 1km from the town centre in a small, wooded park beside the road that leads northeast to the A45. Head down Calle Encarnación from the central Plaza de San Sebastián and follow the signs. Prehistoric people of the Copper Age transported dozens of huge slabs from the nearby hills to construct these burial chambers. The stone frames were covered with mounds of earth. The engineering implications for the time are astonishing. Menga, the larger, is 25m long, 4m high and composed of 32 slabs, the largest of which weighs 180 tonnes. In midsummer the sun rising behind the Peña de los Enamorados hill to the northeast shines directly into the chamber mouth. An information centre is being constructed here.

A third chamber, the **Dolmen del Romeral** (Cerro Romeral; admission free; 9am-6pm Tue-Sat, 9.30am-2.30pm Sun), is further out of town. It is of later construction (around 1800 BC) and features much use of small stones for its walls. To get there, continue 2.5km past Menga and Viera through an industrial estate, then turn left following 'Córdoba, Seville' signs. After 500m, turn left at a roundabout and follow 'Dólmen del Romeral' signs for 200m.

Festivals & Events

Semana Santa (Holy Week) One of the most traditional celebrations in Andalucía, held from Palm Sunday to Easter Sunday; items from the town's treasure-trove are actually used in the religious processions.

Real Feria de Agosto Held in mid-August, this festival celebrates the harvest with bullfights, dancing and street parades.

Sleeping

Antequera hotel prices are refreshingly moderate.

Hospedería Coso San Francisco (☎ 952 84 00 14; Calle Calzada 27-29; s/d €22/35; P ☒ ☐) A friendly place 400m northeast of Plaza de San Sebastián, this 17th-century town house has been completely renovated and refurbished. The 10 rooms are plainly decorated but retain some interesting features from the original building. It has a good restaurant – see right.

Hotel Colón (☎ 952 84 00 10; www.castelcolon.com; Calle Infante Don Fernando 29; s/d €25/40; P ☒ ☐ ☒) A rambling place, Hotel Colón has excellent old-fashioned-style rooms arranged around a flowery inner courtyard. Prices rise a little in August, at Easter and at Christmas. Parking is €7.

Hotel Castilla (☎ 952 84 30 90; www.castillahotel .com in Spanish; Calle Infante Don Fernando 40; s/d €31/42; P ☒ ☒) This place has adequate, clean rooms with TV. The hotel has enthusiastic management and a very lively bar-restaurant downstairs.

Hotel San Sebastián (☎/fax 952 84 42 39; Plaza de San Sebastián 5; s/d €27/43; ☒) Smartly refurbished, this hotel even has a few funky murals, and you can't get much more central. San Sebastián has rather a schizophrenic bar-restaurant downstairs (rustic Spain with game machines and constant pop music) that serves up good fish dishes and local specialities.

Hotel Coso Viejo (☎ 952 70 50 45; Calle Encarnación 9; www.hotelcosoviejo.es; s/d incl breakfast €47/70; P ☒) A converted 17th-century neoclassical palace right in the heart of Antequera, opposite Plaza Coso Viejo where the superb town museum is found. The comfortable and stylish rooms are set around a handsome patio with a fountain and there's a cafeteria and restaurant. This hotel has the same owners as the Hotel Castilla.

Parador de Antequera (☎ 952 84 02 61; www .parador.es; Paseo García del Olmo s/n; s/d €95/118; P ☒ ☒) The Parador is in a quiet area of parkland north of the bullring and near the bus station. It's comfortably furnished and set in pleasant gardens with wonderful views, especially at sunset. However, its

exterior is looking a bit jaded and there are plans to remodel.

La Posada del Torcal (☎ 952 03 11 77; www.la posadadeltorcal.com; Villanueva de la Concepción; r €180; P ☒ ☒ ☒) Outside Antequera, close to El Torcal, this fantastic hilltop *cortijo* is surrounded by wonderful panoramic views. It offers luxurious rooms and facilities including tennis courts, riding treks and a pool with a view.

Eating

Local specialities you'll encounter on almost every Antequera menu include *porra antequerana*, a cold dip that's similar to gazpacho (before the water is added); *bienmesabe* (literally 'tastes good to me'), a sponge dessert; and *angelorum*, a dessert incorporating meringue, sponge and egg yolk. Antequera is also one of the world capitals of the breakfast *mollete* (soft bread roll).

Taberna de Santa María (Calle Encarción 8; tapas €1, raciones €4, salads €5-6) A few doors along from the tourist office, this new bar attracts Antequera's young in-crowd with its creative cookery.

Bar Castilla (☎ 952 84 30 90; Calle Infante Don Fernando 40; platos combinados €8-9) A very busy and popular 100-year-old bar-restaurant serving good-value tapas and meals. Generous helpings of chicken or pork come with chips.

Restaurante Coso San Francisco (☎ 952 84 00 14; Calle Calzada 27-29; mains €7-13) The *simpática* owner of this *hostal*-restaurant has her own vegetable plot which provides fresh ingredients for her dishes. Meat, fish, Antequeran specialities, traditional Spanish egg dishes and crisp salads await you. On Thursday and Friday evenings classical musicians provide entertainment.

Restaurante La Espuela (☎ 952 70 30 31; Calle San Agustín 1; ☒ 1-4pm & 8-11pm Tue-Sun; mains €12-18) Found in a gorgeous cul-de-sac off Calle Infante Don Fernando, elegant La Espuela plays background jazz, and offers a fine selection of Antequeran specialities along with some international fare including pasta dishes. Good smells emanate from the kitchen.

Restaurante Plaza de Toros (☎ 952 84 46 62; Paseo María Cristina s/n; mains €12-22; ☒ closed Sun evening) A long-established Antequera favourite in the bullring at the northwestern end of Calle Infante Don Fernando. It offers traditional Andalucian food with some modern twists, and quirky local dishes.

Getting There & Around

The **bus station** (Paseo Garcí de Olmo s/n) is found 1km north of the centre. **Automóviles Casado** (☎ 952 84 19 57) runs buses to Málaga (€6, 50 minutes, nine to 12 daily). **Alsina Graells** (☎ 952 84 13 65) runs buses to Seville (Prado de San Sebastián; €10.50, two hours, five daily), Granada (€7, 1½ hours, four daily), Córdoba (€8, 1½ hours, two daily), Almería (€18, 4½ hours, two daily) and Málaga (€6, 50 minutes, three daily).

The **train station** (☎ 952 84 32 26; Avenida de la Estación) is 1.5km north of the centre. Two to four trains a day run to/from Granada (€6.50 to €7.50, 1½ hours, six daily), Seville (€12, 1¾ hours, four daily) and Ronda (€5.50, 80 minutes, three daily). For Málaga or Córdoba, change at Bobadilla (€1.50, 15 minutes, three daily).

Antequera can be a traffic nightmare and a team of formidable traffic wardens keeps a tight grip on things. Buy tickets from them at street-side parking spots (per hour €1). There is underground parking on Calle Diego Ponce north of Plaza de San Sebastián (per hour €1, 12 to 24 hours €12). Taxis (€3 to €4 per 2km to 3km) wait halfway along Calle Infante Don Fernando, or you can call ☎ 952 84 55 30.

AROUND ANTEQUERA
Paraje Natural Torcal de Antequera

South of Antequera are the weird and wonderful rock formations of the **Paraje Natural Torcal de Antequera**. A 12-sq-km area of gnarled, serrated and pillared limestone, it formed as a sea bed 150 million years ago and now rises to 1336m (El Torcal). It's otherwordly out here and the air is pure and fresh. A huge new information centre was being built at the time of research. Two marked walking trails, the 1.5km 'Ruta Verde' (green route) and the 3km 'Ruta Amarilla' (yellow route) start and end near the information centre. More-dramatic views are along the restricted 'Ruta Rojo' (red route) for which guided tours should resume once the information centre is completed. For current details, contact Antequera's tourist office. Wear shoes with good tread as the trails are rocky.

To get to El Torcal, you will need your own car or a taxi. By car, leave central Antequera along Calle Picadero which soon joins the Zalea road. After 1km or so you'll see signs on the left to Villanueva de la Concepción. Take this road and, after about 11km, a turn uphill to the right leads 4km to the new information centre. A return taxi costs €29, with one hour at El Torcal. The tourist office will arrange a taxi for you.

Laguna de Fuente de Piedra

About 20km northwest of Antequera, just off the A92 *autovía* (toll-free dual carriageway), is the **Laguna de Fuente de Piedra**. When it's not dried up by drought, this is Andalucía's biggest natural lake and one of Europe's two main breeding grounds for the greater flamingo (the other is in the Camargue region of southwest France). After a wet winter as many as 20,000 pairs of flamingos will breed at the lake. The birds arrive in January or February, with the chicks hatching in April and May. The flamingos stay till about August, when the lake, which is rarely more than 1m deep, no longer contains enough water to support them. They share the lake with thousands of other birds of some 170 species.

The **Centro de Información Fuente de Piedra** (☎ 952 11 17 15; ⏰ 10am-2pm & 4-6pm) is at the lakeside. It gives advice on the best spots for bird-watching. It also sells a range of good maps and hires binoculars (an essential).

Nearby, the well-regarded **Caserío de San Benito** (☎ 952 11 11 03; Carretera Córdoba-Málaga Km 108; menú €15; ⏰ noon-5pm & 8pm-midnight Tue-Sun) is a good place to stop for a quality lunch. A beautifully converted farmhouse, San Benito is stuffed with antiques and serves up exquisitely prepared traditional dishes.

Buses run between Antequera and Fuente de Piedra village (€1, three to six daily).

EAST OF MÁLAGA

The coast east of Málaga, sometimes described as the Costa del Sol Oriental, is less developed than the coast to the west. The suburban sprawl of Málaga extends east into a series of unmemorable and unremarkable seaside towns – Rincón de la Victoria, Torre del Mar, Torrox Costa – which pass in a blur amid huge plastic greenhouses before culminating in the more attractive Nerja, which has a large population of British and Scandinavians.

The area's main redeeming feature is the rugged region of La Axarquía, an interior of mountain villages on the slopes leading up to the border of Granada province. The area is full of great walks, which are less 'discovered' than those in the northwest of the province around Ronda. A 406-sq-km area of these mountains was declared the Parque Natural Sierras de Tejeda, Almijara y Alhama in 1999.

LA AXARQUÍA

The Axarquía region is riven by deep valleys lined with terraces and irrigation channels that date back to Islamic times – nearly all the villages dotted around the olive-, almond- and vine-planted hillsides date from this era. The wild, inaccessible landscapes, especially around the Sierra de Tejeda, made it a stronghold of *bandoleros* who roamed the mountains without fear or favour. Nowadays, its chief attractions include fantastic scenery; pretty white villages; strong, sweet, local wine made from sun-dried grapes; and good walking in spring and autumn.

The 'capital' of La Axarquía, **Vélez Málaga**, 4km north of Torre del Mar, is a busy but unspectacular town, although its restored hilltop castle is worth a look. From Vélez the A335 heads north past the turquoise Embalse de la Viñuela reservoir and up through the **Boquete de Zafarraya** (a dramatic cleft in the mountains) towards Granada. One bus a day makes its way over this road between Torre del Mar and Granada. The highest mountains in Málaga province stretch east from the Boquete de Zafarraya. Around the Embalse de la Viñuela you'll see white houses all over the place. Most are occupied by foreigners, especially British. (One outcome of this foreign concentration has been the creation of a good Tuesday **farmers market** where organic food and handicrafts are sold, at Puente de Don Manuel on the Velez–Boquete de Zafarraya road.)

Some of the most dramatic La Axarquía scenery is up around the highest villages, **Alfarnate** (925m) and **Alfarnatejo** (858m), with towering, rugged crags such as Tajo de Gomer and Tajo de Doña Ana rising to their south.

To sample one of Andalucía's oldest inns, dating from 1690, head north from Alfarnate along the Loja road. Just outside town you will find **Venta de Alfarnate** (☎ 952 75 93 88; Antigua Carretera de Málaga-Granada; mains €8-16; ⏰ 11am-7pm Tue-Thu & Sun, 11am-midnight Fri & Sat). It displays mementos of past visitors including some of the bandits who used to roam these hills. Foodwise, it's renowned for *huevos a la bestia,* a kind of hill-country mixed grill of fried eggs and assorted pork products (€11).

You can pick up information on La Axarquía at the tourist offices in Málaga, Nerja, Torre del Mar or Cómpeta. Prospective walkers should ask for the leaflet on walks in the Parque Natural Sierras de Tejeda, Almijara y Alhama. Rural Andalus and Rustic Blue (see p426) are among agencies renting self-catering houses and apartments here, covering all budgets.

Good maps for walkers are *Mapa Topográfico de Sierra Tejeda* and *Mapa Topográfico de Sierra Almijara* by Miguel Ángel Torres Delgado, both at 1:25,000. Useful guides include *Walk! Axarquía* published by **Discovery Walking Guides** (www.walking .demon.co.uk).

Comares

pop 1500 / 685m

Comares sits like a snowdrift atop its lofty hill. The adventure really is in getting there. You see it for kilometre after kilometre before a final twist in an endlessly winding road lands you below the hanging garden of its cliff. From a little car park you can climb steep, winding steps to the village. Look for ceramic footprints underfoot and simply follow them through a web of narrow, twisting lanes past the Iglesia de la Encarnación and eventually to the ruins of Comares' castle and a remarkable summit cemetery. The village has a history of rebellion, having been a stronghold of Omar ibn Hafsun (see p288), but today there is a tangible sense of contented isolation, enjoyed by locals and many newcomers. The views across the Axarquía are stunning.

For accommodation your best bet is **El Molino de los Abuelos** (☎ 952 50 93 09; d incl breakfast from €55) on the main plaza beside the lookout, a converted olive mill with four double rooms and two apartments. Its restaurant (mains €6 to €14, *menú* €8) has stupendous views and recommended food, especially the lamb.

Other options are on the approach road, just below the village and near the public swimming pool. **Mirador de la Axarquía** (☎ 952 50 92 09; Calle Encinillas s/n; s/d €20/40) has good-value, studio-style rooms and a friendly bar-restaurant that serves up tasty grills (€7 to €10) on a terrace with gorgeous views. Just below is **Hotel Atalaya** (☎ 952 50 92 08; Calle Encinillas 4; s/d €24/42) with adequate rooms and a restaurant that serves mainly meat dishes (mains €5 to €10).

There are a couple of friendly bars at the heart of the village.

On weekdays only, a bus leaves Málaga for Comares at 6pm and starts back at 7am the next morning (€2.20).

Cómpeta
pop 3400 / elevation 625m

The village of Cómpeta is a good base for a stay in La Axarquía. It has some of the area's best local wine, and the popular **Noche del Vino** (Night of the Wine) on 15 August features a programme of flamenco and *sevillana* music and dance in the central and pretty Plaza Almijara, and limitless free wine. It has by and large friendly folk including a large mixed foreign population that contributes to an active cultural scene.

By the bus stop at the foot of the village is a **tourist office** (☎ 952 55 36 85; turismo@competa.es; Avenida de la Constitución; ☺ 10am-2pm & 3-6pm Wed-Sun mid-Sep–Jun, 10am-2pm & 3-6pm Tue-Sat Jul–mid-Sep). There's a car park up the hill from the tourist office. **Marco Polo** (Calle José Antonio 3), just off Plaza Almijara, sells books in English and several other languages as well as a good selection of maps and Spanish walking guides. **Todo Papel** (Avenida de la Constitución

31) sells newspapers and books in English, including guidebooks.

The tourist office has varied information on activities in the area, including horse riding at **Los Caballos del Mosquín** (☎ 608 658108; www.horseriding-andalucia.com), which is 2km from Cómpeta, just above the nearby village of Canillas de Albaida. There are also Spanish classes to be had at **Santa Clara Academia de Idiomas** (☎ 952 55 36 66; www.santa-clara-idiomas.com; Calle Andalucía 6). For good art courses, run by the warm Christa Hillekamp, consult www.artworkshop.eu.

Rooms and houses are available to rent through **Cómpeta Direct** (www.competadirect.com) or you could try the delightful **Las Tres Abejas** (☎ 952 55 33 75; www.lastresabejas.com; Calle Panaderos 43; s/d incl breakfast €35/45), about 150m uphill from Plaza Almijara. The main, three-star hotel in Cómpeta is **Hotel Balcón de Cómpeta** (☎ 952 55 35 35; www.hotel-competa.com; Calle San Antonio 75; s/d €49/67; P 🗙 🖳 🕭), which has comfortable rooms with balconies and great views, a good restaurant, a bar and a large pool and tennis court.

For tasty international lunches (weekends only) and dinners, don't miss **El Pilón** (☎ 952 55 35 12; Calle Laberinto; mains €10-15) or the **Museo del Vino** (Avenida Constitución; raciones €8-15), which serves excellent ham, cheese and sausage *raciones* and wine from the barrel. It's also something of an Aladdin's Cave of regional crafts and produce and Moroccan bits and pieces. Another excellent restaurant, with views to the distant sea, is **Cortijo Paco** (☎ 952 55 36 47; Avenida Canillas 6; mains €10-15; ☺ closed Mon). Funky **Taberna de Oscar** (☎ 952 51 66 31; Plaza Pantaleón Romero 1; media-raciones €3.50-5.50; V) turns out unusual and delicious food. There's something for everyone but vegetarians will appreciate the spinach dish.

THE AUTHOR'S CHOICE

Restaurante Almijara (☎ 952 55 78 31; Calle Estación 19B, Canillas de Albaida; mains €10-15; V) Tucked away in a corner of this picturesque village 2km northwest of Cómpeta is this little gem, the creation of a Scottish woman, Kritz Al-Tayeb, who has lived and worked in Saudi Arabia as well as Spain and Britain and who speaks Arabic (she had a restaurant in the Saudi desert and has plenty of interesting tales).

Her restaurant is decorated in Moroccan style and she prepares largely Arab-based dishes which she describes as Moorish cuisine. Diners can enjoy the relaxed atmosphere and the subtle flavours of falafels, vegetable and meat tagines, and spicy sauces. Kritz supplies the restaurant with fresh produce from her garden so her salads are especially good.

DETOUR: EL LUCERO

Perhaps the most exhilarating walk in La Axarquía region is up the dramatically peaked **El Lucero** (1779m). From its summit on a clear day there are stupendous views as far as Granada in one direction and Morocco in the other. This is a full, demanding day's walking, with an ascent of 1150m from Cómpeta: start by climbing left along the track above Cómpeta football pitch. About 1½ hours from Cómpeta you pass below and west of a fire observation hut on La Mina hill. Four hundred metres past the turning to the hut, turn right through a gap in the rock (not signed, but fairly obvious). This path leads in about one hour to **Puerto Blanquillo** (1200m), from which a path climbs 200m to **Puerto de Cómpeta**.

One kilometre down from the latter pass, past a quarry, the summit path (1½ hours) diverges to the right across a stream bed, marked by a sign board and map. El Lucero is topped by the ruins of a Guardia Civil post that was built after the civil war to watch for anti-Franco rebels.

It's possible to drive as far up as Puerto Blanquillo on a rough mountain track from Canillas de Albaida, a village 2km northwest of Cómpeta.

Cómpeta has a thriving music scene; live-music fans will find something on most Saturday nights at **Bar La Roca** (Avenida de La Constitución) and Sunday afternoons at Taberna de Oscar.

Three buses travel daily from Málaga to Cómpeta (€3.20, 1½ hours), stopping via Torre del Mar.

NERJA

pop 19,000

Fifty-six kilometres east of Málaga with the Sierra Almijara rising behind it, Nerja is older and more charming than the other east-coast towns. At its heart is the perennially beautiful Balcón de Europa, a palm-lined lookout and promenade, from which there are glorious mountain and sea views, and a tangle of old streets nearby. Little coves and attractive town beaches make it a good option for visitors without a car.

The town is increasingly popular with package and independent holidaymakers and 'residential tourists', which has pushed it far beyond its old confines. There are sizable urbanisations, especially to the east. The holiday atmosphere, and sea-water contamination, can be overwhelming from July to September but the place is more 'tranquilo' and the water cleaner the rest of the year. Made famous in Spain during the '80s by the TV series *Verano Azul* (Blue Summer), a kind of Spanish *Neighbours*, Nerja attracts both national and international visitors.

Orientation

Buses stop on the main road, the N340, at the northern edge of the town centre. Just to the southeast of the bus stop is Plaza Cantarero. From here it is little more than 500m to the Balcón de Europa and the tourist office – just head straight down Calle Pintada.

Information

There are plenty of ATMs dotted around the town.

DiGi Ibérica (Calle San Miguel 24; per 30min €1; ◯ 10am-2pm & 5-10pm Mon-Fri, 11am-2pm Sat) Internet access.

Europ@web Cafe (Calle Málaga; per 15min €0.90; ◯ 9am-midnight) Internet access and phone calls.

Municipal tourist office (☎ 952 52 15 31; www .nerja.org; Puerta del Mar; ◯ 10am-2pm & 6-10pm Jul–mid-Sep, 10am-2pm & 5-8pm mid-Sep–Jun) Has plenty of useful leaflets.

Nerja Book Centre (☎ 952 52 09 08; Calle Granada 30-32) Secondhand books in English, Spanish and other languages.

Policía Local (☎ 952 52 15 45; Calle Carmen 1) In the *ayuntamiento*.

Post office (Calle Almirante Ferrandiz; ◯ 9am-8pm Mon-Fri, 9am-2pm Sat)

Smiffs (www.booksaboutspain.com; Calle Almirante Ferrandiz) Well-stocked bookshop specialising in books on Spain, in a small arcade along from the post office.

Sights & Activities

The town centres on the delightful **Balcón de Europa**, built on the base of an old fort, which juts out over the deep, blue water. From the Balcón you can walk east to **Playa Burriana**, Nerja's biggest and best beach, via picturesque Calle Carabeo then down the steps to the beach and along to Burriana.

There are no real sights within Nerja, but there is a lively **market** on Tuesday in town on Calle Almirante Ferrandiz and a Sunday-morning *rastro* north of town in Urbanización Flamingo. There is also a host of activities on offer from outlets such as **Club Nautique Nerja** (☎ 952 52 46 54; www.diving-in-spain.com; Avenida Castilla Pérez 2), which runs diving courses (guided dive/open-water PADI course €40/390), rents out mountain bikes (per one day/week €15/75) and scooters (per one day/week €30/175), and also arranges horse treks (two hours €40) and guided walks. For diving you could also try **Buceo Costa Nerja** (☎ 952 52 86 10; www.nerjadiving.com; Playa Burriana), which organises a 2½-hour taster course for €60 and a PADI open-water course for €450. It also operates snorkelling trips (€30).

Festivals & Events

Nerja celebrates the sea-related festivals – the **Noche de San Juan** (23 June) and the **Virgen del Carmen** (16 July) – with appropriate verve. The annual *feria* is in the second week of October.

Since 2004 Nerja has also hosted a highly successful **Healing Arts Festival** (www.healingartsinternational.com) in early September.

Sleeping

Nerja has a huge range of accommodation, but for the summer period rooms in the better hotels tend to be booked at least two months in advance. Nerja also has many apartments to let; inquire at the tourist office.

Hostal Mena (☎ 952 52 05 41; hostalmena@hotmail; Calle El Barrio 15; s/d €26/39) A short distance west of the tourist office, this friendly *hostal* has immaculate rooms (some with sea views) and a pleasant garden. You pay €5 extra for a terrace.

Hostal Miguel (☎ 952 52 15 23; www.hostalmiguel.com; Calle Almirante Ferrandiz 31; s/d €36/49) Straddled between two streets in the old town, this friendly English-run place is full of youthful vigour. Good rooms with a Moroccan theme occupy several levels of a renovated town house, and there's a roof terrace to enjoy too.

Hostal Marissal (☎ 952 52 01 99; www.hostalmarissal.com; Balcón de Europa; s/d €45/60; ✂ ▢) With

NERJA

0   400 m
0   0.2 miles

INFORMATION	
DiGi Ibérica	1 B1
Europ@web Cafe	2 B3
Municipal Tourist Office	3 C2
Nerja Book Centre	4 B2
Policía Local	5 C2
Post Office	6 C2
Smiffs	7 C2

SIGHTS & ACTIVITIES	
Club Nautique Nerja	8 B2

SLEEPING	
Hostal Alhambra	9 B2
Hostal Marazul	10 B3
Hostal Marissal	11 C2
Hostal Mena	12 B2
Hostal Miguel	13 C2
Hotel Carabeo	14 D2
Hotel Nerja Princess	15 C1
Hotel Plaza Cavana	16 B2

EATING	
A Taste of India	17 C2
Anahi	18 C2
Casa Luque	19 C2
Restaurant 34	(see 14)
Restaurant El Puente	20 B1

ENTERTAINMENT	
Centro Cultural Villa de Nerja	21 B2
Cochran's Irish Bar	22 C2

TRANSPORT	
Bus Stop	23 B1
Underground Car Park	24 C2

To Cueva de Nerja (3km); Almería (169km)

To Torrox Costa (9km); Torre del Mar (21km); Rincón de la Victoria (39km); Málaga (52km)

To Hotel Paraíso del Mar (300m); Playa Burriana (700m); Tropy Sol (800m); Paradise (850m); Buceo Costa Nerja (870m); Merendero Ayo (950m)

MEDITERRANEAN SEA

MÁLAGA PROVINCE

sea views and looking out over the Balcón de Europa, this lovely *hostal* offers great value, comfortable rooms and a reasonable restaurant, ideal for a drink and a snack.

Hotel Nerja Princess (☎ 952 52 89 86; www.hotelnp .com; Calle Los Huertos 46; s/d €61/90; P ✖ ✚) Right in the heart of the old town is this excellent small hotel, with the fabulous bonus of a big pool. Balconied rooms look out over the picturesque streets and are equipped with all mod cons and comfortable furnishings.

Hotel Carabeo (☎ 952 52 54 44; www.hotelcarabeo .com; Calle Carabeo 34; d/ste incl breakfast €91/198; P ✖ ✚ ✚) Full of stylish antiques, this small, family-run, seafront hotel is set above manicured terraced gardens. There's also a good restaurant and the pool is on a terrace overlooking the sea.

Hotel Plaza Cavana (☎ /fax 952 52 40 00; www .hotelplazacavana.com; Plaza Cavana 10; s/d €77/107; P ✖ ✚) With a *Love Boat* interior of mint greens and peach this is probably the smartest hotel in the centre of town, with excellent facilities and much-needed parking space.

Hotel Paraíso del Mar (☎ 952 52 16 21; www .hotelparaisodelmar.com; Calle Prolongación de Carabeo; s/d €104/120; P ✖ ✚) To the east of the centre above one of Nerja's better beaches, Playa Carabeo, the Paraíso del Mar has great sea views and private access to the beach. The hotel also has a range of spa facilities.

In summer, when things get very busy, budget travellers could also try the pleasant **Hostal Alhambra** (☎ 95 252 21 74; Calle Antonio Millón 12; s/d €32/45), with spacious and charming fan-cooled rooms, or **Hostal Marazul** (☎ 952 52 41 91; hmarazul@wanadoo.es; Avenida del Mediterráneo; r €48; ✖ ✚).

Eating

A huge number of restaurants are sprinkled all over town, many with good beach views, but a lot of these are ordinary. Playa Burriana, Nerja's best beach, is backed by a strip of restaurants, coffee and ice-cream shops and bars.

Anahi (☎ 952 52 14 57; Puerta del Mar 6; sandwiches €2.50) A display case of tempting fresh pastries and cakes and a sparkling red-topped bar greet you in this tiny place near the tourist office. Its small terrace is the big attraction as it has one of the best Nerja views. It serves food all day but is best for breakfast and snacks.

A Taste of India (☎ 952 52 00 43; Calle Carabeo 51; mains €8-13) Maybe not the most obvious Spanish choice, but this is a fantastic Goan-style Indian restaurant that serves delicious coconut curry, biryanis, tandooris and a host of other spicy meals cooked on the spot. The hospitable owners are from a former Portuguese colony in Gujarat.

Merendero Ayo (☎ 952 52 12 53; Playa Burriana; mains €9-13) At this open-air place at Playa Burriana you can enjoy a plate of paella cooked on the spot in great sizzling pans over an open fire – and you can go back for a free second helping. It's run by Ayo, the man famed for the discovery of the Cueva de Nerja cave complex and a delightful local character.

Restaurant El Puente (☎ 952 52 58 19; Calle Carretera 4; mains €8-16) A great place despite being awkwardly placed on the west side of town where the old Málaga road crosses a bridge over the Río Chillar. The food makes up for the location, with tapas for €1 and big helpings of everything.

Casa Luque (☎ 952 52 10 04; Plaza Cavana 2; mains €15-19) The attractive and slightly pretentious Casa Luque is on picturesque Plaza Cavana, though it no longer has any tables out there. Instead, for outdoor dining, it has a wonderful panoramic terrace facing the sea. Casa Luque offers an elegant *haute*-Med menu including a long list of excellent tapas. This place has a lot more character than most Nerja eateries.

Restaurante 34 (☎ 952 52 54 44; www.hotel carabeo.com; Hotel Carabeo, Calle Carabeo 34; mains €15-24) A truly gorgeous setting both indoors and outside in the garden, which is gently stepped to its furthest section overlooking the sea. Delicious and exotic food combinations are served but the portions are a bit *nouvelle*.

Drinking

Tropy Sol (☺ 10am-10pm) is Playa Burriana's top place for coffee and ice cream. Nerja also has its own Granada-style *tetería* (tea room) on Calle Carabeo where you can even smoke tobacco in a hookah.

Entertainment

The **Centro Cultural Villa de Nerja** (☎ 952 52 38 63; Calle Granada 45) runs an ambitious annual programme of classical music, theatre, jazz and flamenco, featuring international artists.

Nightlife is focused on the aptly named Tutti-Frutti Plaza, which is Nerja's disco central, and the adjoining Calle Antonio Millón. Things hot up after midnight. **Cochran's Irish Bar** (Paseo Balcón de Europa 6) has live music on weekends and a beautifully sited outdoor bar with great sea views and a tropical-island feel. Over at Playa Burriana a number of places, like **Paradise** (☼ 10am-10pm), serve delicious cocktails and have wide-screen TVs for the football fans.

Getting There & Around

Alsina Graells (☎ 952 52 15 04; Avenida Pescía) runs buses to/from Málaga (€3.50, one hour, at least 18 daily), Almuñécar (€2.30, 30 minutes, up to 13 daily), Almería (€11, 2½ hours, nine daily) and Granada (€8.50, 1½ hours, two to three daily). Nerja's streets are very narrow – for drivers who end up in the heart of the town, there is an underground car park (one/24 hours €1/16) off Calle La Cruz and free parking behind Calle Carabeo in the vacant block where the *feria* is held.

AROUND NERJA

East of Nerja the coast becomes more rugged and with your own wheels you can head out to some great beaches reached by tracks down from the A7/N340. **Playa de Cantarriján**, just over the border in Granada province, and **Playa del Cañuelo**, immediately

before the border, are two of the best, with a couple of summer-only restaurants.

Nerja's really big tourist attraction, the **Cueva de Nerja** (☎ 952 52 95 20; www.cuevadenerja.es; adult/child €7/3.50; ☼ 10am-2pm & 4-6.30pm, later in Jul & Aug), lies 3km east of town, just off the A7, and is extremely busy in summer. The enormous 4km-long cave complex, hollowed out by water around five million years ago and once inhabited by Stone Age hunters, is full of spooky stalactites and stalagmites. Don't miss the huge central column in 'Cataclysm Hall'. Every July, Spanish and international ballet and music stars perform in the cave as part of the **Festival Cueva de Nerja**. Nerja tourist office has programme details.

Seven kilometres north of Nerja and linked to it by several buses daily (except Sunday) is **Frigiliana**, some say the prettiest village in La Axarquía. The **tourist office** (☎ 952 53 42 61; www.frigiliana.org; Plaza del Ingenio; ☼ 9am-8pm Mon-Fri, 10am-1.30pm & 4-8pm Sat & Sun) is helpful. El Fuerte, the hill that climbs above the village, was the scene of the final bloody defeat of the Moriscos of La Axarquía in their 1569 rebellion, and where they reputedly plunged to their death rather than be killed or captured by the Spanish. You can walk up here if you follow the streets to the top of the town and then continue along the dusty track. Frigiliana has loads of bars, restaurants and touristy shops.

CÓRDOBA PROVINCE

Córdoba Province

Once the proud queen of Al-Andalus, with its splendid court and cultured caliphs, Córdoba's opulent and enchanting Islamic heritage resonates with faded glory. Although the city's romanticism and imagination-fuelling history still fascinates travellers, Córdoba today has the added ingredients of modernity and commerce, which give it a contemporary, fun feel. So, some of the epithets used to describe it in its more recent past, such as 'museum city' or 'quiet backwater', are starting to lose their aptness. Córdoba's charm is that one can be intoxicated by architectural and historic beauty during the day, and drop into a happening bar and be intoxicated by various sherry wines and cocktails in the evening.

The Mezquita, Córdoba's greatest monument and the sight that everyone flocks to see, is World Heritage listed and one of the world's architectural wonders. But don't forget that Córdoba, despite all its Islamic elements, is quintessentially Andalucian: it has spawned some of the region's most important bullfighters, it's the home of *salmorejo* (a thick gazpacho) and has some of the best places to eat in the region.

Outside of Córdoba, a vast landscape of olive trees encircles the city like miles of braided hair, and there's a fascinating patchwork of small towns, ranging from introverted Islamic mazes to extravagant baroque showpieces. Then there are magnetic pulls such as the award-winning, velvety olive oil of Baena, and treacly Montilla wine, whose wrinkly vines grow south of Córdoba city. The province also produces some of the tastiest cheese and pork products in Andalucía.

HIGHLIGHTS

- Visit the **Mezquita** (p301) in the early morning for breathtaking architecture in peace
- Explore the labyrinthine alleys of Córdoba's **Judería** (p307) and celebrate the city's secret patios at the festival of **Cruces de Mayo** (p310)
- Sweat buckets at the renovated **Hammam Baños Árabes** (p310), followed by a hookah and tea
- Imagine the short-lived splendour of the **Medina Azahara** (p306) at the ruins of the palace-city
- Enjoy the extravagant baroque architecture of **Priego de Córdoba** (p320)
- Get a great view from the beautiful mountains of **Parque Natural Sierras Subbéticas** (p318) or the wooded hills of **Parque Natural Sierra de Hornachuelos** (p317)

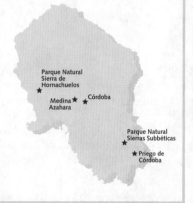

Parque Natural Sierra de Hornachuelos ★

Medina ★ ★ Córdoba
Azahara

Parque Natural Sierras Subbéticas ★

★ Priego de Córdoba

| ■ POPULATION: 1.14 MILLION | ■ CÓRDOBA AV DAILY HIGH: JAN/AUG 11°C/27°C | ■ ALTITUDE RANGE: 55M–1570M |

CÓRDOBA PROVINCE

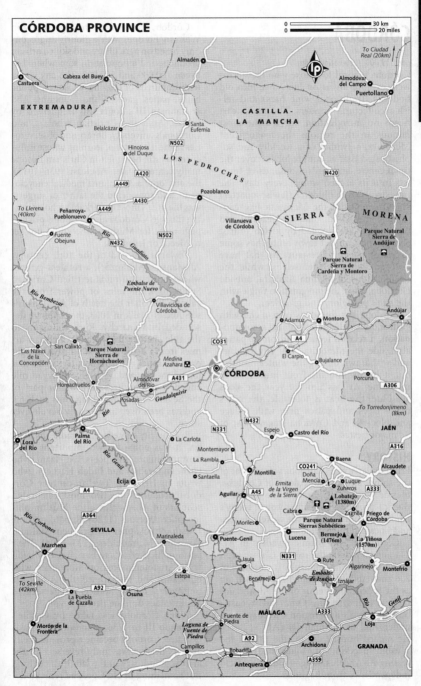

0   30 km
0   20 miles

To Ciudad
Real (20km)

Castuera

Cabeza del Buey

Almadén

Almodóvar
del Campo

Puertollano

EXTREMADURA

CASTILLA-
LA MANCHA

Belalcázar

Santa
Eufemia

Hinojosa
del Duque

N502

LOS PEDROCHES

A420

A449

A430

Pozoblanco

N420

To Llerena
(40km)

Peñarroya-
Pueblonuevo

A449

N502

SIERRA

MORENA

Villanueva
de Córdoba

Cardeña

Parque Natural
Sierra de
Andújar

Fuente
Obejuna

N432

Río Guadiato

Parque Natural
Sierra de
Cardeña y Montoro

Río Bembézar

Embalse de
Puente Nuevo

Villaviciosa de
Córdoba

Adamuz

Montoro

Andújar

Las Navas
de la
Concepción

San Calixto

Parque Natural
Sierra de
Hornachuelos

Medina
Azahara

CO31

A4

El Carpio

Bujalance

Porcuna

A306

Hornachuelos

Almodóvar
del Río

A431

CÓRDOBA

Posadas

Guadalquivir

Río

To Torredonjimeno
(8km)

Palma
del Río

Lora
del Río

Río Genil

N432

Espejo

Castro del Río

JAÉN

A316

La Carlota

Montemayor

Baena

Alcaudete

Écija

A4

La Rambla

Santaella

Montilla

CO241

Doña
Mencía

Luque

Zuheros

A333

A364

Río Corbones

SEVILLA

Aguilar

A45

Ermita
de la Virgen
de la Sierra

Lobatejo
(1380m)

Cabra

Zagrilla

Priego de
Córdoba

Marchena

Marinaleda

Moriles

Parque Natural
Sierras Subbéticas

Bermejo
(1476m)

La Tiñosa
(1570m)

Puente-Genil

Lucena

To Seville
(42km)

A92

Estepa

Osuna

Jauja

Benamejí

N331

Rute

Algarinejo

Montefrío

La Puebla
de Cazalla

Embalse
de Iznájar

Iznájar

Río Genil

Morón de la
Frontera

Fuente de
Piedra

MÁLAGA

A333

Loja

GRANADA

Laguna de
Fuente de
Piedra

A92

Campillos

Bobadilla

Archidona

A359

Antequera

CÓRDOBA

pop 319,000 / elevation 110m

Córdoba is ideal for those who like to eat well, explore towns on foot, dive into old bodegas (traditional wine bars) and relish architectural wonders. The city's heart needs no introduction, for it's the most famous in the region: the magnificent Mezquita, a symbol of a worldly and sophisticated Islamic culture lords it over the town centre, and pulls thousands of tourists into its arched womb every day. The tiny streets of the Judería (Jewish quarter) stretch out from the Mezquita like capillaries, and while some are peaceful and bare, many are clogged by kitsch tourist shops. The compact town centre has some excellent bars and restaurants that have become sights in themselves, while the Islamic ruins of Medina Azahara, outside Córdoba, make the imagination tingle with the site's past glory and grandeur.

Córdoba has found its own niche with gastronomic delights, affordable accommodation, a relaxed feeling and pretty patios alongside the Mezquita. The city is quiet and withdrawn during the winter months, but it bursts into life from mid-April to mid-June. At this time of year the skies are blue, the heat is tolerable, the city's many trees and patios drip with foliage and blooms, and Córdoba stages most of its major fiestas.

HISTORY

From its early years Córdoba was the star of the show. The Roman colony of Corduba, founded in 152 BC, became the capital of Baetica province, covering most of today's Andalucía and bringing the writers Seneca and Lucan to the world.

Córdoba fell to Islamic invaders in AD 711 and soon took the role as Islamic capital on the Iberian Peninsula. It was here in 756 that Abd ar-Rahman I set himself up as the independent emir of the Al-Andalus region, founding the Omayyad dynasty, but the town's and region's heyday came under Abd ar-Rahman III (AD 912–61). He named himself caliph (the title of the Muslim successors of Mohammed) in 929, sealing Al-Andalus' long-standing de facto independence from Baghdad.

Córdoba was by now the biggest city in Western Europe, with a flourishing economy based on agriculture and skilled artisan products, and a population somewhere between 100,000 and 500,000. The city shone with hundreds of dazzling mosques, public baths, patios, gardens and fountains. Abd ar-Rahman III's court was frequented by Jewish, Arab and Christian scholars, and Córdoba's university, library and observatories made it a centre of learning whose influence was still being felt in Christian Europe many centuries later. Abulcasis (936–1013), the author of a 30-volume medical encyclopedia and considered the father of surgery, was the area's most remarkable scholar during this age. Córdoba also became a place of pilgrimage for Muslims who could not get to Mecca or Jerusalem.

Towards the end of the 10th century, Al-Mansur (Almanzor), a ruthless general whose northward raids terrified Christian Spain, took the reins of power from the caliphs. But after the death of Al-Mansur's son Abd al-Malik in 1008, the caliphate descended into anarchy. Rival claimants to the title, Berber troops and Christian armies from Castile and Catalonia all fought over the spoils. The Berbers terrorised and looted the city and, in 1031, Omayyad rule ended. Córdoba became a minor part of the Seville *taifa* (small kingdom) in 1069, and has been overshadowed by Seville ever since.

But the city's intellectual traditions lived on. It was home to two important 11th-century philosopher-poets, Ibn Hazm (who wrote in Arabic) and Judah Ha-Levi (who wrote in Hebrew). Twelfth-century Córdoba produced the two most celebrated scholars of Al-Andalus – the Muslim philosopher Averroës (1126–98; p46) and the Jewish philosopher Moses ben Maimon (known as Maimónides; 1135–1204). Their philosophical efforts to harmonise religion with Aristotelian reason were met with ignorance and intolerance: the Almohads put Averroës in high office, and persecuted Maimónides until he fled to Egypt.

When Córdoba was taken by Castile's Fernando III in 1236, much of its population fled. Córdoba became a provincial city and its decline was only reversed by the arrival of industry in the late 19th century. But something of old Córdoba remained –

one of the greatest Spanish poets, Luis de Góngora (1561–1627) was from the city.

ORIENTATION

The medieval city is immediately north of the Río Guadalquivir. It's a warren of narrow streets surrounding the Mezquita, which is just a block from the river. Within the medieval city, the area northwest of the Mezquita was the Judería, the Muslim quarter was north and east of the Mezquita, and the Mozarabic (Christian) quarter was further to the northeast.

The main square of Córdoba is Plaza de las Tendillas, 500m north of the Mezquita, with the main shopping streets to the plaza's north and west. The train and bus stations are 1km northwest of Plaza de las Tendillas.

INFORMATION
Bookshops

Luque Libros (☎ 957 47 30 34; Calle José Cruz Conde 19) City and Michelin maps half the price of those from the tourist shops near the Mezquita. There are also CNIG and SGE maps, and Editorial Alpina maps.

Emergency

Ambulance (☎ 957 21 79 03, 957 29 55 70)
Policía Nacional (☎ 95 747 75 00; Avenida Doctor Fleming 2) The main police station.

Internet Access

Ch@t (Calle Claudio Marcelo 15; per hr €2; ☑ 10am-1pm & 5-9.30pm Mon-Fri, 10am-2pm Sat) A large internet room in the modern part of town.
Mundo Digital (Calle del Osario 9; ☑ 10am-2pm & 5-10pm Mon-Fri, 11am-2pm & 5-10pm Sat & Sun) Has similar prices to those of Ch@t.

Internet Resources

Info Cordoba (www.infocordoba.com) A useful site with general information on Córdoba.

Left Luggage

Bus station (Plaza de las Tres Culturas; per day €3; ☑ 8am-8pm Mon-Fri) Has a baggage deposit facility in the form of lockers.
Train station (Avenida de América; 8am-8pm Mon-Fri) Also has lockers, which operate similar hours to those at the bus station.

Medical Services

Hospital Cruz Roja (Red Cross Hospital; ☎ 957 29 34 11; Avenida Doctor Fleming s/n) The most central hospital.

Hospital Reina Sofia (☎ 957 21 70 00; Avenida Menéndez Pidal s/n) Nearly 2km southwest of the Mezquita.

Money

Most banks and ATMs are in the newer part of the centre, around Plaza de las Tendillas and Avenida del Gran Capitán. The bus and train stations also have ATMs.

Post

Post office (Calle José Cruz Conde 15)

Tourist Information

Information booth (☑ 10am-2pm & 4.30-8pm Mon-Fri) A kiosk at the train station.
Municipal tourist office (☎ 957 20 05 22; Plaza de Judá Leví; ☑ 8.30am-2.30pm Mon-Fri) A block west of the regional tourist office, with information and maps of Córdoba city.
Regional tourist office (☎ 957 47 12 35; Calle de Torrijos 10; ☑ 9.30am-8pm Mon-Sat, 10am-2pm Sun Apr-Jul, 9.30am-7pm Mon-Sat, 10am-2pm Sun Aug-Mar) In a 16th-century chapel facing the western side of the Mezquita. A good source of information about Córdoba province.

SIGHTS

All of Córdoba's sights can be found in a compact area on the north side of the Río Guadalquivir, with the main tourist activity concentrated around the Mezquita and the adjacent Judería.

Most people take a good half-day to enjoy the Mezquita, and another day or two to explore the city's museums and palaces, which are all a short walk to the northeast. A not-to-be-missed day trip is to the ruins of the palace-city, Medina Azahara, located 8km west of Córdoba.

Mezquita

It's impossible to overestimate the beauty of Córdoba's **Mezquita** (Mosque; ☎ 957 47 05 12; adult/child €8/4; ☑ 10am-7pm Mon-Sat Apr-Oct, 10am-6pm

---

OPENING HOURS

Opening hours for Córdoba's sights change frequently, so check with the tourist offices for updated times. Most places except the Mezquita close on Monday. Closing times are generally an hour or two earlier in winter than summer.

CÓRDOBA

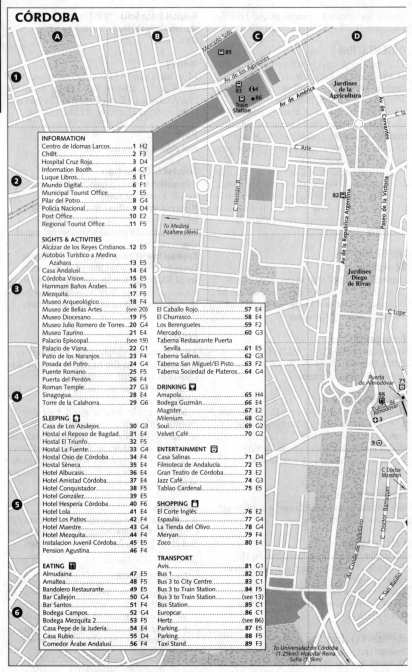

INFORMATION
Centro de Idomas Larcos............**1** H2
Ch@t..**2** F3
Hospital Cruz Roja.....................**3** D4
Information Booth.......................**4** C1
Luque Libros..............................**5** E1
Mundo Digital............................**6** F1
Municipal Tourist Office.............**7** E5
Pilar del Potro............................**8** G4
Policía Nacional.........................**9** D4
Post Office................................**10** E2
Regional Tourist Office.............**11** F5

SIGHTS & ACTIVITIES
Alcázar de los Reyes Cristianos..**12** E5
Autobús Turístico a Medina
    Azahara...............................**13** E5
Casa Andalusí...........................**14** E4
Córdoba Vision.........................**15** E5
Hammam Baños Árabes.............**16** F5
Mezquita..................................**17** F5
Museo Arqueológico.................**18** F4
Museo de Bellas Artes.........(see 20)
Museo Diocesano.....................**19** F5
Museo Julio Romero de Torres..**20** G4
Museo Taurino..........................**21** E4
Palacio Episcopal...............(see 19)
Palacio de Viana.......................**22** G1
Patio de los Naranjos................**23** F4
Posada del Potro.......................**24** G4
Puente Romano.........................**25** F5
Puerta del Perdón.....................**26** F4
Roman Temple..........................**27** G3
Sinagoga...................................**28** E4
Torre de la Calahorra................**29** G6

SLEEPING
Casa de Los Azulejos.................**30** G3
Hostal el Reposo de Bagdad.....**31** E4
Hostal El Triunfo.......................**32** F5
Hostal La Fuente.......................**33** G4
Hostal Osio de Córdoba............**34** F4
Hostal Séneca...........................**35** E4
Hotel Albucasis.........................**36** E4
Hotel Amistad Córdoba.............**37** E4
Hotel Conquistador...................**38** F5
Hotel González.........................**39** E5
Hotel Hesperia Córdoba............**40** F6
Hotel Lola.................................**41** E4
Hotel Los Patios.......................**42** F4
Hotel Maestre...........................**43** G4
Hotel Mezquita.........................**44** F4
Instalacion Juvenil Córdoba.......**45** E5
Pension Agustina......................**46** F4

EATING
Almudaina.................................**47** E5
Amaltea....................................**48** F5
Bandolero Restaurante..............**49** E5
Bar Callejón..............................**50** G4
Bar Santos................................**51** F4
Bodega Campos........................**52** G4
Bodega Mezquita 2...................**53** F5
Casa Pepe de la Judería............**54** E4
Casa Rubio...............................**55** D4
Comedor Árabe Andalusí..........**56** F4

El Caballo Rojo.........................**57** E4
El Churrasco.............................**58** E2
Los Berengueles........................**59** F2
Mercado...................................**60** G3
Taberna Restaurante Puerta
    Sevilla..................................**61** E5
Taberna Salinas........................**62** G3
Taberna San Miguel/El Pisto......**63** F2
Taberna Sociedad de Plateros....**64** G4

DRINKING
Amapola...................................**65** H4
Bodega Guzmán........................**66** E4
Magister...................................**67** E2
Milenium..................................**68** G2
Soul...**69** G2
Velvet Café...............................**70** G2

ENTERTAINMENT
Casa Salinas.............................**71** D4
Filmoteca de Andalucía.............**72** E5
Gran Teatro de Córdoba............**73** E2
Jazz Café..................................**74** G3
Tablao Cardenal.......................**75** E5

SHOPPING
El Corte Inglés..........................**76** E2
Espaluiú...................................**77** G4
La Tienda del Olivo...................**78** G4
Meryan....................................**79** F4
Zoco..**80** E4

TRANSPORT
Avis..**81** G1
Bus 1..**82** D2
Bus 3 to City Centre..................**83** C1
Bus 3 to Train Station................**84** F5
Bus 3 to Train Station..........(see 13)
Bus Station...............................**85** C1
Europcar..................................**86** C1
Hertz..................................(see 86)
Parking.....................................**87** E5
Parking.....................................**88** F5
Taxi Stand................................**89** F3

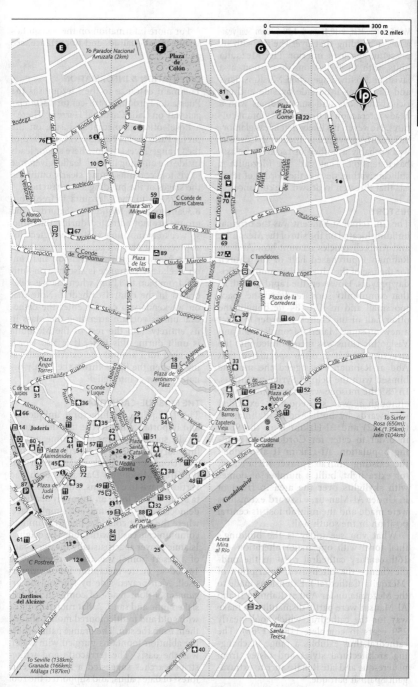

Mon-Sat Nov-Mar, 9-10.45am & 1.30-6.30pm Sun year-round), a building that overwhelms with its peaceful, spacious interior. The Mezquita hints, with all its lustrous decoration, at a lavish and refined age when Muslims, Jews and Christians lived side by side and enriched their city and surroundings with a heady interaction of diverse and vibrant cultures. However, it's likely that a less glamorous reality prevailed – medieval Córdoba was probably a hotbed of racial and class-based tension. That said, the Mezquita is still captivating, despite the hordes of tourists that threaten to drown the romance.

HISTORY

The Church of St Vincent was the original building located on the site of the Mezquita, and Arab chronicles recount how Abd ar-Rahman I purchased half of the church for the use of the Muslim community's Friday prayers. However, the rapid growth of that community soon rendered the space too small and in AD 784 he bought the other half of the church in order to erect a new mosque. Material from Roman and Visigothic ruins was incorporated into the structure and it is often speculated that Abd ar-Rahman I designed the mosque himself with the help of Syrian architects. In 785 the mosque was opened for prayer, although it was subsequently extended southwards by both Abd ar-Rahman II (821–852) and Al-Hakim II in the 960s, in order to cater for Córdoba's expanding population. Al-Hakim II also added the existing mihrab (prayer niche) and, for extra light, built a number of domes with skylights over the area in front of it. Under Al-Mansur, eastward extensions were made and the mihrab lost its central position in the south wall.

What you see today is the building's final form with one major alteration – a 16th-century cathedral right in the middle (hence the often-used description of 'Mezquita-Cathedral'). Extensions made to the Mezquita under Abd ar-Rahman II and Al-Mansur were partly dismantled to make way for the cathedral, which took nearly 250 years to complete (1523–1766). The cathedral thus exhibits a range of changing architectural styles and tastes, from plateresque and late Renaissance to extravagant Spanish baroque.

For more information on the Mezquita's architectural qualities and importance, see p53.

ORIENTATION & INFORMATION

The main entrance to the Mezquita is the Puerta del Perdón, a 14th-century Mudejar gateway on Calle Cardenal Herrero. There's a ticket office immediately inside on the pretty Patio de los Naranjos (Courtyard of the Orange Trees), from where a door leads inside the building itself. A leaflet given free to visitors contains a map clearly outlining the stages of the building's construction.

Entrance to the Mezquita is free from 8.30am to 10am Monday to Saturday and groups are not admitted during this time, so weekday morning visits are perfect for appreciating the Mezquita in peace and quiet. Mass is held at 11am, noon and 1pm on weekdays. Entrance is also free on Sunday from 9am to 11am, when Mass is celebrated in the central cathedral. Note that on weekends you cannot enter the cathedral unless you are attending the Mass in its entirety, and the rest of the Mezquita is unlit during this time. It is also worth taking a turn around the exterior walls at night when the lights throw the highly ornate doorways into relief.

THE MOSQUE-CATHEDRAL

The Mezquita's architectural uniqueness and importance lies in the fact that, structurally speaking, it was for its time, a revolutionary building. It defied precedents. The Dome of the Rock in Jerusalem and the Great Mosque in Damascus both had vertical, nave-like designs, but the Mezquita's aim was to form an infinitely spacious, democratically horizontal and simple space, where the spirit could be free to roam and communicate easily with God. The original Islamic prayer space (usually the open yard of a desert home) was transformed into a 14,400-sq-metre metaphor for the desert itself. Men prayed side by side on the *argamasa*, a floor made of compact, reddish slaked lime and sand. A flat roof, decorated with gold and multicoloured motifs, shaded them from the sun. The orange patio, where the ablution fountains gurgled with water, was the oasis. The terracotta and white-striped arches suggested a hallucinogenic forest of date palms, and supported the roof with 1293 columns (of which only 856 remain). This was truly a mosque – 'a place to prostrate oneself'.

Abd ar-Rahman I's initial mosque was a square split into two rectangular halves – a covered prayer hall and an open ablutions courtyard. The prayer hall was divided into 11 'naves' by lines of two-tier arches striped in red brick and white stone. The columns used for the Mezquita were a mishmash collected from the Visigothic cathedral that had previously occupied the site, Córdoba's Roman buildings and places as far away as Constantinople. This, predictably, presented problems in keeping the ceiling height consistent and making it high enough to create a sense of openness. Inventive builders came up with the idea of using the tall columns as a base and planting the shorter ones on top in order to create the ceiling arches. Later enlargements of the mosque extended these lines of arches to cover an area nearly 120 sq metres and create one of the biggest mosques in the world. The arcades are one of the much loved Islamic architectural motifs. Their simplicity and number give a sense of endlessness to the Mezquita, and imagining this vast space filled with kneeling men, praying in unison, is quite mesmerising.

Originally there were 19 doors, filling the interior of the mosque with light. Nowadays, only one door sheds its light into the dim interior, dampening the vibrant effect of the red-and-white voussoirs of the double arches. Christian additions to the building, such as the solid mass of the cathedral in the centre and the 50 or so chapels around the fringes, further enclose and impose on the airy space.

At the furthest point from the entrance door, on the southern wall of the mosque, the aisles draw you towards qibla (the direction of Mecca) and the mosque's greatest treasure, the mihrab built by Al-Hakim II.

Mihrab & Maksura

Like Abd ar-Rahman II a century earlier, Al-Hakim lengthened the naves of the prayer hall, creating a new mihrab at the south end of the central nave. The bay immediately in front of the mihrab and the bays to each side form the *maksura,* the area where the caliphs and their retinues would have prayed (now enclosed by railings). Inside the mihrab a single block of white marble was sculpted into the shape of a scallop shell, a symbol of the Quran. This formed the dome that amplified the voice of the imam throughout the mosque. The art of the Cordoban caliphate can be seen to have reached maturity here, and many of the intricate decorative effects were carried over into Abd ar-Rahman III's extravagant palace at Medina Azahara (see p306).

The arches within and around the *maksura* are the mosque's most intricate and sophisticated, forming a forest of interwoven horseshoe and bow shapes. Despite their orgy of decoration, these ingenious curves are subtly interwoven to form the strongest elements of the structure. But they were not only physically functional: their purpose was to seduce the eye of the worshipper with their lavish decorations, leading it up to the mihrab – to the focus of prayer and the symbolic doorway to heaven. Equally attractive are the sky-lit domes over the *maksura,* decorated with star-patterned stone vaulting, reminding worshippers of heaven and its promises of beauty. Each dome was held up by four interlocking pairs of parallel ribs, a highly advanced technique in 10th-century Europe.

The greatest glory of Al-Hakim II's extension was the portal of the mihrab itself – a crescent arch with a rectangular surround known as an *alfiz,* surmounted by a blind arcade. For the decoration of the portal, Al-Hakim asked the emperor of Byzantium, Nicephoras II Phocas, to send him a mosaicist capable of imitating the superb mosaics of the Great Mosque of Damascus, one of the great 8th-century Syrian Omayyad buildings. The Christian emperor sent the Muslim caliph not only a mosaicist but also a gift of 1600kg of gold mosaic cubes. These shimmering cubes, shaped into flower motifs and inscriptions from the Quran, decorated the whole *maksura,* giving the Córdoba mihrab area something of the mysterious character of a Byzantine church.

Patio de los Naranjos & Minaret

Outside the mosque, the leafy, walled courtyard and its fountain were the site of ritual ablutions before prayer, while the arcaded walls would have seen much of the ancient city's hustle and bustle. The crowning glory of the whole complex was the minaret, which at its peak towered 48m (only 22m of the minaret still survives) and allowed the call to prayer to echo over the city. Now encased in its 16th-century shell, the original minaret would have looked something like the Giralda in Seville, which was practically a copy. In fact, Córdoba's minaret influenced all the minarets built thereafter throughout the western Islamic world.

The Cathedral

For three centuries following the Reconquista (Christian reconquest) in 1236, the Mezquita remained largely unaltered save for minor modifications such as the Mudejar tiling added in the 1370s to the Mozarabic and Almohad **Capilla Real** (located nine bays north and one east of the mihrab, and now part of the cathedral). In the 16th century King Carlos I gave permission (against the wishes of Córdoba's city council) for the centre of the Mezquita to be ripped out to allow construction of the **Capilla Mayor** (the altar area in the cathedral) and *coro* (choir). However, the king was not enamoured with the results and famously regretted: 'You have built what you or others might have built anywhere, but you have destroyed something that was unique in the world.'

PLEASURE DOME & POWERHOUSE

Legend has it that Abd ar-Rahman III built his palace-city, the **Medina Azahara** (Madinat al-Zahra; ☎ 957 32 91 30; Carretera Palma del Río; non-EU/EU citizen €1.50/free; ☼ 10am-8.30pm Tue-Sat May–mid-Sep, 10am-6.30pm Tue-Sat mid-Sep–Apr, 10am-2pm Sun year-round), for his favourite wife, Az-Zahra. Dismayed by her homesickness and yearning for the snowy mountains of Syria, ar-Rahman tuned into his poetic side; he surrounded his new city with almond and cherry trees, replacing snowflakes with fluffy white blossoms.

More realistically, it was probably the case that Abd ar-Rahman's rivalry with the Abbasid dynasty in Baghdad drove him to build an opulent royal complex outside Córdoba. Building started in AD 936 and chroniclers record some staggering construction statistics: 10,000 labourers set 6000 stone blocks a day, with outer walls extending to 1518m west to east and 745m north to south.

It is almost inconceivable to think that such a city, built over 40 years, was only to last a mere 30 years before the usurper Al-Mansur transferred the seat of government to a new palace complex of his own in 981. Then, between 1010 and 1013, the Azahara was wrecked by Berber soldiers. During succeeding centuries its ruins were plundered repeatedly for building materials. Less than one-tenth of the site has been excavated to date.

Located at the foot of the Sierra Morena, the complex spills down over three terraces with the caliph's palace on the highest terrace overlooking what would have been the court and town. The visitors' route takes you down through the city's original northern gate to the **Dar al-Wuzara** (House of the Viziers) and then to the centrepiece of the site, the **Salón de Abd ar-Rahman III**. Inside, the royal reception hall has been much restored, and the exquisitely carved stuccowork, a riot of vegetal designs, has been painstakingly repaired to cover most of the wall's surface. It gives just a glimpse of the lavishness of the court, which was said to be decorated with gold and silver tiles, and arches of ivory and ebony that contrasted with walls of multicoloured marble. For special effect, a bowl at the centre of the hall was filled with mercury so that when it was rocked the reflected light flashed and bounced off the gleaming decoration.

To reach the site with your own vehicle, follow the signs down Avenida de Medina Azahara, which leads west out of Córdoba onto the A431. The Medina Azahara is signposted 8km from the city centre and there is free parking at the site, although this gets very full. Try to visit before 11am to avoid the buses.

A taxi costs €24 for the return trip, including one hour to view the site, or you can take a bus tour (see p310). The nearest you can get by public transport is the Cruce de Medina Azahara, the turn-off from the A431, from which it's a uninspiring 3km walk, slightly uphill, to the site. City bus 1 will drop you at the Cruce de Medina Azahara – the bus departs from the northern end of Avenida de la República Argentina.

Subsequent additions included a rich 17th-century jasper and red-marble retable (ornamental screenlike structure behind the altar) in the Capilla Mayor, and fine mahogany stalls in the choir, which were carved in the 18th century by Pedro Duque Cornejo.

If you think of the whole building as a cathedral, the forest of arches and pillars provide a superb setting for the central structures. If you see it as a mosque, however, the Christian additions wreck its whole design.

Around the Mezquita

Opposite the Mezquita and next door to the regional tourist office is the **Palacio Episcopal** (Bishops' Palace; Calle de Torrijos), now a conference centre but originally the old Hospital of San Sebastián. A lovely Isabelline-style villa with an internal patio, the palace stages exhibitions, often of regional pottery, to which admission is free if you have a Mezquita ticket. The palace also houses the **Museo Diocesano** (Diocesan Museum; ☎ 957 49 60 85; Calle de Torrijos; admission €1.20; ☉ 9.30am-3pm), which has a collection of religious art. The best of this art is some outstanding medieval woodcarving, including the 13th-century *Virgen de las Huertas*.

Continuing southwest from the Mezquita, down Calle Amador de los Ríos, will bring you to the massive fortified **Alcázar de los Reyes Cristianos** (Castle of the Christian Kings; ☎ 957 42 01 51; Campo Santo de los Mártires s/n; adult/child €4/2, Fri free; ☉ 10am-2pm & 4.30-6.30pm Tue-Sat mid-Oct–Apr, 10am-2pm & 5.30-7.30pm Tue-Sat May, Jun & Sep–mid-Oct, 8.30am-2.30pm Tue-Sat Jul & Aug, 9.30am-2.30pm Sun & public holidays year-round). Built by Alfonso X in the 13th century on the remains of Roman and Arab predecessors, the castle began life as a palace, hosting both Fernando and Isabel. From 1490 to 1821 it became a home for the Inquisition, later being converted into a prison that only closed in 1951. Its large terraced gardens, full of fish ponds, fountains, orange trees, flowers and topiary, were added in the 15th century and are among the most beautiful in Andalucía. They're dotted with fine archaeological remains, including mosaics, marble sarcophagi and Roman statuary. The building itself, much altered, also houses an old royal bathhouse, the Baños Califales.

Situated on the banks of the Río Guadalquivir, the castle overlooks a much restored Roman bridge, the **Puente Romano**. The bridge formed part of the old medieval walls that are reputed to have been some 22km in length. These days, traffic is heavy across the bridge and the pedestrian walkways are narrow. On the other side of the river, the dour-looking **Torre de la Calahorra** (☎ 957 29 39 29; Puente Romano s/n; adult/child €4/2.50; ☉ 10am-2pm & 4.30-8.30pm May-Sep, 10am-6pm Oct-Apr) is the oldest defence tower in the city. Used as a jail for the Cordoban nobility in the 18th century and as a school for women in the 19th century, it now lays extravagant claim to being the 'Living Museum of Al-Andalus' and offers a rather over-the-top multimedia tour (in Spanish), complete with headphones, models and films.

Judería

Córdoba's Judería is a charming maze of narrow streets and small squares, whitewashed buildings with flowers dripping from window boxes, and wrought-iron doorways that give glimpses of plant-filled patios (see Córdoba's Hidden Heart, p308). The Judería is one of Córdoba's main tourist attractions and many of its streets are stuffed with shops selling vast amounts of tacky souvenirs. But there are still quiet residential streets here that offer a glimpse into how the neighbourhood might have been hundreds of years ago.

Spain had one of Europe's biggest Jewish communities, recorded from as early as the 2nd century AD. Persecuted by the Visigoths, they allied themselves with the Muslims following the Arab conquests. By the 10th century they were established as some of the most dynamic members of society, holding posts as administrators, doctors, jurists, philosophers, poets and functionaries. The importance of the community is illustrated by the proximity of the Judería to the Mezquita and the city's centres of power. In fact, one of the greatest Jewish theologians, Maimónides, was from Córdoba. He summarised the teachings of Judaism and completed his magnum opus, the *Mishne Torah*, which systemises all of Jewish law, before fleeing persecution to Fez. He later moved to Egypt, where he became physician to the sultan, Saladin.

CÓRDOBA'S HIDDEN HEART

As you're squeezing yourself down the mini-streets of the Judería, the green, airy patios, partly concealed behind heavy wooden doors and wrought-iron gates, will be stealing your attention at every point. The famed patios of Córdoba have provided shade during the searing heat of summer for centuries. They are a haven of peace and quiet, and a place to talk and entertain.

The origin of these patios probably lies in the Ancient Greek megaron and the Roman atrium, but the tradition, with the addition of a central water fountain, was continued by the Arabs. The internal courtyard was an area for women to go about family life and household chores, and was decorated with potted plants – an idea conceived by desert nomads who carried pots of plants with them on their migrations. The grapevine offered good shade.

In the first half of May you'll notice 'patio' signs in the streets and alleyways, which means that you're invited to enter and view what are for the rest of the year closed to the outside world. At this time of year the patios are at their prettiest, and many are entered in an annual competition, the **Concurso de Patios Cordobeses** (Competition of Cordoban Patios). A map of patios open for viewing is available from the tourist office. Some of the best patios are on and around Calle San Basilio, about 400m southwest of the Mezquita. During the competition, the patios are generally open from 5pm to midnight Monday to Friday, and noon to midnight Saturday and Sunday. Admission is usually free but sometimes there's a container for donations.

Although much diminished, what remains of the old Jewish quarter extends west and northwest from the Mezquita, almost to the beginning of Avenida del Gran Capitán. The most famous street in the area is known as **Calleja de las Flores** (Flower Alley) and gives a picture-postcard view of the Mezquita bell tower framed between the narrow alley walls.

The medieval **Sinagoga** (Synagogue; Calle de los Judíos 20; non-EU/EU citizen €0.30/free; 9.30am-2pm & 3.30-5.30pm Tue-Sat, 9.30am-1.30pm Sun & public holidays), built in 1315, is a beautiful little building, decorated with some extravagant stuccowork that includes Hebrew inscriptions and intricate Mudejar star and plant patterns. There's a solitary menorah, probably where the ark (the cabinet where the Torah is held) used to be. It has a women's gallery upstairs.

The **Casa Andalusí** (Calle de los Judíos 12; admission €2.50; 10am-7pm) is a 12th-century house with a bit of an exaggerated, slightly tacky idea of Al-Andalus. It has a tinkling fountain in the patio and a variety of exhibits, mainly relating to Córdoba's medieval Muslim culture, as well as a Roman mosaic in the cellar, and a shop selling North African items.

Nearby is the **Museo Taurino** (Bullfighting Museum; 957 20 10 56; Plaza de Maimónides; admission €3, Fri free; 10am-2pm & 4.30-6.30pm Tue-Sat Oct-Apr, 10am-2pm & 5.30-7.30pm Tue-Sat May, Jun & Sep, 8.30am-2.30pm Tue-Sat Jul & Aug, 9.30am-2.30pm Sun & public holidays year-round), housed in a 16th-century Renaissance mansion. It celebrates, with grim theatricality, Córdoba's legendary matadors, with rooms dedicated to El Cordobés and Manolete. Exhibits include the rather forlorn, pegged-out hide of Islero, the bull that killed the revered Manolete at Linares in 1947. It was closed for refurbishment during research.

Plaza del Potro, Plaza de la Corredera & Around

Córdoba's famous Plaza del Potro (Square of the Colt) has in its centre a lovely 16th-century stone fountain topped by a rearing *potro* that gave the plaza its name. The plaza is home to an attractive old charity hospital that houses two of the city's most visited museums, the Museo Julio Romero de Torres and the Museo de Bellas Artes. The square's heyday was in the 16th and 17th centuries, when it was the preferred gathering ground for traders, vagabonds and adventurers. On the plaza's western side is the legendary 1435 inn, **Posada del Potro** (957 48 50 18; Plaza del Potro 10; admission free; 10am-2pm & 5-8pm Mon-Fri Aug-May), described in *Don Quixote* as a 'den of thieves'. Cervantes once lived here for a short period, and was no doubt robbed and cheated several times by the rough lot hanging out on the square. The picturesque *posada* (inn), charmingly arranged around a small animal yard, regularly hosts interesting temporary exhibits of art, artefacts and photography.

The **Museo de Bellas Artes** (Plaza del Potro 1; non-EU/EU citizen €1.50/free; 3-8pm Tue, 9am-8pm Wed-Sat, 9am-3pm Sun & public holidays) has a collection of mainly Cordoban artists.

The excellent archaeological museum, **Museo Arqueológico** (957 47 40 11; Plaza de Jerónimo Páez 7; non-EU/EU citizen €1.50/free; 3-8pm Tue, 9am-8pm Wed-Sat, 9am-3pm Sun & public holidays), is housed in a Renaissance mansion that was once the site of an original Roman villa. The museum has a wonderful collection of Iberian, Roman and Muslim artefacts, and provides real insight into pre-Islamic Córdoba. A reclining stone lion takes pride of place in the Iberian section, and there is a huge collection of Roman artefacts – from large mosaics and gladiatorial tombstones to elegant ceramics and tinted glass bowls. The upstairs is devoted to medieval Córdoba, and includes a bronze stag, a gift to Abd ar-Rahman III from the Byzantine emperor Constantine VII, that used to grace one of the fountains at Medina Azahara.

North of Plaza del Potro is the grand 17th-century Plaza de la Corredera, a square with an elaborate history of public entertainment and gory showbiz. This was the site of Córdoba's Roman amphitheatre (where, no doubt, gladiator blood was spilled), and the location for horse races, violent bullfights and horrific Inquisition burnings. Thankfully, all of that is in the past, and nowadays the extensively restored square hosts tame rock concerts and other events (ask at the tourist office for details). A daily fruit market is held here and on Saturday there's a lively flea market selling stuff like secondhand clothes, household items and bric-a-brac.

Some 500m north of Plaza de la Corredera is the stunning Renaissance **Palacio de Viana** (957 49 67 41; Plaza de Don Gome 2; whole house/patios only €6/3; 9am-2pm Mon-Fri, 10am-1pm Sat Jun-Sep, 10am-1pm & 4-6pm Mon-Fri, 10am-1pm Sat Oct-May), which has 12 beautiful patios and a formal garden that are a real pleasure to visit in the spring. The palace was occupied by the Marqueses de Viana until a couple of decades ago. The charge covers a one-hour guided tour of the rooms (packed with art and antiques) and access to the patios and garden. It takes about half an hour to stroll around the garden and patios.

Plaza de las Tendillas & Around

Córdoba's busy main square, Plaza de las Tendillas, features a clock with flamenco chimes, exuberant fountains and an equestrian statue of local lad Gonzalo Fernández de Córdoba, who rose to become Isabel and Fernando's military right-hand man and earned the name El Gran Capitán. You may notice his head is small and white, while the rest of the statue is grey – the town legend goes that someone stole his head and the authorities replaced it with a smaller, colour-clashing version. The mystery gets deflated when you spot his real head (which must have fallen off and broken) in the Museo de Bellas Artes.

The streets running off from here are the main shopping zones. Calle Conde de Gondomar leads west into the broad and

---

ANDALUCÍA'S ARTIST OR CÓRDOBA'S CLICHÉ?

Córdoba's most visited museum, the **Museo Julio Romero de Torres** (957 49 19 09; Plaza del Potro 1; admission €3, Fri free; 10am-2pm & 4.30-6.30pm Tue-Sat mid-Oct–Apr, 10am-2pm & 5.30-7.30pm Tue-Sat May, Jun & Sep–mid Oct, 8.30am-2.30pm Jul & Aug, 9.30am-2.30pm Sun & public holidays year-round), is devoted to the city's beloved painter of the same name and housed in his former studio. Born and bred in Córdoba, Señor Torres (1880–1930) received international recognition and acclaim during his lifetime, but after his death his work lost respect everywhere but in his home town. It won't be long before you notice poster reproductions of his paintings in local shops, bars and restaurants. Romero's art was entirely dedicated to all things passionate, despondent and Andalucian, portraying broken-hearted beauties, jealous bullfighters and proud prostitutes. He was deeply connected to the flamenco world, and is still respected by flamenco musicians – the famous guitarist Paco Peña, a fellow Cordoban, dedicated an entire show to Romero's work and themes. Some have described his work as voyeuristic eroticism and chocolate-box trash, and others as the quintessence of all things Andalucian. Take a look and make up your own mind.

lengthy Avenida del Gran Capitán. The *avenida* is undistinguished architecturally, but is the scene of Córdoba's evening *paseo* (stroll) and is lively enough. To the east of Plaza de las Tendillas, a ruined **Roman temple** on Calle Claudio Marcelo has been partly restored, with 11 columns that remain standing.

ACTIVITIES

When you've had enough of being active, try utter laziness at the newly renovated Arab baths, **Hammam Baños Árabes** (☎ 957 48 47 46; www.hammamspain.com/cordoba in Spanish; Calle Corregidor Luis de la Cerda; bath/bath & massage €12/16; ⏲ 2hr sessions at 10am, noon, 2pm, 4pm, 6pm, 8pm & 10pm). In its glory days Córdoba had 60 of these wonderful baths where you hop from hot pools to tepid and cold pools, sipping mint tea after being pleasantly pummelled and squeezed by the aromatherapy masseuse or masseur. You must wear a swimming costume here, but don't worry if you forget yours, as they rent them on the spot and take hygienic precautions. They also give you a towel, so there's no need to bring one. There's a lovely, cushion-strewn *tetería* (tearoom) upstairs where you can smoke a hookah, drink tea and eat Arabic sweets. Reservations for the baths and massages are required at least a day in advance.

COURSES

Centro de Idiomas Larcos (☎ 957 47 11 03; www .larcos.net; Calle Manchado 9) A private language school offering a range of Spanish courses lasting one or two weeks and longer, plus different accommodation options. A typical two-week course costs €260, and two weeks in a shared apartment costs about an extra €160.

Universidad de Córdoba (☎ 957 21 81 33; www.uco .es/webuco/ceucosa/lenguas in Spanish; 5th flr, Building EU Enfermería, Avenida de Menéndez Pidal, Córdoba) For information on monthly language courses (held every month except August) contact the Servicio de Lenguas Modernas y Traducción Técnica at the university. Course fees are €365 and monthly accommodation can be arranged in shared apartments (€180), university residences (€480) and lodgings with local families (€480).

TOURS

You can book an organised tour to Medina Azahara through many of the hotels, or contact the following places:

Córdoba Vision (☎ 957 23 17 34; Calle Doctor Marañón 1; tour €10; ⏲ tours 4pm Tue-Sat Oct-May, 6pm Tue-Sat Jun-Sep, 10.30am Sat & Sun year-round) Offers a three-hour guided tour to Medina Azahara, conducted in Spanish, French and English. The bus departs from Avenida del Alcázar from in front of the Alcázar de los Reyes Cristianos. It also does a combined tour of the city and Medina for €30.

Autobús Turístico a Medina Azahara (☎ 902 20 17 74; Campo Santo de los Mártires; tour €5; ⏲ tours 11am Tue-Fri, 10am & 11am Sat & Sun) Another good way to get to the Medina. Tickets include a three-hour guided tour and an illustrated book of the site.

FESTIVALS & EVENTS

Spring and early summer are the chief festival times in Córdoba.

Semana Santa (Holy Week) Every evening during the week before Easter Sunday, up to 12 *pasos* (the decorated platforms on which statues are carried in a religious procession) and their processions file through the city, passing along the *carrera oficial* (official trail) – Calle Claudio Marcelo, Plaza de las Tendillas, Calle José Cruz Conde – between about 8pm and midnight. The climax is the *madrugá* (dawn) of Good Friday, when six *pasos* pass between 4am and 6am.

Cruces de Mayo (Crosses of May) During the first few days of May, flower crosses decorate squares and patios, which become a focus for wine and tapas stalls, music and merrymaking. For more information about the patios, see Córdoba's Hidden Heart, p308.

Concurso de Patios Cordobeses (Competition of Córdoban Patios) Held at the same time as the patio festival (see Córdoba's Hidden Heart, p308), this festival has a busy cultural programme that every three years (next in 2007) includes the Concurso Nacional de Arte Flamenco, an important flamenco competition.

Feria de Mayo (May Fair) Held in the last week of May and the first days of June, this is a massive town party with concerts, a big fairground in the El Arenal area southeast of the city centre, and the main bullfighting season in Los Califas ring on Gran Via Parque.

Festival Internacional de la Guitarra (International Guitar Festival) A two-week celebration of the guitar, with live performances of classical, flamenco, rock, blues and more; top names play in the Jardines del Alcázar at night. It's held in late June or early July.

SLEEPING

This is budget traveller's heaven. There are more *hostales* (budget hotels) and *pensiones* (guesthouses) around the Mezquita area than you can shake a pillow at, and those mentioned here are just a selection. The cheapest are towards the east and many of them are built around the charming patios for which the city is famous. There are also some charming midrange and top-end options, some with simple, elegant style and spacious rooms, others laden with antiques and history.

Booking ahead during the main festivals is essential. Córdoba draws increasing numbers of visitors throughout the year, so single rooms at a decent price are in short supply. Prices are generally reduced from November to mid-March; some places also cut their rates in the hot months of July and August. Where stated, hotels do offer parking facilities but these have to be paid for at a rate of around €10 to €12 per day.

Budget

Nearly all of the following places also offer rooms without bathrooms at a cheaper rate.

Instalación Juvenil Córdoba (☎ 957 29 01 66, reservations 902 51 00 00; www.inturjoven.com; Plaza de Judá Leví s/n; dm under 26yr/over 26yr incl breakfast €14/19; 🅿 🖳) Fantastically cheap and perfectly positioned in the Judería, Córdoba's youth hostel accommodates 167 people in double, triple, quadruple and quintuple rooms, all with private bathroom, but beware the screaming school kids who come here on group trips. It can be hellish. One wing is in a converted 16th-century convent.

Pension Agustina (☎ 957 47 08 72; Calle Zapateria Vieja 5; s/d €17/30) A simple, old-fashioned and friendly family-run *hostal* with a plant-filled patio. There are nine simple but pristine rooms.

Hostal el Reposo de Bagdad (☎ 957 20 28 54; www.hostalbagdad.eresmas.com; Calle Fernández Ruano 11; s/d €22/38) Hidden away in a tiny street in the Judería, this place is excellent for anyone wanting an interesting and beautiful place to stay, at bargain prices. The house is over 200 years old, and the en-suite rooms are simple with crisp, white linen. The (dark) ground-floor rooms have lovely Andalucian tiling. There's a guest-only Arabic *tetería* on the ground floor, off a gorgeous leafy patio.

Hostal Osio de Córdoba (☎ /fax 957 48 51 65; Calle Osio 6; d €40; 🅇) This refurbished mansion with two patios has great facilities at a very reasonable price, and has been recommended by Lonely Planet readers. The proprietor speaks English.

Hostal La Fuente (☎ /fax 957 48 78 27; Calle de San Fernando 51; d €45; 🅿 🅇) La Fuente is a 19th-century town house with spacious courtyards, roof terrace and lift. Newly refurbished in 2005, the hostal has 40 compact, pleasant rooms painted in custard yellow, all with TV, heating, and sweet, tiny-tiled bathrooms. Some character and 'class' is added by wrought-iron mirrors and chairs.

Hostal Séneca (☎ /fax 957 47 32 34; Calle Conde y Luque 7; s/d incl breakfast €44/46) A charming and friendly villa with a marvellous pebbled patio filled with greenery. The rambling house has 12 rooms of different sizes and configurations.

Hotel Maestre (☎ 957 47 24 10; www.hotelmaestre .com; Calle Romero Barros 4; s/d €35/49, apt €58; 🅿 🅇) This place has comfortably furnished rooms equipped with all the mod cons, and the helpful reception staff speak English. The same proprietors run an equally good *hostal* a few doors down (No 16) and have a number of attractively furnished apartments that sleep up to four people.

Hostal El Triunfo (☎ 957 49 84 84; reservas@htriunfo .com; Calle Corregidor Luis de la Cerda 79; s/d €29/55; 🅿 🅇) Facing the southern side of the Mezquita, El Triunfo has 70 boxy rooms with yellow walls and blue beds. The biggest thing in the rooms is the spacious wardrobe, so you could spend your time there. Some rooms have views of the Mezquita, but can be noisy. There's also a friendly bar and restaurant.

Hotel Los Patios (☎ 957 47 83 40; www.lospatios .net; Calle Cardenal Herrero 14; s/d €34/59; 🅇) Super friendly but a bit soulless, Los Patios has clean, small rooms with bare walls. You enter through the busy restaurant, so try not to wander to the reception in your pyjamas.

Midrange

Hotel Mezquita (☎ 957 47 55 85; hotelmezquita @wanadoo.es; Plaza Santa Catalina 1; s/d €36/69; 🅇) One of the best value-for-money places in town, the Hotel Mezquita is right opposite the Mezquita itself. The 16th-century mansion has large, elegant rooms, marble floors, tall doors and small balconies; some rooms have views of the great mosque.

Hotel Albucasis (☎ /fax 957 47 86 25; Calle Buen Pastor 11; s/d €47/75; 🅿 🅇) This is a quiet hotel tucked away in the Judería far from the tourist circus and decorated in stern medieval style – though it has to be said that the small driveway promises more than it delivers. The rooms are clean and plain, decorated in melancholy khaki and white.

Hotel González (☎ 957 47 98 19; hotelgonzalez @wanadoo.es; Calle Manriquez 3; d €66; ❷) Located in a building that was once home to the son of Córdoba's favourite artist, Julio Romero de Torres, this hotel has rich baroque décor with golden everything and numerous paintings. There are 16 large, lavishly decorated rooms and the hotel's restaurant serves meals on the pretty flower-filled patio. The friendly proprietors speak fluent English.

Parador Nacional Arruzafa (☎ 957 27 59 00; cordoba@parador.es; Avenida de la Arruzafa s/n; d €113; ❷ ❷ ❷ ❷) Something of a hike if you're not driving, this parador (state-owned luxury hotel) is 3km north of the city centre. But it's fabulously situated on the site of Abd ar-Rahman I's summer palace and is a modern affair set amid lush green gardens where Europe's first palm trees were planted.

Hotel Lola (☎ 957 20 03 05; www.hotelconencan tolola.com; Calle Romero 3; d incl breakfast €114; ❷ ❷) Individualism and quirky style are the prime ingredients here. Each room is named after an Arab princess, and is decorated with large antique beds and other covetable items that you just wish you could stuff into your pockets and take home. What's more, you can eat your breakfast on the roof terrace overlooking the Mezquita bell tower.

Top End

Many of Córdoba's top-end hotels find it difficult to compete in character and location with the cheaper *hostales* and small hotels. However, if you don't want to get embroiled in traffic or are just stopping for a day or two they may be a good option.

Hotel Amistad Córdoba (☎ 957 42 03 35; www .nh-hoteles.com; Plaza de Maimónides 3; s/d €106/130; ❷ ❷ ❷) This bright, spacious hotel spread across two 18th-century mansions has original Mudejar patios and elegant rooms. It is part of the modern NH chain and therefore has all the requisite facilities, including baby sitting and internet access.

Hotel Hesperia Córdoba (☎ 957 42 10 42; www .hesperia.com; Avenida Fray Albino 1; d €115-135;

❷ ❷ ❷ ❷) This place is situated across the river with good views of the Mezquita and the Puente Romano from its rooftop bar. Although the hotel is looking a little tired, it offers a huge range of facilities.

Hotel Conquistador (☎ 957 48 11 02; Calle Magistral González Francés 15; d €118-141; ❷ ❷) An elegant 102-room hotel facing the eastern side of the Mezquita. It is the best-located top-end hotel and offers a good range of facilities and tastefully decorated rooms.

EATING

Food is among Córdoba's greatest draws – it is the best place to eat in the whole of Andalucía. Córdoba's culinary legacy is *salmorejo*, a delicious chilled soup of blended tomatoes, garlic, bread, lemon, vinegar and olive oil, sprinkled with crumbled hard-boiled egg and strips of *jamón* (ham). *Rabo de toro* (oxtail stew) is another juicy favourite. More upmarket restaurants experiment with recipes from Al-Andalus, such as garlic soup with raisins, honeyed lamb, fried aubergine and meat stuffed with dates and pine nuts. People go loco for the wine from nearby Montilla and Moriles. Although similar to sherry, it prides itself on being naturally alcoholic. Like sherry, it comes in *fino*, *amontillado* or *oloroso* (see p83), and there's also the sweet Pedro Ximénez variety made from raisins.

Budget

Córdoba prides itself on its *tabernas* (taverns) – busy bars where you can usually also sit down to eat. A long walk east or north of the Mezquita will produce better options for the budget-conscious or inquisitive gourmand.

Bodega Mezquita (Calle Corregidor Luis de la Cerda 73) This sumptuous place is one of a number of excellent delicatessens in town. It sells a huge selection of olive oils, *jamónes* and wines.

Mercado (market; Plaza de la Corredera) For fresh food and a pleasant wander, this a wonderful food hall with all manner of stalls.

Taberna San Miguel/El Pisto (☎ 957 47 01 66; Plaza San Miguel 1; tapas €1.50, media-raciones €3-6; ✆ closed Sun & August) Full of local characters and open since 1880, El Pisto (the barrel) is one of Córdoba's best *tabernas*, both in terms of atmosphere and food. Traditional tapas and *media-raciones* (half-serves of meal-sized tapas dishes) are done perfectly, and inexpensive Moriles wine is ready in jugs on the bar.

Bar Santos (Calle Magistral González Francés 3; tortilla €2.50) The legendary Santos serves the best *tortilla de patata* (potato omelette) in town – and don't the *cordobeses* (Córdoba locals) know it. They rush here for a tapa of tortilla, and eat it with plastic forks on paper plates while gazing at the Mezquita. Don't miss it.

Taberna Sociedad de Plateros (☎ 957 47 00 42; Calle de San Francisco 6; tapas €2, raciones €8; ✆ closed Sun) Run by the silversmiths' guild, this well-loved restaurant in a converted convent serves a selection of generous *raciones* (meal-sized servings of tapas) in its light, glass-roofed patio.

Taberna Salinas (☎ 957 48 01 35; Calle Tundidores 3; tapas/raciones €2/8; ✆ closed Sun & Aug) A historic *taberna* that dates back to 1879, with a reputation so good the tables are always busy. Try the delicious aubergines with honey, potatoes with garlic, *flamenquín* (rolled pork and *jamón*), and *rabo de toro*.

Comedor Árabe Andalusí (☎ 957 47 51 62; Calle Alfayatas 6; mains €8-11) A stylish Arabic-style eatery with low seating and dim lighting, you can eat *kofte*, falafel, tagines or bowls of fluffy couscous with chicken, lamb, greens and herbs. A great place for indulging in North African tastes.

Bar Callejón (Calle Enrique Romero de Torres; platos combinados €3-6, menú €7.50) On a pedestrian street with tables outside, looking up to

Plaza del Potro, Bar Callejón does tasty omelettes (€4.50) and a range of fish dishes. There's also a *menú* (set meal).

Midrange

Amaltea (☎ 957 49 19 68; Ronda de Isasa 10; mains €6-10; Ⓥ) This place specialises in organic food and wine, serving up excellent meat dishes and a great range of vegetarian fare such as a delicious green salad with avocado and walnuts, and Lebanese-style tabbouleh. A haven in a vegetarian desert.

Los Berengueles (☎ 957 47 28 28; Calle Conde de Torres Cabrera 7; mains €7-14) A fantastic, attractively decorated *azulejos*-lined fish restaurant. Choose your own fresh fish or monster prawns from the cold counter.

Casa Rubio (☎ 957 42 08 53; Puerta de Almodóvar 5; mains €7-15) Dedicating itself to Mezquita arch-imitation, this busy place serves up all the usual tapas and has a *comedor* (dining room) upstairs. Start with *salmorejo* and *cordero a la miel* (lamb in honey).

Taberna Restaurante Puerta Sevilla (☎ 957 29 73 80; Calle Postrera 51; mains €8.50-15; 🔀) This is a restaurant made for intimate lunches and inventive food. It has divided, private salons and a pretty plant-hung patio framed by ancient crenellations. Artistic presentation is important here, as is playfulness; specialities include *bacalao* (cod) tacos and duck in caramel cream.

Bandolero Restaurante (☎ 957 47 64 91; Calle de Torrijos 6; raciones €2.50-8, mains €9-14) This is an attractive *azulejo*-lined bar, facing the western side of the Mezquita. It serves up good traditional dishes (including *media-raciones*) and you can sit in the bar or the restaurant patio at the back.

Casa Pepe de la Judería (☎ 957 20 07 44; Calle Romero 1; mains €9-15) This place has a great rooftop terrace with views of the Mezquita, and a labyrinth of dining rooms that are always packed. Start off with a complimentary glass of Montilla on the patio before choosing any of the delicious house specials, such as *rabo de toro* or venison fillets.

Almudaina (☎ 957 47 43 42; Plaza Campo Santo de los Mártires 1; mains €10-14) An elegant, atmospheric restaurant in a 16th-century mansion, with dark wood and damask tablecloths. Almudaina serves up excellent traditional food in individual dining rooms, including on an ivy-clad patio.

THE AUTHOR'S CHOICE

Bodega Campos (☎ 957 49 75 00; Calle Lineros 32; tapas €5, mains €13-19; ☽ closed Sun evening) One of Córdoba's most atmospheric and famous bodegas, walking in here is like getting lost in a different world. There are dozens of different rooms and patios, and each room is lined with oak barrels that have been signed by local and international celebrities (such as the Spanish queen Sofia and UK prime minister Tony Blair). This bodega produces its own house Montilla, and the restaurant, frequented by swankily dressed *cordobeses*, serves up a delicious array of meals. For a cheaper but no less enjoyable evening, try the huge plates of tapas in the bar.

El Churrasco (☎ 957 29 08 19; Calle Romero 16; mains €12; ☽ closed Aug) One of Córdoba's top-notch restaurants. The food is rich, the portions generous and the service attentive. Meaty dishes include *churrasco* (grilled meat in a tangy sauce) – in this case, barbecued fillet of pork with Arabian sauce.

Top End

El Caballo Rojo (☎ 957 47 53 75; Calle Cardenal Herrero 28; mains €10-18) Busy, big and with a reputation for Mozarabic specialities, El Caballo Rajo serves up heart-warming dishes such as white-bean stew. The upstairs terrace overlooks the Mezquita.

DRINKING

Córdoba's liveliest bars are mostly scattered around the newer parts of town and come alive at about 11pm or midnight on weekends. You'll be lucky to find any action early in the week. Most bars in the medieval centre close around midnight.

Amapola (☎ 957 47 37 40; Paseo de la Ribera 9; ☽ noon-3am) Possibly Córdoba's hippest hang-out, the Amapola is where the young and beautiful lounge and get intoxicated on a selection of elaborate cocktails. Walls are covered with blue tiles on which graphics are projected, a DJ looks busy and inspired in his booth, and people hang out on green leather chairs and sofas. Party in style till late at night.

Soul (☎ 957 49 15 80; Calle de Alfonso XIII 3; ☽ 9am-3am Mon-Fri & 10am-3am Sat & Sun) This DJ bar gets

hot and busy on weekends, and attracts a hip and arty crowd. The music is good and the place is friendly, but perhaps the best thing in this place is the breakfasts (€3 to €4), with bread baked in a wood-fired oven, and fresh orange juice.

Bodega Guzmán (Calle de los Judíos 7) Close to the Sinagoga, this atmospheric local favourite oozes alcohol from every nook. Check out the bullfighting museum and don't leave without trying some *amargoso* Montilla from the barrel.

Magister (Avenida del Gran Capitán 2) This place caters to the more mature drinker, playing soporific background music and brewing beer on the spot to assure patrons the alcohol won't run out. The beer comes in five tasty varieties: blonde *rubia* and *tostada*, the dark *caramelizada* and *morenita*, and the *especial*, which varies from season to season.

Up near the university there are a number of small bar-cafés such as the '60s-style **Velvet Café** (Calle Alfaros 29) or the popular gay haunt **Milenium** (Calle Alfaros 33), which plays a good range of ambient house tunes.

ENTERTAINMENT

The magazines *Qué Hacer en Córdoba?* and *Welcome & Olé!*, issued free by tourist offices, have some what's-on information, as does the daily newspaper *Córdoba*.

Live Music

Fliers for live bands are posted outside music bars and at the Instalación Juvenil Córdoba. Bands usually start around 10pm and there's rarely a cover charge.

Surfer Rosa (☎ 957 75 22 72; Feria El Arenal 4; ☽ 11pm-late Thu-Sat) A riverbank warehouse in the El Arenal (the location of the Feria de Mayo). Live bands play frequently and the recorded music is infectious.

Jazz Café (☎ 957 47 19 28; Calle Espartería s/n; ☽ 8am-late) Black-and-white tiled floors, a dark bar with glittering optics and pictures of jazz legends such as Roberta Flack, Miles Davis and King Curtis set the tone for this fabulous laid-back bar. It's a haven for late-morning coffee away from the tourist hordes and regularly puts on live jazz and jam sessions.

Sala Level (Calle Antonio Maura 58; ☽ 8pm-late) West of the city centre in the Ciudad Jardín suburb is this busy live-band venue. Prices vary depending on the talent.

Flamenco

Tablao Cardenal (☎ 957 48 33 20; www.tablaocardenal.com; Calle de Torrijos 10; show €17; ⏰ 10.30pm-late) This place vibrates with the intoxicating sound of tapping heels when its flamenco shows get going. Performances, which vary in quality, can be enjoyed on the open-air patio. Guitar players and singers also add to the vibe.

Casa Salinas (Calle Fernández Ruano) A cosy bar serving up tapas and Montillas, Casa Salinas quite often also stages flamenco shows. Ask at the tourist office for schedules.

Theatre

Gran Teatro de Córdoba (☎ 957 48 02 37, tickets 901 24 62 46; www.teatrocordoba.com in Spanish; Avenida del Gran Capitán 3) This theatre puts on a busy programme of events ranging from concerts and theatre to dance and film festivals.

Cinemas

Filmoteca de Andalucía (☎ 957 47 20 18; www.cica.es/filmo in Spanish; Calle Medina y Corella 5; tickets €0.90; ⏰ closed Sat & Sun morning & Jul & Aug) An art-house cinema with regular screenings of subtitled foreign films.

SHOPPING

Córdoba is known for its *cuero repujado* (embossed leather) products and silver jewellery (particularly filigree). Shops selling these crafts concentrate around the Mezquita and go for the tourist with mean prices, so shop around for the best deal.

Calle José Cruz Conde is the smartest central shopping street.

Zoco (Calle de los Judíos) In the Judería, Zoco is a group of workshop-showrooms selling good but pricey crafts.

Meryan (☎ 95 747 59 02; Calleja de las Flores) Try this place for embossed leather; you should be able to find a wallet or a pair of slippers for €9 to €12.

Espauliú (Calle Cardenal González 3) A tasteful silver shop that sells modern jewellery.

Museo Regina (Plaza Luis de Venegas 1; admission €3; ⏰ 10am-3pm & 5-8pm) You can buy wonderfully crafted silver pieces from this new place, which has dedicated exhibitions of silver jewellery.

La Tienda del Olivo (☎ 95 747 44 95; Calle de San Fernando 124B) 'The Shop of the Olive Tree' sells fancy soaps made from olive oil, plus oodles of extra virgin olive oil.

El Corte Inglés (Avenida del Gran Capitán) This ubiquitous shop helps to fulfil those shopping whims.

GETTING THERE & AWAY
Bus

The **bus station** (☎ 957 40 40 40; Plaza de las Tres Culturas) is behind the train station. Each bus company has its own terminal. The biggest operator, **Alsina Graells** (www.alsinagraells.es), runs services to Seville (€9.50, 1¾ hours, six daily), Granada (€10.50, three hours, nine daily) and Málaga (€10.50, 2½ hours, five daily). It also serves Carmona (€7.50, two hours, one daily), Antequera (€8.50, 1½ hours, two daily) and Almería (€21.50, five hours, one daily). Bacoma runs to Baeza (€8.50) and Úbeda (€9). Transportes Ureña serves Jaén (€7, 1½ hours, seven daily), while **Secorbus** (www.socibus.es) operates buses to Madrid (€14, 4½ hours, six daily).

Empresa Carrera heads south, with several daily buses to Priego de Córdoba (€6, 1¼ hours) and Cabra (€4.50), and a couple to Zuheros (€4.50, one hour, at least two daily), Rute and Iznájar.

Car

Rental firms include **Avis** (☎ 957 47 68 62; Plaza de Colón 32), **Europcar** (☎ 957 40 34 80) and **Hertz** (☎ 957 40 20 60), with the latter two located at the train station.

Train

Córdoba's modern **train station** (☎ 957 40 02 02; www.renfe.com; Avenida de América) is 1km northwest of Plaza de las Tendillas.

For Seville, there are dozens of Andalucía Exprés regional trains (€7.50, 1½ hours), Alta Velocidad trains (€13.50, 45 minutes) and AVEs (€22, 45 minutes). To Madrid, options include several daily AVEs (€47 to €52, 1¾ hours) and a night-time *Estrecho* (the slower, cheaper train; seat €28, 6¼ hours).

Several trains head to Málaga (€16 to €21, 2½ hours) and Barcelona (€52 to €85, 10½ hours, four daily), and there is a service to Jaén (€8, 1½ hours, one daily). For Granada (€16, four hours) you need to change at Bobadilla.

GETTING AROUND
Bus

City buses cost around €1. Bus 3, from the street between the train and bus stations, runs to Plaza de las Tendillas and down Calle de San Fernando, 300m east of the Mezquita. For the return trip, pick it up on Ronda de Isasa, just south of the Mezquita, or on Avenida Doctor Fleming.

Car & Motorcycle

Córdoba's one-way system is nightmarish, and parking in the old city can be difficult. Metered street parking around the Mezquita and along the riverside is demarcated by blue lines. Charges are €0.30 for 30 minutes or €1.30 for two hours, from 9am to 9pm. Overnight parking outside these hours is free. There is parking across the river, but it is not necessarily secure overnight. A tempting option (metered) is the walled space just below the Mezquita,

abreast of the Puerta del Puente. This is fine by day, but not advised overnight. There is secure parking just off Avenida Doctor Fleming costing €1/6/12/45 for one hour/overnight/12 hours/24 hours. There is an underground car park on Avenida de América that has similar prices.

The routes to many hotels and *hostales* are fairly well signposted, and the signs display a 'P' if the establishment has parking. Charges for hotel parking are about €10 to €12.

Taxi

In the city centre, taxis congregate at the northeastern corner of Plaza de las Tendillas. The fare from the train or bus station to the Mezquita is around €5.

DETOUR: CÓRDOBA'S MYSTERIOUS NORTH

The area north of Córdoba has wild landscapes, dark-green hills and tiny, hard-working pueblos (villages) untouched by the tourist mania of the south. The Sierra Morena rises sharply just north of Córdoba city then rolls back gently over most of the north of the province. The N432 runs northwest into Extremadura, but after 50km, detour onto the lengthy N502, which will take you to the far north along some incredible landscapes in the area of **Los Pedroches**. This sparsely populated area is full of scattered granite-built settlements, occasional rocky outcrops and expanses of *dehesa* (woodland pasture). The area is known for being covered with holm oak, and during the era of Al-Andalus it was called 'the Land of Acorns'. Thanks to the acorns, this area, along with Jabugo in Huelva, is another source of quality *jamón ibérico de bellota* which comes from small black pigs who feast on the October harvest of acorns. The acorns give the meat its slightly sweet, nutty flavour. Salted and cured over a period of six to 12 months, the resulting dark-pink ham is usually served wafer thin with bread and Montilla. And, luckily for you, it can be sampled it in almost every village in this area.

If you enjoy off-the-beaten-track destinations, head to the castles at **Belalcázar** and **Santa Eufemia**. The 15th-century **Castillo de los Sotomayor** looms over remote Belalcázar, and is one of the spookiest fortifications in Andalucía. The castle is in private hands so you can't go inside, but it still provides a dramatic focus amid the low-lying hills. The only place to stay in Belalcázar is the simple **Hostal La Bolera** (☎ 957 14 63 00; Calle Padre Torrero 17; s/d €14/28), which also has a restaurant, although there are also a number of café-bars clustering around the Plaza de la Constitución.

Santa Eufemia, 26km east of Belalcázar across empty countryside, is Andalucía's northernmost village. The originally Islamic **Castillo de Miramontes**, on a crag to the north above the village, is a tumbled ruin, but the 360-degree views are stupendous. To reach the castle turn west off the N502 at Hostal La Paloma in the village, and after 1km turn right at the 'Camino Servicio RTVE' sign, from which it's a 1.5km drive uphill to the castle. The **tourist office** (☎ 957 15 82 29; Plaza Mayor 1; ☼ 9am-2.30pm Mon-Fri) in the *ayuntamiento* (town hall) also has a leaflet (in Spanish) detailing two walks, one up to the castle and the other to the nearby *ermita* (chapel). For comfortable accommodation, book into the village's **Hostal La Paloma** (☎ 957 15 82 42; Calle Calvario 6; s/d €12/24). The *hostal* does a good-value *menú* (set meal) for €8.

The eastern end of Los Pedroches is occupied by the **Parque Natural Sierra de Cardeña y Montoro**, a hilly, wooded area that is one of the last Andalucian refuges of the wolf and lynx.

Buses reach most of Los Pedroches' villages from Córdoba, but to tour freely you will need a vehicle.

WEST OF CÓRDOBA

ALMODÓVAR DEL RÍO

pop 7420 / elevation 123m

Sleepy Almodóvar del Río is best known for its impressive castle. Situated 22km down the Guadalquivir Valley from Córdoba, the town is attractive enough for half a day's visit, best timed after seeing the Medina Azahara. There is a **tourist office** (☎ 957 63 50 14; Calle Vicente Aleixandre 3; �9am-2pm & 4-8pm Mon-Fri, 10am-2pm Sat & Sun Apr-Oct, 9am-2pm & 4-7pm Mon-Fri, 10am-2pm Sat & Sun Nov-Mar) just around the corner from the pretty central square, Plaza de la Constitución.

Almodóvar's monumental and sinister-looking, eight-towered **castle** (☎ 957 63 51 16; admission €3, EU citizen free Wed afternoon; � 11am-2.30pm & 4-8pm, closes 7pm Oct-Mar) dominates the view from miles around. It was built in AD 740 but owes most of its present appearance to post-Reconquista rebuilding. Pedro I ('the Cruel') used it as a treasure store because the castle had never been taken by force. Its sense of impregnability is still potent within the massive walls. The castle has now been over-restored by its owner, the Marqués de la Motilla, and is full of some rather silly exhibits including limp, manacled mannequins. The towers – with names such as 'the Bells', 'the School' and 'the Tribute' – have various stories attached to them and there are information placards in Spanish and English.

If you are driving, the best way to reach the castle (avoiding the crowded town centre) is to ignore the signs ahead for Centro Urbano at the junction as you enter town. Instead, go right and follow the A431 ring road, signed to Posadas and Palma del Río. There is ample parking below the castle, but you can also drive up the stony approach track (there is no official parking space there but you can park). You can easily walk down into the old town centre from the castle.

If you decide to stay in this area, **Hostal San Luis** (☎ 957 63 54 21; Carretera Palma del Río; s/d €24/40) is a decent option alongside the main A431 by the turn-off for Almodóvar coming from Córdoba. It has basic rooms in a separate building attached to its busy restaurant. You can get plentiful *platos combinados* ('combined plates' of seafood,

omelette or meat, with trimmings) for around €7. For accommodation at the opposite end of the spectrum, **Hospedería de San Francisco** (☎ 957 71 01 83; www.casasypalacios.com; Avenida Pio XII 35; d €104; P ☒ ☒) in Palma del Río, 30km southwest, offers luxurious accommodation in a converted 15th-century monastery set around a superb Renaissance patio.

Almodóvar's best and poshest restaurant is **La Taberna** (☎ 957 71 36 84; Calle Antonio Machado 24; mains €9-18; � closed Mon Sep-Jun, Sun Jul & all Aug), which has tasty home-cooked fish and meat dishes.

Autocares Pérez Cubero (☎ 957 68 40 23) runs buses to/from Córdoba (€1.50, 30 minutes, at least five daily).

HORNACHUELOS & PARQUE NATURAL SIERRA DE HORNACHUELOS

The pleasant village of Hornachuelos is the ideal base for spending a couple of days enjoying the quiet charms of Parque Natural Sierra de Hornachuelos. The park is a 672-sq-km area of rolling hills in the Sierra Morena, northwest of Almodóvar del Río. The park is densely wooded with a mix of holm oak, cork oak and ash, and is pierced by a number of river valleys that are thick with willow trees. It is renowned for its eagles and other raptors, and harbours the second-largest colony of black vultures in Andalucía.

Hornachuelos stands above a small reservoir and on its banks is a delightful little picnic area. The **tourist office** (☎ 957 64 07 86; Carretera San Calixto; � 8am-3pm Thu-Tue, 8am-3pm & 4-6pm Wed) is located in the sports complex on Carretera de San Calixto, the main road to the west of the centre. From Plaza de la Constitución, a lane called La Palmera, with a charming palm-tree pebble mosaic underfoot, leads up to the **Iglesia de Santa Maride de las Flores** and a **mirador** (lookout) on Paseo Blas Infante.

Heading 1.5km northwest from Hornachuelos on the road to San Calixto will take you to the **Centro de Visitantes Huerta del Rey** (☎ 957 64 11 40; � 10am-2pm & 4-7pm Mon-Fri, 10am-7pm Sat). This visitors centre features interesting displays on the area and its creatures, has information on visiting the Parque Natural Sierra de Hornachuelos and also sells local produce, including honey. You can get information on any of the numerous walking trails that fan out from the centre and you can book a **guided walk** (☎ 957 33 82 33), hire bikes or arrange horse-riding sessions here. There is a bar-restaurant situated just by the centre car park that serves mains from €5 to €9.

On the main road just west of the centre, **Hostal El Álamo** (☎ 957 64 04 76; Carretera Comarcal 141, aka Carretera de San Calixto; s/d €30/50; ⓟ ⌗) has clean, pleasant rooms. There is also a busy bar and restaurant located in a separate unit. The restaurant does a *menú* for €6.90. Through the *hostal* it is possible to arrange a number of activities such as walking, biking and horse riding.

In the heart of Hornachuelos village, **Casa Rural El Melojo** (☎ 957 64 06 29; Plaza de la Constitución 15; d €50) is a traditionally furnished house with comfortable rooms. There are substantial reductions for groups.

Just south of the road that leads into the village you'll find **Bar Casa Alejandro** (Avenida Guadalquivir 4; raciones €3.60). This bar is very popular with locals and the walls are heavy with hunting trophies; an alarmingly life-like stuffed horse's head protrudes from a bar-side pillar.

Autocares Pérez Cubero (☎ 957 68 40 23) runs buses to/from Córdoba (€3.20, 50 minutes, four times daily Monday to Friday, one to two times daily Saturday and Sunday).

SOUTH OF CÓRDOBA

The south of Córdoba province straddled the Islamic-Christian frontier from the 13th to the 15th centuries, so many towns and villages cluster around huge, fortified castles. The beautiful, mountainous southeast is known as **La Subbética** after the Sistema Subbético range that crosses this corner of the province. The mountains, canyons and wooded valleys of the 316-sq-km **Parque Natural Sierras Subbéticas** (www.subbetica.org in Spanish) offer some enjoyable walks. The CNIG 1:50,000 map *Parque Natural Sierras Subbéticas* is useful; it's best to get a copy before arriving in the area (see p435). The park's **Centro de Visitantes Santa Rita** (☎ 957 33 40 34; A340) is located, not very conveniently, 10km east of Cabra.

The southern boundary of the region is demarcated by the **Embalse de Iznájar**, a long, wriggling reservoir overlooked by the village of Iznájar (see the boxed text, p321). There are some good walks that can be done around the reservoir. The northern section of the park has a number of attractive settlements of which Zuheros and Priego de Córdoba are among the most appealing.

BAENA
pop 18,000

The name 'Baena' is synonymous with fine olive oil. This small market town, surrounded by endless serried ranks of olive trees, produces olive oil of such superb quality, it has been accredited with its own Denominación de Origen (DO; a designation that indicates the product's unique geographical origins, production processes and quality) label. The periphery of the town is dotted with huge storage tanks and it is possible to visit the best oil-producing mill in the province for a guided tour.

The small **tourist office** (☎ 957 67 19 46; Calle Domingo de Henares s/n; ⏰ 9am-2pm & 5-8pm Tue-Fri, 10am-2pm Sat & Sun) has limited information but tries to be as helpful as possible. It stocks a range of leaflets on the town, and a useful map.

The best reason for coming to Baena is to visit the **Museum of Olive Oil** (☎ 957 69 16 41; www.museoaceite.com; Calle Cañada 7; admission €1.50; ⏰ 9am-2pm & 4-6pm Mon-Fri, 10am-2pm Sat), which is devoted to the history and production of Baena's oil. Audiovisual presentations (in Spanish) explain production methods and uses and it is possible to taste and purchase the famous oil from the museum shop.

To experience the best working olive-oil mill in Córdoba, visit **Núñez de Prado** (☎ 957 67 01 41; Avenida de Cervantes s/n; admission free; ⏰ 9am-2pm & 4-6pm Mon-Fri, 9am-1pm Sat), where Paco Núñez de Prado himself will give you a tour of the facilities. Overall, the family owns something like 90,000 olive trees and their organic methods of farming result in a very high quality product. Unlike some other producers, there are no hi-tech gimmicks here; rather, olives are still painstakingly hand-picked to prevent bruising and high acidity and are then crushed in the ancient stone mills. The mill is famous for *flor de aceite*, the oil that seeps naturally from the ground-up olives. It takes approximately 11kg of olives to yield just 1L of oil. The mill shop sells the oil at bargain prices.

Baena also has a number of quaint 16th- and 17th-century churches and a small **archaeological museum** (☎ 957 66 50 10; Casa de la Tercia, Calle Beato Domingo de Henares 5; admission €1; ✹ 10am-1pm & 6-8pm Tue-Fri, 10am-1pm Sat), which exhibits findings from the Baena area from the beginnings of human settlement here.

There are a number of good *hostales* and hotels in town. The best budget option is **Albergue Ruta del Califato** (☎ 957 69 23 59; www .baenarural.com; Calle Coro 7; per person half-/full-board €29/36), located near the Iglesia de Santa María. It has good dorm rooms, a bar-restaurant and some fantastic views. For something more upmarket, try the plush **Casa Grande** (☎ 957 67 19 05; www.lacasagrande.es /hotelbaena/hotelbaena.htm in Spanish; Avenida Cervantes 35; s/d €45/78; ✹), a converted mansion with refurbished accommodation.

ZUHEROS & AROUND

pop 850 / elevation 625m

Rising above the low-lying *campiña* (countryside) south of the C0241, Zuheros is in a dramatic location, crouching in the lee of a craggy mountain. It's approached up a steep road through a series of hairpin bends and provides a beautiful base for exploring the south of the province.

Information

Tourist information is available from **Turismo Zuheros** (☎ 957 69 47 75; Carretera Zuheros-Baena s/n; ✹ 9am-2pm & 5-8pm), a small office at the entrance to the village on the Baena road.

The Turismo has plenty of leaflets and information on walking and bike hire. The staff can also put you in contact with an English-speaking walking guide, Clive Jarman (☎ 957 69 47 96), who lives in Zuheros. There is a **park information point** (☎ 957 33 52 55), open occasionally in summer, a few hundred metres up the road towards the Cueva de los Murciélagos. There is a good car park at the heart of the village below the castle.

Sights & Activities

Zuheros has a delightfully relaxed atmosphere. All around the western escarpment on which it perches are *miradors* with exhilarating views of the dramatic limestone crags that tower over the village and create such a powerful backdrop for Zuheros' **castle**. The ruined Islamic castle juts out on a pinnacle and has a satisfying patina of age and decay in its rough stonework. Near the castle is the **Iglesia de los Remedios**, originally a mosque, and opposite the castle is the **archaeological museum** (☎ 957 69 45 45; Mirador, Zuheros; castle & museum €1.80; ✹ 10am-2pm & 5-8pm Apr-Sep, 10am-2pm & 4-7pm Oct-Mar), which houses some interesting finds from the Cueva de los Murciélagos. Guided tours take place on the hour.

Zuheros is also renowned for its local cheeses and there is a wonderful organic-cheese factory, Fabrica de Queso Biologico, on the road entering the village. Here you can buy delicious varieties of local cheese – some cured with pepper or wood ash – complete hams, wines, olive oil and honey.

DETOUR: ZUHEROS WALK

Behind Zuheros village lies a dramatic rocky gorge, the **Cañon de Bailón**, through which there is a pleasant circular walk of just over 4km (taking about three to four hours).

To pick up the trail find the **Mirador de Bailón**, just below Zuheros on the village's southwestern side, where the approach road C0241 from the A316 Doña Mencía junction bends sharply. There is a small car park here and the gorge is right in front of the *mirador* (lookout). From the car park's entrance – with your back to the gorge – take the broad stony track heading up to the left. Follow the track as it winds uphill and then curves left along the slopes above the gorge. In about 500m the path descends and the valley of the Bailón opens out between rocky walls. The path crosses the stony riverbed to its opposite bank and, in about 1km, a wired-down stone causeway that recrosses the river appears ahead. A few metres before you reach this crossing, bear up left on what is at first a very faint path. It becomes much clearer as it zigzags past a big tree and a twisted rock pinnacle up on the right.

Climb steadily, then, where the path levels off, keep left through trees to reach a superb **viewpoint**. Continue on an obvious path that passes a couple of Parque Natural notice boards and takes you to the road leading up to the Cueva de los Murciélagos. Turn left and follow the road back down to Zuheros.

Some 4km above the village is the **Cueva de los Murciélagos** (Cave of the Bats; ☎ 957 69 45 45; admission €4; ✆ guided tours noon & 5.30pm Mon-Fri Apr-Sep, 12.30pm & 4.30pm Mon-Fri Oct-Mar, 11am, 12.30pm, 2pm & 5.30pm Sat & Sun year-round, extra tours Sat & Sun summer/winter 6.30pm/4pm), which was inhabited by Neanderthals more than 35,000 years ago. It is worth visiting for its Neolithic rock paintings that date back to 6000–3000 BC. Opening times in winter can be unreliable. The drive up to the cave is fantastic, as the road twists and turns through the looming mountains with spectacular views from a number of *miradors*. From one of these you actually get a weird vertiginous, aerial view of the town.

Sleeping & Eating

Hotel Zuhayra (☎ 957 69 46 93; www.zercahoteles.com; Calle Mirador 10; s/d €46/59; ✆ ✆) This hotel is an excellent base for exploring the area. The friendly proprietor, Juan Ábalos (who speaks English), can also provide a great deal of information on walking routes and guided walks. Guests get free use of the village pool and can take part in cheese-making and painting workshops. The hotel's restaurant serves good mains from €4 to €9.

Another good option, recommended by Lonely Planet readers, is the new **Apartamentos de Turismo Rural** (☎ 957 69 45 27; Calle Mirador 2; 4-person apt €60; ✆) just opposite the castle. The apartments are great value and have extremely helpful owners, who arrange excursions. On the same square is the friendly **Mesón Los Palancos** (☎ 95 769 45 38; Calle Llana 43; raciones €3).

Getting There & Away

Empresa Carrera (☎ 957 40 44 14) runs buses to/from Córdoba (€4.50, one hour, at least two daily).

PRIEGO DE CÓRDOBA

pop 23,150 / elevation 650m

Priego de Córdoba is a sophisticated market town full of 18th-century mansions, extravagant baroque churches and fine civic buildings that will turn your head. Perched on an outcrop over the valley, the town looks like a big vanilla cake. It was one of the towns in the 18th century that was famous for its silk production and, like many of the small neighbouring towns, it grew rich on the proceeds. The excruciatingly narrow lanes of the Barrio de La Villa (the old Arab quarter) all converge on the handsome Balcón de Aldarve with its elevated promenade and magnificent views over the Río Salado. Two of the province's highest peaks, 1570m **La Tiñosa** and 1476m **Bermejo**, rise to the southwest.

Orientation & Information

Priego's main square is the busy Plaza de la Constitución, which merges with the smaller traffic junction of Plaza Andalucía. The helpful **tourist office** (☎ 957 70 06 25; Calle del Río 33; ✆ 10am-1.30pm & 5-7.30pm Tue-Sat, 10am-1pm Sun) is a short walk south of the central Plaza de la Constitución. The office's indefatigable chief, José Mateo Aguilera, is an enthusiastic fount of information and the office is in a historic building that you can look around.

Sights & Activities

The town's catalogue of elegant architecture has earned it a reputation as the capital of Cordoban baroque. Golden-hued stonework and whitewashed walls characterise the buildings, and it is easy to lose yourself in the cobbled streets as you move from one sumptuous baroque church to the next.

The most notable church is the **Parroquia de la Asunción** (Calle Plaza de Abad Palomino) with its fantastic **Sagrario chapel** (sacristy) where a whirl of frothy white stuccowork surges upwards to a beautiful cupola. The sacristy (off the left-hand aisle) and the ornate *retablo* (retable) represent a high point in Andalucian baroque and are now considered national monuments. Similarly ornate are the **Iglesia de San Francisco** (Calle Buen Suceso) and **Iglesia de la Aurora** (Carrera de Álvarez), whose brotherhood takes to the streets of the town in a procession each Saturday at midnight. They play guitars and sing hymns in honour of La Aurora (Our Lady of the Dawn). All the churches normally open from 11am to 1pm.

The main area of monuments in Priego lies 200m northeast of Plaza de la Constitución and is reached by following Calle Solana on through Plaza San Pedro. At a junction with Calle Doctor Pedrajas you can turn left to visit the well-preserved 16th-century slaughterhouse, the **Carnicerías Reales** (admission free; ✆ 10am-1pm & 5-7pm). It has an enclosed patio and a wonderful stone staircase; exhibitions of paintings are often held here. Turning right along Calle Doctor Pedrajas takes you to Plaza de Abad Palomino, where you can visit the Parroquia de la Asunción. On the square's northern side is Priego's **castillo**, an Islamic fortress built on original Roman foundations in the 9th century and later rebuilt in the 16th century. Privately owned, and closed to the public, the castle has been the subject of much archaeological investigation, which among other things has turned up dozens of stone cannonballs.

Beyond the castle lie the winding streets of the **Barrio de La Villa**, where cascades of potted geraniums transform the white-washed walls, especially in Calle Real and Plaza de San Antonio. Other pretty alley-ways lead down from the heart of the barrio to the Paseo de Adarve, where there are fine views across the rolling countryside and mountains. On the southern edge of the barrio and ending in a superb **mirador** is the Paseo de Colombia, with fountains, flowerbeds and an elegant pergola.

At the opposite end of town, you will find Priego's extraordinary 19th-century fountain, **Fuente del Rey** (Fountain of the King; Calle del Río), with its large three-tiered basins continually filled with splashing water from 180 spouts. The fountain writhes with classical sculptures of Neptune and Amphitrite and when the level of the water rises to cover Neptune's modesty, the townsfolk know that it will be a good harvest. The fountain is more Versailles than provincial Andalucía and the peaceful leafy square in which it is situated is a popu-lar place to while away an afternoon. Behind the Fuente del Rey is the late-16th-century **Fuente de la Virgen de la Salud**, less flamboyant, but further enhancing the square's delightful tranquillity. If you take the stairs to the left of the Fuente de la Virgen de la Salud you can walk to the **Ermita del Calvario** (Calvary Chapel) from where there are scenic views.

Also worth a visit is the **Museo Histórico Municipal** (☎ 957 54 09 47; Carrera de las Monjas 16; admission free; ☒ 10am-2pm Tue-Fri, 11am-2pm Sat & Sun), just west of Plaza de la Constitución. Here, imaginative displays exhibit artefacts dating from the Palaeolithic to medieval periods. The museum also organises archaeological tours in the area.

Sleeping

There is only a small selection of accom-modation in Priego but places are seldom full.

Hostal Rafi (☎ 957 54 70 27; www.hostalrafi.net; Calle Isabel La Católica 4; s/d €26/40; ☒) Just east of Plaza de la Constitución, Rafi has pleas-ant rooms above a busy, popular restaurant (mains €6 to €9).

Posada Real (☎ 957 54 19 10; www.laposadareal .com; Calle Real 14; d incl breakfast €42; P ☒ ☒) Juan López Calvo and his family have lov-ingly restored this wonderful old house, and decorated the four rooms (each with a balcony) and one apartment with wrought-iron beds and antiques. In the summer, breakfast is served on the quaint patio.

GETTING AWAY FROM IT ALL

South of Priego de Córdoba, stranded on a dramatic promontory above a huge reservoir, is the isolated pueblo of **Iznájar**, which is dominated by its Islamic castle. Despite the poverty of the region, it is a place of outstanding natural beauty and tranquillity, where you can enjoy the beautiful scenery and indulge in a host of outdoor activities.

On the reservoir's **Valdearenas beach** is the province's most scenic camping ground, **Camp-ing La Isla** (☎ 957 53 30 73; www.camping-laisla.com in Spanish; adult/tent/car €4/3.60/3.60; ☒). **Club Nautico** (☎ 957 53 43 04) is close by and hires out dinghies and canoes and runs a variety of courses from its yacht club.

There are also two wonderful rural hotels offering charming accommodation to match the setting. **Cortijo La Haza** (☎ 957 33 40 51; www.cortijolahaza.com; Adelantado 119; s/d €65/75), outside the village, is a 250-year-old Andalucian farmhouse, furnished in typical fashion with wrought-iron beds and rustic furniture, with lovely views from its terraces. Check the website for comprehensive directions (and a map) giving details of how to reach it.

Given the rural beauty and seclusion of this little corner of Andalucía, it is hardly surprising to find one of Spain's most exclusive hotels here – **La Finca Bobadilla** (☎ 958 32 18 61; www .barcelolabobadilla.com; Loja, Granada; s/d €313/332; P ☒ ☒), which is located 20km south of Iznájar in Granada province. Cheaper deals are available for stays of more than two nights.

Río Piscina (☎ 957 70 01 86; www.hotelriopiscina .com; Carretera Monturque-Alcalá La Real Km 44; d €53; **P** **⌘** **⌽**) A '70s hotel with comfortable rooms and some good facilities, including tennis courts, but without much aesthetic appeal.

Villa Turística de Priego (☎ 957 70 35 03; www .villadepriego.com; Aldea de Zagrilla s/n; 2-person apt/cha-let €77/89; **P** **⌘** **⌽**) A modern Islamic-style complex 7km north of Priego on the road to Zagrilla. The 52 self-catering chalets are ar-ranged around a patio and gardens. Guided walks, horse riding and mountain biking can be arranged through the complex.

Eating

Priego has some good restaurants including the one at Hostal Rafi (see p321).

El Aljibe (☎ 957 70 18 56; Calle de Abad Palomino; ra-ciones €4-9, menú €7) Next to the Castillo, El Aljibe has a nice terrace, and part of the downstairs area has a glass floor through which you can view some old Islamic baths.

Bar Cafetería Río (Calle Río; raciones €6-11) This busy central option has *revueltos* (scrambled eggs), fish and meat dishes. The same peo-ple run **Pizzería-Bagueteria Varini** (Calle Torrejón 7) just around the corner, where there's a huge range of pizzas (from €8), pasta dishes (from €4) and baguettes.

Balcón del Adarve (☎ 957 54 70 75; Paseo de Colom-bia 36; mains €8-12) In a wonderful location over-looking the valley, this place is both a good tapas bar and an excellent restaurant. Speci-alities include *solomillo de ciervo al vino tinto con Grosella* (venison in gooseberry and red-wine sauce), and *salmón en supremas a la naranja* (salmon in orange sauce).

Getting There & Around

The centre of Priego can become very busy. There is parking just by the football and basketball pitches on Calle Cava north of Plaza de la Constitución. There is a small car park in Plaza Palenque along Carrera de las Monjas, the street that runs east from Plaza de la Constitución.

Priego's bus station is about 1km west of Plaza de la Constitución on Calle Nuestra Señora de los Remedios. Bus 1 from Plaza Andalucía takes you there. **Empresa Carrera** (☎ 957 40 44 14) runs buses from the station to Córdoba (€6, 1¼ hours, 12 daily Monday to Friday, five daily Saturday and Sunday), Granada, Cabra and elsewhere.

MONTILLA

If you fancy getting closer to wine-making country and tasting some of that sweet wine (see the boxed text, below), Montilla is the

---

TOUGH TREACLE

Pedro Ximénez wine is a treat after dinner and its taste will linger on your tongue for hours. For miles and miles across the rolling *campiña* (countryside) its vines grow in soggy, rain-drenched soil under a glaring sun. Such conditions would destroy other vines, but not Pedro Ximénez (sometimes called Pe Equis in Spanish for PX). This is a toughy, a Rambo of vines: it loves hard-ship and thrives on extreme weather. In fact it is exactly these conditions that give it the unusual flavours, ranging from very thin, dry almost olive tastes through to a sweet, dark treacle.

Originally thought to be a type of Riesling, legend has it that the Ximénez grape was imported to the region in the 16th century by a German called Peter Seimens (the Spanish adapted it to Pedro Ximénez). Its intensely sweet wine is endlessly compared to sherry, much to the irritation of the vintners. The fundamental difference between the Jerez sherries and Montilla is the al-coholic potency – alcohol is added to Jerez wine, while Montilla grapes achieve their own high levels of alcohol (15% proof) and sweetness from the intense summer temperatures experienced by the grapes when they are laid out to dry. Left to darken in the sun, the grapes produce a thick, golden must when crushed. What results from this was traditionally racked off into huge terracotta *tinajas*, now steel vats, for ageing. Wine that is clean and well formed goes on to become the pale, strawlike *fino*; darker amber wines with nutty flavours create the *amontillado*; and full-bodied wines become the *oloroso*. The wines are then aged using a *solera* system, where younger vintages are added to older ones in order to 'educate' the young wine.

You can visit **Bodegas Alvear** (☎ 957 66 40 14; Avenida María Auxiliadora 1; guided tour & tasting weekday/weekend €3.95/2.95; ☺ shop 10am-2pm Mon-Sat) in Montilla but you should call first to book. Tours take place at 12.30pm Monday to Saturday.

place for you. The town itself is not hugely appealing, but it's good enough for a stroll. The **tourist information office** (☎ 957 65 24 62; www.turismomontilla.com; Calle Capitán Alonso de Vergas 3; ☼ 10am-2pm Mon-Fri, 11am-2pm Sat & Sun Jul & Aug, 10am-2pm & 5-7pm Mon-Fri, 11am-2pm Sat & Sun Jun-Sep) has details of wines and bodegas.

There is an interesting and unusual museum, the **Casa Museo del Inca Garcilaso** (☎ 957 65 24 62; Calle Capitán Alonso de Varga 3; admission free; ☼ 10am-2pm Mon-Fri, 11am-2pm Sat & Sun Jul & Aug, 10am-2pm & 5-7pm Mon-Fri, 11am-2pm Sat & Sun Jun-Sep), dedicated to the 16th-century chronicler of Inca civilisation, the Hispano-Inca son of a conquistador.

If you want to stay the night in Montilla, your best choice is out of town in the charming **Finca Buytrón** (☎ 957 65 10 52; www.fincabuytron .com; d from €48; ☒ ☒), a farmhouse with a welcome swimming pool. Advance booking is highly advisable, as sometimes the house gets rented out completely. For food, Montilla's excellent **Las Camachas** (☎ 957 65 00 04; Avenida de Europa 3; mains €8-11) has won prizes for its delicious local specialities, served in the expansive, comfortable restaurant.

AGUILAR

In Aguilar, 10km south of Montilla, life goes along at a slow pace and tourists are pretty uncommon, so don't be unnerved by some of the stares. The town has an unusual octagonal central square, **Plaza de San José**, inspired by a similar square in Archidona which was built by the Salamanca architect Vicente Gutiérrez in 1806. It is rather unfortunate that it's now used as a car park, but despite this, it's possible to appreciate its beauty. Stroll up to the nearby **Torre Civil de Reloj** (Clock Tower), which looks like a missing part of some grandiose castle or church. Thanks to Aguilar's position on top of a hill, there are marvellous views from the site of its old castle, the **Peñon de Moro**. The church of **Santa María del Soterraño** close to the Peñon, was originally built in the Middle Ages, but was entirely replaced in 1530 by the Gothic-Mudéjar building you see today.

Sleeping choices in Aguilar are poor, and the best place, although by no means great, is **Hotel Queen** (☎ 957 66 02 22; Calle Pescaderías 6; s/d €25/40), off Plaza de San José. It has 15 basic rooms decorated with small paintings of Mexicans, fake flowers and a Virgin Mary, plus there is a restaurant on the ground floor, where silent types shoot pool, but the owners are friendly. **Restaurante Guillermo** (☎ 957 66 00 48; Calle Moralejo 47; ración around €6) is a good place to try Andalucian food with a twist of modernity.

Jaén Province

The endless fields of knotted, braided rows of olive trees covering the mountains and hills of this region make a wonderful introduction to Jaén province, especially when accompanied by the lingering scent of olive oil being produced at a nearby factory. In the province's towns, the stern ambience of the nearby region Castilla-La Mancha is more palpably influential than in southern Andalucía; medieval castles and Renaissance mansions prevail, and the simple cheer of bright patios, tiles and plants is replaced by sophistication, elegant art and mahogany wood.

The region is dominated by the towns of Baeza and Úbeda, two Renaissance beauties that look down their chiselled noses on the poorer, more rough 'n' ready regional capital Jaén. They hint at an illustrious past, where aristocratic families hobnobbed with the royal court and splashed out on expensive town planning. The lack of later development, however, and the persistence of a largely agrarian economy controlled by a few wealthy landowning families has led to impoverished modern times. However, the excellent outdoors attractions of the Parque Natural Sierras de Cazorla, Segura y Las Villas, perhaps the most beautiful of all of Andalucía's mountain regions, and the quaint charms of the region's historic towns draw a number of discerning, activity-seeking travellers.

HIGHLIGHTS

- See Andalucía in its classy, aristocratic guise in the gorgeous Renaissance towns of **Úbeda** (p339) and **Baeza** (p334)

- Get those muscles moving in the dreamy, rugged mountains of **Parque Natural Sierras de Cazorla, Segura y Las Villas** (p347)

- Eat in ancient, tourist-free **tapas bars** (p331) in Jaén and then stay in Andalucía's most impressive parador (state-owned luxury hotel), the **Parador Castillo Santa Catalina** (p331)

- Do a castle crawl around **Jaén** (p330), **Baños de la Encina** (p334), **Cazorla** (p346) and **Segura de la Sierra** (p350)

- Shop with a difference: get aristocratic **antiques** (p344) and Andalucian **pottery** (p344) in Úbeda, **olive wood bowls** (p339) in Baeza, and **olive oil** (p332) in Jaén

| ■ POPULATION: 648,000 | ■ JAÉN AV DAILY HIGH: JAN/AUG 9°C/25°C | ■ ALTITUDE RANGE: 323M–2167M |

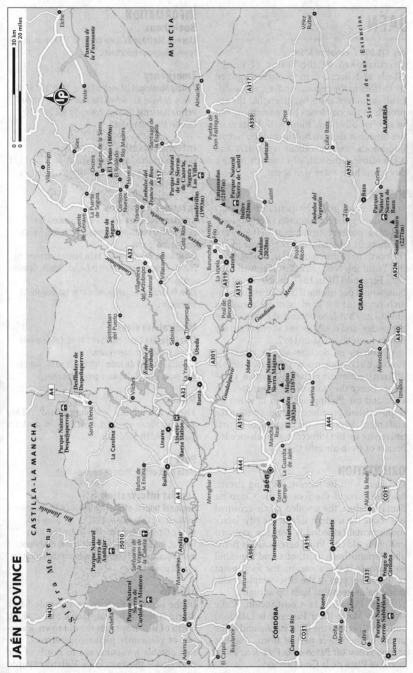

JAÉN PROVINCE

JAÉN

pop 116,000 / elevation 575m

Overshadowed by the beauty of nearby Úbeda and Baeza, Jaén is often forgotten by visitors to the region. And it's not so difficult to understand why, given that the approach to the city looks like something out of an olive oily *Blade Runner*. But this market town has its own bustle, hidden neighbourhoods, some excellent tapas bars and a grandiose cathedral, all of which make a day spent here a day well spent.

HISTORY

Jaén was made grand by its strategic importance during the Reconquista (Reconquest). It was a bone of contention between the Muslims in Granada and the Castilians to the north until the ruling emir, Mohammed ibn Yusuf ibn Nasr, struck a deal with Castile's Fernando III in 1247, which meant ibn Nasr would pay tribute if the Christian monarch respected the borders of his shrinking kingdom. Thus Jaén became the thin end of the wedge, and the Muslims were eventually driven from Granada in 1492.

Centuries of decline set in after the Reconquista, with many *jiennenses* (locals of Jaén) emigrating to the Spanish colonies – hence the existence of other Jaéns in Peru and the Philippines. Jaén now has an impoverished populace struggling to make ends meet. However, the opening of its first university in 1993 injected a much-needed breath of fresh air into the city.

ORIENTATION

Old Jaén, with its narrow, winding streets, huddles around the foot of the Cerro de Santa Catalina, the wooded, castle-crowned hill above the western side of the city. Jaén's monumental cathedral is near the southern end of the old city. From here, Calle de Bernabé Soriano leads northeast and downhill to Plaza de la Constitución, the focal point of the newer part of the city, complete with metal palm trees that light up at night.

From Plaza de la Constitución, Calle Roldán y Marín (later Paseo de la Estación) runs northwest to the train station and is the artery of the newer part of town. The bus station is east off Paseo de la Estación, 250m north of Plaza de la Constitución.

INFORMATION

Bookshops

Librería Metrópolis (Calle del Cerón 17) Sells maps and Spanish-language guidebooks.

Emergency

Policía Municipal (Municipal Police; ☎ 953 21 91 05; Carrera de Jesús) Just behind the *ayuntamiento* (city hall).
Policía Nacional (National Police; ☎ 953 26 18 50; Calle del Arquitecto Berges)

Internet Access

Cyber Cu@k (Calle de Adarves Bajos 24; per 30min €1.20; ☉ 10.30am-12.30pm & 5.30pm-midnight) Found near Plaza de Toros.

Internet Resources

Ayuntamiento de Jaén (www.aytojaen.es) The *ayuntamiento's* website; information in English, French, German and Spanish.
Diputación Provincial de Jaén (www.promojaen.es) Lots of interesting information in English, French, German and Spanish.
Jaén Online (www.jaenonline.com in Spanish) Useful information.

Medical Services

Cruz Roja (Red Cross; ☎ 953 25 15 40; Calle Carmelo Torres) Provides emergency care.
Hospital Ciudad de Jaén (☎ 953 29 90 00; Avenida del Ejército Español) The main general hospital.

Money

There are plenty of banks and ATMs around Plaza de la Constitución and on Calle Roldán y Marín.

Post

Main post office (Plaza de los Jardinillos)

Tourist Information

Regional tourist office (☎ 953 19 04 55; otjaen@andalucia.org; Calle de la Maestra 13; ☉ 10am-7pm Mon-Fri Oct-Mar, 10am-8pm Mon-Fri Apr-Sep, 10am-1pm Sat, Sun & public holidays year-round) Has helpful, multilingual staff and plenty of free information about the city and province.

SIGHTS

In the heart of the city on Plaza de Santa Maria is the cathedral, Jaén's major sight, north of which sprawls the old town, a warren of pleasantly picturesque streets. The two notable museums are to north of the cathedral – the Palacio de Villardompardo

(Villardompardo Palace) on Calle Martínez Molina, and the Museo Provincial on the city's main thoroughfare, Paseo de la Estación. A day or two is needed to really take in these collections and the cathedral, and another full morning could be spent exploring the Castillo de Santa Catalina, finishing off with a memorable lunch at the neighbouring Parador Castillo de Santa Catalina.

Cathedral

They say one should be able to worship God from anywhere, and that proved to be particularly true in Jaén. The Christians worshipped in an old mosque for over 100 years following the Reconquista, and it wasn't until the 16th century that the ambitious plans for Jaén's huge **cathedral** (☎ 953 23 42 33; Plaza de Santa María; ⏰ 8.30am-1pm & 4-7pm Mon-Sat Oct-Mar, 8.30am-1pm & 5-8pm Mon-Sat Apr-Sep, 9am-1pm & 5-7pm Sun & holidays year-round) were conceived and the master architect Andrés de Vandelvira (who was also responsible for many fabulous buildings in Úbeda and Baeza) was commissioned.

Thanks to the grandeur of its design, the magnificent cathedral gave Jaén a confidence boost, especially when compared to its prettier sisters Úbeda and Baeza – finally it, too, had a building that people could gawp at in awe.

Today, its size and opulence still dominates and dwarfs the entire city, and it's fantastically visible from the hilltop eyrie of Santa Catalina. The **southwestern façade**, set back on Plaza de Santa María, was not completed until the 18th century, and it owes more to the late baroque tradition than to the Renaissance, thanks to its host of statuary by Seville's Pedro Roldán. The overall Renaissance aesthetic is dominant, however, and is particularly evident in the overall size and solidity of the internal and external structures, with huge, rounded arches and clusters of Corinthian columns that lend it great visual strength.

During services the cavernous gloom is thick and dark with intense Catholic devotion. The cult of the Reliquia del Santo Rostro de Cristo – the cloth with which St Veronica is believed to have wiped Christ's face on the road to Calvary – has its home behind the main altar, in the **Capilla del Santo Rostro**. The Reliquia reputedly reached Jaén all the way from Constantinople in the 14th century, and a painting of the cloth replaced the original during the Napoleonic Wars. Ironically, having been left alone by Napoleon's army, both the painting and the cloth were stolen during the Spanish Civil War, only to be found years later in a garage outside Paris. Nowadays, they would have undoubtedly turned up on eBay. On Friday at 11.30am and 5pm long queues of the faithful assemble to kiss the cloth. If you're after an excess of religious art and artefacts, visit the **Museo Catedral** (Cathedral Museum; admission €3; ⏰ 10am-1pm & 4-7pm Tue-Sat) in the mausoleum beneath the chapter house.

North of the Cathedral

Northwest of the cathedral, a warren of steep, narrow alleyways disappear into the heart of the old Arab quarter. Calle Madre de Dios, running into Calle Aguilar takes you through the **Arco de San Lorenzo** and up to the handsome Renaissance **Palacio de Villardompardo** (☎ 953 23 62 92; Plaza de Santa Luisa de Marillac; non-EU/EU citizen €1.50/free; ⏰ 9am-8pm Tue-Fri, 9.30am-2.30pm Sat & Sun, closed public holidays & Mon). The *palacio* houses two museums and what are claimed to be the largest Arab baths open to visitors in Spain. There are pamphlets, in French and English, giving some information on the baths and the museums.

The complex is Jaén's most rewarding attraction and houses one of the most intriguing collections of artefacts and archaeological remains found under one roof in Andalucía. The signposted route around the palace leads you first over a glass walkway that reveals Roman ruins, into the bowels of the building and then into the **Baños Árabes** (Arab Baths). The 11th-century baths are in a remarkably good state of preservation, with the usual horseshoe arches and star-shaped skylights lending them an intimate, relaxed atmosphere. After the Reconquista, the Christians, suspicious of what they considered to be a decadent and vice-inducing habit (that also nurtured the Muslim faith), converted the baths into a tannery. The baths then disappeared altogether during the 16th century when the Conde (Count) de Villardompardo built a palace over the site, and were only rediscovered in 1913.

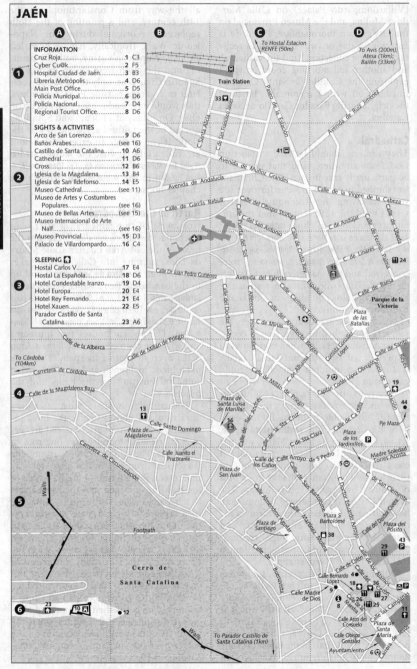

JAÉN

INFORMATION
Cruz Roja	1 C3
Cyber Cu@k	2 F5
Hospital Ciudad de Jaén	3 B3
Librería Metrópolis	4 D6
Main Post Office	5 D5
Policía Municipal	6 D6
Policía Nacional	7 D4
Regional Tourist Office	8 D6

SIGHTS & ACTIVITIES
Arco de San Lorenzo	9 D6
Baños Árabes	(see 16)
Castillo de Santa Catalina	10 A6
Cathedral	11 D6
Cross	12 B6
Iglesia de la Magdalena	13 B4
Iglesia de San Ildefonso	14 E5
Museo Cathedral	(see 11)
Museo de Artes y Costumbres Populares	(see 16)
Museo de Bellas Artes	(see 15)
Museo Internacional de Arte Naïf	(see 16)
Museo Provincial	15 D3
Palacio de Villardompardo	16 C4

SLEEPING
Hostal Carlos V	17 E4
Hostal La Española	18 D6
Hotel Condestable Iranzo	19 D4
Hotel Europa	20 E4
Hotel Rey Fernando	21 E4
Hotel Xauen	22 E5
Parador Castillo de Santa Catalina	23 A6

JAÉN PROVINCE

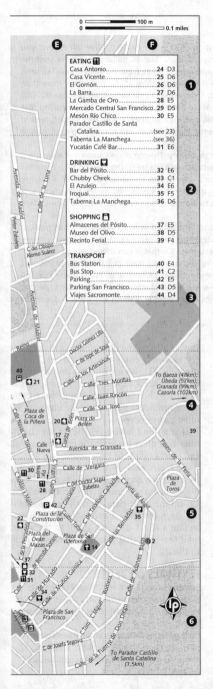

Emerging from the baths, the route takes you through the palace's numerous salons, which are divided into different exhibits of the **Museo de Artes y Costumbres Populares** (Museum of Popular Art & Customs). The collection is wonderfully comprehensive, with a whole range of exhibitions on hideously harsh rural life including shoe making, preindustrial construction, cloth weaving, lace making, ironmongery and every aspect of the Andalucian home. It also sheds light on the very recent hardships endured by the majority of people in the province.

The most recent addition to the *palacio* is the **Museo Internacional de Arte Naïf** (International Museum of Naïve Art). The work and art collection of the museum's founder, Manuel Moral, a native of Jaén province, forms the basis of the display, which complements the folk exhibits of the Museo de Artes y Costumbres Populares. Village life and the countryside are constant themes in the brilliantly coloured and witty paintings.

A short walk west of the Palacio de Villardompardo is Jaén's oldest church, the **Iglesia de la Magdalena** (Calle Santo Domingo; admission free; ⏲ 9am-12.30pm & 5-8pm). Originally a mosque, it now has a Gothic façade and interior. Its tower is the mosque's minaret, which was reworked in the 16th century. The outstanding internal feature is the retable, an ornamental screenlike structure behind the altar. Behind the church is a lovely Islamic courtyard with Roman tombstones and a pool used for ritual ablutions by Muslims before prayer.

Jaén's other most notable museum is the **Museo Provincial** (☎ 953 25 06 00; Paseo de la Estación 27; non-EU/EU citizen €1.50/free; ⏲ 3-8pm Tue, 9am-8pm Wed-Sat, 9am-3pm Sun), which has Spain's finest collection of 5th-century BC Iberian sculptures. Found in Porcuna, the sculptures show a clear Greek influence in their fluidity of form and graceful stylised design. Every year new finds are added and it is hoped that this will eventually become the principal museum of Iberian art in the country. The rest of the exhibits include a collection of Roman and Islamic artefacts, including ceramics, mosaics and sculpture. Admission to the museum also gets you into the upstairs **Museo de Bellas Artes**, which exhibits a supremely mediocre range of 19th- and 20th-century Spanish art.

ESSENTIAL OIL

In Jaén, the *aceituna* (olive) rules. The pungent smell of *aceite de oliva* (olive oil) follows you everywhere you go and perfumes your memories of Jaén. Over 40 million olive trees stud the rolling hills of the province, giving it a strange landscape of what, from a distance, look like rows of green knots. Jaén's olive statistics are pretty staggering: a third of the province – more than 4500 sq km – is devoted to *olivares* (olive groves). In an average year these trees produce 900,000 tonnes of olives, most of which are turned into some 200,000 tonnes of olive oil – meaning that Jaén provides about half of Andalucía's olive oil, one-third of Spain's and 10% of that used in the entire world. You need some of the best Verde Mágina *virgen extra* (extra virgin) oil just to digest those statistics!

The olives are harvested from late November to January. Though there's some mechanisation, much is still done traditionally – by spreading nets beneath the trees, then beating the branches with sticks. The majority of Jaén's (and Andalucía's) olive groves are owned by a handful of large landowners. The dominance of this one crop in the province's economy means that unemployment in Jaén rises from 10% during the harvest to around 45% in summer. An olive picker earns about €30 a day.

Once harvested, olives are taken to oil mills to be mashed into a pulp that is then pressed and filtered. Modern machinery and stainless steel vats have replaced the mule-driven presses that once squeezed the oil through *esparto* (grass) mats. Oil that is considered good enough for immediate consumption is sold as *aceite de oliva virgen* (virgin olive oil), the finest grade, and the best of the best is *virgen extra*. *Aceite de oliva refinado* (refined olive oil) is made from oil that's not quite so good, and plain *aceite de oliva* is a blend of refined and virgin oils. Expect to pay about €5 for a 750mL bottle of Verde Mágina *virgen extra* and about €11 for 2.5L. Specialist shops in Jaén, Baeza and Úbeda sell quality oil.

Some 200m northeast of the cathedral is the huge bulwark of the 13th-century **Iglesia de San Ildefonso** (Plaza de San Ildefonso; admission free; 8.30am-noon & 7-8pm), the 'home church' of Jaén's patron saint, the Virgen de la Capilla, and the second-largest church in the city. An inscription on the northeastern end of its exterior marks the spot where the Virgin is believed to have appeared on 10 June 1430. Her much venerated image stands in a special chapel. Free guided tours can be arranged through the **Guide Organisation** (☎ 953 25 44 42).

Castillo de Santa Catalina

Watching the city from atop the cliff-girt Cerro de Santa Catalina is the former Islamic fortress **Castillo de Santa Catalina** (☎ 953 12 07 33; admission €3; 10am-2pm & 5-9pm Tue-Sun Apr-Sep, 10am-2pm & 3.30-7pm Tue-Sun Oct-Mar). Inside the castle a signposted route takes you around the keep, the chapel and the dungeon, while audiovisual gimmicks explain each point of interest – the best (and most amusing) being the manacled prisoner whose hologrammed face comes to life and tells of his miserable fate at the hands of the evil Napoleonic invaders. There is also a short and shallow film on Jaén's history but the kids may enjoy the 3-D glasses. Unfortunately, all this enjoyment is only to be had in Spanish. Past the castle at the end of the ridge stands a large **cross**, from where there are magnificent views over the city and the olive groves beyond.

If you don't have a vehicle for the circuitous 4km drive up from the city centre, you can take a taxi (€6).

You can also walk (about 40 minutes from the city centre) by heading uphill from the cathedral to join Calle de Buenavista. Go up the right-hand branch before crossing over onto the Carretera de Circunvalación; a short distance along to the right, take the path that heads off steeply uphill to the left.

FESTIVALS & EVENTS

Semana Santa (Holy Week) The week leading up to Easter Sunday is celebrated in a big way, with processions through the old city by members of 13 *cofradías* (brotherhoods).

Feria y Fiestas de San Lucas This is Jaén's biggest party, with concerts, funfairs, bullfights and general merrymaking in the eight days leading up to the saint's day on 18 October.

SLEEPING

Glamour and style are not the leading features of Jaén's hotels. In fact, they are not even an accompanying one. Budget options are very basic and mosquitoes can be a nuisance from May to October, so arm yourself with plenty of insect repellent. Prices in several places rise a bit during Semana Santa and the Feria y Fiestas de San Lucas. Some hotels do offer parking, but this costs around €7 to €10 per day.

Hostal Carlos V (☎ 953 22 20 91; Avenida de Madrid 4, 2º; s/d/tr €21/35/48; ✗) This friendly, family-run *hostal* (budget hotel) is the best budget option in town. The pleasant rooms with wrought-iron beds are in an apartment opposite that of the owners, the bathrooms are shared and there's a TV in each room.

Hostal La Española (☎ 953 23 02 54; Calle Bernardo López 9; s/d €26/32) This hostal is not the most welcoming of places, with a grimly Gothic interior, a creaking spiral staircase and drab furnishings. It's quite cheap and close to the cathedral though, plus it's near some good tapas bars – just as well, since you may need to fortify yourself with a few *vinos tintos* (red wines) to take the edge off this place.

Hostal Estacion RENFE (☎ 953 27 46 14; Plaza de Jaén por la Paz s/n; s/d €29/36; P ✗) Although the exterior of this *hostal* opposite the train station is not the most attractive, inside it offers comfortable accommodation for short stays. It also has its own good restaurant.

Hotel Europa (☎ 953 22 27 00; www.husa.es; Plaza de Belén 1; s/d €34/57; P ✗) Rather overpriced for what it has to offer, Hotel Europa tries to compensate with decent rooms, each with TV and a safe. Its location off Avenida de Granada makes it one of the most convenient options for drivers.

Hotel Xauen (☎ 953 24 07 89; www.hotelxauenjaen .com; Plaza del Deán Mazas 3; s/d €40/55; P ✗ ⧉) Shabbily glamorous receptionists welcome the business crowd and stare out the less well-heeled guests. Despite this, the hotel has good facilities and spacious, well-appointed rooms.

Hotel Rey Fernando (☎ 953 25 18 40; Plaza de Coca de la Piñera 5; P ✗) The modern and comfortable Rey Fernando was under refurbishment during our research.

Hotel Condestable Iranzo (☎ 953 22 28 00; Paseo de la Estación 32; s/d €71/92; ✗) The once grand Condestable is now faded and retro in its glamour, with a plush '70s lobby, dark green leather sofas and a marble reception desk. The friendly, uniformed staff will take your luggage to spacious, modern rooms with caramel marble bathrooms.

Parador Castillo de Santa Catalina (☎ 953 23 00 00; www.parador.es in Spanish; d €113; P ✗ ⧉) If you want character, this is the only place worth checking into. Part of the Castillo de Santa Catalina complex, the hotel has an incomparable setting, theatrical vaulted halls and huge fireplaces. Rooms are incredibly comfortable, with four-poster beds, Islamic tiled details and all the mod cons. There is also an excellent restaurant that's well worth a trip even if you are not a guest.

EATING

Although there aren't many fancy restaurants in Jaén, you won't miss out on excellent food – some of Andalucía's quirkiest tapas bars are here, and the *jiennenses* cherish and preserve them. The best of these are on Calles del Cerón, Arco del Consuelo and Bernardo López, all near the cathedral. The other restaurant strip is the short Calle Nueva, off Calle Roldán y Marín.

Yucatán Café Bar (Calle de Bernabé Soriano; tapas from €1.20) The Yucatán is an old man's hangout with delicious bread and paper-thin *jamón* (ham), excellent *tortilla* (omelette) and incredible chicken livers. Resist going to the toilets here and avoid any of the fast food and sandwiches. You can get breakfast for €2.50.

JAÉN PROVINCE

THE AUTHOR'S CHOICE

El Gorrión (☎ 953 23 22 00; Calle de Arco del Consuelo 7; tapas from €1.20) Atmospheric or old-fashioned is an understatement here: this place *is* the past. Lazy jazz plays on the stereo, old newspaper cuttings are glued to the walls, and mad paintings of bizarre landscapes hang lopsidedly next to oval oak barrels, overlooking old guys who have seemingly been propping up the bar for centuries (or at least since 1888, when it opened). The tapas are simple and traditional, and are best enjoyed with the sherry and wine on offer.

La Barra (Calle del Cerón 7; tapas from €1.30, raciónes €5) If you measured friendliness in a unit, you could call it '1 Barra' – that's how jolly and welcoming this place is. The (friendly) owner has frequent exhibitions of film stills and cartoons; when we were visiting, the (friendly) faces from *Cheers* were smiling at us while we ate traditional tapas and drank beer.

La Gamba de Oro (☎ 953 24 17 46; Calle Nueva 5; raciones €3-6) The rather unattractive La Gamba is a terrific seafood place, despite being miles from the sea. There are baskets underfoot for discarded shells, and a selection of fried fish costs from €4 to €8.

Taberna La Manchega (☎ 953 23 21 92; Calle Bernardo López 12; platos combinados €4; ☯ 10am-5pm & 8pm-1am Wed-Mon) A terrific bar with an atmospheric dining room in the cellar. The taberna is over a century old, and the food is cheap and tasty. Try the simple but unforgettable tapa of baked potato with garlic sauce.

Mesón Río Chico (☎ 953 24 08 02; Calle Nueva 2; menú €8) A top choice, and very popular. The downstairs *taberna* (tavern) serves delicious tapas and *raciones* (meal-sized servings of tapas) of meat, *revueltos* (scrambled eggs) and fish. There is a more expensive restaurant upstairs.

Parador Castillo de Santa Catalina (☎ 953 23 00 00; www.parador.es in Spanish; menú €23) A superb experience akin to travelling back in time. Dine in the authentically recreated medieval dining room amid suits of armour and vast wall tapestries – the atmosphere is solemn and formal, the service dutifully obsequious and the menu suitably traditional.

Casa Vicente (☎ 953 23 28 16; Calle Francisco Martín Mora; menú €30) Located in a restored mansion with a patio, Casa Vicente is one of the best restaurants in town. It has a great bar where you can take a tipple with tapas, or you can sit down in the patio or interior dining room (the best option in winter) to enjoy specialities such as the *cordero mozárabe* (lamb with honey and spices).

Casa Antonio (☎ 953 27 02 62; Calle de Fermín Palma 3; menú €30) Another highly regarded restaurant, rivalling Casa Vicente as the best in town. Serves up *jiennense*-style classics with a more modern twist.

You can buy almost any type of fresh food at the large, modern **Mercado Central San Francisco** (Calle de los Álamos).

DRINKING

The main nightlife zone is towards the train station and university – the students add some zip to the bar life.

For general socialising, several atmospheric old bars are clustered just northwest of the cathedral on Calle del Cerón and narrow Calles Arco del Consuelo and Bernardo López.

El Azulejo (Calle de Hurtado 8; ☯ 10am-midnight) This place is a real surprise in terms of space and style among Jaén's otherwise plain bar choices. Skylights brighten the main drinking area, burnt plum walls add atmosphere, and great paintings of harbours pinch with longing for the sea. The music might be anything from pop, electronic to jazz.

Bar del Pósito (Plaza del Pósito 10; ☯ 10am-midnight) This is a regular hang-out for Jaén's cultural movers and poets – some may even recite quite serious stuff into your ear. Photography exhibitions and other happenings take place here, so check what's on and join in.

Taberna La Manchega (☎ 953 23 21 92; Calle Bernardo López 12; ☯ 10am-5pm & 8pm-1am Wed-Mon) This place has been in action since the 1880s and apart from eating great, simple tapas here, you can drink wine and watch local characters devour hot potatoes. La Manchega has entrances on both Calle Arco del Consuelo and Calle Bernardo López.

Iroquai (☎ 953 24 36 74; Calle de Adarves Bajos 53) Usually has live rock, blues, flamenco or fusion on Thursday nights (look out for its posters about town) and plays good music other nights.

Chubby Cheek (☎ 953 27 38 19; Calle de San Francisco Javier 7) Caters to a slightly older set and has live jazz most weekends.

SHOPPING

Jaén's main shopping areas are centred on Calle Roldán y Marín, Paseo de la Estación and Calle de San Clemente (off Plaza de la Constitución). The province's trademark olive oil can be purchased at **Almacenes del Pósito** (Plaza del Pósito) or the **Museo del Olivo** (Calle Martínez Molina 6). A big and bustling *mercadillo* (flea market) is held every Thursday morning at the **Recinto Ferial** (Exhibition Site; Avenida de Granada), northeast of Plaza de la Constitución.

GETTING THERE & AWAY
Bus
From the **bus station** (☎ 953 25 01 06; Plaza de Coca de la Piñera), Alsina Graells runs buses to Granada (€7, 1½ hours, 14 daily), Baeza (€3.50, 45 minutes, 11 daily), Úbeda (€4.50, 1¼ hours, 12 daily Monday to Saturday) and Cazorla (€7.50, two hours, two daily). The Ureña line travels up to Córdoba (€7, 1½ hours, seven daily) and Seville (€17, three hours, three to five daily). Other buses head for Málaga (€14, one daily), Almería (€26, at least one daily), Madrid (€23, five daily Monday to Saturday) and many smaller places in Jaén province.

Car & Motorcycle
Jaén is 92km north of Granada by the fast A44. This road continues to Bailén, where it meets the Córdoba–Madrid A4. To get to or from Córdoba, take the A306 via Porcuna.

Viajes Sacromonte (☎ 953 22 22 12; Paseo de la Estación 12), in the Pasaje Maza arcade, is a car-rental agent as well as a general travel agent. **Avis** (☎ 953 28 09 37; Avenida de Madrid) and **Atesa** (☎ 953 28 16 40; Calle Ortega Nieto 9) have local offices.

Train
Jaén's **train station** (☎ 953 27 02 02; www.renfe .com; Paseo de la Estacíon) is at the end of a branch line and there are only five departures most days. A train leaves at 8am for Córdoba (€8, 1½ hours, one daily) and Seville (€16, three hours, one daily). There are also trains to Madrid (€22, four hours, four daily).

GETTING AROUND
There's a **bus stop** (Paseo de la Estación) south of the train station; bus 1 will take you to Plaza de la Constitución, the central point for all city buses, for €1.

Driving in Jaén can be stressful due to the one-way road system and the weight of traffic. If you end up in the centre, there is underground parking at Plaza de la Constitución and at Parking San Francisco, off Calle de Bernabé Soriano, near the cathedral. Costs are €0.90 per hour or €12 for 24 hours.

Taxis gather on Plaza de la Constitución, Plaza de San Francisco, near the cathedral, and at the bus and train stations. Call **Radio Taxis** (☎ 953 22 22 22) for taxis.

NORTH OF JAÉN

The A4 north out of Andalucía to Madrid passes through indifferent countryside to the north of Jaén until the hills of the Sierra Morena appear on the horizon. Ahead lies the Desfiladero de Despeñaperros (Pass of the Overthrow of the Dogs), so named because the Christian victors of the 1212 battle at nearby Las Navas de Tolosa are said to have tossed many of their Muslim enemies from the cliffs.

The full drama of the pass is not appreciated until the last minute, when the road from the south descends suddenly and swoops between rocky towers and wooded slopes to slice through tunnels and defiles.

PARQUE NATURAL DESPEÑAPERROS & SANTA ELENA
Road and rail have robbed the Desfiladero de Despeñaperros of much of its historic romance, but the splendid hill country to either side is one of Spain's most beautiful and remote areas. Clothed with dense woods of pine, holm oak and cork trees from which protrude dramatic cliffs and pinnacles of fluted rock, the area around the pass is now a natural park, home to deer and wild boar, and maybe the occasional wolf and lynx. There are no local buses, so you need your own transport to get the most out of the area. The main visitor centre is the **Centro de Visitantes Puerta de Andalucía** (☎ 953 66 43 07; Carretera Santa Elena a Miranda del Rey; ☼ 10am-2pm & 4-8pm Apr-Sep, 10am-2pm & 3-7pm Oct-Mar) on the outskirts of Santa Elena, the small town just south of the pass. The centre has information and maps on walking routes in the area. You can also contact a park guide directly (☎ 610 282531).

Santa Elena is an ideal base for exploring the park, and has shops, bars and cafés. **Hotel El Mesón de Despeñaperros** (☎ 953 66 41 00; meson@serverland.com; Avenida de Andalucía 91; s/d €25/39), at the north end of town, has comfy rooms and a busy restaurant. Alternatively, in La Carolina, 12km south of Santa Elena, there is the more fancy **La Perdiz** (☎ 953 66 03 00; www.nh-hoteles.es in Spanish; Autovía de Andalucía; s/d €74/79; P ⊠ ⌨ ⊠), part of the NH chain, which offers every possible amenity and is set amid lovely gardens. Exit at Km 268.

DETOUR: PARQUE NATURAL SIERRA DE ANDÚJAR

Thirty-one kilometres north of Andújar on the J-5010 is the 13th-century **Santuario de la Virgen de la Cabeza**. It is tucked away in the secluded Parque Natural Sierra de Andújar, and is the scene of one of Spain's biggest religious events, the Romería de la Virgen de la Cabeza. The original shrine was destroyed in the civil war, when it was seized by 200 pro-Franco troops. The shrine was only 'liberated' in May 1937 after eight months of determined Republican bombardment.

On the last Sunday in April nearly half a million people converge to witness a small statue of the Virgin Mary – known as La Morenita (The Little Brown One) – being carried around the Cerro del Cabezo for about four hours from around 11am. It's a festive, emotive occasion: children and items of clothing are passed over the crowd to priests who touch them to the Virgin's mantle.

The park is said to have the largest expanse of natural vegetation in the Sierra Morena. Full of evergreen and gall oaks, the park is home to plenty of bull-breeding ranches, a few wolves, lynx and boars, plus deer, mouflon and various birds of prey. Information is available from the **Centro de Visitantes** (☎ 953 54 90 30), at Km 12 on the road from Andújar to the Santuario de la Virgen de la Cabeza, and from Andújar's **tourist office** (☎ 953 50 49 59; Plaza de Santa María; ☼ 8am-2pm Tue-Sat Jul-Sep, 10am-2pm & 5-8pm Oct-Jun).

There are two small *hostales* (budget hotels), **Pensión Virgen de la Cabeza** (☎ 953 12 21 65; d €35) and **Hotel la Mirada** (☎ 953 54 91 11; d €50), near the sanctuary that provide a good base for exploring the 740-sq-km park.

Buses run daily from Jaén to Andújar (€4, four daily) and there are buses from Andújar to the sanctuary on Saturday and Sunday.

For campers, **Camping Despeñaperros** (☎ 953 66 41 92; campingdesp@navegalia.com; camp site per 2 people, tent & car €12) has a great location among pine trees and the helpful owner can advise on walking in the area.

Several buses from Jaén run on weekdays to La Carolina, from where **La Sepulvedana** (☎ 953 66 03 35) runs about four or five buses to Santa Elena, weekdays only. It's best to check the current schedules.

BAÑOS DE LA ENCINA
pop 2740
One of Andalucía's finest castles, the **Castillo de Burgalimar** (☎ 953 61 32 00; admission free; ☼ 9am-8pm), dominates the quiet ridgetop town of Baños de la Encina. The town is a few kilometres north of unexciting Bailén. Built in AD 967 on the orders of the Cordoban caliph Al-Hakim II, the castle has 14 towers and a large keep entered through a double horseshoe arch. The interior of the castle has an unprotected parapet (not for the faint-hearted!) encircling the walls, with dramatic views across the countryside. The castle fell to the Christians in 1212, just after the battle of Las Navas de Tolosa. For info – and the key to the castle – ask at the **tourist office** (☎ 953 61 41 85; Callejón del Castillo 1; ☼ 8.30am-2pm Mon-Fri).

Several mansions and churches, including the **Ermita del Cristo del Llano**, with its spectacular rococo decoration reminiscent of Granada's Alhambra, make a ramble through Baños' old streets worthwhile. The **Restaurante Mirasierra** (Calle Bailén 6; mains €6-8) serves good fish and meat dishes.

EAST OF JAÉN

This part of the region is where most visitors spend their time, pulled by the allure of Baeza and Úbeda and their Renaissance architecture, and the leafy hills and hiking trails of Cazorla.

BAEZA
pop 15,000 / elevation 790m
If Jaén region is known for anything (apart from olives) it's the twin towns of Baeza (ba-*eh*-thah) and, 9km away, Úbeda, two shining examples of Renaissance beauty. Smaller Baeza makes a good day trip from Úbeda. It has a richness of architecture that defies the notion that there is little of architectural interest in Andalucía apart from structures from the Islamic period. Here, a handful of wealthy, fractious families left a staggering catalogue of perfectly

preserved Renaissance churches and civic buildings.

The town is also famed for its role as the bridgehead of the Christian advance on Muslim Granada. Baeza was one of the first Andalucian towns to fall to the Christians (in 1227), and little is left of its Muslim heritage after years of Castilian influence.

Architecture aside, Baeza is the location of a Guardia Civil training school; in the evenings, when hundreds of prospective policemen from the school hit the streets, the town feels like a set of a strange movie.

Orientation

The heart of town is Plaza de España, with the long, wide Paseo de la Constitución stretching to its southwest.

The bus station is about 700m east of Plaza de España on a street officially called Avenida Alcalde Puche Pardo, though it is more commonly known as Paseo Arco del Agua.

Information

You'll find banks and ATMs on Paseo de la Constitución and to the east of Plaza de España on Calle San Pablo.

Main post office (Calle Julio Burell) East of the plaza.

Speed Informatica (Portales Tundidores 2; per hr €1.80; 10.30am-2pm & 5.30-8pm) Has internet; on the north side of Paseo de la Constitución.

Tourist office (☎ 953 74 04 44; otbaeza@andalucia .org; Plaza del Pópulo; 9am-6pm Mon-Fri, 10am-1pm & 4-6pm Sat Oct-Mar, 9am-7pm Mon-Fri, 10am-1pm & 5-7pm Sat Apr-Sep, 10am-1pm Sun year-round) In a beautiful 16th-century courthouse on Plaza del Pópulo, just southwest of Paseo de la Constitución; has loads of useful information.

Sights

Baeza's sights cluster around the central Plaza de España and Paseo de la Constitución. You can take them all in during a leisurely day's stroll. The opening hours of some of the buildings are unpredictable, so check at the tourist office first.

PASEO DE LA CONSTITUCIÓN & AROUND

Sand-coloured churches and huge mansion palaces that take the afternoon sun so beautifully characterise Baeza's historic centre.

The small Plaza de España is the centre of the town and merges with the sprawling, café-lined Paseo de la Constitución, once Baeza's marketplace and bullring. The lonely **Torre de los Aliatares** (Tower of the Aliatares; Plaza de España) is one of the few remnants of Muslim Bayyasa (as the town was called by the Muslims), having miraculously survived the destructive Isabel la Católica's 1476 order to demolish the town's fortifications. The order was meant to end the feuds between the Benavide and Carvajal noble families.

On Plaza del Pópulo is the old entrance to the city, the **Puerta de Jaén** (Jaén Gate), connected to the huge **Arco de Villalar** (Villalar Arch). The arch was erected by Carlos I in 1526 to commemorate the crushing of a serious insurrection in Castilla that had threatened to overthrow his throne. It dominates Plaza del Pópulo, also called Plaza de los Leones after the **Fuente de los Leones** (Fountain of the Lions) at its centre. The fountain is made of carvings from the Iberian and Roman village of Cástulo and is topped by a statue reputed to represent Imilce, an Iberian princess and the wife of the notorious Carthaginian general Hannibal. On the southern side of the square is the lovely 16th-century **Casa del Pópulo**, formerly a courthouse and now Baeza's tourist office. It was built in the plateresque style, an early phase of Renaissance architecture noted for its decorative façades.

On the eastern side of the square stands the **Antigua Carnicería** (Old Butchery), a beautiful building that must rank as the one of the most elegant tanning sheds in the world.

Through the Puerta de Jaén and along to the Paseo de las Murallas, a path loops around the old city walls to a point near the cathedral. From here, Baeza's fantastic position on the escarpment can be easily appreciated.

PLAZA DE SANTA MARÍA

The most typical of all the town's squares, this plaza was designed to be a focus of religious and civic life, and is surrounded by mansions and churches, such as the **Seminario Conciliar de San Felipe Neri** on the square's northern side, a seminary that now houses the Universidad Internacional de Andalucía.

BAEZA

0 — 200 m
0 — 0.1 miles

INFORMATION
Main Post Office...................... 1 C2
Speed Informatica...................... 2 A3
Tourist Office.......................... 3 A3

To Linares-Baeza
Train Station
(13km)

To Fuentenueva (150m);
Hotel Juanito (600m);
Restaurante Juanito
(600m); La Yedra (4km);
Úbeda (9km)

SIGHTS & ACTIVITIES
Antigua Carnicería...................... 4 A3
Antigua Universidad.................... 5 B3
Arco de Villalar........................ 6 A3
Ayuntamiento.......................... 7 A2
Casa del Pópulo......................(see 3)
Cathedral.............................. 8 B4
Convento de San Francisco...........9 B2
Fuente de los Leones................. 10 A3
Fuente de Santa María.............. 11 B4
Iglesia de la Santa Cruz............ 12 B3
Palacio de Jabalquinto.............. 13 B3
Puerta de Jaén........................ 14 A3
Pópulo Servicios Turísticos.......(see 29)
Seminario Conciliar de San
    Felipe.............................. 15 B3
Torre de los Aliatares................ 16 B3

SLEEPING
Hostal Comercio...................... 17 B2
Hostal El Patio........................ 18 A3
Hotel Palacete Santa Ana........... 19 A2
Hotel Puerta de la Luna............. 20 A4

EATING
Cafetería Mercantil.................... 21 B2
Mesón Restaurante La Góndola... 22 A3
Restaurante El Sali.................... 23 A2
Restaurante Palacete Santa Ana... 24 A2
Restaurante Vandelvira.............. 25 A2

DRINKING
Bar Arcediano......................... 26 B3
Bar Pacos...........................(see 20)
Burladero.............................. 27 B3
Café Central Teatro................... 28 B3

SHOPPING
La Casa del Aceite.................... 29 A3

TRANSPORT
Bus Station............................ 30 D2
Car Park............................... 31 B2
Car Park............................... 32 A3
Taxi.................................... 33 B3

JAÉN PROVINCE

As was the case in all of Andalucía, the Reconquista destroyed the mosque and in its place built Baeza's **cathedral** (Plaza de Santa María; admission free, donations welcome; ☿ 10.30am-1pm & 4-6pm Oct-Mar, 10.30am-1pm & 5-7pm Apr-Sep). This was the first step towards the town's transformation into a Castilian gem. The cathedral itself is an aesthetic hotchpotch, although the overall style is 16th-century Renaissance, clearly visible in the **main façade** on Plaza Santa María. The cathedral's oldest feature is the 13th-century Gothic-Mudejar **Puerta de la Luna** (Moon Doorway) at its western end, which is topped by a 14th-century rose window.

A lavish baroque retable backs the main altar and a 13th-century Romanesque-

Gothic Crucifixion sculpture, rare in Andalucía, stands high on the retable of the adjacent Capilla del Sagrario. At the cathedral's western end, the grille on the **Antiguo Coro** (Old Choir) is one of the masterpieces of Jaén's 16th-century wrought-iron supremo, Maestro Bartolomé. There's a slot to the right of the grille, by an unremarkable painting – if you pop a coin into the slot the painting will slide noisily aside to reveal a large, silver 18th-century **Custodia del Corpus**, used in Baeza's Corpus Christi processions.

Outside the cathedral on the pretty square is the handsome **Fuente de Santa María**, a fountain built in the shape of a miniature triumphal arch in 1569 by *baezano* (Baeza local) Ginés Martínez.

PLAZA SANTA CRUZ

Baeza's most extraordinary palace, the **Palacio de Jabalquinto** (Plaza Santa Cruz; admission free; ☉ 10am-2pm & 4-6pm Thu-Tue, patio only), was probably built in the early 16th century for one of the Benavides clan. It has a spectacularly flamboyant façade typical of Isabelline Gothic style, and a patio with Renaissance marble columns, two-tiered arches and an elegant fountain. A fantastically carved baroque stairway ascends from one side.

Opposite the palace is the tiny **Iglesia de la Santa Cruz** (Plaza Santa Cruz; admission free; ☉ 11am-1.30pm & 4-6pm Mon-Sat, noon-2pm Sun), one of the first churches to be built in Andalucía after the Reconquista. With round-arched portals and a semicircular apse, it's one of Andalucía's few Romanesque-style buildings. Inside are enchanting traces of the mosque that the church replaced. Opening times are not very reliable.

Next door to the Jabalquinto is Baeza's **Antigua Universidad** (Old University; ☎ 953 74 01 54; Calle del Beato Juan de Ávila; admission free; ☉ 10am-1pm & 4-6pm Thu-Tue). It was founded in 1538 and became a fount of progressive ideas that generally conflicted with Baeza's conservative dominant families, often causing scuffles between the highbrows and the well-heeled. It closed in 1824, and since 1875 the building has housed an *instituto de bachillerato* (high school). The main patio, with its elegant Renaissance arches, is open to the public, as is the classroom of poet Antonio Machado (see p47), who taught French at the high school from 1912 to 1919.

NORTH OF PASEO DE LA CONSTITUCIÓN

A block north of the Paseo de la Constitución is the **ayuntamiento** (town hall; ☎ 953 74 01 54; Pasaje del Cardenal Benavides 9), with a marvellous plateresque façade. The four finely carved balcony portals on the upper storey are separated by the coats of arms of the town, Felipe II (in the middle) and the magistrate Juan de Borja, who had the place built. The building was originally a courthouse and prison (entered by the right- and left-hand doors respectively).

A short walk from the *ayuntamiento* is the ruined and controversially restored **Convento de San Francisco** (Calle de San Francisco). One of Andrés de Vandelvira's masterpieces, it was conceived as the funerary chapel of the Benavides family. Devastated by an earthquake and sacked by French troops in the early 19th century, it is now partly restored and converted into a hotel, banqueting hall and restaurant. At the eastern end, a striking arrangement of curved girders traces the outline of its dome over a space adorned with Renaissance carvings. The cloister, occupied by the Restaurante Vandelvira, is worth a look, too.

Activities

Horse riding can be organised through **Hotel Hacienda La Laguna** (☎ 953 76 51 42; Puente del Obispo s/n).

Tours

Guided tours run by **Pópulo Servicios Turísticos** (☎ 953 74 43 70; Plaza de los Leones 1; adult/child under 12yr €6/free; ☉ tours 10am & 5pm Mon-Sat, 11am Sun) take about two hours and start from opposite the tourist office. The tour is pretty ordinary (and your Spanish needs to be pretty good to enjoy it), but in a place with so much history and detail to every building it can really fill in the background.

Festivals & Events

Semana Santa (Holy Week) A typically big, raucous celebration complete with devotional processions. Held in the week before Easter Sunday.

Feria Held in mid-August, this is a Castilian carnival procession of *gigantones* (papier-mâché giants), together with fireworks and a huge funfair.

Romería del Cristo de la Yedra An image of the Virgen del Rosell is carried from the Iglesia de San Pablo through Baeza's streets on 7 October, accompanied by a singing and dancing crowd. In the afternoon, a colourful procession follows the image to La Yedra village, 4km to the north, to continue celebrations there.

Sleeping

Hostal El Patio (☎ 953 74 02 00; fax 953 74 82 60; Calle Conde Romanones 13; d with bathroom €30) Entering this *hostal* is like walking into marshland: the dilapidated 17th-century mansion has a covered patio full of rugged sofas and broken chairs, and tall lush plants hang, stand, lean and generally overflow the place. The grandparents of the house watch the TV incessantly in a corner of the patio, sipping drinks. A Jesus statue stands on a landing, surrounded by flickering candles. The rooms are drab and poorly lit with tiny en suite bathrooms. Cheaper rooms don't have bathrooms. This is a real, dark gem.

Hotel Juanito (☎ 953 74 00 40; juanito@juanitobaeza .com; Paseo Arco del Agua s/n; s/d €34/54; ✖) Next to a petrol station and opposite Baeza's football ground, this is hardly an optimum location. However, the rooms are comfortable, and there is heating and a TV. Its restaurant is one of the most celebrated in the province.

Hospedería Fuentenueva (☎ 953 74 31 00; www .fuentenueva.com; Paseo Arco del Agua s/n; s/d incl breakfast €43/72; ✖ ⊠) This former women's prison is now a beautifully restored small hotel, painted in good-girl colours like subdued oranges and salmon pinks. The 12 rooms are large, comfortable and bright, with modern marble bathrooms.

Hotel Palacete Santa Ana (☎ /fax 953 74 16 57; info@palacetesantaana.com; Calle Santa Ana Vieja 9; s/d €42/66; ✖) This 16th-century converted nunnery is a stylish hotel that prides itself on its art and archaeology collection. The rooms are beautifully decorated with wide beds and luxurious furnishings, and the bathrooms have baths *and* showers. The nearby restaurant of the same name is under the same management.

Hotel Hacienda La Laguna (☎ 953 76 51 42; www .ehlaguna.com/hotel in Spanish; Puente del Obispo s/n; d €64; P ✖ ⊡ ⊠) If you love olive oil, stay in this enormous hacienda (10 minutes' drive from Baeza), where there's a museum of olive oil – the Museo de la Cultura del Olivo – and 18 stylishly furnished rooms. The excellent in-house restaurant, La Campana, is worth visiting even if you are not staying at the hotel. The ranch also has a stable that organises horse riding.

THE AUTHOR'S CHOICE

Hotel Puerta de la Luna (☎ 953 74 70 19; www.hotelpuertadelaluna.com in Spanish; Calle Canónigo Melgares Raya s/n; d incl breakfast €110; P ✖ ⊠) This is no doubt where the Benavides or Carvajals would stay if they were to visit Baeza and didn't already own half the town. Luxurious from start to finish, this mansion hotel has plenty of character to boot. There are manicured hedges on the cobbled Mudejar patio (where you can have breakfast), beautifully furnished salons with welcoming fireplaces, bedrooms full of antiques, and lush damask sheets. There is also a lovely restaurant, modern bar, Turkish bath, spa, gym and library.

Eating

Baeza is good if you want to splash out and eat in elegant restaurants. It is, sadly, short on good tapas bars though. The tourist office can give you small booklet (in Spanish only) detailing a tapas trail, but they won't be as great as in other towns.

Cafetería Mercantil (Portales Tundidores 18, Paseo de la Constitución; raciones €6-9) A unique opportunity to sample *criadillas* (testicles) and *sesos* (brains), at the same time, in the same place. The vast terrace of this busy café spills out onto the Paseo and it's a great spot for watching the machinations of the local clientele. They all range between the ages of 70 and 95 though, so don't expect too much movement.

Restaurante Vandelvira (☎ 953 74 81 72; Calle de San Francisco 14; mains €7-16; ⊕ closed Sun night & Mon) Installed in part of the restored Convento de San Francisco, this is a classy, friendly restaurant. If you want to spoil yourself you might try the partridge pâté salad or the *solomillo al carbón* (chargrilled steak).

Mesón Restaurante La Góndola (☎ 953 74 29 84; Portales Carbonería 13, Paseo de la Constitución; mains €8-14) A terrific local, atmospheric restaurant, helped along by the glowing, wood-burning grill behind the bar, cheerful service and good food. Try *patatas baezanas,* a vegetarian delight that mixes a huge helping of sautéed potatoes with mushrooms.

Restaurante El Sali (☎ 953 74 13 65; Pasaje del Cardenal Benavides 15; menú/mains €12/30; ⊕ closed Wed) Fantastic outdoor tables opposite the imposing *ayuntamiento*. Serves up lots of fresh fish and a tasty Spanish potato and pepper salad.

Restaurante Palacete Santa Ana (☎ 953 74 16 57; Calle Escopeteros 12; menú/mains €15/24) A large restaurant and bar complex that occupies several floors. It serves up regional specialities that are usually complemented by the local olive oil. Reservations are required.

Restaurante Juanito (☎ 953 74 00 40; Paseo Arco del Agua s/n; mains €30; ⊕ closed Sun night & Mon night) The proprietors, Juan Antonio and Luisa Salcedo, have been dishing up traditional Jaén fare for four decades in this acclaimed eatery. People travel far and wide to sample its specialities, but popularity has a price and quality is on the decline. The service is sometimes lacking.

CARMEN LINARES: JAÉN'S CONTRIBUTION TO FLAMENCO

Hailed as the queen of flamenco *cante* (singing), Carmen Linares (1951–), born Mari Carmen Pacheco Rodríguez, started her career singing at private gatherings as a little girl in her native village of Linares, close to Baeza, which is now a growing town. Having seen the reaction she got from singing at home, Carmen moved to Madrid with her family and decided to become a professional *cantaora* (flamenco singer). She broke the male-dominated mould of the flamenco world and appeared on stage with flamenco bigwigs such as Camarón de la Isla and Enrique Morente during the 1970s. Linares was famously invited to sing with the New York Philharmonic Orchestra in the Lincoln Center, a concert which made her a flamenco star throughout the world. She has won awards in Europe and the US, spawned imitators and converted many to the sound of flamenco. For a girl from a tiny Jaén village, it ain't bad.

For more on flamenco see p43. *La Luna en el Río* is a good introduction to the work of Carmen Linares.

Drinking

Nightlife in Baeza is generally limited to a few lively bars.

Burladero (Calle de la Barbacana s/n) Pleasant bar for a decent drink.

Bar Arcediano (☎ 953 74 81 84; Calle de la Barbacana s/n) Another place for a decent drop on the same side of the street as Burladero.

Bar Pacos (☎ 953 74 70 19; Calle Canónigo Melgares Raya 7) A more elegant option in the Hotel Puerte de la Luna.

Café Central Teatro (☎ 953 74 43 55; Calle Obispo Narvaez 19) Often has live bands.

Shopping

La Casa del Aceite (Paseo de la Constitución 9) For good quality oil visit this shop, which sells a huge selection along with other products such as soap, ceramics and olive wood bowls.

Museo de la Cultura del Olivo (☎ 953 76 51 42; Complejo Hacienda la Laguna, Puente del Obispo; adult/child €2.50/1.50; ☺ 10.30am-1.30pm & 4.30-7pm Tue-Sun) This is another good place, and worth the trip to have a look around the museum. It's outside Baeza in the Hotel Hacienda La Laguna.

Getting There & Around

From the **bus station** (☎ 953 74 04 68; Paseo Arco del Agua), Alsina Graells runs daily buses to Jaén (€3.50, 45 minutes, 11 daily), Úbeda (€0.90, 30 minutes, 15 daily) and Granada (€10, five daily). There are also buses to Cazorla (€4, 2¼ hours, two daily), Córdoba (€9), Seville (€17) and Madrid (€21).

The nearest train station is **Linares-Baeza** (☎ 953 65 02 02), 13km northwest of town, where a few trains a day leave for Granada, Córdoba, Seville, Málaga, Cádiz, Almería, Madrid and Barcelona. Buses connect with most trains from Monday to Saturday. A taxi to the train station costs €14.

Parking in Baeza is fairly restricted, but there are parking spots around the Paseo de la Constitución and in Pasaje del Cardenal Benavides.

Taxis wait for fares in Paseo de la Constitución.

ÚBEDA

pop 33,000 / elevation 760m

Úbeda (*oo*-be-dah) is a slightly different proposition to it's little sister, Baeza. Approaching the city you may be put off by the development taking place on the outskirts but, once you enter, the fabulous, elegant centre is enchanting. Aside from the splendour of Úbeda's architecture, fun new tapas bars and restaurants draw in the crowds, and oddities like crazy old junk shops can be found on the city's narrow streets.

Úbeda became a Castilian bulwark on the inexorable Christian march south. As Fernando III reclaimed and reconquered Muslim Andalucía, aristocratic families such as the Molinas, de la Cuevas and Cobos benefited and were rewarded with huge estates. Their ownership moulded the character of the province and still endures today.

Orientation

Most of Úbeda's splendid buildings – the main reason for visiting the town – are in the southeast of the town, among the maze of narrow, winding streets and expansive squares that constitute the *casco antiguo* (old quarter). The cheaper accommodation and the bus station are about 600m away, in the drab new town to the west and north. The better accommodation is concentrated in the *casco antiguo*. Plaza de Andalucía marks the boundary between the two parts of town.

Information

The biggest concentration of banks and ATMs is on Plaza de Andalucía and nearby Calle Rastro.

Centro de Salud (Health Centre; ☎ 953 02 86 00; Calle Explanada s/n) In the new part of town, with an emergency section.

Cybernet World (Calle Niño 22; per 30min €1.20; ⊙ 11am-2pm & 4.30-10pm) Lots of computers, and full of teenagers.

Hospital Comarcal (☎ 953 02 82 00; Carretera de Linares Km 1) The main hospital, found on the northwestern edge of town.

Librería Tres Culturas (☎ 953 75 26 25; Calle Rastro 7) Sells a selection of maps, including maps of Cazorla, and some guidebooks.

Policía Municipal (☎ 953 75 00 23; Plaza de Andalucía) In the busy centre.

Policía Nacional (☎ 953 75 03 55; Plaza Vázquez de Molina) Occupies the Antiguo Pósito.

Post office (Calle Trinidad 4; ⊙ 8.30am-2.30pm Mon-Fri, 9.30am-1pm Sat)

Regional tourist office (☎ 953 75 08 97; otubeda@andalucia.org; Calle Baja del Marqués 4; ⊙ 9am-2.45pm & 4-7pm Mon-Fri, 10am-2pm Sat) Located in the 18th-century Palacio Marqués de Contadero, in the old town.

Sights

Nearly all of Úbeda's main sights are located within the *casco antiguo*, which can be thoroughly explored in a day or two. It is quite helpful to concentrate on the different plazas (Plaza Vázquez de Molina, Plaza del Ayuntamiento and Plaza del 1 de Mayo), with another morning or afternoon set aside to root around Barrio San Millán (the pottery quarter) and do a spot of shopping.

PLAZA VÁZQUEZ DE MOLINA

Following the success of the Reconquista, Úbeda's aristocratic lions lost no time jockeying for power in the Castilian court. In the 16th century, Francisco de los Cobos y Molina secured the post of privy secretary to King Carlos I and was later succeeded by his nephew Juan Vázquez de Molina. Exposed to the cultural influences of the Italian Renaissance that were then seeping into Spain, and benefiting from the wealth and privilege of high office, the Molina family turned their attention to self-aggrandising civic projects in their home town. They commissioned what are now considered to be some of the purest examples of Renaissance architecture in Spain, prompting the Catalan art critic and philosopher Eugenio D'Ors (1881–1954) to later compare the town with the Italian cities of Ferrara and Brescia.

The purity of Renaissance lines is best expressed in the **Capilla del Salvador del Mundo** (☎ 953 75 81 50; adult/child €3/1, last hr free; ⊙ 10am-2pm & 4.30-7pm), the first of many works executed in Úbeda by celebrated architect Andrés de Vandelvira (see Master Builder, p342). A pre-eminent example of the plateresque style, the chapel's **main façade** is modelled on Diego de Siloé's Puerta del Perdón at Granada's cathedral. The classic portal is topped by a carving of the transfiguration of Christ, flanked by statues of St Peter and St Paul. The underside of the arch is an orgy of classical sculpture, executed by French sculptor Esteban Jamete, depicting the Greek gods – a Renaissance touch that would have been inconceivable a few decades earlier. Viewed at night, the whole façade leaps out in dynamic 3-D.

Inside, the sacristy glitters with symbolic carvings, again by Jamete. Having worked on Fontainebleau, Jamete gave the sacristy some French flair with huge swags and medallions, all topped off by the massive frescoed dome modelled on the Capilla Mayor in Granada. The church's main retable, by Alonso de Berruguete, was damaged in the civil war and only one statue, the *Transfiguración del Monte Tabor* (Transfiguration on Mount Tabor), is original. However, the rest have been painstakingly and skilfully restored.

The capilla is the private funereal chapel of the Cobos family (their crypt lies beneath the nave) – a small indication of Francisco's wealth, which at one time exceeded that of King Carlos I himself. Today the church is still privately owned by the Seville-based duques de Medinaceli, descendants of the Cobos, and one of Andalucía's major landowning families.

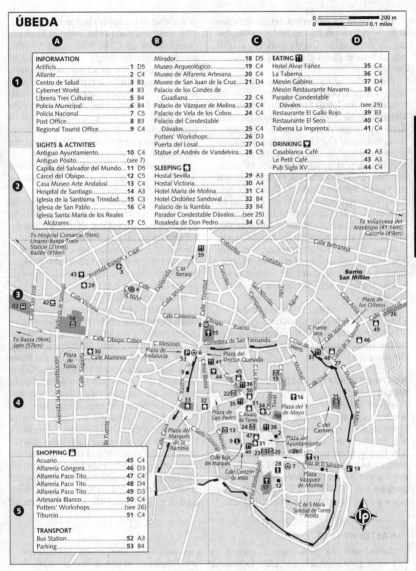

ÚBEDA

0 — 200 m
0 — 0.1 miles

INFORMATION		
Artificis...................................	1	D5
Atlante....................................	2	C4
Centro de Salud........................	3	B3
Cybernet World.........................	4	B3
Librería Tres Culturas.................	5	B4
Policía Municipal.......................	6	B4
Policía Nacional........................	7	C5
Post Office...............................	8	B3
Regional Tourist Office...............	9	C4

SIGHTS & ACTIVITIES		
Antiguo Ayuntamiento................	10	C4
Antiguo Pósito.....................	(see 7)	
Capilla del Salvador del Mundo...	11	D5
Cárcel del Obispo......................	12	C5
Casa Museo Arte Andalusí...........	13	C4
Hospital de Santiago..................	14	A3
Iglesia de la Santísima Trinidad....	15	C3
Iglesia de San Pablo...................	16	C4
Iglesia Santa María de los Reales		
Alcázares............................	17	C5

SLEEPING		
Hostal Sevilla...........................	29	A3
Hostal Victoria..........................	30	A4
Hotel María de Molina................	31	C4
Hotel Ordóñez Sandoval.............	32	B4
Palacio de la Rambla..................	33	B4
Parador Condestable Dávalos....	(see 25)	
Rosaleda de Don Pedro..............	34	C4

Mirador...................................	18	D5
Museo Arqueológico..................	19	C4
Museo de Alfarería Artesana.......	20	C4
Museo de San Juan de la Cruz.....	21	D4
Palacio de los Condes de		
Guadiana...........................	22	C4
Palacio de Vázquez de Molina.....	23	C4
Palacio de Vela de los Cobos......	24	C4
Palacio del Condestable		
Dávalos............................	25	C4
Potters' Workshops....................	26	D3
Puerta del Losal........................	27	D4
Statue of Andrés de Vandelvira...	28	C5

EATING		
Hotel Alvar Fáñez......................	35	C4
La Taberna...............................	36	C4
Mesón Gabino...........................	37	D4
Mesón Restaurante Navarro.........	38	C4
Parador Condestable		
Dávalos...........................	(see 25)	
Restaurante El Gallo Rojo............	39	B3
Restaurante El Seco....................	40	C4
Taberna La Imprenta..................	41	C4

DRINKING		
Casablanca Café........................	42	A3
Le Petit Café............................	43	A3
Pub Siglo XV............................	44	C4

SHOPPING		
Acuario....................................	45	C4
Alfarería Góngora......................	46	D3
Alfarería Paco Tito.....................	47	C4
Alfarería Paco Tito.....................	48	D4
Alfarería Paco Tito.....................	49	D3
Artesanía Blanco.......................	50	C4
Potters' Workshops...............	(see 26)	
Tiburcio...................................	51	C4

TRANSPORT		
Bus Station...............................	52	A3
Parking....................................	53	B4

JAÉN PROVINCE

In fact, the whole beautifully proportioned plaza (180m long), with its excess of architecture, was the Cobos family precinct. Next door to the capilla stands the **Palacio del Condestable Dávalos**, originally the house of the church's chaplain. Partly remodelled in the 17th century, the mansion is now Úbeda's luxurious parador. To the west the

huge **Palacio de Vázquez de Molina** (☎ 953 75 04 40; 10am-2pm & 5-9pm), now Úbeda's *ayuntamiento,* was built by Vandelvira for Juan (Francisco's nephew and successor to the post of privy secretary), whose coat of arms surmounts the doorway. The uncluttered façade, deeply Italian-influenced, has superbly harmonious proportions.

The **Museo de Alfarería Artesana** (admission €1.80; ⏱ 10.30am-2pm & 5-7pm Tue-Sat, 10.30am-2pm Sun) is devoted to Úbeda pottery, a craft whose typical green glaze dates back to Islamic times.

Facing the Palacio de Vázquez de Molina is the site of Úbeda's old mosque, now the location of the **Iglesia Santa María de los Reales Alcázares**, although the picturesque cloisters mark the original site of the Islamic ablutions fountain. The church has been closed for restoration for several years, so check with the tourist office for details of its reopening. Next door to Santa María stands the **Cárcel del Obispo** (Bishop's Prison), where nuns who stepped out of line used to be incarcerated. It is now a courthouse. Under the trees in front is a **statue of Andrés de Vandelvira**, the man who made Úbeda worth visiting. By the statue, fronting the main square, the 16th-century **Antiguo Pósito**, originally a communal store for surplus grain, is now the local headquarters of the Policía Nacional.

East of the square, 150m along Baja de El Salvador, a **mirador** (lookout) gives fine views across the olive fields, overshadowed by the snow-capped Cazorla mountains in the distance.

NORTH OF PLAZA DE VÁZQUEZ DE MOLINA

North of Úbeda's main plaza a warren of winding streets gives way to a series of elegant squares, each lined with ever-increasing numbers of mansions and churches. The first of these is the broad Plaza del Ayuntamiento, overlooked from its northwestern corner by the **Palacio de Vela de los Cobo** (admission free). This palace can be visited by prior arrangement with the tourist office.

Another of the town's best mansions is the 17th-century **Palacio de los Condes de Guadiana**, three blocks up Calle Real (once Úbeda's main commercial street), with some elegant carving around the windows and balconies. For an insight into a typical *palacio* visit the recently opened **Casa Museo Arte Andalusí** (☎ 619 076132; Calle Narvaez 11; admission €1.50; ⏱ 10.30am-2.30pm & 4-8.30pm), which is full of period antiques. It stages flamenco shows every Saturday night from 10pm onwards; prices vary according to the performer.

Northeast of the Plaza del Ayuntamiento is the even bigger Plaza del 1 de Mayo, originally the town's market square and bullring. It was also the site of Inquisition burnings, which local worthies used to watch from the gallery of the **Antiguo Ayuntamiento** (Old Town Hall) in the southwestern corner. Along the northern side of the square is the **Iglesia de San Pablo** (admission free; ⏱ 7am-9pm), which has a fine late-Gothic portal dating from 1511.

Just north of the Iglesia de San Pablo, a 14th-century Mudejar mansion houses the **Museo Arqueológico** (☎ 953 75 37 02; Calle Cervantes 4; admission free; ⏱ 3-8pm Tue, 9am-8pm Wed-Sat, 9am-3pm Sun), with exhibits from Neolithic to Islamic times. A second, smaller museum, the **Museo de San Juan de la Cruz** (☎ 953 75 06 15; Calle del Carmen; admission €1.20; ⏱ 11am-1pm & 5-7pm Tue-Sun) is dedicated to the 16th-century mystic, poet and religious reformer St John of the Cross, who founded the breakaway monastic order of Carmelitos Descalzos (Barefoot Carmelites). He did this, against opposition, in an effort to return to the austerity and contemplative life from which he felt mainstream Carmelites had lapsed. The museum is housed in the Oratorio de San Juan de la Cruz, where St John died of gangrene in 1591. In a reconstructed

---

MASTER BUILDER

Most of what you see in Úbeda, Baeza and Jaén is the work of one man: Andrés de Vandelvira. Born in 1509 in Alcaraz (in Castilla-La Mancha), 150km northeast of Úbeda, Vandelvira almost single-handedly brought the Renaissance to Jaén province. Influenced by the pioneering Renaissance architect Diego de Siloé, Vandelvira designed numerous marvellous buildings and, astonishingly, his work spanned all three main phases of Spanish Renaissance architecture: the ornamental early Renaissance phase known as plateresque, as seen in the Capilla del Salvador del Mundo (p340); the much purer line and classic proportions, which emerged in the later Palacio de Vázquez de Molina (p341); and the austere late Renaissance style called Herreresque, as shown in his last building, the Hospital de Santiago (opposite). With all these achievements under his belt, Vandelvira's was certainly a life well spent.

monk's cell, a lifelike figure of St John sits at his writing table – perhaps musing on 'the dark night of the soul'. Nearby is a cabinet containing his letters, plus a couple of his fingers! Visits, guided by Spanish-speaking monks, last about half an hour.

North of the museum, heading through the impressive **Puerta de Losal** takes you down into the **Barrio San Millán**, Úbeda's famous potters' quarter, with **potters' workshops** located on Calle Valencia. Alternatively, if you turn left at the gate and walk down Calle Fuente Seca and then Calle Cruz de Hierro to link up with Corredera de San Fernando, past the unusual baroque **Iglesia de la Santísima Trinidad** (Corredera de San Fernando), you will eventually reach Vandelvira's last architectural project, the **Hospital de Santiago** (☎ 953 75 08 42; Calle Obispo Cobos; admission free; 🕒 8am-3pm & 4-10pm Mon-Fri, 11am-3pm & 6-10pm Sat & Sun). Completed in 1575, it is a very grand and sober affair, and has often been dubbed the Escorial of Andalucía – a reference to a famous old monastery outside Madrid, which was a precursor to the kind of baroque architecture employed by Vandelvira. It now acts as Úbeda's cultural centre, housing a library, municipal dance school and an exhibition hall.

Tours
Artificis (☎ 953 75 81 50; www.artificis.com in Spanish; Calle Baja de El Salvador 14; adult/child €8/free; 🕒 tours 11am & 5pm year-round, 6pm Jun-Sep) With Artificis, tours of Úbeda's monuments take about two hours (commentary in Spanish). If you ring ahead it is possible to book tours spoken in English, French and Italian. Artificis also runs tours in nearby Baeza.

Atlante (☎ 953 79 34 22; Plaza del Ayuntamiento s/n; adult/child €6/free; 🕒 tours 11am & 5pm year-round, 6pm Jun-Sep) Great theatrical night-time tours are available with Atlante (winter/summer 7pm/10pm), but they also have tours similar to those of Artificis. A combined tour of Úbeda and Baeza is €12.

Festivals & Events
Semana Santa (Holy Week) Solemn brotherhoods, devotional processions and lots of atmospheric drama in the week leading up to Easter Sunday.
Festival Internacional de Música y Danza Ciudad de Úbeda Varied music and dance performances throughout the month of May.
Fiesta de San Miguel Celebrates the capture of the town in 1233 by Fernando III, with firework shows, parades, concerts, a flamenco festival, a bullfighting season and more. It's held from 27 September to 4 October.

Sleeping
Úbeda's budget accommodation is better than Baeza's although it's by no means great. Midrange and top-end hotels, however, make a quantum leap in comfort and character, with many housed in old palaces. Hotel parking usually costs around €9 per day.

Hostal Sevilla (☎ 953 75 06 12; Avenida Ramón y Cajal 9; s/d €20/33) The Sevilla is a pleasant family-run *hostal*, offering good-value rooms with heating.

Hostal Victoria (☎ 953 75 29 52; Calle Alaminos 5; s/d €23/37; 🅿 P) An excellent budget place, this *hostal* is inside a friendly old lady's apartment. The spacious rooms all have TV, and there's heating in the winter.

Hotel María de Molina (☎ 953 79 53 56; www .hotel-maria-de-molina.com in Spanish; Plaza del Ayuntamiento; s/d €52/84; 🅿) This is an attractive hotel housed in a 16th-century *palacio* on the picturesque Plaza Ayuntamiento. The well-appointed rooms are arranged around a patio and the hotel has an excellent restaurant.

Hotel Ordóñez Sandoval (☎ 953 79 51 87; Calle Antonio Medina 1; s/d €53/66; P) The family home of Amalia Perez Ordóñez, this 19th-century *palacio* now has three vast bedrooms open to guests. Amalia is a gracious and helpful hostess, checking on guests at breakfast and trying valiantly with her huge English dictionary to communicate with even the worst Spanish linguists.

Rosaleda de Don Pedro (☎ 953 79 51 47; www .rosaledadedonpedro.com; Calle Obispo Toral 2; s €64-77, d €80-96; P 🅿 📺 🍴 🐕) The effort of a clued-up bunch of friends, the Don Pedro offers good three-star facilities in a central old-town location. The rooms have beautiful custom-made beds, and there's a good restaurant and the only pool in the historic centre. Advance booking means cheaper rooms.

Palacio de la Rambla (☎ 953 75 01 96; Plaza del Marqués de la Rambla 1; d/ste incl breakfast €100/112) Úbeda's loveliest converted palace has eight gorgeous, antique-filled rooms in the home of the Marquesa de la Rambla. The ivy-clad patio is wonderfully romantic and entry is restricted to guests only. Breakfast can be served in your room. The hotel is closed in July and August.

Parador Condestable Dávalos (☎ 953 75 03 45; www.parador.es in Spanish; Plaza Vázquez de Molina; s/d €106/119; P 🅿) As paradors always get the town's best location and building, Úbeda has surrendered its prime spot, looking out over the wonderful Plaza Vázquez de Molina, and has housed the hotel inside an historic monument: the Palacio del Deán Ortega. It has, of course, been comfortably modernised and is appropriately luxurious. It also has the best restaurant in town.

Eating

Úbeda has some good places to eat, starting from tapas, which you get free with your drinks, to excellent nouvelle cuisine restaurants. Calle Real, in the old town, is the best place for tapas bars. An average price of tapas and a drink is between €1 and €1.50.

Mesón Restaurante Navarro (☎ 953 79 06 38; Plaza del Ayuntamiento 2; raciones €4-9) Always crammed, smoky and noisy, the Navarro is a cherished local favourite. Eat your tapas at the bar, or in summer sit out on the sunny plaza. Note that the sign just says 'Mesón Restaurante'.

La Taberna (☎ 953 79 24 70; Calle Real 7; mains €6-10) Children run around screaming, their parents clink glasses and scoff tapas, barmen sweat and work like crazy – a typical Spanish evening scene in this popular tapas bar. Order a drink, get your tapa, and join in.

Mesón Gabino (☎ 953 75 75 53; Calle Fuente Seca; mains €6-10) A wonderfully atmospheric cellar restaurant where the dining room is interrupted by stone pillars. It is a good spot to eat if you have been wandering in the potters' quarter, and it serves up solid fare, including salads and egg dishes.

Restaurante El Gallo Rojo (☎ 953 75 20 38; Calle Manuel Barraca 3; mains €9-12) Just off the northern end of Avenida Ramón y Cajal, this cheerful restaurant is one of the best places in the new part of town. The menú is good value, and there are outdoor tables.

Taberna La Imprenta (☎ 650 375000; Plaza del Doctor Quesada 1; mains €10-13) This wonderful old print shop, done stylishly and frequented by Úbeda's posh noshers, provides free tapas with your drinks. And what tapas they are! You can also sit down and eat baked asparagus, excellent meat and creamy cheesecakes.

Restaurante El Seco (☎ 953 79 14 52; Calle Corazón de Jesús 8; menú €12) Located in the old town, on a pretty square filled with orange trees, El Seco has good traditional dishes such as the steaming carne de monte ('meat of the mountain', usually venison) with a rich

tomato sauce or lightly grilled trout with mixed vegetables.

Parador Condestable Dávalos (☎ 953 75 03 45; Plaza Vázquez de Molina; mains €12-17, menú €25) This deservedly popular restaurant serves up delicious, elegant dishes. Despite the price, this is definitely *the* place to eat in Úbeda and even in the off season the dining room buzzes happily in the evening. Try the local specialities: carruécano (green peppers stuffed with partridge) or cabrito guisado con piñones (stewed kid with pine nuts).

Drinking

Most of the action takes place in the modern town, but the 30-somethings hang out in the tapas bars along Calle Real. Úbeda does not have much of a nightlife and during the off season most of the town's youth seem to hang out at pizza parlours and internet cafés.

Le Petit Café (Avenida Ramón y Cajal 26; ⏰ 7.30am-11pm) A popular café that fills up in the late afternoon with people rushing in for speciality teas, coffees and fruit cocktails, not to mention the huge range of tortas (tarts), biscuits, pastries and ice creams.

Casablanca Café (☎ 953 79 27 88; Redonda de Santiago) If Úbeda had a Hotel California this would be its bar. Jukeboxes, Americana, retro lights, a huge billiard table and an old gas pump create a twilight atmosphere, and on quieter Sunday and Monday nights the bar is full of men contemplating the dregs in their glasses, serenaded by endless sad songs.

Pub Siglo XV (Calle Prior Blanca 5) The only bar in the old town, this atmospheric joint occasionally stages live flamenco or bands. However, in low season it is randomly closed.

Shopping

The typical emerald green glaze on Úbeda's attractive pottery and the tradition of embroidering coloured patterns into the esparto (grass) mats called ubedíes both date back to Islamic times. The potters' quarter still retains three original kilns from this period (there are only six left in the whole of Spain).

The main shopping streets are Calle Mesones and Calle Obispo Cobos, between Plaza de Andalucía and the Hospital de Santiago.

Artesanía Blanco (Calle Real 47) Visit this spot in the old town for *esparto* mats and baskets, which are priced from about €5.

Acuario (Calle Real 61) Close to Artesanía Blanco, this place has some good antiques, and bits and pieces of fine tiling.

Tiburcio (☎ 953 79 10 03; Calle Alvaro de Torres 4; ☿ 11am-3pm & 5-8pm Sat & Sun) A real treasure heap, this is a junk shop where you can find old coffee tins, tiles and ancient pictures. You just have to take your time.

Several workshops sell pottery in Barrio San Millán, northeast of the old town, and the potters are often willing to explain some of the ancient techniques they use. These include adding olive stones to the fire to intensify the heat, which results in a more brilliant glaze. **Alfarería Paco Tito** (Calle Valencia 22, Calle Fuente Seca 17 & Plaza del Ayuntamiento 12) is the largest concern, but nearby **Alfarería Góngora** (Cuesta de la Merced 32) and several others on Calle Valencia are worth a look. Smaller pottery pieces that you could comfortably carry home start at about €6.

Getting There & Around

The **bus station** (☎ 953 75 21 57; Calle San José 6) is located in the new part of town. Alsina Graells runs to Baeza (€0.90, 30 minutes, 15 daily), Jaén (€4.50, 1¼ hours, 12 daily Monday to Saturday), Cazorla (€3.30, 45 minutes, up to 10 daily) and to Granada (€11, seven daily). Bacoma goes to Córdoba (€10, four daily) and Seville (€18, four daily). Other buses head to Málaga (€19) and Madrid (€21), and small places around Jaén province.

The nearest station is **Linares-Baeza** (☎ 953 65 02 02), 21km northwest of town, which you can reach on Linares-bound buses. For information on trains, see p339.

There is now a convenient underground car park in Plaza de Andalucía (one hour €1, 12 hours €8). You can park for free in the narrow streets of the old town and in the streets that radiate from Plaza de Andalucía, although it is not always easy to find a spot.

CAZORLA

pop 8000 / elevation 836m

Cazorla sits on a slope and looks like it may slide off any moment. Huffing and puffing up the steep streets of this fairly large, modern rural town is perfect for those who want to carry on huffing and puffing in the Parque Natural de las Sierras de Cazorla, Segura y las Villas, which begins dramatically amid the cliffs of Peña de los Halcones (Falcon Crag), towering above the town. From here, you can see the passive landscape of the plains, and the great rugged swath of mountains and valleys that unfolds enticingly to the north and east.

Cazorla becomes crowded during Spanish holiday times and on weekends from spring to autumn.

Orientation

The A319 from the west winds up into Cazorla and is known as Calle Hilario Marco. This road ends at Plaza de la Constitución, the often frantically busy main square of the newer part of town. The second important square is Plaza de la Corredera, 150m south of Plaza de la Constitución. It is reached along Calle Doctor Muñoz, Cazorla's narrow, shop-lined main street. Plaza de Santa María, 300m further southeast and reached along even more narrow, winding streets, is the heart of the oldest part of town, and stands directly below the castle and crags.

Information

You'll find several banks with ATMs on and between Plaza de la Constitución and Plaza de la Corredera.

Centro de Salud Dr José Cano Salcedo (☎ 953 72 10 61; Calle Ximénez de Rada 1) Health centre.

Municipal tourist office (☎ 953 71 01 02; Paseo del Santo Cristo 17; ☿ 10am-1pm & 5.30-8pm) Found 200m north of Plaza de la Constitución. It has information on the park and town.

Policía Local (☎ 953 72 01 81) In the *ayuntamiento*, just off Plaza de la Corredera.

Post office (Calle Mariano Extremera 2; ☿ 8.30am-2.30pm Mon-Fri, 9.30am-1pm Sat) Behind the town hall, just off Plaza de la Corredera.

Sights

Here, as in the rest of Jaén province, local history has been shaped by the rich landowning classes, and the town's *palacios* used to or still belong to a few wealthy families. The central square, **Plaza de la Corredera**, is the civic centre of the town, and the elegant **ayuntamiento** dominates the square with its landmark clock tower. The plaza, much like the rest of the town, is full of life.

Canyonlike streets radiate south of the plaza to the **Balcón de Zabaleta**. This little *mirador* is like a sudden window in a blank wall – it has stunning views over the town and up to the **Castillo de la Yedra** (Castle of the Ivy). The dramatic castle is of Roman origin, though it was largely built by the Muslims, then restored in the 15th century after the Reconquista. Much money has been spent on a modern restoration, and the castle now houses the **Museo del Alto Guadalquivir** (Museum of the Upper Guadalquivir; non-EU/EU citizen €1.50/free; 3-8pm Tue, 9am-8pm Wed-Sat, 9am-3pm Sun & public holidays), a mishmash of art and local artefacts. Included are a reconstructed traditional kitchen, models of old oil mills and a chapel featuring a life-sized Roman-esque-Byzantine Crucifixion sculpture.

The shortest way up to the castle is from the attractive **Plaza de Santa María**, starting along the street to the right of the ruined **Iglesia de Santa María**. The devastated church was built by Vandelvira and wrecked by Napoleonic troops in reprisal for Cazorla's tenacious resistance. It is now used for occasional open-air concerts.

In Plaza de Santa María you can while away a pleasant hour or two in the early evening amid the café tables and ancient plane trees overlooking a 400-year-old fountain, the **Fuente de las Cadenas** (Fountain of the Chains).

Festivals

La Caracolá The image of Cazorla's patron saint, San Isicio – a Christian apostle supposedly stoned to death at Cazorla in Roman times – gets carried from the Ermita de San Isicio to the Iglesia de San José on 14 May.

Fiesta de Cristo del Consuelo Fireworks and fair-grounds mark Cazorla's annual fiesta, celebrated between 17 and 21 September. On the first day a 17th-century painting of the Cristo del Consuelo (Christ of Consolation), which was rescued from Napoleonic destruction, is carried in a procession.

Sleeping

As well as the accommodation in Cazorla, more accommodation can be found in or around the nearby village of La Iruela, which is 1km out of Cazorla in the direction of the park.

Camping Cortijo San Isicio (☎ 953 72 12 80; camp site per person/tent/car €3.50/3/2.50; Mar-Oct) A charming camping ground amid pine trees, off the Quesada road 4km southwest of cen-

tral Cazorla. It has room for just 54 people. The access road is narrow and twisting.

Instalación Juvenil Cazorla (☎ 953 72 03 29; www.inturjoven.com; Plaza Mauricio Martínez 6; dm under 26yr/over 26yr €14/19;) Two hundred metres up a steep hill from Plaza de la Corredera and inside a 16th-century convent, Cazorla's sparkling clean youth hostel is run by a friendly bunch of people. It has places for 120 people in rooms holding between two and six, most with shared bathrooms.

Hotel Guadalquivir (☎ 953 72 02 68; www.hguadalquivir.com in Spanish; Calle Nueva 6; s/d €35/47;) Cheap 'n' cheerful, the Guadalquivir has comfortable, blue-hued rooms with pine furniture, TV and heating, though bad views. The singles can be a bit cramped but the hotel is in a decent location and is good value for money.

Hotel Sierra de Cazorla (☎ 953 72 12 25; www.hotelsierradecazorla.com in Spanish; Travesía del Camino de La Iruela 2, La Iruela; s/d €46/62, apt €68-94;) This sprawling modern hotel in La Iruela is redeemed by its scenic surroundings. As is the fashion, furnishings are doomed to pine wood but the pool is fantastic, sited in the shadow of a huge craggy mountain. The hotel also administers the light and airy Don Pedro apartments, which consist of one-, two- and three-bedroom apartments accommodating up to eight people. Be aware that it can get a bit chilly when it rains, although some of the apartments have fireplaces.

Hotel Ciudad de Cazorla (☎ 953 72 17 00; Plaza de la Corredera 9; s/d incl breakfast €63/74;) This modern structure in the middle of mansion-ruled Plaza de Corredera has faced resistance from the traditionally oriented locals. It is, however, an interesting building, with spacious rooms and all the requisite facilities.

Molino la Farraga (☎ 953 72 12 49; www.molinolafarraga.com; Calle Camino de la Hoz s/n; d €64;) Just up the valley from the Plaza de Santa María is the tranquil old mill of La Farraga, nestling in a bucolic idyll of forested slopes crisscrossed by rivers. Inside, the décor is understated comfort, with lots of dark mahogany colours, and the wild, lush garden is heavenly.

Villa Turística de Cazorla (☎ 953 71 01 00; Ladera de San Isicio; 2-/4-person villa incl breakfast €76/128;) Just below the green hill, this is a lovely Andalucian-style tourist village with 32 comfortable villas with living rooms and terrace, but no kitchen. Around the hotel there are pleasant walks into the park, a good-sized swimming pool and a children's play area.

Eating

In late summer or autumn, locals disappear into the woods after rain to gather large, delicious, edible mushrooms that they call *níscalos*. If these appear in your restaurant, get your share.

There are good bars on Cazorla's three main squares, where you can pick out tapas and *raciones*.

A daily market is held in Plaza del Mercado just down from Plaza de la Constitución.

Bar Las Vegas (Plaza de la Corredera 17; raciones €6) The best of Cazorla's bars. You can try tasty prawn-and-capsicum *revuelto* (scrambled eggs), as well as the town's best breakfast *tostadas* (toasted bread with toppings).

La Montería (Plaza de la Corredera 18; tapas €2-4) This place has tapas of *choto con ajo* (veal with garlic) while the *plato olímpico* (Olympic plate) is a good way to sample a selection of its tapas.

La Cueva de Juan Pedro (Plaza de Santa María; raciones €9, menú €10) An ancient, wood-beamed place with dangling *jamones* and clumps of garlic and drying peppers. Taste the traditional Cazorla *conejo* (rabbit), *trucha* (trout), *rin-rán* (a mix of salted cod, potato and dried red peppers), *jabalí* (wild boar), *venado* (venison) and even mouflon. The *menú* includes rabbit in vinaigrette.

Mesón Don Chema (☎ 953 72 00 68; Calle Escaleras del Mercado 2; mains €7-9) Down a lane off Calle Doctor Muñoz, this cheerful place serves up good-value local fare, such as the sizzling *huevos cazorleña*, a mixed stew of sliced boiled eggs and chorizo with vegetables.

Restaurante La Sarga (☎ 953 72 15 07; Plaza del Mercado s/n; mains €8-12, menú €18; ✆ closed Sep) Hailed as Cazorla's best restaurant, with a modern take on traditional food, the quality in this place is unfortunately low. The starter of cod and orange salad was good, but the mains, such as the *caldereta de gamo* (venison stew) or the *lomos de venado con miel* (venison with honey) had a uniform, heavy sauce and badly cooked vegetables.

Other tapas stops:

Café-Bar Rojas (Plaza de la Constitución 2; tapas €1.50-4)

Taberna Quinito (Plaza de Santa María 6; tapas €1.50-4) Down to earth.

Getting There & Around

Alsina Graells runs buses to/from Úbeda (€3, 45 minutes, up to 10 daily), Jaén (€6.50, two hours, two daily) and Granada (€12, 3½ hours, two daily). The main stop in Cazorla is Plaza de la Constitución; the tourist office has timetable information. A few buses run from Cazorla to Coto Ríos (€3, two daily Monday to Saturday) in the park. It makes stops at Arroyo Frío and Torre del Vinagre.

There is a convenient car park in Plaza del Mercado, located below Plaza de la Constitución.

PARQUE NATURAL SIERRAS DE CAZORLA, SEGURA Y LAS VILLAS

One of the biggest draws in the whole of Jaén province is the lushly wooded, 2143-sq-km Parque Natural Sierras de Cazorla, Segura y Las Villas. It is the largest protected area in Spain, and its corrugated, craggy mountain ranges are memorably beautiful, as is the huge, snaking 20km reservoir in its midst. This is also the origin of the Río Guadalquivir, Andalucía's longest river, which rises between the Sierra de Cazorla and Sierra del Pozo in the south of the park and flows northwards into the reservoir, before heading west for the Atlantic Ocean.

The best times to visit the park are in the shoulder seasons of spring and autumn, when the vegetation is at its most colourful and the temperatures are mild. In winter the park is often blanketed in snow. When walking, be sure to equip yourself properly, with enough water and appropriate clothes. Temperatures up in the hills are generally several degrees lower than down in the valleys, and the wind can be cutting at any time.

Exploring the park is a lot easier if you have a vehicle, but some bus services exist and there are plenty of places to stay inside the park. If you don't have a vehicle to get to the more remote places, you do have the option of taking guided excursions to those areas.

The park is hugely popular with Spanish tourists and attracts an estimated 600,000 visitors a year – some 50,000 of those coming during Semana Santa. The other peak periods are July and August, and weekends from April to October.

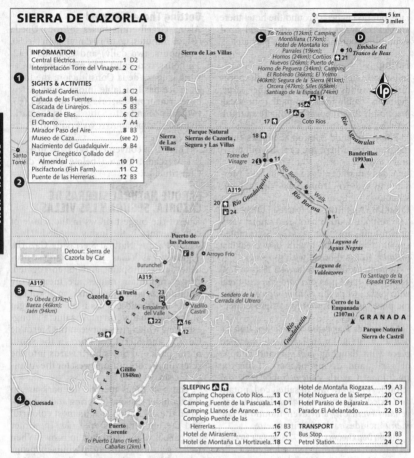

SIERRA DE CAZORLA

INFORMATION	
Central Eléctrica	1 D2
Interpretación Torre del Vinagre	2 C2

SIGHTS & ACTIVITIES	
Botanical Garden	3 C2
Cañada de las Fuentes	4 B4
Cascada de Linarejos	5 B3
Cerrada de Elías	6 C2
El Chorro	7 A4
Mirador Paso del Aire	8 B3
Museo de Caza	(see 2)
Nacimiento del Guadalquivir	9 B4
Parque Cinegético Collado del Almendral	10 D1
Piscifactoría (Fish Farm)	11 C2
Puente de las Herrerías	12 B3

SLEEPING	
Camping Chopera Coto Ríos	13 C1
Camping Fuente de la Pascuala	14 D1
Camping Llanos de Arance	15 C1
Complejo Puente de las Herrerías	16 B3
Hotel de Mirasierra	17 C1
Hotel de Montaña La Hortizuela	18 C2
Hotel de Montaña Riogazas	19 A3
Hotel Noguera de la Sierpe	20 C1
Hotel Paraíso de Bujaraiza	21 D1
Parador El Adelantado	22 B3

TRANSPORT	
Bus Stop	23 B3
Petrol Station	24 C2

Information

The main park information centre, the **Centro de Interpretación Torre del Vinagre** (Information Centre; ☎ 953 71 30 40; Carretera del Tranco Km 51; ◷ 11am-2pm & 5-8pm Apr-Sep, 11am-2pm & 4-7pm Oct-Mar), is at Torre del Vinagre. Built as a hunting lodge for Spain's high and mighty (including General Francisco Franco) in the 1950s, it has a rather dry display on the park's ecology. The centre also has the park's only easily accessible public toilets. There are seasonal tourist offices at Cortijos Nuevos, Hornos, Santiago de la Espada, Segura de la Sierra, Orcera and Siles. The tourism office in Cazorla also provides information on the park.

Good hiking guides are *Walking in Andalucía* by Guy Hunter-Watts, which de-

tails walks of between 5km and 15km, or for Spanish speakers, *Senderos de Pequeño Recorrido – Parque Natural de Cazorla* by Justo Robles Álvarez.

The best maps are Editorial Alpina's 1:40,000 *Sierra de Cazorla*, covering the southern third of the park and *Sierra de Segura*, covering the northern two-thirds. Selected walking and mountain-bike routes are marked and described in accompanying booklets. Quercus produces an excellent driving map (1:100,000), *Parque Natural de las Sierras de Cazorla, Segura y Las Villas*, showing all the park's points of interest.

The *Sierra de Cazorla* map produced by El Olivo is available in English and is sold in the reception of Villa Turística in Cazorla.

You may also be able to get these and other maps and guides at the Torre del Vinagre information centre and at some shops in Cazorla town, but do not rely on it. See p435 for information on buying maps before you arrive.

Sights

THE SOUTH OF THE PARK

The park begins just a few hundred metres up the hill east of Cazorla town. The footpaths and dirt roads working their way between the pine forests, meadowlands, crags and valleys of the park's mountains offer plenty of scope for day walks or drives, with fine panoramas. The park's abrupt geography rising to 2107m at the summit of the **Cerro de la Empanada**, and descending to 460m, makes for rapid and dramatic changes in landscape.

The A319, east from Cazorla, doesn't enter the park until Burunchel, 7km from Cazorla. From Burunchel it winds 5km up to the 1200m Puerto de las Palomas, with the breezy **Mirador Paso del Aire** a little further on. Five twisting kilometres downhill from here is Empalme del Valle, a junction where the A319 turns north towards the park's first major centre, **Arroyo Frío**. From here the road follows the north-flowing Río Guadalquivir.

An interesting detour from Empalme del Valle will take you to the source (see Detour: Sierra de Cazorla by Car, p352). From here you can continue a further 8km to **Cabañas**, which at 2028m is one of the highest peaks in the park. It is a two-hour round-trip walk from the road at Puerto Llano, and the route loops round the southern end of the hill and approaches the summit, which offers superb views from the southeast.

Further good walks in the south of the park are to be had in the **Sierra del Pozo**, which rises above the eastern side of the upper Guadalquivir Valley, and in the **Barranco del Guadalentín**, a deep river valley further east. The latter is particularly rich in wildlife, but you need your own vehicle, or a guide with one, to reach these areas.

Continuing along the A319 from Arroyo Frío, the road continues down the Guadalquivir Valley to Torre del Vinagre, where you will find the park's Centro de Interpretación Torre del Vinagre. In an adjoining building is the **Museo de Caza** (Hunting Museum; admission free; ☉ 11am-2pm & 5-8pm Apr-Sep, 11am-2pm & 4-7pm Oct-Mar), with a welter of stuffed wildlife, plus ibex and deer heads staring dolefully from the walls. A more cheerful place to spend some time is the adjoining **botanical garden**, which exhibits the park's extraordinarily rich flora, including some species that are unique to the area.

Beyond Torre del Vinagre is Coto Ríos and the beginning of the **Embalse del Tranco de Beas** reservoir. This is as far as many people venture from Cazorla. The main concentration of accommodation and visitor facilities in the park is dotted along the road up to this point and the most popular day hike, up the Río Borosa (see Walk the Walk, p350), is accessible from here. The bus from Cazorla only goes this far and to explore the park further you will need your own transport.

THE NORTH OF THE PARK

From Coto Ríos the road follows the edge of the huge, wide reservoir, with tantalising glimpses of the water through the trees. On a sunny day it is quite beautiful. Just 7km north of Coto Ríos, on a spur of land between the A319 and the reservoir, you will find the **Parque Cinegético Collado del Almendral**, a large enclosed game park where ibex, mouflon and deer are kept. A 1km footpath leads from the parking area to three

---

WILD THINGS

If you're a wildlife enthusiast, you have to get yourself to Cazorla. Apart from the excellent walking and hiking opportunities and picturesque villages, this is the place with better prospects of seeing wildlife than almost anywhere else in Andalucía. Creatures such as red and fallow deer, wild boar, mouflon and ibex are all here in good numbers (partly because they are protected in order to be hunted). You may even see deer or boar on some of the roads. And for the bird-watchers among you, some 140 bird species nest in the park, including several types of eagle, vulture and falcon, and efforts are being made to reintroduce the majestic lammergeier (bearded vulture). So get your shoes on, pack those binoculars and off you go.

miradores where you might see animals – your chances are best at dawn and dusk. Fifteen kilometres further north, the A319 crosses the dam that holds back the reservoir near the small village of Tranco. Beyond this the valley widens out and the hills become less rugged.

Twelve kilometres north of the dam at Tranco, the A319 runs into a T-junction from which the A317 winds 4km up to Hornos, a village atop a high rock outcrop with panoramic views. About 10km northeast of Hornos on the A317 is the **Puerto de Horno de Peguera** junction. One kilometre up the road to the north (towards Siles), a dirt road turns left at some ruined houses to the top of **El Yelmo** (1809m), one of the most distinctive mountains in the northern part of the park. It's 5km to the top – an ascent of 360m. At a fork after 1.75km, go right (the left fork goes down to El Robledo and Cortijos Nuevos). The climb affords superb long-distance views. You should see griffon vultures wheeling around the skies and, on the weekend and holidays, paragliders and hang-gliders. The road is OK for cars, if

narrow, but is also a good walk (about six to seven hours round trip).

SEGURA DE LA SIERRA

Easily the most spectacular village in the park, Segura de la Sierra sits perched on a 1000m-high hill crowned by an Islamic **castle**. It's 20km north of Hornos; turn east off the A317 4km after Cortijos Nuevos. Although it's a short distance, the incredibly sinuous road that winds endlessly upwards begins to make you feel like you'll never reach the town. Characterised largely by its Islamic heritage, the village actually dates way back to Phoenician times and ultimately became part of the Christian defensive front line when it was taken from the Muslims in 1214.

As you approach the upper, older part of the village, there's a **tourist office** (☎ 953 12 60 53; ⏰ 10.30am-2pm & 6.30-8.30pm) beside the Puerta Nueva, an arch that was one of four gates of Islamic Saqura. The two main attractions, the **castle** and the **Baño Moro** (Muslim Bath), are normally left open all day every day, but you should

---

WALK THE WALK

The most popular walk in the Parque Natural Sierras de Cazorla, Segura y Las Villas follows the Río Borosa upstream. It goes through scenery that progresses from the pretty to the majestic, via a gorge and two tunnels (a torch is useful) to two beautiful mountain lakes – an ascent of 500m. Although it can get very busy on weekends and at holiday times, this 24km, seven-hour walk (return, not counting stops) is popular for good reason.

A road signed 'Central Eléctrica', east off the A319 opposite the Centro de Interpretacion Torre del Vinagre, crosses the Guadalquivir after about 500m. Within 1km of the river, the road reaches a **piscifactoría** (fish farm), with parking areas close by. The marked start of the walk is on your right, shortly past the fish farm.

The first section is an unpaved road crisscrossing the tumbling, trout-rich river over bridges. After about 4km, where the road starts climbing to the left, take a path forking right. This takes you through a beautiful 1.5km section where the valley narrows to a gorge, **Cerrada de Elías**, and the path changes to a wooden walkway. You re-emerge on the dirt road and continue for 3km to the **Central Eléctrica**, a small hydroelectric station.

The path passes between the power station and the river, and crosses a footbridge, where a 'Nacimiento de Aguas Negras, Laguna de Valdeazores' sign directs you ahead. About 1.5km from the station, the path turns left and zigzags up into a **tunnel** cut into the cliff. This tunnel allows water to flow to the power station. A narrow path, separated from the watercourse by a fence, runs through the tunnel, which takes about five minutes to walk through. There's a short section in the open air before you enter a **second tunnel**, which takes about one minute to get through. You emerge just below the dam of **Laguna de Aguas Negras**, a picturesque little reservoir surrounded by hills and trees. Cross the dam to the other side of the lake then walk about 1km south to reach a similar-sized natural lake, the **Laguna de Valdeazores**.

You can do this walk as a day trip from Cazorla if you take the bus to Torre del Vinagre. Be sure to carry plenty of water with you.

check at the tourist office first (especially for the castle).

You can walk or drive up to the castle, which is at the top of the village. If you're walking, take the narrow Calle de las Ordenanzas del Común to the right after the **Iglesia de Nuestra Señora del Collado**, the parish church. After a few minutes you'll emerge beside Segura's tiny bullring (which has seen famous fighters such as Enrique Ponce during the October festival), with the castle track heading up to the right. Wonderful views of the surrounding countryside unfurl all the way up, and if you climb the three-storey castle keep you get a bird's-eye view across to El Yelmo, about 5km to the south-southwest. You can drive most of the way up to the castle by heading past the parish church and around the perimeter of the village.

Segura's other attraction, the **Baño Moro**, is just off the central Plaza Mayor. Built around 1150, probably for the local ruler Ibn ben Hamusk, it has three elegant rooms (for cold, temperate and hot baths), with horseshoe arches and barrel vaults studded with skylights. Nearby is the **Puerta Catena**, the best preserved of Segura's four Islamic gates; from here you can pick up the waymarked GR-147 footpath to the splendidly isolated village of **Río Madera** (a 15km downhill hike).

Tours

A number of outfits offer guided trips to some of the park's less accessible areas, plus other activities such as horse riding and biking. Nearly all the hotels and camping grounds in the park can arrange these excursions for you.

The main operators:

Excursiones Bujarkay (☎ 953 71 30 11; www .swin.net/usuarios/jcg; Calle Borosa 81, Coto Ríos) Offers walking, 4WD, biking and horse-riding trips with *guías nativos* (local guides). Prices are detailed on the company's website. The company also has a roadside kiosk in Arroyo Frío.

Tierraventura (☎ 953 72 20 11; www.tierraventuraca zorla.com in Spanish; Calle Ximénez de Rada 17, Cazorla) Multiadventure activities including quad biking, canoeing, hiking and rock climbing.

TurisNat (☎ 953 72 13 51; www.turisnat.org in Spanish; Paseo del Santo Cristo 17, Cazorla) Trips include 4WDs with English-speaking guides and cost from €25 per person for a half day to €45 per person for a whole day.

Sleeping & Eating

The park has plenty of accommodation but few places in the budget range, except for camping grounds, of which there are at least 10 (you can get details of these from the Cazorla tourist office). During peak visitor periods it's worth booking ahead. Camping is not allowed outside the organised camping grounds. These don't always stick to their published opening dates, and from October to April you should ring ahead or check with one of the tourist offices. There is very limited accommodation in Segura de la Sierra and it is advisable to book ahead on weekends and in the summer holidays. Most of the restaurants in the park – except small, casual roadside cafés – are part of the hotels or *hostales*. For excellent coverage of nearly all the hotels and camping grounds in the park visit www.turismoencazorla .com (in Spanish).

Complejo Puente de las Herrerías (☎ /fax 953 72 70 90; near Vadillo Castril; camp site per person/tent/car €4/3.60/3.60, 2-/12-person cabins €44/144; P 🞨 🞩) This is the largest camping ground in the park, with room for about 1000 people. It also has a small hotel with 11 double rooms, and self-catering cabins. There's also a restaurant, and you can arrange horse riding, canoeing, canyoning and climbing. It's possible to walk here from the Empalme del Valle bus stop by following the signed paths, Sendero de El Empalme del Valle (1.5km) and Sendero de la Fuente del Oso (1.4km).

Camping Chopera Coto Ríos (☎ 953 71 30 05; camp site with 2 people, tent & car €13) This is a rather cramped but shady camping ground by the side road into Coto Ríos.

Camping Fuente de la Pascuala (☎ 953 71 30 28; camp site with 2 people, tent & car around €14) Beside the A319.

Camping Llanos de Arance (☎ 953 71 31 39; camp site with 2 people, tent & car €15) Just across the Guadalquivir from Camping Chopera Cotos Ríos.

Bar El Cruce (☎ 953 49 50 03; Puerta Nueva 27, Hornos; s/d €12/24) At the entrance to the village of Hornos, this is a cheerful bar with decent rooms to rent. There's a lovely garden terrace where good food is served up. The bar also has information on apartments to rent.

Instalación Juvenil Jorge Manrique (☎ 953 48 04 14; Calle Francisco de Quevado 1, Segura de la Sierra; d with/without bathroom €22/19; 🞨) This is the

DETOUR: SIERRA DE CAZORLA BY CAR

And now for something for the lazy ones among you: a way to see all this nature without sweating a drop. It's a 60km itinerary and a good introduction to the parts of the park nearest to Cazorla town. Much of it is on unpaved roads, but it's all quite passable for ordinary cars, if a little bumpy in places. Allow two hours for the trip – without stops for easy strolls and picnic breaks.

Head first to La Iruela and turn right along Carretera Virgen de la Cabeza soon after entering La Iruela. You reach the **Merenderos de Cazorla** *mirador* (lookout), with fine views over Cazorla, after about 700m. After another 4km you pass the Hotel de Montaña Riogazas; 7km further is **El Chorro**, a gorge that's good for watching Egyptian and griffon vultures.

Keep on the current track, ignoring another dirt road just beyond El Chorro that forks down to the right. The track you are on winds around over the Puerto Lorente (Lorente Pass) and, after 12km, down to a junction. Take the right fork here and after a couple of hundred metres a sign points down some steps towards the river on your left. A plaque on the far bank marks the **Nacimiento del Guadalquivir**, the official source of the Guadalquivir. In dry periods you can apparently identify the stream emerging from underground. The road heads a short distance past the Nacimiento to the **Cañada de las Fuentes** picnic area.

From Cañada de las Fuentes, return to the junction just before the Nacimiento and head northward, with the infant Guadalquivir on your right – a beautiful trip down the wooded valley with the river bubbling to one side and rugged crags rising all around. It's 11km to the **Puente de las Herrerías**, a bridge over the Guadalquivir supposedly built in one night for Queen Isabel la Católica to cross during her campaigns against Granada. Here the road becomes paved, and 3km further on, past the large Complejo Puente de las Herrerías camping ground, you reach a T-junction. Go left and after 400m, opposite the turning to Vadillo Castril village, is the start of the **Sendero de la Cerrada del Utrero**, a beautiful 2km marked loop walk passing imposing cliffs, the **Cascada de Linarejos** (Linarejos Waterfall) and a small dam on the Guadalquivir – a great chance to get out and stretch your legs.

One kilometre further on from the turning to Vadillo Castril is the left-hand turn to the Parador El Adelantado hotel (which is 5km up a paved side road) and after another 2.5km you're at Empalme del Valle junction, from which it's 17km back to Cazorla.

only hostel in Segura de la Sierra, but it is a nice place to stay and caters for a range of budgets. There are also new studio flats. Lunches for hikers are available on request.

Hotel de Montaña Los Parrales (☎ 953 12 61 70; www.turismoencazorla.com/parrales.html in Spanish; Carretera del Tranco Km 78; s/d €25/35; P ⊠) North of Tranco along the road towards Hornos, Los Parrales is a charming hotel with idyllic views of the reservoir. The interior is tastefully decorated in cheerful blues and yellows, with a sweet rustic dining room with chequered tablecloths. Run by Excursiones Bujarkay, you can arrange any number of activities through the hotel.

Hotel de Montaña La Hortizuela (☎ 953 71 31 50; Carretera del Tranco Km 53; s/d €33/55; P ⊠ ⊠) A cosy, 27-room hotel in a tranquil setting 1km off the main road, down a signed track. The hotel has comfortable rooms and a worthwhile restaurant serving a *menú* at €9. The turn-off is 2km north of Torre del Vinagre.

Hotel de Mirasierra (☎ 953 71 30 44; Carretera del Tranco Km 51; s/d €35/45; P ⊠ ⊠) A place with a traditional rustic feel, with woven spreads covering the beds and serving as curtains in the spacious rooms. The pool is great for a dip after lots of walking. Nonguests can stop for lunch at the restaurant, which has a very well-deserved reputation.

El Parral (☎ 953 72 72 65; Carretera del Tranco Km 37, Arroyo Frío; 4-person apt €40; P ⊠ ⊠) Another pleasant complex of attractive stone-faced, self-catering apartments. All apartments have spacious rooms, well-equipped kitchens and bathrooms, and scenic terraces.

Los Enebros (☎ 953 72 71 10; Carretera del Tranco Km 37, Arroyo Frío; s/d €48/78, 4-/12-person apt €93/153; P ⊠ ⊠ ⊠) Located at the northern end of Arroyo Frío, this tourist complex has every type of accommodation that exists: a hotel, apartments, chalets and a small camping ground. It's all a bit rough and ready, but there is a huge range of activities available, from horse riding and hiking to canoeing. There are also two pools and a playground.

Hotel Paraíso de Bujaraiza (☎ 953 12 41 14; www.paraisodebujaraiza.com in Spanish; Carretera del Tranco Km 59; s/d €50/60; P ✕ ᵯ) A lovely small hotel located right on the reservoir. It has its own beach, where you can hire canoes. The rooms are attractive and comfortable, and the restaurant looks out over the huge expanse of water, making it a scenic spot to stop for lunch.

Los Huertos de Segura (☎ 953 48 04 02; www .loshuertosdesegura.com; Calle Castillo 11, Segura de la Sierra; 2-/4-person apt €55/65; P ✕) Excellent, tastefully decorated self-catering studio rooms and apartments with terrific views. The friendly owners are a good source of information about organised tours and walking in the area.

Hotel Noguera de la Sierpe (☎ 953 71 30 21; Carretera del Tranco Km 44.5; s/d €63/97, 4-person chalet €130; P ✕ ᵯ) A paradise for hunting junkies, run by an equally fanatical proprietor who has decorated the place with stuffed animals and suitably proud photos of his exploits. The hotel is housed in a converted *cortijo* (farm house) and overlooks a picturesque lake. There are also five self-contained chalets for rent (four-person chalet costs €130). You can arrange riding sessions at the hotel's stables (first half-hour free, then €12 per hour) and there is a good rustic restaurant.

Parador El Adelantado (Parador de Cazorla; ☎ 953 72 70 75; www.parador.es in Spanish; s/d €81/97; P ✕ ᵯ) This parador is one of the less attractive, but it's redeemed by its lovely setting on a hillside in a pine forest, its grassy garden and a fine pool. The hunters' lodge–style interior has skulls and guns on the walls. Only nine of the 33 rooms have views, so be sure to ask for one of these.

The best restaurants in Segura for tasting good mountain stews, bean and chickpea dishes, chorizo, *jamón*, and quality cheese are **El Mirador Messia de Leiva** (Calle Postigo 2; menú €8), in the upper town near Los Huertos, and **La Mesa Segureña** (☎ 953 48 21 01; www.lamesa desegura.com in Spanish; Calle Postigo 13, Segura de la Sierra; mains €7-12; ᨻ closed Sun night & Mon) run by artist Ana María. La Mesa Segureña also rents out very attractive, good-value apartments in the jigsawlike town for a minimum of two nights (studio apartment €54, two-bedroom apartment €84).

Also recommended:

Camping Montillana (☎ 953 12 61 94; camp site per person/tent/car €3.20/3.40/4.50) Located 4km north of the town, this is the closest camp site to Tranco.

Camping El Robledo (☎ 953 12 61 56; camp site per person/tent/car €3.40/4.50/3.40) Head to this place to camp near Segura de la Sierra. It's about 4km east of Cortijos Nuevos on a road leading up to El Yelmo.

Getting There & Around

Carcesa (☎ 953 72 11 42) runs two buses daily (except Sunday) from Cazorla's Plaza de la Constitución to Empalme del Valle (€1.50, 30 minutes), Arroyo Frío (€1.80, 45 minutes), Torre del Vinagre (€3.50, one hour) and Coto Ríos (€3.50, one hour and 10 minutes). Pick up the latest timetable from the tourist office.

No buses link the northern part of the park with the centre or south, and there are no buses to Segura de la Sierra. However, coming from Jaén, Baeza or Úbeda, you could get an Alsina Graells bus to La Puerta de Segura (leaving Jaén daily at 9.30am and returning from La Puerta at 3pm). From La Puerta the best bet is a **taxi** (☎ 953 48 08 30, 619 060409) onwards to Segura de la Sierra (€12).

If you're driving, approaches to the park include the A319 from Cazorla, roads into the north from Villanueva del Arzobispo and Puente de Génave on the A32, and the A317 to Santiago de la Espada from Puebla de Don Fadrique in northern Granada province. There are at least seven petrol stations in the park.

<p>

354

Granada Province

There are some places in this world that seem to have it all: the looks, the jewels, the sense of fun, a streetwise edge. Granada is one of those places. Millions of people pour into the town just to see its crown gem: the Alhambra, a place that carries with it coffers-full of stories, dreams and mysteries of the last 2½ centuries of a great civilisation. Washington Irving, an unsuspecting diplomat and writer, fell in love with the Alhambra so deeply that he had to move in and live here while he wrote his half-fact, half-fiction *Tales of the Alhambra* back in 1823. His contagious fascination put the magnificent building back among the world's greatest architectural treasures.

But then, Granada is much more than the Alhambra. The old Islamic quarter, the Albayzín, is like a tangled string of pearls with its white-washed houses and narrow streets. The ever-present tapas-mania, hanging out till dawn in flamenco *peñas* or in Andalucía's best nightclub are just some of the highlights of this fabulous city. The growing North African community shows Granada to be more open-minded than any of its Andalucian sisters.

And Granada the province offers more surprises: there's skiing and climbing in the snowy Sierra Nevada, and walking in the amazing Las Alpujarras, where villages house locals, New Age hippies, and expat Brits, simultaneously. You can check out cave life on the Altiplano (high plain) or forget it all and go swimming and eating mangos on Costa Tropical, Granada's Mediterranean coastline.

GRANADA PROVINCE

HIGHLIGHTS

- Imagine the drama and intrigue that once took place in the architectural splendour of the **Alhambra** (p359) and the **Generalife** gardens (p364)
- Walk the white-washed, winding streets of the **Albayzín** (p367), and catch some incredible views of the Alhambra
- Hit the tapas **bars** (p377), **clubs** (p377) and **midnight flamenco** (p378) of Granada's nightlife
- Try out cave living and tourist-free tapas bars at the little-visited **Guadix** (p380)
- Explore the wonderful valleys of **Las Alpujarras** (p386) and climb, walk or ski in the snowy **Sierra Nevada** (p382)
- Dance till dawn at Granada's **Festival Internacional de Música y Danza** (p372) and see pious reverence at **Semana Santa** (p372)

★ Guadix

★ Granada

Sierra Nevada ★

★ Las Alpujarras

■ POPULATION: 828,000	■ GRANADA AV DAILY HIGH: JAN/AUG 11°C/27°C	■ ALTITUDE RANGE: 0M–3479M

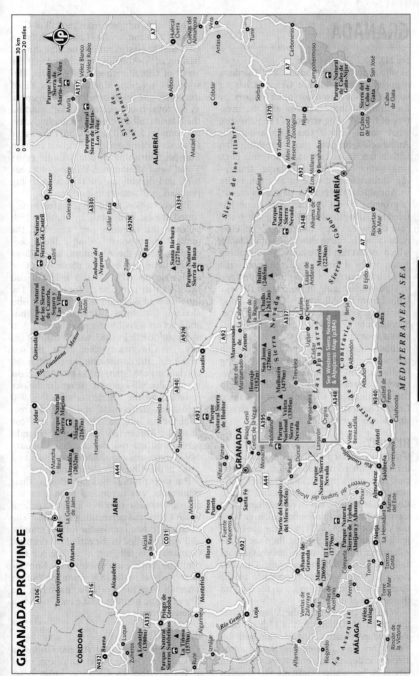

GRANADA PROVINCE

GRANADA

pop 237,000 / elevation 685m

Seville may have the *pasión* and Córdoba a pretty quaintness, but Granada has an edge. Overshadowed for most visitors by the allure of the Alhambra and the mystery of the winding streets of the Albayzín, what you'll find if you stick around is Andalucía's hippest, most youthful city, with a free-tapas culture, innovative bars, tiny flamenco holes, and large, thumping clubs. Here, unlike in any other city in Andalucía, the Islamic past feels recent. A growing North African population has filled the Albayzín with steaming kebab and cake shops, and slipper-and-tea nooks. Granada is also home to thousands of students, which means that there is always something going on, be it the crusty jugglers on Calle de Elvira, skater kids in the university area, or students lounging in the relaxed Realejo. Uphill from the Albayzín is Granada's loud and lively *gitano* (Roma) neighbourhood, Sacromonte, where you can perhaps witness a spot of real flamenco.

In addition, Granada's proximity to both mountain and sea means you can go skiing in the morning in the almost always snow-covered Sierra Nevada and swimming in the afternoon on the ambitiously named Costa Tropical, and be back in the city in time for *la marcha* (nightlife).

HISTORY

Granada's history reads like an excellent thriller, with complicated plots, conspiracies, hedonism and tricky love-affairs. The city began life as an Iberian and then a Roman settlement, but its real development started when Muslim forces took over from the Visigoths in AD 711, with the aid of the Jewish community, around the foot of the Alhambra hill in what was called Garnata al-Jahud, from which the name Granada derives. ('Granada' also happens to be the Spanish word for pomegranate, the fruit on the city's coat of arms.)

With the crumbling of the Almohad state that ruled Al-Andalus in the 13th century, a minor potentate called Mohammed ibn Yusuf ibn Nasr formed the Nasrid emirate, an independent emirate centred on Granada. Soon after, Granada was flooded with Muslim refugees from the fall of Córdoba (1236) and Seville (1248) to Christian Castile. The Nasrid emirate became the last bastion of Al-Andalus, stretching from the Strait of Gibraltar to east of Almería. Despite his isolation, Mohammed ibn Yusuf ibn Nasr went on to develop the Alhambra as his royal court, palace and fortress, and the Nasrids ruled from this increasingly lavish complex for 250 years. Under their rule Granada became one of the richest cities in Europe, flourishing especially under emirs Yusuf I and Mohammed V in the 14th century, and developing the talents of its big population of traders and artisans.

But corruption, ambition and great luxury rotted the heavenly state by the late 15th century: the economy had stagnated, the opulent rulers were leading a life of hedonism inside the Alhambra, and violent rivalry developed over the succession. One faction supported emir Abu al-Hasan and his Christian concubine, Zoraya, and the other backed Boabdil (Abu-Abdullah), Abu al-Hasan's son by his wife Aixa. In 1482 Boabdil set off a civil war and, following Abu al-Hasan's death in 1485, won control of the city. The Christians pushed across the rest of the emirate, devastating the countryside, and laid siege to Granada in 1491. After eight months Boabdil agreed to surrender the city in return for the Alpujarras valleys, 30,000 gold coins and political and religious freedom for his subjects. The Reyes Católicos (Catholic Monarchs) Isabel and Fernando agreed and entered the city on 2 January 1492 ceremonially in Muslim dress, to set up court in the Alhambra for several years.

But their promise was as hollow as their intolerance was fierce and soon after the fall of Granada they set about expelling Spain's Jews and persecuting Muslims. The Muslims revolted across the former emirate and were expelled in the early 17th century. Granada thus fell into a decline for two centuries, but the interest from the Romantic movement in the 1830s brought tourists from all over the world to marvel at the city's Islamic heritage, and gave Granada a renewed breath of life.

ORIENTATION

The two major central streets, Gran Vía de Colón and Calle Reyes Católicos, meet at Plaza Isabel La Católica. From here,

Calle Reyes Católicos runs southwest to Puerta Real, an important intersection, and northeast to Plaza Nueva. The street Cuesta de Gomérez leads southeast from Plaza Nueva towards the Alhambra on its hilltop. The Albayzín rambles over another hill rising north of Plaza Nueva, separated from the Alhambra hill by the valley of the Río Darro. Below the southern side of the Alhambra is the old Jewish district, Realejo.

Newer parts of the city stretch to the west, south and east. From Puerta Real, Acera del Darro, an important artery, heads southeast to the Río Genil. The bus station (northwest) and train station (west) are out of the centre but linked to it by plenty of buses.

INFORMATION
Bookshops
Cartográfica del Sur (Map pp358-9; ☎ 958 20 49 01; Calle Valle Inclán 2) Just off Camino de Ronda; Granada's best map shop, also good for Spanish guidebooks.
Metro (Map p366; ☎ 958 26 15 65; Calle Gracia 31) Stocks an excellent range of English-language novels, guidebooks and books on Spain, plus plenty of books in French and some in German, Italian and Russian.

Emergency
Policía Nacional (National Police; Map p366; ☎ 958 80 80 00; Plaza de los Campos) The most central police station.
Reporting theft (☎ 902 10 21 12) Police hotline; various languages spoken.

Internet Access
Thanks to Granada's 60,000 students, the city's internet cafés are cheap and open long hours daily.
Internet Elvira (Map p366; Calle de Elvira 64; per hr €1.60, students per hr €1; ⊗ 8am-11pm)
N@veg@web (Map p366; Calle Reyes Católicos 55; per hr €1.20; ⊗ 8am-11pm) Excellent internet centre just off Plaza Isabel La Católica. Web-cams, Skype, fax and photocopying.
Net Realejo (Map p366; Plaza de los Girones 3; ⊗ 8am-11pm); Plaza de la Trinidad (Map p366; Calle Buensuceso; ⊗ 8am-11pm)

Internet Resources
Ayuntamiento de Granada (www.granada.org in Spanish) Town hall website with good maps and a broad range of information on what to do, where to stay and so on, with plenty of links. For tourist info, click 'La Ciudad'.

Turismo de Granada (www.turismodegranada.org) Good website of the provincial tourist office, covering the city and other places of interest in the province.

Laundry
Lavandería Duquesa (Map p366; Calle Duquesa 24; ⊗ 9.30am-2pm & 4.30-9pm Mon-Fri, 9.30am-2pm Sat) Wash-and-dry service €10.
Lavomatique (Map p366; Calle Paz 19; ⊗ 10am-2pm & 5-8pm Mon-Fri, 10am-2pm Sat) Wash €5, dry €3.

Medical Services
These are both central hospitals with good emergency facilities:
Hospital Clínico San Cecilio (Map pp358-9; ☎ 958 02 32 17; Avenida del Doctor Oloriz 16)
Hospital Ruiz de Alda (Map pp358-9; ☎ 958 02 00 09, 958 24 11 00; Avenida de la Constitución 100)

Money
Banks and ATMs abound on Gran Vía de Colón, Plaza Isabel La Católica and Calle Reyes Católicos.
American Express (Map p366; ☎ 958 22 45 12; Calle Reyes Católicos 31)

Post
Expendeduría No 37 (Map p366; Acera del Casino 15) If stamps are all you need, avoid the post office queues by slipping around the corner to this *estanco* (tobacconist).
Main post office (Map p366; Puerta Real s/n; ⊗ 8.30am-8.30pm Mon-Fri, 9.30am-2pm Sat) Often has long queues.

Tourist Information
Provincial tourist office (Map p366; ☎ 958 24 71 28; www.turismodegranada.org; Plaza de Mariana Pineda 10; ⊗ 9am-9pm Mon-Fri, 10am-2pm & 4-7pm Sat, 10am-3pm Sun May-Sep, 9am-8pm Mon-Fri, 10am-1pm Sat, 10am-3pm Sun Oct-Apr) A short walk east of Puerta Real, with helpful staff, free maps and bountiful material on Granada and its province.
Regional tourist office Plaza Nueva (Map p366; ☎ 958 22 10 22; Calle Santa Ana 1; ⊗ 9am-7pm Mon-Sat, 10am-2pm Sun & holidays); Alhambra (Map p361; ☎ 958 22 95 75; Pabellón de Acceso, Avenida del Generalife s/n; ⊗ 8am-7.30pm Mon-Fri, 8am-2.30pm & 4-7.30pm Sat & Sun Mar-Oct, 8am-6pm Mon-Fri, 8am-2pm & 4-6pm Sat & Sun Nov-Feb, 9am-1pm holidays) Information on all Andalucía.

SIGHTS & ACTIVITIES
Most major sights are within walking distance of the city centre. There are buses if you get fed up with walking uphill.

GRANADA

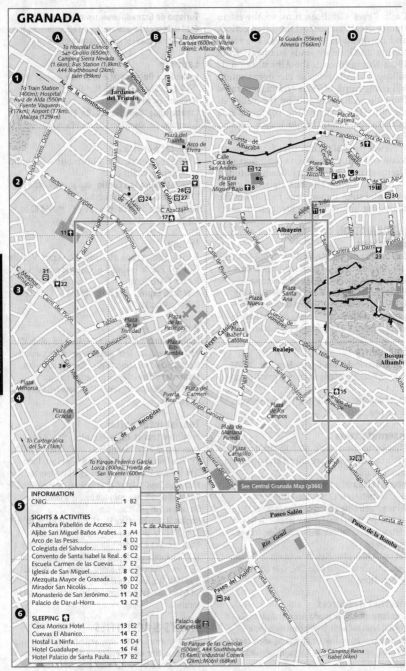

To Monasterio de la
Cartuja (600m); Viznar
(8km); Alfacar (8km)

To Guadix (55km);
Almería (166km)

To Hospital Clínico
San Cecilio (650m);
Camping Sierra Nevada
(1.6km); Bus Station (1.8km);
A44 Northbound (2km);
Jaén (99km)

To Train Station
(400m); Hospital
Ruiz de Alda (550m);
Fuente Vaqueros
(17km); Airport (17km);
Málaga (129km)

Jardines
del Triunfo

Plaza del
Triunfo
Arco de
Elvira

Cuesta de
la Alhacaba

Placeta
Fátima

C Pages

C Panderos

Cuesta de los Chin

San
Agustín

Calle
Coca de
San Andrés

Placeta
de San
Miguel Bajo

Plaza
de San
Nicolás

Cuesta Cabras

C de San Agus

Albayzín

Carrera del Darro

Plaza
Santa
Ana

Plaza
Nueva

Cuesta de
Gomérez

Realejo

Callejón Niño del Royo

Bosque
Alhambr

Monasterio de San Jerónimo

Plaza
de la
Trinidad

Plaza de
las
Pasiegas

Plaza
Bib-
Rambla

Plaza
Isabel La
Católica

Plaza
Menorca

Puerta
Real

Plaza del
Carmen

Plaza
de los
Campos

Campo del
Príncipe

Plaza de
Gracia

Plaza de
Mariana
Pineda

Plaza
Campillo
Bajo

See Central Granada Map (p366)

To Cartográfica
del Sur (1km)

To Parque Federico García
Lorca (400m); Huerta de
San Vicente (600m)

Paseo Salón

Paseo de la Bomba

Río Genil

Cuesta

C de Molinos

Paseo del Violón

Palacio de
Congresos

To Parque de las Ciencias
(500m); A44 Southbound
(1.6km); Industrial Copera
(2km); Mótril (68km)

To Camping Reina
Isabel (4km)

INFORMATION
CNIG................................1 B2

SIGHTS & ACTIVITIES
Alhambra Pabellón de Acceso......2 F4
Aljibe San Miguel Baños Arabes...3 A4
Arco de las Pesas.................4 D2
Colegiata del Salvador............5 D2
Convento de Santa Isabel la Real..6 C2
Escuela Carmen de las Cuevas......7 E2
Iglesia de San Miguel.............8 C2
Mezquita Mayor de Granada.......9 D2
Mirador San Nicolás...............10 D2
Monasterio de San Jerónimo......11 A2
Palacio de Dar-al-Horra...........12 C2

SLEEPING
Casa Morisca Hotel................13 E2
Cuevas El Abanico.................14 E2
Hostal La Ninfa...................15 D4
Hotel Guadalupe..................16 F4
Hotel Palacio de Santa Paula.....17 B2

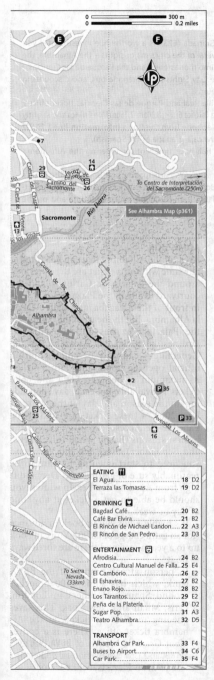

Alhambra

When you've visited the **Alhambra** (Map p361; ☎ 902 44 12 21; www.alhambra-patronato.es; adult/EU senior/Generalife only €10/5/5, disabled & child under 8yr free; ⏰ 8.30am-8pm Mar-Oct, 8.30am-6pm Nov-Feb, closed 25 Dec & 1 Jan) once, you'll spend the rest of your life longing to come back again and again. At first sight the plain walls of the red fortress towers look imposing, rising from woods of cypress and elm. The snowy peaks of the Sierra Nevada are a magnificent backdrop. The Alhambra walls tease you and reveal little, but hint at the size of the complex. This famous trick of Islamic architecture is meant to reward only those who persevere and go inside, where the marvellously decorated emirs' palace, the Palacio Nazaríes (Nasrid Palace), the Generalife (the Alhambra's gardens), and dozens of courtyards, nooks and crannies are all filled with beautiful decorations and fascinating stories from the days of Alhambra's glory. Water is an art form here and even around the outside of the Alhambra the sound of running water and the greenery take you to a different world.

But (and here the soothing music comes to a screeching halt) the tranquillity can be completely shattered by the hordes of visitors who traipse through (an average of 6000 a day), unless you get up early and visit as soon as the Pabellón de Acceso (Ticket Office) opens. Late afternoons are a good time too, but a night visit to the Palacio Nazaríes is a magical experience.

The Alhambra has two outstanding sets of buildings, the Palacio Nazaríes and the Alcazaba (Citadel). Also within the complex are the Palacio de Carlos V, the Iglesia de Santa María de la Alhambra, two hotels (p374), book and souvenir shops and lots of lovely gardens.

There's a small snack bar by the ticket office and another outside the Alcazaba but you're not allowed to bring food inside. There's nowhere to sit down and eat inside the Alhambra except at the two hotels.

HISTORY

The Alhambra takes its name from the Arabic al-qala'at al-hamra (red castle). The first palace on the site was built by Samuel Ha-Nagid, the Jewish grand vizier of one of Granada's 11th-century Zirid sultans (whose own fortress was in the Albayzín).

GRANADA'S BONO TURÍSTICO

Granada's tourist voucher, the Bono Turístico Granada (€23), is a worthwhile investment if you plan to stay a few days. It gives admission to several of the city's major sights – the Alhambra, the cathedral, Capilla Real, La Cartuja and San Jerónimo monasteries, and the Parque de las Ciencias – plus nine rides on city buses, a day pass on the City Sightseeing Granada bus, and discounts in various hotels, restaurants and additional museums.

You can buy the Bono at the Alhambra, Capilla Real and Parque de las Ciencias ticket offices; at the **CajaGranada bank** (Map p366; Plaza Isabel La Católica 6; ⊗ 8.30am-2.15pm Mon-Fri) for the slightly higher charge of €25; by credit card over the telephone from the **Bono information line** (☎ 902 10 00 95; English spoken); or on the internet at www.caja-granada.es (in Spanish).

When you buy your Bono you are given a half-hour time slot for entering the Alhambra's Palacio Nazaríes, as with all Alhambra tickets.

If you stay two nights or more in one of the scheme's participating hotels, paying the hotel's regular room rate, you are entitled to one free Bono per double room. Information on participating hotels (mostly three- and four-star) is available from the Bono information line and on the internet at www.granadatur.com.

The Nasrid emirs of the 13th and 14th centuries turned the Alhambra into a fortress-palace complex, adjoined by a small town of which only ruins remain. The founder of the Nasrid dynasty, Mohammed ibn Yusuf ibn Nasr, set up home on the hilltop, rebuilding, strengthening and enlarging the Alcazaba. His successors Yusuf I (r 1333–54) and Mohammed V (r 1354–59 and 1362–91) built the Alhambra's crowning glory, the Palacio Nazaríes.

After the Reconquista (Christian reconquest) the Catholic Monarchs appointed a Muslim to restore the decoration of Palacio Nazaríes. The Alhambra's mosque was replaced with a church, and the Convento de San Francisco (now the Parador de Granada) was built. Carlos I, grandson of the Catholic Monarchs, had a wing of Palacio Nazaríes destroyed to make space for a huge Renaissance palace, the Palacio de Carlos V.

In the 18th century the Alhambra was abandoned to thieves and beggars. During the Napoleonic occupation it was used as a barracks and narrowly escaped being blown up. In 1870 it was declared a national monument as a result of the huge interest taken in it by Romantic writers such as Washington Irving, who wrote the wonderful *Tales of the Alhambra* during his stay in the Palacio Nazaríes in the 1820s. Since then the Alhambra has been salvaged and heavily restored and has been awarded World Heritage status, together with the Generalife gardens, and the Albayzín. For more on its architectural qualities and importance, see p56.

ADMISSION

Areas of the Alhambra that can be visited at any time without a ticket are the open area around the Palacio de Carlos V and the courtyard inside it, the Plaza de los Aljibes in front of the Alcazaba, and Calle Real de la Alhambra. But the heart of the complex – the Palacio Nazaríes and the adjacent Jardines del Partal, the Alcazaba and the Generalife – can only be entered during official opening hours and with a ticket. A maximum of between 5600 and 6600 tickets is available for each day, depending on the season and day of the week. At least 2000 of these tickets are sold at the Pabellón de Acceso each day, but in the busiest seasons (Easter week, July, August and September) these sell out early and you need to start queuing by 7am to be reasonably sure of getting one. Demand is high from April to October. In winter, you should be able to get a ticket at any time of day or week.

It's highly advisable to book in advance (for an extra charge of €0.90). You can book up to a year ahead and there are three ways to do it:

- In person at any branch of the BBVA bank, which has some 4000 branches around Spain and others in London, Paris, Milan and New York. This saves queuing to pick up tickets at the Alhambra ticket office. There is a convenient Granada branch of **BBVA** (Map p366; ⊗ 8.30am-2.15pm Mon-Fri year-round & 8.30am-1pm Sat Oct-Mar) on Plaza Isabel La Católica.

GRANADA PROVINCE

■ On the internet at www.alhambratickets
.com. The website provides information about tickets for the Alhambra in
English, Spanish, French, German and
Italian.

■ By telephone to **Banca Telefónica BBVA** (☎ in
Spain 902 22 44 60, outside Spain 00-34-91 537 91 78;
⏰ 8am-5.55pm), which offers an English-
speaking service.

For internet or phone bookings you need a
Visa card, MasterCard or Eurocard. The reference number you receive must be shown,
along with your passport, national identity
card and the credit card with which you
paid for the ticket, at the Alhambra ticket
office when you pick up the ticket on the
day of your visit. You may have to queue to
pick up your ticket. You cannot buy same-
day tickets by internet or by phone or from
BBVA, nor can you buy advance tickets at
the Alhambra ticket office.

Every ticket is stamped with a half-hour
time slot during which you must enter the
Palacio Nazaríes. You must enter during

this time, otherwise you'll not be allowed
in if you miss your slot. Once inside the
Palacio Nazaríes, you can stay as long as
you like. Each ticket is also either a *billete de
mañana* (morning ticket), valid for entry up
until 2pm, or a *billete de tarde* (afternoon or
evening ticket), for entry after 2pm. These
are the periods during which you can enter
the Generalife or Alcazaba, where you can
stay as long as you like. If you buy your
ticket on the day of your visit at the ticket
office, in busy seasons your time slot for the
Palacio Nazaríes may be several hours later,
and if it's an afternoon ticket you won't
be able to enter the Alcazaba or Generalife
until 2pm.

The Palacio Nazaríes is also open for
night visits (⏰ 10-11.30pm Tue-Sat Mar-Oct, 8-9.30pm
Fri & Sat Nov-Feb). For each night 400 tickets
are available, at the same prices as daytime
tickets, with the ticket office open from 30
minutes before the palace's opening time
until 30 minutes after it. You can book
ahead for night visits in exactly the same
way as for day visits.

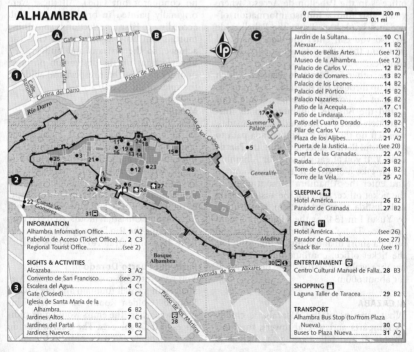

ALHAMBRA

	0 ————— 200 m
	0 ————— 0.1 mi

Jardín de la Sultana.................... 10 C1
Mexuar.. 11 B2
Museo de Bellas Artes..............(see 12)
Museo de la Alhambra..............(see 12)
Palacio de Carlos V.................... 12 B2
Palacio de Comares.................... 13 B2
Palacio de los Leones................. 14 B2
Palacio del Pórtico...................... 15 B2
Palacio Nazaries......................... 16 B2
Patio de la Acequia..................... 17 C1
Patio de Lindaraja...................... 18 B2
Patio del Cuarto Dorado............. 19 B2
Pilar de Carlos V......................... 20 A2
Plaza de los Aljibes..................... 21 A2
Puerta de la Justicia...................(see 20)
Puerta de las Granadas.............. 22 A2
Rauda.. 23 B2
Torre de Comares....................... 24 B2
Torre de la Vela.......................... 25 A2

SLEEPING ⌂
Hotel América.............................. 26 B2
Parador de Granada.................... 27 B2

EATING ⊞
Hotel América............................(see 26)
Parador de Granada..................(see 27)
Snack Bar...................................(see 1)

ENTERTAINMENT ☺
Centro Cultural Manuel de Falla..28 B3

SHOPPING ⌂
Laguna Taller de Taracea........... 29 B2

TRANSPORT
Alhambra Bus Stop (to/from Plaza
     Nueva)...................................... 30 C3
Buses to Plaza Nueva................. 31 A2

INFORMATION
Alhambra Information Office............ 1 A2
Pabellón de Acceso (Ticket Office)..... 2 C3
Regional Tourist Office....................(see 2)

SIGHTS & ACTIVITIES
Alcazaba.. 3 A2
Convento de San Francisco...........(see 27)
Escalera del Agua............................ 4 C1
Gate (Closed)................................. 5 C2
Iglesia de Santa María de la
     Alhambra.................................. 6 B2
Jardines Altos................................. 7 C1
Jardines del Partal.......................... 8 B2
Jardines Nuevos.............................. 9 C2

GETTING THERE & AWAY

Bus

Buses 30 and 32 from Plaza Nueva both run every five to nine minutes from 7.15am to 11pm up Cuesta de Gomérez to the Alhambra, stopping near the ticket office (at the eastern end of the complex). The buses return to Plaza Nueva via a stop near the Puerta de la Justicia. Bus 32 continues from Plaza Nueva on a second loop through the Albayzín. Bus tickets cost €1.

Car & Motorcycle

'Alhambra' signs on the approach roads to Granada will conduct you circuitously to the Alhambra **car parks** (per hr/day €1.40/14), which are just off Avenida de los Alixares, a short distance uphill from the ticket office.

Walking

There are two main ways to walk up to the Alhambra; both take 20 to 30 minutes from Plaza Nueva.

One is the path **Cuesta de los Chinos**, which leads up from Paseo de los Tristes, emerging about 50m from the ticket office. The office is in the Pabellón de Acceso, where you'll also find a tourist information office and bookshop. From the Pabellón de Acceso you can enter the Generalife, and move on from there to other parts of the complex.

The other is **Cuesta de Gomérez**, which leads up through the Puerta de las Granadas (Gate of the Pomegranates), built by Carlos I, and the Bosque Alhambra woods. Immediately after the Puerta de las Granadas, veer left up the Cuesta Empedrada path to a beautiful Renaissance fountain, the **Pilar de Carlos V**. If you already have your Alhambra ticket, take a sharp left after the fountain and enter the Alhambra without going to the ticket office, through the austere **Puerta de la Justicia** (Gate of Justice), constructed by Yusuf I in 1348 as the Alhambra's main entrance. There's an Alhambra information office a short distance inside this gate. For the ticket office, continue outside the Alhambra walls from the Pilar de Carlos V for about 600m.

ALCAZABA

What remains of the Alcazaba is chiefly its ramparts and several towers, the most important and tallest being the **Torre de la Vela** (Watch Tower), with a narrow staircase leading to the top terrace, which has splendid views. The cross and banners of the Reconquista were raised here in January 1492. One of the Alhambra's many dungeons is set in the ground just inside the Alcazaba's eastern walls.

PALACIO NAZARÍES

This is the place in the Alhambra that will stir the desire to own beauty even in the most unpossessive of people. Unfortunately, you can't steal a building, but you can admire the most impressive Islamic structure in Europe and the finest surviving example of Nasrid art and architecture. The perfectly proportioned rooms and courtyards, intricately moulded stucco walls, beautiful tiling, fine carved wooden ceilings and elaborate *muqarnas* (honeycomb or stalactite) vaulting, all worked in mesmerising, symbolic, geometrical patterns, are meant to embody the infinite glory of God, reinforced by the Arabic inscriptions in stuccowork and wood, and the endlessly repeated *Wa la galiba illa Allah* (There is no conqueror but God). All these were originally painted in bright colours. But, according to Islam, perfection is something mortals can only aspire to and God can achieve, so the artisans and builders left imperfections on the designs on purpose, in order to show their respect and abide by the rules of the Quran.

Mexuar

This 14th-century room is the entrance to the palace. It was used as a ministerial council chamber and as an antechamber for those awaiting audiences with the emir. The public would generally not have been allowed beyond here. The chamber has been much altered; it was converted into a chapel in the 16th century, and now contains both Muslim and Christian motifs. At its far end, overlooking the Río Darro, is the small, lavishly decorated Oratorio (Prayer Room).

Patio del Cuarto Dorado

You pass into this courtyard from the Mexuar, with a small fountain and the Cuarto Dorado (Golden Room) on the left. This patio was where the emirs would give audiences to their subjects. The Cuarto Dorado takes its name from its beautiful wooden ceiling, which was gilded and redecorated in the time of the Catholic Monarchs. On the other side of the patio is the entrance to the Palacio de Comares through a beautiful façade of glazed tiles, stucco and carved wood.

Palacio de Comares

This fabulous *palacio* was originally built by Emir Yusuf I, and thereafter served as the private residence for the ruler. It's built around the **Patio de los Arrayanes** (Patio of the Myrtles), and named after the hedges surrounding its rectangular pool and fountains. The rooms along the sides may have been quarters for the emir's many wives. Finely carved arches atop marble pillars form porticos at both ends of the patio. Through the northern portico, inside the Torre de Comares (Comares Tower), is the **Sala de la Barca** (Hall of the Blessing) from the Arabic *al-baraka* for blessing, a word endlessly carved on the walls. This room leads into the square **Salón de Comares** (Comares Hall), also called the Salón de los Embajadores (Hall of the Ambassadors), where the emirs would have conducted their negotiations with Christian emissaries. The stuccowork on the walls again contains repeated inscriptions in praise of God, and the marvellous domed marquetry ceiling contains more than 8000 cedar pieces in a pattern of stars representing the seven heavens of Islamic paradise, through which the soul ascends before reaching the top, where Allah resides.

The southern end of the patio is overshadowed by the walls of the Palacio de Carlos V.

Palacio de los Leones

From the Patio de los Arrayanes you move into the Palace of the Lions, one of the most stunning structures within the Alhambra, and according to some, the royal harem. It was built in the second half of the 14th century under Mohammed V, at the political and artistic peak of Granada's emirate.

The rooms of the palace surround Alhambra's most popular symbol, the **Patio de los Leones** (Lion Courtyard), a marble fountain that channelled water through the mouths of 12 carved marble lions. Carved especially for this palace, the fountain was originally brightly painted, chiefly in gold,

but the originals are now being replaced by copies. The patio's four water channels, running to and from the central fountain, represent the four rivers of Islamic paradise, and the 12 lions are speculated to symbolise any number of things, perhaps the 12 signs of the zodiac, perhaps the 12 hours of the day, ticking from birth to death. The gallery, including the beautifully ornamented pavilions protruding at its eastern and western ends, is supported by 124 slender marble columns. Imagine this entire space covered in vibrant colours and hung with bright textiles – that's how it was during the 14th century.

Of the four halls bordering the patio, the **Sala de los Abencerrajes** on the southern side is the legendary site of the murders of the noble Abencerraj family, who favoured Boabdil in the palace power struggle. The legend tells that the family was massacred because the family's leader dared to get jiggy with Zoraya, Abu al-Hasan's harem favourite. The rusty stains on the floor are said to be the victims' indelible blood. The room's lovely high-domed ceiling features *muqarnas* vaulting in an eight-point star formation. The staircases are supposed to have led to the harem, where blind eunuchs waited on the women who were jealously kept out of sight.

At the very eastern end of the patio is the **Sala de los Reyes** (Hall of the Kings), whose inner alcoves have leather-lined ceilings painted by 14th-century Christian artists, probably Genoans. The room's name comes from the painting on the ceiling of the central alcove, thought to depict 10 Nasrid emirs. On the northern side of the patio is the **Sala de las Dos Hermanas** (Hall of Two Sisters), as beautiful and richly decorated as the Sala de los Abencerrajes, and probably named after the two slabs of white marble sitting on either side of its fountain. This may have been the room of the emir's favourite paramour. It features a fantastic *muqarnas* dome with a central star and 5000 tiny cells, reminiscent of the constellations. At its far end is the **Sala de los Ajimeces** with a beautifully decorated little lookout area, the **Mirador de Lindaraja**. Through the low-slung windows of the *mirador*, the room's occupants could enjoy the luxurious view of the Albayzín and countryside while reclining on ottomans and cushions.

Other Sections

From the Sala de las Dos Hermanas a passageway leads through the **Estancias del Emperador** (Emperor's Chambers), built for Carlos I in the 1520s and later used by Washington Irving. From here you descend to the **Patio de la Reja** (Patio of the Grille), which leads to the pretty **Patio de Lindaraja**, originally created as a lower garden for the Palacio de los Leones. In the southwestern corner of the patio is the entrance (only sometimes open) to the **Baño de Comares**, the Palacio de Comares' bathhouse, with its three rooms lit by star-shaped skylights.

From the Patio de Lindaraja you emerge into the **Jardines del Partal**, an area of terraced gardens created in the early 20th century around various old structures, ruined and standing. The small **Palacio del Pórtico** (Palace of the Portico), from the time of Mohammed III (r 1302–09), is the oldest surviving palace in the Alhambra. You can leave the Jardines del Partal by a gate facing the Palacio de Carlos V (next to the site of the **Rauda** – the emirs' cemetery), or continue along a path to the Generalife, which runs parallel to the Alhambra's ramparts, passing several towers.

PALACIO DE CARLOS V

This huge Renaissance palace sticks out like a sore thumb in the Alhambra, because it clashes spectacularly with the style of its surroundings; were it in a different setting its merits would be more readily appreciated. Begun in 1527 by Pedro Machuca, an architect from Toledo who studied under Michelangelo, it was financed, perversely, from taxes on the Granada area's Morisco (converted Muslim) population. Funds dried up after the Moriscos rebelled in 1568, and the palace remained roofless until the early 20th century. The main (western) façade features three porticos divided by pairs of fluted columns, with bas-relief battle carvings at their feet. The building is square but contains a two-tiered circular courtyard with 32 columns. This circle inside a square is the only Spanish example of a Renaissance ground plan symbolising the unity of heaven and earth.

Inside are two museums. The ground-floor **Museo de la Alhambra** (☎ 958 02 79 00; admission free; ☑ 9am-2.30pm Tue-Sat) has a wonderful collection of Muslim artefacts from the Alhambra, Granada province and Córdoba, with explanatory texts in English and Spanish. Highlights include the elegant Alhambra Vase, decorated with gazelles, and the door from the Sala de las Dos Hermanas.

Upstairs is the **Museo de Bellas Artes** (Fine Arts Museum; ☎ 958 22 14 49; admission free; ☑ 9am-2pm Mon-Fri). Most notable is the mainly Granada-related collection of paintings and sculptures are the carved wooden relief of the Virgin and child (c 1547) by Diego de Siloé, several 17th-century works by Alonso Cano, including the modern-looking *Ecce Homo*, and the portraits and landscapes by Granada's two early-20th-century José Marías – López Mezquita and Rodríguez Acosta.

OTHER CHRISTIAN BUILDINGS

The **Iglesia de Santa María de la Alhambra** was built between 1581 and 1617 on the site of the Islamic palace mosque. The **Convento de San Francisco**, now the Parador de Granada hotel (p374), was erected over a small Islamic palace. Isabel and Fernando were laid to rest in a sepulchre here while their tombs in the Capilla Real were being built.

GENERALIFE

The term Generalife comes from the Arabic *yannat-al-arif* or 'Architect's Garden'. Planted on a hillside facing the Alhambra, this is a beautiful, soothing composition of pathways, patios, pools, fountains, trimmed hedges, tall, ancient trees and, in season, flowers of every imaginable hue. It is the perfect place to end an Alhambra visit and to sit and enjoy the peace and contemplate the extent of luxury enjoyed by those who lived here. The Muslim rulers' summer palace is in the corner furthest from the entrance. On the way to it you pass through the Generalife's 20th-century **Jardines Nuevos** (New Gardens). Within the palace, the **Patio de la Acequia** (Court of the Water Channel) has a long pool framed by flowerbeds and 19th-century fountains whose shapes sensuously echo the arched porticos at each end. Off this patio is the **Jardín de la Sultana** (Sultana's Garden), a lovely little garden with the stump of a 700-year-old cypress tree trunk. When this was a flourishing tree, Zoraya, Abu al-Hasan's favourite concubine, flirted with the head of the Abencerraj clan under its thick shade. Unfortunately, this is where she was also caught flirting, which led to the murders in the Sala de los Abencerrajes of the Palacio Nazaríes.

Above are the modern **Jardines Altos** (Upper Gardens), with the **Escalera del Agua** (Water Staircase) – a set of steps with water running down beside them.

Capilla Real

Adjoining the cathedral, the **Capilla Real** (Royal Chapel; Map p366; ☎ 958 22 92 39; www .capillarealgra nada.com; Calle Oficios; admission €3; ⏰ 10.30am-1pm & 4-7pm Apr-Oct, 10.30am-1pm & 3.30-6.30pm Nov-Mar, from 11am Sun year-round, closed Good Friday) is Granada's outstanding Christian building. Spanish-history fans will enjoy its connection with the Catholic Monarchs Isabel and Fernando, who commissioned it as their own mausoleum, to be built in elaborate Isabelline Gothic style. Since it wasn't finished until 1521, several years after their deaths, they had to be temporarily interred in the Alhambra's Convento de San Francisco.

The monarchs lie with three relatives in simple lead coffins in the crypt, beneath their marble monuments in the chancel. The chancel is divided from the chapel's nave by a gilded screen made in 1520 by Maestro Bartolomé de Jaén – a masterpiece of wrought-iron artisanry. The coffins, from left to right, belong to Felipe El Hermoso (Philip the Handsome; the husband of the monarchs' daughter Juana la Loca, or Joanna the Crazy), Fernando, Isabel, Juana la Loca and Miguel, the eldest grandchild of Isabel and Fernando.

The marble effigies reclining above the crypt were a tribute by Carlos I to his parents and grandparents. The slightly lower of the two monuments, representing Isabel and Fernando and with a Latin inscription lauding them (scarily) as 'subjugators of Islam and extinguishers of obstinate heresy', was carved by a Tuscan, Domenico Fancelli. The other monument (1520), to Felipe and Juana, is higher, apparently because Felipe was the son of Holy Roman Emperor Maximilian. This is the work of Bartolomé Ordóñez from Burgos.

The chancel's densely decorated plat' eresque retable (1522), with a profusion of gold paint, is by Felipe de Vigarni. Note its kneeling figures of Isabel (lower right, with the name 'Elisabeth') and Fernando (lower left), attributed to Diego de Siloé, and the

brightly painted bas-reliefs below depicting the defeat of the Muslims and subsequent conversions to Christianity.

The sacristy contains an impressive small museum with Fernando's sword and Isabel's sceptre, silver crown and personal art collection, which is mainly Flemish but also includes Sandro Botticelli's *Prayer in the Garden of Olives*. Also here are two fine statues of the Catholic Monarchs at prayer by Vigarni.

Cathedral

Adjoining the Capilla Real but entered separately, from Gran Vía de Colón, is Granada's cavernous Gothic and Renaissance **cathedral** (Map p366; ☎ 958 22 29 59; admission €2.50; ⏰ 10.45am-1.30pm & 4-8pm Mon-Sat, 4-8pm Sun, closed 7pm daily Nov-Mar). Construction of the cathedral began in 1521 and lasted until the 18th century. It was directed from 1528 to 1563 by Renaissance pioneer Diego de Siloé, and the main façade on Plaza de las Pasiegas, with four heavy square buttresses forming three great arched bays, was designed in the 17th century by Alonso Cano. De Siloé carved the statues on the lavish Puerta del Perdón on the northwestern façade, and much of the interior is also his work, including the gilded, painted and domed Capilla Mayor. The Catholic Monarchs at prayer (one above each side of the main altar) were carved by Pedro de Mena in the 17th century. Above the monarchs are busts of Adam and Eve by Cano. In the cathedral museum, be sure to see Cano's fine *San Pablo* sculpture and the golden Gothic monstrance given to Granada by Isabel La Católica.

La Madraza

Opposite the Capilla Real is part of the old Muslim university, **La Madraza** (Map p366; Calle Oficios). Now with a painted baroque façade, the much-altered building retains an octagonal domed prayer room with stucco lacework and pretty tiles. The building is part of the modern university but you can take a look inside whenever it's open.

Centro José Guerrero

Just along the street from La Madraza, the **Centro José Guerrero** (art museum; Map p366; ☎ 958 22 51 85; www.centroguerrero.org; Calle Oficios 8; admission free; ⏰ 11am-2pm & 5-9pm Tue-Sat, 11am-2pm Sun)

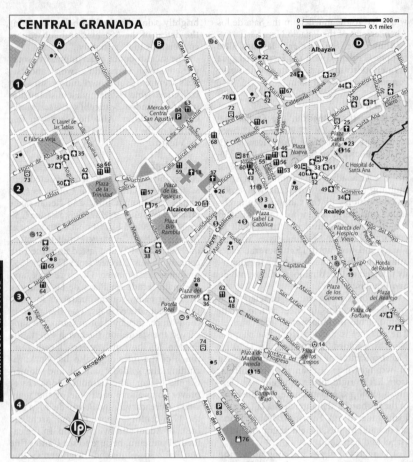

CENTRAL GRANADA

is dedicated to the most celebrated artist to come out of Granada – abstract expressionist José Guerrero (1914–91), who was born in the city but found fame in New York in the 1950s. The centre, which opened in 2000, exhibits good temporary shows as well as a permanent collection of Guerrero's dramatic and colourful canvases. It's well worth a visit.

Alcaicería, Plaza Bib-Rambla & Plaza de la Trinidad

The **Alcaicería** (Map p366) was the Muslim silk exchange but what can be seen here now is a 19th-century restoration that is filled with tourist shops. It's best in the early morning light and quiet. Its buildings, divided by

narrow alleys, are just south of the Capilla Real. Southwest of the Alcaicería is the large **Plaza Bib-Rambla** (Map p366), another tourist haunt with restaurants, flower stalls and a central fountain with statues of giants. Its square has seen jousting, bullfights and Inquisition burnings during its lifetime. Pedestrianised Calle Pescadería and Calle de los Mesones lead northwest to the leafy **Plaza de la Trinidad** (Map p366), which has a couple of good tapas bars.

Corral del Carbón

You can't miss the lovely Islamic façade and elaborate horseshoe arch of the **Corral del Carbón** (Map p366; Calle Mariana Pineda), which began life as a 14th-century inn for merchants.

GRANADA PROVINCE

It has since been used as an inn for coal dealers (hence its modern name, meaning 'Coal Yard') and later a theatre. It is home to government offices and a government-run crafts shop, Artespaña (see p378).

Albayzín

Stretching and twisting its way up the hill that faces the Alhambra across the Darro Valley, the **Albayzín** (Map pp358-9) is one of Granada's most fabulous treasures. The steep winding streets with the gorgeous *carmen* houses (large mansions with walled gardens, from the Arabic *karm,* for garden) reveal the best views of the Alhambra, and in fact it's almost as if the Albayzín and the Alhambra secretly fancy each other: the Albayzín doesn't look as enchanting from anywhere as it does from the Alhambra's tiled chambers, and the Alhambra looks like it rules the world when seen from one of the miradors of the Albayzín. But despite all this charm and beauty, this neighbourhood is still a work-in-progress and is being refurbished

more each year, and, unfortunately, its narrow streets are often havens for thieves and muggers. We have had reports of muggings, some violent, in the Albayzín so if you are alone try to avoid this area during siesta time (3 to 5pm) and after dark.

Albayzín was once Granada's 'cradle' as an Iberian settlement in about the 7th century BC, and was where its Muslim rulers dwelt before they started to develop the Alhambra in the 13th century. The Albayzín's name derives from events in 1227, when Muslims from Baeza (Jaén province) moved here after their city was conquered by the Christians. It became a densely populated residential area with 27 mosques, and it survived as the Islamic quarter for several decades after the Reconquista in 1492. Islamic ramparts, houses, gates, fountains and cisterns remain, and Islamic relics are incorporated in many of the churches and villas of the Albayzín.

Buses 31 and 32 both run circular routes from Plaza Nueva around the Albayzín

A SNIPPET OF LIFE IN THE MUSLIM COMMUNITY

After walking down the Albayzín's Calles Calderería Nueva and Vieja and peeking into all the slipper and hookah shops and the tea houses with their belly dancers, and tea-drinkers reclining on the sparkling cushions, I get myself a *shwarma* (kebab in pitta bread) and a bite of baklava. Then, in one of the *teterías* (teahouses) I light up a hookah and get talking to a man called Abdeselam, a 26-year-old PhD student from Ceuta. I wonder how life is in Granada for young Muslims like himself.

'I study here, I am doing a PhD in Arab Philology and Islamic Archaeology at Granada University. I'm a fluent Spanish speaker, so it wasn't so hard to fit in, language-wise.' But what about culturally? Granada's streets are full of students behaving badly. Was that a shock for him when he came over? 'Well, yes and no. I don't drink, I go out to places where generally alcohol is not served, in *teterías* and so on, so it doesn't bother me. But some other Muslims have integrated more in that respect. They go out clubbing and drinking.'

I meet a man from Iraq, working in a souvenir shop. We talk about his life – he left during Saddam's regime, and his family is still in Iraq. He was expelled from the country for being an outspoken journalist, ridiculing the system in the press. Now, apart from working in the shop, he teaches at Granada University about the power of the media. In between, he writes poetry and wishes he could work as a journalist in Iraq again. He's about to publish a poetry book in Spanish, his first.

Both men agree that real integration with the Spanish population is pretty much nonexistent – *granadinos* do have a reputation for being unfriendly – but it's much better than in most other parts of Spain.

Abdeselam likes to hang out in **Kasbah** (p376) *tetería*, and gets his *shwarma* from **King of Shwarma** on Plaza Albert Einstein, around the university area.

(Paseo de los Tristes, Cuesta del Chapiz, Plaza del Salvador, Plaza de San Nicolás, Placeta de San Miguel Bajo, Arco de Elvira) and back to Plaza Nueva about every seven to nine minutes. Bus 32 follows this with another loop up to the Alhambra and back. Eight times a day bus 31 detours to Sacromonte midroute. Bus 32 runs from 7.20am to 11pm, while bus 31 goes from 7.30am to 11.05pm.

ALBAYZÍN WALKING TOUR

This tour of the Darro Valley and the Albayzín, starting from Plaza Nueva, should take four or five hours, including visits to some of the sights and a stop for something to eat and drink.

Plaza Nueva extends northeast into Plaza de Santa Ana, where the **Iglesia de Santa Ana (1)** incorporates a mosque's minaret in its bell tower (as do several churches in the Albayzín). Along narrow Carrera del Darro, have a look at the 11th-century Islamic bathhouse, the **Baños Árabes El Bañuelo (2**; ☎ 958 02 78 00; Carrera del Darro 31; admission free; ☺ 10am-2pm Tue-Sat), one of Granada's oldest buildings. Further along is the fascinating **Museo Arqueológico (3**; Archaeological Museum;

☎ 958 22 56 40; Carrera del Darro 43; non-EU/EU citizen €1.50/free; ☺ 3-8pm Tue, 9am-8pm Wed-Sat, 9am-2.30pm Sun), housed in a Renaissance mansion, the Casa de Castril. On display are finds from Granada province from Palaeolithic to Islamic times.

Just past the museum, Carrera del Darro becomes Paseo de los Tristes (also called Paseo del Padre Manjón). Several cafés and restaurants here have outdoor tables and, with the Alhambra's fortifications looming above, it makes a good spot to pause, keeping in mind that many of them cater very much for tourists. Several narrow lanes head up into the Albayzín – try Calle Candil, which leads up into Placeta de Toqueros, where the **Peña de la Platería (4)** flamenco club is located (see Granada's Top Five Flamenco Haunts, p378).

If you turn right at the top of Placeta de Toqueros, left at the fork soon afterwards, then left again, you emerge on Carril de San Agustín. Go left and after about 100m the street turns 90 degrees to the right. Continue 200m (initially uphill) to Plaza del Salvador, dominated by the **Colegiata del Salvador (5**; ☎ 958 27 86 44; admission €0.80; ☺ 10am-1pm & 4-7.30pm Mon-Sat Apr-Oct, 10.30am-

12.30pm & 4.30-6.30pm Mon-Sat Nov-Mar), a 16th-century church on the site of the Albayzín's main mosque. The mosque's patio, with three sides of horseshoe arches, survives at the church's western end. From here Calle Panaderos leads west to **Plaza Larga (6)**, home to some lively bars.

Leave Plaza Larga through the **Arco de las Pesas (7)**, an impressive Islamic gateway in the Albayzín's 11th-century defensive wall, and take the first street to the left, Callejón de San Cecilio. This leads to the **Mirador San Nicolás (8)**, a lookout with fantastic views of the Alhambra and the Sierra Nevada. You might like to come back here later for sunset (you can't miss the trail then!), but at any time of day keep a tight hold on your belongings. Skilful, well-organised wallet-lifters and snatchers of bags and cameras operate here. One of their tactics is to distract people with 'impromptu' flamenco dance routines; another is for pillion riders on passing motorbikes to stand up and grab bags lying on the side walls of the *mirador*.

The Albayzín's first new mosque in 500 years, the **Mezquita Mayor de Granada (9**; ☎ 958 20 23 31; ☽ gardens 11am-2pm, 6-9.30pm), has been built just east of Mirador San Nicolás, off Cuesta de las Cabras, to serve modern Granada's growing Muslim population. Opened in 2003, it includes an Islamic centre and gardens that have a direct view of the Alhambra and are open to the public. This open-door policy has defused opposition from some quarters to the opening of a new mosque in Granada.

Take the steps down beside the south end of Mirador San Nicolás, turn right and follow the street down to Camino Nuevo de San Nicolás. Turn right, which takes you down to the **Convento de Santa Isabel la Real** (**10**; Convent of St Isabel the Monarch; ☎ 958 27 78 36; Calle Santa Isabel la Real 15; admission €5; ☽ guided tours 4.30pm Fri, 10am & 11.30am Sat), founded in 1501 and with a Gothic chapel. A few more steps down the street is **Placeta de San Miguel Bajo (11)**, with many cafés and restaurants with outdoor tables. The plaza's **Iglesia de San Miguel (12)** is another church on the site of a former mosque. Leave Placeta de San Miguel Bajo by Callejón del Gallo, turn right at the end of this short lane and you'll come to the door of the 15th-century **Palacio de Dar-al-Horra (13**; Callejón de las Monjas s/n; admission free; ☽ 10am-2pm Mon-Fri), which was home to Aixa, the mother of Granada's last Muslim ruler, Boabdil. With its patio, pool, arched doorways, coffered ceilings, and friezes with decorative inscriptions, it's like a mini-Alhambra.

Return to Placeta de San Miguel Bajo and head down Placeta Cauchiles de San Miguel, which becomes Calle San José, where the lovely little **Alminar de San José (14**; San José Minaret) survives from the 11th-century mosque that stood here before the neighbouring Iglesia de San José was built in the 16th century. Calle San José meets the top of **Calle Calderería Nueva (15)**, lined by *teterías* (tea houses), and shops brimming with slippers, hookahs, jewellery and North African pottery. The atmosphere is relaxed and there's no pressure to buy, so stop here for a sweet Moroccan mint tea or head on down to Calle de Elvira and then back to Plaza Nueva.

Alternatively, from Placeta de San Miguel Bajo, take Calle Cruz de Quirós, the street parallel to Placeta Cauchiles de San Miguel. After a couple of hundred metres this will bring you to **El Ojo de Granada (16**; ☎ 958 20 24 73; www.elojodegranada.com; admission €5; ☽ 10.30am-8.30pm Jun-Aug, 10.30am-6.30pm Mar-May, Sep & Oct,

WALKING TOUR

Distance	5½km
Duration	4-5 hours

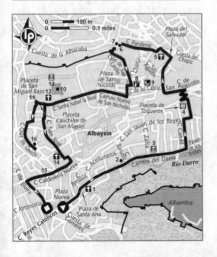

GRANADA'S SACRED MOUNTAIN

Fancy some fresh air? Then make your way up to the Sacromonte district, the cave-dwelling neighbourhood of *gitanos* (Roma), northeast of the Albayzín. Once deemed a danger to public order and still largely on society's margins except for the area of music (mainly flamenco), the *gitanos* probably started inhabiting the caves before the 14th century. General poverty made many poor peasants who'd come to live in Granada move to the caves in the 19th century. To this day, 80% of the caves are inhabited, and you'd be surprised at how flashy some of them are. But be advised: don't accept invitations to look at a private house (unless you know the person) since a hefty fee may be demanded after.

If you wish to see the *gitanos'* way of life and traditional crafts – metalwork, pottery, weaving, and basket-making – go to the **Centro de Interpretación del Sacromonte** (Map pp358-9; ☎ 958 21 51 20; www.sacromontegranada.com; Barranco de los Negros s/n; ⏲ 10am-2pm & 5-9pm Tue-Fri, 10am-9pm Sat & Sun Jun-Oct, 10am-2pm & 4-7pm Tue-Fri & 10am-7pm Sat & Sun Nov-May), a place that makes a trip to Sacromonte really worthwhile. This wide-ranging ethnographic and environmental museum and arts centre is set in large grounds planted with all manner of herbs where you can also see art exhibitions and attend a herbal-remedy workshop. Morning is the best time to see the artists at work. The centre has an outdoor flamenco music, dance and film programme starting at 10pm on Wednesday and Friday from June to September.

To get here, hop off the Sacromonte bus at the Venta El Gallo Flamenco School, 250m along the road from El Camborio cave disco (p377), and follow the signs up Barranco de los Negros to the centre. It's about a 200m uphill walk. Bus 31 (see p367) detours along Camino del Sacromonte eight times daily; times are posted at its stops.

The best views of the Alhambra, Sierra Nevada and the Albayzín are from the Iglesia de San Miguel Alto, at the top of the hill. Make sure you're not hanging around the uninhabited parts by nightfall. Some caves on or near Sacromonte's main street, Camino del Sacromonte, are venues for expensive tourist-oriented flamenco shows or lively dance clubs (see p377). Be discerning so that you don't get ripped off.

10.30am-5.30pm Nov-Feb), which has a camera-obscura system projecting live, 360-degree views of Granada onto a screen. There's a running commentary in Spanish, English and French.

Monasterio de San Jerónimo

Five hundred metres west of the cathedral, the 16th-century **Monasterio de San Jerónimo** (Map pp358-9; ☎ 958 27 93 37; Calle Rector López Argüeta 9; admission €3; ⏲ 10am-1.30pm & 4-7.30pm Apr-Oct, 10am-1.30pm & 3-6.30pm Nov-Mar) features some beautiful stone carving and a spectacularly decorated church. In the cloister are two lovely plateresque doorways carved by the monastery's chief architect, the talented Diego de Siloé. The church, in a combination of Isabelline Gothic and Renaissance styles, features an incredible profusion of brightly painted sculpture on the enormous retable and the towering vaults at the eastern end. Before it, at the foot of the steps, is the tombstone of El Gran Capitán (the Great Captain) – Gonzalo Fernández de Córdoba, the military right-hand man of the Catholic Monarchs. Statues of El Gran Capitán and his wife, the Duquesa de Sesa, at prayer stand either side of the retable.

Monasterio de la Cartuja

Another architectural gem stands 2km northwest of the centre, reached by bus 8 from Gran Vía de Colón. **Monasterio de la Cartuja** (☎ 958 16 19 32; Paseo de la Cartuja; admission €3; ⏲ 10am-1pm & 4-8pm Apr-Oct, 10am-1pm & 3.30-6pm Nov-Mar, 10am-noon Sun year-round), with an imposing, sand-coloured stone exterior, was built between the 16th and 18th centuries. It's the lavish baroque monastery church that people come to see, especially the Sagrario (Sanctuary) behind the main altar, a confection of red, black, white and grey-blue marble, columns with golden capitals, profuse sculpture and a beautiful frescoed cupola; and, to the left of the main altar, the Sacristía (Sacristy), the ultimate expression of Spanish late baroque, in effusive 'wedding-cake' stucco and brown-and-white Lanjarón marble (resembling a melange of chocolate mousse and cream).

The Sacristía's cabinets, veneered and inlaid with mahogany, ebony, ivory, shell and silver by Fray José Manuel Vázquez in the 18th century, represent a high point of Granada marquetry art.

Huerta de San Vicente

The great *granadino* writer Federico García Lorca (see the boxed text, p48) spent summers and wrote some of his best-known works at the **Huerta de San Vicente** (Map pp358-9; ☎ 958 25 84 66; Calle Virgen Blanca s/n; admission €1.80, free Wed, admission only by guided tour in Spanish; ☒ 10am-12.30pm & 4-7pm Tue-Sun Oct-Mar, 10am-1pm & 5-8pm Apr-Jun, 10am-3pm Jul-Aug). The house is a 15-minute walk from the city centre and was once surrounded by orchards. Today, the **Parque Federico García Lorca** separates the house from whizzing traffic in an attempt to recreate the tranquil environment that inspired him.

The folksy house contains some original furnishings, including Lorca's writing desk and piano, some of his drawings and other memorabilia, and exhibitions connected with his life and work. A cheeky Salvador Dalí drawing of a short-haired blonde woman smoking a pipe catches the eye.

To get here, head 700m down Calle de las Recogidas from Puerta Real, turn right along Calle del Arabial then take the first left into Calle Virgen Blanca.

Hammams

Granada has two *Baños Árabes* (Arabic Baths) and a visit to one of these is a must-do for the sheer lazy pleasure of it. Both baths offer a similar deal: a bath and aromatherapy massage that lasts for two hours (bath 1¾ hours, massage 15 minutes) and both need advance reservations. Sessions start on the hour every two hours from 10am until 10pm. Swimwear is obligatory (you can rent it here), a towel is provided, and all sessions are mixed.

The better of the two is the **Aljibe San Miguel Baños Árabes** (Map pp358-9; ☎ 958 52 28 67; www.aljibesanmiguel.es; San Miguel Alta 41; bath/bath & massage €15/22) with seven pools of different temperatures, wonderful tiled nooks and arches. The pools feel private and there is a relaxed, silent atmosphere inside, and only six people are allowed in a session, so it never gets crowded. The semidarkness and the drops of condensation from the curved ceilings are ideal for relaxation. Sweet mint tea is included in your bathing time.

The older but smaller **Hammam** (Map p366; ☎ 958 22 99 78; www.hammamspain.com/granada in Spanish; Calle Santa Ana 16; bath/bath & massage €16/25) is in the Albayzín, just below the Alhambra. It has wonderful geometric mosaics, arches and latticework decorations, and soothing background music, but only two pools: one hot and one cold. You can have tea in the *tetería* from 3pm and there's a rooftop restaurant.

Parque de las Ciencias

Granada's fun, modern **Parque de las Ciencias** (Map pp358-9; ☎ 958 13 19 00; Avenida del Mediterráneo s/n; adult/child under 18yr museum €4.50/3.50, planetarium €2/1.50; ☒ 10am-7pm Tue-Sat, 10am-3pm Sun, closed 15-30 Sep), a science museum 2km south of the centre, has plenty of hands-on exhibits and a special room for children to explore basic scientific principles. The planetarium has sessions roughly every hour. Take buses 1, 4, 5, 10 or 11 from the centre.

COURSES

With its many attractions and youthful population, Granada is a good place to study Spanish; it also has several Spanish dance schools. The provincial tourist office can provide lists for all types of schools. For more information check out www.granada spanish.org, www.spanishcourses.info and www.granadainfo.com.

Centro de Lenguas Modernas (Modern Languages Centre; Map p366; ☎ 958 21 56 60; www.clm-granada .com; Placeta del Hospicio Viejo s/n) Granada University's modern languages department, in the historic Realejo district, offers a variety of Spanish language and culture programmes, from intensive beginners' courses to classes for teachers of Spanish. Its teachers are highly qualified. Intensive language courses at all levels start at 10 days (40 hours' tuition) for €305.

Escuela Carmen de las Cuevas (Map pp358-9; ☎ 958 22 10 62; www.carmencuevas.com; Cuesta de los Chinos 15, Sacromonte) This private school gets good reports. It teaches Spanish language and culture, and flamenco dance and guitar, all at several levels. A two-week intensive language course (40 hours' tuition) costs €284.

TOURS

Cicerone Cultura y Ocio (☎ 670 541669; www.cicero negranada.com) Offers guided walking tours in English (2½ hours, €10) from Plaza del Carmen, in front of the *ayuntamiento*, at 10.30am daily.

City Sightseeing Granada (☎ 902 10 10 81) Granada's double-decker city tour bus. It has 20 stops outside the main sights, including the cathedral and the Alhambra. You hop on and off where you like and the ticket (€15) is valid for 24 hours. There's a smaller minibus that does a miniroute. You can travel on either bus with the same ticket.

Granavisión (☎ 902 33 00 02) Offers guided tours of the Alhambra and the Generalife (€38), Historic Granada tours (€43) and excursions further afield.

FESTIVALS & EVENTS

Festival Internacional de Tango (www.eltango .com) Dancing cheek-to-cheek in the street, in dance halls and listening to the wonderful melancholy of tango; held each year from 21 to 26 March. Tickets go on sale at the beginning of the year at the **festival box office** (Map p366; ☎ 958 22 18 44; www.granadafestival.org; Corral del Carbón, Calle Mariana Pineda s/n) and can be purchased online.

Semana Santa (Holy Week) This and Feria de Corpus Cristi are Granada's big two popular festivals; during the week leading up to Easter Sunday, benches are set up in Plaza del Carmen for viewing the Semana Santa processions.

Día de la Cruz (Day of the Cross) On 3 May, squares, patios and balconies are adorned with floral Cruces de Mayo (May Crosses). These become the focus for typical Andalucian revelry – drinking, horse riding, polka-dot dresses and *sevillanas* (traditional Andalucian dances with high, twirling arm movements).

Feria de Corpus Cristi (Corpus Christi Fair) Granada's big annual fair – a week of fairgrounds, drinking, bullfights and *sevillanas*; held early June 2007, mid-May 2008.

Festival Internacional de Música y Danza First-class 2½-week festival of mainly classical music and dance, with many events held in the Palacio Nazaríes, Generalife, Palacio de Carlos V and other historic sites; held late June to early July.

SLEEPING

Granada has a great range of places to stay all around the central areas, especially around Plaza Nueva. The best places to lay your head are in the renovated Albayzín *carmen* houses, usually with Alhambra views of some kind, mostly in the midrange and top-end brackets, although there are some good hostels in the area, too.

You should have no problem finding a room except during Semana Santa and at Christmas. At busy times rooms tend to fill up before noon, especially on Cuesta de Gomérez, so from March to October book ahead to secure your choice. Most places

keep more or less the same prices year-round except for a few days over Easter. Parking, where offered, costs €8 to €12 per day. For apartments, check out www.granada .info.com.

Near Plaza Nueva
BUDGET

Oasis Backpackers' Hostel (Map p366; ☎ 958 21 58 48; www.oasisgranada.com; Placeta Correo Viejo 3; dm €15, d €36; ☐ ✕) Granada's top hostel, in a renovated *carmen* house, is seconds away from the Caldererías and bars on Calle de Elvira. This place is designed for serious backpackers and word spreads fast, so book ahead to enjoy its little luxuries: happy staff, free internet access, rooftop terrace, personal safes, tapas tours, and a tip-top central location.

Hostal Landázuri (Map p366; ☎ /fax 958 22 14 06; Cuesta de Gomérez 24; s/d/tr/q €28/45/50/60, s/d with shared bathroom €20/28; P) This folksy place boasts a terrace with Alhambra views and a café. The 20 rooms have been updated and a few have a TV; triples and quads are large, bright and comfortable. It's well heated in winter.

Hostal Britz (Map p366; ☎ /fax 958 22 36 52; Cuesta de Gomérez 1; s/d €32/44, with shared bathroom €25/34) The friendly, efficient Britz has 22 clean, plain rooms with double glazing, gleaming wooden surfaces and central heating. There's also a lift.

The **Hostal Austria** (Map p366; ☎ 958 22 70 75; www.hostalaustria.com; Cuesta de Gomérez 4; s/d/tr/q €35/45/60/70; P ✕) and **Hostal Viena** (Map p366;

THE AUTHOR'S CHOICE

Hostal Venecia (Map p366; ☎ 958 22 39 87; Cuesta de Gomérez 2; r €32, s/d/tr/q with shared bathroom €15/28/39/52) A lovely *hostal* (simple guesthouse) where the friendly hosts are as sweet as the flower-and-picture-filled turquoise corridors. The nine rooms are all different and brim with character. The owners bring you a soothing herbal infusion to drink each morning. Relaxing background music plays, incense wafts, and it's warm in winter. There are overhead fans for the hot summer months. The owners run Hostal Patagonia, a similar, comfortable place in the university area, where you are more independent but still looked after.

☎/fax 958 22 18 59; Calle Hospital de Santa Ana 2; s/d €35/45, with shared bathroom €25/37) are both run by the same Austrian-Spanish family. The Austria has better, though still uninspiring, rooms with attractive wooden doors and shutters. Some of the rooms are on the thigh-achingly high 4th floor, so watch out if you have heavy bags.

Half-a-dozen *hostales* (simple guesthouses or small places offering hotel-like accommodation) are strung along Cuesta de Gomérez, between Plaza Nueva and the Alhambra. The streets between Calle de Elvira and Gran Vía de Colón, west of Plaza Nueva, also have several more *hostales* worth a look if you're having difficulty finding a room.

MIDRANGE

Hotel Maciá Plaza (Map p366; ☎ 958 22 75 36; www .maciahoteles.com; Plaza Nueva 4; s/d €49/73; P ✱ ◻) One of four Maciás in Granada, this hotel has 44 comfy rooms with attractive enough décor in an excellent location. Try for a double overlooking the plaza. Its single rooms are small, but you can have a double to yourself for €58. Rates drop to €50 for a double on weekends in winter, July and August.

Hotel Anacapri (Map p366; ☎ 958 22 74 77; www .hotelanacapri.com; Calle Joaquín Costa 7; s/d €78/105; ✱) Just a minute's walk from Plaza Nueva, the Anacapri has 49 pretty rooms in varied colours, with floral bedspreads, cork floors and satellite TV. Its 18th-century patio is fitted out with cane chairs and palms. Buffet breakfast is €7.50 and the reception staff make you feel welcome.

Hotel Puerta de las Granadas (Map p366; ☎ 958 21 62 30; www.hotelpuertadelasgranadas.com; Cuesta de Gomérez 14; s/d €77/97, superior r €107-180; ✱ ◻) One of the renovated *carmen* houses, decorated in a gorgeous modern minimalist style with wooden shutters and elegant furnishings. The more expensive, luxurious rooms have a number of windows that catch divine views of the Alhambra and/or the old-city roofline. Prices drop significantly midweek. The hotel also has a lift.

Albayzín

MIDRANGE

Casa del Capitel Nazarí (Map p366; ☎ 958 21 52 60; www.hotelcasacapitel.com; Cuesta Aceituneros 6; s/d €73/91; ✱ ◻) A 16th-century patio is the focus of this beautiful building, with understated décor, wooden balconies, ancient pillars and classy rooms.

Casa del Aljarife (Map p366; ☎/fax 958 22 24 25; www.granadainfo.com/most; Placeta de la Cruz Verde 2; r €95; ✱) The best place to stay for those who want to feel at home, this beautifully restored 17th-century house has just four spacious rooms and a pretty patio where you can take breakfast.

Hotel Zaguán (Map p366; ☎ 958 21 57 30; www.hotel zaguán.com; Carrera del Darro; s €50, r €80-100; ✱ ◻) A risen-from-ruins and tastefully restored 16th-century *carmen* house. Its 13 rooms are all different; some look out over the Río Darro. There's a bar-restaurant too.

TOP END

The following hotels in the Albayzín all have English-speaking staff and offer breakfast for €10. Each one is sumptuously decorated and has its individual stamp.

El Ladrón del Agua (Map p366; ☎ 958 21 50 40; www.ladrondeagua.com; Carrera del Darro 13; s €76-115, d €99-149; ✱ ◻) Smooth, simple and elegant, 'The Water Thief' mixes modern pleasures with antique beauty, crisp sheets, abstract paintings and a slightly snooty attitude.

Casa Morisca Hotel (Map pp358-9; ☎ 958 22 11 00; www.hotelcasamorisca.com; Cuesta de la Victoria 9; s/d interior €90/119, exterior €120/150; ✱) This place occupies a late-15th-century mansion that's centred on a patio with an ornamental pool and wooden galleries. It has 14 rooms, which aren't huge but compensate in style.

Hotel Carmen de Santa Inés (Map p366; ☎ 958 22 63 80; www.carmensantaines.com; Placeta de Porras 7; s/d €95/105, ste €125-200; ✱) This Islamic-era house that was extended in the 16th and 17th centuries is furnished with antiques, and the lovely patio opens onto a garden of myrtles, fruit trees and fountains.

Around Plaza Isabel La Católica

Hotel Palacio de Santa Paula (Map pp358-9; ☎ 902 29 22 93; www.ac-hotels.com; Gran Vía de Colón; r from €205; P ✱ ◻) This opulent and beautiful five-star hotel occupies a former 16th-century convent, some 14th-century houses with patios and wooden balconies, and a 19th-century aristocratic house, all with a contemporary overlay. The rooms sport every top-end luxury you might desire and the hotel also has a fitness centre, sauna and Turkish bath.

Plaza Bib-Rambla & Around

BUDGET

Hostal Lisboa (Map p366; ☎ 958 22 14 14; www
.lisboaweb.com; Plaza del Carmen 27; s/d €32/44, with
shared bathroom €19/29) On the pretty little
Plaza del Carmen and next to the bars
of Calle Navas, this friendly place has 28
clean rooms and funny silver-and-pink
promo key chains. The rooms are large
and basic with granny chequered throws
adorning the beds. All rooms have fans
and winter heating.

Hostal Sevilla (Map p366; ☎ 958 27 85 13;
hostalsevilla@telefonica.net; Calle Fábrica Vieja 18; r €35,
s/d with shared bathroom €18/27; P) Set inside a
young family's house, this friendly, clean,
14-room *hostal* has pretty tilework and
lampshades and a great, large double-room
attic. All rooms have heating.

Hostal Zurita (Map p366; ☎ 958 27 50 20; Plaza
de la Trinidad 7; r €38, s/d with shared bathroom €18/30;
P ⊠) Friendly, super-clean Zurita has 14
quiet, bright and sparkly rooms with winter heating. Nearly all rooms have a little
balcony.

Hostal Meridiano (Map p366; ☎ /fax 958 25 05 44;
www.hostalpensionmeridiano.com; Calle Angulo 9; r €38,
s/d with shared bathroom €18/32, 4-/6-person apt €35/40;
P ⊠ 🖳) Yellow-walled Meridiano has
plants dotting the friendly reception and a
rocking horse looking nostalgic in the corridor. It's run by a helpful couple tuned to
travellers' needs, like internet access and
homely rooms. Six of the 18 rooms have
a bathroom; the rest share a bathroom between two rooms.

Hostal Mesones (Map p366; ☎ 958 26 32 44; Calle
de los Mesones 44; d €40, s/d with shared bathroom €20/32)
Mesones is a top family-run *hostal* with
impeccably clean rooms, power-shower
bathrooms, cute yellow chequered beds
and curtains, and balconies that overlook
the super-central pedestrianised shopping
street below.

Hostal Lima (Map p366; ☎ 958 29 50 29; Calle Laurel
de las Tablas 17; s/d €30/40, apt €50, 2-person ste €55;
P ⊠) Possibly the winner of Granada's
most kitsch *hostal*, this place bombards
with medieval motifs, paintings of Greek
goddesses, chubby cherubs playing flutes,
Cuban sweet-sellers, and Andalucian tiles
here and there. The rooms are in oranges
with lovely new bathrooms and brass bedsteads. It may not have style, but it certainly
has character.

MIDRANGE

Hotel Los Tilos (Map p366; ☎ 958 26 67 12; www.hotel
lostilos.com; Plaza Bib-Rambla 4; s/d €41/65; ⊠) Excellent spacious rooms overlooking Plaza
Bib-Rambla, the cathedral or the Alhambra –
the choice is yours. The reception and
several bathrooms were being renovated
during our research. There's a small but
panoramic roof terrace.

Hotel Reina Cristina (Map p366; ☎ 958 25 32 11;
www.hotelreinacristina.com; Calle Tablas 4; s/d €66/98;
P ⊠) The Reina Cristina is a renovated
19th-century mansion that once belonged
to the Rosales family, friends of Lorca. The
writer spent his last days here before being
arrested and subsequently murdered by the
Nationalists during the civil war. Rooms
are very comfortable and have satellite TV.
There is also a good restaurant.

Hotel Navas (Map p366; ☎ 958 22 59 59; www
.hotelesporcel.com; Calle Navas 22; s/d €72/96; ⊠) An
adequate but unexciting city-centre hotel.
With 44 rooms, it's on a manageable scale,
and all rooms have an external window,
pastel tones, satellite TV and a safety box.
Prices tumble in July and August.

Realejo

Hostal La Ninfa (Map pp358-9; ☎ 958 22 79 85; Campo
del Príncipe s/n; s/d €45/65; ⊠) You'll be bowled
over by the dozens of funny, colourful ceramic stars on the hotel's façade. The place
has tons of character, a pretty foyer-cum-
breakfast-room and 10 clean, cosy rooms.

Hotel Molinos (Map p366; ☎ 958 22 73 67; www
.eel.es/molinos; Calle Molinos 12; s/d €50/73; P ⊠)
The luminous Molinos is neat and clean,
with nine sunny rooms. It once made it
into the *Guinness Book of Records* as the
world's narrowest hotel. Rooftop views are
360-degree.

Alhambra

MIDRANGE

Hotel América (Map p361; ☎ 958 22 74 71; www
.hotelamericagranada.com; Calle Real de la Alhambra 53;
s/d €70/106; ⊙ Mar-Nov; ⊠) This has certainly
got the best location in town if you can't
tear yourself from the Alhambra – it's in its
grounds. Alas, there are only 17 rooms, and
reservations are essential. There's a leafy
patio where good lunches are served.

Hotel Guadalupe (Map pp358-9; ☎ 958 22 34
23; www.hotelguadalupe.es; Avenida Los Alixares s/n;
€76/104; P ⊠) On the Alhambra's doorstep

and with views of the Alhambra or the beautiful olive groves behind, the jolly Guadalupe has 42 spacious, beautifully fitted-out rooms and friendly, efficient staff.

TOP END

Parador de Granada (Map p361; ☎ 958 22 14 40; www .parador.es; Calle Real de la Alhambra s/n; s/d €182/228; **P ☒**) This is the Alhambra's San Francisco monastery, converted into a hotel. Originally built in the time of the Catholic Monarchs, whose initial burial place was here, it's the most expensive parador in Spain. You can't beat its location within the Alhambra and its historical connections. Book ahead.

Sacromonte

Cuevas El Abanico (Map pp358-9; ☎ /fax 958 22 61 99, 608 848497; www.el-abanico.com; Vereda de Enmedio 89, Sacromonte; s/d/tr €58/58/73, 4-person 2-bedroom cave €88; **P**) For something different, try the cave lodgings in the Sacromonte *gitano* neighbourhood. The five cave apartments are comfortable and kitted out with heating, a kitchen, a bathroom, hot water and outdoor terraces. There's normally a two-night minimum stay.

Around Granada

Camping Reina Isabel (Map pp358-9; ☎ 958 59 00 41; Carretera Granada-La Zubia Km 4; camping per adult/tent/car €4/4/4; **☒**) About 5km south of the centre, Reina Isabel is clean, with good bathrooms. Take La Zubia exit from the Ronda Sur ring road.

Camping Sierra Nevada (Map pp358-9; ☎ 958 15 00 62; Avenida de Madrid 107; camping per adult/tent/car €5/5.50/5.50; **☒**) A short walk from the bus station, 2.5km northwest of the centre, this camping ground has big, clean bathrooms and a laundry. Bus 3 runs between here and Gran Vía de Colón in the city centre.

EATING

Here's a place where gastronomy stays down to earth, but still experiments. Granada is one of the last bastions of that fantastic practice of free tapas with every drink. Take note: the more you drink, the better the tapas become. After you order each drink, you'll hear the barman shouting: '*primera!*', '*segunda!*' or '*tercera!*' which means your first, second, and third tapas are on their way. Depending on where you are, you can get Spanish beans, Arabic couscous, Brazilian chicken or *haute cuisine* tapas, served in dinky dishes.

Top tapas areas include the streets off Calle de Elvira (near Plaza Nueva), south of the cathedral and Calle Navas. The terrace tables on Plaza Nueva, Paseo de los Tristes and Plaza Bib-Rambla are decent, but often very touristy. Alternatively, get some North African nosh up or down the incense-infused Calle Calderería Nueva/Vieja.

A mesmerising experience is dining in the Albayzín. The reward for finding a restaurant with a terrace is a spectacular view of the Alhambra, floodlit at night, though the food may not be as amazing as the views and the prices can be high.

Calle de Elvira, Plaza Nueva & Around

Al Andalus (Map p366; ☎ 958 22 67 30; Calle de Elvira; mains €3-6) The first in a range of over-the-counter, Arabic fast-food-feast kebab houses. This place looks onto Plaza Nueva and does a mean parcel of falafel in pitta (€3).

Café Central (Map p366; ☎ 958 22 97 06; Calle de Elvira; raciones €4.50-8.50) At the beginning of the Calle de Elvira trail, this is a good place for perking up with a strong morning coffee (€1.60) for breakfast, or after a night out.

Bodegas Castañeda (Map p366; Calle Almireceros s/n; raciones from €6) An institution among locals and tourists alike, this place whips up traditional food in a typical bodega (traditional wine bar) setting. Get yourself some Spanish tortilla and *alioli* (aïoli; garlic mayonnaise).

Antigua Bodega Castañeda (Map p366; Calle de Elvira s/n; raciones €6.90-13.50) If the barrels of potent 'Costa' wine from the Sierra de la Contraviesa tempt you to the point of befuddlement, then sober up with a few *montaditos* (small sandwiches; €3.20 to €4.50).

THE AUTHOR'S CHOICE

Los Diamantes (Map p366; ☎ 958 22 70 70; Calle Navas 26; media-raciones €6) This place is reason alone to come to Granada: it's a heaven for anyone who loves fish and seafood. The plates are heaped with an amazing mix of *pescado frito* (fried fish) and prawns to die for. A little *caña* (small glass of beer) makes perfect company.

GRANADA PROVINCE

Vía Colón (Map p366; ☎ 958 22 98 42; Gran Vía de Colón 13; mains €10-17; ◷ 8am-1am) A great place for a rich breakfast, where apron-clad, rushing waiters are overlooked by cherubs and angels. There are also meaty mains, such as the delicious *jamón ibérico de bellota* (ham made from pigs fed on *bellotas*, or acorns; €17).

Jamones Castellano (Map p366; cnr Calles Almireceros & Joaquín Costa) This is a perfect delicatessen for picnic preparation – get some *jamón serrano* (mountain-cured ham), *pimientos del piquillo* (preserved charred peppers) and some cheese for a perfect, rhyming *bocadillo* (filled roll).

For fresh fruit and veg head for the large, covered **Mercado Central San Agustín** (Map p366; Calle San Agustín), a block west of the cathedral. Inhale the lingering aroma of the herb and spice stalls along the Calle Cárcel Baja side of the cathedral. The bulging sacks contain everything from sage to saffron.

Alhambra

Parador de Granada (Map p361; ☎ 958 22 14 40; Calle Real de Alhambra s/n; sandwiches from €5; ◷ 11am-11pm) The charming Parador de Granada is a swanky place to indulge in fine fare or a juicy *bocadillo* as you contemplate the Alhambra's magnificence. The whole experience will leave you feeling rather special – as intended.

Albayzín

The labyrinthine Albayzín contains a wealth of eateries, all tucked away in the narrow streets – some behind gates with inconspicuous bells and missable signs.

Kasbah (Map p366; Calle Calderería Nueva 4; teas €1.80-2.40) Belly-dancing spectacles take place in this candlelit tea den, among glimmering cushions and customers, invisible through the sweet smoke of the hookah. Match cream-topped Arabic special tea (€2.40) with a doubly fattening cream-and-chocolate crepe (€2.30) and dance the calories off later.

Tetería As-Sirat (Map p366; Calle Calderería Nueva 4; teas €2-3) For a lung-filling hookah and tea experience try this little place next door to Kasbah. Among a head-spinning variety of teas you'll find Cocktail Cleopatra (€3) or a fruity mango infusion (€2), which complements the honey-and-orange crepe (€3) nicely.

Restaurante Arrayanes (Map p366; ☎ 958 22 84 01; Cuesta Marañas 4; mains €7-17; ◷ from 8pm) An excellent North African restaurant that will make you weep with joy over its lamb tagine, where wrinkly dates snuggle next to the tender meat and the whole affair is sprinkled with blanched almonds (€10). The chicken couscous melts like snowflakes in your mouth. The décor is a healthy mix of cushions and little mirrors and there's no alcohol.

El Agua (Map pp358-9; ☎ 958 22 33 58; Plaza Aljibe de Trillo 7; fondues per person €14-19, minimum 2 people; ◷ 1.30-3.30pm & 8-11.30pm Wed-Mon, 8-11.30pm Tue) Wild fondue feasts are the mainstay of this first-rate restaurant. Melt along with the cheese as you dunk your chunks of juicy *jamón* and take in the fabulous Alhambra views.

Terraza las Tomasas (Map pp358-9; ☎ 958 22 41 08; Carril de San Agustín 4; mains €16-20; ◷ 1.30-3.30pm Mon-Tue, 1.30-3.30pm & 8.30-11pm Wed-Sat) For a touch of adventure and exclusivity, ring the little bell to get in here and enjoy the romantic views of the Alhambra, impeccable service and commendable food. Try the *granadino* favourite, tortilla Sacromonte (€9 for starter).

Plaza Bib-Rambla & Around

Poë (Map p366; Calle Paz; media-ración €3) Imagination, Brazilian influence and a desire for something different has resulted in a great mix of excellent free tapas, such as *feijoada* (bean and rice stew) or chicken stew with polenta, and a trendy international vibe. Hang out at the bar, chat to others and enjoy this gem.

Om-Kalsum (Map p366; Calle Jardines 17; media-ración €3) Just around the corner from Poë and even more exciting, Om-Kalsum is a tapas bar gone North African, so you get mini-lamb tagines, gorgeous bite-sized chicken kebabs in pitta bread, and a stomach-full of couscous with caramelised onion and swollen sultanas. A satisfied international crowd reclines full on the cushioned seats.

Guerrero (Map p366; ☎ 958 28 14 60; Plaza de la Trinidad 7; raciones €5.50-6.50) A low-key café-bar and many a hungover person's breakfast choice, this is where you come for *tostadas* (€1.50), freshly squeezed orange juice and a tall glass of *café con leche* (café latte).

Reca (Map p366; ☎ 636 891189; Plaza de la Trinidad s/n; mains €8) Relatively new and already one of Granada's top tapas places, Reca is always packed with people hungering after their wonderfully presented, modern dishes. Miraculously and thankfully it is about the only bar in the area that serves food until 5pm, without a break in the middle of the day.

Cunini (Map p366; ☎ 958 25 07 77; Calle Pescadería 14; menú €18) A good reputation surrounds this little upmarket seafood bar and restaurant on the old Fishmonger Square, where you can get first-class fish and seafood as tapas, standing at the bar, or sit down and really indulge in the restaurant at the back.

DRINKING

Granada buzzes with floorboard-bashing flamenco dancers, bottle-clinking travellers and grooving students out on the pull. The best areas for drinking are Calle de Elvira and around the university. Other chilled bars line the Río Darro at the base of the Albayzín, and Campo del Príncipe attracts a sophisticated bunch.

El Rincón de Michael Landon (Map pp358-9; Calle Rector García Duarte 2; beer €1.50; ⏰ noon-4pm & 8pm-1am Mon-Sat, 8m-1am Sun) In the midst of Granada's student life, this funny bar is dedicated to retro kitsch and the bizarrely cult star of *The Little House on the Prairie*. The hip bunch that hangs out here comes for the simple tapas (with names such as JR – *Jamón* & Roquefort), beer, and music blasting from the small stereo.

Anaïs Café (Map p366; Calle Buensuceso 13; glass of house wine €1.50; ⏰ 9am-1pm) This is a bar for bookworms with a penchant for imbibing, literary evenings and tarot readings, as well as mindless fun.

Bodegas Castañeda (Map p366; Calle Almireceros; glass of house wine €1.50) and **Antigua Bodega Castañeda** (Map p366; Calle de Elvira; glass of house wine €1.50) are the most inviting bars, with out-of-the-barrel wine and bites of tapas to keep things going.

El Círculo (Map p366; Calle de Elvira; beer €1.50) One of Calle de Elvira's treasures, El Círculo is a calm and unpretentious tapas bar with a slightly retro feel. After one of the large spirit measures you might be wishing there were more seats, though.

Bagdad Café (Map pp358-9; Coca de San Andrés; glass of house wine €1.50; ⏰ from 6pm) A dirty side street and a derelict feel won't put off those hunting for Granada's alternative scene.

Strain to hear the pulsing beat through the black door and then make your way into the chilled den.

Café Bar Elvira (Map pp358-9; Calle de Elvira 85; beer €1; ⏰ from noon) A hang-out for dreadlocks, whistle and dog-on-a-bit-of-string–type crowd, the café's atmosphere is jolly and there's drinking, singing and shouting all day – partly thanks to the large spirit measures and the popular mixers.

El Rincón de San Pedro (Map pp358-9; Carrera del Darro 12; ⏰ from noon) Turquoise walls and slate tiles give this hip bar a cooling feel to complement the sound of the Río Darro trickling past. Gaze out of the back doors onto the greenery at the base of the Alhambra as you sip a refreshing gin and tonic (€4.50).

ENTERTAINMENT

There's lots to get you dancing in Granada: it's home to Andalucía's best nightclub, and the city's large university population includes plenty of aspiring musicians who keep the gig circuit alive. Look out for posters and leaflets advertising live music and nontouristy flamenco. The bi-weekly flyer *Yuzin* (www.yuzin.com) lists many live-music venues, some of which are also dance clubs where DJs spin the latest tracks. The excellent monthly *Guía de Granada* (€1), available from kiosks, lists entertainment venues and places to eat, including tapas bars.

Posters listing forthcoming cultural events can be viewed on the notice board in the foyer of **La Madraza** (Map p366; Calle Oficios), located opposite the Capilla Real.

Nightclubs

Granada 10 (Map p366; Calle Cárcel Baja; admission €6; ⏰ from midnight) A glittery converted cinema is now Granada's top club for the glam crowd, who recline on the gold sofas and go crazy to cheesy Spanish pop tunes.

Enano Rojo (Map pp358-9; Calle de Elvira 91; ⏰ from 10pm) Gritty and grungy Enano Rojo, with its toadstool emblem, plays jazz and funk to a hip crowd on weekends. Midweek it's a little tamer and the later you get here the better.

Industrial Copera (☎ 958 25 84 49; www.industrial copera.net; Carretera Armilla, Calle la Paz, warehouse 7; admission varied; ⏰ 11pm-late) The award-winning Industrial Copera has been voted Andalucía's best club. It is a warehouse where serious clubbers go for serious all-nighters. The

GRANADA'S TOP FIVE FLAMENCO HAUNTS

It's difficult to see flamenco that's not geared to tourists but some shows are more authentic than others and attract Spaniards as well as foreigners.

Centro de Interpretación de Sacromonte (Map pp358–9; ☎ 958 21 51 20; www.sacromontegranada .com; Barranco de los Negros s/n; ☻ 10am-2pm & 5-9pm Tue-Fri, 10am-9pm Sat & Sun summer, 10am-2pm & 4-7pm Tue-Fri & 10am-7pm Sat & Sun winter) In summer the flamenco nights here are well worth catching. For more information on the centre, see the boxed text, p370.

El Eshavira (Map pp358–9; ☎ 958 29 08 29; www.eshavira.com; Postigo de la Cuna 2) Top local performers come to bash the guitar strings or floorboards in this boho hang-out in the Albayzín.

El Upsetter (Map p366; ☎ 958 22 72 96; Carrera del Darro 7; admission €10) Live flamenco on Saturday nights and a good chance to miss the tourists.

Los Tarantos (Map pp358–9; ☎ day 958 22 45 25, night 958 22 24 92; Camino del Sacromonte 9; admission €21) Though it's geared towards tourists, the midnight shows on Friday and Saturday can still be promising and draw fewer foreigners. For these shows, you can prebook tickets through hotels and travel agencies. Wear your dancing shoes if you want to sit in the first few rows: you'll be pulled up on stage before you know it!

Peña de la Platería (Map pp358-9; ☎ 958 21 06 50; Placeta de Toqueros 7) Buried deep in the Albayzín warren, Peña de la Platería is a genuine aficionados' club with a large outdoor patio. Catch a 9.30pm performance on Thursday or Saturday.

music is varied, so look out for posters or check their site, but count on lots of techno, a fair dose of hip-hop, and DJs from Ibiza, Madrid and Barcelona. Get a cab there and keep their number for the return journey.

Planta Baja (Map p366; www.plantabaja.net; Calle Horno de Abad 11; admission €5; ☻ 12.30am-6am Tue-Sat) Planta Baja's popularity never seems to wane, and it's no wonder since it caters to such a diverse crowd *and* has top DJs like Vadim. There's old school, hip-hop, funk and electroglam downstairs, and lazy lounge sessions on the top floor.

Afrodisia (Map pp358-9; www.afrodisiaclub.com; Calle Almona del Boquerón; admission free; ☻ 11pm-late) If you dig Granada's ganja-driven scene, this is where you'll find a like-minded lot. Lots of groovin' and lovin' takes place on the dancefloor and DJs spin 'original black sounds' aka hip-hop, ska and reggae, funk and even jazz on Sundays.

Sugar Pop (Map pp358-9; Calle del Gran Capitan 25; admission €5; ☻ 11pm-late) This place has a good vibe and draws a young, studenty crowd that loves indie music and quality pop DJs.

El Camborio (Map pp358-9; ☎ 958 22 12 15; Camino del Sacromonte 47; admission €6; ☻ from 11pm Sat & Sun) Mixing modern sounds with prehistoric surroundings, El Camborio has two dance floors with one at cave level.

Live Music
El Eshavira (Map pp358-9; ☎ 958 29 08 29; www.eshavira.com; Postigo de la Cuna 2; ☻ from 10pm) Just off

Calle Azacayas, duck down the spooky alley, battle with the hefty door and adopt the *granadino* penchant for dark, smoky haunts that ooze cool jazz and sultry flamenco.

El Upsetter (Map p366; ☎ 958 22 72 96; Carrera del Darro 7; admission for flamenco show €10; ☻ 11pm-late) For a decent Saturday-night flamenco show head to El Upsetter, which doubles as a dreadlock-swinging reggae bar for the rest of the week.

Tetería del Hammam (Map p366; ☎ 958 22 99 78; www.hammamspain.com/granada in Spanish; Calle Santa Ana 16; ☻ 8pm-late) If heel-banging is not your thing and you prefer midriff movement, there's belly dancing here on Thursday nights.

Concerts & Theatre
Centro Cultural Manuel de Falla (Map p361; ☎ 958 22 00 22; Paseo de los Mártires s/n) A haven for lovers of classical music, this venue right near the Alhambra presents weekly orchestral concerts.

The **Teatro Alhambra** (Map pp358-9; ☎ 958 22 04 47; Calle de Molinos 56) and the more central **Teatro Isabel La Católica** (Map p366; ☎ 958 22 15 14; Acera del Casino) both have ongoing programmes of theatre and concerts (and sometimes flamenco).

SHOPPING
Excellent, classic pots with their distinctive *granadino* blue-and-white glazing can be bought at **Cerámica Fabre** (Map p366; Calle Pescadería s/n). A distinctive local craft is *taracea*

(marquetry), used on boxes, tables, chess sets and more – the best have shell, silver or mother-of-pearl inlays. Marquetry experts can be seen at work in **Laguna Taller de Taracea** (Map p361), opposite the Iglesia de Santa María in the Alhambra. Places to look out for Granada handicrafts include the Alcaicería, the Albayzín and Cuesta de Gomérez. Also try the government-run Artespaña in the Corral del Carbón (p366). The Plaza Nueva area is awash with jewellery vendors, selling from rugs laid out on the footpath, and ethnic-clothes shops.

Get a handmade guitar for those flamenco classes from **Manuel L Bellido** (Map p366; Calle Molinos) or just see the *guitarrero* (guitar maker) at work.

For general shopping, trendy clothes and ever-delightful Spanish shoes, try pedestrianised Calle de los Mesones, or **El Corte Inglés** (Map p366; Acera del Darro).

GETTING THERE & AWAY

Air

Iberia (Map p366; ☎ 958 22 75 92; Plaza Isabel La Católica 2) has flights daily to/from Madrid and Barcelona.

From the UK, two low-cost, web-based airlines fly to Granada daily: **Ryanair** (www.rynanair.com) and **Monarch Airlines** (www.flymonarch.com).

Bus

Granada's **bus station** (Map pp358-9; Carretera de Jaén) is almost 3km northwest of the city centre. All services operate from here except for a few to nearby destinations such as Fuente Vaqueros. **Alsina Graells** (☎ 958 18 54 80) runs buses to the following destinations:

Destination	Cost	Duration	Daily Frequency
Baza	€8	2hr	up to 8
Córdoba	€12	3hr	9
Guadix	€4.50	1hr	up to 14
Málaga	€9	1½hr	16
Mojácar	€15	4hr	2
Seville	€18	3hr	10

Alsina also handles buses heading to Las Alpujarras (p387), as well as destinations in Jaén province and on the Granada, Málaga and Almería coasts, and to Madrid (€15, five to six hours, 10 to 13 daily).

Alsa (☎ 902 42 22 42; www.alsa.es) runs buses up the Mediterranean coast as far as Barcelona (€60 to €70, seven to 10 hours, five daily). It also runs buses to many international destinations.

Car & Motorcycle

ATA Rent A Car (Map p366; ☎ 958 22 40 04; Plaza Cuchilleros 1) has small cars for one/two/seven days for €71/83/219.

Train

The **station** (Map pp358-9; ☎ 958 20 40 00; Avenida de Andaluces) is 1.5km west of the centre, off Avenida de la Constitución. Four trains

DRIVING IN GRANADA: IT WILL DRIVE YOU AROUND THE BEND

Granada's traffic system has been designed to give the uninitiated a nervous breakdown. Vehicle access to the Plaza Nueva area (and therefore to the narrow streets leading up from Plaza Nueva to the Alhambra and the Albayzín) is restricted by red lights and little black posts known as *pilonas*, which block certain streets during certain times of day. Residents and other authorised drivers slot cards into a box, causing the posts to slide down into the ground to let one car (only) pass. You'll see the warning sign *'Obstáculos en calzada a 20 metros'* and will have to detour. The only exception is if you are going to stay at one of the Plaza Nueva area hotels – in which case, press the button by your hotel's name beside the *pilonas* to speak with your hotel's reception, which will be able to lower the *pilonas* for you.

It's a good idea to ask advice beforehand from your hotel about parking. Some hotels have their own parking facilities for which they might charge you anything from €7.50 per day. Alternatively, there are underground car parks such as **Parking San Agustín** (Map p366; Calle San Agustín; per hr/day €1/16), just off Gran Vía de Colón, and **Parking Plaza Puerta Real** (Map p366; Acera del Darro; per hr/day €1/12), as well as the Alhambra car parks (see p362). Free parking can be found in the little streets across the river, on the eastern side of town, but you'll have to search, remember where you parked, and walk back.

GRANADA PROVINCE

run daily to/from Seville (€20, three hours) and Almería (€13, 2¼ hours) via Guadix. Three go to Ronda (€11, three hours) and Algeciras (€17, four to 4½ hours). For Málaga (€12, 2½ hours) or Córdoba (€14, four hours) take an Algeciras train and change at Bobadilla (€7, 1½ hours). Five trains go to Linares-Baeza daily (€10 to €19, three hours), and one or two each to Madrid (€31 to €35, six hours), Valencia (€42 to €62, 7½ to eight hours) and Barcelona (€52 to €125, 12 to 14½ hours).

GETTING AROUND
To/From the Airport
The **airport** (Map pp358-9; ☎ 902 40 05 00) is 17km west of the city on the A92. At least five daily buses (€3), operated by **Autocares J González** (☎ 958 49 01 64), run between the airport and a stop near the Palacio de Congresos, stopping in the centre on Gran Vía de Colón, where a schedule is posted at the outbound stop, opposite the cathedral (see the Central Granada map, p366). A taxi costs around €18 to €20.

Bus
City buses cost €0.90. Tourist offices give out a leaflet showing routes. The Bono Turístico voucher (see p360) includes nine bus rides.

Bus 3 runs between the bus station and Gran Vía de Colón in the centre. To reach the centre from the train station, walk straight ahead to Avenida de la Constitución and pick up buses 4, 6, 7, 9 or 11 going to the right (east). From the centre (Gran Vía de Colón) to the train station, take No 3, 4, 6, 9 or 11.

Taxi
Taxis line up on Plaza Nueva. Most fares within the city cost between €4.50 and €7.50. To call a taxi, ring **Teleradio taxi** (☎ 958 28 06 54).

AROUND GRANADA

Granada is surrounded by a fertile plain known as La Vega, planted with poplar groves and crops ranging from potatoes and corn to melons and tobacco. La Vega has always been vital to the city and was an inspiration to the writer Federico García

Lorca, who was born and died here. The **Parque Federico García Lorca**, a memorial park between the villages of Víznar and Alfacar (about 2.5km from each), marks the site where Lorca and hundreds – possibly thousands – of others are believed to have been shot and buried by the Nationalists at the start of the civil war.

FUENTE VAQUEROS
The house where Lorca was born in 1898, in Fuente Vaqueros village, 17km west of Granada, is now the **Museo Casa Natal Federico García Lorca** (☎ 958 51 64 53; www.museogarcia lorca.org; Calle Poeta Federico García Lorca 4; admission €1.80; ☺ guided visits hourly 10am-1pm & 5-7pm Tue-Sun Apr-Jun, 10am-2pm & 6-8pm Tue-Sun Jul-Sep, 10am-1pm & 4-6pm Tue-Sun Oct-Mar). The place brings his spirit alive, with numerous charming photos, posters and costumes for plays that he wrote and directed, and paintings illustrating his poems. A short video captures him in action with the touring Teatro Barraca.

Buses to Fuente Vaqueros (€1.50, 20 minutes) by **Ureña** (☎ 958 45 41 54) leave from Avenida de Andaluces in front of Granada train station. Departures from Granada at the time of writing were at 9am and 11am, then hourly from 1pm to 8pm except 4pm, Monday to Friday, and at 9am, 11am, 1pm and 5pm on Saturday, Sunday and holidays.

EAST OF GRANADA

The A92 northeast of Granada crosses the forested, hilly Parque Natural Sierra de Huétor before entering an increasingly arid landscape. Outside Guadix the A92 veers southeast towards Almería, crossing the Marquesado de Zenete district below the northern flank of the Sierra Nevada, while the A92N heads northeast across the Altiplano, Granada's 'High Plain', which breaks out into mountains here and there and affords superb long-distance views on the way to northern Almería province.

GUADIX
pop 20,135 / elevation 915m
Guadix (gwah-*deeks*), 55km from Granada, is a place mainly famous for the fact that it has the biggest concentration of cave dwellings in eastern Granada – not prehistoric

remnants but the homes of about 3000 present-day townsfolk. It's a great place to stay the night (in a cave) and try out the town's excellent, tourist-free tapas bars.

Information

There's a **tourist office** (☎ 958 66 26 65; Carretera de Granada s/n; ☺ 9am-3pm Mon, 9am-4pm Tue-Fri, 10am-2pm Sat) on the Granada road leaving the town centre and an **information office** (☎ 670 20 83 53; ☺ 9am-3pm Mon, 9am-4pm Tue-Fri, 10am-2pm Sat) by the cathedral, where multilingual German-born Tania provides general information and takes you around on walking tours (€10 per person).

Sights

At the centre of Guadix is a fine sandstone **cathedral** (Calle Santa María del Buen Aire; admission €2; ☺ 10.30am-1pm & 2-7pm Mon-Sat, 9.30am-1pm Sun), built between the 16th and 18th centuries on the site of the town's former main mosque in a mix of Gothic, Renaissance and baroque styles. Nearby, **Plaza de las Palomas** is beautiful when floodlit at night.

A short distance south you'll find the 10th- and 11th-century Islamic castle, the **Alcazaba** (Calle Barradas 3; admission €1.20; ☺ 11am-2pm & 4-6.30pm Tue-Sat, 10am-2pm Sun), which gives views over the main cave quarter, the Barriada de las Cuevas, some 700m south.

The typical 21st-century cave has a whitewashed wall across the entrance, a chimney and TV aerial protruding from the top, and all mod cons inside. Some have many rooms. The caves maintain a comfortable temperature of around 18°C year-round. The **Cueva Museo Municipal** (☎ 958 66 08 08; Plaza de Padre Poveda; admission €1.50; ☺ 10am-2pm & 4-6pm Mon-Sat, 10am-2pm Sun & holidays), in the Barriada de las Cuevas, recreates typical cave life.

Sleeping & Eating

Cuevas Pedro Antonio de Alarcón (☎ 958 66 49 86; www.cuevaspedroantonio.com; Barriada San Torcuato; s/d/q €40/61/104; P ☒) The genuine Guadix experience (ie sleeping in a cave) is best at this comfy, modern cave-apartment-hotel with a pool and restaurant, 3km from the town centre, along the Murcia road heading towards the A92 (look for 'Alojamiento en Cuevas' signs).

Hotel Comercio (☎ 958 66 05 00; www.hotelcomercio.com; Calle Mira de Amezcua 3; s €48.15, d €55-64; ☒)

DETOUR: ORCE

The dusty Altiplano village of Orce styles itself as the 'Cradle of European Humankind'. A fossilised bone fragment possibly between one and two million years old, found in 1982 at nearby Venta Micena, may be part of the skull of an infant *Homo erectus*, an ancestor of *Homo sapiens*. If so, the bit of bone would be the oldest-known human remnant in Europe. The many sceptics, however, say the 'Hombre de Orce' (Orce Man) fragment more likely came from a horse or deer and could be less than a million years old. Even so, Orce can still claim Spain's oldest evidence of human presence in the form of stone tools that are 1.3 million years old.

For most of the last four million years, much of the Hoya de Baza, the now arid basin in which the Baza–Orce area lies, was a lake. Wildlife drinking at the edge of the lake was vulnerable to attack by larger animals, and the relics of such encounters, between one and two million years ago, have been found at Venta Micena and nearby sites. The uncovered fossilised bones include dozens of species, including the mammoth, rhinoceros, sabre-tooth tiger, hippopotamus, giant hyena, wolf, bear, elephant and buffalo.

A good selection of the finds – including enormous mammoths' teeth and a replica of the 'Hombre de Orce' fragment (the original is under lock and key in Orce town hall – are on show in Orce's interesting **Museo de Prehistoria y Paleontología** (☎ 958 74 61 01; admission €1.50; ☺ 11am-2pm Tue-Sun year-round, 6-8pm Tue-Sun Jun-Sep, 4-6pm Tue-Sun Oct-May), in an Islamic castle just off the village's central square.

Orce makes an interesting detour if you are driving between Granada/Guadix/Baza and the Los Vélez area of northern Almería province. Eighteen kilometres east of Baza on the A92N, turn north along the A330 towards Huéscar. After 23km, turn east along the SE34 for Orce (6km away).

Continuing east from Orce it's a further 30km to María, the first Los Vélez village. As you cross the empty plains between Orce and María, it's quite a thrill to know that this landscape was once roamed by the likes of mammoths, sabre-tooth tigers and elephants.

If caves don't rock your boat, check into this long-standing central hotel with comfy rooms and a fine restaurant.

Churrería Serrano (Puerta del Parque; ☽ breakfast) For breakfast, get takeaway *churros con chocolate* (doughnuts and hot chocolate; €1 to €2) or sit inside and check out the characters who run this place.

La Bodeguita (Calle Doctor Pulido 4; drink & tapa €1) Guadix also has some remarkable tapas bars, but La Bodeguita is one of the best. Here, old men and families enjoy delicious tapas in simple surroundings and eat baked spuds, and raw *habas* (broad beans) when in season.

Bodega Calatrava (Calle La Tribuna s/n; drink & tapa €1.50, ración €5) The other top tapas spot in town, where you can have excellent tapas such as juicy fried prawns, or sit down and order some *raciones*.

Getting There & Away

Guadix is about one hour from Granada (bus €4.50, train €6) and 1½ hours from Almería (bus €7.50, train €6 to €14); there are at least nine buses and four trains daily in each direction. At least two daily buses head to Baza (€4, one hour) and Mojácar (€11, three hours). The **bus station** (☎ 958 66 06 57; Calle Concepción Arenal) is off Avenida Medina Olmos, about 700m southeast of the centre. The train station is off the Murcia road, about 2km northeast of the town centre.

MARQUESADO DE ZENETE

This bleak, flat area between Guadix and the Sierra Nevada was a prosperous agricultural district in Islamic times, awarded to Cardinal de Mendoza, chief adviser to the Catholic Monarchs during the war against Granada in the Reconquista times. His illegitimate son Rodrigo de Mendoza became its first *marqués* (marquis).

The main town, Jerez del Marquesado, is a starting point for ventures into the high Sierra Nevada. Thirteen kilometres east of Jerez, the forbidding **Castillo de La Calahorra** (admission €3; ☽ 10am-1pm & 4-6pm Wed, other times by appointment with caretaker Antonio Trivaldo ☎ 958 67 70 98) looms above the village of La Calahorra. The castle was built between 1509 and 1512 by Rodrigo de Mendoza, whose tempestuous life included a spell in Italy unsuccessfully wooing Lucrezia Borgia. The

building's domed corner towers and blank walls enclose an amazingly elegant Italian Renaissance courtyard which has a staircase of Carrara marble. There are at least two *hostales* and one hotel to be found in La Calahorra village, from which the A337 heads south over the Puerto de la Ragua pass to Las Alpujarras.

BAZA
pop 21,000 / elevation 850m
The market town of Baza, 44km northeast of Guadix, dates back to Iberian times. Its attractive Plaza Mayor is dominated by the 16th-century **Iglesia Concatedral de la Encarnación**. Baza's **tourist office** (☎ 958 86 13 25; Plaza Mayor 2; ☽ 10am-2pm & 4-6.30pm except holidays) is in the same building as the town's good **Museo Municipal** (☎ 958 70 35 55; admission €1.20; ☽ 10am-2pm & 4-6.30pm except holidays), whose mainly archaeological collection includes a copy of the *Dama de Baza*, a person-sized Iberian goddess statue unearthed locally in 1971 (the original is housed in Madrid's Museo Arqueológico Nacional).

In town, about 500m south of Plaza Mayor, is the friendly **Hostal Anabel** (☎ 958 86 09 98; Calle María de Luna s/n; s/d €22/38; ✂), but the real treat is the mini-cave resort **Cuevas Al Jatib** (☎ 958 34 22 48; www.aljatib.com; Arroyo Cúrcal s/n; 2-person cave €75-95, 4-/6-person cave €89/143; P 🚹) on the edge of town, with comfortable accommodation in five well-equipped caves, plus Arab baths, a tearoom, a restaurant, a play-cave for kids and a cave adapted for wheelchair users.

The **bus station** (☎ 958 70 21 03; Calle Reyes Católicos) is 200m north of Plaza Mayor. There are about 15 buses a day to/from Guadix (€3.50, one hour) and Granada (€8, two hours) in one direction and Vélez Rubio (€4.50, 1½ hours) in the other.

SIERRA NEVADA

The Sierra Nevada range, with mainland Spain's highest peak, Mulhacén (3479m), forms an almost year-round snowy backdrop to Granada. The range extends about 75km from west to east, crossing from Granada into Almería province.

All the highest peaks (3000m or more) are towards the range's western (Granada) end, and the Estación de Esquí Sierra Nevada (Sierra Nevada Ski Station), Europe's most southerly and one of Spain's best, stands on its northern flank. In the warmer seasons the mountains and the valleys beneath them (especially Las Alpujarras, to the south) offer wonderful walking.

The best overall maps of the area are Editorial Alpina's *Sierra Nevada, La Alpujarra* (1:40,000) and Editorial Penibética's *Sierra Nevada* (1:50,000). Both come with booklets, in English or Spanish, describing walking, biking and skiing routes.

The ideal period for walking in the high mountains is early July to early September: only then is the high ground reliably snow-free and the weather relatively settled. Unfortunately this doesn't coincide with the most comfortable months down in the valleys (see p387). Late June/early July and the first half of September are the best compromise periods. The Sierra Nevada is a serious mountain range: temperatures on the summits average 14°C less than in the highest Alpujarras villages. You should come well equipped, and prepared for cloud, rain or strong, icy winds at *any* time.

Nearly all the upper reaches of the Sierra Nevada are included in the 862-sq-km Parque Nacional Sierra Nevada, the biggest of Spain's dozen national parks. This rare high-altitude environment is home to 2100 of Spain's 7000 plant species, among them unique types of crocus, narcissus, thistle, clover, poppy and gentian. Andalucía's largest ibex population (about 5000) is here, too – in summer, walkers may come across ibex anywhere above about 2800m.

Surrounding the national park at lower altitudes is the 848-sq-km Parque Natural Sierra Nevada, with a lesser degree of protection.

ESTACIÓN DE ESQUÍ SIERRA NEVADA

The **ski station** (☎ 902 70 80 90; www.sierranevadaski .com in Spanish), at Pradollano, 33km from Granada on the A395, is an ugly modern construction and very crowded on weekends and holidays in the ski season (when it has a thumping nightlife), but the skiing and facilities are good enough to have hosted the World Alpine Skiing championships in 1996 and now a World Cup event every year. Snow conditions and weather are frequently better than in more northerly Spanish ski resorts.

Information

About 10km before the ski station is the **Centro de Visitantes El Dornajo** (☎ 958 34 06 25; ⏱ 10am-2pm & 6-8pm Apr-Sep, 10am-2pm & 4-6pm Oct-Mar), with plenty of Sierra Nevada information, and maps for sale.

Activities

The ski season normally lasts from December to April or early May. *Forfaits* (lift passes; one day for €27 to €35) and accommodation cost the least in the 'promotional' periods at the beginning and end of the season, and cost the most around Christmas/New Year and other holiday periods, and on Saturday and Sunday from January to March.

The station has 85 marked downhill runs – five graded black (very difficult), 36 red (difficult), 35 blue (easy) and 10 green (very easy). The highest start almost at the top of 3395m Veleta, the second-highest peak

---

NOT JUST FOR SKIERS

The ski station is not just for skiers. You can ice-skate (€7.50 per hour, including skate rental), ride a dog-sled (€40 per person per half-hour), go snowshoeing (€34 per two hours) and even toboggan on giant inner tubes (€15 per half-hour). Remember that nonskiers need to wrap up just as warmly as skiers!

The Al-Andalus cable car has wheelchair access, and skiing equipment for the disabled is available near its upper station.

Outside the ski season the **Sierra Nevada Activa programme** (www.sierranevadaactiva.com) lays on a host of warmer-weather activities. Options include mountain biking to Trevélez (one day €78) or the coast (two days €170); a four-day trek to several of the range's 3000m-plus peaks (€346); a day's horse ride to the Cañada de Siete Lagunas (€80); and canyoning on the Río Verde above Almuñécar (€75 per day). In winter it offers cross-country skiing expeditions and guided ascents of the high peaks.

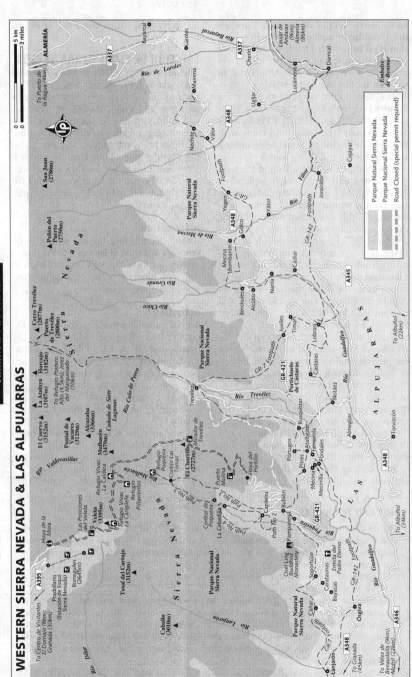

WESTERN SIERRA NEVADA & LAS ALPUJARRAS

in the Sierra Nevada. Cable cars (€10 return for nonskiers) run up from Pradollano (2100m) to Borreguiles (2645m); other lifts go higher. There are cross-country routes, too, and a dedicated snowboard area above Borreguiles.

Kit yourself out at the resort's numerous ski-hire shops. Skis, boots and poles cost €21 for one day; a snowboard and boots cost €24. The resort has several ski and snowboard schools: a six-hour weekend course is €60.

Sleeping & Eating

The ski station has around 20 hotels, *hostales* and apartment-hotels. None is cheap (double rooms start at around €80) and reservations are always advisable. The best deals are ski packages, bookable through the station's website or phone number, which start at around €150 per person for two days and two nights with half-board and lift passes. Book two weeks ahead, if you can.

There are only a limited number of places to stay and eat that remain open outside of the ski season.

Albergue Juvenil Sierra Nevada (☎ 958 48 03 05; Calle Peñones 22; adult/under 26yr incl breakfast ski season €18/14, rest of year €12.25/9.05; 🖳) A youth hostel near the top of the ski station, with 341 places in dorm rooms holding two to four people, including six doubles that are adapted for the disabled.

Hotel Ziryab (☎ 958 48 05 12; www.cetursa.es; Plaza de Andalucía; r €119; 🕑 late Nov-early May; P 🐾) This top-end hotel near the foot of the resort is reasonably attractive, with a lot of stone and wood.

El Lodge (☎ 958 48 06 00; www.ellodge.com; Calle Maribel 8; s/d €230/250; 🕑 year-round; P) This luxurious log-cabin 20-room hotel was constructed with Finnish (!) pine, and has a great Basque restaurant.

These are some of the slightly less expensive hotel/*hostal* options:

Hostal El Ciervo (☎ 958 48 04 09; www.eh.etursa.es; Edificio Penibético; r €84; 🕑 Dec-Apr)

Hotel Apartamentos Trevenque (☎ 958 48 08 62; www.cetursa.es; Plaza de Andalucía 6; r €105; 🕑 year-round; P)

For out-of-the-hotel food, take your pick from 30 varied eateries in the resort and nine up on the slopes.

Getting There & Away

In the ski season **Autocares Bonal** (☎ 958 46 50 22) operates three daily buses (four on the weekends) to the ski resort from Granada's bus station (€4/7 one-way/return, one hour). Outside the ski season there's just one daily bus (9am from Granada, 5pm from the ski station). A taxi from Granada costs about €40.

MULHACÉN & VELETA

The Sierra Nevada's two highest peaks – Mulhacén (3479m) and Veleta (3395m), even in summer usually marked out by patches of snow – rise to the southeast of the ski station. They also crown the head of the Poqueira Valley in Las Alpujarras on the southern flank of the range. The summit of the towering Mulhacén supports a small shrine and a roofless chapel, a few metres from the edge of a near-perpendicular 500m drop to the Hoya de Mulhacén basin. The views, on a good day, take in such incredibly distant ranges as the Rif Mountains of Morocco and the Sierra de Cazorla.

A road climbs right over the Sierra Nevada from the ski station to Capileira, the highest village in the Poqueira Valley, but it's closed to motor vehicles (except with a special permit) between Hoya de la Mora (2550m), some 3km up from Pradollano, and Hoya del Portillo (2150m), 12km above Capileira. From about late June to the end of October (depending on the snow cover) the Parque Nacional Sierra Nevada operates a shuttle bus service, called the Servicio de Interpretación Ambiental Altas Cumbres (High Peaks Environmental Interpretation Service), giving walkers access to the upper reaches of the range. The bus service runs about 6km up the road from Hoya de la Mora (to Las Posiciones del Veleta, at 3020m), and some 21km up from Capileira (to the Mirador de Trevélez, at 2680m). Tickets (€4/6 one-way/return on either route) and further information are available from the national park information posts at **Hoya de la Mora** (☎ 630 95 97 39; 🕑 about 8.30am-2.30pm & 3.30-7.30pm in bus-service season) and **Capileira** (☎ 958 76 34 86, 686 414576; 🕑 about 9am-2pm & 4.30-7.30pm year-round).

Many exciting walks start from near the top end of the bus routes; the national park information posts have leaflets summarising them. From the Posiciones del Veleta it's about 4km to the top of Veleta, an ascent of about 370m with 1½ hours' walking (plus stops); or 14km to the top of Mulhacén, with four to five hours' walking; or about 15km (five or six hours) all the way over to Mirador de Trevélez (avoiding the summits). From the Mirador de Trevélez it's around three hours to the top of Mulhacén (6km, 800m ascent), or you could reach the **Cañada de Siete Lagunas**, a lake-dotted basin below the eastern side of Mulhacén, in 1½ to two hours.

If you want to make more than a day trip of it, there are four high-mountain refuges where you can spend the night.

The **Refugio Poqueira** (☎ 958 34 33 49; per person €9; ☺ year-round) is a modern 87-bunk refuge with a restaurant (breakfast €3.50, dinner €10) and hot showers, towards the top of the Poqueira Valley at 2500m. Phone ahead, if possible. You can get here by walking 4km from the Mirador de Trevélez (about one hour), or following the Río Mulhacén for 2.3km down from the road beneath the western side of Mulhacén, then veering 750m southeast along a path to the refuge.

Sleeping in the three *refugios vivac* (simple stone or brick shelters with boards for around 12 people to sleep on) is free, and they are always open, but reservations are not possible. Refugio Vivac La Caldera is below the western flank of Mulhacén, a 1½-hour walk up from Refugio Poqueira; Refugio Pillavientos is about a 20-minute walk southwest along the road from Refugio La Caldera; Refugio Vivac La Cariguela is at the 3200m Collado del Veleta pass below the summit of Veleta.

Overnight camping in the mountains is permitted, but only above 1600m, at least 50m from high-mountain lakes and at least 500m from staffed refuges and vehicle tracks. You must give prior notification by email, fax or letter to the park authorities: check the latest regulations at a park information office.

You can also reach the refuges and high altitudes under your own steam, without using the shuttle service. From Capileira, path No 3 with yellow marker posts (see the boxed text, p389) makes its way up the Poqueira Valley to Cortijo Las Tomas, from which it is about 45 minutes further up to the Refugio Poqueira – about five hours' walking from Capileira in all. A good route from Trevélez is to head northwestward up to the Cañada de Siete Lagunas, from which you can ascend Mulhacén via the rocky Cuesta del Resuello ridge – around seven hours' walking from Trevélez.

MONACHIL
pop 6000 / elevation 810m

Climbers swamp this attractive village in the foothills just 6km southeast of Granada for the spectacular gorge, **Los Cahorros**, just to its east. There are 300 sport and classical routes here, though Los Cahorros is also good for short walks, with a nearby suspension bridge and waterfalls. Monachil is also the home of British-run **Ride Sierra Nevada** (☎ 958 50 16 20; www.ridesierranevada.com), a recommended mountain-bike tour firm. It offers guided biking holidays with self-catering accommodation from UK£110 (long weekend) or from UK£175 (one week). Prices include airport transfers.

Buses to Monachil (€0.80, 15 minutes) run 20 times a day (10 on Saturday, four on Sunday) from Paseo del Salón in Granada.

LAS ALPUJARRAS

Las Alpujarras or La Alpujarra, a 70km-long jumble of valleys along the southern flank of the Sierra Nevada, is a beautiful, diverse and, dare we say it, slightly strange place. Heavenly in its landscape of arid slopes, deep crags and egg-white villages that look as if they were spilled by accident onto the mountain side, the towns on the mountain's lower belts simmer with New Age hippies hoping to get spiritual in front of confused locals. Menus in English and tons of traditional rugs and jugs on display mean that the term 'unspoilt' is not entirely appropriate here. A recent upsurge in tourism and foreign (mainly British) settlers has given the area a new dimension.

Still, there are villages in Las Alpujarras where tourists rarely set foot, and you'll know those places by the narrow car-unfriendly roads and incredible silence. The villages were built in Berber-style during the area's flourishing Islamic past. Winding lanes of flat-roofed, two-storey houses (the lower storey is still often used for storage and animals), and the terraced and irrigated

SILKWORMS & ROUGH TIMES

Berber migrants introduced silkworms (the mulberry leaf–eating caterpillars of the silk moth) to Las Alpujarras in Muslim times. Thread spun from the silkworms' unravelled cocoons was the raw material of the thriving silk workshops of 10th- and 11th-century Almería and, later, Nasrid Granada. Together with irrigation-based agriculture, the production of silk thread supported a population of probably over 150,000 in at least 400 villages and hamlets in Las Alpujarras by the late 15th century.

On his surrender to the Catholic Monarchs in 1492, the last emir, Boabdil, settled at Laujar de Andarax in the eastern Alpujarras (Almería province), but left for Africa the next year, leaving behind an oppressed and dissatisfied Muslim population in the mountain villages. Muslim riots in 1500 and continuing unrest between the Muslim population and the Christian rulers, plus a new repressive decree by Felipe II in 1567 that forbade the use of Arabic names and dress and even the Arabic language, provoked another revolt in 1568. The revolt was led by an Alpujarras Morisco (Muslim convert to Chirstianity) named Aben Humeya. Two years of vicious guerrilla war in Las Alpujarras ended only after Don Juan of Austria, Felipe's half-brother, was brought in to quash the insurrection and Aben Humeya was assassinated by his cousin Aben Aboo.

Almost the whole Alpujarras population was then deported to Castile and western Andalucía, and some 270 villages and hamlets were re-peopled with settlers from northern Spain. The other villages were abandoned. Over the following centuries, the silk industry fell by the wayside and swaths of Las Alpujarras' woodlands were lost to mining and cereal growing.

hillsides offer a unique look into this once-remote area's way of life.

It's a delightful area to explore on foot and is the starting point for some of the best routes up into the Sierra Nevada.

The main road into the Alpujarras from the west is the A44 (C333 on some signs), which leaves the N44 34km south of Granada. The GR-421 turns north off the A348 just west of Órgiva to wind along the northern slopes of the Alpujarras, rejoining the A348 a few kilometres north of Cádiar.

Many Alpujarras villages are within the Parque Natural Sierra Nevada but none are within the Parque Nacional Sierra Nevada.

Walking

The best times for walking in Las Alpujarras are April to mid-June, and mid-September to early November, when the temperatures are just right and the vegetation at its most colourful.

An infinite number of good walks connect valley villages or head up into the Sierra Nevada. *Holiday Walks in the Alpujarras* by Jeremy Rabjohns is a useful English-language guide available locally, as is the **Discovery Walking Guides** (www.walking.demon.co.uk) guide to Las Alpujarras. Two long-distance footpaths traverse Las Alpujarras. One is the GR-7, which crosses Europe from Greece to Tarifa (Cádiz province): you could follow it

through the Granada Alpujarras from La-roles to Lanjarón in one week. The 144km GR-142 runs east from Lanjarón along the length of Las Alpujarras, then curves northwest to Fiñana on the northern flank of the Sierra Nevada in Almería province. See p382 for information on maps.

Sleeping & Eating

It's worth booking ahead for rooms in Las Alpujarras during Semana Santa and from July to September. Many villages have apartments and houses for short-term rental; ask in information offices or check websites such as **Turgranada** (www.turgranada.com).

Most Alpujarras food is what good Spanish food is all about: beans, lentils and grains, combined with good meat and local trout. Trevélez is famed for its *jamón serrano*, which some say is the best in Spain. A *plato alpujarreño* consists of fried potatoes, fried eggs, sausage, ham and maybe a black pudding (sound like an English breakfast to you?), and usually costs around €6.

'Alpujarras' or 'Costa' wine comes from the Sierra de la Contraviesa, on the south flank of Las Alpujarras, and tends to be strong and fairly raw.

Getting There & Away

Buses to the Alpujarras are run by **Alsina Graells** (☎ Granada 958 18 54 80, Órgiva 958 78 50 02,

Málaga 95 234 17 38, Almería 950 23 51 68). From Granada, buses leave three times daily for the following destinations:

Destination	Cost	Duration	Daily Frequency
Bérchules	€7.50	3¾hr	3
Bubión	€5.50	2¼hr	3
Cádiar	€7	3hr	2
Capileira	€5.50	2½hr	3
Pampaneira	€5	2hr	3
Pitres	€5.50	2¾hr	3
Órgiva	€4	1½hr	3
Trevélez	€6.50	3¼hr	3
Válor	€8	3¾hr	2
Yegen	€8	3½hr	2

Return buses start from Bérchules at 5am and 5pm and from Pitres at 3.30pm. There is a Málaga–Órgiva bus (€9, 3¼ hours, once daily except Sunday), and a daily Almería–Bérchules service (€8, 3¾ hours).

ÓRGIVA

pop 5370 / elevation 725m

The main town of the western Alpujarras, Órgiva is a scruffy but bustling place. The Thursday morning market in Barrio Alto, the upper part of town, is a funny mix of locals and the New Age hippies that form the town's international populace, who gather to buy and sell everything from vegetables and cheese to bead necklaces.

The landmark 16th-century twin-towered **Iglesia de Nuestra Señora de la Expectación** (Plaza García Moreno) stands beside Órgiva's central traffic lights. The **Alsina Graells bus stop** (Avenida González Robles 67) is about 300m down the street from here. You'll find banks and ATMs on and around Plaza García Moreno.

Sleeping & Eating

Camping Órgiva (☎ 958 78 43 07; www.descubre laalpujarra.com; A348 Km 18.9; camping per adult/tent/car €4.50/5/3.60, cabins/bungalows €35/55; P ⚑) This smallish camping ground, 2km south of the centre on the A348 towards the Río Guadalfeo, has a nice pool area and a reasonably priced restaurant, and some nice stilt-standing cabins.

Hotel & Hostal Mirasol (☎ 958 78 51 08/59; Avenida González Robles 5 & 3; s/d hostal €17/28, hotel €35/45; ⚑) Near the bridge over the Río Chico on the western side of town, the Mirasol provides plain but adequately comfortable

rooms with tiled floors and all-white walls. Those in the hotel section are larger and newer and have TV.

Hotel Taray (☎ 958 78 45 25; www.turgranada .com/hoteltaray; A348 Km 18.5; r from €73; P ⚑ ⚑) A rural idyll with a wild garden, massive pool, two good restaurants and white-washed walls. The rooms are in pleasant pastels, with traditional bedspreads. The hotel sits about 1.5km south of the centre on the A348 running down towards the Río Guadalfeo.

Café Baraka (Calle Estación 12A; snacks & light meals €2-3) The spicy aromas tell you this pleasantly spacious café has been touched by the New Age generation. There are herbal teas, milk shakes and *shwarmas*, or a variety of sandwiches. You'll find it beside the municipal car park in the upper part of town.

Mesón Casa Santiago (Plaza García Moreno; mains €6-12) Good for grilled meats at indoor or outdoor tables, right in the heart of town.

PAMPANEIRA, BUBIÓN & CAPILEIRA

When seen from a distance, these three almost Portuguese-sounding villages look like splatters of white paint, Jackson Pollock–style, against the grey arid land that surrounds them. Pampaneira (1050m), Bubión (1300m) and Capileira (1440m) are the Alpujarras' most beautiful and touristy villages, clinging to the side of the deep Barranco de Poqueira ravine, 14km to 20km northeast of Órgiva, with good restaurants and decent hotels. Capileira, the highest of the three, is the best base for walks.

Information

You'll find ATMs just outside the car park entrance in Pampaneira, and in Capileira at **La General** (Calle Doctor Castilla) bank.

Punto de Información Parque Nacional de Sierra Nevada (☎ 958 76 31 27; Plaza de la Libertad, Pampaneira; ☼ 10am-3pm Sun & Mon year-round, 10am-2pm & 5-7pm Tue-Sat, afternoon hours 4-6pm about mid-Oct–Easter) Plenty of information about Las Alpujarras and Sierra Nevada; maps and books for sale.

Servicio de Interpretación de Altos Cumbres (☎ 958 76 34 86, 686-414576; ☼ about 9am-2pm & 4.30-7.30pm) By the main road in Capileira (information mainly about the national park, but also on Las Alpujarras.

Sights

All three villages – like many others in Las Alpujarras – have solid 16th-century **Mude-**

WALK LIKE AN ALPUJARRAN

Eight trails ranging from 4km to 23km (two to eight hours) are marked by colour-coded posts in the beautiful **Barranco de Poqueira**. Although their starting points can be a little hard to find, they are marked and described on the recommended Editorial Alpina map (see p382). Most routes start from Capileira.

Path No 2, a 4km circuit down into the valley and back up again, starts at the end of Calle Cerezo in Capileira. Path No 4 (8km, 3½ hours) takes you from Capileira up to the hamlet of La Cebadilla, then down the western side of the valley and back up to Capileira. To find its start, walk down Calle Cubo from Plaza Calvario at the northern end of Capileira, turn right where the street takes its second turn to the left, and follow the street out into the countryside. Fork up to the right 125m after the last village building on your right. Path No 3 continues up the valley from La Cebadilla to Cortijo Las Tomas (from which it's a steep half-hour walk up to Refugio Poqueira) then returns to Capileira following a path high on the eastern side of the valley (the full round-trip from Capileira is 19km, about eight hours).

Nevadensis (☎ 958 76 31 27; www.nevadensis.com), at the information office in Pampaneira, offers hikes and treks with knowledgeable guides, including a combined 4WD and foot ascent of Mulhacén for €35 per person.

---

jar churches (mass times are posted on the doors). They also have small **weaving workshops** that you can peek at: an interesting little one in Bubión is the French-owned **Taller del Telar** (Calle Santísima Trinidad; 🕙 11am-2.30pm & 5-8.30pm), with ancient looms from Granada. Also in Bubión, don't miss the **Casa Alpujarreña** (Calle Real; admission €1.80; 🕙 11am-2pm Sun-Thu, 11am-2pm & 5-7pm Fri, Sat & holidays), beside the church. This is an excellent little folk museum in a village house that was left untouched from the 1950s until its recent adaptation – a marvellous glimpse of bygone Alpujarras life!

Activities

Nevadensis (see the boxed text, above) is a highly experienced local firm offering a host of guided activities in the area, including mountain biking, climbing, canyoning, horse riding and even snowshoeing. Horseriders recommend rides with **Rafael Belmonte** (☎ 958 76 31 35; www.ridingandalucia.com) and **Dallas Love** (☎ 958 76 30 38; dallaslove@arrakis.es); both are Bubión-based, speak English and offer trail rides lasting anywhere up to a week. **Horizonte Vertical** (☎/fax 958 76 34 08; www.granadainfo .com/hv; Calle Nivel 6, Bubión) will take you paragliding over some of this thrilling topography.

Sleeping & Eating

For self-catering accomodation try **Rustic Blue** (Barrio la Ermita, Bubión; ☎ 958 76 33 81; www.rusticblue .com), an agency that rents out cottages, farmhouses and village houses in the region.

PAMPANEIRA

Hostal Ruta del Mulhacén (☎ 958 76 30 10; www .rutadelmulhacen.com; Avenida Alpujarra 6; s €25-35, d €30-45) Most of the cosy rooms at this *hostal* at the entrance to the village have balconies, and a few have their own terraces with views down the valley.

Hostal Pampaneira (☎ 958 76 30 02; Avenida Alpujarra 1; s/d €26/36) Opposite Hostal Ruta del Mulhacén, this place has a friendly local owner and clean, good-sized rooms. Its Restaurante Alfonso is one of the village's best-value eateries (trout €5.50, menú €9).

Restaurante Casa Diego (☎ 958 76 30 15; Plaza de la Libertad 3; mains €5-9) Good trout with ham, or local ham and eggs are great for lunch or dinner on the upstairs terrace.

BUBIÓN

Hostal Las Terrazas (☎ 958 76 30 34; www.terrazas alpujarra.com; Plaza del Sol 7; s/d €22/29, 2-/4-/6-person apt €48/59/77) Rustic rooms, caramel bathrooms and excellent views of the valley from the terraces (hence the name) on each floor. The wood-reception area is decorated with farming tools and little plants. Signposted off the main road.

Teide Restaurant (☎ 958 76 30 84; Carretera de Sierra Nevada; menú €8) A good, traditional, local people's restaurant by the road, with a *menú del dia* that includes generous portions of lentils for starters, meat in a tomato sauce, plus salad and coffee, while local characters flood in and out for some *jamón* and wine.

CAPILEIRA

Campileira (☎ 958 76 34 19; Carretera de Sierra Nevada; camping per person/site €3.50/6.50, dm €12, d €27; P) Some 500m up the Sierra Nevada road from the top of the village, Campileira provides clean dorms in a spacious stone building, hot showers, inexpensive meals (breakfast €2.15, dinner €8.55), camping on a grassy terrace and fabulous views.

Hostal Atalaya (☎ 958 76 30 25; www.hostal atalaya.com; Calle Perchel 3; s/d incl breakfast with view €22/36, without view €17/32) The Atalaya, just 100m down the road from Mesón Poqueira, is friendly and geared to travellers, with simple but pleasant rooms and plenty of information on offer.

Mesón Poqueira (☎ 958 76 30 48; Calle Doctor Castilla 11; s/d €18/24, 2-/4-/6-person apt €48/80/90) A good mountain-lodge hotel, just off the main road, with spacious, simple rooms and a friendly owner who'll give you any information you want, though in Spanish only. A good breakfast is included, and there's the option of a doggie bag breakfast if you're going walking.

Finca Los Llanos (☎ 958 76 30 71; www.hotelfinca losllanos.com; Carretera de Sierra Nevada; s/d €45/72; P ⓩ) Recently refurbished, Los Llanos now has some pretty nifty suites and tasteful rooms with terracotta-tile floors and folksy textiles, *and* a library by the restaurant. It's at the top of the village, which means that the views from the pool are excellent.

Cortijo Catifalarga (☎ 958 34 33 57; www.cati falarga.com; Carretera de Sierra Nevada; s €58-69, d €73-90, apt from €73; P) This charmingly renovated old farmstead is the choicest base in the Poqueira Valley. The signposted 500m driveway begins 750m up the Sierra Nevada road from the top of Capileira. Chestnut beams, stone floors and Moroccan rugs decorate the spacious rooms, and some have their own terrace. You can dine indoors or out, and hear live music some nights. The views are fabulous and so is the food – a mix of Andalucian, Arabic, Catalan, vegetarian and more (mains €6 to €12).

Bar El Tilo (☎ 958 76 31 81; Plaza Calvario; raciones €4-6) The village tavern is on a lovely white-washed square with a terrace where you can have good-value *raciones* such as melon and ham or *patatas a lo pobre*, potatoes with peppers and garlic.

Restaurante Ibero-Fusión (☎ 958 76 32 56; Calle Parra 1; salads €5-9, mains €7-10; ⓨ 7-10.45pm) This long-established restaurant just below the church is a bizarre but brilliant find in the middle of the Alpujarras – a gastronomic fusion of Andalucian, Arabic and Indian, excellent for vegetarians. Think couscous, dhal and, ehm, Saharan turkey with dates and apples.

Shopping

All three villages have many craft shops selling, among many other things, colourful, inexpensive, homespun Alpujarras cotton rugs. In Capileira **J Brown** (☎ 958 76 30 92; Calle Doctor Castilla) sells quality handmade leather and suede clothing at good prices, including waistcoats from €50.

PITRES & LA TAHA

Pitres (1250m) is a true break from the tourists and souvenirs you'll find in the Poqueira gorge villages, although not as beautiful. But the five lovely villages in the valley just below Pitres – **Mecina**, **Mecinilla**, **Fondales**, **Ferreirola** and **Atalbéitar** – are a treat for those looking for quiet tradition. They are grouped together in a municipality called La Taha, the old Arabic name for the administrative units into which Las Alpujarras was divided. Ancient paths between these hamlets wend their way through lush woods and orchards, while the tinkle of running water provides the soundtrack. A few minutes' walk below Fondales is an old Islamic bridge over the deep gorge of the Río Trevélez, with a ruined Islamic mill beside it (ask for the *puente árabe*). For those of you with vehicles, narrow roads mean slow driving is recommended.

Sleeping & Eating

Balcón de Pitres (☎ 958 76 61 11; www.balcondepitres .com; Carretera GR-421 Km 51, Pitres; camping per adult/ tent/car €5.50/5.50/5, cabins & cottages from €45; P ⓩ) Just above the main road on the western side of Pitres, this camping ground is shady and fairly spacious. It has a decent, inexpensive restaurant and some nice wooden cabins. You pay extra to use the pool.

Refugio Los Albergues (☎ 958 34 31 76; Pitres; dm €7-8; ⓨ closed mid-Dec–mid-Feb) Los Albergues is a small, simple walkers' hostel in a beautiful setting 200m (signposted) off the GR-421 main road on the eastern side of Pitres. It has an equipped kitchen, hot showers and interesting outdoor toilets. The friendly

GRANADA PROVINCE

THE AUTHOR'S CHOICE

Sierra y Mar (☎ 958 76 61 71; www.sierraymar.com; Calle Albaicín, Ferreirola; s/d incl breakfast €36/56) Hidden away along the sun-bleached alleys of the gorgeously quiet village of Ferreirola, this place is a true marvel. Bought and decorated over 20 years by the welcoming, multilingual Danish and Italian owners, the small houses and the garden just keep on getting more beautiful. It has a wild, grassy garden, white walls, sea-blue coffee tables and great views of the valley, plus stylish, earthy rooms with writing desks under the windows that frame the views delightfully. If you want to plan walks in the district, the hosts are super-knowledgeable. There is a preference (not a rule) for stays of more that one night.

German owner is full of information on the area's many good walks. There's one double room (€24/21 with/without heating).

L'Atelier (☎ 958 85 75 01; www.ivu.org/atelier; Calle Alberca 21, Mecina; s/d €29/42, incl breakfast €30/45) A little French-run vegetarian guesthouse in a centuries-old village house, L'Atelier serves gourmet meatless meals and has six cosy rooms and an art gallery next door. Vegetarian cookery courses happen here, too. The restaurant is open from 7pm to 11pm, Wednesday to Monday.

Hotel Albergue de Mecina (☎ 958 76 62 41; Calle La Fuente s/n, Mecina; r €65; **P** **②**) A tasteful 21-room hotel, modern and comfortable but with touches of traditional Alpujarras style.

TREVÉLEZ

pop 840 / elevation 1476m

Trevélez, set in a gash in the mountainside almost as impressive as the Poqueira gorge, is famous for three reasons: it's a starting point for routes into the high Sierra Nevada; it produces some of Spain's best *jamón serrano*, with hams trucked in from far and wide for curing in the dry mountain air; and it claims to be the highest village in Spain. Other villages actually have better claims to the 'highest' title, but the Trevélez municipality is certainly the highest on the mainland, as it includes the summit of Mulhacén.

Along the main road you're confronted by a welter of ham and souvenir shops, but an exploration of the upper parts reveals a lively, typically Alpujarran village. La General bank, just above the main road, has an ATM.

Sleeping & Eating

Camping Trevélez (☎ /fax 958 85 87 35; www.camping trevelez.net; Carretera Trevélez-Órgiva Km 1; camping per adult/tent/car €4.50/5/3.50, 2-/4-person cabins from €19/39; **P** **②**) Eco-aware and among lots of trees, the camping ground slopes on a terraced hillside. There's a good-value restaurant that serves up tasty veg dishes (€2.50 to €4), as well as meat and fish dishes (€6 to €7.50).

Hotel La Fragua (☎ 958 85 86 26; Calle San Antonio 4; s/d €23/35) The rooms at La Fragua are pine-furnished and comfortable, but if a walking group decides to clatter forth at 6am, you stand little chance of sleeping through it. The hotel is towards the top of town, a 200m walk (signposted) from Plaza Barrio Medio. Its restaurant, Mesón La Fragua (mains €6 to €9), a few doors away, is one of the best in town, with items including partridge in walnut sauce, fig ice cream, excellent pork *solomillo* (sirloin) and some good vegetarian dishes.

Hotel Pepe Álvarez (☎ 958 85 85 03; Plaza Francisco Abellán s/n; s/d €23/41) Some rooms have a terrace overlooking the busy plaza, which spills out by the main road at the foot of the village.

Mesón Joaquín (☎ 958 85 89 04; GR-421; 3-course menú €7) This is one of Trevélez' better restaurants, but mind your head on the hanging hams! The Joaquín is on the western side of the village.

Restaurante González (☎ 958 85 85 31; Plaza Francisco Abellán s/n; mains €5-13) A good-value place by the main road at the foot of the village, this restaurant serves trout, *jamón, plato alpujarreño* and other local fare.

EAST OF TREVÉLEZ

Seven kilometres south of Trevélez the GR-421 road crosses the low Portichuelo de Cástaras pass and turns east into a harsher, barer landscape, yet still with oases of greenery around the villages. The central and eastern Alpujarras have their own magic but see fewer tourists than the western villages.

Bérchules

pop 805 / elevation 1350m

This village 17km from Trevélez is set in a green valley that stretches a long way back into the hills. The area around here offers attractive walks.

La Posada (☎ 958 85 25 41; Plaza del Ayuntamiento 7; per person with private/shared bathroom €18/15) provides simple but comfortable lodgings – two sturdy old village houses adapted by villager Miguel, which are geared to walkers but open to all. Vegetarian breakfast and dinner are available.

By the main road at the bottom of Bérchules the **Hotel Los Bérchules** (☎ 958 85 25 30; www.hotelberchules.com; Carretera s/n; r €42-45; P) has good, clean, bright rooms (all with bathtub), helpful English-speaking hosts who can help you set up all manner of activities, the best restaurant in town (mains €6 to €11; try the local lamb with mint) and a cosy lounge area with a bookcase full of books on Spain.

Cádiar

pop 1600 / elevation 850m

Down by the Río Guadalfeo 8km south of Bérchules, Cádiar is one of the bigger Alpujarras villages. The **Alquería de Morayma** (☎ 958 34 32 21; www.alqueriamorayma.com; d €49-59, 4-person apt €84; P), 2km south of Cádiar just off the A348 towards Órgiva, is one of the most charming, and progressive, places to stay in Las Alpujarras – an old farmstead lovingly renovated and expanded by its *granadino* owners to provide 19 comfortable rooms and apartments, all unique. There's excellent, moderately priced food, a library of Alpujarras information, great views, fine walking available nearby and fascinating art and artefacts everywhere. The Alquería also hosts classes in tai chi, reiki, yoga and other disciplines.

Yegen

pop 400 / elevation 1100m

Yegen, where writer Gerald Brenan made his home in the 1920s, is about 12km east of Bérchules. Parts of the valley below Yegen have a particularly moonlike quality. **Brenan's house**, just off the village square, is marked by a plaque. Several **walking routes** have been marked out locally, including a 2km 'Sendero de Gerald Brenan'.

El Rincón de Yegen (☎ 958 85 12 70; www.aldearural.com/rincondeyegen; s/d €25/36, 4-person apt €65; P) is a small hotel on the eastern edge of the village with old-fashioned furnishings and an excellent, medium-priced restaurant (mains €7 to €13). Succumb to the pears in Contraviesa wine and hot chocolate.

Válor

pop 735 / elevation 900m

Válor, 5km northeast of Yegen, was the birthplace of Aben Humeya, leader of the 1568 rebellion, and is the setting for the biggest of several annual Moros y Cristianos (Moors & Christians) festivities in Las Alpujarras that recreate the historical clash. On 14 and 15 September, colourfully costumed 'armies' battle it out noisily from midday to evening.

Mairena

pop 300 / elevation 1050m

The unspoiled village of Mairena, 6km from Válor, enjoys superb views from its elevated position. **Las Chimeneas** (☎ 958 76 03 52; www.alpujarra-tours.com; Calle Amargura 6; d incl breakfast €70;) is something of an institution: a village house renovated in charming, uncluttered style by helpful young British owners who are also keen walkers. They offer guided walks, mountain biking, horse riding and painting excursions, serve good dinners (€15) using local organic produce, and can organise transport from Granada or Guadix.

East of Mairena you'll encounter the A337, which crosses the Sierra Nevada by the 2000m Puerto de la Ragua pass (occasionally snowbound in winter) to La Calahorra.

COSTA TROPICAL

The ambitiously named coast of Granada is in fact a true Mediterranean landscape with barren hills, aromatic herbs and wiry pomegranate trees, but the suggestion of tropical lushness comes thanks to the hot-climate crops such as custard apples, avocados and mangoes that are grown in the area. Although this stretch of the coast has not been nearly as exploited by developers as that of the neighbouring Malaga and Almería provinces, there are signs that things are heading that way as land runs out elsewhere.

The 80km coastline has spectacular views from the N340 as it winds up and down between scattered seaside towns and villages. East of Motril, the mountains often come right down to the sea, making for some of Andalucía's better scuba diving (especially around the towns of Calahonda and Castell de Ferro, although the settlements are drab and the beaches pebbly). West of Motril the terrain is less abrupt and there are three quite attractive beach towns.

SALOBREÑA

pop 11,750

Salobreña's huddle of white houses rises on a crag between the N340 and the sea. It's not a breathtaking town, though there is an impressive Islamic castle and below is a long, wide dark-sand beach. It's a low-key place for most of the year but jumps in August.

Orientation & Information

Avenida García Lorca, the easterly entrance into Salobreña from the N340, leads 200m straight to the helpful **tourist office** (☎ 958 61 03 14; Plaza de Goya; 🕙 9.30am-1.30pm & 4-7pm Tue-Sat). The Alsina Graells bus stop is diagonally across the street from the tourist office and the beach is 1km further on.

Sights & Activities

The **Castillo Árabe** (Arab Castle; admission incl Museo Histórico €3; 🕙 10.30am-1.30pm & 4-8pm), a 20-minute walk uphill from the tourist office, dates from the 12th century, though the site was fortified as early as the 10th century. The castle was used as a summer residence by the Granada emirs, but a dark legend has it that Emir Mohammed IX had his three daughters, Zaida, Zoraida and Zorahaida, held captive here. Washington Irving throws in his own angle on the story in *Tales of the Alhambra*. The inner Alcazaba, a setting for many cultural events, retains much of its Nasrid structure. You can walk along parts of the parapets. Just below the castle is the 16th-century Mudejar **Iglesia de Nuestra Señora del Rosario**, with an elegant tower and striking arched doorway. The **Museo Histórico** (Plaza del Ayuntamiento; admission incl Castillo Árabe €3;

🕙 10.30am-1.30pm & 4-8pm) is nearby, in the former *ayuntamiento,* below the church. The museum exhibits artefacts and documents on Salobreña's history, with archaeological findings going back around 6000 years.

The old Muslim town spills out below the castle, ending on one side in steep cliffs. There's a **mirador** on Paseo de las Flores, below the castle.

It is possible to drive to this upper part of town (follow the 'Casco Antigua' and 'Castillo Árabe' signs) but parking can be difficult. There's also an urban bus from the lower part of town up to the Iglesia de Nuestra Señora del Rosario a few times a day (except Sunday).

Salobreña's long **beach** is divided by a rocky outcrop, El Peñón. Playa de la Charca, the eastern part, is grey sand; the western Playa de la Guardia is more pebbly.

Sleeping

Pensión Mari Carmen (☎ 958 61 09 06; Calle Nueva 30; s/d €20/39, d with shared bathroom €24; 🅟) The Mari Carmen has beautifully bright and clean pine-furnished rooms, some with their own terrace, and a communal terrace with great views. It is a 10-minute uphill walk from Plaza de Goya.

Hostal San Juan (☎ 958 61 17 29; www.hotel-san-juan.com; Calle Jardines 1; d €42; 🅟) A lovely tiled and plant-dotted patio-lounge welcomes you as you enter this sparkly *hostal* on a quiet street about 400m from the tourist office. The rooms have wrought-iron bedsteads and dizzying red-and-white bathroom tiling, plus a large roof terrace.

Hotel Avenida (☎ 958 61 15 44; www.hotelavenidatropical.com; Avenida Mediterráneo 35; s €35-55, d €50-80; 🅟 🅧 🖵) This is a family-oriented hotel and the best place to rest your head in town. It's equipped with 30 comfortable elegantly simple rooms with phone, satellite TV, bathtub and safe – plus its own restaurant, elegantly decked-out bar, Jacuzzi and sun terrace, you may never see the town. The hotel is between the town centre and beach.

Eating & Drinking

There are loads of restaurants, beachside *chiringuitos* (small open-air eateries) and bars, and a spot of nightlife, on and near the beachfront.

Restaurant El Peñón (☎ 958 61 05 38; Paseo Marítimo s/n; mains €6-12; 🕙 closed Mon) Just by El

Peñón, the big rock dividing Salobreña's beach, this place has good medium-priced seafood and meat, best enjoyed as you sit outside, almost on top of the waves.

Restaurante Tropical (☎ 958 61 25 84; Paseo Marítimo; mains €7.50-15; 🕙 closed Tue) This popular semi-open-air steakhouse has some bizarre sauces with the meat, like pineapple and curry. It's right on the corner when you hit the beachfront road coming from town.

Also recommended is **La Bodega** (☎ 958 82 87 39; Plaza de Goya; menú €8, meat & fish mains €10-20), by the tourist office, with outdoor tables and good service.

Getting There & Away

Alsina Graells (☎ 958 61 25 21) has at least six daily buses to Almuñécar (€1, 20 minutes), Granada (€5.50, one hour), Málaga (€7 1½ hours) and Nerja (€3, 40 minutes), plus four to Almería (€8, 1½ hours) and one (except Sunday) to Órgiva (€2.50, 30 minutes).

ALMUÑÉCAR
pop 24,700

Heading 15km west of Salobreña, Almuñécar is pretty uninviting, save for the attractive old section around its 16th-century castle. Popular with Spanish tourists and a growing community of northern Europeans, it's bright and not too expensive, although the beaches are mainly pebbly.

Orientation & Information

The N340 runs across the northern part of town, with the bus station just to its south. Plaza de la Constitución, the main square of the old part of town, is a few minutes' walk southwest of the bus station, with a maze of narrow streets dotted with galleries and interesting boutiques, spreading to its south and southeast.

The beachfront is divided by a rocky outcrop, the Peñón del Santo, with Playa de San Cristóbal – the best beach (grey sand and small pebbles) – stretching to its west, and Playa Puerta del Mar to the east.

There's a **tourist information kiosk** (☎ 958 63 11 25; Avenida Fenicia; 🕙 10am-2pm & 5-8pm, afternoon hours 4-7pm approx Oct-Apr) along the street from the bus station near the roundabout on the N340. The **main tourist office** (☎ 958 63 11 25; www.almunecar.info; Avenida Europa s/n; 🕙 10am-2pm & 5-8pm, afternoon hours 4-7pm approx Oct-Apr) is 1km southwest of the kiosk and the roundabout

in the Palacete de La Najarra, just back from Playa de San Cristóbal.

Sights & Activities

Just behind the Peñón del Santo is a 'sexy' tropical bird aviary, **Parque Ornitológico Loro-Sexi** (☎ 958 63 02 80; adult/child €2/1.50; 🕙 11am-2pm & 5-7pm, afternoon hours 4-6pm approx Oct-Apr). The **Castillo de San Miguel** (☎ 958 63 12 52; adult/child incl Museo Arqueológico €2/1.50; 🕙 10.30am-1.30pm & 5-7.30pm Tue-Sat approx Nov-Mar, 10.30am-1.30pm & 4-6.30pm Tue-Sat approx Oct-Apr, 10.30am-1.30pm Sun year-round) tops the hill, and was built by the conquering Christians over Islamic and Roman fortifications. The sweaty, circuitous climb up to the entrance rewards with excellent views and an informative little museum. The **Museo Arqueológico** (☎ 958 63 12 52; Calle Málaga; 🕙 10.30am-1.30pm & 5-7.30pm Tue-Sat approx Nov-Mar, 10.30am-1.30pm & 4-6.30pm Tue-Sat approx Oct-Apr, 10.30am-1.30pm Sun year-round) a few streets northeast, is set in 1st-century Roman underground galleries called the Cueva de Siete Palacios. It displays finds from local Phoenician, Roman and Islamic sites plus a rare 3500-year-old Egyptian amphora, probably brought by the Carthaginians. One hundred metres along Avenida de Europa from the main tourist office is **Parque Botánico El Majuelo** (admission free; 🕙 9am-10pm), where you'll find the **Factoría de Salazones de Pescado**, which is the remains of a Carthaginian and Roman fish-salting workshop. The park hosts Andalucía's only summer jazz festival, the international **Festival de Jazz en la Costa**, in early July.

You can paraglide, windsurf, dive, sail, ride a horse or bicycle, walk, or descend canyons in and around Almuñécar and nearby La Herradura. The tourist office's website and its leaflet *Sport Tourism* have information.

Sleeping

The town has a whopping 40 hotels, *hostales* and holiday apartments.

Hostal Altamar (☎ 958 63 03 46; Calle Alta del Mar 21; s €16-25, d €50) On a narrow street lined with internet cafés in the old part of the centre, the Altamar's rooms are plain brown and white, but comfy; there's a pleasant lounge-cafeteria where you can get breakfast.

Hotel California (☎ 958 88 10 38; www.hotelcaliforniaspain.com; Carretera N340 Km 313; s/d €33/48; P) Shame about the name but the Andalucian-Moroccan interior makes things better with

10 colourful rooms all with a private balcony, prettily tiled bathrooms and great views of the town and sea. The hotel is just off the N340 on the northwestern edge of Almuñécar, and the friendly young English and Belgian owners, one of them an experienced and enthusiastic paraglider, offer packages for paragliders combining accommodation, breakfast, car hire, guiding and retrieval for around €400 per person per week.

Hostal Plaza Damasco (☎ /fax 958 63 01 65; Calle Cerrajeros 16; s €20-30, d €60) This is a spotlessly clean *hostal* in the older part of the town centre, prettily adorned with flowers and tiles. All 17 rooms have a bathtub.

Hotel Casablanca (☎ 958 63 55 75; www.almunecar.info/casablanca; Plaza San Cristóbal 4; s/d €45/64; P ☼) Islamic arches, bright rooms with carved wooden beds and wardrobes, beautiful lamps, balconies or picture windows – you can't get much better than this in Almuñécar. The tall, slimline hotel overlooks the Peñón del Santo and is almost opposite the monument to Abd ar-Rahman I on Playa de San Cristóbal.

Eating

La Trastienda (Plaza Kelibia; canapés €4-5) The wonderful smoked salmon, caviar and cheese canapés come with a delicious salad, or you might fancy some *tablas* (platters) of cold meats, cheeses and smoked fish for €6 to €10.

La Galería (☎ 958 63 41 18; Paseo Puerta del Mar 3; mains €13-18, lunch menú €15 & €25; ☼ closed Wed) A talented young Belgian chef has upped the eating standards in Almuñécar by serving up tasty duck, meat and fish dishes and inventive concoctions such as wild mushroom and foie-gras lasagne. Find it above Playa Puerta del Mar on the eastern side of town.

Restaurante Calabre (☎ 958 63 00 80; Playa de San Cristóbal; mains €9-15; ☼ closed Tue) A great place for seafood on the beach, at the eastern end of Playa de San Cristóbal. There's an open-air terrace facing the waves and a nice bright glassed-in area for cooler days. Beware of items priced by the kilogram!

For tapas, head to Plaza Kelibia, a pedestrianised plaza in the old town filled with tables from several bars.

Drinking & Entertainment

In summer Plaza Kelibia and the beach bars along Playa Puerta del Mar buzz all night.

Musical events, theatre, poetry readings and a cine club happen at the **Casa de la Cultura** (☎ 958 83 86 05; Calle Angustias Viejas).

Getting There & Away

From the **bus station** (☎ 958 63 01 40; Avenida Juan Carlos I 1), at least six buses a day go to Almería (€10, two hours), Granada (€7, 1½ hours), La Herradura (€0.90, 15 minutes), Málaga (€6, 1½ hours), Nerja (€2.30, 30 minutes), and Salobreña (€1, 20 minutes), and one (except on Sunday) to Órgiva (€4, 1¾ hours).

LA HERRADURA
pop 4300

The little resort town of La Herradura, 7km west of Almuñécar along the coast, is like the Tarifa of Costa Tropical with its endless appeal to water-sports enthusiasts, and paragliders who ride the thermals that rise around the hills backing its pretty, horseshoe-shaped bay. It's also popular locally for good seafront restaurants. The sheltered town beach is packed in July and August, but a few kilometres to the west, down a 1km side road beyond the towering Cerro Gordo headland, is a popular 'clothing-optional' beach, Playa Cantarriján. On the far side of Punta de la Mona, which forms the eastern side of La Herradura's bay, is an attractive pleasure-boat harbour, Marina del Este.

Orientation & Information

The Alsina Graells bus stop is at the top of Calle Acera del Pilar, by the N340. This street heads south to the seafront Paseo Andrés Segovia (also called Paseo Marítimo), which runs along the bay. There's a **tourist information kiosk** (☼ 10am-2pm & 5-7pm Mon-Fri, 10am-2pm Sat) a few steps west of this junction along the Paseo: it's a branch of the Almuñécar tourist office, whose website, www.almunecar.info, also covers La Herradura.

Activities

For rentals, outings, classes and courses:
Buceo La Herradura (☎ 958 82 70 83; www.buceolaherradura.com; Marina del Este) Diving.
Club Adventure (☎ 958 64 07 80; www.club-adventure.com; Calle Olmos 3) Paragliding, canyoning, mountain biking.
Club Nautique (☎ 958 82 75 14; www.clubnautique.com; Marina del Este) Diving, yachting.
Granada Sub (☎ 958 64 02 81; www.granadasub.com; Paseo Andrés Segovia 6) Diving.

DETOUR: CARRETERA DEL SUSPIRO DEL MORO

If you're OK with narrow, winding mountain roads then, for a truly spectacular alternative to the normal N323 up from the coast to Granada, take the Carretera del Suspiro del Moro from Almuñécar, with the option of stopping off for a good walk en route. From the N340 main road through Almuñécar, turn into town at the roundabout by the tourist information kiosk. Pass McDonald's on your left and follow the street around to the right, then take the first turn-off to the right – Calle Suspiro del Moro (you may notice a small 'Otívar' sign pointing in the direction you must go). The road passes under the N340 and heads northward out of Almuñécar up the Río Verde valley. You reach the village of Otívar after 13km. Make a note of your car's kilometre reading here.

From Otívar the road winds its way endlessly upwards with ever more breathtaking panoramas and ever higher, more jagged crags appearing above. In 13km from Otívar the road ascends 1000m before, relatively speaking, levelling off for the next 7km to its highest point.

Sixteen kilometres from Otívar, the signed 7.35km Sendero Río Verde walking trail starts on the western side of the road. This circular route of around 3½ hours descends nearly 400m into the deep valley of the Río Verde, with fine views and a good chance of sighting ibex as you go. At the highest point of the road, 3.5km later, another marked walk branches off to the Pico de Lopera (1485m), 2.5km west. Beyond here the landscape is generally gentler and after around 15km you start to get views of the often snowcapped Sierra Nevada to the east.

Turn left 35km from Otívar onto a road signed 'Suspiro del Moro' and in five minutes you emerge in front of the Suspiro del Moro restaurant, with Granada in view 12km to the north. You're at the Puerto del Suspiro del Moro, the 'Pass of the Moor's Sigh,' where, legend has it, the last Muslim emir of Granada, Boabdil, looked back and wept as he left the city for the final time in 1492. Follow the 'Granada' signs to continue to the city.

Windsurf La Herradura (☎ 958 64 01 43; www .windsurflaherradura.com; Paseo Andrés Segovia 34) Windsurfing, kitesurfing, canoeing, kayaking.

Some of the best dive sites are around Punta de la Mona and Cerro Gordo at the bay's eastern and western ends respectively, and the Grutas de Cantarriján further west.

Sleeping

Hotel Sol Los Fenicios (☎ 958 82 79 00; www.trypnet.com; Paseo Andrés Segovia; s €69-128, d €95-174; P ⊗ ☆) The best hotel in town, towards the eastern end of the beach, with 42 rooms. Nearly all have a sea view and terrace or balcony, and are set around an interior patio. The restaurant and café-bar overlook the beach, too.

Also recommended:

Nuevo Camping La Herradura (☎ 958 64 06 34; Paseo Andrés Segovia; camping per 2 adults, tent & car €20) Fairly basic camping ground across the street from the western part of the beach.

Hostal Peña Parda (☎ 958 64 00 66; Paseo Andrés Segovia 65; d €48) At the western end of the beach, with a good restaurant.

Hostal La Caleta (☎ 958 82 70 07; Paseo Andrés Segovia s/n; d €60-72) Towards the eastern end of the beach, also with a good restaurant.

Eating

Most restaurants on Paseo Andrés Segovia serve good food at reasonable prices, although they mark up drinks.

El Chambao de Joaquín (☎ 958 64 00 44; Paseo Andrés Segovia; paella €6) Paella is dished out from a giant pan at 2.30pm every Saturday and Sunday in the beachside garden here at the far eastern end of the beach. You need to book for Sunday.

Chiringuito La Sardina (☎ 958 64 01 11; Paseo Andrés Segovia; mains €9-16) Situated right on the beach, La Sardina is a top place for seafood.

Mesón El Tinao (☎ 958 82 74 88; Edificio Bahía II, Paseo Andrés Segovia; mains €12-20; ☽ closed Mon) El Tinao prepares excellent Alpujarras food and unusual dishes such as duck with raspberries.

Getting There & Away

Plenty of Alsina Graells buses head east and west along the coast and a few go to Granada. Buses go to Almería (€9.50, 3½ hours, five daily), Almuñécar (€0.90, 15 minutes, 10 daily), Granada (€7, two hours, five daily), Málaga (€5, 1¾ hours, six daily) and Nerja (€1.60, 20 minutes, 10 daily). Catch them from the Alsina Graells bus stop at the top of Calle Acera del Pilar, by the N340.

Almería Province

Almería's big draw is sun, sand and ehm, sun again – over 3000 hours of it a year. Stretches of green golf courses in this dry part of Europe bring in sun-seekers and settlers on low-cost flights from Europe. The region is a bit of a contradiction: on the one hand, it's overdeveloped in places and vastly populated by postretirement Brits, Germans and Scandinavians looking for a cheap place to live and enjoy the sun; on the other hand, it is one of the least explored coastal areas in Andalucía, with excellent beaches hiding in the Parque Natural Cabo de Gata-Níjar. Up-and-coming coastal pueblos along Cabo de Gata, such as the village of Agua Amarga, are something like the Hamptons for Madrid's trendy, young professionals.

Inland, the wooded Alpujarras give way to a succession of mountain ranges. Vast parts of the province are mountainous semidesert, with beautiful landscapes and Spaghetti Western film sets. Paradoxically, this arid region is the 'garden of Europe', ie a top area for greenhouse fruit and vegetables, which are then sold all over the EU.

Things change still in Almería city, the coastal capital, a place that many say is an 'extension' of Morocco, with signposting in Spanish and Arabic and ferry-loads of immigrant labourers filling the streets down by the seafront and along Calle Real. Despite its lack of major sights, save for the Alcazaba, the city has an unpolished, promising vibe, a couple of good restaurants and tapas bars, and is refreshingly untouristy.

HIGHLIGHTS

- Experience silence and solitude on the rugged, sandy beaches along the **Parque Natural Cabo de Gata-Níjar** (p410)
- Get into shabby chic with the trendy *madrileños* at **Agua Amarga** (p415)
- See the sea of mountainous desert and Wild West film sets amid the arid mountains of the **Tabernas** (p407)
- Explore Almería's biggest Islamic monument, the **Alcazaba** (p401)
- Go underground at the **Cuevas de Sorbas** (p408) for one of the best caving excursions in Andalucía
- Check out the magnificent views from **Mojácar Pueblo** (p416)

ALMERÍA PROVINCE

| ■ POPULATION: 546,000 | ■ ALMERÍA AV DAILY HIGH: JAN/AUG 13°C/25°C | ■ ALTITUDE RANGE: 0M–2609M |

ALMERÍA

pop 177,000

This is Andalucía in its up-and-coming guise. Almería, a town known mainly for the sunny province that surrounds it, has much too tough a competition to deal with: with Granada and Seville lording over the region, poor Almería is not given the time of day by many. But if you want to get off the beaten track, this is the place to visit. Almería is something like the Marseilles of Spain, or how Valencia was a decade ago. It has been described as a 'rough diamond' and 'rough around the edges', but with the efforts of Almería's proud citizens, and the agri-dollars that come in from the plastic agriculture, Almería is now experiencing something of a cultural and architectural resurrection.

There's already plenty in Almería for a couple of days' stay: the enormous Alcazaba (citadel) is a major historical site; the old quarter is dotted with charming marble squares, churches and a cathedral, shaded by tall palms; the wide boulevard is forever full of people, and there are old-style tapas bars and innovative, modern-cuisine restaurants. Chic bars and clubs are packed and stay rocking till dawn. This city is definitely a great place to get a touch of Andalucía with an edge that is getting smoother by the year.

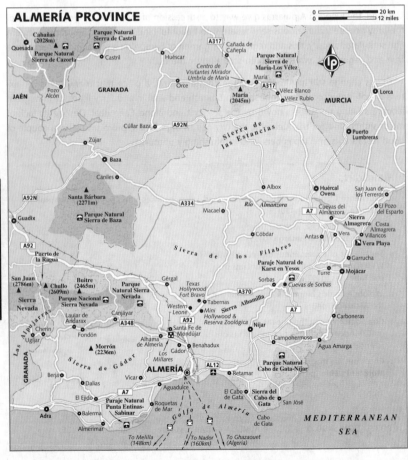

ALMERÍA PROVINCE

HISTORY

Almería's watchtower, the grand Alcazaba, is the only remaining Islamic monument in town and a reminder of the city's former historical importance. The name 'Almería' comes from the Arabic *al-mariyya* (the watchtower), in reference to the Alcazaba, but it has also been suggested that it may come from *al-miraya* (the mirror) – reflecting North Africa back to itself.

This monument harks back to the time when merchants from Egypt, Syria, France and Italy thronged the city's streets. Initially a port for the Cordoban caliphate, it soon became the most important outlet of Al-Andalus, being both the headquarters of the Omayyad fleet and its admiral. Almería once raked in revenues that far surpassed any other Andalucian seaport. Following the Reconquista (Christian reconquest), the city began a long, slow decline, exacerbated by the shifting of naval interests to the Atlantic ports and the Americas. Following a devastating earthquake, a census revealed that in 1658 the city had only 500 inhabitants. Things never really picked up for Almería, but it seems that finally the fortunes are turning and the flush of agri-dollars coming in from the controversial, yet booming, *plasticultura* industry is being streamed towards a concerted drive to market the region as an alternative to the Costa del Sol.

ORIENTATION

Old and new Almería lie either side of the Rambla de Belén, a *paseo* (walk) that runs down the centre of Avenida de Federico García Lorca. A broad, airy boulevard, Rambla de Belén descends gently towards the sea. East of the Rambla lies Almería's architecturally bland commercial district; to its west is the city centre, the cathedral, the Alcazaba and the oldest and most interesting streets and plazas. The old city's main artery, Paseo de Almería, leads diagonally north from Rambla de Belén to a busy intersection called Puerta de Purchena. The bus and train stations sit side by side on the Carretera de Ronda, a few hundred metres east of the seaward end of Rambla de Belén.

INFORMATION
Bookshops

El Libro Picasso (☎ 950 23 56 00; Calle de los Reyes Católicos 17 & 18) An excellent bookshop with two branches across the street from each other. General interest books and maps of all kinds.

Emergency

Policía Local (Local Police; ☎ 950 21 00 19; Calle Santos Zárate 11) Just off Rambla de Belén.
Policía Nacional (National Police; ☎ 950 22 37 04; Avenida Mediterráneo 201) At the northern end of Avenida Frederico García Lorca.
Red Cross (Cruz Roja; ☎ 950 22 22 22) Call this number to request an ambulance.

Internet Access

Internet (Avenida de Pablo Iglesias ☼ 8am-2am; per hr €2) A small shop-cum-internet café, with plenty of terminals and good connections. Very central.
Voz y Datos (bus terminal, Carretera de Ronda; per hr €2 ☼ 9am-2pm & 4.30-8.30pm Mon-Fri, 9.30am-2pm Sat) Two handy computers in the main bus terminal.

Internet Resources

Andalucia.com (www.andalucia.com) A generic regional site with several pages dedicated to information about Almería.

Medical Services

Hospital Torrecárdenas (☎ 950 01 61 00; Pasaje Torrecárdenas) The the main public hospital, located 4km northeast of the city centre.

Money

There are numerous banks on Paseo de Almería. There is also a Banco de Andalucía with an ATM in the bus terminal.

Post

Post office (Plaza de Juan Cassinello 1; ☼ 9am-8pm Mon-Fri & 9am-1.30pm Sat) Just off Paseo de Almería.

Tourist Information

Municipal tourist office (☎ 950 28 07 48; Rambla de Belén, Avenida de Federico García Lorca s/n; ☼ 10am-1pm & 5.30-7.30pm Mon-Fri, 10am-noon Sat) Found below ground level, but not very well signedposted. It has a very useful range of information and helpful staff.
Regional tourist office (☎ 950 27 43 55; Parque de Nicolás Salmerón s/n; ☼ 9am-7pm Mon-Fri, 10am-2pm Sat & Sun) Provides more free leaflets and brochures.

SIGHTS

Almería's enormous Alcazaba is the city's main sight and can be explored thoroughly in a good halfday. Almería is not a monumental city, but there are plenty of interesting distractions in its meandering streets.

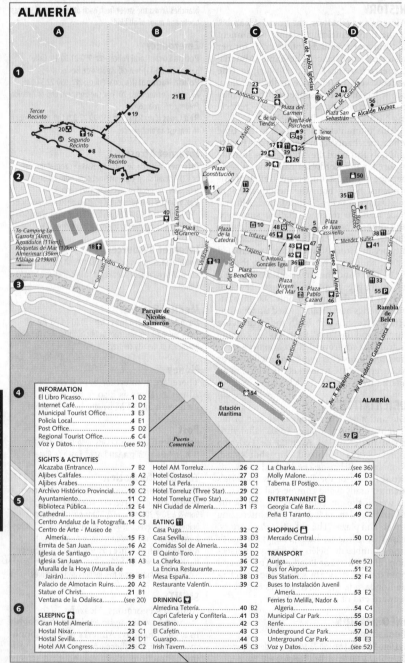

ALMERÍA

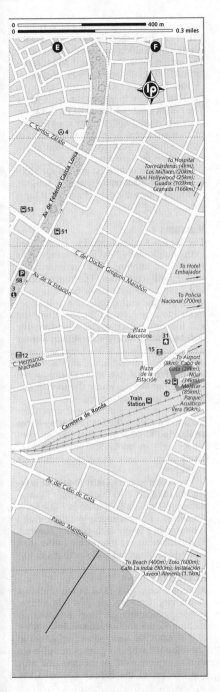

To Hospital
Torrecárdenas (4km);
Los Millares (20km);
Mini Hollywood (25km);
Guadix (109km);
Granada (166km)

To Hotel
Embajador

To Policía
Nacional (700m)

Plaza
Barcelona

To Airport
(8km); Cabo de
Gata (28km);
Níjar
(34km);
Mojácar
(85km);
Parque
Acuático
Vera (90km)

Plaza
de la
Estación

Train
Station

Carretera de Ronda

Av del Cabo de Gata

Paseo Marítimo

To Beach (400m); Eolo (600m);
Café La India (900m); Instalación
Juvenil Almería (1.1km)

ALMERÍA PROVINCE

The old town tumbles down its eastern slope and is the location of most of the city's cafés and bars. Other notable sights are the cathedral to the south, and the archaeological collections in the Biblioteca Pública and Archivo Histórico Provincial to the east.

Almería's beach is a good kilometre out of the centre of town but can be crowded in summer. A better alternative is a day or two in the Parque Natural Cabo de Gata-Níjar (p410), an easy day trip from Almería.

Alcazaba

The **Alcazaba** (☎ 950 27 16 17; Calle Almanzor s/n; EU/non-EU citizen free/€1.50; ☒ 10am-2pm & 5-8pm May-Sep, 9.30am-1.30pm & 3.30-7pm Oct-Apr, closed 25 Dec & 1 Jan) is Almería's premier attraction: a monstrous fortress that rises austerely from impregnable cliffs to dominate the city. Built in the 10th century by Abd ar-Rahman III, the greatest caliph of Al-Andalus, the simple 'watchtower' transformed the seaport into a major metropolis and a flourishing locus for trade. Even though its interior doesn't measure up to the Alhambra (p359), having been shaken by a dramatic earthquake and ravaged by time, it is nonetheless an interesting place.

The huge interior is divided into three separate compounds and originally contained the civic centre in the lowest area, the **Primer Recinto**. Houses, baths, water storage chambers and all the necessities for city life have now been replaced by windswept rose gardens. From the battlements you can see the **Muralla de la Hoya** (also known as the Muralla de Jairán) – a fortified wall built in the 11th century by Jairán, Almería's first *taifa* (small kingdom) ruler – which descends the valley on the northern side of the Alcazaba and climbs the slopes of Cerro de San Cristóbal opposite, a parched and barren hill crowned with a ruined church and a giant **statue of Christ**.

Deeper within the fortified walls is the **Segundo Recinto**. On the northern side of the enclosure you will find the ruins of the Muslim rulers' palace, **Palacio de Almotacín**. It's named after Almotacín (r 1051–91), under whom medieval Almería reached its peak. Inside, the **Ventana de la Odalisca** (Concubine's Window) is romantically named after a slave girl who, legend says, leapt to her death after her Christian lover had been thrown from the same window.

Also within the compound are the pre-served **Aljibes Califales** (Caliphal Water Cis-terns) and a chapel, the **Ermita de San Juan**, converted from a mosque by the Reyes Católicos (Catholic Monarchs).

At the highest point of the Alcazaba, within the **Tercer Recinto**, is a fortress that was added by the Catholic Monarchs. It has been well restored and from its walls there are breathtaking views across the city and the sea.

The Cathedral & Around

Almería's fortresslike **cathedral** (Plaza de la Catedral; admission €2; ☺ 10am-5pm Mon-Fri, 10am-1pm Sat) is shaded by tall palms and fronted by a peaceful square. With its embattled walls and six formidable towers, the struc-ture was designed to withstand constant piratical raids. Its one notable decorative feature is the exuberant **Sol de Portocarrero**, a splendid 16th-century relief of the sun carved on the eastern (Calle del Cubo) end of the building. The vast, spacious inte-rior – dominated by three huge naves – is trimmed with jasper and local marble. The chapel behind the main altar contains the tomb of the cathedral's founder, Bishop Diego Villalán. The bishop's broken-nosed image is a work of 16th-century architect and sculptor Juan de Orea, as are the choir, with its walnut stalls, and the Sacristía Mayor. A door in the south wall opens onto a small Renaissance courtyard crammed with shrubs and flowers. The cathedral's architect built another fascinating build-ing: the **Iglesia de Santiago** (St James' Church; Calle de las Tiendas; ☺ hours of service). Erected in the 1550s, this is now the centre of a hip area, full of bars and restaurants.

Remains of Almería's Islamic past are evident in several buildings. The **Iglesia San Juan** (Calle San Juan; ☺ hours of service), the city's old mosque, still has its 11th-century mihrab. The old Arab *souq* (market) where livestock, fruits and vegetables were sold and no doubt lots of tea was drunk, is now **Plaza Constitución** (also known as Plaza Vieja), a charming 17th-century arcaded square hung with vivid bougainvillea. The centre of the plaza is filled with tall palm trees that encircle the bone-white **Monumento a los Colorgos** (Monument to the Redcoats), which commemorates the execution in 1824 of 24 liberals who took part in a rebel-lion against the despotic rule of Fernando VII. The city's theatrical-looking **ayunta-miento** (city hall) is on its northwest side. The extremely well preserved **Aljibes Árabes** (☎ 950 27 30 39; Calle Tenor Iribarne 20; admission free; ☺ 10am-2pm Mon-Fri), were built by Jairán in the 11th century to supply the city's water. The old city gate of **Puerta de Purchena**, the place where Al-Zagal, the city's last Muslim ruler, surrendered here to the Christians in 1490, is now a busy road junction at the heart of the modern city.

Other places of interest are the spectacu-lar covered **mercado central** (market; ☺ 8am-2pm), surrounded by some of the town's best tapas bars.

Museums

The Museo Arqueológico has been closed to the public since 1993 and the saga of its notable collection of Los Millares archaeo-logical finds continues. The tourist office will have up-to-date news but it is most likely that the entire collection will be re-located to a new site. In the meantime you will have to scatter yourself between the **Biblioteca Pública** (Calle Hermanos Machado; admission free; ☺ 9am-2pm Mon-Fri, 9.30am-1.30pm Sat), hous-ing some prehistoric finds, and the **Archivo Histórico Provincial** (Calle Infanta 12; admission free; ☺ 9am-2.30pm Mon-Fri), where the Iberian and Roman artefacts are located.

To see the city's permanent art collec-tion, take a visit to the **Centro de Arte – Museo de Almería** (☎ 950 26 64 80; Plaza Barcelona; admis-sion free; ☺ 11am-2pm & 6-9pm Mon-Fri, 6-9pm Sat, 11am-2pm Sun), which also stages temporary exhibitions.

The contemporary **Centro Andaluz de la Fo-tografía** (☎ 950 00 27 00; Calle Conde Ofalia 30; admis-sion free; ☺ 11am-2pm & 6-9pm Mon-Fri, 7-10pm Sat) is Andalucía's first photography museum and is housed in a lovely 18th-century convent. The exhibitions are interesting rather than ground-breaking, but still worth going to.

ACTIVITIES

Almería's long, grey-sand beach southeast of the city, fronting the Paseo Marítimo, is not particularly exciting. But what *is* exciting is the well-organised **Eolo** (☎ 950 26 17 35, 670-391480; www.eolo-wind.com; Avenida del Cabo de Gata 187), which organises out-of-town trips to explore some of the dramatic cliffs and beaches of the Parque Natural Cabo de Gata-Níjar by windsurfing, kayaking, catamaran and other water-related activities. Eolo has English-speaking staff and its trips range from €39 to €90. You can learn or perfect your windsurfing with a 10-hour course for €72. Or you can simply rent equipment (one hour/one day for €9/€30) and Eolo will even deliver it to the park for you.

WALKING TOUR

The main arterial road leading from the south to the Alcazaba, called Calle de la Reina, once divided the old Muslim medina and the quarter of La Musalla, which was originally a large orchard. Turn right into Calle Bailén and walk about 150m to reach Almería's impressive **cathedral (1)**. Head back to Calle de la Reina and take a turn west along Calle Almedina, which will take you deep into a narrow labyrinth of original Muslim-era streets to the **Iglesia San Juan (2)**. From here it is just a five-minute walk to the entrance of the **Alcazaba (3)** on Calle Almanzor.

Calle Almanzor heads east to the beautiful **Plaza Constitución (4)** and the city's **ayuntamiento (5)**. At the centre of the plaza is the **Monumento a los Colorgos (6)**. From the

plaza, walk about 300m northeast up Calle de las Tiendas. Here, you'll pass the lovely **Iglesia de Santiago (7)**, before arriving at the **Aljibes Árabes (8)**. A stone's throw from here, further along Calle de las Tiendas, is the old city gate of **Puerta de Purchena (9)**.

To take a break for lunch, walk about 200m from the gate down Rambla del Obispo Orbera, turning right at Calle de los Reyes Católicos to get to the covered **mercado central (10**; ⏰ 8am-2pm). There are some good eateries nearby, including Comidas Sol de Almería (p405) and El Quinto Toro (p405). After lunch wander down the Paseo de Almería, and after about 500m turn right into Calle General Tamayo, walking one block to reach the contemporary **Centro Andaluz de la Fotografía (11)** for a cultural pick-me-up.

FESTIVALS & EVENTS

Feria de Almería (late August) runs for 10 days and nights with live music, bullfights, fairground rides, exhibitions and full-on partying.

SLEEPING

Almería's bunking choices are pretty uninspiring, especially on the budget end. Things improve as prices rise, and in midrange rooms you can count on satellite TV, air-con in summer and heating in winter.

Budget

Camping La Garrofa (☎ 950 23 57 70; www.lagarrofa .com; camping per person/tent/car €4/4/4, bungalow €75;

WALKING TOUR	
Distance	2.6km
Duration	3–4 hours

ALMERÍA PROVINCE

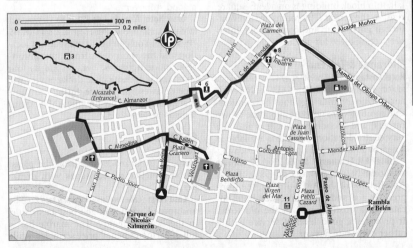

year-round) An attractive camping ground on the coast, 4km west of town on the Aguadulce road. In addition to the camping ground there are some two-bedroom self-catering bungalows (sleeping up to five people) and you can arrange a host of activities at the site.

Albergue Juvenil Almería (☎ 950 26 97 88; fax 950 27 17 44; Calle Isla de Fuerteventura s/n; under/over 26yr €14/19) Clean and well-kept, the Albergue can accommodate 170 people, nearly all in double rooms. It's 1.5km east of the city centre, beside the stadium and three blocks north of Avenida del Cabo de Gata. Take Bus 1 'Universidad' from the eastern end of Rambla del Obispo Orbera and ask the driver for the *albergue* (hostel) or for the stadium.

Hostal Nixar (☎ /fax 950 23 72 55; Calle Antonio Vico 24; s/d €27/45) Time stands still at this gloomy hotel where a grim man welcomes you without a smile. The rooms are adequate, however, for a night's stay and the place is central enough. You have to ring for entrance, even in the middle of the day.

Hostal Sevilla (☎ 950 23 00 09; Calle de Granada 23; s/d €34/54; ⚡) This small, friendly place is Almería's best *hostal* (budget hotel), with old-fashioned grey telephones as the peak of its design features. It's clean and efficient and the rooms have TVs with flickering domestic channels.

Hotel La Perla (☎ 950 23 88 77; fax 950 27 58 16; Plaza del Carmen 7; s/d €45/65; ⚡ 🖳) La Perla's tall, thin block building is on a leafy square, right in the centre. The rooms are uneventful but good value and comfortable. Internet access is free for guests.

Midrange & Top End

Hotel Costasol (☎ /fax 950 23 40 11; www.hotelcosta sol.com; Paseo de Almería 58; s/d €52/71; ⚡) This fairly ordinary midrange hotel has comfortable rooms (we're not sure about the brown carpets) and friendly service. It is also in a very central location. Parking is available in a nearby municipal car park (€7 per day).

Hotel AM Congress (☎ 950 23 49 99; www.am torreluz.com; Plaza de las Flores 5; s/d €56/60; P ⚡) An offshoot of the AM Torreluz, the Congress is a brand-new three-star hotel located in a bustling part of the old town. It provides a good level of service with a rather corporate flavour.

Hotel AM Torreluz (☎ 950 23 49 99; www.am torreluz.com; Plaza de las Flores 5; s/d €69/92; P ⚡ ⚡) A grand four-star place with lots of brass and marble and a huge sweeping staircase. It's definitely a favourite with business clientele and has all the trimmings. Note that it's under different management to its namesake neighbours (the two- and three-star hotels of Hotel Torreluz). Prices are reduced by up to 40% on weekends.

NH Ciudad de Almería (☎ 950 18 25 00; nhciudad -dealmeria@nh-hotels.com; Calle Jardín de Medina s/n; d €80-131; P ⚡) Bordering on the quietly stylish modern look and characterless anonymity, the NH is a well-appointed chain hotel, even if it doesn't quite pull off the style-statement of the year. As it's opposite the bus and train stations it also makes for a good stopover.

Gran Hotel Almería (☎ 950 23 80 11; www.gran hotelalmeria.com; Avenida Reina Regente 8; s/d €108/135; P ⚡ ⚡) You can't beat the seafront location and the wide views from the comfortable, modern rooms, but, despite its four stars and a website that declares you will receive 'awesome' service during your time there, you'll probably find the AM Torreluz hotel is better value.

EATING
Tapas

Here, as in Granada and Jaén, the pleasurable practice of free tapas with drinks persists.

Casa Puga (Calle Jovellanos 7; drink & tapa €1) The undisputed winner of the best tapas title, in the heavy category. The marble bar is full of barmen's pencil price scribbles, while fat *jamónes* (hams) hang suspended from wrought-iron hooks in bunches, like meaty chandeliers. Shelves of ancient wine bottles and traditional *azulejo* wall tiles set the tone for a roaring lunch.

El Quinto Toro (☎ 950 26 15 21; Calle de los Reyes Católicos; drink & tapa €1.50) Close to the market, this dark, bullfight-loving, atmospheric bar is always full of faithful tapas devotees.

La Charka (☎ 950 25 60 45; Calle Trajano 8; drink & tapa €1.50) A very popular tapas bar in Almería's busiest evening spot. A big bar, wooden chairs and tables and real 'saucers' of tapas (rather than plates) provide just the right amount of nibbles to keep the clientele guzzling. A great spot to graze before moving on to some late-night bars.

Mesa España (☎ 950 27 49 28; Calle Mendez Nuñez 19; drink & tapa €1.80, fondue €20) This busy bar and restaurant has seating up-front for tapas eaters and red *comedor* (dining room) banquettes at the back for serious dining. A great stop in the evening, especially for a fondue melting session.

Restaurants

Comidas Sol de Almería (Calle Circunvalación, Mercado Central; menú €9; closed Sun & Mon evenings;) A fun little restaurant opposite the busy covered market. At lunch, hungry shoppers stream in here to tuck into the extensive and hearty daily *menú* (set menu). There is also a large patio out the back, dotted with flowering oleanders.

Restaurante Valentín (☎ 950 26 44 75; Calle Tenor Iribarne 19; mains €10-15; Tue-Sun Oct-Aug) A secluded little restaurant with stylish service. Dark wood and exposed brickwork create an intimate atmosphere and the food is good. If you really want to splash out and

> **THE AUTHOR'S CHOICE**
>
> **La Encina Restaurante** (☎ 950 27 34 29; Calle Marín 3; mains €11-21; closed Sun & Mon evening) Almería's most exciting restaurant for inventive cuisine. Get yourself some deer cutlets with caramel treacle (€21), see-through thin *carpaccio* (€12) or pork medallions with mushrooms, pine nuts and sweet *moscatel* wine. If there's space, finish with a fondue of fresh fruit and chocolate. Alternatively, have some tapas and relax al fresco on the terrace.

eat in style, the *langosta* (lobster) will set you back €52.

Casa Sevilla (☎ 950 27 29 12; Calle Rueda López; menú €24; closed Sun & 1st-15th Aug) A *tour de force* of Andalucian cuisine and wine (the same people own La Vinoteca next door). Specialities include *bacalao a la almeriense* (cod in a spicy tomato sauce) and Argentinian beef, and there are over 8000 bottles of wine from which to choose. The restaurant is inside the Galería Almericentro shopping centre.

DRINKING

Capri Cafetería y Confitería (☎ 950 23 76 85; Calle Méndez Núñez 14) If you need to put up your feet late in the afternoon, prop up the chrome bar at the Capri where you can tuck into a range of delicious pastries or enjoy a cool granita.

Almedina Tetería (Calle Paz 2, off Calle Almedina; 11am-11pm Wed-Sun) Inside the Islamic centre and in a tiny street, the lovely Almedina serves mint teas and good couscous; if you're feeling wild, get a henna tattoo.

Guarapo (☎ 950 268 188; Calle Antonio González Egea; 4.30pm-late) Shiny, modern and trendy, the youngsters devour the endless cocktail combinations and stay up very, very late.

Desatino (Calle Trajano 14; 8pm-late) A trendy bar with mirrored windows, playing Cuban rumbas. It doesn't fill up until late.

Molly Malone (Paseo de Almería 56; 8am-11pm) A massive tree shades the front terrace of this fun bar. Inside it's all spit-and-sawdust décor – lots of dark wood and old London theatre posters – bathing in the fog of cigarette smoke. It is also a great spot for breakfast (€2.50).

La Charka (☎ 950 25 60 45; Calle Trajano 8; 8pm-2am) This tiny but packed tapas bar is opposite Desatino.

Other popular bars on Calle Antonio González Egea include El Bicho, the Irish Tavern and Taberna El Postigo.

ENTERTAINMENT

A dozen or so music bars are clustered in the streets between the post office and the cathedral. Some of them open from late afternoon.

Peña El Taranto (☎ 950 23 50 57; Calle Tenor Iribarne 20) Almería's top flamenco club hides in the renovated Aljibes Árabes (Arab Water Cisterns). Live performances (€20), open to the public, often happen on weekends. Ring for details or check at the tourist office.

Georgia Café Bar (☎ 950 25 25 70; Calle Padre Luque 17; ☺ 8pm-late) The Georgia Café Bar has a terrific ambience. It has been open for more than 20 years and stages the occasional live-jazz gig, although even the piped music is great.

GETTING THERE & AWAY
Air

Almería's **airport** (☎ 950 21 37 00; www.aena.es) receives charter flights from several European countries. You can get cheap flights from several British and European cities (see p441). Scheduled services go to/from Düsseldorf with **LTU** (☎ 950 21 37 80; www.ltu.de), to London Gatwick with **GB Airways** (☎ 950 21 38 98; www.gbairways.com) and to Barcelona, Madrid and Melilla with **Iberia** (☎ 950 21 37 90; www.iberia.com). You can pick up inexpensive outbound international fares from agencies such as **Viajes Cemo** (airport ☎ 950 21 38 47; Roquetas de Mar ☎ 950 33 35 02) or **Tarleton Direct** (airport ☎ 950 21 37 70; Mojácar ☎ 950 47 22 48; Roquetas de Mar ☎ 950 33 37 34).

Boat

From Almería's Estación Marítima (passenger port), **Trasmediterránea** (☎ 950 23 61 55, 902 45 46 45; www.trasmediterranea.es) sails to/from Melilla three times daily Tuesday to Friday and twice daily Saturday to Monday, from June to September, with daily sailings from October to May. The trip takes up to eight hours. The cheapest passenger accommodation, a *butaca* (seat), costs €29 one way; the fare for a car starts at €123 for a small vehicle.

The Moroccan lines **Ferrimaroc** (☎ 950 27 48 00; www.ferrimaroc.com), **Comarit** (☎ 950 23 61 55; www.comarit.com in Spanish) and **Limadet** (☎ 950 27 07 71) sail to/from Nador, the Moroccan town neighbouring Melilla, with similar frequency to Trasmediterránea. Prices vary between €28 to €33 for a one-way adult fare and €128 to €139 for a car.

You can buy tickets for all sailings at the Estación Marítima. See the Transport chapter for more information regarding services to Morocco (p448).

Bus

Daily departures from the **bus station** (☎ 950 26 20 98) include buses to the following destinations:

Córdoba (€22, 5 hours) One daily.
Guadix (€7.50, 1¼ hours) Nine daily.
Granada (€10-12.20, 2¼ hours) Up to 10 daily.
Jaén (€19, 5 hours) One or two daily.
Madrid (€23, 7 hours) Five daily.
Málaga (€15, 3¼ hours) Up to 10 daily.
Murcia (€5, 2½ hours) Ten or more daily.
Seville (€28-29, 5 hours) Two daily.
Valencia (€31-38, 8½ hours) Five daily.

For buses to places within Almería province, see left for information on individual destinations.

The bus station is extremely efficient and clean. There are clean toilets, an ATM, internet access (p399) and automatic left-luggage lockers (per day €5). Renfe has a travel centre in the terminal, where you can book onward tickets, and there is a helpful **information desk** (☺ 6.45am-10.45pm) that will direct you to the right ticket booth for your destination.

Train

You can buy tickets at the town centre **Renfe** (☎ 950 23 18 22; www.renfe.es; Calle Alcalde Muñoz 7; ☺ 9.30am-1.30pm Mon-Fri & 9.30am-1pm Sat) office, as well as at the **train station** (☎ 902 24 02 02). Direct trains run to/from Granada (€14 2¼ hours, four daily), Seville (€32, 5½ hours, four daily) and Madrid (€33 to €38, 6¾ to 10 hours, twice daily).

GETTING AROUND
To/From the Airport

The airport is 8km east of the city, off the AL12; bus 20 (the 'Alquián' bus; €1) runs between the city (from the western end of Calle del Doctor Gregorio Marañón) and the airport every 30 to 45 minutes from 7am to 10.30pm, but less frequently on Saturday and Sunday. It runs from the airport to the city every 30 to 45 minutes from 7am to 10.08pm Monday to Friday, and from 7am to 11.03pm on Saturday and Sunday.

Car & Motorcycle

There are several car-rental agencies in the city. Avis, Europcar and Hertz have desks at the airport. A good-value local company, **Auriga** (☎ 902 20 64 00; www.aurigacar.com), has an office in the bus terminal.

Almería has the same difficult streetside parking as most Andalucian cities. Parking for 30 minutes will cost you €0.20 and an hour is €1.05. There are, however, large underground car parks beneath the Rambla de Belén and on the eastern side of the Rambla at its seaward end. Fees at these car parks are €1 for one hour and €10 for 24 hours.

Taxis

There are **taxi stands** (☎ 950 22 61 61; night taxis ☎ 950 42 5757) on Puerta de Purchena and Paseo de Almería and at the bus and train stations.

NORTH OF ALMERÍA

LOS MILLARES

You need to be an archaeology enthusiast to consider a visit to **Los Millares** (☎ 608 903404; admission free; ❤ 9.30am-4pm Tue-Sat Apr-Sep, 10am-2pm Wed-Sat Oct-Mar), 20km northwest of Almería between the villages of Gádor and Santa Fé de Mondújar. Your own transport is necessary as there is no viable public transport and the site is a 1.5km trek from the main road.

The site covers 190,000 sq metres and stands on a 1km-long spur between the Río Andarax and Rambla de Huéchar. It was a town that was possibly occupied from around 2700 BC to 1800 BC, during a period when the Río Andarax was navigable from the sea. The town's metalworking people may have numbered up to 2000 during optimum periods of occupation. They hunted, bred domestic animals and grew crops; their skills included pottery and jewellery-making, and certain finds indicate trading links with other parts of the Mediterranean.

The site is enclosed within four lines of defensive walls reflecting successive enlargements of the settlement. Inside lie the ruins of the stone houses typical of the period. Outside the living area are the ruins – and some reconstructions – of typical passage graves (domed chambers entered by a low passageway) of the Neolithic and pre-Bronze Age period.

Do not be discouraged by a notice on the roadside wall of the gatehouse stating that you should contact the Delegación de Cultura de Almería for permission to enter the site. It is essential, however, that before you leave for the site you check that someone will be on duty at Los Millares **gatehouse** (☎ 608 95 70 65) to let you in. To get here, take the A92 north from Almería to Benahadux,

---

THE WILD WEST

When you go north of Benahadux, into Almería's savage semidesert landscape, you'd never think you were on ground that was once walked on by Clint Eastwood, Raquel Welch and Charles Bronson – the squinting, the pouting and the moustachioed stars of Spaghetti Westerns. But what the area may lack in water, it certainly doesn't lack in a history of film stars. In the 1960s and '70s, makers of Western movies spotted the resemblance between this area and the 'badlands' of the American West, and shot dozens of films here, including *A Fistful of Dollars*, *The Magnificent Seven* and *The Good, the Bad and the Ugly*. Locals played Indians, outlaws and cavalry, while Eastwood, Welch and Bronson took centre stage. Movie-makers come here less often now, but the surviving shells of three Wild West sets remain as bizarre and excellent tourist attractions.

Mini Hollywood (☎ 950 36 52 36; adult/child €17/9, ticket includes Reserva Zoológica; ❤ 10am-9pm Apr-Oct, 10am-7pm Tue-Sun Nov-Mar; shows at 5pm year-round, & 8pm from mid-Jun to mid-September), the best-known and most expensive of these sets, is 25km from Almería on the Tabernas road and has bank hold-ups, shoot-outs and hangings, plus men saying: 'This town ain't big enough for both of us, hombre' (in Spanish, of course). Rather bizarrely, adjoining the Wild West town is a wildlife town, the **Reserva Zoológica**, with lions, elephants, buffalo and other species.

Three kilometres further towards Tabernas, then a few minutes along a track to the north, **Texas Hollywood Fort Bravo** (☎ 950 16 54 58; www.texashollywood.com; adult/child €10.50/6.50; ❤ 10am-10pm) is another Western town, with a stockaded fort, a Mexican village and Indian tepees. There's also **Western Leone** (☎ 950 16 54 05; admission €9; ❤ 9.30am-sunset Apr-Sep, 9.30am-sunset Sat & Sun year-round) on the A92, about 1km north of the A370 turning. Both of these sights played a part in some of the same films as Mini Hollywood and have a more authentic if slightly worn-out air (which extends itself to their approach tracks, so it's best to drive slowly).

SOMETIMES IT'S HARD TO BE A COWBOY

'We just want to entertain, we want the audience to have a good time, you know?' A cowboy called Domingo speaks to me in a hoarse voice, while a dreamy film score plays in the background and shy kids ask for autographs. We're in Texas Hollywood Fort Bravo. He'd just done an array of somersaults, acrobatics, free falls and displayed a mastery of weapons, all on horseback. 'You have to be brave to do this job' says he. You certainly do – especially if your job involves mounting a horse at breakneck speed, and sometimes even jumping off balconies, straight into your saddle. 'I was once filming with a top star here on the set, and I was riding a horse so fast I fell off – seven stitches above one eye, five on the cheek.' But his injuries are not a hardship. In fact Domingo has worked hard to earn his right to be a cowboy: 'I came to see the show back in '86, and I loved it so much I asked to take part. They told me I could, but that I'd have to pay and bring my own horse. So I turned up with my horse and took part in the shows over the years, until I learned the trade and they started to pay me.' And the rest is history, so to speak. 'I've done loads of films and TV series, from WWII films to action films, doing stunts. But I love working here the most. I'm with the horses, the people like it, and we have fun. The Wild West is where I love to be.' He gets on his horse, shouts 'Yeeehaaa!' and rides off into a dusty Spanish sunset.

---

then head northwest on the A348. Signs indicate the Los Millares turning, shortly before Alhama de Almería.

NÍJAR

The small mountain town whose real-life story of forbidden love and revenge gave Federico García Lorca (p48) the inspiration for his poetic drama, *Blood Wedding*, is a beautiful though touristy town with narrow, uphill streets, and gleaming white houses whose flat roofs stand unforgivingly against the blue sky. Níjar's other claim to fame is the production of some of Andalucía's most attractive and original glazed pottery, and colourful striped rag rugs known as *jarapas*.

From the top end of Calle García Lorca, the narrow Calle Carretera leads into the heart of old Níjar and to **Plaza la Glorieta** and the church of **Santa María de la Anunciación**. Beyond Plaza la Glorieta, up Calle Colón, is the delightful **Plaza del Mercado**, with a huge central plane tree and a superb blue-tiled fountain with large fish-head taps.

Accommodation is limited, but **Hostal Asensio** (☎ 950 36 10 56; Calle Parque 2; s/d €20/38) has bright, pleasant rooms. Cheap eats can be had in the popular **Café Bar La Curva** (Calle Parque; platos combinados €6), which is diagonally opposite Hostal Asensio. For a more picturesque spot, though not great food, head for **Café Bar Glorieta** (Plaza la Glorieta; platos combinados €5) or across the plaza to **Bar Restaurante El Pipa** (Plaza la Glorieta; bocadillos €2.50).

Shops and workshops selling pottery and rugs line the main street, Calle García Lorca, and are dotted along the adjoining **Barrio Alfarero** (Potters' Quarter) along Calle Las Eras, off Calle García Lorca. Most notably, **La Tienda de los Milagros** (Calle Lavadero 2) is the workshop of British ceramicist Matthew Weir and his wife, who produces quality *jarapa* rugs.

Níjar is served by two buses a day (one only on Saturday), but the scheduled times make a return day trip from Almería impossible. By car, Níjar is 4km north of the A7, 31km northeast of Almería. There are parking bays all the way up Calle García Lorca, but check for parking restriction signs.

SORBAS

Another pottery town, Sorbas lies about 34km by road from Níjar and can be reached from here by a pleasant drive through the compact mountains of the Sierra de Alhamilla. More excitingly, Sorbas stands along the edge of a dramatic limestone gorge in the Paraje Natural de Karst en Yesos, where water erosion over millions of years has resulted in the stunning **Cuevas de Sorbas** (☎ 950 36 47 04; www.cuevasdesorbas.com; adult/child €10.50/6.50; ♥ guided tours 10am-8pm Apr-Oct). The excellent guided tours, complete with pit helmets and lights, can be organised through the town's **tourist office** (☎ 950 36 44 76; Calle Terraplén 9; ♥ 10.30am-2.30pm Wed-Sun) or through the **Centro de Visitantes Los Yesares** (☎ 950 36 44 81; Calle Terraplén s/n; ♥ 11am-2pm & 5-8pm). Both of these are located on the road into town. Tours are only run on request and at least a day's notice is required.

The only accommodation option is the bland, motel-style **Hostal Sorbas** (☎ 950 36 41 60; s/d €25/40; P) on the main road right at the entrance to the village. For food, the best options are **Cafetería Caymar** (Plaza de la Constitución; tapas €1.80) or the good-quality **Restaurante el Rincón** (☎ 950 36 41 52; Plaza de la Constitución; mains €8-14) next door. Both are on the charming central plaza.

There are buses from Almería to Sorbas and back (€4, 1¾ hours, four daily Monday to Friday).

LAS ALPUJARRAS

West of the small spa town of Alhama de Almería, the A348 winds up the Andarax Valley into the Almería section of Las Alpujarras (for more details on the Alpujarras, see p386).

The landscape is at first relentlessly barren, with arid, serrated ridges stretching to infinity. However, it gradually becomes more vegetated as you approach Fondón, where the small **Camping Puente Colgante** (☎ 950 51 42 90; camping per person/tent/car €2/2/2; year-round) is located.

For information on walking routes and refuges in the Sierra Nevada mountains, which rise from the north side of Las Alpujarras, visit the **Centro de Visitantes Laujar de Andarax** (☎ 950 51 35 48; 10.30am-2.30pm Thu & Fri, 10.30am-2.30pm & 6-8pm Sat & Sun), on the A348, just west of Laujar de Andarax.

Laujar de Andarax

pop 1800 / elevation 920m

This pleasant 'capital' of the Almería Alpujarras is where Boabdil, the last emir of Granada, settled briefly after losing Granada. It was also the headquarters of Aben Humeya, the first leader of the 1568–70 Morisco uprising, until he was assassinated by his cousin Aben Aboo. Today the town produces Almería's best wine.

SIGHTS & ACTIVITIES

To sample some of the local *vino* (wine), pop into the shop at **Cooperativo Valle de Laujar** (8.30am-noon & 3.30-7.30pm Mon-Sat) where you can sample the cooperative's own wines and *digestifs* and buy good local produce. You'll find it 2km west of town on the A348.

Laujar de Andarax itself is not remarkable but there is a handsome **Casa Consistorial** (town hall) on the central Plaza Mayor de la Alpujarra, with three tiers of arches crowned by a distinctive belfry. Otherwise, the large 17th-century brick **Iglesia de la Encarnación** is the only other building of note, with its minaretlike tower and a lavish golden retable.

A signposted road leads 1km north to **El Nacimiento**, a series of waterfalls in a deep valley, with a couple of restaurants nearby. On weekends the falls are full of weekending Spaniards who rock up to use the purpose-built barbecues under the trees. It's possible to buy meat and wood at the falls although most people usually bring their own.

The falls are the starting point for some walking trails that the Centro de Visitantes can tell you about.

SLEEPING & EATING

Hostal Fernández (☎ 950 51 31 28; Calle General Mola 2; s/d €16/31) Just off the main square, Plaza Mayor de la Alpujarra, this is a friendly place overlooking the square and the valley. It also has an excellent restaurant (mains €9) that serves local wines.

Hotel Almirez (☎ 950 51 35 14; almihost@larural .es; s/d €32/42) About 1km west of town on the A348, the Almirez is a nicely situated modern hotel with comfortable rooms. It has a bar and a large restaurant that offers a reasonable *menú* for €9.

A popular bar-restaurant is the **Fonda Nuevo Andarax** (☎ 950 51 31 28; Calle General Mola 4; d €33; raciones €3.50), which also has rooms above the restaurant.

GETTING THERE & AWAY

A bus to Laujar (€5, 1¼ hours, one daily) leaves Almería bus station at 9am Sunday to Friday, starting back from Laujar at 3.45pm. To get from Laujar to the Granada Alpujarras, take a bus to Berja, then another to Ugíjar or beyond.

COSTA DE ALMERÍA

AROUND ALMERÍA

Here is where Almería's coast becomes divided between noisy package-tourist resorts, such as **Aguadulce**, 11km from Almería, and, 6km further down the road,

ALMERÍA PROVINCE

THE PLASTIC SEA

The sea of plastic-fantastic greenhouses along Spain's most arid soil shows that with a bit of imagination, effort and no scruples, anything is possible. What was once a land where even olives struggled to grow has now become Europe's fruit 'n' veg garden. Beneath the steaming polythene swell tomatoes, lettuce and peppers, all irrigated by underground aquifers. Their production and sale has brought untold wealth to parts of Almería province since the 1970s. The prime example of this growth is the town of El Ejido, west of Almería: it has Spain's highest ratio of bank branches to population.

But these riches are starkly contrasted by terrible racism, particularly in El Ejido where in 2000, race-riots broke out against the African workers who labour at the greenhouses. Many of them are illegal immigrants who arrive on the infamous *pateras* (small, wooden boats) and hope to find work in Almería's greenhouses. Despite the fact that the industry wouldn't be what it is without their work, they get less than €20 a day and live and work in appalling conditions. Since 2004, many Eastern European workers have been brought to Almería's greenhouses to replace the African labour force, which has worsened both living and working conditions and decreased wages. The opening chapter of the travelogue *Andalus: Unlocking the Secrets of Moorish Spain,* by Jason Webster, describes the situation vividly.

The environmental price is also high: there are 20,000 tons of nonbiodegradable rubbish produced annually here, and the aquifers are diminishing. The real state of Almería's precious water resources became evident when the Partido Popular (PP) national government (1996–2004) planned to divert water from the Río Ebro in northern Spain to keep the show on the road. This was strongly opposed by Ebro area inhabitants and by ecologists concerned about the large Ebro delta. The plan has since been shelved under the Partido Socialista Obrero Español (PSOE) government. Instead, the world's second-largest desalination plant is being built at Carboneras on Almería's east coast, to ensure that Europe's driest desert continues to produce.

To see for yourself you can take the bizarre 'Plastic-fantastic' tour offered by **Hola-Almería** (☎ 627 46 03 01; sergitocv@yahoo.es; tours in English & Spanish €15), which takes you to a good old veg auction in El Ejido before commencing a tour of greenhouses in the locality and ending with tapas on the beach at Balerma.

Roquetas de Mar, and the quiet, isolated beaches to be sought out within the **Parque Natural Cabo de Gata-Níjar**, where there is a refreshing lack of big hotels and mass tourism. Then there are old seaside towns with stylish small hotels and gourmet restaurants by the beach, where trendy *madrileños* (residents of Madrid) come to spend their holidays, such as **Agua Amarga**. For those of you seeking some water sports fun, try **Almerimar**, a town popular with Spanish holidaymakers. It has the best windsurfing conditions on Andalucía's Mediterranean coast.

The extensive wetlands of the **Paraje Natural Punta Entinas-Sabinar**, located between Roquetas and Almerimar, are a good place for bird-watchers to spot greater flamingos and other water birds – around 150 species have been recorded there. A vast area to the west of Almería and a lesser one to its east are covered in plastic-sheeted greenhouses.

PARQUE NATURAL CABO DE GATA-NÍJAR

The wild rugged landscape of volcanic hills tumbling down into a sparkling turquoise sea around the Cabo de Gata peninsula is a delight to lovers of nature, silence and solitude. Some of Spain's most preserved and least crowded beaches are strung beautifully between the stark cliffs and capes of the dramatic Parque Natural Cabo de Gata-Níjar. With just 100mm of rain in an average year, Cabo de Gata is the driest place in Europe, yet the area supports over 1000 varieties of animal and plant wildlife that thrive in the arid, salty environment. The scattered settlements of whitewashed, flat-roofed houses add to its haunting character. This is one of the highlights of not only Andalucía, but the whole of Spain.

You can walk along the coast for 61km all the way from Retamar (east of Almería city) around the southern tip of Cabo de

Gata and then northeast to Agua Amarga, but in summer there's very little shade. This place gives you the feeling of being in real wilderness – nature here is still largely untouched and you are likely to be walking in splendid isolation amid some extraordinary scenery.

It's recommended to call ahead for accommodation anywhere on Cabo de Gata during Easter and July and August. Camping is only allowed in official camping grounds.

The Editorial Alpina 1:50,000 map *Cabo de Gata-Níjar Parque Natural* is the best for the area. See right for information on getting to the various villages on the peninsula.

Information

About 2.5km before Ruescas on the road from Almería is **Centro de Interpretación Las Amoladeras** (☎ 950 16 04 35; Carretera Cabo de Gata-Almería, Km 7; ☉ 10am-2pm & 5.30-9pm mid-Jul–mid-Sep, 10am-3pm Tue-Sun mid-Sep–mid-Jul), the main information centre for the Parque Natural Cabo de Gata-Níjar, which covers Cabo de Gata's 60km coast plus a thick strip of

hinterland. The centre has displays on the area's fauna, flora and human activities, as well as tourist information and maps.

Getting There & Away

Buses run from Almería to El Cabo de Gata (€2, 30 minutes, 10 daily), San José (€2.50, 1¼ hours, four daily Monday to Saturday), Las Negras (€3.50, 1¼ hours, one daily Monday to Saturday) and Agua Amarga (€4, 1¼ hours, one daily Monday to Friday). Bus schedules can be obtained from Almería city tourist offices or from Almería bus station.

To reach Faro de Gata you will need your own car. Alternatively you can hire bicycles in El Cabo de Gata at the **Oficina de Información** (☎ 950 38 00 04; Avenida Miramar 88; ☉ 10am-2.30pm & 5.30-9pm) for an easy ride. If you are touring the park by car, the only petrol station is halfway along the Ruescas–San José road. San José has a couple of car-rental agencies.

El Cabo de Gata

When people dreamily talk of Cabo de Gata, they are usually referring to the natural park,

rather than the village itself. A summer holiday resort for Almería's day-trippers who prostrate themselves on the coarse, sandy beach, out of season, the place is windswept, shuttered and deserted.

South of the town are the **Salinas de Cabo de Gata**, an area of soupy salt-extraction lagoons. In spring, many greater flamingos and other water birds call in at the salt pans while migrating from Africa to breeding grounds further north. With more arrivals in August there can be as many as 1000 flamingos on the pans. Autumn brings the largest numbers of birds as they pause on their return south. A good place to watch the birds is in the hide that's found in a wood-fenced area just off the road 3km south of the village.

Another flamingo-viewing spot, where you'll probably get closer to the birds, is the small lagoon where the stream **Rambla de Morales** reaches the beach, 2km northwest of El Cabo de Gata village.

A good way to explore the wide, flat area is on a bike, which can be hired in El Cabo de Gata at the **Oficina de Información** (☎ 950 38 00 04; Avenida Miramar 88; 2hr/1 day €4/13; ☉ 10am-2.30pm & 5.30-9pm).

An extremely well run camp site, **Camping Cabo de Gata** (☎ /fax 950 16 04 43; camping per person/site €4/8, bungalow €6; ☉ year-round; P ᵫ) is close to the beach, and probably the best place to stay in El Cabo de Gata. It has all the necessary amenities, including a restaurant and 250 sites. You will find it 2km down a signposted side road southwest of Ruescas.

Hostal Las Dunas (☎ 950 37 00 72; www.lasdunas.net; Calle Barrio Nuevo 58; s/d €36/51; P) is a friendly family house with well-kept, modern rooms and crazy balustraded balconies in carved marble.

Right at the entrance to the village, **Blanca Brisa** (☎ /fax 950 37 00 01; www.blancabrisa.com; Las Joricas 49; s/d €39/65; P), a big peach-coloured hotel, has clean and comfortable rooms with no décor to speak of. It has a large, decent restaurant (one of the few restaurants in town) with *platos combinados* (mixed plates) for about €5.

At the southern end of town, **La Goleta** (☎ 950 37 02 15; mains €5-20; ☉ closed Mon Oct-Jun & Nov) has good seafood and great sunset views from the beach tables.

El Naranjero (☎ 950 37 01 11; Calle Iglesia 1; mains €10-25; ☉ closed Sun) is one of the closest things you'll find to a proper restaurant in El Cabo de Gata, right at the entrance to the village. The Naranjero specialises in fish and seafood and gets busy at lunch time.

Faro de Cabo de Gata & Around

Salt collected from the *salinas* (salt lagoons) is piled up in great heaps at La Almadraba de Monteleva. This desolate-looking village has an equally desolate-looking church, the **Iglesia de las Salinas**, whose extremely tall tower dominates the area for miles around.

South of La Almadraba the coast becomes abruptly more rugged and the perilously narrow road winds airily around the sharp cliffs. It soon reaches the lonely lighthouse of the **Faro de Cabo de Gata** on the southern tip of the peninsula. From here a *mirador* (lookout) has a view over the jagged reefs of the **Arrecife de las Sirenas** (Reef of the Mermaids).

There is an **information cabin** (☉ 10am-2pm & 4.30-8.30pm May-Sep, 10am-3pm Oct-Apr) that has some information on the park, but it is randomly closed in the off-season. You can pick up information here about the boat trips around the peninsula that are run by

---

TOP BEACHES ALONG EL CABO DE GATA

- Cala Carbón – Fine sand, gorgeous sea
- Cala de la Media Luna – More fabulous swimming and sunbathing
- Playa Mónsul – As featured in *Indiana Jones and the Last Crusade*
- Playa del Barronal – Get in your birthday suit
- Calas del Barronal – The four seductive Calas are a dream
- Playa de los Genoveses – 1km of fine sand
- Playa San Pedro – A ruined hamlet beach now housing New Age hippies

El Cabo a Fondo (reservations ☎ 637 44 91 70). The trips are a wonderful way to view the dramatic coastline.

San José

Almería's attempts at creating a new Costa del Sol along its own coastline have resulted in places like San José or Mojácar Playa (p416), where, as in other resort towns, life happens mostly in the summer. San José does have a more tastefully executed appearance, with low-rise developments, a neat little marina, and a couple of good places to stay. Situated on the edge of the Parque Natural Cabo de Gata-Níjar, there are a host of healthy outdoor activities available, which is one of the reasons Spaniards flock here for the holidays and long weekends. The resort centres around a small sandy bay with a harbour at its eastern end, representing the village's origins as a fishing cove.

Drivers from El Cabo de Gata will have to head inland and turn off in an easterly direction towards Ruescas. After about 61km you will hit the San José–Níjar road. Turn right and after a further 7km you will reach San José.

ORIENTATION & INFORMATION

The road that enters the town eventually becomes San José's main street, Avenida de San José, with the beach, Playa de San José, a couple of blocks down to the left. On Avenida de San José, in the main block of shops and cafés, just before the central Plaza Génova, you'll find a **natural park information office and visitors centre** (☎ 950 38 02 99; ☽ 10am-2pm & 5-9.30pm Mon-Sat, 10am-2pm Sun). It sells maps and a range of books, souvenirs and craft work.

Also on Avenida de San José, in the village centre, are a Caja Rural bank, an ATM and a Spar supermarket.

ACTIVITIES

The information office can tell you about bicycle rental, boat trips, 4WD tours and diving. For horse riding, book a 45-minute lesson (€21.05) at the **Hotel Cortijo el Sotillo** (right), or take a cross-country ride to Playa de los Genoveses (€45, 2½ hours) or further into the *parque natural* (€64, 3½ hours). Almería's **Eolo** (☎ 950 26 17 35, 670-391480; www .eolo-wind.com; Avenida del Cabo de Gata 185, Almería)

also organises activity trips to the *parque natural*.

SLEEPING

Camping Tau (☎ /fax 950 38 01 66; e@parquenatural .com; camping per adult/child/tent/caravan €4/3.50/5/5.50; ☽ Apr-Sep) A cool, wooded camping ground, set 250m back from the beach, Tau has room for 185 people and is very popular with families. Follow the 'Tau' sign pointing left along Camino de Cala Higuera as you approach central San José from the north.

Instalación Juvenil de San José (☎ 950 38 03 53; fax 950 38 02 13; Calle Montemar s/n; bunks €8; ☽ Apr-Sep) A friendly, non-Inturjoven youth hostel run by the local municipality, which stays open over the Christmas and New Year period and long weekends. To find it, head towards Camping Tau but turn right after crossing a dry river bed, then take the first left up the hill.

Hostal Sol Bahía (☎ 950 38 03 07; fax 950 38 03 06; Avenida de San José; d €70; ✴) and its sister establishment **Hostal Bahía Plaza** (Avenida de San José) across the street, are bright, modern buildings in the centre of San José with 34 simple but decent and clean rooms with TV.

Hotel Cortijo el Sotillo (☎ 950 61 11 00; Carretera Entrada a San José s/n; s/d €120/141; P ✴ ☎) Depending on the season, this ranch-style complex can be a romantic getaway for couples, or a family spot to release shouting children. The house is an authentic 19th-century *cortijo* (country property) with rural-style rooms and on-site riding. It has an excellent restaurant serving regional cuisine.

Hotel Doña Pakyta (☎ 950 61 11 75; fax 950 61 10 62; Calle del Correo; d with sea view €151; P ✴) This place has an unparalleled sense of space, with huge picture windows framing magnificent sea views that greet you as you enter the cool, white lobby. Rooms are large and spacious, in sea blues and whites and there's a beach right below the hotel. A room with a terrace is a must (those without are only €10 cheaper) to enjoy the wonderful views.

Plenty of apartments are available for rent (ask at the tourist office or look for signs); two people can pay as little as €18 a day for a few days' stay in the off-season, though it costs more like €60 during July and August.

EATING

Restaurante El Emigrante (☎ 950 38 03 07; Avenida de San José; fish & meat mains €6-12) Under the same ownership as the Bahía *hostales* (p413), Emigrante is a somewhat ordinary but dependable option in the centre of town. A breakfast of orange juice, toast and coffee costs €3.

Hotel Cortijo el Sotillo (☎ 950 61 11 00; Carretera Entrada a San José s/n; mains €8-14) Almost always full thanks to its honest and hearty regional food, the huge, echoing dining room of the *cortijo* has satisfied diners eating lunch up to 5pm in the afternoon. Reservations are recommended.

La Gallineta (☎ 950 38 05 01; Pozo de los Frailes; mains €8-18; 🕒 8pm-late Tue-Sun, closed mid-Jan–end-Feb) A small, elegant restaurant 4km north of San José where urbanites on weekend escapes come for the inventive food with an international twist. Try the prawns in mango purée (€7.50) or the fillet of beef in a thick Pedro Ximénez gravy (€18).

Mesón El Tempranillo (☎ 950 38 00 59; Puerto de San José 6-7; mains €9-15) One of a number of good fish restaurants found beneath a string of colourful awnings near the harbour. Eat out on the shaded veranda that overlooks the beach.

Also try **La Cueva** (☎ 950 38 01 54; Puerto Deportivo 3, 4 & 5; mains €8-14), another good fish eatery, next door to Méson El Tempranillo.

GETTING AROUND

There is a reasonable amount of parking on Avenida de San José, on the north side of the main beach, and at the harbour. Taxis can be contacted on ☎ 950 38 97 37 or 608 056255.

San José to Las Negras

The rugged coast northeast of San José has only two small settlements, the odd fort and a few beaches before the village of Las Negras (17km northeast from San José, as the crow flies). The road can be confusing as it spends most of its time diverting inland.

The hamlet of **Los Escullos** has a short, mainly sandy beach and a restored old fort, the Castillo de San Felipe. You can walk here from San José along a track from Cala Higuera. **La Isleta del Moro**, 1km further northeast, is a gorgeous, tiny fishing village on the western arm of a wide bay, with the **Playa del Peñón Blanco** stretching to its east. The beach is small but relatively quiet.

From here, the road climbs to a good viewpoint, the **Mirador de la Amatista**, before heading inland past the former gold-mining village of Rodalquilar. About 1km past Rodalquilar is the turning for **Playa del Playazo**, 2km away along a level track. This attractive, sandy beach stretches between two headlands, one topped by the Batería de San Ramón fortification (now a private home). From here you can walk along the coast to Camping La Caleta and the village of Las Negras.

The tiny village of **Las Negras** stands above a pebbly beach that runs north towards Punta del Cerro Negro, an imposing headland of volcanic rock, and has a small population of young hippies giving it some oomph.

SLEEPING & EATING
Los Escullos

Camping Los Escullos (☎ 950 38 98 11; camping per 2 people, tent, car & electrical hook-up €19; 🕒 year-round; 🅿 🐾) This large, moderately shaded place is 900m back from the Los Escullos beach. It has a pool, restaurant, grocery store and ATM, and bikes for hire.

Hotel Los Escullos (☎ 950 38 97 33; d incl breakfast €85; 🐾) A small hotel near the beach with reasonable rooms (all with TV). It also has a restaurant serving limited fare for between €8 and €15.

La Isleta del Moro

Hostal Isleta del Moro (☎ 950 38 97 13; fax 950 38 97 64; s/d €21/43) This *hostal* is in a superb

---

THE AUTHOR'S CHOICE

Casa Café de la Loma (☎ 950 38 98 31; www.degata.com/laloma; La Isleta del Moro; s/d €30/45 Sep-Jul, s/d €35/52 Aug) This is true Mediterranean heaven in an old *cortijo* (farm house) that has been kept simple and beautiful, with a large, wild garden, terrific views of the sea and the village beach, and friendly owners. The 6 airy rooms have rustic and North African mementos and mosquito nets hang over each bed. In the summer months, a restaurant opens with vegetarian and meaty dishes, and there are jazz and flamenco concerts once a week in the garden, under candle light. The Casa is not far from La Isleta del Moro along the road to Las Negras.

DETOUR: LAS NEGRAS TO AGUA AMARGA

There's no road along this cliff-lined and se-cluded stretch of the Cabo de Gata coast, but walkers can take an up-and-down path of 11km (four to five hours). **Playa San Pedro**, one hour's walk from Las Negras, is the site of a ruined hamlet whose buildings (including a castle) once housed an inter-national colony of two or three dozen hip-pies and the occasional wandering naturist. It's 1½ hours' walk on from San Pedro to **Cala del Plomo**, a beach with another tiny settlement. You could stop at the little **Cala de Enmedio** beach, half an hour after Cala del Plomo, before heading on for about one hour to reach Agua Amarga.

---

location overlooking La Isleta del Moro's harbour. It also has a good restaurant that serves fresh seafood.

Las Negras

The largest settlement along this stretch of coast is the hamlet of Las Negras, which has good *hostal* accommodation, camping facilities and one or two eateries.

Camping La Caleta (☎ 950 52 52 37; camping per adult/child/tent/car €5/5/4.50/5; ☻ year-round; P ☻) This place lies in a valley 1km south of Las Negras, in a separate cove. It can be fiercely hot in summer, but there is a good pool.

Hostal Arrecife (☎ 950 38 81 40; Calle Bahía 6; s/d €26/38) A very well maintained small *hostal* on the main street in Las Negras. The rooms are cool and quiet and some of them have sea views from their balconies.

Other accommodation in Las Negras consists of holiday apartments and houses to let, but you may find a few signs of-fering rooms by the night. For food, try **Restaurante La Palma** (☎ 950 38 80 42; mains €5-10), a relaxed shack overlooking the beach, for good music and excellent fish at medium prices.

Another option is **Pizza y Pasta** (☎ 950 38 80 97; Calle San Pedro; mains €5-6; ☻ Mar-Nov), a friendly Italian restaurant with checked tablecloths and a small patio. Pop across the road to the perpetually busy **Cerro Negro** (Calle San Pedro), whose outside tables are invariably occupied by hippies or bright young things chilling out with a cold beer.

Agua Amarga

Agua Amarga is to trendy Madrid profes-sionals what the Hamptons is to New York's darlings. Well, almost. The style is suitably understated here. The unassuming village has a low-key, relaxed feeling, with the emphasis on quality, chic and expensive accommoda-tion and inventive-cuisine restaurants. House prices have soared in the past few years with everyone wanting their own authentic village house. Sandy streets, surfer shops and boho-chic make this just about the most fashion-able fishing village on the coast.

There are boats for hire on the long sandy beach and 3km east (up the Carbo-neras road) is a turning to a cliff-top light-house, the **Faro de la Mesa Roldán** (1.25km away), from where there are spectacular views. From the car park by the turning you can walk down to the naturist **Playa de los Muertos**.

Drivers from Las Negras to Agua Amarga must head inland through Hortichuelas. From the bus shelter on the eastern side of the road in Fernán Pérez, you head north-east for 10km on a new tarmac road until you meet the N341. Turn right here for Agua Amarga.

SLEEPING & EATING

Hostal Restaurante La Palmera (☎ 950 13 82 08; Calle Aguada s/n; d €90; ☻) With a breezy, beachfront location in the middle of the action, La Palm-era has 10 bright rooms with rocking chairs and half-moon balconies. The restaurant (mains €7 to €15) has a nice beach terrace and is the locals' favourite for lunch.

Hostal Familia (☎ 950 13 80 14; fax 950 13 80 70; Calle La Lomilla; d with breakfast with/without sea views €120/80; ☻) A relaxed place, set amid trees, with prices that don't quite match the ef-fort: the rooms are big and comfortable, but their décor is patchy at times and the baths are quite run-down. The *hostal* is re-nowned for its excellent three-course North African–influenced *menú* (€18).

Hotel El Tio Kiko (☎ 950 13 80 80; www.eltiokiko .com; Calle Embarque; d €150; P ☻ ☻) El Tio Kiko is a top-of-the-range large hotel where all rooms enjoy lovely views over the bay. The style is something akin to Mexican adobe with lots of wood and white.

MiKasa (☎ 950 13 80 73; www.mikasasuites.com; Car-retera Carboneras s/n; s €85, d incl breakfast €105-190, ste €219-235 P ☻ ☻) The slick and chic MiKasa has understated, elegant décor with super-comfortable rooms, some with fresh floral patterns and others in Oriental-style opulence, coir matting, colonial recliners and discreet balconies. A savvy crowd of professionals rush down here from Madrid for long weekends. Cold and heated swimming pools, Jacuzzi baths and a small health spa make this Almería's most romantic hideaway.

Café Bar La Plaza (☎ 950 13 82 14; Calle Ferro-carril Minero; platos combinados €6) Located in the village square, this is a cheerful, down-to-earth favourite of the locals. Try the delicious fish soup.

La Villa (☎ 950 13 80 90; Carretera Carboneras s/n; mains €18-20; ☺ 8.30am-late, closed Wed) Right next door to MiKasa and run by the same family, La Villa offers the same stylish environment and a quality international *menú* influenced by the family's extensive travels. Meals can be taken outside around the atmospheric pool.

MOJÁCAR
pop 6000

There are two Mojácars: old Mojácar Pueblo, a village that looks like a multilevel wedding cake melting down the cliff, with its jumble of white, cube houses on top of a steep hill 2km inland. Then there is Mojácar Playa, a soulless modern coastal resort 7km long but only a few blocks wide. Mojácar Pueblo is dominated by tourism, but retains its picturesque charms and can still captivate with its mazelike streets, and balconies swathed in bougainvilleas. Mojácar Playa is a relentless strip of hotels, apartments, shops, bars and restaurants, and is home to northern European retirees and year-round caravan-dwellers seeking sunshine. There is a good, long beach and a lively summer scene, but life slows down from October to Easter.

From the 13th to the 15th century, Mojácar Pueblo stood on the Granada emirate's eastern frontier and suffered several Christian attacks, including a notorious massacre in 1435, before finally succumbing to the Catholic Monarchs in 1488. Tucked away in an isolated corner of one of Spain's most backward regions, it was decaying and almost abandoned by the mid-20th century before its mayor lured artists and others with giveaway property offers.

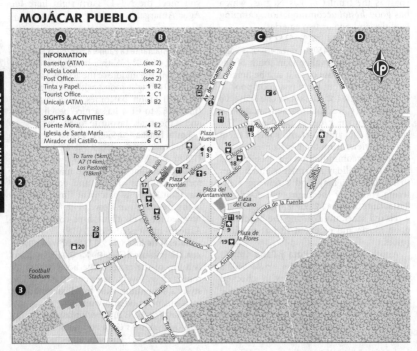

MOJÁCAR PUEBLO

INFORMATION
Banesto (ATM)................................(see 2)
Policía Local...................................(see 2)
Post Office......................................(see 2)
Tinta y Papel.......................................**1** B2
Tourist Office.......................................**2** C1
Unicaja (ATM).......................................**3** B2

SIGHTS & ACTIVITIES
Fuente Mora.......................................**4** E2
Iglesia de Santa María.......................**5** B2
Mirador del Castillo...........................**6** C1

Orientation

Mojácar is divided into two distinct areas: the *playa*, the developed beachfront, running for several kilometres, and the pueblo, the old village located on a hilltop 2km inland. To reach the pueblo from the *playa* turn inland at the roundabout by the huge shopping centre, Parque Comercial. Regular buses run from the pueblo to the *playa* and vice versa.

Information

In Mojácar Pueblo, both Banesto and Unicaja (across the square) have ATMs, as does Banco de Andalucía, which is located in the Parque Comercial.

Centro Medíco (medical centre; ☎ 950 47 51 05; Parque Comercial, Mojácar Playa; ☯ 10am-1pm & 5.30-8pm) General medical help. English and French are spoken.

Information booth (☎ 950 47 87 26; Paseo del Mediterráneo, Mojácar Playa; ☯ 10am-2pm & 5-7.30pm Mon-Fri, 10.30am-1.30pm Sat Apr-Sep) Opposite the Parque Comercial.

Policía Local (☎ 950 47 20 00; Calle Glorieta, Mojácar Pueblo) In the same building as the tourist office.

Post office (Calle Glorieta, Mojácar Pueblo; ☯ 12.30-2.30pm Mon-Fri & 10am-noon Sat) In the same building as the tourist office.

Tinta y Papel (☎ 950 47 27 92; Centro Comercial, Plaza Nueva, Mojácar Pueblo) Located on the 1st floor of the shopping centre; there are maps of the region and some tourist books.

Tito's (☎ 950 61 50 30; Playa de las Ventánicas, Mojácar Playa; per hr €3; ☯ 10am-8.30pm, closed when raining) Internet access; a lively outdoor bar overlooking one of the beaches along Mojácar Playa.

Tourist office (☎ 950 47 51 62; info@mojacar.es; Calle Glorieta, Mojácar Pueblo; ☯ 10am-2pm & 5-7.30pm Mon-Fri, 10.30am-1.30pm Sat) Just north of Plaza Nueva; a very helpful office.

Sights & Activities

The best way to see the pueblo is to wander around the quaint streets with their flower-decked balconies, and browse through the boutiques. There are great views from the public terraces of **Mirador del Castillo**, located at the top of the village. The fortress-style **Iglesia de Santa María** (Calle Iglesia) is just south of Plaza Nueva and dates from 1560. On Calle La Fuente is the remodelled, though still expressive **Fuente Mora** (Moorish Fountain), a fine example of the Spanish-Islamic tradition of enhancing function with artistry. An inscription records the last Muslim governor's noble plea for Mojácar Muslims to be allowed to remain in their home. The plea was made to the Catholic Monarchs, who usurped the governor in 1488.

Apart from Mojácar Playa's long, sandy main beach, a number of more secluded beaches are strung out to the south of the town. Some of those beyond the **Torre de Macenas**, an 18th-century fortification, are naturist beaches. For good windsurfing equipment (per hour €12), canoeing, sailing and water-skiing (per session €20), check out **Samoa Club** (☎ 666 442263, 950 47 84 90; Playa de las Ventánicas, Mojácar Playa), on one of the beaches on Mojácar Playa. For some exciting quad biking (one hour €35) in the Cabrera mountains contact **Mojácar Quad Treks** (☎ 600 258385, 637 925505; Paseo del Mediterráneo).

Festivals & Events

On the weekend nearest 10 June, see Mamabel's (p418) costumes in action for the re-enactment of the Christian conquest of Mojácar, **Moros y Cristianos**. There's dancing, processions and other festivities.

ALMERÍA PROVINCE

THE MOORS' LAST SIGH

Driven from the heady heights of Granada in 1492, the remaining Andalucian Muslims retreated east to Almería's and Granada's Alpujarras valleys, Mojácar, Murcia and Valencia. However, over the next century they were inexorably pressured to convert to Christianity or emigrate to North Africa.

During Inquisition times, members of the Muslim community were banned from reading or writing Arabic and were forced into mass conversions in the 1490s. Many did convert (becoming known as Moriscos), but this conversion was superficial and revolts ensued over the years. In 1609 the Inquisition finally sought the official expulsion of the Moriscos and over the next few years some 300,000 (some say three million) Muslim Spaniards were expelled from Al-Andalus. The refugees were only permitted to take belongings that they could carry, and they arrived at the ports, 'tired, in pain, lost, exhausted, sad, confused, ashamed, angry, crestfallen, irritated, bored, thirsty and hungry' as Father Áznar Cardona observed. Children under seven were not allowed to travel directly to Islamic lands, forcing many families to give them up to Christian orphanages. The arrival of the refugees in the ancestral homeland was far from comfortable – dressed as Europeans, with many of them having forgotten their Arabic mother-tongue, they were quickly labelled the 'Christians of Castile'.

Interestingly, when photographer Kurt Hielscher arrived in Mojácar in the early 20th century he found the local women dressed in black, wearing veils over their faces. At the entrance to the village there was a sign stating 'Mojácar, Kingdom of Granada' as though the last 400 years had never happened.

Sleeping

MOJÁCAR PUEBLO

Hostal Arco Plaza (☎ 950 47 27 77; fax 950 47 27 17; Calle Aire Bajo 1; s/d €36/52; 🖃) Bang in the centre of the village, this *hostal* has spacious bathrooms, sky-blue rooms with wrought-iron beds, crisp white linen, and great views of the Plaza Nueva and the valley below. Bedrooms also have TVs, and the management is incredibly friendly and efficient.

La Fonda del Castillo (☎ 950 47 30 22; www.el castillomojacar.com; Mirador del Castillo; d €48-54; 🖃) This laid-back *hostal* manages to stay just the right side of characterful. Peeling paint and a bit of damp do nothing to eclipse the bohemian atmosphere. Bedrooms and bathrooms are neat and all have fantastic views. There is a bar, Café Bar Mirador del Castillo (opposite), in front of the house, with some rooms above it. More rooms are around a courtyard (with a pool in the middle) at the back.

Pensión El Torreón (☎ 950 47 52 59; Calle Jazmín 4; d with shared bathroom €60) A breathtakingly beautiful little *hostal* with a bougainvillea-clad terrace overlooking the village. The five rooms are almost English-countryside quaint, with lace-work linen and antique bits and bobs. The new, English owners are promising en-suite rooms. The house is allegedly the birthplace of Walt Disney, who

was, according to the locals, the love-child of a village girl and a wealthy landowner.

Hostal Mamabel's (☎ /fax 950 47 24 48; www.mama bels.com; Calle Embajadores 5; d/ste €65/87) Mamabel is quite a character and her *hostal* almost serves like a showcase for her handmade dolls and exquisitely decorated rooms, individually styled with antiques. She also makes costume dresses for the Moros y Cristianos festival, if you're in town. Some rooms have fantastically precipitous views from their windows and terraces.

MOJÁCAR PLAYA

Almost everything here is on Paseo del Mediterráneo, the main road running along the beach.

Hotel Río Abajo (☎ 950 47 89 28; www.mojacar.info /rio-abajo in Spanish; Calle Río Abajo; d €57; P 🖃) Nestling amid trees in a residential cul-de-sac on the edge of the Lagunas del Río Aguas, this has to be the most tranquil hotel on the *playa*. Nineteen blue and white pueblo-style chalets are dotted among lush gardens, with direct access to the broad, sandy beach. It's a fantastic place for kids and there are even swings in the gardens.

Hotel Felipe San Bernabé (☎ 950 47 82 02; fax 950 47 27 35; Playa Las Ventanicas; d €66; P 🖃) Completely different from the Río Abajo, this is a swish (and good-value) hotel with well-appointed rooms. Set back from one of the better beaches, the hotel's main feature is its excellent restaurant (right).

Hotel El Puntazo (☎ 950 47 82 65; Paseo del Mediterráneo 257; 1-star d €57, 3-star d €116; P ❄ ᪥) The sprawling Puntazo comprises separate but adjacent hotels of one and three stars, under the same management. It has comfortable (if soulless) modern rooms and arranges plenty of activities, making it popular with families.

Parador de Mojácar (☎ 950 47 82 50; www.para dor.es; Paseo Mediterráneo; s/d €79/99; P ❄ ᪥) A few hundred metres south of the Parque Comercial, Mojácar's *parador* (one of the Paradores de Turismo, a chain of luxurious hotels, often in historic buildings) is a modern building with lavish gardens and is well located for the golf course.

Eating

MOJÁCAR PUEBLO

La Taberna (☎ 647 72 43 67; Plaza del Cano 1; tapas & platos combinados from €4) Good tapas and tasty vegetarian bites get everyone cramming into this thriving little restaurant inside a warren of intimate rooms, full of chatter and belly-full diners. There's also an enormous house kebab that arrives on its own scaffolding!

Restaurante El Viento del Desierto (Plaza Frontón; mains €5-6) A good-value Moroccan restaurant just by the church. It is well regarded by the locals and makes a nice change from tapas, although it also does standard Spanish dishes such as pork fillet with mushrooms or rabbit in mustard.

Pizzeria Pulcinella (Cuesta del Castillo; pizzas €6, pasta from €7) For cheap eats you should check out this cheerful place which has good views over the *playa*.

Sinaloa Fanny's (☎ 950 47 22 73; Rincón Zahori; meat & fish mains €8; ᪥ closed Wed Oct-May) This laid-back Mexican joint is run by the affable Steve, who has lived in Mojácar for 20 years. Reputed to have the largest selection of tequilas in Spain, the restaurant also has slow internet access, a pool table and vertiginous terraces.

El Horno (☎ 950 47 24 48; Calle Embajadores 5; menú €13, mains €11-16) The stylish restaurant of Hostal Mamabel's (opposite) is the best place for home-cooked food in Mojácar, including a tasty couscous dish. The location also has excellent views. Definitely not to be missed.

MOJÁCAR PLAYA

Maskó (☎ 950 47 22 47; Parque Comercial; pastries €1.50-2 ᪥ 8am-late) A real Italian-run café with strong espresso and foamy cappuccinos, plus a huge selection of pastries, cakes, ice creams, sandwiches and snacks. Open almost all the time, this place is the main rendezvous in town and is perpetually busy.

Hotel Restaurante Felipe San Bernabé (☎ 950 47 82 02; Playa Las Ventanicas; mains €11-16) A plush conservatory-style restaurant decked out in cool whites and greens, with big wine glasses and pristine white tablecloths getting dirty with some excellent Spanish cooking. There's a good selection of fish dishes and good-value tapas.

Los Pastores (☎ 950 46 80 02; Cortijo Cabrera, Turre; mains €9-16; ᪥ Tue-Sun) It's an epic journey to reach this modest eatery, but it is worth it, especially on the weekends (when it is advisable to book two days in advance). The cosy publike interior belies the excellent cooking – home-made pastas, grilled sea breams, giant king prawns – and a commendable wine list. From Mojácar head towards the A7 *autovía* (toll-free dual carriageway). Turn left (through a large stone gateway) after about 10km, at the sign for Cortijo Grande. Drive a further 8km past the golf course and up to Cabrera at the top of the hill. There are occasional signs for the restaurant en route.

Drinking & Entertainment

Classical music, live comedy acts and jazz concerts are staged at the lively **Café Bar Mirador del Castillo** (☎ 950 47 30 22; Mirador del Castillo, Mojácar Pueblo; ᪥ 11am-11pm or later). There's a throng of busy summer bars in Mojácar Pueblo but some of the better ones include the following:

Bar La Sartén (Calle Estación Nueva) Keeps going even longer than Time & Place, with a terrific stir of conversation and character.

Budú Pub (Calle Estación Nueva) Has a great roof-terrace.

Caipirinha Caipirosa (Calle Horno) Mexican style.

La Muralla (Calle Estación Nueva) Has the most romantic views from its *mirador* terrace.

Reggae Azul Marino (Calle Enmedio)

Time & Place (Plaza de la Flores) For good conversation and late-night drinking; a stylish place that keeps going to the early hours.

Unless indicated, all the bars are open evenings only from 8pm until late. Bars on Mojácar Playa include the following:

La Mar Salada (Paseo del Mediterráneo 62, Mojácar Playa; ☺ 10am-late Mon-Fri, 11am-late Sat) The beach-front bar of the moment.

Tito's (☎ 950 61 50 30, Playa de las Ventánicas; ☺ Apr-Oct) Lively and long-established. On one of the beaches on Mojácar Playa, Tito's features live music, including jazz.

Getting There & Away

BUS

Long-distance buses stop at the Parque Comercial and at the Fuente bus stop at the foot of Mojácar Pueblo. The tourist office has bus timetables.

Alsa Enatcar (☎ 902 42 22 42; www.alsa.es) runs daily buses to/from Murcia (€9, 2½ hours, four daily), Almería (€5.50, 1¾ hours, two daily), Granada (€15, four hours, two daily) and Madrid (€29, eight hours, two daily). There's a bus to Málaga daily except Sunday and holidays. For Almería, Granada and Murcia you buy tickets on the bus; for Málaga and Madrid you must book at a travel agency such as **Viajes Cemo** (☎ 950 47 28 35; Paseo del Mediterráneo, Mojácar Playa), 2km south of the Parque Comercial (Pueblo Indalo bus stop). Buses to Alicante, Valencia and Barcelona go from Vera, 16km north, which is served by several daily buses from Mojácar (€1.20, 50 minutes, nine daily).

CAR & MOTORCYCLE

Mojácar is 14km east of the A7. A wind-ing, scenic coastal road approaches Mojácar from Agua Amarga and Carboneras to the south.

Getting Around

A local bus service (€1) runs a circuit from the southern to the northern end of Mojácar Playa, then back to the Parque Comercial, up to the pueblo (stopping near the tourist office), then back down to the *playa*. It runs every half-hour from 9am to 11.30pm, April to September, and every hour from 9.30am to 7.30pm, October to March, reaching the pueblo in 15 minutes.

Parking in Mojácar Playa is along the seaward side of the main road. In Mojácar Pueblo you should follow the one-way system along Avenida de Paris to reach the main car park, at Plaza Rey Alabez. Mojácar's Wednesday market takes over the car park. It is not advisable to leave your car in this car park overnight on Tuesday night, when parking is transferred to the nearby football stadium for the duration of the market. **Taxis** (☎ 950 47 81 84) hang about in Plaza Nueva. There are several car-rental offices strung out along Mojácar Playa.

VERA & AROUND

Vera pop 6500 / elevation 102m

Almería's once neglected stretch of coast from Mojácar to the provincial border with Murcia is now attracting many holiday-makers, some wearing nothing but their birthday suits. They are especially drawn to the big sandy beaches either side of the Río Almanzora. Here, one of the largest naturist resorts in Europe is still developing within a vast complex of apartments, villas and hotels. Further north is the darkly dramatic Costa Almagrera, backed by the brooding hills of the Sierra Almagrera, where few lo-cals and visitors set foot.

Mojácar to Cuevas de Almanzora

Five kilometres north of Mojácar is the fishing port of **Garrucha**, a bustling holiday resort with a fun harbour where there is a clutch of good fish restaurants such as **Restaurante Rincón del Puerto** (☎ 950 13 30 42; Puerto Deportivo s/n; raciones €6-10). There are beaches at the southern entrance to the town. The cosmopolitan **Hotel Tikar** (☎ 950 61 71 31; www.hoteltikar.com; Carretera Garrucha-Vera s/n; d €89/115; P ☒), with its excellent restaurant and modern rooms in burnt orange and blue, is the best place to stay, even if it is set back off the beach.

Just beyond Garrucha the main road heads inland for 8km to **Vera**. There is little to interest the visitor in Vera itself other than the handsome **Iglesia de la Encarnación**. In front of the church is a charming, pe-destrianised square, a haven amid Vera's otherwise traffic-logged streets. The town has a complicated one-way traffic system and, if you plan to stop off during the busy morning period, it's best to park on the outskirts and walk in.

For some child-friendly fun, head in-land to the **Parque Acuático Vera** (☎ 950 46 73 37; www.aquavera.com in Spanish; Carretera Vera-Villaricos; adult/child €13/8; ☺ 11am-6pm 18 May–end Jun & 1-17 Sep, 10.30am-7.30pm Jul & Aug). Children will also enjoy poking around in the troglodyte dwellings at **Cuevas de Almanzora**, a busy ag-ricultural town lying 6km north of Vera. The caves, which are known properly as the

Cuevas del Calguerín (☎ 950 45 66 51, 639 101948; admission €5; ☺ guided visits 11am, 2pm, 4pm & 9pm, in Spanish only), pock-mark several layers of cliff-face on the northern outskirts of the town (follow the signs for 'Cuevas Históricas'). The price for the cave tour does not quite match what you get, but it is fascinating nevertheless. There are 8600 caves (some permanently inhabited), and the tour provides an insight into cave life.

The town's other big attraction is the handsome **Castillo Marqúes de Los Vélez** at the heart of the town, which houses a **Museo Arqueologíco** and the **Museo Antonio Manuel Campoy** (☎ 950 45 80 63; admission free; ☺ 10am-1.30pm & 5-8pm Tue-Sat, 10am-1.30pm Sun). The latter exhibits a large and fascinating selection of artworks, from the outstanding private collection of Antonio Manuel Campoy, a native of Cuevas who was one of Spain's greatest 20th-century art critics.

There is not much accommodation in Cuevas itself, but the large **Cuatro Vientos** (☎ 950 45 62 28; Avenida Atrales 21; s/d €20/40; [P] [☒]), opposite the bus station, has reasonable rooms.

Vera Playa & the Sierra Almagrera

Back on the coast, Vera Playa comprises the good beaches to either side of the mouth of the Río Almanzora and is exuberantly naturist. The big **Camping Almanzora** (☎ /fax 950 46 74 25; Carretera de Garrucha a Villaricos; camping per adult/child/tent/car €4/3.50/4/4) has a *zona naturista* for naturists and a *zona textiles* for the clothed, although the beach is healthily all-embracing.

There is big money to be made in putting a roof over the unclothed, it seems. Pretty unsightly, large developments are springing up, and complexes such as **Vera Playa Club** (☎ 950 46 74 75; Carretera de Garrucha a Villaricos; d from €180) and a clutch of equally expensive apartments shut off the beaches from the main road, although there are access points for all.

Just to the north is the pleasant village of Villaricos, which heralds a sudden return to traditional buildings after the vast architectural confections of Vera Playa. It has a pebbly beach and a smart little harbour at its northern end. Close by, **Diving Vivariva** (☎ 950 46 75 72; Puerto de la Esperanza 7) runs diving trips and courses in the crystal-clear waters of the Almagrera coast. Hire of a boat and

equipment costs around €45 while a 'Discover Scuba' course is around €85.

The **Hostal Restaurante Don Tadeo** (☎ /fax 950 46 71 05; Calle Baria 37; s/d €24/36), has decent rooms, although **Hostal Restaurante Playa Azul** (☎ 950 46 70 75; Calle Barea 62; s/d €24/48) is a better offer, with balconied rooms and an excellent restaurant.

You'll need your own transport to explore further north from here. The road winds on for 8km between the coast and the gaunt, wrenched-looking slopes of the Sierra Almagrera. There is a rare sense of isolation along the coast until the road reaches the village of El Pozo del Esparto. Beyond El Pozo, San Juan de los Terreros is the last resort before the border with Murcia.

Getting There & Away

There are plenty of buses between Almería and Vera (€6.50, 2¾ hours, 10 daily) and between Mojácar, Garrucha (€0.80, 30 minutes, nine daily) and Vera (€1.20, 50 minutes, nine daily). Several buses also travel between Mojácar, Vera and Cuevas de Almanzora (€2, 15 minutes) but there are no regular bus connections to Villaricos and north along the Almagrera coast. In July and August there are infrequent connections to Villaricos from Vera. Schedules change each year so it's best to contact **Vera bus station** (☎ /fax 950 39 04 10).

LOS VÉLEZ

VÉLEZ BLANCO & AROUND
Vélez Blanco pop 2300 / elevation 1070m

The beautiful, sparse landscape of Los Vélez district lies 60km inland from Vera. Its main settlements are the three small towns Vélez Rubio, Vélez Blanco and María, which nestle in the shadow of the remote Sierra de María range. Much of the range is protected, in the Parque Natural Sierra de María-Los Vélez. The most attractive and interesting of the towns is Vélez Blanco, with its dramatic castle overlooking a scramble of red-tiled houses.

Information

At Vélez Blanco's **Centro de Visitantes Almacén del Trigo** (☎ 950 41 53 54; Avenida del Marqués de los Vélez; ☺ 10am-2pm Tue, Thu & Sun, 10am-2pm & 4-6pm Fri & Sat), information on walking routes, refuges and general attractions is available. The centre is on the northern edge of town. If arriving by car from the south, reaching it is easier by following the main road that by-passes Vélez Blanco, then entering the town by its northern access road. Another natural park visitor centre, the **Centro de Visitantes Mirador Umbría de María** (☎ 950 52 70 05) is 2km west of María off the A317 and has similar opening times to the Vélez Blanco office.

In Vélez Blanco there is a post office on Calle Clavel and an ATM at the start of Calle Vicente Sánchez, at the eastern end of Calle La Corredera (the main street). The ATM is behind a solid metal grille, so don't get your hand stuck.

Sights

Vélez Blanco's pride and joy is the very imposing **Castillo de los Fajardo** (☎ 607 41 50 55; adult/child €1/0.50; ☒ 11am-2pm & 5-7pm Mon, Tue, Thu & Fri, 11am-4pm Sat, Sun & holidays), a castle that seems to spring naturally from its rocky pinnacle. It confronts the great sphinxlike mountain butte of La Muela across the tiled roofs of the village, as if on a bizarre duel. The castle is built over an earlier Islamic fort and dates from the 16th century. The interior is now rather bare, as the impoverished owners sold off the decorations (including the fabulous carved white marble Patio de Honor) in 1904 to American millionaire George Blumenthal. Next time you're in New York, you can see the lovely patio reconstructed in The Metropolitan Museum of Art.

A stroll around Vélez Blanco is rewarding, not least for its delightful maze of streets and its many attractive houses. From the far end of the tree-lined main street, Calle La Corredera, you can head up Calle Vicente Sánchez to reach the castle. On the way, Calle Palacio, the first left, is a good example of Vélez Blanco's stylish domestic architecture, all overhanging tiles and handsome wrought-iron balconies.

Just south of Vélez Blanco on the road from Vélez Rubio, signs point to the **Cueva de los Letreros** (road A317; admission free). The district has several groups of 7000-year-old rock paintings, but it's at this ancient rock shelter that you'll find the most outstanding of them. They include the now ubiquitous Indalo figure (used all over the province as a sign of good luck). For a close-up look,

contact the **Centro de Visitantes Almacén del Trigo** (☎ 950 41 53 54; Avenida del Marqués de los Vélez; ☒ 10am-2pm Tue, Thu & Sun, 10am-2pm & 4-6pm Fri & Sat) and arrange a time for them to open the iron fence around the shelter for you. From the A317 you can drive 500m along the signposted dirt track, then it's a 10-minute walk up to the shelter.

The upland town of **María** is a plain little place but has a fine position against the awesome backdrop of the Sierra de María. It's a good base from which to explore the mountains. The town is surrounded by almond groves that are a glorious froth of pink and white blossom in spring.

About 6km west of María, the A317 heads north onto a high plateau towards the lonely village of **Cañada de Cañepla**, from where it continues, by a superbly scenic road, into the Parque Natural Sierras de Cazorla, Segura y las Villas (p347).

Sleeping & Eating

Hostal La Sociedad (☎ 950 41 50 27; Calle Corredera 5, Vélez Blanco; d €30) Right in the centre of Vélez Blanco, this *hostal* has comfortable rooms run by the same management as the popular **Bar Sociedad** (Calle Corredera; tapas €1.50, menú €9) just across the road.

Casa de los Arcos (☎ 950 61 48 05; Calle San Francisco 2, Vélez Blanco; d/ste €45/65) Located close to the information office in Vélez Blanco, this converted mansion has comfortably renovated rooms that overlook a scenic gorge. The hotel also runs tours to the Cueva de los Letreros (these tours are also open to nonguests).

Hotel Velad Al-Abyadh (☎ 950 41 51 09; www .hotelvelad.com; Calle Balsa Parra 28, Vélez Blanco; s/d with view €45/70; ☒ ☒) A mock hunting-lodge with almost medieval rooms and incredible views over the valley, the hotel is at the entrance to Vélez Blanco from Vélez Rubio. Rustic artefacts and exposed brickwork give the place an intimate atmosphere. The hotel also has a good restaurant.

Restaurante Los Vélez (Calle Balsa Parra 15, Vélez Blanco; mains €8-10) Along the street from Hotel Velad, this place does satisfying meals.

Mesón el Molino (☎ 950 41 50 70; Calle Curtidores 1, Vélez Blanco; fish & meat mains €12-15; ☒ closed Thu evening) Tucked away up a narrow lane near the centre of Vélez Blanco is this superb restaurant, with big displays of raw beef and hung hams. The patio has a gurgling stream channelled through it. Choice ranges from partridge and duck to steak and hake.

In Vélez Rubio and María the following two hotels are the best accommodation options, although it would be preferable to stay in Vélez Blanco, if you can.

Hotel Jardín (☎ 950 41 01 06; N342, Vélez Rubio; s/d €18/30) A huge 1960s building on the old main road at the eastern end of Vélez Rubio. Although rather ugly, it's the best hotel in town and has a friendly bar that serves food.

Hotel Sierramaría (☎ 950 41 71 26; www.hotelsierra maria.com; Paraje la Moratilla, Maria; s/d €36/58) The Sierramaría is a large, modern motel-style place in María, with superb mountain views. It is reached by turning into Paraje la Moratilla, which is just before Hostal Torrente.

Getting There & Away

Alsina Graells (☎ 968 29 16 12) runs buses each way through Vélez Rubio to Granada (€11, 3½ hours, three daily), Guadix (€7.50, 2½ hours, three daily) and Murcia (€7, 2¼ hours, four daily).

Enatcar (☎ 902 42 22 42) has a bus that runs services from Almería to Vélez Rubio (€11, 2¼ hours, one daily), Vélez Blanco (€11, 2½ hours, one daily) and María (€11, 2½ hours, one daily).

Autobuses Giménez García (☎ 968 44 19 61) has a bus from María to Vélez Blanco, Vélez Rubio and Lorca.

The bus stop in Vélez Rubio is on Avenida de Andalucía at the junction by Hostal Zurich.

ALMERÍA PROVINCE

Directory

CONTENTS

ACCOMMODATION

The Sleeping sections for larger towns and cities in this book are split into Budget, Midrange and Top End sections. The budget bracket covers places where a typical room for two people costs under €65 in high season; midrange is for places where rooms for two cost between €65 and €120; and the top end is for places where rooms for two cost more than €120.

The budget range includes the more economical hotels as well as most *hostales*, *hospedajes* and *pensiones* (all types of guesthouses), hostels and camping grounds. There are plenty of attractive and comfort-

able places to stay in this range. Most rooms, in all types of establishment, now have a private bathroom (with at least a toilet, a washbasin and either a shower or a bathtub). All accommodation listed in this book provides private bathrooms unless stated otherwise.

Midrange covers lodgings whose rooms are generally a bit bigger and more attractively designed and furnished, with more touches of comfort. They are also likely to have larger and better-equipped public areas and facilities – swimming pools, gardens, lounges, bars, cafés, restaurants. Top-end establishments will have all these facilities and standards in higher degree. The midrange and top-end categories include many places whose charming design or architecture (from ancient palaces to hip contemporary minimalism), or their spectacular location, add greatly to their attractions – these characterful lodgings are the ones you are most likely to remember after your trip.

Most places to stay have separate prices for *temporada alta* (high season), *temporada media* (shoulder season) and *temporada baja* (low season). Every hotel in Andalucía seems to have its own unique twist to seasonal prices, but in most places high season is some part of the summer. On the coast, July and August is the typical high season; inland, it's more likely to be May, June and September, when temperatures are more pleasant. In many places the Christmas–New Year period, Semana Santa (Holy Week) and local festivals that attract lots of visitors are also high season – or even *temporada extra* (extra-high season). Low season is typically November to February, and shoulder season whatever is neither high nor low.

BOOK ACCOMMODATION ONLINE

For more accommodation reviews and recommendations by Lonely Planet authors, check out the online booking service at www.lonelyplanet.com. You'll find the true, insider lowdown on the best places to stay. Reviews are thorough and independent. Best of all, you can book online.

PRACTICALITIES

- Spain uses the metric system for weights and measures.

- Like other Continental Europeans, the Spanish indicate decimals with commas and thousands with points.

- Most prerecorded video tapes on sale in Spain use the PAL image registration system common to most of Western Europe and Australia. PAL is incompatible with the NTSC system used in North America and Japan.

- Electric current in Spain is 220V, 50Hz, as in the rest of Continental Europe. Plugs have two round pins.

- Among the major daily national newspapers, the liberal-left *El País* is hard to beat for solid reporting. Every sizable Andalucian city has at least one daily paper of its own.

- Dozens of commercial radio stations fill the FM band, but you might prefer the several stations of Radio Nacional de España (RNE): RNE3 plays a variety of pop and rock, RNE2 is classical. *El País* publishes province-by-province wavelength guides in its *Cartelera* (What's-On) section.

- Switch on the TV in your hotel room and you'll probably get six or eight free-to-air channels including the state-run TVE1 and TVE2, the national independent channels Antena 3 and Tele 5, and a couple of local channels. International satellite channels crop up on some TVs.

Accommodation prices given in this book are high-season prices unless stated otherwise – so you can expect some pleasant surprises at other times. Differences between low- and high-season prices vary from place to place: you might pay 40% less in winter in one place, or 10% less in another.

Most places to stay display an official chart of room prices according to season in the reception area or somewhere reasonably prominent. But they can also vary their prices according to demand and are free to charge less than the posted prices, which they quite often do, or more, which happens less often.

In the low season there's generally no need to book ahead, but when things get busier it's advisable to do so, and at peak periods it can be essential if you want to avoid a wearisome search for a room. Often, all that's needed is a phone call with an indication of what time you'll arrive. Occasionally you'll be asked for a credit card number: this is a safeguard for the hotel in case you fail to show without having cancelled.

The official Andalucía tourism website, **Andalucía te Quiere** (www.andalucia.org), has a directory of over 4000 officially registered establishments of all types, often with links to their websites.

Camping

Andalucía has over 130 officially registered *campings* (camping grounds). Some are

well located in woodland or near beaches or rivers, others are stuck away near main roads on the edges of towns and cities. Some cater for under 100 people, others can take over 5000. None are near city centres.

Camping grounds are officially rated 1st class (1ªC), 2nd class (2ªC) or 3rd class (3ªC). Facilities range from reasonable to very good, though any camping ground is likely to get crowded and noisy at busy holiday times. Even a 3rd-class place is likely to have hot showers, electrical outlets and a cafeteria. The best *campings* have heated pools, supermarkets, restaurants, laundry service and children's playgrounds.

Camping grounds usually charge per person, per tent and per vehicle – typically around €5 for each. Children usually cost a bit less. Some places close from around October to Easter.

With certain exceptions – such as many beaches and environmentally protected areas – it is permissible to camp outside camping grounds (though not within 1km of official ones). Signs may indicate where camping in wilderness areas is not allowed. You'll need permission to camp on private land.

Hospedajes, Hostales & Pensiones

These places are mainly inexpensive guesthouses or budget hotels, typically a town or city house with between six and 12 rooms.

Hostales – not to be confused with hostels – are generally a grade better than *hospedajes* and *pensiones,* and the best *hostales* are as good as some midrange hotels, though they rarely provide meals of any kind.

Most rooms have private bathrooms, though there are still places where some rooms share bathrooms.

Hostels

International backpackers hostels have not yet taken off in a big way in Andalucía. So far there are just a few in places such as Granada, Seville and Cádiz. Most of Andalucía's 30 or so hostels are *instalaciones juveniles* (youth hostels) affiliated to the official Andalucian youth-hostel organisation **Inturjoven** (Instalaciones y Turismo Joven; ☎ reservations & information 902 510000; www.inturjoven.com). Inturjoven hostels are mostly modern places with a large number of twin rooms as well as small dormitories with bunks. Though they are sometimes full of large, noisy school groups, they provide decent accommodation for travellers with tight budgets.

Most rooms have private bathrooms. Hostels don't have cooking facilities but they do have *comedores* (dining rooms), usually serving meals at low prices. You can book places in any Inturjoven hostel through the Inturjoven website, on Inturjoven's reservations line or through the hostel itself.

Prices for bed and breakfast in any Inturjoven hostel for the low/mid/high season are €9.50/12.50/14.50 for under-26s and €13/17/19 for people aged 26 or over. The periods of the different seasons vary from hostel to hostel; see the website for full details.

To stay in an Inturjoven hostel you need a youth-hostel card. If you don't already have one from your own country, you can get a Hostelling International (HI) card, valid for the calendar year in which you buy it, at any Inturjoven hostel or any of the 140 or so other hostels in the Red Española de Albergues Juveniles (REAJ), the Spanish HI affiliate. For the HI card, you pay in instalments of €3.50 for each of the first six nights you spend in a hostel, up to €21.

SELF-CATERING ACCOMMODATION

Renting self-catering accommodation is a popular way to cut costs and be your own boss. It's particularly worthwhile for families or other groups of three, four or more, and when you plan to stay at least several days in one place.

Andalucía's holiday *costas* (coasts) are thick with apartments and villas for rent – many of them owned by non-Spaniards – and inland there are plenty of tourist apartments in the cities and *casas rurales* (country houses) available in villages in the countryside. The latter are usually comfortably renovated village houses or farmhouses.

A typical straightforward, well-equipped, two-bedroom coastal apartment for four people ranges from around €300 a week in winter to around €550 in July or August. A two-bedroom coastal villa with private pool, or a *casa rural* for four, might run from €400 to €800 a week.

An internet search for 'apartment', 'villa' or 'self-catering' plus the name of a town or village will usually throw up plenty of options, many of them with online booking. **Andalucía te Quiere** (www.andalucia.org) and **Andalucia.com** (www.andalucia.com) are two general websites with lots of leads to self-catering (and other) accommodation. The following organisations are strong on rural accommodation:

Red Andaluza de Alojamientos Rurales (Andalucian Country Lodgings Network; ☎ 950 28 00 93; www.raar.es) About 150 rural accommodation possibilities throughout Andalucía.

Rural Andalus (☎ 952 27 62 29; www.ruralandalus.es) Around 450 rural properties in most parts of Andalucía, especially Málaga province.

Rustic Blue (☎ 958 76 33 81; www.rusticblue.com) Cottages, farmhouses and village houses, mainly in inland areas of Granada and Málaga provinces (Las Alpujarras, La Axarquía, the Ronda area and so on).

Tourist offices and their websites can supply lists of places for rent; in Britain the travel sections of the broadsheet press carry private ads for such places.

British-based house and villa agencies include **Individual Travellers Spain** (☎ 08700 780194; www.indiv-travellers.com) and **Travellers' Way** (☎ 08456 129001; www.travellersway.co.uk).

OLD-FASHIONED LUXURY

Spain's paradors, officially Paradores de Turismo, are a state-owned chain of 91 high-class hotels dotted all around the country (16 of them in Andalucía). Most are in beautiful locations and a good number, such as those at Carmona, Jaén, Úbeda and Granada, are in historic and atmospheric buildings such as castles, mansions or monasteries. The network, founded in 1928 to help preserve Spain's historical heritage, is still expanding, and many paradors – some of which had become a little dowdy – have recently been modernised and improved. Singles/doubles in the low season range from €77/96 to €120/150, and in the high season from €94/118 to €128/160 – even more at the Parador de Granada (p375), which is the most expensive parador in Spain. Special offers can make paradors more affordable and there are deals for the over-60s and people in their 20s. Check out the offers at www.parador.es, or by contacting the paradors' central reservation service, the **Central de Reservas** (☎ 91 516 66 66; reservas@parador.es; Calle Requena 3, 28013 Madrid) or one of its 22 overseas booking offices (listed on the website).

Hotels

Hoteles range from simple places where a double room could cost €40, up to super-luxury places where you would pay €300. Officially they're classified from one to five stars, depending on their facilities. Even in the cheapest hotels, there is usually a restaurant (if there isn't, the establishment will be called a *hotel-residencia*).

Some of Andalucía's most charming and atmospheric lodgings are small- or medium-sized hotels occupying old town houses or mansions, or country properties with attractive gardens and pools. The manageable scale of such establishments makes for more personal attention. For our top 10 Andalucian hotels based in beautifully converted properties, see p16.

Some places offer a range of rooms at different prices – standard rooms, suites, rooms with or without terrace or sea view, interior and exterior rooms, and so on. Many places have rooms for three, four or more people where the per-person cost is much lower than in a single or double – good news for families. Ask for an *habitación familiar* if you want a family room. Note that *una habitación doble* (a double room) might have one *cama matrimonial* (double bed) or two *camas individuales* (single beds). If one or the other option is important to you, specify it.

Checkout time is nearly always noon.

ACTIVITIES

You can do it all in Andalucía, from wind-surfing off Europe's southern tip to scaling the highest peak in mainland Spain. Classes and courses are available in many outdoor activities. See the Andalucía Outdoors chapter (p71) for details.

ADDRESSES

In Spain, in an address such as 'Edificio Sevilla 2, 8°, the symbol after the 8 indicates the equivalent of the English 8th; in this case it refers to the 8th floor of the building. The letters s/n following a street name (such as Calle Beatriz s/n) stand for *sin número* (without number), which indicates that the building has no street number.

BUSINESS HOURS

Banks generally open from 8.30am to 2pm Monday to Friday and 9am to 1pm Saturday, and post offices from 8.30am to 8.30pm Monday to Friday and 9am to 1.30pm Saturday. There are of course some local and seasonal variations.

Most shops and nongovernment offices (such as travel agencies, airline offices and tour companies) open from 9am or 10am to 1.30pm or 2pm and 5pm to 8pm or 9pm, Monday to Saturday, though some skip the Saturday evening session. Large supermarkets, department stores and *centros comerciales* (large, purpose-built shopping centres) normally stay open all day, from 9am to 9pm, Monday to Saturday.

Restaurants and tapas bars typically open from between 12.30pm and 1.30pm to between 3.30pm and 4pm, and in the evening from 7.30 or 8.30pm to 11pm or midnight. Many have one weekly closing day (often Monday).

Night-time bars generally open in the early evening, but get kicking from between 11pm and midnight to between 2am and

4am – the later in the week, the later they stay open.

CHILDREN

Travelling with children in Andalucía is easy. You can get just about everything you need, and Andalucians as a rule are very warm towards children. Any child whose hair is less than jet black will get called *rubia* (blonde) if she's a girl, *rubio* if he's a boy. Children accompanied by adults are welcome at all kinds of accommodation, and in virtually every café, bar and restaurant. Andalucian children stay up late and at fiestas it's commonplace to see even tiny ones toddling the streets at 2am or 3am. Visiting kids like this idea too, but can't always cope with it quite so readily.

Cots are usually available in hotels, though highchairs in restaurants are not so common. Safety seats are available for hire cars: you're certainly given the option when booking a hire car on the internet. Safety seats in taxis are rarer. Andalucians still have a slack attitude to using safety seats and wearing seat belts, though this is slowly changing with improved traffic law enforcement.

Some top-end hotels will be able to help arrange childcare. Nappy-changing facilities are rare and breast-feeding in public is unusual, though discreet breast-feeding is no problem.

As well as the obvious attraction of the beaches, playgrounds are plentiful. Special attractions such as water parks and aquariums are spread over the region but abound in Málaga province and especially along the Costa del Sol; see the Andalucía for Kids itinerary (p21) for details. Another feature of Andalucía that excites many young 'uns is the visibility of wildlife such as dolphins, apes, deer, vultures and wild boar: to find out more, check the Top 10 Wildlife Spotting Sites box (p62) in the Environment chapter.

Along the coasts many older kids will enjoy water sports – see p73 for an introduction to what they can do and where. The generally gentler winds on the Mediterranean make it more suitable for beginners in some sports than the Atlantic coast, but more adventurous young adults can try windsurfing or kitesurfing on the Atlantic, and even have a go at surfing at El Palmar (see p210). Andalucía has plenty more adventurous activities on offer; see Andalucía Outdoors (p71) for more ideas.

Children benefit from cut-price or free entry at many sights and museums. Those under four years of age travel free on Spanish trains and those aged four to 11 normally pay 60% of the adult fare. Lonely Planet's *Travel with Children* has lots of practical advice and first-hand stories from many Lonely Planet authors and others.

CLIMATE CHARTS

There's a difference between the coastal and interior climates. Inland, the weather can be pretty inclement from November to February and frying hot in July and August. On the coasts, temperatures are more temperate in winter and not quite so hot in summer. And with the prevailing winds coming from the Atlantic Ocean, western Andalucía is damper than the east.

Andalucian weather is less predictable than you might imagine. Only June, July and August are certain to be more or less rain-free. Winter (November to February) can be predominantly dry and warm (raising the danger of drought) or subject to weeks of rain, with the possibility of flooding.

For tips on the best times to travel in Andalucía, see p14.

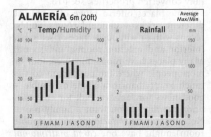

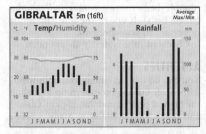

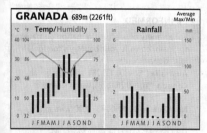

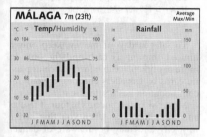

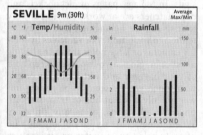

COURSES

Taking a course in Andalucía is a great way not only to learn something but to also meet people and get an inside angle on local life. Many of the universities and schools offering language courses (see right) also offer other courses in Spanish history, literature and culture.

Alternative Lifestyles

Andalucía has a big alternative scene, with members of its large international community at the forefront of activities. A variety of classes and courses, from tai-chi and chigung to oriental dance and holistic medicine, is available if you know where to look for them, especially in areas like Las Alpujarras (p386). A good source of information is the bilingual (English and Spanish) magazine *La Chispa*, dedicated to 'natural living in Andalucía', and available in places like

health-food shops, vegetarian restaurants and *teterías* (oriental-style tearooms), and also online at www.lachispa.net. See p285 for a recommended yoga school.

Cooking

Courses in creative Spanish cookery are increasingly popular – see p85 for our list of recommendations.

Dance

Andalucía is dance-mad and a good place both for professional dancers to hone their skills or for beginners to try a little flamenco or other styles of dance. See Seville (p111) and Granada (p371) for information on courses in Spanish dance and/or guitar. The magazine *El Giraldillo* (available from tourist offices) carries ads for dance classes and courses. You can learn salsa or tango in Granada, flamenco in Nerja, or Bollywood in Vejer de la Frontera with **Dance Holidays** (www.danceholidays.com).

Language

Teaching Spanish to foreigners is a booming business in Andalucía and new language schools are springing up all the time. The **Instituto Cervantes** (www.cervantes .es in Spanish) has a great deal of information on Spanish-language courses in Andalucía. With branches in more than 30 cities around the world, it exists to promote the Spanish language and the cultures of Spanish-speaking countries.

Spanish Directory (www.europa-pages.com/spain) is another good internet source on language courses.

Seville (see p112), Granada (p371), Málaga (p248) and Cádiz (p179) are the most popular places in Andalucía to study Spanish, but there are schools in many other attractive and interesting towns such as Córdoba (p310), and even in some mountain villages such as Cómpeta (p293) in Málaga province. Courses sections in this book point to recommended schools, and tourist offices can usually supply plenty more information.

University courses offer some of the best value, with a typical four-week course of 20 one-hour classes a week for around €500 to €600. These courses can range from as little as two weeks to as long as a year. Private language schools are generally more flexible about when you can start and how long you study. Most places cater for a wide range of levels, from beginners up.

Many schools offer accommodation with families, in student lodgings or in flats – generally from around €300 a month with no meals to €700 to €1000 for full board. Shared apartments are often the cheapest option at around €180 a month.

Things to think about when choosing a course include how intensive it is (this varies at different schools), class sizes, who the other students are likely to be and whether you want organised extracurricular activities. Recommendations from previous students count for a lot in selecting your school. It's also worth asking whether a course will lead to any formal certificate. The Diplomas Oficiales de Español como Lengua Extranjera (DELEs) are internationally recognised diplomas at initial, intermediate and superior levels awarded by Spain's Ministry of Education & Science. For a complete beginner, approximately 40 hours of classes are required to achieve the most basic DELE qualification.

It's easy to arrange private classes in many places; check notice boards in universities and language schools, or small ads in the local press. Expect to pay around €15 per hour for individual private lessons.

Outdoor Activities

You can do plenty of courses in a gamut of active pursuits from diving to skiing – see Andalucía Outdoors (p71) for more details.

CUSTOMS

Duty-free allowances for entering Spain from outside the EU include 2L of wine, 1L of spirits and 200 cigarettes or 50 cigars. Duty-free allowances for travel between EU countries were abolished in 1999. Limits on imports and exports of duty-paid goods between other EU countries and Spain include 110L of beer, 90L of wine, 10L of spirits, 800 cigarettes and 200 cigars.

DANGERS & ANNOYANCES

Andalucía is generally a pretty safe place. The main thing you have to be wary of is petty theft (which of course may not seem so petty if your passport, money and camera go missing).

> **BE INFORMED**
>
> For a variety of useful information on travel to Spain, consult your country's foreign affairs department:
>
> **Australia** (☎ 1300 139 281; www.dfat.gov.au)
> **Canada** (☎ 800 267 6788; www.dfait-maeci .gc.ca)
> **New Zealand** (☎ 04-439 8000; www.mft .govt.nz)
> **UK** (☎ 0845 850 2829; www.fco.gov.uk)
> **USA** (☎ 888-407-4747; travel.state.gov)

To safeguard your money, keep only a limited amount as cash and the bulk in more easily replaceable forms such as plastic cards or travellers cheques. If your accommodation has a safe, use it.

Most risk of theft occurs in tourist resorts and big cities, and when you first arrive in a city and may be unaware of danger signs. In Málaga, gangs of pickpockets and bag snatchers are at work relieving unwary tourists of their belongings. Don't draw attention to your money or valuables by waving cameras or large notes around or having a wallet bulging in your pocket. Keep hold of your baggage and watch out for people who touch you or seem to be getting unwarrantedly close at bus or train stations, on crowded streets, or in any situation. When using ATMs be wary of anyone who offers to help you, even if your card is stuck in the machine. Don't leave anything that even looks valuable visible in a parked car.

Anyone driving away from Málaga airport should be aware of a tyre-puncture scam perpetrated on some tourists there; see p244.

If you want to make an insurance claim for anything stolen or lost, you'll need to report it to the police and get a copy of the report. For help replacing a lost or stolen passport, contact your embassy or consulate.

Terrorism

The Basque terrorist organisation Euskadi Ta Askatasuna (ETA; Basques & Freedom) has occasionally exploded bombs or committed murders in Andalucía, as in other parts of Spain. The country has of course also been victim to Islamic terrorism. Before travelling to Spain, you can consult your country's foreign-affairs department for any current warnings.

DISCOUNT CARDS

Student, teacher and youth cards can get you worthwhile discounts on airfares and other travel as well as reduced prices at some museums, sights and entertainment venues.

The International Student Identity Card (ISIC), for full-time students, and the International Teacher Identity Card (ITIC), for full-time teachers and academics, are issued by colleges and student-travel organisations such as STA Travel. The ISIC gives access to discounted air and train fares, 50% off national museums in Spain and up to 20% off trips with the Alsa bus company.

Anyone under 26 can get a Euro<26 card (Carnet Joven in Spain), which is available in Europe to people of any nationality, or an International Youth Travel Card (IYTC or GO25 card), available worldwide. These give similar discounts to the ISIC and are issued by many of the same organisations. Benefits for Euro<26 card holders in Andalucía include 20% or 25% off many train fares, 20% off some car hires and bus fares with the Socibus company, 10% to 15% off rooms at accommodation and discounts at a few museums and tourist attractions.

For more information, including places you can obtain the cards, see www.istc.org and www.euro26.org.

EMBASSIES & CONSULATES
Spanish Embassies & Consulates

Following is a list of Spanish embassies and consulates in selected countries:

Australia Canberra (☎ 02-6273 3555; www.embaspain .com; 15 Arkana St, Yarralumla, ACT 2600); consulate in Melbourne (☎ 03-9347 1966); consulate in Sydney (☎ 02-9261 2433)

Canada Ottawa (☎ 613-747 2252; www.embaspain.ca; 74 Stanley Ave, Ontario K1M 1P4); consulate in Montreal (☎ 514-935 5235); consulate in Toronto (☎ 416-977 1661)

France Paris (☎ 01 44 43 18 00; www.amb-espagne.fr; 22 Ave Marceau, 75008); consulate in Paris (☎ 01 44 29 40 00; www.cgesparis.org; 165 Blvd Malesherbes, 75840); consulate in Lyon (☎ 04 78 89 64 15); consulate in Marseille (☎ 04 91 00 32 70); consulate in Toulouse (☎ 05 61 52 05 50)

Germany Berlin (☎ 030-254 00 70; www.spanischebots chaft.de; Lichtensteinallee 1, 10787); consulate in Düsseldorf

(☎ 021-143 90 80); consulate in Frankfurt am Main (☎ 069-959 16 60); consulate in Munich (☎ 089-998 47 90)

Ireland (☎ 01-269 1640; www.mae.es/embajadas/dub lin; 17A Merlyn Park, Ballsbridge, Dublin 4)

Italy Rome (☎ 06-684 04 01; www.amba-spagna.com; Palacio Borghese, Largo Fontanella di Borghese 19, 00186); consulate in Rome (☎ 06-687 14 01; Via Campo Marzio 34, 00186); consulate in Genoa (☎ 010-56 26 69); consulate in Milan (☎ 02-632 88 31); consulate in Naples (☎ 081-41 11 57)

Japan (☎ 3-3583 8531; embespjp@mail.mae.es; 1-3-29, Roppongi, Minato-ku, 106-0032, Tokyo)

Morocco Rabat (☎ 07-633900; ambespma@mail.mae .es; Rue Aïn Khalouiya, Rte Des Zaërs Km 5.3, Suissi); consulate in Casablanca (☎ 02-220752); consulate in Tangier (☎ 09-937000)

Netherlands The Hague (☎ 070-302 49 99; ambespnl@correo.mae.es; Lange Voorhout 50, 2514 EG); consulate in Amsterdam (☎ 020-620 38 11)

New Zealand See Australia.

Portugal Lisbon (☎ 213-472 381; embesppt@correo .mae.es; Rua do Salitre 1, 1269); consulate in Porto (☎ 225-363 915); consulate in Vila Real de Santo António (☎ 281-544 888)

UK London (☎ 020-7235 5555; embespuk@mail.mae.es; 39 Chesham Pl, SW1X 8SB); consulate in London (☎ 020-7589 8989; www.conspalon.org; 20 Draycott Pl, SW3 2RZ); consulate in Edinburgh (☎ 0131-220 18 43); consulate in Manchester (☎ 0161-236 1233)

USA Washington DC (☎ 202-452 0100; www.spainemb .org; 2375 Pennsylvania Ave NW, 20037); consulate in Washington (☎ 202-728 2330; 2375 Pennsylvania Ave NW, 20037); consulate in Boston (☎ 617-536 2506); consulate in Chicago (☎ 312-782 4588); consulate in Houston (☎ 713-783 6200); consulate in Los Angeles (☎ 323-938 0158); consulate in Miami (☎ 305-446 5511); consulate in New Orleans (☎ 504-525 4951); consulate in New York (☎ 212-355 4080); consulate in San Francisco (☎ 415-922 2995)

Embassies & Consulates in Spain

All foreign embassies are in Madrid, but many countries also have consulates in Andalucian cities, especially Seville. Embassies and consulates include the following:

Australia Madrid (☎ 91 353 66 00; www.spain.embassy .gov.au; Plaza del Descubridor Diego de Ordás 3); honorary consulate in Seville (Map pp102–3; ☎ 954 22 09 71; Calle Federico Rubio 14)

Canada Madrid (☎ 91 423 32 50; www.canada-es.org; Calle de Núñez de Balboa 35); consulate in Málaga (Map p243; ☎ 952 22 33 46; 1st fl, Plaza de la Malagueta 2)

France Madrid (☎ 91 423 89 22; www.ambafrance-es .org; Calle Salustiano Olózaga 9); consulate in Seville (Map pp102–3; ☎ 954 29 32 00; www.consulfrance-seville .org; Plaza de Santa Cruz 1)

Germany Madrid (☎ 91 557 90 00; www.embajada -al emania.es; Calle de Fortuny 8); consulate in Málaga (Map p243; ☎ 952 36 35 91; Edificio Eurocom, Calle Mauricio Moro Pareto 2)

Ireland Madrid (☎ 91 436 40 93; Paseo de la Castellana 46); consulate in Fuengirola (☎ 952 47 51 08; Galerías Santa Mónica, Avenida de los Boliches); honorary consulate in Seville (Map pp102–3; ☎ 954 21 63 61; Plaza de Santa Cruz 4)

Italy Madrid (☎ 91 423 33 00; www.ambmadrid.esteri .it; Calle Lagasca 98); consulate in Seville (Map pp102–3; ☎ 954 22 85 76; Calle Fabiola 10)

Japan Madrid (☎ 91 590 76 00; www.es.emb-japan .go.jp; Calle de Serrano 109)

Morocco Madrid (☎ 91 563 10 90; www.maec.gov.ma /madrid; Calle de Serrano 179); consulate in Algeciras (Map p225; ☎ 956 66 18 03; Calle Teniente Maroto 2); consulate in Seville (Map pp94–5; ☎ 954 08 10 44; Pabellón de la Naturaleza, Camino de los Descubrimientos s/n, Isla de la Cartuja)

Netherlands Madrid (☎ 91 353 75 00; www.embaja dapaisesbajos.es; Avenida del Comandante Franco 32, Madrid); consulate in Seville (Map pp102–3; ☎ 954 22 87 50; Calle Placentines 1); consulate in Torremolinos (☎ 952 38 08 88; Edificio San Andrés 1F, Avenida Carlota Alessandri 33)

New Zealand Madrid (☎ 91 523 02 26; Plaza de la Lealtad 2)

Portugal Madrid (☎ 91 782 49 60; www.embajadapor tugal-madrid.org; Calle Pinar 1); consulate in Madrid (☎ 91 577 35 85; Calle Lagasca 88); consulate in Seville (Map pp94–5; ☎ 954 23 11 50; Avenida del Cid 1)

UK Madrid (☎ 91 700 82 00; www.ukinspain.com; Calle de Fernando el Santo 16); consulate in Málaga (Map p243; ☎ 952 35 23 00; Edificio Eurocom, Calle Mauricio Moro Pareto 2)

USA Madrid (☎ 91 587 22 00; www.embusa.es; Calle de Serrano 75); consular agency in Fuengirola (☎ 952 47 48 91; Apartment 1C, Avenida Juan Gómez 8); consular agency in Seville (Map pp102–3; ☎ 954 21 87 51; Plaza Nueva 8-8)

FESTIVALS & EVENTS

Andalucians indulge their love of colour, noise, crowds, pageantry, dressing up and partying at innumerable exuberant local fiestas. Every little village and every city *barrio* (district or quarter) holds several festivals every year, each with its own unique twist. Many fiestas are religion-based but still highly festive.

Most places hold their *feria* (main annual fair) in summer, with concerts, parades, fireworks, bullfights, fairgrounds, dancing and an all-night party atmosphere. You'll find information on the most important local

events in city and town sections throughout this book, and tourist offices can supply detailed information. The following are the outstanding regionwide celebrations:

January

Día de los Reyes Magos (Three Kings' Day) On 6 January each year, children receive gifts in commemoration of the gifts brought by the Three Kings to the baby Jesus; in many towns, Reyes Magos *cabalgatas* (cavalcades) tour the streets the evening before, tossing sweets to the crowds.

February/March

Carnaval (Carnival) Fancy-dress parades and general merry-making happen in many places (wildest in Cádiz), usually ending on the Tuesday 47 days before Easter Sunday.

March/April

Semana Santa (Holy Week) The biggest event of Spain's religious calendar. The week leading up to Easter Sunday sees parades of lavishly bedecked holy images, long lines of *nazarenos* (penitents), and big crowds lining the streets, in almost every city, town and village. In major cities there are daily processions from Palm Sunday to Easter Sunday. Seville's celebrations are the most lavish and intense; Málaga, Granada, Córdoba, Arcos de la Frontera, Jaén, Baeza and Úbeda also stage spectacular processions.

May

Cruces de Mayo (May Crosses) Crosses are placed in squares and patios in many towns, notably in and around Granada and Córdoba. Decorated with flowers, the crosses become the focus for temporary bars, food stalls, music and dancing. It's held on 3 May and around.

June

Hogueras de San Juan (Bonfires of San Juan) Bonfires and fireworks, especially on beaches, are the heart of this midsummer celebration held 23 June; many thousands of people camp overnight along Andalucía's beaches.

July

Día de la Virgen del Carmen On this feast day of the patron of fisherfolk on 16 July, the Virgin's image is carried into the sea, or paraded upon a flotilla of small boats, at many coastal towns.

FOOD

The Eating sections for some larger towns and cities in this book are split into Budget, Midrange and Top End sections. The budget bracket covers places where a typical main dish is under €9; midrange is where a typical main dish is between €9 and €15;

and the top end covers places where typical mains cost more than €15.

Restaurants normally open for lunch between 12.30pm and 1.30pm, closing at 4pm; for dinner they open around 7.30pm to 8.30pm and close between 11pm and midnight. Variations to these hours are given in reviews in this book. For an introduction to Andalucian food, see p79.

GAY & LESBIAN TRAVELLERS

Andalucía's liveliest gay scenes are in Málaga, Torremolinos, Seville and Granada, but there are gay- and lesbian-friendly bars or clubs in all major cities.

Websites such as www.andalucia.com, www.gayinspain.com, www.guiagay.com (in Spanish) and www.cogailes.org have good listings of gay and gay-friendly accommodation, bars, clubs, beaches, cruising areas, health clubs and associations. Gayinspain and Cogailes have message boards too. Cogailes is the site of the Coordinadora Gai-Lesbiana, a Barcelona-based gay and lesbian organisation that operates a free national information telephone line in English, Spanish and Catalan on ☎ 900 60 16 01, from 6pm to 10pm daily.

The **Asociación Andaluza de Lesbianas y Gais** (Calle Lavadero de las Tablas 15, Granada) runs the **Teléfono Andaluz de Información Homosexual** (☎ 958 20 06 02). The **Federación Colega** (www.colegaweb .net) works for Andalucian gay and lesbian solidarity, rights and acceptance, and has branches in all eight provincial capitals.

Even though gay marriage was legalised in Spain in 2005, some hotel receptionists still have difficulty understanding that two people of the same sex might want to share a double bed. One traveller suggested that to avoid wasted time, it can be a good idea for one of the pair to do the checking in before the other appears.

HOLIDAYS

Everywhere in Spain has 14 official holidays a year – some are holidays nationwide, some only in one village. The list of holidays in each place may change from year to year. If a holiday date falls on a weekend, sometimes the holiday is moved to the Monday. If a holiday falls on the second day following a weekend, many Spaniards take the intervening day off too – a practice known as making a *puente* (bridge).

The two main periods when Spaniards go on holiday are Semana Santa (Holy Week, leading up to Easter Sunday) and the six weeks from mid-July to the end of August. At these times accommodation in resorts can be scarce and transport heavily booked.

There are usually nine official national holidays:

Año Nuevo (New Year's Day) 1 January
Viernes Santo (Good Friday) 6 April 2007, 21 March 2008
Fiesta del Trabajo (Labour Day) 1 May
La Asunción (Feast of the Assumption) 15 August
Fiesta Nacional de España (National Day) 12 October
Todos los Santos (All Saints' Day) 1 November; traditional day for paying respect to the dead.
Día de la Constitución (Constitution Day) 6 December
La Inmaculada Concepción (Feast of the Immaculate Conception) 8 December
Navidad (Christmas) 25 December

In addition, regional governments normally set three holidays, and local councils a further two. The three regional holidays in Andalucía are usually these:

Epifanía (Epiphany) or **Día de los Reyes Magos** (Three Kings' Day) 6 January – see opposite
Día de Andalucía (Andalucía Day) 28 February
Jueves Santo (Holy Thursday) 5 April 2007, 20 March 2008

The following are often selected as local holidays by town halls:

Corpus Christi 7 June 2007, 22 May 2008
Día de San Juan Bautista (Feast of St John the Baptist, King Juan Carlos I's saint's day) 24 June
Día de Santiago Apóstol (Feast of St James the Apostle, Spain's patron saint) 25 July

INSURANCE

A travel-insurance policy to cover theft, loss and medical problems is a good idea. Travel agents will be able to make recommendations. Check the small print: some policies specifically exclude 'dangerous activities', which can include scuba diving, motorcycling, even trekking. You may prefer a policy that pays doctors or hospitals directly, rather than you having to pay on the spot and claim later. If you have to claim later, make sure you keep all documentation. Check whether the policy covers ambulances or an emergency flight home.

Buy travel insurance as early as possible. If you buy it in the week before you leave home, you may find, for example, that you are not covered for delays to your trip caused by strikes.

Paying for your airline ticket with a credit card often provides limited travel accident insurance, and you may be able to reclaim payment if the operator doesn't deliver.

See p455 for more information on health insurance and p452 for motor insurance.

INTERNET ACCESS

There are plenty of internet cafés in large and small towns throughout Andalucía, with a typical charge of around €1.50 per hour. Some are equipped with CD burners, webcams, headphones and so on. But they may not have card readers, so bring your own or the camera-to-USB cable if you plan on burning photos to CD along the way.

For those travelling with a laptop or hand-held computer, a growing number of hotels in Andalucía provide wi-fi access, and some have modem connections in rooms (accommodation with any kind of internet access for guests receives an 🖳 icon in this book). Be aware that your modem may not work once you leave your home country. The safest option is to buy a reputable 'global' modem before you leave home, or buy a local PC-card modem if you're spending an extended time in any one country. For lots of useful stuff on connecting to the web while travelling, visit www.kropla.com.

LEGAL MATTERS

Article 17 of the Spanish constitution determines that anyone who is arrested must be informed immediately, in a manner understandable to them, of their rights and the grounds for the arrest. Arrested people are entitled to the assistance of a lawyer during police inquiries or judicial investigations. If an arrested person does not appoint their own lawyer, they must be allotted a duty lawyer. For many foreign nationalities including British citizens, the police are also obliged to inform an arrested person's consulate immediately. Arrested people are likely to be held in a police cell until a formal statement answering the charges against them is taken, although by article 17 they may not be compelled to make a statement. Within 72 hours of arrest, the person must be brought before a judge or released. A lawyer to safeguard the arrested person's rights, and if necessary an interpreter, must be present when the statement is taken and when the arrested person goes before the judge.

Further useful information on Spanish legal procedures and lawyers is published on the website of the UK embassy in Madrid (www.ukinspain.com) under the 'Information Leaflets' section.

Drugs

Spain's once liberal drug laws were severely tightened in 1992. The only legal drug is cannabis, and then only for personal use – which means very small amounts. Public consumption of any drug is illegal. It would be very unwise to smoke cannabis in hotel rooms or guesthouses.

Travellers entering Spain from Morocco, especially with a vehicle, should be prepared for intensive drug searches.

Police

Spain has three main types of police. The **Policía Nacional** (National Police; ☎ 091) cover cities and bigger towns, sometimes forming special squads dealing with drugs, terrorism and the like. A further contingent is to be found shuffling paper in bunkerlike police stations called *comisarías*. The **Policía Local** (Local Police; ☎ 092), also known as Policía Municipal, are controlled by city and town halls and deal mainly with minor matters such as parking, traffic and bylaws. They wear blue-and-white uniforms. The responsibilities of the green-uniformed **Guardia Civil** (Civil Guard; ☎ 062) include roads, the countryside, villages and international borders.

If you need to go to the police, any of them will do, but you may find the Policía Local are the most approachable.

LEGAL AGE

- Voting: 18
- Driving: 18
- Drinking: 16
- Sex: 13 (for both heterosexual and homosexual, but sex between under-15s and over-18s is illegal)

MAPS

Michelin's 1:400,000 *Andalucía* is excellent for overall planning and touring, with an edition published each year. It's widely available in and outside Andalucía – look for it at petrol stations and bookshops.

Maps provided by tourist offices are often adequate for finding your way around cities and towns. So are those in phone directories, which come with indexes of major streets. For something more comprehensive, most cities are covered by one of the Spanish series such as Telstar, Escudo de Oro, Alpina or Everest, all with street indexes – available in bookshops. Check the publication dates, though.

On the internet, **Multimap** (www.multimap.com) and **Andalucía** (www.andalucia.com) have searchable street maps of Andalucian cities and towns.

If you're going to do any walking in Andalucía you should arm yourself with the best possible maps. Good commercially published series, all usually accompanied by guide booklets, come from Editorial Alpina, Editorial Penibética and Britain's Discovery Walking Guides. Spain's **Centro Nacional de Información Geográfica** (CNIG; www.cnig.es), the publishing arm of the Instituto Geográfico Nacional (IGN), produced a useful *Mapa Guía* series of national and natural parks, mostly at 1:50,000 or 1:100,000, in the 1990s. The CNIG also covers about three-quarters of Andalucía in its 1:25,000 *Mapa Topográfico Nacional* maps, most of which are up to date. Both the CNIG and the Servicio Geográfico del Ejército (SGE; Army Geographic Service) publish 1:50,000 series: the SGE's, called *Serie L*, tends to be more up to date (most of its Andalucía maps have been revised since the mid-1990s). CNIG maps may be labelled CNIG, IGN or both.

The Junta de Andalucía, Andalucía's regional government, also publishes a range of Andalucía maps, including a *Mapa Guía* series of natural and national parks. These have been published recently and are widely available, although perhaps better for vehicle touring than for walking, with a scale of 1:75,000. Their covers are predominantly green, as opposed to the CNIG *mapas guía* that are mainly red or pink. Other Junta maps include 1:10,000 and 1:20,000 maps covering the whole of Andalucía – there are good maps but sales outlets for them are few.

Local availability of maps is patchy, so it's a good idea to try to obtain them in advance. **Stanfords** (☎ 020-7836 1321; www.stanfords.co.uk; 12-14 Long Acre, London WC2E 9LP, UK) has a good range of Spain maps and you can order them online. In Spain, seek out any specialist map or travel bookshops; several are recommended in this book's destination chapters. LTC in Seville (see p93) is the best map shop in Andalucía, selling most Junta maps as well as SGE and CNIG maps.

The CNIG has sales offices in Andalucía's eight provincial capitals, including the following:

Granada (Map pp358–9; ☎ 958 90 93 20; Avenida Divina Pastora 7 & 9)

Málaga (☎ 952 21 20 18; Calle Ramos Carrión 48)

Seville (Map pp94–5; ☎ 955 56 93 20; Avenida San Francisco Javier 9, Edificio Sevilla 2, 8°, módulo 7)

MONEY

Spain's currency is the euro (€), made up of 100 cents. It comes in coins of one, two, five, 10, 20 and 50 cents and one and two euros, and notes of five, 10, 20, 50, 100, 200 and 500 euros. See the inside back cover for exchange rates.

You can get by very well in Andalucía with a credit or debit card enabling you to make purchases direct and to withdraw cash euros from *cajeros automáticos* (ATMs), which are extremely common. But it's wise to take more than one card (if you have them) and preferably a few travellers cheques too. The combination gives you a fall-back if you lose a card.

See p15 for an introduction to costs in Andalucía.

Cash & Travellers Cheques

Cash and travellers cheques can be exchanged at virtually any bank or exchange office. Banks are plentiful and tend to offer the best rates. Exchange offices – usually indicated by the word *cambio* (exchange) – exist mainly in tourist resorts. Generally they offer longer opening hours and quicker service than banks, but worse exchange rates.

Travellers cheques usually bring a slightly better exchange rate than cash, though that is often offset by the charges for buying

DIRECTORY

them in the first place. Thomas Cook, Visa and American Express (Amex) are widely accepted brands with efficient replacement policies. Amex offices cash their own travellers cheques commission-free, but exchange rates may be more favourable at a bank or exchange office.

In many places, the more money you change, the better the exchange rate you'll get. Check commissions first, and confirm that posted exchange rates are up to date. A typical commission is 2% to 3%, with a minimum of €4 or €5. Places that advertise 'no commission' usually offer poor exchange rates. In Spain you usually can't use travellers cheques like money to make purchases.

Credit & Debit Cards

Not every establishment accepts payment by card. You should be able to make payments by card in midrange and top-end accommodation and restaurants, and larger shops, but you cannot depend on it elsewhere. When you pay by card, you may be asked for ID such as your passport. Don't forget to memorise your PIN numbers as you may have to key these in as you pay, and do keep a note of the numbers to call for reporting a lost or stolen card.

Visitors from outside the euro zone will get most value for their pound, dollar or whatever by making purchases by credit card or debit card, with ATM withdrawals as second-best value. After you take into account commissions, handling fees, exchange-rate differentials, etc, obtaining euros by exchanging cash or travellers cheques generally gives less value for your money.

Taxes & Refunds

Spanish value-added tax (VAT) is called IVA (ee-ba; impuesto sobre el valor añadido). On accommodation and restaurant prices, it's 7% and is usually (but not always) included in the prices that you'll be quoted. On retail goods and car hire, IVA is 16%. As a rule, prices given in this book include IVA. Some accommodation places will forget about IVA if you pay cash and don't require a receipt. To ask 'Is IVA included?', say '¿Está incluido el IVA?'

Visitors resident outside the EU are entitled to a refund of the 16% IVA on any purchases costing more than €90.15 from any shop if they are taking them out of the EU within three months. Ask the shop to give you an invoice showing the price and IVA paid for each item and the name and address of the vendor and purchaser. Then present both the invoice and goods to the customs booth for IVA refunds at the airport, port or border from which you leave the EU. The officer will stamp the invoice and you hand it in at a bank in the airport or port for the reimbursement. Some retailers offer a slightly simplified version of this procedure via refund services such as **Global Refund** (www.globalrefund.com) or **Premier Tax Free** (www.premiertaxfree.com).

Tipping

Spanish law requires menu prices to include the service charge, and tipping is a matter of personal choice – most people leave some small change if they're satisfied, and 5% is usually plenty. Porters will generally be happy with €1.50. Taxi drivers don't have to be tipped but a little rounding up won't go amiss.

POST

At 2006 rates, a postcard or letter weighing up to 20g costs €0.57 from Spain to other European countries, and €0.78 to the rest of the world. Certificado (registered) mail costs an extra €2.20. Urgente service, which means your mail may arrive two or three days quicker than normal, costs around €2 extra for international mail.

Stamps are sold at estancos (tobacconist shops with 'Tabacos' in yellow letters on a maroon background), as well as at oficinas de correos (post offices). It's quite safe to post mail in the yellow street buzones (postboxes) as well as at post offices. Mail to or from other Western European countries normally arrives within a week; to or from North America within 10 days; to or from Australia and New Zealand within two weeks.

Poste restante mail can be addressed to you at Poste Restante (or better, Lista de Correos, the Spanish name for it), anywhere in Spain that has a post office, with the name of the province following that of the town. This will be delivered to the place's main post office unless another one is specified in the address. Take your pass-

---

SPAIN'S 'ANTI-TOBACCO' LAW

In 2006 smoking was banned in many public places throughout Spain including offices, shops, schools, hospitals and on public transport, largely in response to the country's 50,000 annual smoking-related deaths. Under the January 2006 'anti-tobacco' law, bars and restaurants larger than 100 sq metres must create separate smoking areas with their own ventilation systems. Smaller bars and restaurants can choose whether or not to allow smoking – hence all the signs on bar doors saying whether or not people can smoke in there. Hotels are supposed to set aside at least 70% of their rooms for non-smokers – though this is one part of the law that seems to be widely ignored.

---

port when you go to pick up mail. Every Spanish address has a five-digit postcode, use of which may help your mail arrive a bit quicker.

SOLO TRAVELLERS

Unfortunately for solo travellers, a single room normally costs well over half the price of a double room. Budget travellers have the option of cutting costs by staying in youth hostels in some places, but backpacker hostels, real gathering places for international travellers, are thin on the ground.

Despite Andalucians' reputation for being gregarious, it is possible for solo travellers to feel left out of some of the fun. You can't expect the locals to want to get to know every foreigner who passes through, and Andalucian accommodation is not, in general, terribly conducive to getting to know other guests. Bars can be a good place to meet people but women need to be wary as many bars are the domain of macho males or those on the lookout for female tourists. This obviously is less the case in sophisticated places such as central areas of Málaga, Granada and Seville. Of course, if you're gregarious, self-assured and can speak a bit of Spanish, you'll get by just fine.

Solo travellers need to be watchful of their luggage when on the road and should stay in places with safe boxes for their valuables so as not to be burdened with them when out and about. One big drag of travelling alone is when you want to take a quick

dip in the sea and there's no-one to keep an eye on your valuables!

TELEPHONE & FAX

Spain has no telephone area codes. Every phone number has nine digits and for any call within Spain you just dial all those nine digits. If calling Spain from another country, dial your international access code, followed by Spain's country code ☎ 34, followed by all nine digits of the local number. The international access code for calls from Spain is ☎ 00.

The first digit of all Spanish fixed-phone numbers is ☎ 9. Numbers beginning with ☎ 6 are mobile phones.

Many towns now have cheap-rate call offices known as *locutorios*, where you can make international calls for low rates (eg around €0.20 a minute to the USA or €0.30 a minute to Australia), although calls within Spain are generally at similar rates to street payphones. Even cheaper (to fixed phones) are internet phone calls, available at some *locutorios* and internet cafés.

Andalucía is fairly well provided with blue payphones, which (as long as they are in working order) are easy to use for both international and domestic calls. They accept coins and/or *tarjetas telefónicas* (phonecards) issued by the national phone company Telefónica. Phonecards come in €6 and €12 denominations and are sold at post offices and *estancos*. Coin payphones inside bars and cafés – often green – are normally a little more expensive than street payphones. Phones in hotel rooms may be a good deal more expensive: managements set their own rates, so ask about costs before using one.

Costs

A three-minute payphone call to a fixed phone costs €0.20 within your local area, around €0.30 to other places within the same province, around €0.40 to other Spanish provinces, about €1 to other EU countries or the USA, and about €2 to Australia – though for international calls you're usually better off finding a *locutorio*. Payphone calls are generally 10% to 20% cheaper from 8pm to 8am Monday to Friday, and all day Saturday and Sunday. Payphone calls to most Spanish mobile phones (which are numbers starting with ☎ 6) cost around €1 for three minutes.

Calls to Spanish numbers starting with ☎900 are free. Numbers starting with ☎901 to ☎906 are pay-per-minute numbers and charges vary; a common one is ☎902, for which you pay about €0.35 for three minutes from a payphone.

Calls from private lines cost about 25% less than calls from payphones.

Fax

Most main post offices have a fax service: sending one page costs €1.90 within Spain, €8 elsewhere in Europe and €15 to North America or Australasia. However, you'll often find cheaper rates at shops or offices with 'Fax Público' signs.

Mobile Phones

If you're going to make lots of calls within Spain, it's worth considering buying a Spanish mobile. Shops on every main street and in every shopping centre sell phones at bargain prices and Amena, Movistar and Vodafone are widespread and reputable brands. You need to understand the detail of advertised deals, however. For example if a phone with a call credit of €50 is on sale for €40, you will usually have to buy more credit at normal rates to qualify for the €50 free credit.

If you're considering taking a mobile from your home country to Spain, you should find out from your mobile network provider whether your phone is enabled for international roaming, and what the costs of calls, text and voicemail are likely to be. Don't forget to take a Continental adaptor for your charger plug.

Ofcom (www.ofcom.org.uk; go to 'Advice for Consumers') and **Steve Kropla's Help for World Travelers** (www.kropla.com) have useful advice on using your mobile abroad; **GSM World** (www.gsmworld .com) provides coverage maps, lists of roaming partners and links to phone companies' websites.

Reverse-charge & Information Calls

Dial ☎1009 to speak to a domestic operator, including for a *llamada por cobro revertido* – a domestic reverse-charge (collect) call.

To make an international reverse-charge call via an operator in the country you're calling to, dial the following numbers:
Australia (☎900 990061)
Canada (☎900 990015)

France (☎900 990033)
New Zealand (☎900 990064)
UK (☎900 990044)
USA AT&T (☎900 990011); MCI (☎900 990014); Sprint (☎900 990013)

Codes for other countries are often posted up in payphones. Alternatively, you can usually get an English-speaking international operator on ☎1008 to call Europe and ☎1005 for the rest of the world.

For Spanish directory inquiries you need to dial ☎11822; these calls cost €0.22 plus €0.01 per second.

For international directory inquiries dial ☎11825. Warning: the cost is €1 plus €0.75 per minute.

TIME

All mainland Spain is on GMT/UTC plus one hour during winter, and GMT/UTC plus two hours during the country's daylight-saving period, which runs from the last Sunday in March to the last Sunday in October. Most other Western European countries have the same time as Spain year-round, the major exceptions being Britain, Ireland and Portugal. Add one hour to these three countries' times to get Spanish time.

Spanish time is normally USA eastern time plus six hours, and USA Pacific time plus nine hours. But the USA tends to start daylight-saving time a week or two later than Spain, so you must add one hour to the time differences during the intervening period.

In the Australian winter subtract eight hours from Sydney time to get Spanish time; in the Australian summer subtract 10 hours. The difference is nine hours for a few weeks in March.

Morocco is on GMT/UTC year-round, so is two hours behind Spain during Spanish daylight-saving time, and one hour behind at other times of the year.

For further information see World Time Zones, pp486–7.

TOILETS

Public toilets are not common, but it's OK to wander into many bars and cafés to use the toilet even if you're not a customer. It's worth carrying some toilet paper with you as many toilets lack it.

TOURIST INFORMATION
Tourist Offices in Spain

All cities and many smaller towns and even villages in Andalucía have at least one *oficina de turismo* (tourist office). Staff are generally knowledgeable and increasingly well versed in foreign languages. Offices are usually well stocked with printed material. Opening hours vary widely.

Tourist offices in Andalucía may be operated by the local town hall, by local district organisations, by the government of whichever province you're in, or by the regional government, the Junta de Andalucía. There may also be more than one tourist office in larger cities, each offering information on the territory it represents. The Junta de Andalucía's environmental department, the Consejería de Medio Ambiente, also has visitors centres located in many of the environmentally protected areas (*parques naturales* and so on).

You'll find details of useful tourist offices in the Information sections of destination chapters throughout this book.

Spain's national tourism authority is **Turespaña** (☎ 91 343 35 00, tourist information 901 300600; www.spain.info; Calle José Lázaro Galdiano 6, 28071 Madrid). The Andalucian regional tourism authority is the Junta de Andalucía's **Consejería de Turismo, Comercio y Deporte** (☎ 955 06 51 00; www .juntadeandalucia.es/turismocomercioydeporte; Torretriana, Isla de la Cartuja, 41092 Seville). Marketing, promotion and planning are handled by **Turismo Andaluz** (☎ 951 29 93 00, tourist information 901 20 00 20; www.andalucia.org; Calle Compañía 40, 29008 Málaga).

Tourist Offices Abroad

You can get information on Andalucía from Spanish national tourist offices in 23 countries, including the following:

Canada (☎ 416-961 3131; www.tourspain.toronto .on.ca; Suite 3402, 2 Bloor St W, Toronto M4W 3E2)

France (☎ 01 45 03 82 57; www.espagne.infotourisme .com; 43 rue Decamps, 75784 Paris, Cedex 16)

Germany (☎ 030-882 6036; berlin@tourspain.es; Kurfürstendamm 63, 5.0G, 10707 Berlin) Also branches in Düsseldorf, Frankfurt am Main and Munich.

Italy (☎ 06 692 00 453; www.turismospagnolo.it; Piazza di Spagna 55, 00187 Rome)

Japan (☎ 03-3432 6141; www.spaintour.com; Daini Toranomon Denki Bldg, 4F, 3-1-10 Toranomon, Minato-ku, Tokyo 105)

Netherlands (☎ 070-346 59 00; www.spaansverkeers bureau.nl; Laan Van Meerdervoor 8a, 2517 AJ The Hague)

Portugal (☎ 213 541 992; lisboa@tourspain.es; Avenida Sidónio Pais 28-30 Dto, 1050-215 Lisbon)

UK (☎ 020 7486 8077; www.tourspain.co.uk; 2nd flr, 79 New Cavendish St, London W1W 6XB)

USA (☎ 212-265 8822; www.okspain.org; 35th fl, 666 Fifth Ave, New York, NY 10103) Also branches in Chicago, Los Angeles and Miami.

You'll find details of the other offices on the Turespaña website.

TRAVELLERS WITH DISABILITIES

Some Spanish tourist offices in other countries (see left) provide a basic information sheet with useful addresses for travellers with disabilities, and can give details of accessible accommodation in specific places.

Wheelchair accessibility in Andalucía is improving as new buildings meet regulations requiring them to have wheelchair access. The Spanish-language guidebook for people with disabilities, *Guía de los Hoteles mas Accesibles para Viajeros en Sillas de Ruedas* (sold at www.valinet.org) lists over 300 recommended Spanish hotels with wheelchair access, many of them in Andalucía. Many midrange and top-end hotels are now adapting rooms and accesses for wheelchair users. Nearly all Andalucian youth hostels have rooms adapted for the disabled, but accessibility is poorer at other budget accommodation. In this book we indicate with a wheelchair icon (♿) where a sight or accommodation option is particularly well set up for wheelchair users.

Accessible Travel & Leisure (☎ 01452-729739; www.accessibletravel.co.uk) is a travel agency specialising in holidays for the mobility-impaired. It can book you into accessible hotels, villas and apartments in Spain. The following UK-based organisations have further travel information for travellers with disabilities:

Holiday Care (☎ 0845 124 9971; www.holidaycare.org .uk) Produces an information pack on Spain for people with special needs, including accommodation with disabled access.

Radar (☎ 020-7250 3222; www.radar.org.uk) Run by and for disabled people. Its excellent website has links to travel and holiday-specific sites.

VISAS

Citizens of EU countries, Switzerland, Norway, Iceland and Liechtenstein need only carry their passport or national identity

DIRECTORY

document in order to enter Spain. Citizens of many other countries, including Australia, Canada, Japan, New Zealand, Singapore and the USA, do not need a visa for visits of up to 90 days but must carry their passport.

At the time of writing, nationalities required to obtain a visa to visit Spain included South Africa, Russia, Morocco, India and Pakistan. Consult a Spanish consulate well in advance of travel if you think you need a visa. The standard tourist visa issued when necessary is the Schengen visa, which is valid not only for Spain but for all the 14 other countries that are party to the Schengen agreement, which abolished controls at borders between these countries in 2000. The other Schengen countries are Austria, Belgium, Denmark, Finland, France, Germany, Greece, Iceland, Italy, Luxembourg, the Netherlands, Norway, Portugal and Sweden. You normally have to apply for the visa in person at a consulate in your country of residence. In the UK, visas cost UK£24.15.

VOLUNTEERING

Spain doesn't offer the opportunities for volunteer work that a developing country might, and the majority of openings that exist are in the country's north. But the following sources are worth checking out if you're keen to volunteer or do an internship in Andalucía:

Adelante Abroad (www.adelanteabroad.com) Arranges internships with private-sector companies in Seville, including some language study. A two-month internship costs around US$3000.

Best Programs (www.bestprograms.org) Nine-to-12-week internships with Spanish NGOs, including some language study, for around US$1600 to US$2000.

Earthwatch (www.earthwatch.org) Seeks volunteers for 12-day dolphin research projects off Andalucía's coasts (volunteers usually pay around UK£1000 or more).

Idealist.org (www.idealist.org) Good place to look for Spanish volunteer possibilities.

Oasis Project (www.aulapolis.com/oasis/oasising.htm) Internships in nonprofit organisations.

Transitions Abroad (www.transitionsabroad.org) Good source on volunteering and internships worldwide, including in Spain.

Volunteer Abroad (www.volunteerabroad.com) Details on a range of volunteer openings in Spain.

WOMEN TRAVELLERS

Women in Spain are just about on an equal footing with men these days. By and large women work, contribute to the family purse, and have their own money to spend and share in decision-making in the home. Sexual equality has been slower coming to Spain than in many other parts of the Western world but this new-found confidence among Spanish women is striking. Women now occupy positions of power and authority in all sectors. Young women generally hold their own and are unafraid to stand up for themselves, although this sometimes results in unpleasant consequences. Spain has its share of abused girls and women – something the PSOE government under José Luis Rodríguez Zapatero has made a priority of tackling since it was elected in 2004.

Men under about 35, who have grown up in the post-Franco era, are less sexually stereotyped than their older counterparts whose thinking and behaviour towards women is still directed by machismo.

Though harassment is not frequent, women travellers should be ready to ignore any stares, catcalls and comments. Avoid plunging necklines, short skirts and bare shoulders to spare yourself unwanted attention. Remember the word for help (socorro) in case you need to use it. You do still need to exercise common sense about where you go solo. Think twice about going alone to isolated stretches of beach or country, or down empty city streets at night. A lone woman, for example, would be better to forget wandering around the uninhabited parts of Granada's Sacromonte area. It's highly inadvisable for a woman to hitchhike alone – and not a great idea even for two women together.

Skimpy clothes are the norm in many coastal resorts, but people tend to dress more modestly elsewhere. As in France and Italy, many Spanish women like to get really dressed up and made up. You can feel rather conspicuous on a Sunday when they take to the plazas and promenades for the afternoon paseo (walk) and you're in your casual gear.

Each province's national police headquarters has a special Servicio de Atención a la Mujer (SAM; literally Service of Attention to Women). The national **Comisión para la Investigación de Malos Tratos a Mujeres** (Commission for Investigation into Abuse of Women; emergency ☎ 900 10 00 09; www.malostratos.org in Spanish; ⏰ 9am-9pm) maintains an emergency line for victims of physical abuse anywhere in Spain. In Andalucía the **Instituto Andaluz de la Mujer** (☎ 900 20 09 99; ⏰ 24hr) also offers help.

Transport

THINGS CHANGE...

The information in this chapter is particularly vulnerable to change. Check directly with the airline or a travel agent to make sure you understand how a fare (and ticket you may buy) works and be aware of the security requirements for international travel. Shop carefully. The details given in this chapter should be regarded as pointers and are not a substitute for your own careful, up-to-date research.

GETTING THERE & AWAY

Most vacationers fly to Andalucía, which has five airports with direct flights from several European countries as well as Spanish domestic services. Gibraltar receives flights from the UK. Andalucía's busiest airport, Málaga, also has flights from Morocco. From other countries, you'll need to change planes en route, usually at Madrid or Barcelona or in another European country.

Andalucía is well connected by train and bus with the rest of Spain, and there are direct bus services from several European countries and Morocco (though flying is often no more expensive from Europe). Rail routes to Andalucía from other European countries involve a change of train in Madrid or Barcelona.

Drivers can reach Andalucía from just about anywhere in Spain in a single day on the country's good-quality highways. The main routes run down the centre of the country from Madrid and along the Mediterranean coast from Barcelona. Popular vehicle ferries run from the UK to Bilbao and Santander in northern Spain, from which you can drive to Andalucía via Madrid. Ferry routes also connect Andalucía with Tangier and Nador in Morocco and with Ceuta and Melilla, the Spanish enclaves on the Moroccan coast.

ENTERING THE COUNTRY

Citizens of many countries need no visa to enter Spain but must carry a passport (or, for many European nationalities, a national identity document) – see p439 for further information. Immigration formalities for travellers entering Spain from other European Union countries are minimal – a quick glance at your identity document if you arrive by plane and often no checks at all if you arrive overland from France or Portugal. If you're flying into Spain from outside the EU, officials might take a little more interest in your passport and luggage.

Travellers coming by ferry from Morocco should be prepared to receive more attention: vehicles in particular may be subject to rigorous searches when reaching Spanish territory.

AIR
Airports & Airlines

Málaga airport (code AGP; ☎ 952 04 88 38) is the main international airport in Andalucía. **Almería** (code LEI; ☎ 950 21 37 00), **Seville** (code SVQ; ☎ 954 44 90 00), **Granada** (code GRX; ☎ 958 24 52 07), **Jerez de la Frontera** (code XRY; ☎ 956 15 00 00) and **Gibraltar** (code GIB; ☎ 73026) also receive international flights. For useful information on all Spanish airports, visit www.aena.es.

Airlines flying into Andalucía, with local telephone numbers in Andalucía or Spain, include the following:

Aer Lingus (airline code EI; ☎ 902 50 27 37; www.aer lingus.com; hub Dublin)

Air Europa (airline code UX; ☎ 902 40 15 01; www.air-europa.com; hub Madrid)

Air Nostrum See Iberia.

Air-Berlin (airline code AB; ☎ 901 11 64 02; www.air berlin.com; hub Palma de Mallorca)

Alitalia (airline code AZ; ☎ 902 10 03 23; www.alitalia.it; hubs Milan, Rome)

Bmibaby (airline code WW; ☎ 902 10 07 37; www.bmibaby.com; hubs Birmingham, Cardiff, Durham Tees Valley, London Heathrow, Manchester, Nottingham East Midlands)

British Airways (airline code BA; ☎ 902 11 13 33, in Gibraltar 79300; www.ba.com; hub London Heathrow)

Condor (airline code DE; ☎ 902 51 73 00; www.condor.com; hub Frankfurt)

Finnair (airline code AY; ☎ 952 13 61 77; www.finnair.com; hub Helsinki)

Flybe (airline code BE; ☎ 952 10 54 88; www.flybe.com; hubs Birmingham, Exeter, Norwich, Southampton)

Flyglobespan (airline code GSM; ☎ 952 04 84 84; www.flyglobespan.com; hubs Glasgow, Edinburgh)

GB Airways (airline code BA; ☎ 902 11 13 33, in Gibraltar 79300; www.gbairways.com; hub London Gatwick)

Germanwings (airline code 4U; ☎ 91 625 97 04; www.germanwings.com; hub Cologne)

Hapagfly (airline code HF; ☎ 902 39 04 00; www.hapagfly.com; hubs Frankfurt, Mallorca, Munich)

Iberia (airline code IB; ☎ 902 40 05 00; www.iberia.com; hub Madrid)

Jet2 (airline code LS; ☎ 902 02 02 64; www.jet2.com; hubs Leeds-Bradford, Manchester)

Lauda Air (airline code; ☎ 902 25 70 00; www.aua.com; hub Vienna)

LTU (airline code LT; ☎ 901 33 03 20; www.ltu.de; hubs Düsseldorf, Munich)

Lufthansa (airline code LH; ☎ 902 22 01 01; www.lufthansa.com; hub Frankfurt)

Monarch Airlines (airline code ZB; ☎ 800 09 92 60, in Gibraltar 47477; www.flymonarch.com; hubs London Gatwick, London Luton, Manchester)

Portugália Airlines (airline code NI; ☎ 952 04 83 50; www.flypga.com; hub Lisbon)

Regional Air Lines (airline code RGL; ☎ 902 18 01 51; www.royalairmaroc.com; hub Casablanca)

Royal Air Maroc (airline code AT; ☎ 91 548 78 00; www.royalairmaroc.com; hub Casablanca)

Ryanair (airline code FR; ☎ 807 22 00 32; www.ryanair.com; hubs Dublin, Liverpool, London Stansted)

Scandinavian Airlines (airline code SK; ☎ 902 11 71 92; www.scandinavian.net; hubs Copenhagen, Stockholm)

SN Brussels Airlines (airline code SN; ☎ 902 90 14 92; www.flysn.com; hub Brussels)

Spanair (airline code JK; ☎ 902 13 14 15; www.spanair.com; hubs Barcelona, Madrid)

Sterling (airline code NB; ☎ 91 749 66 43; www.sterlingticket.com; hubs Copenhagen, Oslo, Stockholm)

Swiss (airline code LX; ☎ 901 11 67 12; www.swiss.com; hub Zürich)

Thomas Cook Airlines (airline code TCX; ☎ 952 04 82 14; www.flythomascook.com; hubs Birmingham, Glasgow, London Gatwick, Manchester, Newcastle)

Thomsonfly (airline code TOM; ☎ 91 414 14 81; www.thomsonfly.com; hubs Bournemouth, Bristol, Doncaster, Manchester, London Gatwick, London Luton, Newcastle)

Transavia (airline code HV; ☎ 902 11 44 78; www.transavia.com; hub Amsterdam)

Virgin Express (airline code TV; ☎ 902 88 84 59; www.virginexpress.com; hub Brussels)

Vueling (airline code VY; ☎ 902 33 39 33; www.vueling.com; hub Barcelona)

Tickets

The best-value tickets to Andalucía are usually found on the internet (direct from budget airlines, or through agencies). International online booking agencies worth a look include **CheapTickets** (www.cheaptickets.com) and, for students and travellers under the age of 26, **STA Travel** (www.statravel.com).

Tickets on budget airlines of course get more expensive nearer departure date: low-season flights (especially mid-September to mid-December and mid-January to just before Easter) and weekday flights (Monday to Friday) generally fill up slower, so bargains are more readily available at these times.

For flights heading out of Andalucía, including last-minute and standby seats, it's worth checking the ads in local foreign-language papers such as *Sur in English*, or trying the following local travel agencies with offices at Málaga airport:

Flightline (☎ 902 20 22 40; www.flightline.es)
Servitour (☎ 902 40 00 69; www.servitour.es)
Travelshop (☎ 952 46 42 27; www.thetravelshop.com)
Viajes Mundial Schemann (☎ 902 10 06 05) For flights to Germany.

Several Spanish online booking agencies, including **Rumbo** (☎ 902 12 39 99; www.rumbo.es) and **eDreams** (☎ 902 88 71 07; www.edreams.es) offer good fares too.

Australia & New Zealand

There are no direct flights from Australia or New Zealand to Spain. You fly to Europe via Asia, the Middle East or (less often) America, changing flights at a major European airport to reach Spain. Return fares from Sydney or Auckland to Málaga normally start at somewhere around A$2000 or NZ$2500, plus a few hundred dollars if you're travelling in the high seasons, especially European summer. Round-the-world tickets can sometimes be cheaper.

The following are well-known agents for cheap fares, with branches throughout both countries:

Flight Centre Australia (☎ 133 133; www.flightcentre .com.au); New Zealand (☎ 0800 243 544; www.flight centre.co.nz)

STA Travel Australia (☎ 1300 733 035; www.statravel .com.au); New Zealand (☎ 0508 782 872; www.statravel .co.nz)

For online fares try www.travel.com.au or www.zuji.com from Australia, and www .travel.co.nz or www.zuji.co.nz from New Zealand.

Continental Europe

Except for very short hops, air fares usually beat overland alternatives on cost. For online bookings throughout Europe, try **Opodo** (www.opodo.com) or **Ebookers** (www.ebookers.com).

FRANCE

Air Europa has daily flights from Paris (Charles de Gaulle) direct to Málaga and to Seville via Barcelona, both for as little as €110 if booked in good time. Iberia flies Paris–Seville direct, and can take you from a range of French cities to any Andalucian airport with a connection in Barcelona or Madrid. Return fares start just under €100 but you'll often have to pay more than that.

Recommended ticket agencies:

OTU Voyages (www.otu.fr) Student and youth travel specialist.

Voyageurs du Monde (☎ 01 40 15 11 15; www.vdm .com)

GERMANY

Several budget airlines typically provide flights for €100 to €200 each way when booked one to two months in advance. Partners Air-Berlin and Hapagfly fly from around 15 German airports to Almería, Jerez de la Frontera, Málaga and Seville, usually with a stop at Palma de Mallorca. Condor flies to Málaga and Jerez from many German airports; LTU heads to Almería

and Málaga from Düsseldorf, Frankfurt, Hamburg, Munich and Stuttgart; Spanair connects many German cities with Jerez, Málaga and Seville via Frankfurt and Madrid; EasyJet flies to Málaga from Berlin and Dortmund; and Germanwings runs an inexpensive Cologne–Jerez service.

With a connection at Barcelona or Madrid Iberia will take you to any Andalucian airport from seven German cities, and Lufthansa flies to Jerez, Málaga and Seville from most German airports. Return fares booked in good time can be as low as €200.

Recommended ticket agencies:

Expedia (www.expedia.de)

Just Travel (☎ 089 747 3330; www.justtravel.de)

STA Travel (☎ 01805 456 422; www.statravel.de) For travellers aged under 26.

NETHERLANDS & BELGIUM

Transavia (Amsterdam to Almería, Málaga and Seville; Rotterdam–Málaga) and Virgin Express and Ryanair (both Brussels–Málaga) have some of the best fares, typically €200 to €250 return if booked a month or two ahead. SN Brussels Airlines (Brussels–Seville) typically charges a little more. Iberia often has competitive fares from Amsterdam or Brussels to any Andalucian airport. A recommended ticket agency is **Airfair** (☎ 070-3076110; www.airfair.nl).

PORTUGAL

Portugália Airlines flies daily nonstop between Lisbon and Málaga. Return fares, typically in the region of €200, are worth considering.

SCANDINAVIA

Sterling, flying from all four Scandinavian capitals to Málaga, consistently has some of the best fares, often in the €200 to €300 region for return flights a month or two ahead. Some fares on Iberia and Spanair are pretty competitive, too. Other airlines linking Scandinavia with Andalucía include Finnair, Scandinavian Airlines and Virgin Express.

Morocco

Royal Air Maroc, with some flights operated by Regional Air Lines, flies direct between Málaga and Tangier (daily), and Málaga and Casablanca (several days weekly), with typical return fares in the region of €350 for Tangier and €500 for Casablanca. Iberia and Air Europa often offer better fares via Madrid. Iberia also flies daily nonstop from Málaga, Almería and Granada to Melilla, the Spanish enclave on the Moroccan coast, with return fares under €100 if booked far enough ahead. These flights are operated by Air Nostrum.

Spain

Flying within Spain is most worth considering if you're in a hurry and you're making a longish one-way trip or a return trip.

Spain's biggest airline, Iberia, flies daily (in some cases several times a day) nonstop from Madrid and Barcelona to all five Andalucian airports. One-way/return fares from Madrid or Barcelona to Málaga or Seville are often below €50/100 if booked sufficiently in advance. Other direct routes include Asturias, Bilbao, Santander, Santiago de Compostela, Valencia and Vigo to Seville and Málaga, and Alicante and San Sebastián to Seville. With a connection in Madrid or Barcelona, Iberia will fly you to any Andalucian airport from any airport in Spain.

Air Europa flies nonstop on the following routes: Madrid–Málaga, Barcelona–Seville, Palma de Mallorca–Granada, Palma de Mallorca–Seville, Bilbao–Málaga and Palma de Mallorca–Málaga. Spanair's nonstop routes include Barcelona to Málaga and Seville, and Madrid to Málaga, Seville and Jerez de la Frontera. Both these airlines offer connections at Madrid to and from many other Spanish cities. Their fares are similar to Iberia's.

Vueling flies from Barcelona to Málaga and Seville, and from Valencia to Seville. Fares can be under €50 each way.

UK & Ireland

An ever-growing array of budget or semi-budget airlines flies to Andalucía, especially Málaga. Return fares range between about UK£80 and UK£300 on most routes year-round and depend on how far ahead you book. (Advertised fares of two quid and the like don't include taxes or booking charges.) Budget airlines flying to Málaga from the following airports include:

Aberdeen Monarch
Belfast EasyJet, Thomsonfly
Birmingham Bmibaby, Flybe, Monarch, Thomas Cook Airlines
Blackpool Monarch
Bournemouth Thomsonfly
Bristol EasyJet, Thomsonfly
Cardiff Bmibaby
Cork Aer Lingus
Doncaster Sheffield Thomsonfly
Dublin Aer Lingus, Ryanair, Spanair
Durham Tees Valley Bmibaby
Edinburgh Flyglobespan, Thomsonfly
Exeter Flybe
Glasgow EasyJet, Flyglobespan, Thomas Cook Airlines, Thomsonfly
Humberside Thomsonfly
Leeds-Bradford Jet 2, Thomsonfly
Liverpool EasyJet, Thomsonfly
London (Gatwick/Heathrow/Luton/Stansted) EasyJet, GB Airways, Monarch, Thomas Cook Airlines, Thomsonfly
Manchester Bmibaby, GB Airways, Jet 2, Monarch, Thomas Cook Airlines, Thomsonfly
Newcastle EasyJet, Thomas Cook Airlines, Thomsonfly
Norwich Flybe, Thomsonfly
Nottingham East Midlands Bmibaby, EasyJet
Shannon Ryanair
Southampton Flybe

Services to Seville go from Dublin (Aer Lingus), Liverpool (Ryanair), London Gatwick (GB Airways) and London Stansted (Ryanair); to Granada from Liverpool (Ryanair), London Gatwick (Monarch) and London Stansted (Ryanair). To Jerez de la Frontera you can fly from London Stansted (Ryanair) or Manchester (Thomas Cook Airlines). Flights to Almería go from Birmingham (Monarch), Dublin (Aer Lingus), London Gatwick (EasyJet, Thomas Cook Airlines), London Stansted (EasyJet, Ryanair) and Manchester (Monarch, Thomas Cook Airlines). And you can fly to Gibraltar from London Gatwick (GB Airways), London Luton (Monarch) and Manchester (Monarch).

British Airways and Iberia fly to all Andalucian airports (usually with connections at London, Madrid, or Barcelona) from London, Aberdeen, Birmingham, Edinburgh, Glasgow, Manchester and Newcastle, plus Belfast (British Airways) and Dublin (Iberia), often with competitive fares.

Recommended travel agencies include the following:

Airline Network (☎ 0870-700-0543; www.airline
-network.co.uk)

Avro (☎ 0870-458-2841; www.avro.com) Charter and scheduled flights.

Dial A Flight (☎ 0870-333-4488; www.dialaflight.com)

Expedia.co.uk (☎ 0870-050-0808; www.expedia.co.uk)

First Choice (☎ 0870-850-3999; www.firstchoice.co.uk) Mainly charter flights.

Flight Centre (☎ 0870-890-8099; http://flightcentre.co.uk)

Lastminute.com (www.lastminute.com)

Quest Travel (☎ 0870-442-3542; www.questtravel.com)

Sky Deals (☎ 0800-975-5477; www.skydeals.co.uk)

STA Travel (☎ 08701-630-026; www.statravel.co.uk) For travellers under the age of 26.

USA & Canada

There are no direct flights between North America and Andalucía at the time of writing, but plenty of flights with transfers in Madrid or another European city are available. Fares via Barcelona, London, Paris or Frankfurt are not necessarily more expensive than via Madrid. Booking ahead, you should be able to get a New York–Málaga round-trip ticket for about US$500 to US$700 in low season or US$1000 to US$1200 in high season. Round trips from Montreal or Toronto to Málaga range from about C$1000 to C$1700.

The following agencies are recommended for online bookings from the USA:

www.cheaptickets.com
www.expedia.com
www.lowestfare.com
www.orbitz.com
www.sta.com (for travellers under 26)
www.travelocity.com

Travel Cuts (☎ 800 667 2887; www.travelcuts.com) is Canada's national student travel agency. For online bookings from Canada try www.expedia.ca and www.travelocity.ca.

LAND

For information on the paperwork needed for taking a vehicle to Spain and general information on driving in Spain, see p450. For a summary of routes through Spain to Andalucía, see p446.

Continental Europe

BUS

Bus travel to Andalucía from other countries except Portugal often works out no cheaper than flying. **Eurolines** (www.eurolines.com), a grouping of 32 bus companies from different countries, runs to several Andalucian cities from France, Germany, Switzerland, Italy, the Czech Republic and Portugal. The Spanish company **Alsa** (www.alsa.es) is the Eurolines operator on many of these routes. A Paris–Granada trip, for example, costs €118/213 one-way/return (24 hours each way).

From Portugal, Eurolines/Alsa has daily services from Lisbon's Terminal Oriente to Seville (€36, seven hours) via Evora and Badajoz, and to Málaga (€53, 12 hours) via Faro, Huelva and Seville. **Anibal** (www.anibal.net) runs six times weekly from Lisbon to Seville (€30, seven hours) via Faro and Huelva, and Spain's **Casal** (www.autocares casal.com) has a daily service between Seville and the border at Rosal de la Frontera (west of Aracena), where you can connect with Portuguese buses to/from Lisbon for a total Seville–Lisbon journey time of 10 hours, costing €22. There's also a twice-daily service (except Saturday, Sunday and holidays from October to May) from Lagos to Seville (€18, 5½ hours) via Albufeira, Faro and Huelva, run jointly by Portugal's **Eva Transportes** (☎ 289-899 700 in Portugal; www.eva-bus.net) and Spain's **Damas** (www.damas-sa.es).

TRAIN

All routes from France to Andalucía involve at least one change of train (usually in Madrid). The only direct train between France and Madrid is the overnight 'Francisco de Goya' sleeper train, No 409, from Paris Austerlitz to Madrid Chamartín, taking 13½ hours. Standard one-way/return tourist-class fares are €137/220, though special offers can cut those by half. Trains from Madrid (usually Atocha station) get you to the main Andalucian cities in a few hours for between €28 and €70.

No railway crosses from Portugal into Andalucía, but trains run along the Algarve to Vila Real de Santo António, where there's a ferry across the Río Guadiana to Ayamonte in Andalucía. To travel all the way by train from Lisbon to any Andalucian city you need to transfer in Madrid (and change from Chamartín to Atocha station there): tourist-class seats on the overnight Lisbon–Madrid 'Lusitania' train (11 hours) are €55.

Direct trains run at least three times a week to Barcelona from cities in Switzerland and northern Italy, and daily from Montpellier in southern France. You can transfer to an Andalucía-bound train at Barcelona.

Rail companies serving international routes to Andalucía include the following:

Caminhos de Ferro Portugueses (Portuguese Railways; ☎ 808 208 208 in Portugal; www.cp.pt)

Renfe (Red Nacional de los Ferrocarriles Españoles; Spanish National Railways; ☎ 902 24 02 02 in Spain; www.renfe.es)

SNCF (French National Railways; ☎ 36 35 in France; www.sncf.com)

Morocco
BUS
Eurolines and Alsa run several weekly buses between Moroccan cities such as Casablanca, Marrakesh and Fès, and Andalucian destinations such as Seville, Marbella, Málaga, Granada, Jerez de la Frontera and Almería, via Algeciras–Tangier ferries. The Málaga–Marrakesh trip, for example, takes 19 to 20 hours for around €95/165 one-way/return.

Spain
BUS
Bus is sometimes quicker or cheaper than the train, sometimes slower or more expensive – it depends on the route.

From Madrid, buses running to Cádiz, Córdoba, Huelva, Jerez and Seville are operated by Socibus/Secorbus; to Málaga, the Costa del Sol and Algeciras by Daibus; to Granada by Continental Auto; and to Jaén by La Sepulvedana. Most leave from Madrid's **Estación Sur de Autobuses** (☎ 91 468 42 00; Calle Méndez Álvaro; metro Méndez Álvaro). The trip from Madrid to Seville, Granada or Málaga, for example, takes around six hours for between €15 and €20. The Barcelona–Granada trip takes 12 to 15 hours for between €62 and €73.

Services down the Mediterranean coast from Barcelona, Valencia and Alicante to Almería, Granada, Jaén, Córdoba, Seville, Málaga and the Costa del Sol are mainly provided by Alsa. The other main route into Andalucía, covered by Alsa and Dainco, is from northwestern Spain (Galicia, Asturias and Cantabria) via Castilla y León and

Extremadura to Seville and Cádiz. Damas runs from Badajoz (Extremadura) to Seville and Huelva.

All these services go at least daily, often several times daily.

The following are the main bus companies serving Andalucía from other parts of Spain:

Alsa (☎ 902 42 22 42; www.alsa.es)

Continental Auto (☎ 902 33 04 00; www.continental-auto.es)

Daibus (☎ 902 27 79 99 in Madrid, 95 231 52 47 in Málaga; www.daibus.es in Spanish)

Dainco (☎ 902 42 22 42; www.dainco.es)

Damas (☎ 959 25 69 00; www.damas-sa.es in Spanish)

La Sepulvedana (☎ 902 22 22 82; www.lasepulvedana.es in Spanish)

Secorbus/Socibus (☎ 902 22 92 92; www.socibus.es in Spanish)

CAR & MOTORCYCLE
Spain's main roads are good and you could drive to Andalucía in a day, if you wish, from any corner of the country.

The main highway from Madrid to Andalucía is the A4/AP4 to Córdoba, Seville and Cádiz. For Jaén, Granada, Almería or Málaga, turn off at Bailén.

From the ferry ports at Santander or Bilbao or the French border at Irún, the most direct route is to head for Burgos, from which it's a pretty straight 240km to Madrid.

The AP7/A7 leads all the way down the Mediterranean side of Spain from La Jonquera on the French border as far as Algeciras, except for a couple of stretches in Andalucía where the old, unmodernised N340 remains. There are tolls totalling around €50 between La Jonquera and Alicante, and €12 between Málaga and Algeciras, and toll-free alternative roads on these stretches tend to be quite busy and slow. Branch off the A7 along the A92N for Granada; this is also the quickest approach to Málaga and beyond, until further stretches of the N340 are replaced between Almería and Málaga. It is possible to drive from Barcelona to Málaga in eight hours (though at a sane pace it's closer to 11 hours).

The A66/AP66/N630 heads all the way down to Seville from Gijón on Spain's north coast, through Castilla y León and Extremadura.

APPROACHES TO ANDALUCÍA

TRANSPORT

TRAIN

Spain's national railway company **Renfe** (Red Nacional de los Ferrocarriles Españoles; Spanish National Railways; ☎ 902 24 02 02; www.renfe.es) provides quick, comfortable, reliable direct trains to Andalucía from Madrid and points along the Mediterranean coast, plus more basic regional train services linking western Andalucía with neighbouring Extremadura. From most other parts of Spain you can reach Andalucía by train in one day, usually with a connection in Madrid. The fastest services are the AVE (Alta Velocidad Española) trains covering the 471km from Madrid to Seville, via Córdoba, in around 2½ hours, reaching speeds of 280km/h.

Most long-distance trains have *preferente* (1st-class) and *turista* (2nd-class) carriages. They go under various names indicating standards of comfort and time of travel. An InterCity is a straightforward, limited-stop, daytime train on the Madrid–Córdoba–Málaga route. More comfortable and more expensive daytime trains may be called Altaria, Arco, Talgo, Talgo 200, or AVE. The fastest and most expensive way to go is to take the AVE itself on the Madrid–Córdoba–Seville line. An AVE branch to Málaga is under construction: in the meantime, most Madrid–Málaga trains are Talgo 200s, which use the existing AVE line for part of their journey. Overnight trains are classed as Estrella (with seats, couchettes and sleeping compartments) or the more comfortable Trenhotel. Both types offer seats, couchettes, and single or double compartments with and without shower.

It's best to buy your ticket in advance as trains can get fully booked. You can do so in English by both telephone and internet, though there are a couple of complications. Phone-booked tickets must be collected and paid for at a Renfe ticket office within 72 hours of booking and more than 24 hours before the train's departure from its starting point. Internet tickets can be paid for online. For the first online purchase with any individual credit card, tickets must be picked up at a Renfe ticket office at least one hour before the train's departure from its starting point; for further purchases, tickets can also be printed online or, for many trains, collected on board.

The fare you pay between two places depends on the type of train, the class you travel in, and sometimes the time of day. Examples of one-way *turista*-class seat fares include the following:

Route	Fare (€)	Duration (hr)
Barcelona-Granada	53	11½
Mérida-Seville	12	5
Madrid-Córdoba	28-52	1¾-5½
Madrid-Málaga	35-58	4¼-7¼
Madrid-Seville	55-70	2½-3¼

Return fares on long-distance trains are 20% less than two one-way fares. Children aged under four years travel free; those from four to 11 (to 12 on some trains) get 40% off the cost of seats and couchettes. The Euro<26 card (see p431) gives 20% or 25% off long-distance and regional train fares.

UK
BUS
Bus travel to Andalucía often works out no cheaper than flying. Eurolines runs two or three times weekly from London's Victoria coach station to all the main Andalucian cities. The trip takes 31½ hours to Granada and 32½ hours to Seville or Málaga, for around UK£120/170 one-way/return in each case.

CAR & MOTORCYCLE
If you just want to drive *in* Andalucía, it's normally easier and cheaper to fly and rent a car there. But if you plan to stay for several weeks and want a car most of the time, driving from home might work out cheaper. The options for getting your vehicle from Britain to continental Europe are threefold: you can use **Eurotunnel** (www .eurotunnel.com; France ☎ 08 10 63 03 04, Spain 902 30 73 15, UK 0870 535 3535), the Channel Tunnel car train from Folkestone to Calais; or put your vehicle on a cross-channel ferry to France; or use the direct vehicle ferries from England to Bilbao or Santander in northern Spain (from which it's possible to reach Andalucía in one long day).

Using Eurotunnel or a ferry to France, then driving pretty hard to Andalucía, should cost between UK£600 and UK£800

there and back for two people, including petrol, food and one night's accommodation each way en route. To this, add about UK£80 each way for road tolls if you use the quickest routes. Eurotunnel runs around the clock, with up to four crossings (35 minutes) an hour. You pay for the vehicle only. Standard one-way fares range from about UK£50 and UK£130 for a car and UK£25 to UK£65 for a motorcycle, depending when you travel and how far ahead you book. See opposite for details of the ferry options.

In the UK, further information on driving in Europe is available from the **RAC** (☎ 0870 572 2722; www.rac.co.uk) or the **AA** (European breakdown cover inquiries ☎ 0800 085 2840; www .theaa.com).

TRAIN
The simplest and quickest route from London to Andalucía (about 24 hours) involves **Eurostar** (☎ 0870 518 6186; www.eurostar.com), the Channel Tunnel service from Waterloo to Paris, a change in Paris from the Gare du Nord to the Gare d'Austerlitz, an overnight sleeper-only train to Madrid's Chamartín station, and a change there to Atocha station for a fast train to Andalucía. This costs around UK£300 return to Seville, Málaga or Granada with a reclining seat (the cheapest option) on the Paris–Madrid leg.

For information and bookings on rail travel from Britain, contact **Rail Europe** (☎ 0870 837 1371; www.raileurope.co.uk) or Eurostar.

SEA
Morocco & Algeria
You can sail to Andalucía from the Moroccan ports of Tangier and Nador, as well as Ceuta or Melilla (Spanish enclaves on the Moroccan coast) and Ghazaouet (Algeria). The routes are: Melilla–Almería, Nador–Almería, Ghazaouet–Almería, Melilla–Málaga, Tangier–Gibraltar, Tangier–Algeciras, Ceuta–Algeciras and Tangier–Tarifa. All routes usually take vehicles as well as passengers. The most frequent sailings are to/from Algeciras. Usually, at least 10 sailings a day ply the routes between Algeciras and Tangier (1¼ to 2½ hours) and 16 between Algeciras and Ceuta (45 minutes). Extra services are added at busy times, especially during the peak summer period (mid-June to mid-September) when hundreds of thou-

sands of Moroccan workers return home from Europe for holidays.

Anyone travelling to Morocco for the first time should consider sailing to Ceuta or Melilla rather than Tangier. The hustlers around the port at Tangier can be hard to handle and it's more painless to sail to Ceuta or Melilla. The border crossing into Morocco itself is more straightforward from Melilla than from Ceuta, but sailings to Melilla can take eight hours and are much less frequent (just one a day from Almería and one a day from Málaga for most of the year). Passenger seat fares to Melilla are little more than to Algeciras or Ceuta, but if you want a cabin or are taking a car, it gets more costly.

The most prominent ferry company, with sailings from Tangier and Ceuta to Algeciras, Melilla to Málaga and Melilla to Almería, is the Spanish-owned **Trasmediterránea** (www.trasmediterranea.es; Spain ☎ 902 45 46 45,Tangier 039-931133, UK 0870 499 1305). The other main operators to Algeciras are **EuroFerrys** (☎ 902 19 50 14; www.euroferrys.com) and, from Ceuta only, **Buquebus** (☎ 902 41 42 42; www.buquebus.es). There's little price difference between the rival lines. One-way passenger fares from Algeciras are around €32 to Tangier and €25 to Ceuta. Two people with a small car pay around €160 to Tangier and €130 to Ceuta.

If you're taking a car, book well ahead for July, August or Easter travel. Anyone crossing from Morocco to Spain with a vehicle should be prepared for rigorous searches on arrival at Ceuta and Melilla and on the mainland.

For further details see the Getting There & Away sections for Algeciras (p226), Almería (p406), Gibraltar (p238), Málaga (p263) and Tarifa (p223).

UK

PORTSMOUTH–BILBAO
P&O Ferries (www.poferries.com; Spain ☎ 902 02 04 61, UK 0870 598 0333) operates a ferry from Portsmouth to Bilbao. As a rule, there are two sailings a week except for a few weeks in January (when there's no service) and the month of February (when it's once weekly). Voyage time varies between 29 and 34 hours.

Standard return fares for two people with a car range from around UK£430 to UK£750 depending on the season, including the cheapest cabin accommodation. The ferries dock at Santurtzi, about 14km northwest of central Bilbao.

PLYMOUTH–SANTANDER
Brittany Ferries (www.brittanyferries.com; Spain ☎ 942 36 06 11, UK 0870 366 5333) operates a twice-weekly car ferry from Plymouth to Santander (19 to 23 hours sailing time), between March and November. For two people with a car, return fares range from about UK£350 to UK£800 with reclining seats, or around UK£520 to UK£970 with the cheapest type of cabin.

VIA FRANCE
The busiest and quickest (1¼ to 1½ hours) ferry route, with around 60 crossings daily at peak times, is Dover–Calais, operated by **P&O Ferries** (www.poferries.com; France ☎ 0825 120 156, UK 0870 598 0333) and **SeaFrance** (www.seafrance.com; France ☎ 0825 082 505, UK 0870 571 1711). Fares are volatile and you should research the latest offers. In August a Dover–Calais return ferry ticket for a car and two people can cost UK£150 to UK£250. Winter fares are lower.

Other routes include Newhaven–Dieppe, operated by **Transmanche Ferries** (www.transmancheferries.com; France ☎ 0800 650 100, UK 0800 917 1201), and Portsmouth–Caen and Portsmouth–Cherbourg, which are both operated by **Brittany Ferries** (www.brittanyferries.com; France ☎ 0825 828 828, UK 0870 366 5333).

Ferrysavers (☎ 0870 990 8492; www.ferrysavers.com) offers an online booking service and comparisons of cross-Channel sailing options.

GETTING AROUND

AIR
There are no internal flights operating between Andalucian cities.

BICYCLE
Andalucía is good biking territory, with wonderful scenery and varied terrain. Plenty of lightly trafficked country roads, mostly in decent condition, enable riders to avoid the busy main highways. Road biking here is as safe as anywhere in Europe provided you make allowances for some drivers' love of speed. Off-road, thousands of kilometres of tracks, including old railway lines adapted

for bikers and hikers, await. Day rides and touring by bike are particularly enjoyable in spring and autumn, avoiding weather extremes. See p77 for an introduction to cycling and mountain biking in Andalucía.

If you get tired of pedalling, it's often possible to take your bike on a bus (you'll usually just be asked to remove the front wheel). You can take bikes on overnight sleeper trains (not long-distance daytime trains), and on most regional and suburban trains, but there are various conditions to comply with. On overnight sleepers, you have to remove the pedals and pack the bike in a specially designed container. Check the regulations and details before buying tickets.

Bicycles are quite widely available for hire in main cities, coastal resorts and inland towns and villages that attract tourism. They're often *bicis todo terreno* (mountain bikes). Prices range from €10 to €20 a day.

Bike lanes on main roads are rare, but cyclists are permitted to ride in groups up to two abreast. Helmets are obligatory outside built-up areas.

BUS

Buses, mostly modern, comfortable and inexpensive, run almost everywhere in Andalucía, including along some unlikely mountain roads to connect remote villages with their nearest towns. The bigger cities are linked to each other by frequent daily services. On the less busy routes services may be reduced (or occasionally nonexistent) on Saturday and Sunday.

Larger towns and cities usually have one main *estación de autobuses* (bus station) where all out-of-town buses stop. In smaller places, buses tend to operate from a particular street or square, which may be unmarked. Ask around; locals generally know where to go.

During Semana Santa (Holy Week) and July and August it's advisable to buy long-distance bus tickets a day in advance. On a few routes, a return ticket is cheaper than two singles. Travellers aged under 26 should ask about discounts on intercity routes.

Buses on main intercity routes average around 70 km/h, for a cost of around €1 per 14km. For detail on services, see this book's city and town sections.

CAR & MOTORCYCLE

Andalucía's good road network and inexpensive rental cars make driving an attractive and practical way of getting around.

Bringing Your Own Vehicle

Bringing a vehicle of your own to Andalucía makes the most sense if you plan to stay more than a couple of weeks. For information on routes from the UK and through Spain to Andalucía, see p446. Petrol (around €1 per litre in Spain) is widely available. In the event of breakdowns, every small town and many villages will have a garage with mechanics.

When driving a private vehicle in Europe proof of ownership (a Vehicle Registration Document for UK-registered vehicles),

MAIN BUS COMPANIES

Company	Website	Telephone	Main destinations
Alsina Graells	www.alsinagraells.es	☎ 954 41 88 11 Seville ☎ 958 18 54 80 Granada ☎ 952 34 17 38 Málaga	Almería, Córdoba, Granada, Jaén, Málaga, Seville
Casal	www.autocarescasal.com	☎ 954 99 92 90	Aracena, Carmona, Seville
Comes	www.tgcomes.es	☎ 902 19 92 08	Algeciras, Cádiz, Granada, Jerez, Málaga, Ronda, Seville
Damas	www.damas-sa.es	☎ 959 25 69 00	Huelva, Seville, Ayamonte
Linesur	www.linesur.com	☎ 954 98 82 20	Algeciras, Écija, Jerez, Osuna, Seville
Los Amarillos	www.losamarillos.es	☎ 902 21 03 17	Cádiz, Jerez, Málaga, Ronda, Seville
Portillo	www.ctsa-portillo.com	☎ 902 14 31 44	Algeciras, Costa del Sol, Málaga, Ronda
Transportes Ureña	-	☎ 957 40 45 58	Córdoba, Jaén, Seville

ROAD DISTANCE CHART (KM)

	Almería	Barcelona	Bilbao	Cádiz	Córdoba	Gibraltar	Granada	Huelva	Jaén	Madrid	Málaga	Seville
Almería	---											
Barcelona	809	---										
Bilbao	958	620	---									
Cádiz	463	1284	1058	---								
Córdoba	316	908	796	261	---							
Gibraltar	339	1124	1110	124	294	---						
Granada	162	868	829	296	160	255	---					
Huelva	505	1140	939	214	241	289	346	---				
Jaén	220	804	730	330	108	335	93	347	---			
Madrid	547	621	395	654	396	662	421	591	335	---		
Málaga	207	997	939	240	165	134	125	301	203	532	---	
Seville	410	1046	933	126	143	201	252	95	246	534	209	---

driving licence, roadworthiness certificate (MOT), and either an insurance certificate or a Green Card (see Insurance, p452) should always be carried. Also ask your insurer for a European Accident Statement form, which can greatly simplify matters in the event of an accident.

If the car is from the UK or Ireland, remember to adjust the headlights for driving in mainland Europe (motor accessory shops sell stick-on strips which deflect the beams in the required direction).

In the UK, further information on driving in Europe is available from the **RAC** (☎ 0870 572 2722; www.rac.co.uk) or the **AA** (European breakdown cover inquiries ☎ 0800 085 2840; www .theaa.com).

Driving Licence

All EU countries' licences (pink or pink-and-green) are accepted in Spain. (But note that the old-style UK green licence is not accepted.) Licences from other countries are supposed to be accompanied by an International Driving Permit, but in practice your national licence will suffice for renting cars or dealing with traffic police. The International Driving Permit, valid for 12 months, is available from automobile clubs in your country.

Hire

If you plan to hire a car in Andalucía, it's a good idea to organise it before you leave. As a rule, local firms at Málaga airport

or on the Costa del Sol offer the cheapest deals. You can normally get a two-door air-con economy-class car from local agencies for around €130 to €140 a week in August or €100 to €110 a week in January. A larger four-door, family-size vehicle should be around €260 to €300 in August or €200 to €230 in January. Many local firms offer internet booking and you simply go to their desk in or just outside the airport on arrival. In general, rentals away from the holiday *costas* (coasts) are more expensive.

Well-established local firms with branches at Málaga airport (and other Andalucian airports and coastal towns too) include the following:
Centauro (☎ 902 10 41 03; www.centauro.net)
Crown Car Hire (☎ 952 17 64 86; www.crowncarhire .com)
Helle Hollis (☎ 952 24 55 44, UK 0871 222 7245; www .hellehollis.com)
Holiday Car Hire (☎ 952 24 26 85; www.holidaycar hire.com)
Niza Cars (☎ 951 01 35 20; www.nizacars.es)

Major international rental companies give assuredly high standards of service:
Avis (☎ 902 13 55 31; www.avis.com)
Europcar (☎ 913 43 45 12; www.europcar.com)
Hertz (☎ 917 49 90 69; www.hertz.es)
National/Atesa (☎ 902 10 01 01; www.atesa.es)

An alternative is to go through online brokers such as **Holiday Autos** (www.holidayautos

.co.uk), **Transhire** (www.transhire.com), **Carjet** (www.carjet.com), **TravelAutos** (www.travelautos.com) and **Sunny Cars** (www.sunnycars.de, www.sunnycars.nl). These firms act as intermediaries between you and the agencies, offering a wide variety of vehicle options and pick-up locations. You'll usually wind up paying a bit more than if you rent direct.

Spain's national tourism authority, **Turespaña** (www.spain.info), has useful town-by-town listings of car-rental companies on its website.

To rent a car you need to be aged at least 21 (23 with some companies) and to have held a driving licence for a minimum of one year (sometimes two years). Under-25s have to pay extra charges with many firms.

It's much easier, and often obligatory, to pay for your rental with a credit card.

As always, check the detail of exactly what you are paying for. Some companies will throw in extras such as child seats and the listing of additional drivers for free; others will charge for them. See the following section for some tips on rental-car insurance.

Insurance

Third-party motor insurance is a minimum requirement throughout Europe. If you live in the EU, your existing motor insurance will probably provide automatic third-party cover throughout the EU. But check with your insurer about whether you will also be covered for medical or hospital expenses or accidental damage to your vehicle. You might have to pay an extra premium if you want the same protection abroad as you have at home. A European breakdown assistance policy such as the AA's or RAC's European Breakdown Cover, or the policies offered by Eurotunnel and many cross-Channel ferry companies, is also a good investment, providing services such as roadside assistance, towing, emergency repairs and 24-hour telephone assistance in English.

The Green Card is an internationally recognised document showing that you have the minimum insurance cover required by law in the country visited. It is provided free by insurers. If you're carrying an insurance certificate that gives the minimum legal cover, a Green Card is not essential, but it has the advantage of being easily recognised by foreign police and authorities.

If you are renting a vehicle in Andalucía, the routine insurance provided may not go beyond basic third-party requirements. For cover against theft or damage to the vehicle, or injury or death to driver or passengers, you may need to request extra coverage.

Road Conditions

Spanish roads have one of the highest death rates in Europe, and some drivers' love of high speed has to be a factor in the casualty rate. Be prepared for other road users to be travelling faster than you might be accustomed to, especially on *autovías* (toll-free dual carriageways) and even in heavy traffic.

One-way systems, heavy traffic and poor signposting can make urban driving a frustrating headache, especially on arrival in a new city. Keep your patience, use maps to get close to your destination, and park. You can always move the car later if a better spot comes up.

PARKING

Street parking space can be hard to find during working hours (about 9am to 2pm Monday to Saturday and 5pm to 8pm Monday to Friday). You'll often have to use underground or multistorey car parks, which are common enough in cities, and well enough signposted, but not cheap (typically around €1 per hour or €10 to €15 for 24 hours) – though generally more secure than the street. City hotels with their own parking usually charge for the right to use it, at similar rates to underground car parks.

Blue lines along the side of the street usually mean you must pay at a nearby meter to park during working hours (typically around €0.50 an hour). Yellow lines mean no parking. It's not sensible to park in prohibited zones, even if other drivers have (you risk your car being towed and paying around €60 to have it released).

Road Rules

As elsewhere in continental Europe, drive on the right and overtake on the left. The minimum driving age is 18 years. Rear seat belts, if fitted, must be worn. Children under three must sit in child safety seats. The blood-alcohol limit is 0.05% (0.03% for drivers with a licence less than two years old) and breath-testing is carried out on occasion. The police can, and do, carry out spot checks on drivers so it pays to have all your papers in order. Nonresident foreigners may be fined on the spot for traffic offences. You can appeal in writing (in any language) to the Jefatura Provincial de Tráfico (Provincial Traffic Headquarters) and if your appeal is upheld, you'll get your money back – but don't hold your breath for a favourable result. Contact details for each province's traffic headquarters are given on the website of the **Dirección General de Tráfico** (www.dgt.es). Click on 'Direcciones y Teléfonos,' then select the province you are in.

The speed limit is 50km/h in built-up areas, 90km/h or 100km/h outside built-up areas, and 120km/h on *autopistas* (toll highways) and *autovías*.

In Spain it's compulsory to carry two warning triangles (to be placed 100m in front of and 100m behind your vehicle if you have to stop on the carriageway), and a reflective jacket, which must be donned if you get out of your vehicle on the carriageway or hard shoulder outside built-up areas.

It's illegal to use hand-held mobile phones while driving.

LOCAL TRANSPORT

Cities and larger towns have efficient bus systems, but you often won't need to use them because accommodation, attractions and main transport terminals are usually within fairly comfortable walking distance of each other. All Andalucía's airports are linked to city centres by bus – in Málaga's case also by train. Gibraltar airport is within walking distance of downtown Gibraltar and of the bus station in La Línea de la Concepción, Spain.

Taxis are plentiful in larger places and even most villages have a taxi or two. Fares are reasonable – a typical 2km to 3km ride should cost about €3 to €4 (airport runs are a bit extra). Intercity runs are around €0.60 per kilometre. You don't have to tip taxi drivers.

TRAIN

Renfe (☎ 902 24 02 02; www.renfe.es), Spain's national railway company, has an extensive and efficient rail system in Andalucía linking all the main cities and many smaller places. Trains are at least as convenient, quick and inexpensive as buses on many routes.

See p447 for information on long-distance trains linking Andalucía with other parts of Spain. Some of these are good for journeys within Andalucía as well, on routes such as Córdoba–Málaga, Córdoba–Seville –Cádiz, and Córdoba–Ronda–Algeciras. Generally more frequent services between Andalucian destinations are provided by the cheaper, one-class *regional* and *cercanía* trains. *Regionales*, some of which are known as Andalucía Exprés, run between Andalucian cities, stopping at towns en route. *Cercanías* are commuter trains that link Seville, Málaga and Cádiz with their suburbs and nearby towns.

Good or reasonable train services, with at least three direct trains running each way daily (often more), run on the following routes: Algeciras–Ronda–Bobadilla–Antequera–Granada, Córdoba–Málaga, Málaga–Torremolinos–Fuengirola, Seville–Jerez de la Frontera–El Puerto de Santa María–Cádiz,

TRANSPORT

LUXURY AT AN OLD-FASHIONED PACE

If you like trains and believe journeys can be as much fun as arriving, and you find that today's superefficient trains often get there a little too soon – and you have a couple of thousand euros to spend – consider riding the **Alandalus Express** (www.alandalusexpreso.com). This luxurious privately run train is definitely not an express – it takes six days to toddle from Seville to Granada and back – but it provides its passengers with a supercomfortable holiday on rails, complete with luxurious sleeping compartments, restaurant cars serving quality food and wine, and a bar and lounge all in impeccable leather-upholstered, glass lamp–fitted, belle-époque style. The international, mainly retired clientele are treated to tours of selected stops along the way. At the time of writing the standard trip was a six-day venture from Seville to Córdoba, Granada, Jerez de la Frontera and back to Seville, for €2700 per person in a double cabin.

Seville–Córdoba, Seville–Huelva, Seville–Bobadilla–Málaga and Seville–Antequera–Granada–Guadix–Almería.

Services on other routes tend to be infrequent and they often involve changing trains at the small junction station of Bobadilla in central Andalucía, where lines from Seville, Córdoba, Granada, Málaga and Algeciras all meet. But with a little perseverance you can reach a surprising number of places by train, including Jaén, the Sierra Norte of Sevilla province and the Sierra de Aracena.

Regional trains average around 75km/h, for a cost of around €1 per 15km. For more information see this book's city and town sections.

Health Dr Caroline Evans

CONTENTS

BEFORE YOU GO

Prevention is the key to staying healthy while abroad. Some predeparture planning will save you trouble later on. See your dentist before a long trip, carry a spare pair of contact lenses and glasses, and take your optical prescription with you. Bring medications in their original, clearly labelled, containers. A signed and dated letter from your physician describing your medical conditions and medications, including generic names, is also a good idea. If carrying syringes or needles, be sure to have a physician's letter documenting their medical necessity.

INSURANCE

If you're an EU citizen, the free EHIC (European Health Insurance Card) covers you for most medical care in Spain, including maternity care and care for chronic illnesses such as diabetes (though not for emergency repatriation). You will, however, normally have to pay for medicine bought from pharmacies, even if prescribed, and perhaps for some tests and procedures. The EHIC does not cover private medical consultations and treatment in Spain; this includes nearly all dentists, and some of the better clinics and surgeries. In the UK, you can apply for an EHIC online at www.dh.gov.uk/travellers,

by telephone on ☎ 0845 606 2030, or on a form available at post offices. Non-EU citizens should find out if there is a reciprocal arrangement for free medical care between their country and Spain.

If you do need health insurance, strongly consider a policy that covers you for the worst possible scenario, such as an accident requiring an emergency flight home. Find out in advance if your insurance plan will make payments directly to providers or reimburse you later for overseas health expenditures. The former option is generally preferable, as it doesn't leave you out of pocket.

RECOMMENDED VACCINATIONS

No vaccinations are necessary for Spain; however, the WHO recommends that all travellers should be covered for diphtheria, tetanus, measles, mumps, rubella and polio, regardless of destination. Since most vaccines don't produce immunity until at least two weeks after they're given, visit a physician at least six weeks before departure to be safe.

INTERNET RESOURCES

The WHO's publication *International Travel and Health* is revised annually and is available online at www.who.int/ith. Other useful websites:

www.ageconcern.org.uk Advice on travel for the elderly.
www.fitfortravel.scot.nhs.uk General travel advice for the layperson.
www.mariestopes.org.uk Information on women's health and contraception.
www.mdtravelhealth.com Travel health recommendations for every country; updated daily.

IN TRANSIT

DEEP VEIN THROMBOSIS (DVT)

Blood clots may form in the legs during plane flights, chiefly because of prolonged immobility. The chief symptom of Deep Vein Thrombosis (DVT) is swelling or pain of the foot, ankle or calf, usually but not always on just one side. When a blood clot

HEALTH

travels to the lungs, it may cause chest pain and breathing difficulties. Travellers with any of these symptoms should seek medical attention immediately.

To prevent the development of DVT on long flights you should walk about the cabin, contract the leg muscles while sitting, drink plenty of fluids and avoid alcohol and tobacco.

IN ANDALUCÍA

AVAILABILITY OF HEALTH CARE

If you need an ambulance call ☎ 061. For emergency treatment go straight to the *urgencias* (casualty) section of the nearest hospital.

Good health care is readily available and *farmacias* (pharmacies) offer valuable advice and sell over-the-counter medication. In Spain, a system of *farmacias de guardia* (duty pharmacies) operates so that each district has one open all the time. When a pharmacy is closed, it posts the name of the nearest open one on the door.

TRAVELLER'S DIARRHOEA

If you develop diarrhoea, be sure to drink plenty of fluids, preferably an oral rehydration solution such as Dioralyte. If diarrhoea is bloody, persists for more than 72 hours or is accompanied by a fever, shaking, chills or severe abdominal pain, you should seek medical attention.

ENVIRONMENTAL HAZARDS
Altitude Sickness

Lack of oxygen at high altitudes (over 2500m) affects most people to some extent. Symptoms of Acute Mountain Sickness (AMS) usually develop during the first 24 hours at altitude but may be delayed up to three weeks. Mild symptoms include headache, lethargy, dizziness, difficulty sleeping and loss of appetite. AMS may become more severe without warning and can be fatal. Severe symptoms include breathlessness, a dry, irritable cough (which may progress to the production of pink, frothy sputum), severe headache, lack of coordination and balance, confusion, irrational behaviour, vomiting, drowsiness and unconsciousness. There is no hard-and-fast rule as to what is too high: AMS has been

fatal at 3000m, although 3500m to 4500m is the usual range.

Treat mild symptoms by resting at the same altitude until recovery, usually a day or two. Paracetamol or aspirin can be taken for headaches. If symptoms persist or become worse, however, *immediate descent is necessary;* even 500m can help. Drug treatments should never be used to avoid descent or to enable further ascent.

Diamox (acetazolamide) reduces the headache caused by AMS and helps the body acclimatise to the lack of oxygen. It is only available on prescription and those who are allergic to sulfonamide antibiotics may also be allergic to Diamox.

In the UK, fact sheets are available from the **British Mountaineering Council** (www.thebmc .co.uk; 177-179 Burton Rd, Manchester, M20 2BB).

Bites & Stings

Bees and wasps only cause real problems to those with a severe allergy (anaphylaxis). If you have a severe allergy to bee or wasp stings carry an 'epipen' or similar adrenaline injection.

In forested areas you should watch out for the hairy reddish-brown caterpillars of the pine processionary moth. They live in silvery nests up in the pine trees and, come spring, leave the nest to march in long lines (hence the name). Touching the caterpillars' hairs sets off a severely irritating allergic skin reaction.

Some Andalucian centipedes have a very nasty, but nonfatal sting. The ones to watch out for are those composed of clearly defined segments, which may be patterned with, for instance, black-and-yellow stripes.

Jellyfish, with their stinging tentacles, generally either occur in large numbers or hardly at all, so it's fairly easy to know when not to go in the sea.

The only venomous snake that is even relatively common in Spain is Lataste's viper. It has a triangular-shaped head, is grey with a zigzag pattern and up to 75cm long. It is found in dry, rocky areas, usually away from humans. Its bite can be fatal and needs to be treated with a serum, which state clinics in major towns keep in stock.

Mosquitoes are found in most parts of Europe. They may not carry malaria but can cause irritation and infected bites.

Sandflies are found around the Mediterranean beaches. They usually cause only a nasty itchy bite, but can also carry a rare skin disorder called cutaneous leishmaniasis. Use a DEET-based insect repellent to prevent both mosquito and sandfly bites.

Scorpions are found in Spain and their sting can be distressingly painful but is not considered fatal.

Check for ticks if you have been walking where sheep and goats graze as these parasites can cause skin infections and other more serious diseases.

Heat Exhaustion & Heat Stroke

Heat exhaustion occurs following excessive fluid loss with inadequate replacement of fluids and salt. Symptoms include headache, dizziness and tiredness. Dehydration is already happening by the time you feel thirsty – aim to drink sufficient water to produce pale, diluted urine. Replace lost fluids by drinking water and/or fruit juice, and cool the body with cold water and fans. Treat salt loss with salty fluids such as soup or add a little more table salt to foods than usual.

Heat stroke is a much more serious condition, resulting in irrational and hyperactive behaviour and eventually loss of consciousness and death. Rapid cooling by spraying the body with water and fanning is ideal treatment, and emergency fluid and electrolyte replacement by intravenous drip is recommended.

Water

Tap water is generally safe to drink in Spain, but the city of Málaga is one place where many people prefer to play it safe by drinking bottled water. Do not drink water from rivers or lakes as it may contain bacteria or viruses that can cause diarrhoea or vomiting.

TRAVELLING WITH CHILDREN

Make sure children are up to date with routine vaccinations, and discuss travel vaccines well before departure as some vaccines aren't suitable for children under one year old.

WOMEN'S HEALTH

Travelling during pregnancy is usually possible but always seek a medical check-up before planning your trip. The most risky times for travel are during the first 12 weeks of pregnancy and after 30 weeks.

SEXUAL HEALTH

Condoms are widely available but emergency contraception may not be, so take the necessary precautions. When buying condoms, look for a European CE mark, which means they have been rigorously tested. Remember also to keep them in a cool, dry place so that they don't crack and perish.

HEALTH

Language

CONTENTS

Spanish, or Castilian (castellano) as it's often and more precisely called, is spoken throughout Andalucía. English isn't as widely spoken as many travellers might expect, though you're more likely to find people who speak some English in the main cities and tourist areas. Generally, however, you'll be much better received if you make some attempt to communicate in Spanish.

For a more comprehensive guide to the Spanish language than we're able to offer in this book, pick up a copy of Lonely Planet's handy pocket-sized Spanish Phrasebook.

ANDALUCIAN PRONUNCIATION

Andalucians don't pronounce Spanish in quite the same way as do speakers from other parts of Spain, or as it is taught to foreigners. Local accents vary too, but whether you choose to use mainland pronunciation or learn the following rules, you're sure to get your message across. The pronunciation guides included with the words and phrases below reflect the local Andalucian pronunciation, which should make things even simpler still.

Vowels

a	as in 'father'
e	as in 'met'
i	as in 'marine'
o	as in 'or' (with no 'r' sound)
u	as in 'rule'; the 'u' is not pronounced after **q** and in the letter combinations **gue** and **gui**, unless it's marked with a diaeresis (eg *argüir*), in which case it's pronounced as English 'w'

Consonants

While the consonants **ch**, **ll** and **ñ** are generally considered distinct letters, **ch** and **ll** are now often listed alphabetically under **c** and **l** respectively. The letter **ñ** is still treated as a separate letter and comes after **n** in dictionaries.

c	as 'k' before **a**, **o** and **u**; as 's' when followed by **e** or **i** (not the lisped 'th' of standard Castilian)
ch	as in 'choose'
d	as in 'dog' when initial or preceded by **l** or **n**; elsewhere as the 'th' in 'then', and sometimes not pronounced at all – thus *partido* (divided) becomes 'partio'
g	as in 'go' when initial or before **a**, **o** and **u**; elsewhere much softer. Before **e** or **i** it's a harsh, breathy sound, similar to the 'ch' in Scottish *loch* (**kh** in our guides to pronunciation).
h	always silent
j	as the 'ch' in the Scottish *loch* (**kh** in our guides to pronunciation)
ll	similar to the 'y' in 'yellow' but often closer to a 'j' in Andalucía
ñ	as the 'ni' in 'onion'
s	often not pronounced at all, especially when it occurs within a word; thus *pescados* (fish) can be pronounced 'pecao' in Andalucía
x	as the 'x' in 'taxi' when between two vowels; as the 's' in 'sound' before a consonant
z	pronounced as 's' (not 'th' as in standard Castilian); **z** is often silent when at the end of a word

Word Stress

Stress is indicated by italics in the pronunciation guides included with all the words and phrases in this language guide. In general, words ending in vowels or the letters **n** or **s** have stress on the next-to-last syllable, while those with other endings have stress on the last syllable. Thus *vaca* (cow) and *caballos* (horses) both carry stress on the next-to-last syllable, while *ciudad* (city) and *infeliz* (unhappy) are both stressed on the last syllable.

Written accents indicate a stressed syllable, and will almost always appear in words that don't follow the rules above, eg *sótano* (basement), *porción* (portion).

GENDER & PLURALS

In Spanish, nouns are either masculine or feminine, and there are rules to help determine gender (there are of course some exceptions). Feminine nouns generally end with -**a** or with the groups -**ción**, -**sión** or -**dad**. Other endings typically signify a masculine noun. Endings for adjectives also change to agree with the gender of the noun they modify (masculine/feminine -**o**/-**a**). Where both masculine and feminine forms are included in this language guide, they are separated by a slash, with the masculine form first, eg *perdido/a*.

If a noun or adjective ends in a vowel, the plural is formed by adding **s** to the end. If it ends in a consonant, the plural is formed by adding **es** to the end.

ACCOMMODATION

I'm looking for ...	Estoy buscando ...	e·stoy boos·kan·do ...
Where is ...?	¿Dónde hay ...?	don·de ai ...
a hotel	un hotel	oon o·tel
a boarding house	una pensión/ residencial/ un hospedaje	oo·na pen·syon/ re·see·den·syal/ oon os·pe·da·khe
a youth hostel	un albergue juvenil	oon al·ber·ge khoo·ve·neel

I'd like a ... room.	Quisiera una habitación ...	kee·sye·ra oo·na a·bee·ta·syon ...
double	doble	do·ble
single	individual	een·dee·vee·dwal
twin	con dos camas	kon dos ka·mas

How much is it per ...?	¿Cuánto cuesta por ...?	kwan·to kwes·ta por ...
night	noche	no·che
person	persona	per·so·na
week	semana	se·ma·na

Does it include breakfast?
¿Incluye el desayuno? een·kloo·ye el de·sa·yoo·no

May I see the room?
¿Puedo ver la habitación?	pwe·do ver la a·bee·ta·syon
I don't like it.	
No me gusta.	no me goos·ta
It's fine. I'll take it.	
OK. La alquilo.	o·kay la al·kee·lo
I'm leaving now.	
Me voy ahora.	me voy a·o·ra

MAKING A RESERVATION

To ...	A ...
From ...	De ...
Date	Fecha
I'd like to book ...	Quisiera reservar ... (see 'Accommodation' for bed and room options)
in the name of ...	en nombre de ...
for the nights of ...	para las noches del ...
credit card ...	tarjeta de crédito ...
number	número
expiry date	fecha de vencimiento
Please confirm ...	Puede confirmar ...
availability	la disponibilidad
price	el precio

full board	pensión completa	pen·syon kom·ple·ta
private/shared bathroom	baño privado/ compartido	ba·nyo pree·va·do/ kom·par·tee·do
too expensive	demasiado caro	de·ma·sya·do ka·ro
cheaper	más económico	mas e·ko·no·mee·ko
discount	descuento	des·kwen·to

CONVERSATION & ESSENTIALS

When talking to people familiar to you or younger than you, it's usual to use the informal form of 'you', *tú*, rather than the polite form *Usted*. The polite form is always given in this guide; where options are given, the form is indicated by the abbreviations 'pol' and 'inf'.

Hello.	Hola.	o·la
Good morning.	Buenos días.	bwe·nos dee·as
Good afternoon.	Buenas tardes.	bwe·nas tar·des
Good evening/ night.	Buenas noches.	bwe·nas no·ches
Goodbye.	Adiós.	a·dyos
Bye/See you soon.	Hasta luego.	as·ta lwe·go
Yes.	Sí.	see
No.	No.	no

Please.	Por favor.	por fa·*vor*
Thank you.	Gracias.	*gra*·syas
Many thanks.	Muchas gracias.	*moo*·chas *gra*·syas
You're welcome.	De nada.	de *na*·da
Pardon me.	Perdón/	per·*don*
	Discúlpeme.	dees·*kool*·pe·me

(before requesting information, for example)

Sorry.	Lo siento.	lo see·*en*·to

(when apologising)

Excuse me.	Permiso.	per·*mee*·so

(when asking permission to pass, for example)

How are things?
¿Qué tal?   ke tal

What's your name?
¿Cómo se llama Usted?   *ko*·mo se *ya*·ma *oo*·ste (pol)
¿Cómo te llamas?   *ko*·mo te *ya*·mas (inf)

My name is ...
Me llamo ...   me *ya*·mo ...

It's a pleasure to meet you.
Mucho gusto.   *moo*·cho *goos*·to

Where are you from?
¿De dónde es/eres?   de *don*·de es/e·res (pol/inf)

I'm from ...
Soy de ...   soy de ...

Where are you staying?
¿Dónde está alojado?   *don*·de es·ta a·lo·*kha*·do (pol)
¿Dónde estás alojado?   *don*·de es·tas a·lo·*kha*·do (inf)

May I take a photo?
¿Puedo hacer una foto?   *pwe*·do a·*sair* *oo*·na *fo*·to

DIRECTIONS

How do I get to ...?
¿Cómo puedo llegar a ...? *ko*·mo *pwe*·do lye·*gar* a ...

Is it far?
¿Está lejos?   es·ta *le*·khos

Go straight ahead.
Siga/Vaya derecho.   *see*·ga/*va*·ya de·*re*·cho

Turn left.
Doble a la izquierda.   *do*·ble a la ees·*kyer*·da

SIGNS	
Entrada	Entrance
Salida	Exit
Abierto	Open
Cerrado	Closed
Información	Information
Prohibido	Prohibited
Prohibido Fumar	No Smoking
Comisaría	Police Station
Servicios/Aseos	Toilets
Hombres	Men
Mujeres	Women

EMERGENCIES

Help!   *¡Socorro!*   so·*ko*·ro
Fire!   *¡Incendio!*   een·*sen*·dyo
Go away!   *¡Vete!/¡Fuera!*   ve·te/*fwe*·ra

Call ...!
¡Llame a ...!   *ya*·me a
 an ambulance
 una ambulancia   oo·na am·boo·*lan*·sya
 a doctor
 un médico   oon *me*·dee·ko
 the police
 la policía   la po·lee·*see*·a

It's an emergency.
Es una emergencia.   es oo·na e·mer·*khen*·sya

Could you help me, please?
¿Me puede ayudar,   me *pwe*·de a·yoo·*dar*
 por favor?   por fa·*vor*

I'm lost.
Estoy perdido/a.   es·toy per·*dee*·do/a

Where are the toilets?
¿Dónde están los baños?   *don*·de es·tan los *ba*·nyos

Turn right.
Doble a la derecha.   *do*·ble a la de·*re*·cha

I'm lost.
Estoy perdido/a.   es·toy per·*dee*·do/a

Can you show me (on the map)?
¿Me lo podría indicar   me lo po·*dree*·a een·dee·*kar*
 (en el mapa)?   (en el *ma*·pa)

---

here	aquí	a·*kee*
there	allí	a·*yee*
traffic lights	semáforos	se·*ma*·fo·ros
north	norte	*nor*·te
south	sur	soor
east	este	*es*·te
west	oeste	o·*es*·te

HEALTH

I'm sick.
Estoy enfermo/a.   es·toy en·*fer*·mo/a

I need a doctor (who speaks English).
Necesito un médico   ne·se·*see*·to oon *me*·dee·ko
 (que habla inglés).   (ke *a*·bla een·gles)

Where's the hospital?
¿Dónde está el hospital?   *don*·de es·ta el os·pee·tal

I'm pregnant.
Estoy embarazada.   es·toy em·ba·ra·*sa*·da

I'm ...	Soy ...	soy ...
asthmatic	asmático/a	as·*ma*·tee·ko/a
diabetic	diabético/a	dya·*be*·tee·ko/a
epileptic	epiléptico/a	e·pee·*lep*·tee·ko/a

I'm allergic to ...	Soy alérgico/a a ...	soy a·ler·khee·ko/a a ...
antibiotics	los antibióticos	los an·tee·byo·tee·kos
nuts	las nueces	las nwe·se
peanuts	los cacahuetes	los ka·ka·we·tes
penicillin	la penicilina	la pe·nee·see·lee·na
I have ...	Tengo ...	ten·go ...
diarrhoea	diarrea	dya·re·a
a fever	fiebre	fee·eb·ray
a headache	un dolor de cabeza	oon do·lor de ka·be·sa
nausea	náusea	now·se·a

LANGUAGE DIFFICULTIES

Do you speak (English)?

¿Habla/Hablas (inglés)?   a·bla/a·blas (een·gles) (pol/inf)

Does anyone here speak English?

¿Hay alguien que hable inglés?   ai al·gyen ke a·ble een·gles

I (don't) understand.

Yo (no) entiendo.   yo (no) en·tyen·do

How do you say ...?

¿Cómo se dice ...?   ko·mo se dee·se ...

What does ... mean?

¿Qué quiere decir ...?   ke kye·re de·seer ...

Could you please ...?	¿Puede ..., por favor?	pwe·de ... por fa·vor
repeat that	repetirlo	re·pe·teer·lo
speak more slowly	hablar más despacio	a·blar mas des·pa·syo
write it down	escribirlo	es·kree·beer·lo

NUMBERS

1	uno	oo·no
2	dos	dos
3	tres	tres
4	cuatro	kwa·tro
5	cinco	seen·ko
6	seis	says
7	siete	sye·te
8	ocho	o·cho
9	nueve	nwe·ve
10	diez	dyes
11	once	on·se
12	doce	do·se
13	trece	tre·se
14	catorce	ka·tor·se
15	quince	keen·se
16	dieciséis	dye·see·says
17	diecisiete	dye·see·sye·te
18	dieciocho	dye·see·o·cho
19	diecinueve	dye·see·nwe·ve
20	veinte	vayn·te
21	veintiuno	vayn·tee·oo·no
22	veintidós	vayn·tee·dohs
30	treinta	trayn·ta
31	treinta y uno	trayn·ta ee oo·no
32	treinta y dos	trayn·ta ee dos
40	cuarenta	kwa·ren·ta
50	cincuenta	seen·kwen·ta
60	sesenta	se·sen·ta
70	setenta	se·ten·ta
80	ochenta	o·chen·ta
90	noventa	no·ven·ta
100	cien	syen
101	ciento uno	syen·to oo·no
200	doscientos	do·syen·tos
1000	mil	meel
5000	cinco mil	seen·ko meel

SHOPPING & SERVICES

I'd like to buy ...

Quisiera comprar ...   kee·sye·ra kom·prar ...

I'm just looking.

Sólo estoy mirando.   so·lo es·toy mee·ran·do

May I look at it?

¿Puedo mirar(lo/la)?   pwe·do mee·rar·(lo/la)

How much is it?

¿Cuánto cuesta?   kwan·to kwes·ta

That's too expensive for me.

Es demasiado caro para mí.   es de·ma·sya·do ka·ro pa·ra mee

Could you lower the price?

¿Podría bajar un poco el precio?   po·dree·a ba·khar oon po·ko el pre·syo

I don't like it.

No me gusta.   no me goos·ta

I'll take it.

Lo llevo.   lo ye·vo

I'm looking for the ...	Estoy buscando ...	es·toy boos·kan·do
ATM	el cajero automático	el ka·khe·ro ow·to·ma·tee·ko
bank	el banco	el ban·ko
bookstore	la librería	la lee·bre·ree·a
chemist/ pharmacy	la farmacia	la far·ma·sya
embassy	la embajada	la em·ba·kha·da
laundry	la lavandería	la la·van·de·ree·a
market	el mercado	el mer·ka·do
post office	los correos	los ko·re·os
supermarket	el supermercado	el soo·per·mer·ka·do
tourist office	la oficina de turismo	la o·fee·see·na de too·rees·mo

LANGUAGE

Do you accept ...?	¿Aceptan ...?	a·sep·tan ...
credit cards	tarjetas de crédito	tar·khe·tas de kre·dee·to
travellers cheques	cheques de viajero	che·kes de vya·khe·ro

less	menos	me·nos
more	más	mas
large	grande	gran·de
small	pequeño/a	pe·ke·nyo/a

What time does it open/close?
¿A qué hora abre/cierra? a ke o·ra a·bre/sye·ra

I want to change some money/travellers cheques.
Quiero cambiar dinero/ kye·ro kam·byar dee·ne·ro/
cheques de viajero. che·kes de vya·khe·ro

What is the exchange rate?
¿Cuál es el tipo de kwal es el tee·po de
cambio? kam·byo

I want to call ...
Quiero llamar a ... kye·ro lya·mar a ...

airmail	correo aéreo	ko·re·o a·e·re·o
letter	carta	kar·ta
registered mail	correo certificado	ko·re·o ser·tee·fee·ka·do
stamps	sellos	se·lyos

TIME & DATES

What time is it?	¿Qué hora es?	ke o·ra es
It's one o'clock.	Es la una.	es la oo·na
It's seven o'clock.	Son las siete.	son las sye·te
midnight	medianoche	me·dya·no·che
noon	mediodía	me·dyo·dee·a
half past two	dos y media	dos ee me·dya
now	ahora	a·o·ra
today	hoy	oy
tonight	esta noche	es·ta no·che
tomorrow	mañana	ma·nya·na
yesterday	ayer	a·yer

Monday	lunes	loo·nes
Tuesday	martes	mar·tes
Wednesday	miércoles	myer·ko·les
Thursday	jueves	khwe·ves
Friday	viernes	vyer·nes
Saturday	sábado	sa·ba·do
Sunday	domingo	do·meen·go

January	enero	e·ne·ro
February	febrero	fe·bre·ro
March	marzo	mar·so
April	abril	a·breel
May	mayo	ma·yo

June	junio	khoo·nyo
July	julio	khoo·lyo
August	agosto	a·gos·to
September	septiembre	sep·tyem·bre
October	octubre	ok·too·bre
November	noviembre	no·vyem·bre
December	diciembre	dee·syem·bre

TRANSPORT
Public Transport

What time does ... leave/arrive?	¿A qué hora sale/llega ...?	a ke o·ra sa·le/ye·ga ...?
the bus	el autobús	el ow·to·boos
the plane	el avión	el a·vyon
the ship	el barco	el bar·ko
the train	el tren	el tren

the bus station	la estación de autobuses	la es·ta·syon de ow·to·boo·ses
the bus stop	la parada de autobuses	la pa·ra·da de ow·to·boo·ses
the left luggage room	la consigna	la kon·seeg·na
taxi	taxi	tak·see
the ticket office	la taquilla	la ta·kee·lya
the train station	la estación de tren	la es·ta·syon de tren

The ... is delayed.
El ... está retrasado. el ... es·ta re·tra·sa·do

I'd like a ticket to ...
Quiero un billete a ... kye·ro oon bee·lye·te a ...

Is this taxi free?
¿Está libre este taxi? e·sta·lee·bre es·te tak·see

What's the fare to ...?
¿Cuánto cuesta hasta ...? kwan·to kwes·ta a·sta ...

Please put the meter on.
Por favor, ponga el por fa·vor pon·ga el
taxímetro. tak·see·me·tro

a ... ticket	un billete de ...	oon bee·lye·te de ...
one-way	ida	ee·da
return	ida y vuelta	ee·da ee vwel·ta
1st class	primera clase	pree·me·ra kla·se
2nd class	segunda clase	se·goon·da kla·se
student	estudiante	es·too·dyan·te

Private Transport

I'd like to hire a/an ...	Quisiera alquilar ...	kee·sye·ra al·kee·lar ...
4WD	un todoterreno	oon to·do·te·re·no
car	un coche	oon un ko·che
motorbike	una moto	oo·na mo·to
bicycle	una bicicleta	oo·na bee·see·kle·ta

ROAD SIGNS

Acceso	Entrance
Aparcamiento	Parking
Ceda el Paso	Give Way
Despacio	Slow
Desvío	Detour
Dirección Única	One-way
Frene	Slow Down
No Adelantar	No Overtaking
Peaje	Toll
Peligro	Danger
Prohibido Aparcar/	No Parking
No Estacionar	
Prohibido el Paso	No Entry
Vía de Accesso	Exit Freeway

Is this the road to ...?
¿Se va a ... por   se va a ... por
esta carretera?   es·ta ka·re·te·ra

Where's a petrol station?
¿Dónde hay una   don·de ai oo·na
gasolinera?   ga·so·lee·ne·ra

Please fill it up.
Lleno, por favor.   ye·no por fa·vor

I'd like (20) litres.
Quiero (veinte) litros.   kye·ro (vayn·te) lee·tros

diesel	diesel	dee·sel
petrol/gas	gasolina	ga·so·lee·na

(How long) Can I park here?
¿(Por cuánto tiempo)   (por kwan·to tyem·po)
Puedo aparcar aquí?   pwe·do a·par·kar a·kee

Where do I pay?
¿Dónde se paga?   don·de se pa·ga

I need a mechanic.
Necesito un mecánico.   ne·se·see·to oon me·ka·nee·ko

The car has broken down (in ...).
El coche se ha averiado   el ko·che se a a·ve·rya·do
(en ...).   (en ...)

Also available from Lonely Planet:
Spanish Phrasebook

The motorbike won't start.
No arranca la moto.   no a·ran·ka la mo·to

I have a flat tyre.
Tengo un pinchazo.   ten·go oon peen·cha·so

I've run out of petrol.
Me he quedado sin   me e ke·da·do seen
gasolina.   ga·so·lee·na

I've had an accident.
He tenido un accidente.   e te·nee·do oon ak·see·den·te

TRAVEL WITH CHILDREN

I need ...
Necesito ...   ne·se·see·to ...

Do you have ...?
¿Hay ...?   ai ...

a car baby seat
un asiento de seguridad   oon a·syen·to de se·goo·ree·da
para bebés   pa·ra be·bes

a child-minding service
un servicio de cuidado   oon ser·vee·syo de kwee·da·do
de niños   de nee·nyos

a children's menu
un menú infantil   oon me·noo een·fan·teel

(disposable) diapers/nappies
pañales (de usar y tirar)   pa·nya·les (de oo·sar ee tee·rar)

an (English-speaking) babysitter
un canguro (de   oon kan·goo·ro
habla inglesa)   (de a·bla een·gle·sa)

infant formula (milk powder)
leche en polvo   le·che en pol·vo

a highchair
una trona   oo·na tro·na

a potty
un orinal de niños   oon o·ree·nal de nee·nyos

a stroller
un cochecito   oon ko·che·see·to

Do you mind if I breast-feed here?
¿Le molesta que dé   le mo·les·ta ke de
de pecho aquí?   de pe·cho a·kee

Are children allowed?
¿Se admiten niños?   se ad·mee·ten nee·nyos

LANGUAGE

Glossary

For terms for food, drinks and other culinary vocabulary, see p86. For additional terms and information regarding the Spanish language, see the Language chapter on p458.

alameda – *paseo* lined (or originally lined) with *álamo* (poplar) trees
alcázar – Islamic-era fortress
artesonado – ceiling with interlaced beams leaving regular spaces for decorative insertions
autopista – toll highway
autovía – toll-free dual carriageway
AVE – Alta Velocidad Española; the high-speed train between Madrid and Seville
ayuntamiento – city or town hall
azulejo – tile

bahía – bay
bailaor/a – flamenco dancer
bandolero – bandit
barrio – district or quarter (of a town or city)
biblioteca – library
bici todo terreno (BTT) – mountain bike
bodega – winery, wine bar or wine cellar
buceo – scuba diving
bulería – upbeat type of flamenco song
buzón – postbox

cabalgata – cavalcade
cajero automático – automated teller machine (ATM)
calle – street
callejón – lane
cama individual – single bed
cama matrimonial – double bed
cambio – currency exchange
campiña – countryside (usually flat or rolling cultivated countryside)
camping – camping ground
campo – countryside, field
cantaor/a – flamenco singer
cante jondo – 'deep song', the essence of flamenco
capilla – chapel
capilla mayor – chapel containing the high altar of a church
carnaval – carnival; a pre-Lent period of fancy-dress parades and merrymaking
carretera – road, highway
carril de cicloturismo – road adapted for cycle touring
carta – menu

casa de huéspedes – guesthouse
casa rural – a village house or farmhouse with rooms to let
casco – literally 'helmet'; used to refer to the old part of a city (*casco antiguo*)
castellano – Castilian; the language also called Spanish
castillo – castle
caza – hunting
centro comercial – shopping centre
cercanía – suburban train
cerro – hill
cervecería – beer bar
chiringuito – small, often makeshift bar or eatery, usually in the open air
choza – traditional thatch hut
Churrigueresque – ornate style of baroque architecture named after the brothers Alberto and José Churriguera
cofradía – see *hermandad*
colegiata – collegiate church, a combined church and college
comedor – dining room
comisaría – station of the Policía Nacional
consigna – left-luggage office or lockers
converso – Jew who converted to Christianity in medieval Spain
copla – flamenco song
cordillera – mountain chain
coro – choir (part of a church, usually in the middle)
corrida de toros – bullfight
cortes – parliament
cortijo – country property
costa – coast
coto – area where hunting rights are reserved for a specific group of people
cruce – cross
cuenta – bill (check)
cuesta – sloping land, road or street
custodia – monstrance (receptacle for the consecrated Host)

dehesa – woodland pastures with evergreen oaks
Denominación de Origen – a designation that indicates the unique geographical origins, production processes and quality of wines, olive oil and other products
duende – the spirit or magic possessed by great flamenco performers
duque – duke
duquesa – duchess

embalse – reservoir
ermita – hermitage or chapel

escalada – climbing

estación de autobuses – bus station

estación de esquí – ski station or resort

estación de ferrocarril – train station

estación marítima – passenger port

estanco – tobacconist

estrella – overnight train with seats, couchettes and sleeping compartments

farmacia – pharmacy

faro – lighthouse

feria – fair; can refer to trade fairs as well as to city, town or village fairs

ferrocarril – railway

fiesta – festival, public holiday or party

finca – country property, farm

flamenco – means flamingo and Flemish as well as flamenco music and dance

frontera – frontier

fuente – fountain, spring

gitano – the Spanish word for Roma people

Guardia Civil – Civil Guard; police responsible for roads, the countryside, villages and international borders. They wear green uniforms. See also *Policía Local, Policía National*.

hammam – Arabic-style bathhouse

hermandad – brotherhood (which may include women), in particular one that takes part in religious processions; also *cofradía*

hospedaje – guesthouse

hostal – simple guesthouse or small place offering budget hotel-like accommodation

infanta – daughter of a monarch but not first in line to the throne

infante – son of a monarch but not first in line to the throne

instalación juvenil – youth hostel or youth camp

IVA – *impuesto sobre el valor añadido*; the Spanish equivalent of VAT (value-added tax)

jardín – garden

judería – Jewish barrio in medieval Spain

Junta de Andalucía – executive government of Andalucía

latifundia – huge estate

lavandería – laundry

levante – easterly wind

librería – bookshop

lidia – the modern art of bullfighting on foot

lista de correos – poste restante

lucio – pond or pool in the Doñana *marismas*

madrugada or **madrugá** – the 'early hours', from around 3am to dawn; a pretty lively time in some Spanish cities!

marismas – wetlands, marshes

marisquería – seafood eatery

marqués – marquis

medina – Arabic word for town or inner city

mercadillo – flea market

mercado – market

mezquita – mosque

mihrab – prayer niche in a mosque indicating the direction of Mecca

mirador – lookout point

morisco – Muslim converted to Christianity in medieval Spain

moro – 'Moor' or Muslim (usually in a medieval context)

movida – the late-night bar and club scene that emerged in Spanish cities and towns after Franco's death; a *zona de movida* or *zona de marcha* is an area of a town where people gather to drink and have a good time

mozárabe – Mozarab; Christian living under Islamic rule in medieval Spain

Mudejar – Muslim living under Christian rule in medieval Spain; also refers to their decorative style of architecture

muelle – wharf, pier

muladí – Muwallad; Christian who converted to Islam, in medieval Spain

nazareno – penitent taking part in Semana Santa processions

nieve – snow

nuevo – new

oficina de correos – post office

oficina de turismo – tourist office

olivo – olive tree

palacio – palace

palo – literally 'stick'; also refers to the categories of flamenco song

panadería – bakery

papelería – stationery shop

parador – one of the Paradores Nacionales, a state-owned chain of luxurious hotels, often in historic buildings

paraje natural – natural area

parque nacional – national park

parque natural – natural park

paseo – avenue or parklike strip; walk or stroll

paso – literally 'step'; also the platform an image is carried on in a religious procession

peña – a club; usually for supporters of a football club or flamenco enthusiasts (*peña flamenca*), but sometimes a dining club

pensión – guesthouse

pescadería – fish shop

picadero – riding stable

pícaro – dice trickster and card sharp, rogue, low-life scoundrel

pinsapar – forest of *pinsapo*

pinsapo – Spanish fir

piscina – swimming pool

plateresque – early phase of Renaissance architecture noted for its decorative façades

playa – beach

plaza de toros – bullring

Policía Local – Local Police; also known as Policía Municipal. Controlled by city and town halls, they deal mainly with minor matters such as parking, traffic and bylaws. They wear blue-and-white uniforms. See also *Guardia Civil, Policía Nacional.*

Policía Municipal – Municipal Police; see *Policía Local*

Policía Nacional – National Police; responsible for cities and bigger towns, some of them forming special squads dealing with drugs, terrorism and the like.

poniente – westerly wind

pozo – well

preferente – 1st-class carriage on a long-distance train

provincia – province; Spain is divided into 50 of them

pueblo – village, town

puente – bridge

puerta – gate, door

puerto – port, mountain pass

puerto deportivo – marina

puerto pesquero – fishing port

punta – point

rambla – stream

Reconquista – the Christian reconquest of the Iberian Peninsula from the Muslims (8th to 15th centuries)

refugio – shelter or refuge, especially a mountain refuge with basic accommodation for hikers

regional – train running between Andalucian cities

reja – grille; especially a wrought-iron one over a window or dividing a chapel from the rest of a church

Renfe – Red Nacional de los Ferrocarriles Españoles; Spain's national rail network

reserva – reservation, or reserve (eg nature reserve)

reserva nacional de caza – national hunting reserve

reserva natural – nature reserve

retablo – retable (altarpiece)

ría – estuary

río – river

romería – festive pilgrimage or procession

ronda – ring road

s/n – *sin numero* (without number); sometimes seen in addresses

sacristía – sacristy, the part of a church in which vestments, sacred objects and other valuables are kept

salina – salt lagoon

Semana Santa – Holy Week; the week leading up to Easter Sunday

sendero – path or track

sevillana – a popular Andalucian dance

sierra – mountain range

Siglo de Oro – Spain's cultural 'Golden Century', beginning in the 16th century and ending in the 17th century

taberna – tavern

tablao – flamenco show

taifa – one of the small kingdoms into which the Muslim-ruled parts of Spain were divided during parts of the 11th and 12th centuries

taquilla – ticket window

taracea – marquetry

tarjeta de crédito – credit card

tarjeta telefónica – phonecard

teléfono móvil – mobile telephone

temporada alta – high season

temporada baja – low season

temporada extra – extra-high season

temporada media – shoulder season

terraza – terrace; often means an area with outdoor tables at a bar, café or restaurant

tetería – Middle Eastern-style tearoom with low seats around low tables

tienda – shop, tent

tocaor/a – flamenco guitarist

torre – tower

trenhotel – sleek, expensive, sleeping-car-only train

turismo – means both tourism and saloon car; *el turismo* can also mean the tourist office

turista – 2nd-class carriage on a long-distance train

v.o. – *versión original*; foreign-language film

v.o.s. – *versión original subtitulada*; foreign-language film subtitled in Spanish

valle – valley

zoco – large market in Muslim cities

zona de protección – protected area

zona restringida – restricted area

Behind the Scenes

THIS BOOK

This is the 5th edition of *Andalucía*. The first two editions were written by John Noble and Susan Forsyth, who were joined by Des Hannigan and Heather Dickson on the 3rd edition. The 4th edition was written by John, Susan, Heather and Paula Hardy. This edition was written by John Noble, Susan Forsyth and Vesna Maric. The Health chapter was written by Dr Caroline Evans. It was commissioned in Lonely Planet's London office, and produced by the following:

Commissioning Editors Sally Schafer, Paula Hardy
Coordinating Editor Rosie Nicholson
Coordinating Cartographers Andrew Smith, Jolyon Philcox
Coordinating Layout Designer Jacqueline McLeod
Managing Editor Bruce Evans
Managing Cartographer Mark Griffiths
Assisting Editors Elisa Arduca, Gennifer Ciavarra, Adrienne Costanzo, Andrea Dobbin, Susan Paterson, Laura Stansfeld
Assisting Cartographers Hunor Csutoros, Matthew Kelly, Valentina Kremenchutskaya, Julie Sheridan, Amanda Sierp, Simon Tillema
Assisting Layout Designers Laura Jane, Indra Kilfoyle, Wibowo Rusli
Cover Designer Jane Hart
Project Manager Rachel Imeson
Language Content Coordinator Quentin Frayne

Thanks to Sally Darmody, Trent Paton, Celia Wood

THANKS

FROM JOHN NOBLE & SUSAN FORSYTH

Many thanks to Karen Abrahams, Irene and Joy Lucas, Pepa and Alan in El Puerto, Monika Schroeder, Jan Stendahl, and Craig Balmain for showing John the way out of (and back to, and back out of again) Castaño del Robledo.

FROM VESNA MARIC

The biggest thanks go to Rafael, as always, for making every trip so much better than it already is. Thank you to Gabriel, too. Big thanks also to Susana Perez Aguilar (¡Muchas gracias, Susa!), to Carlos Melguizo and his family in Córdoba, to *tía* Cris in Mojácar Playa, to Martín for letting us stay in his lovely flat and showing us fun places, and to Pablo for joining in the fun and offering to drive us to Lisbon on a whim. *Gracias* and *hvalas* to Minja and Constancio for driving many kilometres to come and see us. And thank you always to my mother who met me at the airport and made everything more fun.

OUR READERS

Many thanks to the travellers who used the last edition and wrote to us with helpful hints, useful advice and interesting anecdotes:

Lisa Adams, Steve Akeroyd, Cecilia Anderhub, Sven Armbrust, Sarah Armstrong, Joan Barry, Susan Bolsover, Robert Braiden, Philip Candy, Rosanna Clarelli, Mona Clark, Marie-Aude Danguy, Tracy & Ian Davis, Regine Denaegel, Omar do Nascimento, Aaron

---

THE LONELY PLANET STORY

The story begins with a classic travel adventure: Tony and Maureen Wheeler's 1972 journey across Europe and Asia to Australia. There was no useful information about the overland trail then, so Tony and Maureen published the first Lonely Planet guidebook to meet a growing need.

From a kitchen table, Lonely Planet has grown to become the largest independent travel publisher in the world, with offices in Melbourne (Australia), Oakland (USA) and London (UK). Today Lonely Planet guidebooks cover the globe. There is an ever-growing list of books and information in a variety of media. Some things haven't changed. The main aim is still to make it possible for adventurous travellers to get out there – to explore and better understand the world.

At Lonely Planet we believe travellers can make a positive contribution to the countries they visit – if they respect their host communities and spend their money wisely. Every year 5% of company profit is donated to charities around the world.

Forshaw, Chris Gilmartin, Natalie Godfrey, Alex Hammond, Margaret Hazellsmith, Kimberly Herrick, Ursula Hockauf, Reginald Hurren, Catie Inches-Ogden, Lorna Keeler, Patrick le Vaguerèse, Diane Macrae, Manuel Marino, Angelique Meul, Sarah Miller, Miriam & Hendriks, Barry North, Bonn Poland, Esther Schreur, Marianne Segeler, Lisa Shafer, Keith Tadhunter, David Tatman, Freek van Gijn, Andrew & Marilyn Vasilevich, Annie Watson, Gero Wedemann, Pauline Wilkinson, Maggie Willsher

Index

000 Map pages
000 Photograph pages

INDEX

INDEX

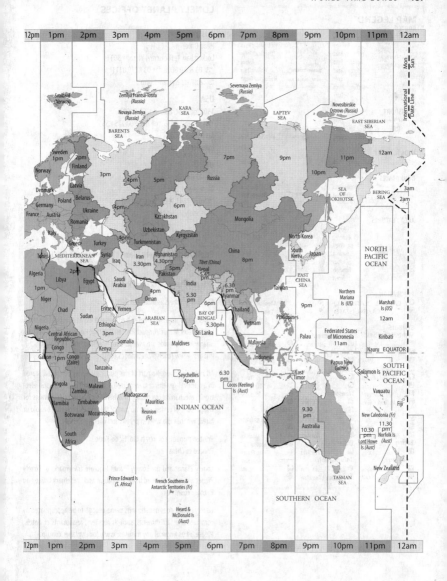

MAP LEGEND
ROUTES

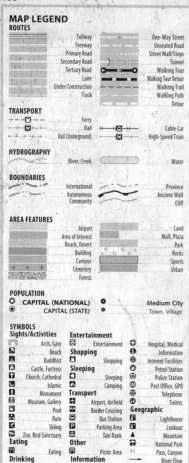

Tollway
Freeway
Primary Road
Secondary Road
Tertiary Road
Lane
Under Construction
Track

One-Way Street
Unsealed Road
Street Mall/Steps
Tunnel
Walking Tour
Walking Tour Detour
Walking Trail
Walking Path
Detour

TRANSPORT

Ferry
Rail
Rail (Underground)

Cable Car
High-Speed Train

HYDROGRAPHY

River, Creek
Water

BOUNDARIES

International
Autonomous
Community

Province
Ancient Wall
Cliff

AREA FEATURES

Airport
Area of Interest
Beach, Desert
Building
Campus
Cemetery
Forest

Land
Mall, Plaza
Park
Rocks
Sports
Urban

POPULATION

○ **CAPITAL (NATIONAL)**   ● **Medium City**
◉ CAPITAL (STATE)   ○ Town, Village

SYMBOLS

Sights/Activities
Arch, Gate
Beach
Buddhist
Castle, Fortress
Church, Cathedral
Islamic
Monument
Museum, Gallery
Pool
Ruin
Skiing
Zoo, Bird Sanctuary
Eating
Eating
Drinking
Drinking
Café

Entertainment
Entertainment
Shopping
Shopping
Sleeping
Sleeping
Camping
Transport
Airport, Airfield
Border Crossing
Bus Station
Parking Area
Taxi Rank
Other
Picnic Area
Information
Bank, ATM
Embassy, Consulate

Hospital, Medical
Information
Internet Facilities
Petrol Station
Police Station
Post Office, GPO
Telephone
Toilets
Geographic
Lighthouse
Lookout
Mountain
National Park
Pass, Canyon
River Flow
Shelter, Hut
Waterfall

LONELY PLANET OFFICES

Australia
Head Office
Locked Bag 1, Footscray, Victoria 3011
☎ 03 8379 8000, fax 03 8379 8111
talk2us@lonelyplanet.com.au

USA
150 Linden St, Oakland, CA 94607
☎ 510 893 8555, toll free 800 275 8555
fax 510 893 8572
info@lonelyplanet.com

UK
72–82 Rosebery Ave,
Clerkenwell, London EC1R 4RW
☎ 020 7841 9000, fax 020 7841 9001
go@lonelyplanet.co.uk

Published by Lonely Planet Publications Pty Ltd
ABN 36 005 607 983

© Lonely Planet Publications Pty Ltd 2006

© photographers as indicated 2006

Cover photograph: Woman in traditional dress at a festival, Seville, Spain, Peter Menzel/Impact Photos/Heritage-Images. Many of the images in this guide are available for licensing from Lonely Planet Images: www.lonelyplanetimages.com.